Bible Commentary

Bible Commentary
JEREMIAH

By

Theo. Laetsch, D. D.

CONCORDIA PUBLISHING HOUSE

SAINT LOUIS, MISSOURI

Concordia Paperback Edition 1965

Printed in U. S. A.   ISBN 0-570-03218-0   15-2003

To my former teachers at Concordia Seminary, St. Louis, Mo., in grateful memory, and to the faculty of Concordia College at Adelaide, Australia, in sincere appreciation of their kindness to me.

Preface to Commentary

The study of Scripture must never lag. God speaks to each new generation through His Word, the Bible. The message of the prophets is as significant for our day as it was to Israel of old. The Law of Sinai is as binding upon us as it was upon the Old Testament people under Moses, the Judges, and the kings. The Psalms express the heart cry of the ages and bring comfort to those who at the present moment sit in the valley of the shadow of death.

We still must know the Way, Christ Jesus of the Gospel, if we are to find peace and hope in a world which is in despair. We must go to the cross and look up to Him who was pierced for our transgressions. And to us still is given the challenging commission to preach the Gospel to the whole world with unrelinquishing zeal and undying fervor, as we have the pattern set for us in the Book of Acts and the Epistles of the New Testament.

But no one will grow in grace, be filled with a burning desire to serve and share who keeps this Sacred Book closed and sealed. Jesus urges us to "search the Scriptures." Only then shall we know the truth which makes us wise unto salvation.

To create in Bible students an eager desire to increase their understanding of Scripture, a new commentary of the Bible is in the making by scholars of The Lutheran Church — Missouri Synod and is being published by Concordia Publishing House, St. Louis, Mo., under the direction of the Church's Literature Board.

The first of these volumes is herewith presented.

THE PUBLISHERS

Foreword

The BOOK OF JEREMIAH is not as well known as it deserves to be. Jeremiah is generally called the Weeping Prophet. That name creates the impression that he was an effeminate person, lacking manly strength of character, lamenting in season and out of season, like the mourning women of Israel always ready to shed tears on the slightest occasion. It is true that Jeremiah was of a warmhearted, sympathetic nature. He did shed tears when he saw the ever-increasing wickedness and stubborn self-hardening of his people, whose salvation he so fervently desired, or when he realized that the horrible judgments of the just God were drawing ever closer and finally saw them poured out like a devastating flood on people and country. Yet by the grace of God he became a tower of strength, a real man's man, one of God's outstanding heroes. Not once did he break down in public. Facing his people, he was invariably the man of God, the messenger of the Lord's mercy, calling to repentance the nation he loved with a love as tender as that of a mother, as sincere as that of a faithful friend, sticking closer than a brother. His love of his people, however, did not interfere with his sense of duty, his love and obedience toward God. Unsparingly he pronounced God's judgments upon the impenitent without respect of persons. Like walls of brass he stood firm against frenzied prophets, fanatic priests, frantic people, furious kings. Calmly he faced this pack of snarling wolves ready to murder him. Neither defamation, nor persecution, nor imprisonment, nor threats of death kept him from speaking whatever God commanded him. Only when alone with himself and his God did he give voice to his agonized feelings, his doubts and fears, his heartaches and gnawing grief, his bitterness and his maledictions. And from every battle he rose more than a conqueror by the grace and power of Him who was the LORD, his Strength, his Fortress, and his Refuge in the day of affliction, because this LORD was Jehovah, his Righteousness.

Jeremiah the Prophet spoke and wrote by inspiration of the Holy Ghost, the Spirit of Christ testifying through him, 1 Peter 1:11. As such divinely inspired revelation of God we accept this book *in toto*, John 10:35; 2 Tim. 3:16; 2 Peter 1:21. The prophetic message is God's; the shortcomings in its presentation in this volume are the author's. May the Lord graciously grant His blessing to this effort to make the Prophet speak to our present generation. THEO. LAETSCH

Table of Contents

Complete Destruction!

PART II

The Prophecies Against the Nations, Chapter 46—52

THE LAMENTATIONS OF JEREMIAH

Jeremiah

JEREMIAH

Introductory Remarks

Historical and Religious Background of Jeremiah's Time

Pious King Hezekiah had energetically and quite successfully removed the outer evidences of idolatry, the high places, the images, the "groves," or *asherim* (2 Kings 18:4), which under wicked Ahaz had been erected throughout the land and even in the house of the Lord (2 Kings 16). Hezekiah had not succeeded in eradicating that strange hankering after other gods which had been the prevailing sin of Israel and Judah from the days of the Exodus (Ex. 32:1; Num. 25: 1-2; Judg. 2:1-13). When young Manasseh at the age of twelve years ascended the throne of his father, every trace of Hezekiah's reform was wiped out and Judah was reduced to the level of a heathen country.

"All the idolatrous, licentious, cruel, and superstitious rites in use among the surrounding nations, which had been strictly prohibited during the reign of Hezekiah, came back, rushing in with a flood that carried everything before it." (G. Rawlinson, in *The Bible Commentary,* on Kings, p. 120.) Read the horrible tale as recorded 2 Kings 21:1-16; 2 Chron. 33:1-10. In punishment of his atrocious wickedness the Lord gave Manasseh into the power of the Assyrian king, probably Esarhaddon (681—668), or Ashurbanipal (668—626), who took him captive to Babylon. Here in prison Manasseh turned to the Lord, who heard his petition and restored him to his kingdom. Manasseh now strengthened the fortifications of Jerusalem, placed garrisons into the chief cities of Judah, removed the idols out of the house of the Lord and Jerusalem, repaired the altar, and commanded Judah to serve the Lord God (2 Chron. 33:12-16).

Amon, who succeeded Manasseh on the throne of David, reinstated idol worship as the official religion of Judah and increased the guilt resting like a heavy burden on the land (2 Chron. 33:23). For some reason not stated the court officials assassinated him, but were put to death by the people (v. 25).

There seemed to be a hope of a national wholehearted return to the Lord, when, after Amon's short reign of two years, his eight-year-old son Josiah succeeded him on the throne. This lad, unlike his

1

wicked father and grandfather, walked in the ways of pious King David and did that which was right in the sight of the Lord. In the morass of idolatry and immorality and wickedness at the royal court, a beautiful branch, a real tree of righteousness, had sprouted by the power of divine grace out of the seemingly hopelessly corrupt root of David: a ruler of exemplary godliness, to whom the Searcher of hearts Himself gives that remarkable testimony recorded 2 Kings 23:25. Sixteen years old, he began to seek after the God of David, his father. At the age of twenty he began to remove every evidence of idolatry in Jerusalem and Judah. His reform extended beyond the confines of Judah to the cities of Manasseh and Ephraim and Simeon, even unto Naphtali (2 Chron. 34:1-7).

In the eighteenth year of Josiah's kingdom, 622, necessary and long-delayed repairs were begun in the house of the Lord. They were financed by freewill offerings of the people of Judah and Benjamin and of the remaining tribes of Israel still dwelling in the land of Canaan (2 Chron. 34:8-13). In the course of these repairs the ancient Temple copy of the Law of Moses, the Pentateuch, was found under the rubbish which had accumulated during the long years that the Temple had been transformed into a house of idolatrous worship and heathenish practices. On the basis of this ancient Code, Josiah and his people renewed the covenant in solemn assembly (2 Chron. 34: 29-33), continued the reformation (2 Kings 23:4-20; 2 Chron. 34:33) in a serious endeavor to stem the tide of idolatry threatening ruin and disaster to the people (2 Chron. 34:24ff.). They celebrated the Passover in the exact manner prescribed in the Book of the Law (2 Kings 23:21-23; 2 Chron. 35:1-19).

Yet even this reformation, though carried out with a fervent zeal and the burning desire to save Israel from the impending judgment, failed to eradicate the evil effects of Manasseh's and Amon's wickedness. So thoroughly had the sin of Manasseh (2 Kings 24:3; Jer. 15:4) penetrated the warp and woof of Judah's national and religious life, so firmly had it taken hold of the hearts and minds of the people, that as soon as the curb of Josiah's reform was removed, it broke out afresh in open rebellion against God and His faithful prophets and followers. Therefore God could not turn from His wrath provoked by Manasseh, and the time drew near that He would fulfill His threat to wipe Jerusalem as a man wipeth a dish, wiping it and turning it upside down (2 Kings 21:11-13).

Pious Josiah was by the grace of God gathered to his fathers in peace, so that his eyes did not have to see all the evil, the horrible days, that by God's just judgment were soon to come upon the corrupt apostates (2 Chron. 34:28). After he had ruled thirty-one years, he

2

met a sudden death when he endeavored to halt Pharaoh Necho's campaign to assist Assyria in its final efforts to re-establish its power. Mortally wounded at Megiddo in the valley of Jezreel, he was brought to Jerusalem, where he died. So great was the esteem in which he was held that the anniversary of his death was commemorated as a day of fasting and lamentation (2 Chron. 35:25).

After Josiah's death, the people in an effort to maintain their independence chose not Eliakim, the older son of Josiah (2 Kings 23:36, twenty-five years), but the two-years-younger Jehoahaz (2 Kings 23:31). He is to be identified with Shallum (see notes on Jer. 22:11). The reasons for this preference are not stated. Perhaps they had already learned the vicious character of Eliakim. Proud Necho resented their action, summoned Jehoahaz to Riblah, sent him bound to Egypt, where he died (2 Kings 23:33; Jer. 22:11-12). After imposing a heavy tribute on Judah (2 Kings 23:33), Necho placed Eliakim on the throne, changing his name to Jehoiakim. Jehoiakim was a wicked man (2 Kings 23:37; 2 Chron. 36:5, 8). In his brief characterization of Jehoiakim, Jeremiah presents the picture of an inordinately vain and ambitious, covetous, bloodthirsty, violent oppressor and tyrant (Jer. 22:13-17). He was bitterly opposed to Jehovah and His worship, reinstating the abominations removed by Josiah (2 Chron. 36:8; 2 Kings 23:37). Equally determined was he in his hatred against the true prophets, slaying Uriah (Jer. 26:20-23), burning Jeremiah's scroll after cutting it to pieces, and seeking to kill Jeremiah and Baruch (ch. 36:22-26). Nothing positive can be stated concerning the dating of the events recorded 2 Kings 24:1-2 and 2 Chron. 36:6-7. 2 Kings 24:7 places this campaign in connection with the disastrous defeat of Necho at Carchemish, 605. At that time Nebuchadnezzar made Jehoiakim tributary, but the latter revolted three years later, 602. The Babylonian king sent bands of Chaldeans against him and incited the neighboring nations to harass Judah (2 Kings 24:2). Whether 2 Chron. 36:6-7 refers to this same campaign or must be dated later, we cannot tell. Jer. 52:28 speaks of a deportation of 3,023 Jews in the seventh year of Nebuchadnezzar, the year before Jehoiachin was deported (2 Kings 24:12) and therefore may refer to another campaign of Nebuchadnezzar against Jerusalem, at which time the dread prophecy Jer. 22:18-19 may have been fulfilled.

After Jehoiakim's death his son Jehoiachin (cp. notes on Jer. 22:24) ruled three months and ten days (2 Chron. 36:9). By some unrecorded action he roused the suspicions of the Babylonian king, who sent an army against Jerusalem. Without offering resistance, Jehoiachin surrendered to Nebuchadnezzar, who plundered the royal palace and the Temple and deported the king, his mother, the princes,

3

and other officials, together with ten thousand soldiers and artisans, the cream of the population (Jer. 24: 5), leaving only the lower classes, the rabble. The last son of Josiah, Mattaniah, twenty-one years old, was placed on the throne by Nebuchadnezzar, who changed his name to Zedekiah and to whom Zedekiah pledged allegiance (2 Kings 24: 17-20; 2 Chron. 36: 10-13). On the character of Zedekiah see p. 276 f.; 290 to 300.

In the ninth year of Zedekiah's reign the constantly repeated threat of Jer. 1: 13-15 was at last beginning to be fulfilled. God's mills, grinding slowly but thoroughly, were now ready to inaugurate the final crushing of the wicked nation. The Babylonian hosts were advancing toward Jerusalem. Already the Judean armies had clashed with them in fanatical but ineffective efforts to stem the tide which threatened to overwhelm Jerusalem and all the land of Judah. Realizing that only a miracle could save the nation from destruction, the king sent a delegation to Jeremiah with the fervent plea to ask the Lord for such a miracle (Jer. 21:2). Jeremiah frankly told the delegates that such a miracle was not to be hoped for. He foretold in the plainest language possible the destruction of Jerusalem by fire and the deportation of the people to Babylon. He repeated his plea that the king and his people surrender before more people would needlessly perish. When the king hesitated, the Lord sent Jeremiah to meet Zedekiah privately in order to impress upon him the folly and wickedness of further resistance, since the Lord Himself had decreed the inevitable destruction of the city and nation. In order to embolden the king to surrender, He promised him escape from the sword, a peaceful death, and an honorable burial, even though he would have to go into exile (ch. 34: 1-7). And still the king refused to follow the advice and plea of the prophet. The Babylonians came ever closer. With two exceptions all the fortified cities had fallen (ch. 34: 7). Jerusalem was encircled by the enemy's army. Wavering between despair and hope, the vacillating king, willing to strike a bargain with God as long as he did not have to humble himself by an unconditional surrender, sought to gain God's favor by persuading the people to do away by a solemn covenant a long-standing injustice (ch. 34: 6-10), the enslavement of their poverty-stricken brethren, a flagrant violation of God's Law (Ex. 21: 2f.). The shameful hypocrisy of this "reform" became apparent at once. When the Babylonians raised the siege in order to repel the army of Hophra of Egypt marching to the aid of Zedekiah, the people at once revoked the manumission (ch. 34: 11, 16ff.), since they felt that they no longer needed the Lord's help. Again Jeremiah is sent to announce the speedy return of the victorious Babylonian armies, the complete destruction of the city, and the deportation of the people (v. 17ff.).

4

JEREMIAH

Before the return of the army, Zedekiah sent a second delegation to Jeremiah with an appeal to pray for them. Jeremiah once more repeats the threat of complete destruction (ch. 37: 3-10).

In the absence of the Babylonian army, Jeremiah decided to transact some business in his native town of Anathoth. While passing through the gate, he was arrested by one of the guards, who charged him with the intention to desert. In spite of the prophet's denial he was brought to the princes, who gladly accepted the opportunity to vent their spite on the aged prophet, beat him, and cast him into one of the subterranean cells in the house of Jonathan, the secretary, which had been converted into a prison. Their hope that he would perish there before long was frustrated. King Zedekiah summoned the prophet, hoping that Jeremiah had experienced a change of heart. The prophet repeated the threat of deportation and asked the king not to send him back to the dungeon "lest I die there." Zedekiah, disappointed and angry when the prophet refused to change his message, did not dare to aid in the murder of God's prophet and therefore ordered his transfer to the Court of the Guard in the royal palace, where the royal guard was quartered. Here the prophet was protected from further maltreatment and received a loaf of bread daily as long as it was available. While in the Court of the Guard, Jeremiah bought the field of his uncle and there in the presence of witnesses executed the necessary legal formalities (ch. 32: 6-14). Evidently he had opportunity to speak to the people coming to the royal palace, perhaps had received permission even to appear in public (ch. 38: 1). Because of his repeated efforts to persuade the people to surrender, the prophet finally was formally denounced by the princes as a public enemy fomenting dissatisfaction and war weariness within the city. In order to save himself, Zedekiah turned Jeremiah over to his murderous enemies, who at once lowered him into a cistern partly filled with mud. No one dared to lift a finger for his rescue except a foreigner, an Ethiopian, one of the king's eunuchs. He asked for and received the king's permission to save the life of the prophet, who was returned to the Court of the Guard (ch. 38: 1-13). Once more Zedekiah in a secret conversation asked the prophet for information. When the prophet did not change his message, but remaining loyal to the Word of his Lord, pleaded once more with the king to surrender before it was too late, the king kept him under guard in the palace Court of the Guard.

On the ninth day of the fourth month of the eleventh year of Zedekiah, July, 586 (Jer. 39: 2; 52: 4; 2 Kings 25: 3), the walls of the city were breached, and the enemy entered Jerusalem. Under cover of darkness the king and his army sought to escape to Transjordania, but he was overtaken in the plains of Jericho. Zedekiah and his family

5

were brought to Nebuchadnezzar at Riblah. The Babylonian king, exasperated at the treachery and stubborn resistance of this petty king, ordered the sons of Zedekiah to be slain before his eyes. Then he was blinded, bound with two brazen chains, and deported to Babylon.

At the command of Nebuchadnezzar, Nebuzaradan, the chief of the Babylonian army, released Jeremiah and gave him into the charge of Gedaliah, whom Nebuchadnezzar had appointed as governor of Judah (ch. 39:11-14). Through some misunderstanding, Jeremiah was placed among the captives at Jerusalem, bound with chains, and deported as far as Ramah, where somehow the mistake was discovered and Jeremiah was released to go "whither it seemed good and convenient for him to go" (ch. 40:1-4). For his further history see notes on ch. 40—44.

Shallum and Zedekiah were full brothers, born thirteen years apart: 631 and 618. Jehoiakim was their half brother, older than they, born 634.

Jehoahaz is not to be identified with Johanan, the first-born son of Josiah (1 Chron. 3:15); Jehoahaz was not the first born, but was two years younger than Jehoiakim (cp. 2 Kings 23:31, 36; 2 Chron. 36:2, 5). Jehoahaz is to be identified with Shallum, the fourth son of Josiah (1 Chron. 3:15), who according to Jer. 22:11 succeeded his father, Josiah. He was dethroned and deported and never saw his native land again. This corresponds exactly with the history of Jehoahaz (2 Kings 23:30-34; 2 Chron. 36:1-4), and not with the history of any other son of Josiah. Hence Jehoahaz is the name taken by Shallum, probably when he became king.

According to 2 Kings 24:8 Jehoiachin was eighteen years old when he ascended the throne, hence seven years old when his grandfather, Josiah, was slain, 609. 2 Chron. 36:9 states that he was eight years old, evidently a copyist's error (LXX, A has 18; B, 8), since Jehoiachin had wives (2 Kings 24:15). Jehoiachin was released from prison by Evil-Merodach, the successor of Nebuchadnezzar in 561 (2 Kings 25:27-30).

Zedekiah was Jehoiachin's uncle, *dod* (2 Kings 24:17), the brother of Jehoiachin's father, Jehoiakim. In 2 Chron. 36:10 Zedekiah is called Jehoiachin's "brother," "brother" used here in the wider sense of *ach*, "brother"; cp. Gen. 13:8; 14:16, where Lot, Abraham's nephew (Gen. 11:27), is called Abraham's brother. Similarly, Rebecca, the granddaughter of Nahor, Abraham's brother (Gen. 22:20-23), is called Nahor's daughter (Gen. 24:48). Or the original text may have been *achi abiw*, his father's brother, as LXX, Syrian, Itala, read, and *abiw* may have dropped out owing to a scribal error.

The Family of Josiah

Josiah, King of Judah, Son of Amon and Jedidah (2 Kings 22:1)
Born 648/7, Ruled 640/39—609/8

1. Johanan	2. Eliakim	3. Mattaniah	4. Shallum
Only mentioned 1 Chron. 3:15	2 Kings 23:34 2 Chron. 36:4	2 Kings 24:17	1 Chron. 3:15 Jer. 22:11
	Called Jehoiakim 1 Chron. 3:15 2 Chron. 36:4 2 Kings 23:34	Called Zedekiah 1 Chron. 3:15 2 Kings 24:17	Called Jehoahaz 2 Kings 23:30-34 2 Chron. 36:1ff.
	Mother: Zebudah 2 Kings 23:36	Mother: Hamutal 2 Kings 24:18	Mother: Hamutal 2 Kings 23:31
	Born: 634	Born: 619/18	Born: 632/1
	Enthroned by Pharaoh Necho, 609	Enthroned by Nebuchadnezzar, 597 2 Kings 24:17-20 2 Chron. 36:10	Enthroned by people, 609/8 2 Kings 23:30 2 Chron. 36:1
	Died: 598/7; 36 years old	Deposed and deported to Babylon, 586; 32 or 33 years old 2 Kings 25:1-7 2 Chron. 36:12-21	Deposed by Pharaoh Necho, 609/8 2 Kings 23:32ff. 2 Chron. 36:3-4
	His character, cp. Jer. 22:13-19	His character, cp. Ezek. 19:5-9	His character, cp. Ezek. 19:1-4
	Jehoiachin, son of Jehoiakim 2 Kings 24:6-16 1 Chron. 3:15 2 Chron. 36:8-10		
	Mother: Nehushta 2 Kings 24:8		
	Born: 616/5		
	Succeeded his father 598/7 2 Kings 24:6 2 Chron. 36:8		
	Dethroned and deported by Nebuchadnezzar, 597 2 Kings 24:10-16 2 Chron. 36:10 18 years old		
	Released from prison and honored by Evil-Merodach, king of Babylon, 561, at age 55 2 Kings 25:27-30		

7

Chronology of Events in the History of the Last Days of Judah-Jerusalem

Assyria	Year	Judah	Regnal Year	Age	Jeremiah's Activity	Egypt
Sennacherib	705	Hezekiah	27	52		
	698	Hezekiah's death	29	54		
		Manasseh king	1	12		
Esarhaddon 681—668	681					Psammetich 663—609
Assurbanipal 668—626	668					Thebes sacked by Assurbanipal, 663
	664	Amon born				
	648	Josiah born				
	643	Manasseh's death	55	66		
		Amon king (2 Kings 21:19f.; 2 Chron. 33:21)		22		
	641	Amon's death (2 Kings 21:23f.; 2 Chron. 33:24)	2	24		
		Josiah crowned (2 Kings 22:1; 2 Chron. 34:1)	0	8		
	633	Josiah seeks the Lord (2 Chron. 34:3a)	8	16		
	629	Reform begun (2 Chron. 34:3b)				
	628	Jeremiah called (Jer. 1)	13	21	1	
Assurbanipal died	626		15	23	3	
Babylon independent						
Nabopolassar king	626/5					
	623/2	Book of Law found (2 Kings 22:3ff.; 2 Chron. 34:8ff.)	18	26	6	
Nineveh destroyed	612		29	36	17	
Nabopolassar conquers Haran	610					
	609	Megiddo. Josiah slain by Necho (2 Kings 23:29-30; 2 Chron. 35:20-25) The people choose Jehoahaz, who rules three months, summoned by Necho to Riblah, taken	31	39	20	Necho, 609 to 594, comes to aid of Assyria; establishes headquarters at Riblah

Assyria	Year	Judah	Regnal Year	Age	Jeremiah's Activity	Egypt
		captive to Egypt (2 Kings 23:30-34; 2 Chron. 36:1-4; Jer. 22: 10-12)				
	608	Necho places Jehoiakim on the throne	1	25	21	
	606	Nebuchadnezzar takes Jerusalem, takes hostages and Temple vessels (Dan. 1:1-2)	3			
	605	Nebuchadnezzar defeats Necho at Carchemish, Jer. 46:1ff., pursues him to Egypt. Jehoiakim made tributary (2 Kings 24:1; 2 Chron. 36:6; (or must this be dated later?). Jeremiah's speech (Jer. 25:1ff.); he writes his prophecies on a scroll (ch. 36:1-8); Baruch's complaint (ch. 45)	4	28	24	
Babylon						
Nabopolassar dies	605					
Nebuchadnezzar succeeds him 605:0						
1	604	Baruch reads the scroll. Jehoiakim burns it, ninth month (December) (Jer. 36:9-26); Jeremiah in hiding (ch. 36:26 b). Scroll rewritten (vv. 27-32)	5	29	25	
4	602/1	Jehoiakim rebels (2 Kings 24:1b). Nebuchadnezzar sends Chaldeans and others against him (2 Kings 24:2)	8	32	28	
7	598/7	Jehoiakim's death (2 Kings 24:6; Jer. 22: 18-19) probably in a Babylonian campaign against Jerusalem, in which 3,023 Jews were deported in the seventh year of Nebuchadnezzar (Jer. 52:28)	11	35	31	

9

Babylon	Year	Judah	Regnal Year	Age	Jeremiah's Activity	Egypt
8	597	Jehoiachin succeeds his father, rules three months, ten days, is deported with 10,000 captives (2 Kings 24: 10-16; 2 Chron. 36: 9-10; Jer. 29:1-2)	1	18	30	
	596	In the early years of Zedekiah, Jeremiah wrote his prophecy of the good and bad figs (Jer. 24:1-10) and against Elam (Jer. 49: 34-39). Zedekiah also sends an embassy to Babylon, to whom Jeremiah entrusts his letter to the exiles (Jer. 29:1-3). Shemaiah demands that Jeremiah be silenced (vv. 24-32)	1	21	32	
	593	In Zedekiah's fourth year envoys of Tyre and other neighboring nations meet at Jerusalem. Jeremiah warns them against rebellion (Jer. 27:1-22). In fifth month (Ab, August) Hananiah opposes Jeremiah and dies in the seventh month (Tisri, October) (Jer. 28:1-17)	4	24	35	
	588/7	Egypt succeeds in inciting Zedekiah to rebel against Nebuchadnezzar (Ezek. 17:3-21), who at once attacks Judah (Jer. 34:7). Jeremiah urges surrender (ch. 34:1-6), Zedekiah refuses. Tenth month (January), tenth day, siege of Jerusalem begins (2 Kings 25:1; Jer. 39:1; 52:4; Ezek. 24:2). Zedekiah's delegation (Jer. 21:2-14); slaves released (ch. 34:8-10), re-enslaved on report of Hophra's approach and the lifting of the siege (ch. 34:11-22; 37:5). Probably now the deportation of 832	9	29	40	Hophra, Pharaoh of Egypt, 588—569

Babylon	Year	Judah	Regnal Year	Age	Jeremiah's Activity	Egypt
		from Jerusalem (ch. 52:29). Jeremiah's arrest and imprisonment; interview with Zedekiah, transfer to Court of Guard (ch. 37:6-21).				
18	587	Purchase of Hanameel's field (ch. 32:1ff.). Princes demand his death, confine him in a pit; rescued by Ebedmelech (ch. 38:6-13). Last interview with Zedekiah (ch. 38:14-28)	10	31	42	
	586	4th month (Tammuz, July), ninth day, walls breached. Zedekiah's flight, capture, trial at Riblah, exiled to Babylon (2 Kings 25:4-7; Jer. 39:1-7; 52:5-11) 5th month (Ab, August), seventh day, Nebuzaradan comes to Jerusalem with orders to protect Jeremiah, commits him to Gedaliah (Jer. 39:11-14). 7th to 10th day, city and Temple plundered and burnt (2 Kings 25:8-21; 2 Chron. 36:13-21; Jer. 39:8; 52:12-27). Gedaliah appointed governor over Judah (2 Kings 25:22-24; Jer. 40:5-12). Jeremiah released at Rama (Jer. 40:1-6). 7th month (Tisri, October), Gedaliah slain and avenged (ch. 40:13 to 41:15). Flight into Egypt (ch. 41:16—44:30)	11	32	43	
23	582	745 Jews deported (ch. 52:30)				
Nebuchadnezzar died, ruled 43 years	562/1					
Amel-Marduk	561	Jehoiachin released from prison (2 Kings 25:27-30; Jer. 52:31-34)		55		

11

JEREMIAH

The Divisions of the Book of Jeremiah

The Book of Jeremiah may be divided into two chief parts: ch. 2—45 and ch. 46—51, with an introductory and a concluding chapter, ch. 1 and ch. 52.

The first part contains chiefly prophecies and narratives concerning Judah and Jerusalem, though a number of prophecies concerning the surrounding nations are interspersed; while the second part consists of oracles directed against nine foreign nations.

Ch. 52 narrates the siege and destruction of Jerusalem, the deportation of the Jews, and the deliverance of Jehoiachin by Evil-Merodach (Amel-Marduk) in 562/1.

I. Prophecies Relating to the Theocracy

Chapters 1—45

Ch. 1, narrating the call of the prophet, is divided into three parts: vv. 1-10; 11-16; 17-19, the leading thoughts of which influenced the logical arrangement of the prophecies and narratives of Part I, ch. 2—45.

1. Ch. 1: 4-10 narrates how Jeremiah was called to be the prophet of the Lord, who in complete disregard of his personal feelings and desires was to proclaim to Jews and Gentiles whatever the Lord would tell him to speak. He is promised God's protection.

2. In vv. 11-16 the Lord foretells the complete destruction of Judah by an enemy from the north, later identified as Babylon (chap. 20: 4-6; 25: 1, 9-12).

3. Vv. 17-19. In spite of ever-increasing unbelief and opposition on the part of rulers and people, Jeremiah is to proclaim God's message fearlessly and is promised God's unfailing aid and deliverance.

In Part I the prophet three distinct times calls attention to the fourth year of Jehoiakim: ch. 25: 1; 36: 1; 45: 1; the only passages in which this year is mentioned in ch. 2—45. We shall see that each of these three chapters links with one of the three sections of ch. 1, and that each at the same time summarizes the preceding chapters, thus dividing Part I, ch. 2—45, into three sections (ch. 2—25; 26—36; 37—45), each having as its summarizing conclusion a chapter referring to the fourth year of Jehoiakim and linking with ch. 1.

The Importance of Jehoiakim's Fourth Year

The fourth year of Jehoiakim, 605 B. C., ushered in the fatal crisis in the political and religious life of Judah, as clearly indicated in ch. 25, 36, and 45. In this year, Pharaoh Necho, Babylon's only remaining rival for world supremacy after the fall of Nineveh (612), was decisively defeated by Nebuchadnezzar at Carchemish (cp. 2 Chron. 35:20; Jer. 46:2-12; 2 Kings 24:7).

In the fourth year of Jehoiakim, Nebuchadnezzar ascended the throne of Babylon as successor to his father, Nabopolassar, news of whose death reached Nebuchadnezzar in Egypt shortly after the battle of Carchemish, 605. Him the Lord had chosen to execute God's judgment upon Jerusalem, whose total destruction was foretold by Jeremiah in this fourth year of Jehoiakim (ch. 25:9-11); in the same year Jeremiah's previous prophecies were written on a scroll to be publicly read (ch. 36:1-4) and revealed to Baruch in the same year as unalterable (ch. 45).

The fourth year was also the critical year in the religious life of Judah. For in this year Jeremiah was commanded to put his prophecies in writing as a last test for King Jehoiakim, who rejected the Word of God and sought to slay the prophet (ch. 36), when the book was read in the ninth month of the fifth year of Jehoiakim (ch. 36:9), 604.

Chapters 25, 36, 45 Are Fitting Conclusions to Preceding Chapters

1. *Ch. 25.* Here the prophet calls attention (v. 3) to his faithfulness in carrying out God's commission (ch. 1:4-10) irrespective of his own personal feelings and desires. This sums up his activity as described ch. 2—24. This section alone shows us the inner conflicts disturbing the prophet, his personal desires and hopes so often at variance with God's plans; acquaints us with his efforts to induce the Lord to change His plans; reveals his disappointments, his doubts and misgivings as to God's justice and mercy, pictures his moments of deepest anguish to the point of stark despair (ch. 4:10, 19; 6:10; 9:1-2; 10:19; 11:19-20; 12:1-4; 14:7—15:21; 20:7-10, 14-18). Yet from the year of his call to the fourth year of Jehoiakim, for twenty-three years, he had been faithful to the Lord's commission (ch. 25:3) and continued to speak what the Lord told him to speak (ch. 1:7), to the last year of Zedekiah (ch. 21—22). In obedience to the Lord's command he had torn down and destroyed (ch. 1:10), and he had built and planted (ch. 1:10b; cp. the wonderful promises, ch. 3:12-25; 23:3-8). He had experienced the fulfillment of the Lord's promise of deliverance, comfort, consolation. He still lived to do the Lord's will. While, therefore, ch. 2—24 are not chronologically arranged, yet ch. 1:4-10; ch. 2—24; ch. 25, stand in close logical relation. They picture the prophet throughout his long career as the faithful servant of the Lord, the prophet of the nations (cp. ch. 25:8-38 with ch. 1:10), tearing down and building up, following not his own inclinations, but doing the Lord's will and speaking the Lord's message.

13

2. *Ch. 36.* This chapter links with ch. 1:17-19. In Jehoiakim's fourth year God commanded Jeremiah to write all his prophecies in a book in order to put Jehoiakim to a final test (ch. 36:1-8). Continuing in his violent opposition to the Lord and the prophet, Jehoiakim cuts the scroll to pieces and burns it (vv. 9-25) and orders Jeremiah and Baruch to be imprisoned. The Lord hid them (v. 26), and at His command the scroll is rewritten and enlarged (vv. 27-32). God fulfills His promise of protection against violent opposition (ch. 1: 17-19).

Ch. 36 also climaxes the contents of ch. 26—35. Jeremiah's courageous iteration of his prophecy against the city and the Temple (ch. 26:1-6) meets with fierce opposition on the part of priests, prophets, and people, who demand his death (vv. 7-11). Undaunted, he defends himself (vv. 12-15) and is set free (vv. 16-19, 24). Uriah is slain by Jehoiakim (vv. 20-23). In the days of Zedekiah, Jeremiah's prophecy of the Babylonian captivity (ch. 27) rouses Hananiah's opposition (ch. 28:1-11), but the prophet is vindicated by the Lord (vv. 12-17). Jeremiah's courageous letter to the exiles (ch. 29:1-23) inflames Shemaiah, who demands his imprisonment, but again the Lord foils the plans of the enemies (vv. 24-32). In fulfillment of His promise (ch. 1:18-19) the Lord strengthens His prophet by a series of most remarkable revelations (ch. 30—33). But before these promises can be fulfilled, the present kingdom must be destroyed, because in glaring contrast to the Rechabites' faithfulness in keeping a human command (ch. 35) the Jews had flagrantly violated God's covenant (ch. 34), an act of rebellion rivaling that of Jehoiakim (ch. 36). Hence ch. 36 speaking of Jeremiah's faithfulness and God's protection in days of violent opposition links with ch. 1:17-19 and climaxes ch. 26—35.

3. *Ch. 45.* For the third time reference is made to the fourth year of Jehoiakim (ch. 45:1). Baruch is told that it is the Lord's fixed determination to destroy the whole land of Judah.

This oracle links with ch. 1:11-16, foretelling this destruction, and sums up ch. 37—44, which vividly depict the death of the Jewish commonweatlh. Significantly there are no Messianic prophecies in ch. 37—45. Destruction only!

II. The Prophecies Against the Nations
Chapters 46—52

Ch. 46—51 list nine of the prophecies spoken by Jeremiah as the prophet "set over the nations" by the Lord (ch. 1:10). In the fourth year of Jehoiakim, Jeremiah had been told to send the cup of God's wrath to Judah (ch. 25:18) and to all the surrounding nations, twenty of which are named. In ch. 46—51 nine of these nations are listed:

Egypt; Philistia (in which prophecy the defeat of Tyre and Sidon is incorporated, ch. 47:4); Moab (ch. 48); Ammon (ch. 49:1-6); Edom (vv. 7-22); Damascus (vv. 23-27), representing the northern kingdoms named ch. 25:26a; Kedar and Hazor (vv. 28-33), comprehending the Arabian tribes listed ch. 25:23-25a; Elam, including Media (vv. 34-39), and Babylon (ch. 50—51). Egypt is very properly placed at the head, because by the defeat of Egypt, Babylon gained her world supremacy, enabling her to crush all opposition (cp. ch. 25:9; 27:2-11). The prophecies against Egypt and Babylon end with a promise to Judah, because these two world powers were the chief enemies of Judah, and their destruction was for the believing Jews a cause of special comfort.

PART 1

Prophecies Relating to the Theocracy
Chapters 1—45

SECTION ONE

The Selfless Faithfulness of the Prophet

Chapters 1—25

I. Introduction, Ch. 1

CHAPTER 1

1. The Superscription, Vv. 1-3

1 The words of Jeremiah, the son of Hilkiah, of the priests which lived at Anathoth in the land of Benja-
2 min, that came as the word of the LORD to him in the days of Josiah, the son of Amon, king of Judah, in the thirteenth year of his reign.

3 It came also in the days of Jehoiakim, the son of Josiah, king of Judah, unto the end of the eleventh year of Zedekiah, the son of Josiah, king of Judah, when Jerusalem was deported in the fifth month.

Grammatical Notes

V. 1. The etymology and meaning of the name Jeremiah is not quite certain. Jerome derived it from רום, to exalt, and has found many followers. Yet in analogy to such names as Jaaziah (1 Chron. 24: 26), Ibneiah (1 Chron. 9: 8), Ismaiah (1 Chron. 12: 4; 27: 19), etc., the derivation from רמה, to fling, throw down (cp. Ex. 15: 1), seems to be preferable, being indicative of the doom he was to foretell.

V. 1. "The words of Jeremiah, the son of Hilkiah." The name "Jeremiah" apparently was quite common among the Jews (cp. 2 Kings 23: 31; 1 Chron. 5: 24; 12: 4, 10, 13; Neh. 10: 2; Jer. 35: 3).

"Of the priests that were in Anathoth" does not refer to Hilkiah, but to Jeremiah ben Hilkiah. The identity of Jeremiah's father, Hilkiah, with the high priest named 2 Kings 22: 3ff.; 2 Chron. 34: 8ff., cannot be proved. The high priests generally dwelt at Jerusalem, and the statement "of the priests," etc., may have been inserted in order to prevent an identification of Jeremiah's father with the high priest Hilkiah.

"In Anathoth." This is a village about two and a half to three miles northeast of Jerusalem on the eastern slope of the ridge extending from Jerusalem in a northeasterly direction, its slopes gradually descending some 3,800 feet in fifteen miles to the Jordan River near the Dead Sea. It was named in pre-Israelite times for the Phoenician goddess Anath (cp. Beth Anath, Judg. 1: 33). It lay within the territory of the tribe of Benjamin and was one of the thirteen cities set aside for the priests in the territories of Judah, Simeon, and Benjamin (Joshua 21: 13-19; 1 Chron. 6: 57-60). In the division of the kingdom, 977, Anathoth remained within the Southern Kingdom. Its modern name is Anata.

19

"In the land of Benjamin." Like Paul, the great Apostle of the New Testament unto Jews and Gentiles, Jeremiah, the Old Testament prophet unto Jews and Gentiles (Jer. 1: 5, 10, 18), was a Benjamite, an heir to the marvelous promise given to his ancestral tribe centuries before (Deut. 33: 12). He was, indeed, beloved of the Lord, dwelling safely with Him, who carried him through all the ups and downs of his arduous career, as a father carries his son on his shoulders.

V. 2. "To whom the Word of the LORD *came.*" This expression is a favorite one with Jeremiah. It means more than that the Word of God was spoken to, and heard by, him. The term connotes an influence exercised, a taking possession of, a placing under obligation. Cp. on this use 1 Sam. 16: 16, 23; 19: 9, 20, 23. In Ezek. 45: 16-17 the phrase is used in the sense of being under obligation: "All the people of the land *shall be under obligation to* this oblation for the prince. And *it shall be the prince's part (obligation)* to give burnt offerings." During all the years of Jeremiah's prophetical activity, the extent of which is described in vv. 2 and 3, he was under obligation to the Word of Jehovah. Every one of these words took hold of him, directing his views, his emotions, his character, his life, his whole self. (Cp. Jer. 15: 15-21; 20: 7-18; 23: 29; Amos 3: 8 b.) This divine Word strengthened and sustained him in the performance of that almost superhuman task imposed upon him by God's call. Though at times the struggle grew very bitter, yet from every battle with his enemies, from every conflict with his own flesh and blood, from every wrestling with his God, he finally issued forth more than a conqueror, because the Word of God possessed him, held him in its strong and loving, persuasive embrace, supplying to him strength, endurance, patience, unceasing faithfulness.

V. 3. "In the days of Josiah . . . fifth month." On the history of the three kings named here, see Introductory Remarks, pages 1—6. Jehoahaz and Jehoiachin are not included in the superscription because of the brevity and relative unimportance of their rule.

"Unto the end of the eleventh year." Zedekiah's eleventh regnal year came to a premature but complete end in its fifth month.

---

2. Jeremiah is Called to Be the Lord's Prophet, Vv. 4-19

A. Disregarding your personal feelings, go where I send you! Vv. 4-10

4 And the word of the LORD came
5 to me, saying: Before I formed you in the womb, I knew you, and before you came forth from the womb, I sanctified you. I ordained you a
6 prophet to the nations. Then I said: Ah, Lord LORD! I have no experience in speaking; for I am only

7 a youth. And the LORD said to me, Do not say: I am a youth; for wherever I send you, you shall go; and whatever I command you, you 8 shall speak. Be not afraid of them, for with you am I to deliver you, 9 is the oracle of the LORD. Then the LORD stretched forth His hand and touched my mouth. And the LORD said to me: Behold I have put My words into your mouth. 10 See, I have appointed you this day over the nations and over the kingdoms to root up and tear down, and to destroy and to throw down, to build and to plant.

Grammatical Notes

V. 5. "Formed thee," "camest forth." The imperfects describe the gradual development. "I knew thee." יָדַע denotes 1) the knowledge gained by experience (cp. Jer. 1:6); 2) a knowledge both affectionate and effective, embracing intellect, emotion, and will (Ex. 33:17; 2 Sam. 7:20; Amos 3:2; Nah. 1:7 of God; Jer. 2:8; 4:22 of man). "I sanctified thee." The root meaning of קָדַשׁ is disputed. Some prefer "to be clean, pure"; others, "to be separated, set apart." This latter seems to agree better with the usage in Hebrew.

V. 5. "Formed thee." On the formation of the embryo see Job 10:8-12; Ps. 139:14-16. "I knew thee." Before God began to form Jeremiah, He knew him, took an interest in him, lovingly considered him. "Sanctified." Because God was interested in Jeremiah, God decided to separate, segregate him, put him in a class into which not all children of men belong. The exact nature of this consecration is stated in the third clause, unconnected by any conjunction: "as a prophet unto, or for, the nations have I given, appointed thee." On this sense of give with double accusative see Gen. 17:5; Ex. 7:1; etc.

"Prophet," nabi. The etymology is disputed. Some regard it as the passive form of a Babylonian-Assyrian root, nibu, "to sweep away," hence, one who is swept away by his emotions, by fanatic frenzy. Others arrive at the same result by deriving it from a root "to bubble up," "to boil over." The prophets, they say, were in a state of ecstasy, variously defined. "The intelligent consciousness retreated, was reduced by a violent (gewaltsam) influence of the divine Spirit to a state of passivity." (Hengstenberg, Christologie, I, 294.) "He [the prophet] might be mingling with the crowd. . . . Suddenly something would happen to him. His eye would become fixed, strange convulsions would seize upon his limbs, the form of his speech would change. Men would recognize that the Spirit had fallen upon him. The fit would pass, and he would tell to those who stood around the things which he had seen and heard." (Theodore Robinson, quoted in Harvard Theological Review, Vol. 38, 1945, p. 4.) "It is clear that this band from Gibeah" (1 Sam. 10:9ff.) "in their involuntary manifestations of orgiastic frenzy, resembled rather a band of dancing and

21

frantic dervishes . . . than that preconceived notion which we moderns have of prophets." (Kittel, *The Religion of the People of Israel,* translated by R. Caryl Micklem, 1925.) These extreme theories have never been generally accepted, though tenaciously held in various forms by many liberals. Its chief support, based on 1 Sam. 19:23-24, does not prove their point. Saul's frenzy was not "prophetic frenzy." The Lord's Spirit had left Saul, surrendering him to the evil spirit (1 Sam. 16:14f.). This spirit incited him to jealousy of David (1 Sam. 18:8-9), to several efforts to kill David (ch. 18:10-29; 19:1-17). When David fled to Samuel at Ramah, Saul three times sent messengers to take David. The Spirit of God caused them to prophesy (ch. 19:18-21). Infuriated at the failure of his plans, Saul came to Ramah with the firm intention to kill David. God showed him that He was stronger than Saul by causing the king also to prophesy. Struggling in frenzied efforts against the power of God, completely under the influence of Satan, Saul tore his clothes in furious anger and remained in this pitiable condition all that day and night, a psychopath rather than a prophet seized by "prophetic frenzy."

We prefer the etymology adopted by Koenig, offered also by Gesenius-Buhl, deriving the word from a root *naba,* נבא, to bring news, to utter, speak; hence, the speaker. With this etymology agrees the definition of a prophet by the Lord in Jer. 1:9; and in Ex. 7:1. Aaron, who was to be Moses' "spokesman," "mouth," by divine direction (Ex. 4:16), is because of this fact called Moses' prophet. So God's prophets are called His "mouth" (1 Kings 8:15; 2 Chron. 6:4, compared with 2 Sam. 7:4 ff., "unto" Nathan; Is. 30:2; Jer. 15:19); or "interpreter" (teacher, A. V., Luther) (Is. 43:27). Reading the records of the activity of God's prophets from the first time this title is used (Gen. 20:7), we must come to the conclusion that God's prophets were not frenzied fanatics, nor deprived of their self-consciousness. The prophets of the Lord retained their consciousness; they knew what they were doing; they voiced their objections (Ex. 3:11; Jer. 20:14-18; Jonah 1:3; 4:1-3, 8), their doubts and fears (Jer. 1:6; 15:10ff.; Hab. 1:2-4, 12ff.), their willingness (Is. 6:8), their joy (Jer. 31:26), their astonishment (Jer. 32:16-27); they asked questions if they did not understand the vision (Zech. 1:19, 21; 4:4, 12-13; 5:6, 10; 6:4), they took an active part (Zech. 3:5), they proclaimed their visions to the people after the vision had passed away (Isaiah 6; Ezek. 11:24-25; cp. 8:1ff.).

While the years of service for the Kohathites were fixed by the Lord from the thirtieth to the fiftieth year (Num. 4:3, 23, 30-35, 47), for Levites in general from the twenty-fifth to the fiftieth year (Num. 8:23-25), later by King David from age twenty to fifty (1 Chron. 23: 24-32), the prophetic office was not limited to any definite number of years. God called the prophets when He pleased and retained them in His service as long as He desired.

To this prophetic office God had appointed Jeremiah before He had formed him in his mother's womb. An artist seeks a suitable piece of marble which he can shape into that object his mind has conceived. God does not need to seek His material, He creates it to suit His purpose. He was determined to have a prophet unto the nations, and with that in mind, He formed and shaped Jeremiah's body and soul. While not changing the manner in which sinful parents beget sinful children, He gave to this child the character, the temperament, the gifts and talents which would qualify him for his high and important office. "A prophet unto the nations," not only to his own comparatively small nation, under vassalage to Egypt, Assyria, Babylon, but to all the nations living at his time, small and great. Compare the list of nations Jer. 25:18-26. And as long as nations shall exist on earth, so long will Jeremiah be the prophet ordained by the Lord unto these nations. He has lessons for our nation and our Church also, lessons as timely and as important today as they were 2,500 years ago. In v. 5 we have the Lord's biography of Jeremiah's life and activity compressed into eleven short words. Note the majestic roll and rhythm of the words, fit raiment for the wonderful content of this remarkable life history; a biography extending from eternity to beyond the end of time; reaching back into the timeless eons before the world began and stretching forward to the time when there shall be no more nations to preach to.

Jeremiah is an intensely human personality, a man whom we can understand and love, and yet a person endowed with such mysterious power from on high that we at times are overawed by his grandeur. Jeremiah, so humanly weak, and yet so divinely firm; his love so humanly tender, and at the same time so divinely holy; his eyes streaming with tears at beholding the affliction about to come upon his people, yet sparkling with fiery indignation against their sins and abominations; his lips overflowing with sympathy for the daughter of Zion, only to pronounce upon her almost in the same breath the judgment and condemnation she so fully deserved. Truly so remarkable and powerful a personality, at the same time so lovable, that we cannot fail to recognize in him an instrument especially chosen and prepared by the God of grace and strength and wisdom.

V. 6. "Ah, Lord LORD!" Alas! Woe is me! a cry of consternation (cp. Joshua 7: 7; Judg. 6: 22; Jer. 4: 10; 32: 17). He shudders at the very thought of becoming a prophet. He feels so unworthy, so incompetent for the office. "I cannot," literally, do not know. The Hebrew word here denotes a knowledge gained by experience (Gen. 30: 29; Deut. 1: 39). "Speak," דַּבֵּר, is used quite commonly of the proclamation of God's message (Ex. 6: 29; Jer. 1: 7; 35: 2), or it implies the ability to speak publicly (Ex. 4: 14). Like Moses, Jeremiah feels that he lacks the necessary qualifications for the work he was to do. "I am a child." The Hebrew term denotes a young person, from the age of infancy (Ex. 2: 6, three months) to the period of manhood, including all who are not yet able to take the full responsibility of a given profession, hence inexperienced (Judg. 8: 20; 1 Sam. 17: 33; 1 Kings 3: 7). It was not customary for youths to speak publicly or in the presence of older men unless asked to do so (Job 12: 12; 32: 4-7; Ecclus. 7: 14; 32: 7-9).

V. 7. The Lord encourages and strengthens the young man. There is no reason why he should be afraid or reluctant to become the Lord's prophet. "You do not have to worry what you shall do, nor be under obligation to choose your own way. Leave that to Me." He is chosen as God's ambassador, and God will map out his paths and his work. "And you need not worry about your inexperience in public speaking. What you shall speak and how you shall speak, is My business. I will attend to that!" What a marvelous promise! What a burden did that lift off the young man's shoulders! We hear no further word of protest or uncertainty from Jeremiah. He is willing to go and speak at the Lord's behest. But the Lord deals fairly with His ambassador. Before sending him out, He tells Jeremiah of the trials awaiting him and promises deliverance.

V. 8. "Be not afraid of their faces." There will not be smooth sailing at all times. There will be opposition, fiercest antagonism, such as might cause your heart to tremble with fear. Yet be unafraid. They that oppose you are men; while "with thee," at thy side, "I," Jehovah, the unchanging God and Ruler of the world. I am with you, not to preserve you from all trials, but "to deliver you," liberate you, saith the Lord, your Covenant God, on whom you can rely, whose word you may trust. This promise is repeated with a slight, but very effective, change in v. 19, and in ch. 15: 20.

V. 9. As Isaiah felt the touch of the glowing coal on his lips and heard the voice of the seraphim (Is. 6: 6-7), so here Jeremiah saw the

Lord put forth His hand; he felt the touch of the Lord's hand upon his mouth and heard the word of the Lord speaking. "Touched," caused to touch. The Hiphil (as in Is. 6:7) stresses the purposiveness, the deliberateness of the act, the meaning of which is at once explained to the prophet. "Behold, I have put My words in thy mouth." The perfect describes the putting of the word as a completed act, the action is "presented in a condition of rest," no matter how often it may be repeated. Throughout your lifetime I put My words in your mouth. From your mouth shall issue the words that I have placed in them. How useless therefore to worry about his inexperience! How useless to fear his opponents! Resisting Jeremiah's word, they resist Jehovah's Word, Jehovah Himself, who is with Jeremiah and causes him to speak what God wants His audience to be told, no more, no less. Jeremiah's prophetic activity is comprehended in this symbolic act of dedication and consecration. The exact manner in which the Lord here appeared, whether it was the Son of God who had assumed some visible form, as Calov and others regard possible without definitely deciding the question, we do not know nor need we know.

God's prophets in Israel certainly were not unemotional beings, without any will or feeling of their own, like mechanical automatons or phonographic records. Moses rebels against God's will; Isaiah at once offers himself to the Lord: Here I am, send me, send me; he goes willingly. Jeremiah must fight down his own reluctance before he wholeheartedly accepts the call extended to him. But in each case God creates the willingness to serve Him before He actually sends them as His messengers. God does not want unwilling servants in His kingdom. And yet God demands unconditional surrender to His will; and works that by His Word, by removing the fears, the doubts, the objections, and persuading, convincing, convicting the man called, willingly to go wherever the Lord sends him, to speak whatever the Lord tells him.

V. 10. "I have set thee." The Hebrew term means to seek, visit, inspect, supervise; the Hiphil is causative, to make one an inspector. The *Bible Commentary* (p. 329) makes this pertinent comment: "God's dealings may be viewed either from above or from below (Phil. 2:12-13). Viewed from God's side, the prophet is a mere messenger, speaking what he is told, doing what he is bid. From man's side, he is God's viceregent, with power 'to root out and to pull down.'" God is the Ruler of the universe; He it is that shapes the destinies of the nations, and He appoints Jeremiah as His representative on earth, places him, the young man, "over the nations and over the kingdoms." He is placed over them for a twofold purpose, that of destruction and that of construction. The destruction of the proud nations must come first; their self-satisfaction, their pride, their opposition to the true God, must be utterly destroyed before really constructive work can be begun. The destruction is described by four words, each describing destruction from a different viewpoint, the sum total bringing out very vividly the idea of complete ruin. "Root out," "to uproot," like a noxious weed is uprooted and thrown on the compost pile; "pull down," to tear down, break down; "destroy," to cause to be ruined, hopelessly lost, as a harvest is ruined by locusts (Joel 1:11); a plant by a worm (Jonah 4:10); "throw down," as a wall (Ezek. 13:14), a tower (Ezek. 26:4), closely approximating "pull down." Four words are used, because the prophecies threatening destruction far outnumber those promising construction, which is described by only two terms: to build, namely, what was torn down; and to plant. These two words express the exact opposite of the first two; the second pair having been added for the sake of emphasizing total destruction. Destruction, complete and thorough, precedes construction.

The kings and rulers, the nations and empires, boast of their prowess and sovereignty. Cf. Is. 10:13-14; 36:15ff.; Ps. 2:1-3. Yet it is God and His prophet who rule them, who decide their destiny, who destroy if it is His will, who build when His time has come. Cp. Jer. 25:13-38; ch. 46—51. See also ch. 18 (potter and clay) and the many dire threats and numerous gracious promises concerning Judah and Jerusalem.

B. Complete destruction! Vv. 11-16

11 The word of the LORD came to me, saying: What do you see, Jeremiah? And I said: I am seeing an
12 almond branch. Then the LORD said to me: You have seen aright, for I am watching over My word
13 to do it. And the word of the LORD came to me a second time, saying: What do you see? And I said: I am seeing a pot blown upon, and its face is from the north.
14 Then the LORD said to me: Out of the north shall be released the evil upon all inhabitants of the land.

15 For, behold, I am ready to call all the families, the kingdoms of the north, is the oracle of the LORD; and they shall come, and every one shall place his throne at the entrance of the gates of Jerusalem and on all her walls round about and upon all the cities of Judah.
16 And I will pronounce My judgments upon them for all their wickedness, because they have forsaken Me and have sacrificed to other gods and have worshiped the works of their hands.

Grammatical Notes

V. 11. "Rod of an almond tree," מַקֵּל שָׁקֵד. מַקֵּל does not merely designate a rod (for punishment) or a staff (for traveling). It is used also in the sense of branch or bough (cp. Gen. 30:37–39). "Almond tree," the root meaning of שָׁקֵד is "to be awake, watchful, alert" (cp. Ps. 127:1; Jer. 31:28; 44:27). It denotes the almond (Gen. 43:11; Num. 17:8; Eccl. 12:5). The almond tree was called by this name because it was the first shrub to awake from its winter sleep, putting forth its pink flowers while its leaves were not yet unfolded. It flowered in January and matured its fruit in March, thus serving as "a very expressive emblem of wakefulness and activity" (*Bible Commentary*). Luther translates: "ein wackerer Stab," a watchful, alert staff; Volz: "ein Zweig vom wachen Baum," a bough from the wakeful tree, or the tree awake.

V. 16. Burn incense, קִטֵּר, the Piel always used of illegitimate sacrifices by Gentiles or Jews.

V. 11. "What seest thou?" See Grammatical Notes. It will be difficult to decide whether God showed the almond branch (v. 11) and the seething caldron (v. 13) to His prophet in a vision, or whether Jeremiah saw them at some place. At any rate, the Lord's purpose in calling the attention of the prophet to these objects was to convey an important revelation to him.

V. 12. As it was the Lord who had caused Jeremiah to see the almond branch, so it was the Lord who interpreted this vision to the prophet. "I will hasten," literally, waking am I; watchfully ready. That is characteristic of Me, I watch over My Word to do it, to fulfill it. The Lord expressly assures Jeremiah of this fact by a special vision in order to give His prophet that unflinching courage which only divinely engendered certainty of the truthfulness and unfailing fulfillment of one's proclamation can create. No preacher should ever forget that he is the messenger of Him who watches over His Word; who will suffer no promise to fall to the ground, who will with equal wakefulness watch over the fulfillment of His threats. A Christian preacher is an ambassador of the Lord.

V. 13. "Pot," a vessel, kettle, caldron, used as a receptacle for ashes (Ex. 27:3), as a washbasin (Ps. 60:10; A. V., v. 8), for boiling (2 Kings 4:38ff.; Ezek. 11:3, 7, 11). "Seething," literally, blown upon. The prophet sees a caldron, "the face thereof," its open side, "toward the north," rather "from the north," see v. 15; ch. 23:8. It is tilted toward the south, and as the wood is gradually consumed by the fire blown to fierce intensity with a bellows, it tilts farther and farther until it finally is overturned and its boiling, death-dealing waters pour out over the land. The Lord Himself explains the vision.

27

V. 14. "Out of the north an evil shall break forth," be opened, and destroy the whole land as seething water kills all it overflows. Though Babylon lay due east, yet all Babylonian and Assyrian invasions came from the north via the "Fertile Crescent." The city of Jerusalem could be attacked successfully only from the north, as the west, south, and east sides were rendered practically impregnable by the deep valleys of Hinnom and Kidron.

The prophet is not told who this enemy is. At the time of his call, Assyria was still the world power, and while signs of decadence were in evidence, the empire had in its long history repeatedly manifested a remarkable power of rejuvenation, and Isaiah's prophecy of a deportation to Babylon (Is. 39: 6-7) did not specify whether the ruler of Babylon would be an Assyrian, a Babylonian, or a member of some other nation. In the fourth year of Jehoiakim, 606, Nebuchadnezzar is named for the first time as the conqueror of Jerusalem (Jer. 25: 9-12).

In vv. 15-16 the prophet is given a panoramic view of the world events during the next four decades, the outpouring of the seething waters of God's wrath upon the apostate nation of Judah. In vivid, lifelike colors the prophet portrays the chief actors in one of the great crises in the history of the world and of the Church of God. We see the enemy from the north, as yet unnamed; we see Judah and Jerusalem, the object of his attack; we see Jeremiah, the prophet, his activity, the opposition he must endure. And over and above all we see the Lord God of Hosts directing the history of His world and His Church according to His wise and just and gracious will.

V. 15. "Families," tribes, denotes the genealogical groups; the "kingdoms" the political divisions of the vast world empire in the north. Savage hordes, semicivilized peoples, highly cultured nations, all are united in that vast army marching against Judah and Jerusalem. Every one of these nations sets his throne "at the entering of the gates." The city gates naturally held an important part in the defense of the city. For this purpose they were strongly fortified and usually flanked by massive towers of stone. The gates proper were constructed of heavy timbers, usually covered with metal and closed with locks and heavy metal bars (Deut. 3: 5; Jer. 51: 30; Lam. 2: 9; Neh. 3: 3, 6, 13-15). The gateways were usually very spacious. At Gezer the northern passageway was forty feet wide; the southern, forty-two feet long, nine feet wide. These large spaces are called "broad places" in A. V., squares, courts. This term denotes also the wide places in other parts of the city (Deut. 13:16; 2 Sam. 21:12; Jer. 5:1; 9:20, etc.), similar to our "courts," "squares," small "parks." In these squares young and old congregated for social entertainment and play (Zech. 8:4-5); travelers found a night's lodging (Gen. 19:2; Judg. 19:15, 17, 20); people met for hearing or telling news (2 Sam. 3:27; 15:2; 18:4, 24); for public assemblies (Prov. 1:20); for judicial sessions (Deut. 17:5; 21:19; Ruth 4:1); for buying and selling (2 Kings 7:1). At the entering of these gates and "against," rather, "upon," all the walls of Jerusalem and all the cities of Judah the enemies "shall set every one his throne"; symbolic language, denoting their purpose to establish and manifest their authority over these cities, to exercise judgment upon this rebellious country that had dared to revolt against its sovereign to whom it had solemnly pledged loyalty. On the use of "throne" in the sense of judgment throne cp. Neh. 3:7; Ps. 9:4; 122:5; Prov. 20:8; Is. 16:5. These nations march at the command of a human emperor whose purpose is chiefly political, the firm establishment of his sovereignty, the merciless throttling of all opposition. The prophet sees more than a campaign of one nation against another, of man against man, of Gentile against Jew. He can see what God alone sees, the plans and purposes of the Lord of the universe, as they slowly but surely develop in the events of history, which often seem only chaos to the minds of men. It is the Lord that is calling these nations to carry out His will. Already in the year of Jeremiah's call, forty years before the final judgment, He is calling the families of the earth, He is shaping the course of history, of individual nations, of individual persons, so that His will may be done in due time.

V. 16. "I will utter My judgments." As Keil observes, this phrase is peculiar to Jeremiah (cp. ch. 4:12; 12:1; 39:5; 52:9). It occurs in only one more passage (2 Kings 25:6). It includes the entire judicial proceedings, from the indictment to the execution of the final judgment. The Lord is the supreme Judge, who is at the same time the testifying Witness, the prosecuting Attorney, the Executor of His judgment. He it is who institutes, conducts, and carries into effect the legal proceedings. The enemies from the north wreaking their vengeance upon Judah are merely pawns in His hands. Now He calls them to be His associate or assisting judges, using their passion and bloodthirsty cruelty as instruments of His justice, to execute His verdict. In this manner the just Judge punishes "their wickedness," Judah's evil. They bring evil (v. 14) upon Judah because of the evil

29

committed by Judah. "They have forsaken Me." That is the wickedness of which Judah has become guilty. All their apostasies throughout the centuries are comprised in that one word, the perfect tense. "They have burned . . . and worshiped"; two imperfects denote the ever repeated acts as the consequence of their apostasy. "Burn incense," see Grammatical Notes. Here used of illegitimate sacrifice by Gentiles or Jews. Israel, the nation to whom God had revealed Himself in so marvelous a manner, whom He had chosen as His own people, runs away from their God, casts Him off. And having forsaken the Lord, they sink deeper and deeper into sin and superstition. (Cp. Rom. 1:21-32.)

C. Let no opposition deter you! I am with you! Vv. 17-19

17 And you! Gird your loins, and so arise and speak to them all that I will command you. Do not be dismayed before them, lest I dismay 18 you before them. And I — behold, today I establish you as a fortified city and as an iron pillar and as walls of bronze against the whole land, against the kings of Judah and its princes and its priests and 19 against the common people. And they shall fight against you, but they shall not overcome you; for with you am I, is the oracle of the LORD, to deliver you!

V. 17. Three of the outstanding figures in the history of Judah during the next four decades have been introduced: Judah, the northern enemy, the Lord. Now a fourth appears, Jeremiah. "And thou, gird up thy loins." The girdle was used to fasten the undergarment (a close-fitting shirt reaching to the knees) to the body; also to draw up the upper garment so that it would not be in the way while walking or working. On the girdle the sword was fastened (Judg. 3:16; 2 Sam. 20:8). A strong and well-fastened girdle was an essential necessity to the soldier (1 Kings 2:5; Is. 5:27). The girdle, therefore, "was a symbol of preparation and implied also firm purpose and some degree of alacrity" (*Bible Commentary*), and to gird oneself signified getting ready for work (Prov. 31:17; Luke 17:8), or for debate (Job 38:3; 40:7), or for battle (1 Sam. 25:13; Is. 8:9). Whether it was for the work of preaching; or the wearying, nerve-straining argumentation with his opponents, who were always ready to challenge him with questions and who were masters at twisting words and employing sophistries or hurling stinging calumnies, scurvy charges at him; or the actual suffering of persecution, hunger, thirst, imprisonment — Jeremiah is to be ready, prepared for anything that might happen. Such readiness, such constant preparedness was essential for his life's work, which is now described in two short words: Stand! Speak! Against all opposition he is to stand calm and fearless, firm and steadfast. And unmoved by flattery or bitter enmity, he is to speak whatever God commands him. He is not to suppress one single threat, no matter what a storm of outraged protest or fierce persecution it might provoke. He is not to omit or qualify a single promise, no matter how inopportune it might seem to the prophet, no matter how unworthy the hearers might be; and if it seems like casting pearls before the swine, speak what I tell you, and speak it as I tell you!

"Be not dismayed at their faces." "Dismayed," literally, to be downcast, broken, to tremble with fear. The prophet is never to permit himself to break down before his audience, never to show any signs of fear, nor let his fear of the people induce him to change any one word of the Lord's message. Such breaking down would be a very serious matter and of disastrous consequences for his person and his office. "Lest I confound thee," cause thee to break down. If the prophet breaks down at seeing the faces before him distorted with rage and fury, at hearing their angry shouts, at seeing their hands stretched out to grasp him, to murder him, then God will cause him to break down utterly and completely! The Lord makes stern demands on His prophet and threatens dire punishments to him if he will not measure up to these demands. He is no respecter of persons. The unchanging Lord remains the Lord of unalterable holiness also when dealing with His prophets. If the fear of men's threats or the love of men's flattery causes them to add or detract from His holy Word, He will cause them to be filled with fear, to change more and more of His words, to sink deeper into sin, become the more unworthy of their office, be disavowed by the Lord. "Das ist der Fluch der boesen Tat, dass sie fortzeugend immer Boeses muss gebaeren!" That is the curse pronounced by the unchanging Lord upon all prophets who shirk to do their full duty.

The Lord does not demand too much of His messenger. He will supply to His prophet all that is necessary to do his duty. He asks much, and gives more.

V. 18. "I have made thee this day." God does not only begin to establish Jeremiah, but at this very moment He completely equips him for his office. "A fenced city." The Hebrew term denotes something inaccessible, as a well-fortified, impregnable city (cp. Jer. 5:17; 8:14), against which even great multitudes battle in vain. "And

31

an iron pillar," standing firm and unmovable in storm and tempest. "And brazen walls." "Brass" in ancient times was an alloy of copper and tin, bronze, not, like the modern brass, an alloy of copper and zinc. It was the toughest metal known to the ancients. The plural pictures vividly the impossibility of overthrowing him. Even if one wall has fallen, there are others just as strong, exhausting the strength of the enemy. Jeremiah shall be walls not of wood, to which fire can be applied; nor of stone, which could be battered down; but of solid brass, against which all weapons of ancient days were ineffective. Picture a wall of ten to twelve feet of brass, backed up by other walls of equal strength, and you will understand the problem confronting the enemy, Satan, and his allies, endeavoring to overthrow Jeremiah, the one man.

"Against the whole land." Even if the whole nation storms and rages against you, you shall stand firm and fast against all their attacks. The Lord enumerates the various classes constituting "the whole land." 1) "The kings of Judah," the sons of Josiah, who, unlike their father, were notoriously wicked, are named first as the opponents of Jeremiah. — 2) "The princes," called *sarim*," appear in the history of Israel first as civic officers, judges, chosen by Moses on the advice of his father-in-law to assist him (Ex. 18:13-26). Perhaps these men also became the military commanders in time of war, or else the system was adopted by Moses also in organizing the military forces (Deut. 20:9). In the time of the Judges we find *sarim* as officials in cities (Judg. 8:6; 9:30) and tribes (ch. 5:15). So in the time of the kings (1 Kings 22:26; 2 Kings 23:8), where we meet also *sarim* of provinces (1 Kings 20:14, 19). Solomon chose eleven *sarim*, civic, military, and religious officials, most likely for mutual consultation and planning (1 Kings 4:2-6). These princes gradually gained more power and influence, at times an evil influence (cp. 2 Chron. 24:17-23). Hezekiah seems to have taken no important action without prior consultation with the *sarim* and their full co-operation (cp. 2 Chron. 30:2, 6; 31:8; 32:3). Josiah also had *sarim* as his advisers (2 Chron. 35:8). In the early days of Jehoiakim the *sarim* were still men who had been trained by Josiah to put loyalty to the Lord and His Word above all other considerations. They refused to take sides with the priests and prophets who, like Jehoiakim, were bitter opponents of Jeremiah. When they had charged the prophet with treasonable action, the princes defended Jeremiah and succeeded in persuading the people to liberate him (Jer. 26:1-24). When Jehoiakim's son and successor,

Jehoiachin, was deported to Babylon, all the *sarim,* together with all the better class of people, were taken to Babylon, and only "the poorest sort of people" were left in the land (2 Kings 24:12-16), the rabble, the underworld characters, the dregs of society, so corrupt that the Searcher of hearts compares them to rotten, worthless figs (Jer. 24:8-10). These parvenus, taking over the offices and homes of the deported citizens, made use of every means to enrich themselves and, while boldly and outrageously transgressing every law of God, still proudly regarded themselves as God's people and their city and Temple as God's habitation and a guarantee of their political security. They were the inveterate enemies of Jeremiah and sought every possible means to make life miserable for the aged loyal spokesman of God. — 3) A third class are the priests, the religious leaders of the people (cp. Jer. 20:1-4; 26:7-9). — 4) "The people of the land," the common people blindly following their fanatical leaders.

V. 19. The Lord does not deceive His prophet, He tells him that the future history of his life is that of an uninterrupted warfare (the perfect). Yet this dreary outlook need not discourage the prophet. "They shall not prevail against thee!" Every effort to stop you, to silence you, to overcome you, will fail! "For with you — I!" They — you — I. They, no matter how numerous, how powerful, how cunning, how bloodthirsty, they fight without Me. You, weak and frail and seemingly alone, yet with you — I. A fortified city might be stormed, an iron pillar might be smashed, even brazen walls might be broken down. But I am with you, the great I AM THAT I AM, the Invincible Lord, with you! That is "the oracle of the LORD," sure, reliable, trustworthy! "To deliver thee!" While the order of the words in v. 8 emphasized "the LORD," here the last word is "to deliver thee," a word of comfort and of strength. On the part of man, incessant enmity, battle, warfare; on the Lord's part, ever-repeated deliverance! What a remarkable life history do these brief words reveal! "To deliver thee!" Let that word sound in your ear continually! Just as in the Aaronic blessing the last word of the Lord to the Israelite returning to his daily task was "Peace!" (Num. 6:26), so here the assurance of deliverance and final peace is the last word, the farewell, the good-by of the Lord as He sends His chosen prophet forth to his mission.

II. Israel Must Repent of Its Apostasy, Ch. 2:1—3:5

CHAPTER 2

1. God's Loving-Kindness and Israel's Sin, Vv. 1-8

1. 2 The word of the LORD came to me, saying: Go and proclaim in the hearing of Jerusalem, saying: Thus says the LORD, I recall your youthful affection, your bridal love, how you followed Me in the desert, in
3 an unsown land. Israel was holiness to the LORD, the first fruit of His harvest; all that devoured him were held guilty; evil came to them,
4 is the oracle of the LORD. Hear the word of the LORD, O house of Jacob, and all the families of the
5 house of Israel! Thus says the Lord: What perverseness have your fathers found in Me that they departed far from Me and followed
6 vanity and became vanity? And they did not say: Where is the LORD that has brought us up out of the land of Egypt, that led us through the desert, through a land of steppes and pits, through a land of drought and shadow of death, through a land through which no man travels, where no human being
7 lives? I brought you to a garden land to eat its fruit and its good things, and then you went and defiled My land, and changed My
8 heritage into an abomination. The priests asked not: Where is the LORD? Those who handled the Law cared nothing about Me; the shepherds rebelled against Me, and the prophets prophesied by Baal and followed things that were unprofitable.

Grammatical Notes

V. 2. "I remember thee"; לָךְ is dative commodi, for your sakes, in your interest (Neh. 5:19; 12:22).

Vv. 1-2a (A. V.). "Moreover . . . Jerusalem." Jeremiah did not run without being sent (Jer. 23:21; 1:7). — There can hardly be any doubt that ch. 2—3:5 is a digest of his first message or messages to the people of Jerusalem. He reminds his people of their first love (ch. 2:2), of the faithfulness with which the Lord of the Covenant has fulfilled His promises (vv. 3-7a), calls attention to the shameful ingratitude of Judah, and tells them that the Covenant God, the Lord of infinite love, is also the God of unchanging justice and holiness who will fulfill the conditions of His covenant even if the people have broken it (ch. 2:7b—3:5; cp. Ex. 20:5; 34:7; Deuteronomy 28). Therefore, "Turn!" (Ch. 3:1, last clause.)

V. 2b. In words of divine love and exquisite beauty the Lord invites Judah and Jerusalem to return to Him. "The kindness," *chesed*, occurs some 245 times and denotes tender, kind, merciful, condescending love on the part of God toward man; on the part of man to man, that loving-kindness clinging to its object with tender affection and mercy in complete self-forgetfulness, as the loving bride clings to her beloved bridegroom.

"The kindness of thy youth, the love of thy espousal," might be understood of God's loving-kindness and affection for His youthful bride. So the Vulgate and a number of commentators. Yet the third item, "thy walking after Me," refers to Israel's faith and obedience, and therefore it is better to regard the love and affection as Israel's love toward God. The state of betrothal comprises the period from the deliverance out of Egypt to the establishment of the Sinaitic Covenant (Exodus 3—24). God Himself commends the love and loyalty of His people at this time (cp. Deut. 5:28-29). When Moses came to Israel in bondage, they believed and worshiped the Lord (Ex. 4:29-31; cp. also Ex. 12:22-28, 34-41, 50-51; 14:9-22; 19:8-25; 24:1-18). While at times Israel voiced complaints (Ex. 14:11ff.; 15:24; 16:2ff.; 17:2ff.), yet these complaints were due to weakness of faith rather than to apostasy, and the Lord sent immediate help. See also Hos. 2:15b; 9:10. The first apostasy of Israel occurred after the establishment of the Covenant (Ex. 32:1ff.) and was immediately followed by the Lord's threat of annihilation, averted only by the intercession of Moses (Ex. 32:7—34:10; cp. Num. 11:1-35; 14:1-45).

Therefore we translate: I remember for thy sake thy youthful affection, thy bridal love, thy following Me into the barren wilderness, where there were no visible means of support. Their trust was not in vain. Like a faithful bridegroom He watched zealously over His beloved and loving bride.

V. 3. "Israel was holiness unto the LORD." This term here is used in the peculiar ritual sense of Num. 18:8-19, 26-29, according to which certain offerings were called "holiness," "hallowed things," because they were to be separated from common use, reserved for the Lord, for the sustenance of the priests (cp. Lev. 22:16). One of these holy things were the first fruits of Israel's products (cp. Lev. 23:9-21; Num. 15:17-21). God had declared Israel to be a holy nation (Ex. 19:5-6; Deut. 7:6; 14:2; 26:19). He had called Israel His first-born (Ex. 4:22; cp. Jer. 31:9). Therefore Israel was to enjoy the privileges of the holy things of the first fruits, the special protection of the Lord, who would punish all that dared to "devour" His people. "Evil shall come upon them." (See Exodus 7—14; 17:8-15; Numbers 31.)

Vv. 4-5. This speech is addressed "to the entire people of Israel of all times and places, to all those whose common ancestors had become guilty of the sins reproved in the following verses and had bequeathed this guilt to their descendants" (Naegelsbach in loc.).

"What iniquity have ye found in Me?" "God judges not as a judge, but advances an apology as though He were accountable" (Theodoret). (Cp. Is. 5:3-4; Micah 6:3.) Surely the Lord was not to blame for the sins and apostasy of which Israel became guilty. Even a thorough search would fail to find any fault in Him who is without perverseness (Deut. 32:4). Hence there was not the slightest justification for their complete apostasy from their Lord. Neither did the nature of the gods chosen by them in preference to the Lord, nor any advantage gained by their turning away from the Lord, justify their apostasy. They walked after "vanity," literally, breath, symbol of evanescence, impotence, incompetence. This is one of Jeremiah's favorite titles for idols. Their idols had no existence of their own (1 Cor. 8:4; 10:19); they are fictions, creations of their own mind (Deut. 32:16-17, 21). Therefore, instead of being profited by their change to idols, they are harmed. Their choice of vanities resulted in their becoming like their gods, worthless, unable to help themselves and others from sinking deeper into sin and shame and ruin.

V. 6 adds another fact for which the Lord is not responsible, the black ingratitude of Israel. They did not say: "Where is the LORD?" etc. They did not seek the Lord in their distress nor in their days of prosperity. The very form in which the question is cast by the prophet shows the wickedness and ingratitude of forgetting Jehovah. He had brought them up out of Egypt and led them through the "wilderness." The Hebrew term may designate an actual desert, waterless, uninhabited, arid; or a steppe, suitable for pasture land, a prairie. The wilderness is therefore further described as a land of "deserts," a waterless region; of "pits," full of fissures, rents, precipitous gulleys, making travel dangerous; a land that is "drought," an arid land offering neither drink nor food and therefore very appropriately called a land of the shadow of death, where death lurks on every side. To lead a whole nation (Ex. 12:37) through the wilderness and sustain them for forty years is so stupendous a task that Fosdick calls it "an appalling strain upon credulity" and believes "that something is seriously the matter with the Biblical figures" (*A Pilgrimage to Palestine,* p. 66). Yet the Lord did it, and did it in a miraculous manner (Deut. 8:4, 14-16; 29:5-6).

V. 7. He had brought them into "a plentiful country," a *"karmel,"* a garden, a park, whose fruits and goodness (cp. Deut. 7:13; 8:7-13) they had now enjoyed for many centuries. In black ingratitude they defiled what God calls "My land," and "My heritage," My own. Here they lived in the same sins and unnatural vices for which the heathen were spewn out of the land (Lev. 18: 24-29). And the Lord has in mind here not merely such atrocious transgressions. He regards the very fact that they despised His Law as a defilement and desecration of His land.

V. 8. The defiling of God's land was caused primarily by the spiritual leaders of the nation. Four classes are named: 1) the priests, who were the divinely appointed teachers of the people (Lev. 10:11) and for this purpose were to seek the Law at the Lord's mouth (Mal. 2: 7). They did not ask: Where is the Lord? but changed the Law at will. 2) Those who handle the Law, either the teaching Levites (2 Chron. 17: 7-9; 35:3) or some other students of the Law, perhaps the forerunners of the scribes. They knew not the Lord, were blind leaders of the blind. 3) The pastors, shepherds, perhaps the kings and rulers, who were to be not merely civic leaders, but were to shepherd the flock of God, watch over the worship and cult, and keep its sacred character inviolate against idolatrous practice (Deut. 17: 18-20; Joshua 1: 7-8). 4) The prophets, who were to be the spokesmen of God, but prophesied by Baal and followed the idols that were of no help or profit to the people.

2. God's Judgment upon the Ungrateful Nation, Vv. 9-19

9 Therefore I am again indicting you, is the oracle of the LORD, and I am continuing to indict the children of
10 your children's children. For pass over to the coastlands of Cyprus and see, and send to Kedar and observe closely and see whether anything like this ever has oc-
11 curred. Has a nation changed its gods? And they are not gods! Yet My people has changed its Glory
12 for a useless thing! Be amazed, O heavens, at this, and shudder! Be utterly dried up! is the oracle
13 of the LORD. For My people commit a twofold wickedness; Me they forsake, the Fountain of living waters, in order to hew for themselves cisterns, broken cisterns
14 which cannot hold water. Is Israel a slave? or a home-born servant? Why then has he fallen a prey?
15 Against him roar young lions, they have lifted up their voice. They make his land desolate; his cities they destroy and leave without in-
16 habitant. Also the sons of Memphis and Tahpanhes shall pasture clean
17 the crown of your head. But have you not brought this upon yourself by forsaking the LORD your God at the time He was your Leader in
18 the way? And now, why do you choose the way to Egypt to drink the waters of Shichor? And why do you choose the way to Assyria to drink the waters of the River?
19 Your own wickedness will teach you, and your apostasy will convict you, and you will realize and see how bad and bitter it is to forsake the Lord, your God, and not to make My fear a matter of your concern, is the oracle of the Lord, the LORD of Hosts.

Grammatical Notes

V. 9. "Plead with you." רִיב, to quarrel, to institute a suit, used very frequently of disputes between God and man, either of God calling man to account and listing His charges against the sinner, or of man quarreling with God.

V. 10. "If there be," הֵן, "behold," is sometimes used in the conditional sense, e. g., Ex. 4:1; Jer. 3:1, but never as an interrogative. Kittel, Bibl. Hebr., therefore suggests to read הֲנִהְיָ֖תָה Niphal of היה, which occurs quite frequently in the sense of "to be brought about, to be done," with the interrogative הֲ. This reading necessitates no change of the consonants and is therefore acceptable, particularly since v. 11 begins with the same interrogative.

V. 9. Here God is the plaintiff about to set forth His accusation, and He is at the same time the Judge with whom to accuse is to condemn and from whose condemnation there is no escape (cp. ch. 1:16). For centuries He has striven with them; and He will continue to strive with the children's children, because they will continue in their rebellion.

Vv. 10-11. "For pass over the isles. . . ." Judah degrades herself below the Gentiles she so despised. Neither the isles of the Chittim, originally Kition on Cyprus, from where the Chittim settled on the islands and coasts of the Mediterranean Sea, west of Palestine, nor the land of Kedar in the Syrian-Arabian desert in the East, change their gods. Go to the west or to the east, and you will not find any people that does what Judah does!

V. 12. Judah's sin is so horrible that in a remarkable personification the very heavens are called upon to "be astonished," show their stupefaction; they are to "be horribly afraid," to shudder, their hairs are to stand on end. "Be very desolate" may mean either to be ruined, withered away, as sudden and great fright causes one to wither away; or it may mean to become dry, lose their moisture, i. e., wither away (cp. Ps. 102:26), wax old.

V. 13. "Two evils." The first, they have forsaken the living Fountain; the second, they have done that for the purpose of digging in its stead broken cisterns. On "Fountain of living water" cp. Ps. 36:9; Prov. 10:11; 13:14; 16:22; Is. 55:1; John 4:10-14; 7:37-39; Zech. 13:1. The eternal Fountainhead of life is God, the Lord, who makes His Son the Fountainhead of everlasting life for all sinners. What a wicked thing to leave this Fountain and to imagine that man can produce something better! What wicked folly to labor hard and long, to hew out of solid rock cisterns which at best can furnish only the stale water collected from dirty roofs or from the dusty soil and in the time of

38

drought soon are emptied! And every one of these man-made cisterns made in proud and wicked defiance of God's fountain, is a broken one, its walls full of fissures and cracks, through which all of the water (the Hebrew has the article!) they contain seeps away and leaves the digger of the cistern waterless when he needs water most. It is not only the height of folly, it is supreme wickedness, when man, the tiny creature, the lost sinner, endeavors to work out his own salvation and rejects the free grace of God in Christ Jesus.

V. 14. "A home-born slave" was one born in the household by slave parents, born unto slavery. Slaves, even in Israel, were under bondage and often shamefully treated. Was Israel such a slave? No! Israel was holiness to the Lord (v. 3), the beloved bride of the heavenly Bridegroom (v. 1)! Why, then, has Israel become a spoils to the nations? The extent of her spoliation is described in the verses following.

V. 15. "The young lion," in youthful strength and vigor, is here used figuratively to denote the enemies, particularly the Assyrians, attacking the Northern Kingdom (2 Kings 15:19-29; 17:4-26) and Judah (2 Kings 18:19; 2 Chron. 33:11; Is. 10:28-32).

V. 16. Egypt also would add to the ruin of Judah. *"Noph"* (Is. 19:13; Jer. 2:16; 44:1; 46:14, 19; Ezek. 30:13, 16), spelled *Moph* (Hos. 9:6), is Memphis, the ancient capital of lower Egypt. Its ruins are situated twenty-five to thirty miles south of Cairo. The kings of Memphis were the pyramid builders. "Tahpanhes," LXX: *Taphanai,* Greek: *Daphne,* now: Tell el Defenneh, a fortress southwest of Pelusium near the northeast boundary of Egypt. Both cities were ancient capitals. "Have broken," rather shall depasture. "The crown of thy head," the pate, the uppermost part of the head, symbolic of greatest glory. Judah's head was the king, and Josiah was one of the noblest of kings (cp. 2 Kings 23:25). Quite evidently, this is a reference to Josiah's premature death by the hand of the Egyptian Pharaoh (2 Kings 23:29).

V. 17. Judah has only herself to blame for her destruction. The people had left the way pointed out to them by the divinely sent messengers (cp. Jer. 6:16; 7:23; 32:39). On this way the Lord was willing to lead them, yet they had refused to walk on it.

V. 18. Shichor, the name of various canals and arms of the Nile Delta; here, the Nile. To drink water is, like "to eat bread" with a person, a symbolism of practicing fellowship, entering into alliances, adopting the ways and customs and vices of foreign countries. Judah left her loving Bridegroom and sought the love and friendship of paramours. What was greater, Judah's wickedness or Judah's folly?

V. 19. "Correct," teach, chastise; "reprove," judge, reprimand, chastise. Since you will not listen to the Lord and His prophets, you will have to learn the hard way. Sin and apostasy is a harsh schoolmaster, a stern judge, knowing no pity, showing no mercy. Having chosen sin as their teacher, its pupils make ever greater and ever faster progress in forsaking the Lord, in rooting out of their heart the fear of the Lord. And the final lesson? Deut. 28:15-68; James 1:14-15; Rom. 6:21, 23. Surely a bad and bitter thing the graduate of sin's school will receive as the reward of his diligence in following the precepts of his teacher.

---

3. Israel's Idol Worship, Vv. 20-37

A. Its universality and incurableness, vv. 20-22

20 For from ancient times I have broken your yoke and removed your bonds; and you said: I will not serve! For on every high hill and under every green tree you lay

21 down and played the harlot. Yet I Myself planted you as a noble vine, of perfectly pure seed. How, then, have you changed to base

22 shoots of a wild vine? Even if you would wash yourself with niter and would take for yourself much lye, your iniquity stands before Me in deeply engraved letters, is the oracle of the Lord Jehovah.

Grammatical Notes

V. 20. שָׁבַרְתִּי. The A. V., "I have broken"; Luther, thou hast broken, following LXX and Vulgate. Quite frequently the second person feminine ends in תִּי instead of תְּ, particularly in Jeremiah and Ezekiel. Naegelsbach lists Jer. 2:33; 3:4,5; 4:19; 22:23; 31:21; 46:11; Ezek. 16:18, 20, 22, 31, 36, 43, 44, 47, 51, etc.; Micah 4:13; Ruth 3:3, 4. In our passage and Micah 4:13 both K'tib and Q'ri demand the first person singular.

V. 20 proves the wickedness of Judah's apostasy. It is blackest ingratitude. In response to God's ever-repeated deliverance they kept on saying: I will not serve! They may not always have voiced their disobedience, but their actions spoke louder than words. "Every high hill," etc. Under the shade of the green trees surrounding the idol altars erected on the high hills (1 Kings 14:23; 2 Kings 16:4; Jer. 3:6,13) they practiced spiritual adultery, idolatry, usually connected with coarse immoralities. "Wanderest," literally, stretched yourself out as a harlot inviting passers-by.

V. 21. God had planted Judah as a "noble vine," a choice dark-red grape, "wholly" a right seed, of pure stock, true offspring of Abraham and Israel (Gen. 15:6; 32:26-28). Judah had turned into wild shoots of the strange vine. A twofold change: Instead of a true offspring of the noble vine, Judah is a "strange vine" that God did not plant and does not recognize as His planting, and of this strange vine Judah is a wild shoot, growing rank, but bearing no fruit. Compare the charge that Judah was worse than the heathen (2 Chron. 33:9; Jer. 3:10-11; 18:13).

V. 22. "Niter," also Prov. 25:20, natron, a mineral alkali deposited on the shores and beds of certain lakes in Egypt, where it was gathered to make lye for washing purposes. "Soap," also Mal. 3:2, vegetable alkali, potash, made by pouring water through wood ashes. We see a woman trying to wash filthy clothes, stained with blood (cp. v. 34), vainly trying to remove the spots, which will yield neither to mineral nor to vegetable lye. (Cp. Lady Macbeth, in *Macbeth*, Act 5, Scene 1.) All the efforts of man to clear himself from his guilt, to hide his stains, are in vain (Ps. 90:8). The guilt is "marked," deeply engraved, indelibly marked before God. Judah did not even make an effort to cleanse herself. In boldest effrontery she denied her sins, her pollution.

B. Its brazen hypocrisy, vv. 23-25

23 How can you say: I am not defiled! I do not follow Baalim! Look at your ways in the valley! Recognize what you are doing, you swift dromedary crisscrossing her paths!
24 You wild ass, accustomed to the desert, gasping in the desire of her soul, sniffing at the wind, that no one can turn from her trysting place; no one will tire himself in seeking her; in her month they will
25 find her. Guard your feet from losing their sandals and your throat from thirst. But you say: Hopeless! No! For I love strangers and after them will I go!

Grammatical Notes

V. 23. "Dromedary," בִּכְרָה, the young female dromedary that has not foaled.
V. 24. "Wild ass," פֶּרֶה, usually masculine, therefore the masculine לִמֻּד "accustomed to," and נַפְשׁוֹ. Then female suffixes are used, since the term is here used to designate the female. 89 Mss., Q'ri, LXX read נַפְשָׁה.
"Occasion," תַּאֲנָה, from אנה, to meet accidentally.

V. 23. On the polluting character of Baal worship cp. Hos. 5:3; 6:10. The Lord is astonished at her denial. "How canst thou say that?" It takes a brazen front to deny your guilt. See your way in the valley, i. e., the valley of Hinnom (2 Chron. 28:3; 33:6; Jer. 7:31). Way is here either literally, the way leading to the valley, or figuratively, the cult (cp. Jer. 12:16; Amos 8:14; Acts 9:2).

"Thou art a swift dromedary," see Grammatical Notes, the young

41

female dromedary which has not yet foaled. "Swift," rushing headlong, vehemently; "traversing," literally, to cross one's way, run back and forth and in every direction, interlace. The phrase is to be translated as a vocative addressed to Judah, "You swift dromedary! . . ."

V. 24. "A wild ass," see Grammatical Notes. The wild ass, accustomed as she is to the steppe, the uninhabited prairies or wildernesses, where she can roam as she pleases, "in the desire, pleasure of her soul," is the type of an untamed and reckless person. "Snuffeth up," breathes, pants, desires (Jer. 14:6). She snuffs up the wind which carries the scent of the male to her eager nostrils. "In her occasion," meeting by agreement, tryst, hence coming together, copulation. Who shall turn her back from her tryst? Such a wild, ruttish ass, that any male can find without tiring himself in the search, is Judah at all times; offering herself to all that are willing to use her.

V. 25. "Withhold thy foot. . . ." Be careful lest in running after lovers you lose your shoes and be obliged with your tender, dainty feet to trod the hot sands and the sharp stones of the wilderness. "Thy throat from thirst." You will be in danger of perishing with thirst if you wander from home in your quest of paramours! God warns, but Israel refuses to listen to the warning. Nothing doing! Never! No! I love those strangers, as You call them, and after them will I go! The old God of Israel with His insistence on holiness seemed so outmoded. They wanted a change. The surrounding nations with their laxer morals, their gayer festivities, appealed to them, particularly since in serving these gods they could pamper their own flesh and its desires. "After them we will go!"

C. Its folly, vv. 26-28

26 As a thief is ashamed when he is discovered, so the house of Israel is ashamed, they, and their kings, and their princes, and their priests, 27 and their prophets. Who are saying to the wood: My father are you! and to the stone: You have borne me. For they turn toward Me their back, and not their face. But in the time of their distress they say: 28 Arise, and help us! Where are your gods which you have made for yourself? Let them arise if they can help you in the time of your distress. For as many cities, so many gods have you, Judah!

Vv. 26-27. Judah is depicted as a thief caught in the act of stealing, standing shamefaced, not because he stole, but because he must now face the consequences: ridicule, punishment, imprisonment. All the people, rulers and ruled, had paid homage to wood and stone, saying to a stock (the Hebrew word is masculine, tree): My father! and to

42

stone (feminine in Hebrew): Thou hast borne me! had turned to Me, faced Me, with their back and not with their face, which they kept turned to their idols. Yet in the day of trouble they turn back to the Lord, asking not for forgiveness, but shouting, shrieking at Him: Arise! Get up! Help us! They seek not God's grace and forgiveness, but help in need. Their god is their ego; whoever satisfies that will be their god for so long as they are satisfied with Him.

V. 28. In bitter irony God asks them: "Where are thy gods which thou hast made thee?" You have gods aplenty, you ought to have helpers aplenty, "for as the number of thy cities have become thy gods, Judah!" What a terrible charge! (Cp. Deut. 6:4-5.) Every city had its gods whom the inhabitants loved, and the only unloved one was Jehovah, their Creator, their Redeemer! "The stick and the stone would themselves laugh their worshipers to scorn" (Cowles).

D. Its ingratitude, vv. 29-32

29 Why do you quarrel with Me? All of you have rebelled against Me, is 30 the oracle of the LORD. In vain did I smite your children. They would not accept My training. Your sword devoured your prophets 31 like a killer lion. What a generation you are! Behold the sword of the LORD! Have I been a wilderness unto Israel? Or a densely dark land? Why, then, do My people say: We roam about and 32 will no longer come to You? Can a virgin forget her ornament? a bride her girdle? Yet My people have forgotten Me, days without number!

Grammatical Notes

V. 31. O generation: אַתֶּם is to be connected with הַדּוֹר

Vv. 29-30. Wherefore will ye plead. . . ." When God did not at once help the apostates, they began to quarrel with Him, charging God with unfaithfulness, injustice, cruelty. God resents such shameful behavior. His smitings were not cruelties, nor inflicted unjustly. They had deserved them, and He had sent them in order to induce His wayward children to return in sincere repentance to their Savior-God. Yet the children of Mother Judah did not learn their lesson, but continued stubbornly in their sin and rebellion. Like bloodthirsty lions, they turned against the prophets that warned them and silenced these unwelcome messengers by murdering them. (Cp. 2 Kings 21: 14-16; Jer. 26:20-23.)

V. 31. "O generation!" The generation that you are! In indignation and disgust the Lord is almost ready to turn away from the apostate nation and leave them to their doom. Yet once more He turns to them, makes another effort to win them back. "See the word of the LORD!" You blind, deluded people, open your eyes and behold My Word. Have I ever broken it? Consider what I have done in the past. He certainly had not been a "wilderness" to them, providing neither food nor shelter, nor a land of darkness, leaving them without light (cp. Ps. 119:105; Prov. 6:23). Why, then, do My people shun Me as one shuns desert and darkness? Why do they say: We are lords!? Targum, Syriac, Vulgate, and most recent commentaries derive the word from a root "to rove," roam. We go our own ways. We go and come and do as we please! If that was not the language of their lips, their actions spoke louder than words their absolute refusal to return to their God. Cp. Hos. 11:12 (Masoretic text and Luther: 12:1). "Judah runs wild as to God," as a wild beast broken loose (Cowles), unbridled (Keil).

V. 32. Judah had been a "maid," a virgin, pure and chaste, chosen by the Lord as His bride (v. 2), yet while a maiden does not forget her ornaments nor a bride her wedding girdle, perishable things, God's people had forgotten Him (cp. ch. 2:13), "days without number!"

E. Its punishment, vv. 33-37

33 How well have you planned your ways to seek love! Therefore I will also make your ways accustomed to 34 evils. On your skirts is also found the lifeblood of poor innocents; one need not break through the walls to find them, for it is over all these 35 things! And you keep on saying: I am innocent! Surely His wrath will turn away from me! Behold I am ready to prosecute you because you say: I have not sinned. 36 Why do you wear yourself out in changing your policy? You will be put to shame by Egypt also as you were put to shame by Assyria. 37 Also from there will you go forth with your hands upon your head, for the LORD has rejected your supports and has not granted them success.

V. 33. "Why trimmest thou thy way?" Literally, Why do you make good, do something in a good, thorough manner? While they forgot Jehovah, their Husband, Judah took great pains in learning and practicing ways and means of seeking love, illicit love, the favor of the surrounding lovers. Alliance with foreign nations implied religious unionism, syncretism, at least tolerance of idolatry. One did not dare to offend "friendly" nations, or nations whose friendship seemed politically helpful, by condemning their idolatry and wickedness. (Cp. 2 Kings 16:8-18.) "Therefore hast thou also taught. . . ." Here as in v. 20 the K'tib is the better reading: Therefore I have taught your ways, made them acquainted with, the evils, the misfortunes you are now suffering. (Cp. Deut. 28:16ff.) You insisted on making your bed; now I make you sleep in it. It is a bed of evil actions and of evil consequences.

V. 34. Your lack of love of Me has resulted in lack of love to My people. Your skirts are spattered with the blood of innocents (2 Kings 21:16). "Not by secret search" (cp. Ex. 22:2), literally, by breaking through a wall into a house, by burglary. I did not have to break into a home; murder was committed not only in secret, but openly; I found blood on "all these," pointing to the city, its streets, its homes, its inhabitants; all are guilty.

V. 35. Stubbornly Judah persists in protesting her innocence. Self-righteously she contends that God cannot retain His anger against His people. He will speedily deliver them from the enemies. God cuts off all hope of such deliverance. He is ready to forgive sins, but if a sinful people continually protests its innocence, there can be only punishment.

Vv. 36-37. The Lord refers to their constant efforts to gain the favor of one or both of the world powers. Powerful Psammetich II (663—610) had succeeded in gaining Egypt's independence from Assyria, while Assurbanipal was having trouble with revolutionaries. The time seemed auspicious for an alliance with Egypt against Assyria. God tells them that they would fare no better with Egypt than they had fared with Assyria, whose aid Ahaz has sought against Pekah (2 Kings 16:5-18; 2 Chron. 28:16, 20-21; on Egypt cp. Jer. 42:11-22; 46:1-26), for the Lord had rejected "their confidences," here the objects of their confidence, as in ch. 17:7; 48:13.

CHAPTER 3

4. God's Call to Repentance, Ch. 3:1-5

1 Saying: If a man divorce his wife and she leave him and become the wife of another man, will he return to her again? Would not this land be thoroughly desecrated? But you have played the harlot with many paramours! Yet, turn to Me, is 2 the oracle of the LORD. Lift up your eyes to the bare heights, and see where you have not lent yourself to prostitution. You sat at the wayside for them as the Arab in the desert and have desecrated the land by your whoredom and by 3 your wickedness. The showers were withheld, and there was no late rain. You have an harlot's brow, 4 you refuse to be ashamed. Are you not at this very moment crying to Me: My Father! The Friend of my 5 youth art Thou! Will He keep anger forever or retain it everlastingly? Behold, you speak, while you are doing evil of every sort and gain your end!

45

Grammatical Notes

V.1. "They say." The לֵאמֹר seems out of place. LXX, Syrian, and 1 Ms. omit it. Aquila, Targum, Ancient Latin, read it. Luther, Keil, and others, following Kimchi, connect it with the preceding context, particularly with "rejected" (ch. 2:37). Keil regards vv.1-3 as the wording of the decree of rejection, introduced by "saying." Yet this construction (while not intolerably harsh, as Naegelsbach says) is rather improbable, since לֵאמֹר is separated by a complete sentence from "rejected"; and the passages quoted as supporting this construction (Joshua 22:11; Judg. 16:2; Is. 9:8; 44:28) are not analogous. Others transpose the date, v. 6a, to v.1, since in v. 6 "lemor" is omitted. The problem remains unsolved.

V.1. "If," הֵן here not "behold," but the conditional conjunction "if," as, e. g., Ex. 8:22; Is. 54:15; etc. G.-K. 159w.

V. 1. In order to bring Judah to a consciousness of her iniquity, the Lord calls her attention to a constitutional requirement of the commonwealth of Israel, recorded Deut. 24:1-4. When a husband has put away his wife, and she has married another man, and her second marriage is severed by divorce or death, then the first husband is forbidden to again take her as his wife, for that remarriage would "pollute," desecrate, paganize, the land (cp. vv. 2, 6; Num. 35:33; Is. 24:5; Dan. 11:32). The question is not: May the wife return to him? It is: May the former husband take her back? Even if she is willing to return to him, and even if he is willing to take her back, he cannot do it unless he willfully transgresses God's Law. This law is applied by the Lord to His relation to Judah, His espoused wife (Jer. 2:2). Judah had forgotten her Husband (v. 32); had played the harlot with many lovers (ch. 3:1); she was no longer the wife of the Lord (cp. Hos. 2:2-5). What does God tell her? Interpreters differ radically in their conception of God's reaction. The Targum, Peshito, Jerome, Luther, Calvin, A. V., Naegelsbach, and others translate: Yet return again to me! The LXX, Theodoret, and most modern exegetes render the words as an interrogative: "And shalt thou return to Me?" Grammatically both translations are possible. Much depends on the tone in which they were originally spoken, either as a gracious invitation or as a threatening question. The chief reasons why modern commentators declare for the interrogative are (a) the context which speaks of sins, the very nature of which makes a reunion impossible, and (b) the fact that God's refusal to take back His wife would be in keeping with the law of Deuteronomy 24. From a twofold viewpoint the interrogative interpretation does not seem acceptable: 1) It would declare a reunion of Judah with the Lord as contrary to God's will irrespective of what Judah's attitude might be; else the application of the law of Deuteronomy 24 would not be in accordance with the Law itself, which positively and absolutely forbids the husband to take back the wife under the circumstances described. Such an absolute refusal on the part of the Lord to re-establish the union with Judah would be contrary to the context, which pleads with Judah to repent and return, and in general with the universal grace of God (Is. 1:18; Ezek. 18:21-23; 33:11). 2) It would seem strange that the impossibility of the wife's return is emphasized, while both Deut. 24:4: "May not take her again," and Jer. 3:1: "Shall he return?" prohibit the husband's return, the wife's willingness or unwillingness to return being left out of consideration. Hence the translation of our Authorized Version is, after all, the preferable one. The urgent need for such return is brought out in vv. 2-5, the conclusion of the speech beginning ch. 2:1 with a reference to "the kindness of Judah's youth and the love of her espousal."

V. 2. "Lift up . . . thy wickedness," impresses upon Judah the need of such repentance, by again stressing the manifest wickedness and detestable hypocrisy of Judah. Not only on all hills covered with green trees (ch. 2:20) nor only in the beautiful Valley of Hinnom (ch. 2:23) did Judah commit spiritual adultery. Her insatiable lust for idol worship and the carnal indulgences and gross immoralities connected with it urged her to build altars on even the driest and hottest "high place." The Hebrew term used here and ch. 3:21; 4:11; 7:29; 12:12; 14:6; Is. 41:18; 49:9; Num. 23:3, denotes a hill with a bare summit, or entirely destitute of vegetation, a bald knob, without water springs (Is. 41:18; 49:9); also the sand dunes and bare rocks in the wilderness, as well as hills denuded of their trees by the ax. The heat reflected by these hills from the burning sun was so intense that the very winds blowing from them brought no refreshing coolness, but served only to make the heat still more unbearable and burnt up all vegetation (Jer. 4:11; 14:6). Yet so eager were the people to worship their idols that they flocked in great numbers to these uninviting hills, just as in our day not only the luxuriously furnished clubs, but crude buildings, hovels lacking every comfort, draw capacity crowds eager to pamper their flesh and satisfy their lusts.

"Thou hast been lain with." The Hebrew term, "to debauch," "prostitute," was regarded by the Masoretes as an obscene word, and wherever this word occurs, they suggested to read the corresponding form of another verb, "to lie with." The Lord purposely uses

47

strong language in order to show them how far they have strayed, how urgent the need of turning!

"In the ways hast thou sat for them." (Cp. Gen. 38: 14, 16, 21; Prov. 7: 11, 12.) You did not wait for an invitation, but sat like public harlots on the streets and highways and invited others to debauch you, to participate in the idolatrous festivities inaugurated by yourself (cp. 2 Kings 21: 2-7; 23: 4-15).

"As the Arabian in the wilderness," the marauding Bedouin, "as eager as the desert tribes were for plunder, so was Israel for idolatry" (R. Payne Smith). On "polluted" see v. 1. They had changed God's land into a pagan country by living in heathen vices.

V. 3. "Therefore the showers . . . no latter rain." God's actions had proved His displeasure. He was the God of the Covenant who would bless His obedient children, but who had also threatened dire penalties to the covenant breakers, such as withholding the rain showers, so essential to a land like Canaan (cp. Deut. 11: 10-17). This is the general term, beside which the "latter rain" is especially mentioned, falling in March and April, without which the harvest could not mature properly. Judah refused to see the hand of God in these rainless seasons, refused to be ashamed of her immoral and idolatrous conduct. With the unabashed effrontery of a harlot she covered her wicked ways with the cloak of external piety.

Vv. 4-5. "Wilt thou not." The negative interrogative here introduces an assured fact and is best translated "Are you not?" "Yes, indeed; yes, surely," G.-K. 150e (Joshua 1: 9; 1 Sam. 23: 19; 2 Kings 15: 36; etc.). "From this time," from now on, at this very time, refers to the reform instituted by Josiah (2 Kings 23: 2-24; 2 Chronicles 34 and 35). They came to the Temple, they used the terms which pious teachers taught them. They called the Lord "my Father, "the Husband, the devoted, beloved, loving Friend and Husband, art Thou!" Yet all these pious words came from a hypocritical heart. They demanded their rights as God's children without the least intention to fulfill their duties as children. They expected their Husband to live up to His obligations without the least thought of their own responsibilities as God's bride and spouse. Holding God to His promises, they charge Him with anger, cruelty, tyranny, with retaining His wrath needlessly. Their heart remains unchanged, that is set on doing evil "as thou couldest"; they are determined to carry out their wicked thoughts.

III. God Is Ready to Reject His People, Ch. 3:6—6:30

1. God Calls His Apostate and Treacherous People to Repentance
Ch. 3:6—4:4

**A. Treacherous Judah refuses to learn the lesson of apostate Israel's rejection
ch. 3:6-10**

6 In the days of King Josiah the LORD spoke to me: Have you seen what Apostasy Israel has done? She has gone to every high hill and under every green tree, and there you played the harlot.
7 I thought that after she had done all these things she would return, but she did not return! And Treachery Judah, her sister, saw it.
8 And when I had put away Apostasy Israel for all the adulteries she had committed and had given her a letter of divorce, I saw that treacherous Judah, her sister, undaunted, also went and played the harlot,
9 and so by her boisterous harlotry she desecrated the land, committing adultery with stone and with wood.
10 And even in all these things Treachery, her sister Judah, did not turn to Me in full sincerity, but deceitfully, is the oracle of the LORD.

Grammatical Notes

V. 6. "Backsliding," מְשֻׁבָה, apostasy, occurs twelve times in the Old Testament; once in Proverbs (ch. 1:32), twice in Hosea (ch. 11:7; 14:5), nine times in Jeremiah (ch. 3:6, 8, 11, 12, where it is used as a proper name for Israel; in ch. 8:5 it is applied to Judah; the plural ch. 2:19; 3:22; 5:6; 14:7).

V. 7. "Treacherous," בָּגוֹדָה. Gesenius-Buhl and Gesenius-Kautzsch, in 84 a, k, list it as an adjective, "the masculine of which does not occur; feminine only Jer. 3:7, 10." In 84 a, k, G.-K. lists masculine abstracts of like formation, such as כָּבוֹד, honor; שָׁלוֹם, peace (originally, short vowel in first syllable, long in second). He calls bagodah an abnormal form because of the retention of long qamez in the first syllable. Since the Masoretes in Jer. 3:7, 10 retained the long qamez, may we not safely assume that Jeremiah regarded bagodah as a feminine abstract noun "Treachery" and intentionally used this abstract as the proper name for Judah, to correspond to the abstract "Apostasy" used of Israel? The root word, בגד = to cover, compare בֶּגֶד, garment.

V. 9. "Defiled," חָנֵף is a stronger term than טָמֵא.

V. 9. "The lightness," קֹל. The A. V. derives the term from קלל, to be light; the ancient versions concur, because of the defective writing, but this occurs also Gen. 45:16; Ex. 4:8. Luther translates, das Geschrei, the clamor. Since the word does not occur elsewhere in the sense of "lightness," and since "the clamor" is the more expressive, we prefer the latter.

Addressing Jeremiah, the Lord first speaks of Israel in the third person (ch. 3:6-11), but His call to repentance (vv. 12-14a) and His marvelous promise (vv. 14b-17) are addressed to Israel directly. In like manner God first speaks of Judah in the third person (vv. 10-11, 18a), then addresses the reunited people in His words of promise (vv. 18b-19). Using the second person in v. 20, He changes to the third in v. 21, and back to the second in v. 22; ch. 4:1-2. Compare the similar change from the third person to the second and back again to the third in Hos. 2:6-15, and again in ch. 2:16-23.

V. 6. "The LORD said also unto me in the days of Josiah, the king." It seems best to restrict this dating to the chapters immediately following (Jer. 3:6—6:30), since a new superscription is placed ch. 7:1. As the prophet later summarizes his preaching extending over twenty-three years in two verses (ch. 25:5-6), so this section characterizes his preaching under Josiah as a call to repentance, showing its urgent need, the dire consequences if this call is neglected, and the wonderful blessings in store for a repentant people.

The sin of Israel was apostasy, an open, flagrant turning away from God for the purpose of committing the lascivious idolatry of the Canaanite in worshiping Baal and his consort, Asherah (cp. ch. 7:18). The whole country, every high mountain, on which they seemed closer to heaven, the abode of the gods, and every green tree, which afforded refreshing shade for the practice of their lustful desires, were desecrated by being put into the service of idols and man's lust. "Hast thou seen?" Israel's sin was manifest, practiced openly for all to see. The prophets of Baal in Israel called themselves by that name and were fanatical in their loyalty to Baal (1 Kings 18:25-30). King Ahab made Baal worship the official religion of Israel (1 Kings 16:31-33; 18:18), while all the other kings persisted in the idolatrous calf worship instituted by Jeroboam in direct opposition to the true worship of Jehovah (1 Kings 12:26-33; 13:33f.; 2 Kings 17:7-17).

V. 7. The Lord's repeated calls to repentance were ignored (2 Kings 17:13-15); compare the prophecies of Elijah, Hosea, and Amos. Her treacherous sister, Judah, rather: And Treachery, her sister, Judah, saw all these abominations. Did she warn her sister? No! While Israel was outspoken in her rejection of the worship of Jehovah, Judah still retained the outer correct form, the elaborate Temple ritual. That was only the beautiful cloak with which she covered her apostasy, and thus she was truly Treachery.

V. 8. "And I saw," the object is added in the "yet" clause, v. 10. Judah had not warned and pleaded with her sister to return, but had followed in the footsteps of her sister, Apostasy. Even when God had finally divorced His unfaithful spouse, when Samaria was destroyed in 722, Judah continued in her hypocrisy. Judah was called Treachery in v. 7, here God calls her "treacherous," the participle denoting habitual treachery as a characteristic trait of Judah.

V. 9. See Grammatical Notes. By her loud, boisterous idol festivities she "defiled," desecrated, paganized (by impious, wicked actions) God's Holy Land (cp. Num. 35:33; Is. 24:5; Jer. 3:1-2; Dan. 11:32). "With stock and stone." Bitter irony. Forsaking her Bridegroom (Jer. 2:2), the Fount of living water (ch. 2:13), she chose as her gods wood and stone (cp. ch. 2:27). What was greater, her wickedness or her folly?

V. 10. Judah, the treacherous spouse, is like an adulterous wife that seeks to deceive her husband by promising faithfulness while she continues in her relations with other men. On Judah's hypocritical worship compare Is. 1:10-15; Jer. 6:20; 7:4-19; Amos 5:22; on reforms instituted by pious kings and priests, to a great extent only partial, superficial, short-lived, see 1 Kings 15:11-14; 2 Chronicles 19; ch. 23: 16-21; ch. 29—31. Never once did the nation as such return to the Lord wholeheartedly. Their sacrifices were deliberate deception; their weepings, crocodile tears; their hymns, lip service; their avowals of faithfulness, perfidious dissembling.

B. God calls Israel to repentance and promises her reacceptance and glorification
vv. 11-17

11 So the LORD said to me: Apostasy Israel has caused herself to appear more righteous than treacherous
12 Judah. Go and cry out these words towards the north, and say: Return, O Apostasy Israel! is the oracle of the LORD. I will not be angry with you, for I am merciful, is the oracle of the LORD; I will not retain
13 anger forever. Only acknowledge your guilt, that you have rebelled against the LORD, your God, and have wandered in every direction to alien gods under every green tree, and have not obeyed My voice, is the oracle of the LORD. Return,
14 you apostate children, is the oracle of the LORD, for I am wedded unto you, I will take you, one from a city and two from a tribe, and I will
15 bring you to Zion. And I will give you shepherds according to My heart, and they shall shepherd you with knowledge and understanding.
16 And it shall come to pass, when you shall have multiplied and become fruitful in the land in those days, is the oracle of the LORD, then you shall no more say: Ark of the Covenant of the LORD, and it shall not come to your mind, and you shall not remember it and shall not miss it, and it shall
17 not be made again. At this time they shall call Jerusalem "the throne of the LORD," and all nations shall be gathered unto her, to the name of the LORD, to Jerusalem, and they shall no more follow the stubborn inclinations of their wicked heart.

Grammatical Notes

V. 15. "Feed," רעה, not merely "to feed"; it denotes the full work of a shepherd. In this sense the Hebrew term is never used with the accusative of food. Hence, "with knowledge and understanding" is not the instruction they give. דֵעָה וְהַשְׂכֵּיל are absolute infinitives used adverbially in connection with any form of the finite verb in order to define in which manner or under which circumstances the action or state described by the finite word takes place (G.-K. 113h; cp. Jer. 22:19; Is. 7:11; 57:17); hence, in a knowing and understanding manner.

V. 16. "Remembered," זָכַר לְ, denotes a remembrance "clinging to," לְ, its object. "Visit it," פָּקַד, to seek, is also used in the sense to regret the loss, to miss it, hence, seek it (1 Sam. 20:6, 18; 25:15; 1 Kings 20:39; Is. 34:16; Ezek. 23:21). "Be done any more," יֵעָשֶׂה. עשׂה is used of the construction of the Ark and its

component parts (Ex. 25:10, 13, 17, 18, 19; 37:1, 4, 6, 7. Letteris points יֵעָשֶׂה, one shall make. "Any more" here: once more, again, a second time (Gen. 4:25; 24:20; Judg. 13:8).

V. 17. "Dwell," ישׁב, is frequently used of sitting on a throne as a king, to "throne." Koenig vindicates this sense for the simple ישׁב in the following passages: Is. 10:13; Amos 1:5, 8 ("inhabitant"); Ps. 2:4; 9:8a (A. V., 7a "endureth"); 22:4(3); 29:10; 55:20 (A. V., v. 19, "abideth"). (Koenig, *Das Buch Jesaia,* p. 148.)

V. 11. "Justified" here used in the sense of causing oneself to appear as righteous (cp. Ezek. 16:51, 52). Israel was not guiltless. Her wickedness had caused her rejection. Yet as a dirty garment appears cleaner when placed beside a filthy rag, so Israel's undeniable guilt appears less horrible if placed side by side with the guilt of Treachery Judah. God bluntly tells Judah that she has sunk lower than rejected Israel and that she is in sore need of returning to the Lord if she hopes to escape a punishment even more severe than that of apostate Israel.

V. 12. We expect God's announcement of the dissolution of His covenant with His former people. Instead, the Lord, whose ways and actions pass understanding, unfolds one of the most marvelous manifestations of His unlimited grace found in the Old Testament (vv. 12-19). His prophet, who was to deliver so many messages of God's wrath to the people he loved, is now granted the honor of transmitting this message of purest grace to the whole house of Israel. He is told to direct his proclamation to captive Israel in order to encourage her to return to her Covenant God; and he is to speak in the hearing of Judah, in order to make her ashamed of her past treachery and to urge her also to return wholeheartedly to the God of everlasting grace.

"Turn, thou ever-turning Israel!" For once turn in the right direction, back to Me! That is the call which not merely demands, but as the Word of life works the return it calls for. You need not be afraid to come back to Me. I will not cause My anger, literally, "My face," to fall upon you (cp. Gen. 4:5-6), the opposite of "lift

52

up one's face" (Num. 6:26). The Lord had caused His face to fall upon them when He had sent them into the Assyrian captivity 722 B.C. Returning to Him, they will no longer find a Lord with a fallen face, He will extend a glad welcome to His returning children (cp. Luke 15:7, 10). For I am merciful, loving, kind (cp. Is. 54:7-8).

V. 13. "Only acknowledge," come to understand and to feel keenly (*nosse cum affectu et effectu*) "your iniquity," here in the sense of guilt (cp. Gen. 15:16; Ex. 20:5; Ps. 32:5; Is. 1:4; etc.). This is not a condition of God's grace. His grace had called them and was willing to forgive their sin even while they were still turning their back to Him. He had in fact, for the sake of the promised Woman's Seed (Gen. 3:15; Isaiah 53; Heb. 9:14-15), forgiven their sin. The obstacle to their reacceptance is not, therefore, their sin, but their refusal to accept this forgiveness, the refusal to acknowledge their sinful depravity. In order to lead them to thorough recognition and confession of their guilt, the Lord describes their sin in three clauses: 1) "Thou hast transgressed," rebelled, against the Covenant God of grace and mercy (Ex. 34:6-7; Deut. 32:4-6; Is. 1:2-4), who is I AM THAT I AM, the God of unalterable justice and eternal power (Deut. 28:15-68; 32:39-41). 2) "Scattered thy ways to the strangers," idols (cp. Deut. 32:16; Jer. 2:25), wandered in all directions in search of gods whose service seemed more pleasant and profitable than that of Jehovah (cp. Hos. 2:5, 12-13). "Green tree," see Jer. 2:20; 3:6. 3) "Not obeyed My voice," rejecting God's Law and spurning His Gospel.

V. 14. Still the Lord of the Covenant calls His apostate people back to Himself. While they are "backsliding" (v. 14), disobedient, rebellious idolaters (v. 13), He still loves them with a father's love, calls them "children," although unworthy of this name. He addresses them as individuals, willing to acknowledge every single one as His child, to give to every one the precious privilege of calling Him Father. "For I am married unto you"; the perfect denotes this marriage as an action resulting in a permanent state. Again He uses the plural, you, the individuals constituting His people. God is the Father and the Husband of every Israelite (cp. on this terminology Hos. 2:1-6). This twofold relationship had been broken shamefully by His people, yet He, the faithful Covenant God, the Father and Husband, still is willing to continue this relation. To that end He calls them to return; and as a Husband and Father He promises: "I will take you one of a city and two of a family." "Family" here denotes a tribe, a clan, in which there are a number of cities (cp. Gen. 10:5, 18, 20, 31, 32; Jer. 1:15; Judg. 13:2; etc.). The Lord is not looking for a mass conversion, a return of all descendants of Jacob, or of the northern tribes. He knows that most of them will refuse to return to Him. Yet that will not invalidate His invitation. If the converted Israelite is the only Israelite within a city, or the only repentant Israelite in a city teeming with Israelites, the Lord will not overlook this one solitary Israelite; He will take him and bring him to Zion (cp. Luke 15:1-10). Zion was the Lord's dwelling place (Ps. 74:2; 132:13-14; Is. 8:18; etc.), where He dwelt among His people (Ex. 25:8; 29:45), whom He had chosen as His own (Ex. 19:5-6). Here the Lord promises to Israel, the northern tribes, carried into captivity in fulfillment of God's threat (Deut. 28:36ff.; Hos. 3:4), that He will bring back to Zion everyone who will return to Him in sincere repentance. For the duration of the Sinaitic Covenant the Lord had pledged Himself to do that very thing (Deut. 30:1-5). As a faithful Husband and Father He will fulfill this promise if they return to the Lord. And therefore He pleads with them: Return, thou backsliding Israel (vv. 12, 14). For there is no return to Zion, unless they first return to the Lord.

V. 15. "Pastors," shepherds. This term cannot be restricted to civic rulers. Jeremiah calls himself a "pastor," a shepherd (Jer. 17:16). The "wicked shepherds" of Ezekiel 34, certainly refer chiefly, if not exclusively, to spiritual leaders, false prophets, to be supplanted by the Lord (vv. 11-22), the spiritual Ruler, and His Messiah (vv. 23-31), the spiritual Savior. Cp. also Zech. 10:2; ch. 11. "Feed," pasture, never used with the accusative of food. "With knowledge and understanding." See Grammatical Notes. The shepherds will shepherd you in a knowing and understanding manner, as Christ knows and loves both the content of His teaching (Matt. 11:27; John 6:35-63; 8:12-32, 49-56), and those whom He teaches (John 10:11-18, 27-29). "Understanding" is closely related in meaning to knowledge, literally, to look at, have insight, so as to clearly understand the nature of the person or object observed, and be able to teach intelligently, realizing the needs of the situation, the difficulties to be expected, knowing and using the means to overcome the obstacles and alleviate the needs.

V. 16. "Be multiplied and increase." This increase is one of the characteristic traits of Messianic prophecy (cp. Gen. 15:5-6; 17:2; 28:14; Jer. 23:3; Ezek. 36:11; Hos. 1:10; 2:23; on the latter two passages see Rom. 9:24-26; 1 Peter 2:9-10). To this Messianic era also the next phrase refers, "in those days." See Jer. 30:24—31:38, where practically all the chronological terms describing the days of the Messiah are found. "In the latter days" (Jer. 30:24); "the days are coming (ch. 31:27, 31, 38); "in those days" (ch. 31:29); "after those days" (ch. 31:33). Jer. 31:31-34 is quoted Heb. 8:8-12; 10:15-18 as referring to the New Testament era; Jer. 31:15 in Matt. 2:17-18.

In the Messianic era Israel shall multiply (cp. Acts 1:15, 120 souls; Acts 2:41, 3,000; Acts 4:4, 5,000), and they, the multitudinous seed of Israel, shall no longer say: The Ark of the Covenant of Jehovah! That is an exclamation denoting desire, love, esteem, joy because of its presence, or sorrow for its loss. In no such sense will the expression be used. "Come to mind," literally, upon the heart. (Cp. Is. 65:17; Jer. 7:31; 51:50; 1 Cor. 2:9.) "Not be remembered," denotes here a remembrance that clings to the Ark in affectionate longing. "Visit it" = to regret the loss of something, to miss an object. "Be done any more," rather, neither shall the Ark be made again, a second time. (On these expressions see Grammatical Notes.) The Ark, being lost, destroyed, shall not again be constructed.

The vital importance of the Ark for the religious and civic life may be gathered from its purpose and symbolism. 1) It was the Ark of the Testimony (Ex. 40:3, 5), since the testimony of the Lord, His Law (Ex. 31:18; 34:28), the witness of His unalterable holiness and justice, was deposited in it (Ex. 25:21b; 40:20). 2) A testimonial of the Lord's unchanging grace and mercy; on it was placed the Mercy Seat, the Kapporeth (Ex. 25:17, 21), the atonement cover (cp. Lev. 16: 14-19). 3) The place of God's revelation (Ex. 25:22; 29:42; Num. 7:89). 4) God's dwelling place, where He dwelt between the cherubim (1 Sam. 4:4; 2 Sam. 6:2; 2 Kings 19:15; Ps. 80:1; 99:1) and where the prayers of Israel and their symbol, the incense (Ps. 141:2; Rev. 5:8; 8:3-4), were offered to the Lord, who "inhabited," dwelt amidst, the praises of Israel (Ps. 22:4 [A. V., v. 3], cp. Joshua 7:6; 2 Kings 19: 14-15).

Clearly and unmistakably the prophet announces to Judah that the days were coming in which there would be no more Ark of the Covenant; that Ark which had played so prominent a part in the worship of the Old Covenant would be forgotten; there would be no longing for its restoration. This announcement, the first of its kind in the history of Israel, must have come as a shock to the Jews, for whom the Ark was the very center of their Sanctuary, round which their entire worship was built up by the ordinance of the Covenant God Himself. This same truth was revealed to Ezekiel several years later (sixth year of Zedekiah, ca. 593/2), when in a vision he saw the glory of the Lord depart from off the threshold of the Temple (Ezek. 10:18), and finally leave the city (Ezek. 11:23).

The very fact that the returning exiles no longer possessed the Ark, was to be to them a lesson teaching them that the complete dissolution of the Old Covenant was approaching. Already the kinghood was lost; their independence a thing of the past, Urim and Thummim was no more (Ex. 28:15-30; Neh. 7:65). Josephus, *Ant.*, III, 8. 9 states that the breastplate left off shining 200 years before he wrote his book. With Malachi, prophecy ceased. The Old Covenant, decaying and waxing old, was ready to vanish away (Heb. 8:13). This gradual disappearance of Israel's Old Testament glory before the coming of the Messiah was a punishment for Israel's externalizing the worship of Jehovah. They had substituted ceremony for loyalty to the Lord; legalism for the Gospel of grace; ritual for return to God; penances for repentance. They had cast away the essence and were gradually being deprived of the outward form, the shadows, until these also completely passed away. Now nothing remains to them of what was once the glory of Israel (Rom. 9:4).

But while the outer form which characterized the Old Covenant and was essential to it gradually disintegrated and was finally annihilated, this annihilation of the outer form at the same time according to the eternal counsel of God served to bring to its highest culmination the real essence of the Old Testament Covenant, God's plan of salvation through His own Son. The death of the Old Covenant was like that of the seed which dies only to bring forth much fruit; like the passing away of the shadow to make place for the body; like the death of our body, which is sown in corruption and weakness to be raised in power and incorruption (Hengstenberg).

The return of such only as had been made willing by the Lord to leave Babylon and go back to the ruins of Jerusalem (Ezra 1:5), who willingly built the Temple (Ezra 2:68) and refused to fraternize with the adversaries (ch. 4:1-3; 6:21; 7:26; 8:22), was the foreshadowing, the beginning, of the fulfillment of this promise of the deliverance and restoration of God's people, the fruit of Messiah's victory over the powers of darkness. Without Messiah's redemption, no reconciliation, no restoration!

V. 17. "The throne of the LORD." While the Ark of the Covenant is never directly called God's throne, yet it was in fact no less than that. It was called "the Ark of the Covenant of the LORD of

Hosts, which dwelleth between the cherubim" (1 Sam. 4:4, etc.). "Dwell," see Grammatical Notes. Quite evidently the Most Holy Place was regarded as the throne room of God, where above the Mercy Seat, between and above the cherubim, the Lord throned. We must of course dissociate from the term "throne of the LORD" every idea of a physical or material local presence. The Ark was both the throne and the "footstool" (1 Chron. 28:2; Ps. 99:5; 132:7) of the Lord, where He whom the heaven of heavens cannot contain (1 Kings 8:27) condescended to dwell.

The Ark of the Covenant of the Old Testament was not to be restored "in those days" (v. 16), in the New Testament era. Yet the Jerusalem of the new era was not to be the poorer for lack of this Ark. The throne of God shall not be removed from Jerusalem. "They," the people of Jerusalem (vv. 16-18), shall call it "the throne of God." The imperfect describes the ever-renewed naming of this city as constantly new believers are added to the New Testament Church. Shall, then, either in the New Testament era or in the millennium, physical Jerusalem be the throne of God from which Messiah shall rule His kingdom? Scripture gives us God's own answer, an emphatic No! Paul states clearly that the Jerusalem of the New Testament, "the mother of us all," all believers to the end of time, is not physical Jerusalem, that is now "in bondage with her children," in the self-chosen bondage of the Law. It is rather "Jerusalem which is above," spiritual Jerusalem, of which all believers are children (Gal. 4:24-31). The Jerusalem of the New Covenant is the holy Christian Church, the communion of saints. The Israel of God in the New Covenant (Gal. 6:16) is composed of all that walk according to the rule outlined in v. 15. (Cp. Heb. 12:18-24.) Christ, sitting on the throne of God, rules His Church and sits in the midst of His Church, which is not only His throne, but His body, the fullness of Him that filleth all in all (Eph. 1:20-23).

That the New Testament Church is to be identified with Jerusalem is evident also from the next words of Jeremiah: "All the nations shall be gathered unto it," to Jerusalem, of course, "to the name of the LORD, to Jerusalem." We must not translate: "because of the LORD'S name at Jerusalem" (Keil), nor supply "which is" before "Jerusalem" (Naegelsbach). We have here an identification of the name of Jehovah with Jerusalem, and to make that identification emphatic, Jerusalem is twice referred to, once by the pronoun "to it," pointing back to "Jerusalem," called the throne of God, and then a second time by the phrase "to Jerusalem." Because Jerusalem is called God's throne, the Gentiles shall be gathered, assemble themselves, at Jerusalem, and in so doing they assemble themselves to "the name of Jehovah." What is the meaning of this phrase? The Lord Himself has defined this term (Ex. 20: 24). Wherever God makes mention of His name to His people, He Himself comes to them with all His blessings. The manner of God's proclamation of His name may vary. The context of Ex. 20: 24 speaks of altars, on which sacrifices were to be offered as a means of "recording" the name of God, revealing Him to Israel as the God of salvation through the sacrifice of the Woman's Seed (Gen. 3: 15), Abraham's Seed (Gen. 15: 5-6; cp. Gal. 3: 16). To Moses, God recorded His name on Moses' request (Ex. 3: 14-15); and later, again at Moses' plea (Ex. 33: 18-23; 34: 5-7), granted him a visible and audible revelation of God's name, God's essence and being. God's name is revealed also in the Angel of the Lord (Ex. 23: 21, "My name is in Him"). Cp. John 10: 30; 14: 9. God records His name through His prophets, His "mouths" (Jer. 15: 19; 1: 9; 5: 14), in the Holy Scriptures, by the word of preaching (Gen. 4: 26; 12: 8; Luke 10: 16; John 17: 20). Irrespective of the manner in which God records His name, He Himself in and by such recording comes to men to bless them (cp. Num. 6: 23-27). In revealing His name, God reveals Himself. The presence of His name posits His own personal presence, not God as an abstract idea, but as a living, active Being He records His name, He comes, He blesses.

To Jerusalem one must go in order to know the name of God as the Covenant God of infinite grace through the merits of the Redeemer. And whatever is called Jerusalem by the Lord, there His name can be found, there is God Himself ready to bless all who come. Wherever the name of Jehovah is recorded, wherever the revelation of His loving-kindness is proclaimed, there is **Jerusalem, the** Church of God; there the nations can assemble; there they can become fellow citizens with the saints, children of Jerusalem.

This gathering of the Gentiles to the Church of the Lord is characteristic of the New Testament era (Isaiah 60; 62; Eph. 2: 11—3: 11). Having come to Jerusalem, the nations no longer "shall walk after the imagination of their evil heart." On "evil heart" see Jer. 17: 9. "Imaginations," שְׁרִירוּת, occurs also Deut. 29: 19; Ps. 81: 14; Jer. 7: 24; 9: 14; 11: 8; 16: 12; 18: 12; 23: 17. Gesenius-Buhl derives it from שרר, to be firm, hard; hence, hardness, stubbornness. While the phrase, wherever else it occurs, is used in connection with the Covenant people, yet the heart of the Gentiles is by nature no better than that of the Jews, and in the New Testament converted Gentiles are embodied in God's Covenant people who no longer walk in the stubbornness of their own mind, but bring into captivity every thought to the obedience of Christ (2 Cor. 10:5).

Vv. 12-17 are indeed a marvelous revelation of the loving-kindness of the Covenant God of Israel; an invitation manifesting unscalable heights and unfathomable depths of divine grace and mercy and long-suffering.

C. God calls Judah to repentance by promising her a place of honor among His children, vv. 18-20

18 In those days the house of Judah shall go to the house of Israel, and together they shall be going out of the land of the north to the land which I have caused their fathers 19 to inherit. And I Myself have said: Oh, how will I set you among the children! I will give you a desirable land, an inheritance of the most glorious beauties of the heathen. And I say: They shall call Me: My 20 Father and shall no more turn away from Me. Surely, as a wife is unfaithful to her friend, so you have been unfaithful to Me, O house of Israel! is the oracle of the LORD.

Grammatical Notes

V. 18. "Shall walk," יֵלְכוּ, "shall come," יָבֹאוּ, the imperfects describe the progressive return of Judah and Israel throughout the centuries.

V. 19. "Hosts of nations," צְבָאוֹת גּוֹיִם, A. V. and Luther ("Heer der Heiden") derive צְבָאוֹת from צָבָא, host, which lexicographically is a correct translation and has the support of the accents. Yet just as correctly צְבָאוֹת may be regarded as the plural of צְבִי, glory, splendor. Nouns formed with final י sometimes add an א or change י to א. Gesenius-Kautzsch, 93 x, lists among others

מְלָאִים (sing. מְלִי), lamb (1 Sam. 15:4; Is. 40:11); צְבָאִים (1 Chron. 12:8) and צְבָאוֹת (Cant. 2:7; 3:5), sing. צְבִי, gazelle. So the clause may be translated as above. We prefer the second translation, since the phrase "hosts of nations" in this form does not occur in the Old Testament, while the superlative is quite commonly expressed in the form of a singular construct and plural of same word, here צְבִי צְבָאוֹת (cp. Gen. 9:25; Ex. 26:33; Num. 3:32; Deut. 10:17; Cant. 1:1).

V. 18. "In those days," the New Testament era, when there shall be no more Ark (v. 16), when the shadows and types shall have vanished, because in Christ the body has come (Col. 2:17; Heb. 9: 8-12); then also the house of Judah shall walk (see Grammatical Notes) with the house of Israel, with those whom the Lord has taken, one of a city, and two of a family, those converted Israelites who shall in the course of centuries be brought to Zion, the Church of

God, by the Lord of the Church (v. 14). Israel, the northern tribes, never returned to Jerusalem as a nation.

If at all Judah would return to the Lord, their God, they would have to return like despised Israel (cp. Ezek. 11:15) out of like exile in like repentance. Yet this divine description of the reunion of the two estranged sisters, equally estranged from their God, extends to both a sincere and urgent invitation to be reunited in common sorrow for their sin, in common faith in the promised Savior, in common return to the Covenant God. The converted Israelites together with the Jews (of Judah) and the Gentiles joining repentant Israel constitute the true house of Israel (Rom. 2:28-29), who no longer disgrace the glorious name of their forefather Israel, but, like him, cling to God with the arms of faith and will not let Him go except He bless them (Gen. 32:26).

V. 19. While the message of vv. 12-17 was to be addressed by the prophet to exiled Israel (v. 12), it was spoken in the hearing of Judah. From v. 19 onward the Lord turns to both sister nations in a plea to return to Him. The charge of treachery, four times raised against Judah (vv. 7, 8, 10, 11), is now applied to the house of Israel (v. 20). Both houses are one in apostasy and in treachery, and both Israel and Judah are invited to return as one to their one Lord and God, who promises a marvelous blessing to the reunited Israel.

"But [rather "and"] I have said." The perfect simply presents this declaration of God as an accomplished fact" (Naegelsbach). It is God's eternal decree. "How," usually an interrogative, here as in ch. 9:7 an interjection. How highly will I honor you! "Among the children," not the nations, who are never called children of God, but the members of the Church, among whom God has by eternal decree given the seat of honor to Israel (Ex. 4:22; Amos 3:2; Deut. 18:15-18; Matt. 15:24; John 4:22; Acts 3:26; 10:36-39; Rom. 9:4-5). Because God's Messianic promises to Israel had not yet been fulfilled in the days of the Babylonian exile, He reaccepted repentant Israel into His Sinaitic covenant (cp. Deut. 30:1-10). After Messiah had come and Israel had stubbornly rejected Him, the Lord rejected Israel as a nation (1 Thess. 2:15-16), only individual members of which shall enter His Kingdom of Grace and Glory (Jer. 3:14). Yet to the end of time and throughout eternity it will be true: Salvation is of the Jews, whose are the fathers, of whom Christ came, who is God blessed forever, our only Savior! (Rom. 9:5-6.) The assurance of divine grace and forgiveness, the adoption of sons, the confident hope of the resurrection of the body unto life everlasting, all has become a reality through an Israelite, a Jew! What a place of honor God has given to Israel! What an inducement for them to turn to Him in sincere repentance and faith!

"A pleasant land," literally, a land of longing. So the Land of Promise was called (Ps. 106:24; Zech. 7:14). On Israel's longing for the land, cp. Jer. 51:50-51; Ps. 42; 122; 137:5-6. "A goodly heritage of the hosts of nations," all the Gentile nations shall be the heritage, the possession of Israel (cp. Is. 60:1-16). See Grammatical Notes. It is preferable to render this clause: "an inheritance of glory of glories," superlative glory of the nations, the greatest glory known to the nations; God's Kingdom of Grace on earth passing over into the Kingdom of Glory, than which there is nothing more glorious, the pearl of great price (Matt. 13:45-46; Is. 54:11-14; 51:11; Phil. 3:8-14; Revelation 21—22). That is Jerusalem, the city fair and high, toward which we nightly pitch our moving tent, a day's march nearer home! That is the true homeland, for which the believers of the Old Covenant longed (Heb. 11:13-16).

"Thou shalt call," the imperfect of progressive duration. As often as the Church as a unit or in its individual members shall call upon God, they shall call Me: My Father! The filial relation, dear children of a dear Father, shall always be uppermost in their mind (Rom. 8: 14-17). "Shall not turn away from Me." The Una Sancta is ever faithful, will never apostatize (Jer. 31:22b; John 10:27-29; Rom. 8: 29-39). These decrees of the Lord (v. 19) make it impossible to interpret this passage (vv. 12-18) in a millennialistic sense, of a physical return of all Israelites to Palestine and the establishment of a visible kingdom of Israel under the rulership of Christ. As long as His particular covenant with the people of Israel continued, the Lord faithfully fulfilled His promises of temporal and material blessings given to the faithful covenant keepers (Ezra 1:1-11; ch. 3—7; Nehemiah 1—13; Hag. 2:11-19; Mal. 3:10). With the disestablishment of the Old Covenant, naturally its specific temporal and material blessings, the possession of the land, peace, and prosperity, as rewards promised for fulfillment of certain stipulations, ceased.

V. 20. The realization of the happy reunion pictured by the Lord (vv. 12-19) still lies in the distant future, and as He views the present state, He sees only unfaithfulness and apostasy. "The remembrance of Israel's past conduct rises unbidden in the mind of God to cross like a dark cloud this bright hope of Israel's return to God" (*Bible*

Commentary). "Surely, as a wife treacherously departeth from her husband," literally, friend, companion. "The choice of the word seems to indicate the inner hollowness of the married life. The woman sees in her husband only the companion, behind whose back she can follow her own inclinations." (Cheyne.) Yet the invitation of the divine Husband to His treacherous, apostate wife is not altogether futile.

D. Penitent return of Israel and Judah, vv. 21-25

21 A voice is heard on the bare hills, weeping lamentation of the Children of Israel; for they have perverted their ways; they have for-
22 gotten the LORD, their God! Turn, you turning children! I will heal, cure, your turnings! Behold, we are coming to Thee, for Thou art
23 the LORD, our God. Surely for naught were the hills, the noise of the mountains! Surely in the LORD, our God, is the salvation of
24 Israel! And Shame has eaten the product of our fathers from our youth! Their flocks and their herds,
25 their sons and their daughters! Let us lie prostrate in our shame, and let our reproach cover us! For against the LORD, our God, we have sinned, we and our fathers from our youth up to this day, and we have not listened to the voice of the LORD, our God!

Grammatical Notes

V. 23. "In vain," literally, "unto vanity, deceit." "From the hills," מִגְּבָעוֹת. Naegelsbach suggests to strike the dagesh and read מִגְעָוֹת, that which is high, heights. He maintains that while this word occurs only as the term for the priestly headgear ("bonnets," A. V.) (because of its height), there is no reason why the prophet here may not have used it in its etymological sense, heights, hills. This seems a more plausible explanation than other suggestions. LXX, Syrian, Vulgate translate "the hills," reading the article instead of the preposition. "From the multitude," הָמוֹן never has this meaning, it denotes noise, tumult.

V. 21. The grace and loving-kindness of the Covenant God finally breaks down their stubborn denial of their guilt (ch. 2:35) and their refusal to return (ch. 2:31-32). On the "high places," rather, dry hills (cp. ch. 3:2), once the scene of their idolatrous festivities, a voice is heard, far more pleasing to God than their ribald shouts at their boisterous festivities. It is the voice of weeping, of supplications, of prayers pleading for forgiveness for having perverted their ways and forgotten the Lord.

V. 22. At once the Lord strengthens their spiritual life to keep them from despair. Backsliding, apostasy, had been their sin; yet still He calls them children and bids them return. He is still their gracious Father, whose house is still open for them, whose arms are still extended to them (Luke 15:20-24). Come to Me! "I will heal your backslidings." He who has called them (v. 12), whose call has turned them (v. 21), He will also heal them, give them a faithful heart which will not turn from Him. Conversion *in toto* is God's work. We hear their joyous response (v. 21b) and a frank confession of their sin.

V. 23. The hills were unto deceit, deceived us; the mountains were noise. When the shouting and tumult and revelry were past, only guilt remained. On the nature of these noisy festivities cp. 1 Kings 14:23-24; 15:11-13; 2 Kings 23:4-15; Ps. 106:35-40; Is. 28:7-8; Hos. 4: 9-14; Amos 2:7b-8. Nowhere but in Jehovah is salvation to be found.

V. 24. "Shame," disgrace, *boshet*. This word was frequently used as a derisive name for Baal (Jer. 11:13; cp. Hos. 9:10); Jerubbaal (Judg. 6:32) = Jerubbosheth (2 Sam. 11:21); Ishbosheth (2 Sam. 2:8) = Ishbaal (1 Chron. 8:33). Baal worship, idolatry, has devoured the labors of our fathers. People usually spend far more money in serving their idols, in the maintenance of false religions, in service of the triple deity of this world (1 John 2:16), than God's children would think of sacrificing for their Savior and His Church. And in penalty of their idolatry God sent His judgments, droughts, famines, pestilence, war (Amos 4:4-12). Idolatry is expensive business, and its net results are an accusing conscience, a heavy burden of guilt, death, and damnation.

V. 25. "Confusion," burning shame "covereth us." The imperfect describes the ever-recurring feeling of shame surging up at every memory of their past sins. The more thoroughly the repentant realizes the true nature of sin and the loving-kindness of that God against whom his sin is directed, the more ashamed will he be of his past sins and the more determined to fight against this mistress of a thousand wiles. This is the godly sorrow of 2 Cor. 7:9-11; cp. also Jer. 31:19. — Note the long-drawn-out syllables in v. 25 (Hebrew) vividly picturing the sobbing and wailing of the repentant people. How different a spirit and language from that of ch. 2:25, 27, 31, 35!

CHAPTER 4

E. Such repentance must be wholehearted and effective of good works, vv. 1-4

1 If you will turn, Israel, is the oracle of the LORD, turn to Me! And if you remove your abominations from before Me, and do not roam about,
2 and swear by the living LORD truthfully in judgment and in jus-

tice, then nations will cause themselves to be blessed in Him and make Him the object of their praise.
3 For thus says Jehovah to the citizens of Judah and to Jerusalem: Break up the fallow ground, do not

4 sow among the thorns. Circumcise yourselves unto the LORD, and remove the foreskins of your heart, you citizens of Judah and inhabitants of Jerusalem; lest My wrath go forth as the fire and burn unquenchably because of the wickedness of your deeds.

Grammatical Notes

V. 1. תָּשׁוּב is 2. masculine, cp. וְנִשְׁבַּעְתָּ, v. 2, and the masculine suffix in "thy abominations." Israel and Judah, regarded as feminine in ch. 3, are now construed as masculine.

אִם with imperfect denotes that the condition is being fulfilled or that there is a possibility or probability of its future fulfillment. G.-K. 159 b.

Keil, following Ewald, construes all the clauses of ch. 4:1-2a as conditional, v. 2b as the apodosis. The LXX omits "then shalt thou not remove" and treats v. 1a as one conditional sentence: "If Israel would return, saith the LORD, let him return unto Me!" and vv. 1b-2 as a second conditional sentence in which the last clause "and the nations," etc., forms the apodosis. The A. V. has still a different construction. We prefer the construction of the LXX, retaining, however, "if thou wilt not remove," or "roam," as one of the conditions. So R. P. Smith in *Bible Commentary;* Cuerliss, A. R. Gordon in *The Complete Bible,* and others. "Remove." נוּד, to move to and fro, to waver, roam, rove.

Vv. 1-2. The picture of Israel's return to the Lord as presented ch. 3:21-25 was that of a future ideal still far removed from the present reality. Therefore the Lord once more appeals to His people: "If you turn, then to *Me* turn." Thou turning Israel (compare ch. 3:14, 22), constantly turning after strange gods, cease turning to those that cannot help you, and to Me turn, to Jehovah, to the unchanging God of the Covenant, to the almighty Savior, turn! And do that in the manner just described (ch. 3:21-25).

He adds a remarkable promise, based on certain conditions: 1) Remove your abominations, idolatry, and other atrocities, from My sight; 2) Thou shalt not roam, rove, run to and fro to other gods, but remain true to Me; 3) Swear by the life of Yahweh, the living Lord. Renew on your part the covenant you have broken, which still stands as far as God is concerned. "The Lord liveth" was the common form of the Jewish oath. On renewal of the covenant compare Deut. 26:17f.; 2 Kings 23:3; Neh. 9:1—10:39. Such swearing loyalty to God must be performed "in truth," not feignedly (Jer. 3:10), hypocritically, lyingly, deceitfully. It must be a swearing not only by word of mouth, but in "truth," in sincerity, in steadfastness; the truthfulness of which is manifested in all your actions. Your whole life must be in conformity with your oath, a life "in judgment," in keeping with what is right, what is laid down in the Law as the correct life pleasing to God, and "in righteousness," coupled with love, which is the chief

64

demand of God's Law (Deut. 6:5, 24-25; 10:12-13; Micah 6:8). And now the promise! Then shall the heathen, now offended by your life of sin and shame, bless and glorify the Lord God, whom now they blaspheme because of your wickedness (cp. Ezek. 36:20-23; Rom. 2:24). Then shall the promise of Jer. 3:17 be fulfilled. Israel's whole-hearted repentance shall be a blessing to themselves and to the world (cp. Gen. 12:3; 18:18; 22:18). Their apostasy, wickedness, treachery, shuts out themselves and causes others to be shut out from God's kingdom. For the Lord's sake, for your own sake, for the sake of the heathen world, repent! Turn! Wholeheartedly! In truth and in judgment and in righteousness! That is impossible, unless you change your entire life and begin anew with My help, who alone can heal you (Jer. 3:22). That is the thought brought out in the next verse.

V.3. Break up! Fallow! The English term "fallow," like the Hebrew *nir*, designates the act of plowing and working virgin soil, land that has not yet been broken, and then leaving it unseeded until the weeds or brambles have been killed by repeated and thorough plowing. To break virgin soil, to clear land that for centuries was woodland, covered with heavy timber or dense bramble, is hard work, and to plow such ground time and again seems such a waste of time and energy that one may be inclined to hurry this work and put the land to seed after the first superficial plowing. Yet to seed land that has been covered with weeds, thistles and thorns, quack grass, etc., is practically throwing the seed away and wasting one's labor. The weeds will grow faster than the grain and will choke it, or if it will not be choked entirely, only a small yield of inferior quality will be produced, and chances are that the next sowing will fare no better or even worse.

Therefore, before sowing, before looking for a harvest, break up for yourselves, for your own welfare, what fallow ground still is to be found within yourselves. Each individual must do that for himself, and all together for themselves. It is personal work for personal blessing; and common work for common weal. The more thoroughly the plowing and working is done, the richer the harvest.

Sow not among thorns (cp. Matt. 13:7). The weeds and brambles of sin and evil desires must be exterminated, relentlessly killed, if an abundant harvest of good works is to be gathered from the field of our hearts. The more thoroughly we root out every evil thought, the more luxuriantly will good desires grow up into good words and good deeds. That is hard work, but absolutely essential. It can be

65

done, if we remember the love of Him who has taken us by the hand and brought us to Zion (Jer. 3:14), and if we keep in remembrance the name of Jehovah (ch. 3:17), our Redeemer God, who has purchased us with the price of His own blood and death. This Word demanding repentance is the Word of the Lord, the Covenant God (v. 3a), a living Word, a power of God unto salvation, calling forth that very repentance it calls for.

V. 4. "Circumcise yourselves." The same truth is impressed by another figure, that of circumcision.*

The prophet turns again to the men of Judah and the inhabitants of Jerusalem of his day. They need this admonition as much as did Israel in captivity; and unless they heed the command, disaster and ruin shall surely come upon the nation. The Lord sees what Judah tried to cover and hide under the cloak of externalism, of outward obedience to the ritual and ceremonies prescribed in the Law of God. God does not tell them that they should neglect the cult; that ritual and ceremonies are man-made customs to be rejected and repudiated in the true worship of God. No, God had *commanded* Israel conscientiously and meticulously to perform all the rites and ceremonies prescribed by Him, and all the prophets insist on the observance of these rites. But God had also demanded that these rituals be carried out in the right spirit, that Israel circumcise not only the foreskin of their flesh, but of their hearts (Deut. 10:16); only such a circumcision, possible only by God's almighty grace (Deut. 30:6), would enable them to love God and keep His Commandments (Deut. 30:6). That is the lesson so easily forgotten, therefore so constantly repeated by the prophets and apostles. (Cp. Ezek. 11:19f.; 36:26f.; Rom. 2:29; Phil. 3:3; Col. 2:11; also Jeremiah's constant warning against walking in the imagination of their evil heart.) Mere outward circumcision makes them members of the commonwealth of Israel. Circumcision to Jehovah makes them Jehovah's true children, the true Israel, for whose sake God still remained the God of the nation. Refusal to turn to the Lord with their whole heart, to remove all uncleanness, refusal

---

* The ancient Jews distinguished various forms of circumcision. Pirke R. Elieser, c. 29: Rabbi Seira has said: There are five species of foreskins in the world, four in man, one in trees (Lev. 19:23). On the four in man remember this: Jer. 6:10 speaks of the foreskin of the ears; Ex. 6:12, 30, of the foreskin of the lips; Deut. 10:16, of the foreskin of the heart; Gen. 17:14, of the foreskin of the flesh (cp. Jer. 9:25). The foreskin of the heart is not able to do the will of its Creator.

to accept the Gospel and live in the Law of God would cause the wrath of the Lord to come forth like fire and burn with unquenchable fury.

2. God's Wrath is Poured Out on Judah and Jerusalem, Vv. 5-31

5 Publish in Judah, and announce in Jerusalem and say: Blow the trumpet in the land, and cry with a loud voice and say: Assemble! And let

6 us go to the fortified cities! Raise signals toward Zion! Flee! Do not tarry! For I am about to bring evil from the north and great ruin!

7 A lion has gone forth from his thicket, and a destroyer of nations has broken loose and gone forth from his place to make your land desolate, your cities will be demolished, rendered uninhabitable!

8 Therefore gird yourselves with sackcloth, lament, and shriek; for the burning wrath of the LORD

9 does not turn from us! On that day, is the oracle of the LORD, the courage of the king shall fail, and the courage of the princes shall fail, and the priests stand abashed, and the prophets be paralyzed with

10 fear. And I said: Ah! Lord Jehovah! Thou hast certainly deceived this people and Jerusalem, saying: Peace shall be unto you! while now the sword touches their very soul!

11 At this time shall it be said of this people and of Jerusalem: A hot wind from the bare hills directly toward the daughter of My people, not to winnow, not to cleanse!

12 A wind stronger than these shall come at My will! Now I also will

13 speak judgments with them! Behold! He comes up like clouds, and as a whirlwind are His chariots! Swifter than eagles His horses! Woe unto us! For we are ruined!

14 Wash your heart of wickedness, O Jerusalem, in order that you may be saved! How long will you harbor thoughts of wickedness in your

15 heart? For hark! A messenger from Dan, and an announcer of bad

16 news from Ephraim! Call it to the attention of the nations! Behold! announce it at Jerusalem! Watchmen are coming from a land afar off and raise their cry against the

17 cities of Judah! Like field guards they shall surround her, because she has revolted against Me, is the

18 oracle of the LORD. Your conduct and your action have brought this on you; it is your wickedness that causes you grief, that strikes your

19 heart. My heart! My heart! I must writhe in pain! The walls of my heart! My heart pounds within me! — I cannot keep silence! For my soul hears the blare of the

20 trumpet, the shout of battle! "Ruin upon ruin" is the cry! For destroyed is the whole land; swiftly are ruined my tents, in a moment

21 my curtains. How long must I see signals, hear the alarm of trum-

22 pets? Surely, My people is perverted; Me they do not know; foolish children they are; they are without understanding. Wise they are to do wickedness, but not how

23 to do good. I looked at the earth, and, behold, a void and formless mass! at the heavens, and their

24 light is gone! I looked at the mountains, and, behold, they quaked! And all the hills were

25 trembling. I looked, and, behold, all mankind was gone! And all the birds of the heavens had fled!

26 I looked, and, behold, the parkland was a desert! And all its cities were destroyed by the LORD and by His

27 burning wrath! For thus says the LORD: Desolation shall all the land become! Yet I will not com-

28 pletely annihilate it. Because of this shall the earth sorrow, and the heavens above shall be shrouded in darkness. Because I have spoken, I have planned and shall

not revoke it; and I will not turn
29 back from her. At the rumor of
horsemen and archers every city
takes to flight. They go into the
thickets and climb the crags. Every
city is deserted, no one remains
30 dwelling in them. And you —
O ruined one! — of what use was it
that you clothed yourself in scarlet
and decked yourself with golden
finery? that you widened your
eyes with eye paint? In vain did
you beautify yourself! Your lovers
despise you! Your soul they seek!
31 Hark! I hear a cry as of a woman
in travail, of anguish like that of
one that brings forth her first-born
child; it is the cry of the daughter
of Zion as she gasps for breath, as
she spreads out her hands: Oh,
woe is me! My soul must succumb
to murderers!

Grammatical Notes

V. 7. "His thicket," סָבְכוֹ, from סְבָךְ, something interwoven, with *dagesh forte euphonicum,* G.-K. 20 h.

V. 12. "Toward," דֶּרֶךְ, is the accusative used as locative. In connection with a genitive it often indicates the direction toward which the way leads, assumes prepositional force, "toward." (Compare Deut. 1: 19; Ezek. 8: 5; 40: 44.)

"Give sentence against," cp. note on Jer. 1: 16; אוֹתָם = אֶתָּם, G.-K. 103 b.

V. 19. אֹחִילָה, K'tib אָחוּלָה (47 Mss.), Q'ri אָחִילָה. The Q'ri is an abnormal form; the K'tib, cohortative of חוּל, to labor in childbirth, to writhe in pain. Like אֶשְׁמָעָה (v. 21), the cohortative here expresses a necessity, compulsion to a certain act. Gesenius-Kautzsch, 108 g, denies this usage. He asserts that in the passages usually listed in support of this usage the form of the cohortative was still retained for the usual imperfect because of its fuller sound, while its real meaning had completely vanished. This argumentation is not convincing, because in Jeremiah and in Psalms the cohortative is still being used in its original force, to express a self-exhortation (Jer. 18: 18), a wish (Jer. 9: 1; 40: 15), an intention (Jer. 20: 10). We therefore translate: I must writhe. How long must I hear?

V. 22. "For," כִּי, originally a demonstrative pronoun, may here be best translated as a particle of asseveration, Indeed! Surely! (Cp. Gen. 6: 5; 26: 9;

27: 20; Ex. 3: 12; etc. G.-K. 157 b. Cp. also Gen. 18: 20; 33: 11; Is. 7: 9; etc. G.-K. 148 d; 159 ee.)

"Foolish," אֱוִיל, from the stem אוּל, one of the various meanings of which is "to be at the front," a leader. The אֱוִיל is one who desires to be first, puts his own self into the foreground, the self-conceited (Prov. 12: 15), "prating" person ("fool of lips") (Prov. 10: 8, 10). The adjective and its noun usually have the connotation of sinfulness (cp. Job 5: 2-3; Ps. 38: 5; Prov. 1: 7) and at times that of incurableness (Prov. 26: 11; 27: 22).

V. 22. "Sottish," סְכָלִים, foolish, also frequently with the connotation of sinfulness, wickedness. So the Hiphil of the verb is used (Gen. 31: 28; 1 Sam. 26: 21), the Niphal (1 Sam. 13: 13; 2 Sam. 24: 10; 1 Chron. 21: 8; 2 Chron. 16: 9), the adjective (Jer. 5: 21; Eccl. 7: 17). In this sense of sinful folly, or sin as folly, we take it here, as the context evidently demands this connotation.

V. 22. "Understanding," נְבוֹנִים, is the plural participle Niphal of בִּין, the root idea of which is that of separation, distinction, differentiation. בִּינָה is the faculty to see clearly the distinguishing marks which differentiate one object from another and constitute its own peculiar nature; a faculty which is the very basis of true knowledge. (Cp. Prov. 14: 6 b; 17: 24 a.)

V. 30. אַתְּ. The original of the second feminine personal pronoun was אַנְתִּי, contracted to אַתִּ. The י later was dropped in speech and writing, but in seven passages the ending still occurs in the K'tib while the Q'ri points אַתְּ to indicate the current pronunciation. "Lovers," עֹגְבִים, the verb is used only of illicit love and occurs only here and Ezek. 23:5, 7, 9, 12, 16, 20.

Vv. 5-9a. At the approach of the enemy consternation and despair seizes the people who had refused to believe the prophet's warning. The alarm (v. 5a); the flight of the people to the fortified cities, particularly Jerusalem, standards everywhere pointing out the shortest and quickest route to the shelter (vv. 5b-6). From the north, like a killer lion, comes the enemy, depopulating and laying waste the land (vv. 6b-7). The lament of the people (v. 8). "Sackcloth," coarse cloth, such as is used for sacks (Gen. 42:25; Joshua 9:4), worn by mourners (Joel 1:13) on the hips (Jer. 48:37), or under the other garments (2 Kings 6:30). V. 9. The consternation and despair of the leaders, civic and spiritual. "The heart perishes," the seat of life, of intellect, emotion and will, here particularly the first and last, perishes. The rulers are paralyzed with fear, are completely helpless. Even the ready-tongued prophets (cp. Jer. 23:25-32) can only repeat, I have dreamed!

V. 10. Jeremiah's lament. Since the people in obstinate disobedience refused to listen to God's Word, the Lord not only permitted, but sent false prophets to deceive the hardened hearts by their ever-repeated "Ye shall have peace!" (Cp. Jer. 14:13; 23:17; 1 Kings 22: 20-23; also v. 18.)

Vv. 11-12. God's answer. He "gives sentence," pronounces judgment, by sending a stormwind, which will no longer aid in winnowing and cleansing the threshed grain, but will scatter, disperse the entire nation.

V. 13. The enemy's advance, swift and unrestrainable. He comes swiftly as a sudden thunderstorm, as an eagle swooping down on his unsuspecting prey, as a destructive whirlwind, three vivid pictures.

V. 14. A final warning. The cry of the people: We are lost! (v. 13b) is answered by the prophet: There is still hope! Repent! But do not delay!

Vv. 15-17. The necessity of immediate repentance is brought out by the rapid approach of the enemy, swiftly drawing ever nearer. Dan in the north, then through Ephraim, then Judah and Jerusalem.

V. 18. The guilt of the nation.

Vv. 19-21. Jeremiah speaks as the representative of the people. The land is laid waste! Incessant war alarms, sound of trumpet; innumerable standards marching past; destruction upon destruction, farms, gardens, homes, villages, cities, the whole land spoiled, laid waste; and still more troops coming; renewed destruction, pillaging. What a horrifying scene!

V. 22. Jehovah's lament over His people. A play upon words. The mystery is made still greater by the fact that sons, beloved, favored sons, *banim*, have become self-conceited fools, *lo nebonim*, lacking the power to distinguish; altogether unlike their Father. Apostatizing from the Fount of Wisdom, only folly and lack of understanding can be the result. "Sottish," the wicked fool (cp. Jer. 5:21; Eccl. 7:17).

Vv. 23-26. The desolate condition of Judah during the years of exile as foreseen by the prophet. I beheld, four times. Earth again is a *tohu wabohu* (Gen. 1:2). The heavens are turned into darkness. As though the final Judgment had come, earthquakes! Not a man! Not a bird! No more fruitful gardens! No more cities! All, all is laid waste, destroyed by the wrath of God. Compare 2 Kings 17:25-26 (Northern Israel); Jer. 52:4-30; Lamentations 1—5, on the ruthless destruction by the enemy. The threat (Deut. 28:47-68) will be fulfilled.

Vv. 27-28. God will punish without mercy, yet not make a full end. Judah is not yet finally rejected (cp. 1 Thess. 2:16).

V. 29. Deathlike silence after the swift conquest. The people have fled into thickets and hills, the cities are deserted. Quiet! Death!

Vv. 30-31. A final appeal to Jerusalem, pointing out her folly and its dismal results in a last effort to bring her to her senses.

"And when . . . thou do?" Rather, And thou, O destroyed thing, what did you get or profit? The omniscient God already sees Judah and Jerusalem, the whole land as a destroyed thing, a dead, lifeless object. In bitter irony (cp. Gen. 3:22; Ps. 2:4; Prov.1:24-26) He asks them what all their efforts to gain the favor of the world powers profited them. Judah played the part of an adulterous woman who seeks to keep the attentions of her paramour, wastes her time trying to cover with cosmetics the wrinkles and crow's feet, telltale evidence of beauty ravaged by age and a life of sin, and wastes her money for gaudy dress and flashy finery in a vain attempt to keep her friend's love by youthful appearance. So Judah did all in her power to gain the favor of the powers of this world. For them she became unfaithful to her divine Spouse and Redeemer, adopted the worship, the manners, the sins and abominations, of the heathen nations. And now she suffers the well-deserved fate of the unfaithful wife. Her Husband, the everlasting Lord of Hosts, has turned against her, and her lovers who used her while they found it profitable and satisfying, but all the time despised her, even while flattering her, grow tired of the self-seeking, self-willed, useless hag and do away with her.

Again Jeremiah shows his masterful skill in making words picture a scene vividly, impressively, indelibly to our mind's eye. We see Jerusalem in her death agony. Finally — alas too late! — are the eyes of the daughter of Zion opened to the actual situation confronting her because of her own folly. Now at last she recognizes her "lovers," Hebrew: *hogebim*, as her murderers, *horegim*. Like a woman in childbirth she shrieks in the agony of her soul. Alas, it is not her sinful folly that she bewails, but only the agony she must endure. She still remains the self-centered fool. Woe is me now! she cries, as with outstretched hands she sinks exhausted to the ground. The agony chokes her, she tries to catch her breath (the Hithpael "bewaileth herself," is causative reflexive), makes herself gasp, but all in vain; she must yield her wearied soul to murderers. She did not want God as her Husband, but sought paramours; she refused to have God beautify her, she insisted on beautifying herself and not for God, but for her lovers. She left God, the Fountainhead of life, and chose murderers as her friends. Three times her efforts to please these friends are described: You are constantly arraying yourself in scarlet; you deck yourself with gold; you "rend" your face with painting. The last refers to the custom of women of applying antimony, or stibium, a silver-white metallic element, the base for a black rouge with which women dyed the upper and under eyelids in order to "rend," widen, increase the apparent size of the eyes and to give them unnatural brilliancy (cp. Ezek. 23:40). And three times the futility of all these measures is stated: "In vain shalt thou make thyself fair; thy lovers despise thee; they seek thy life." Note the contrast, "Thou makest thyself fair," *tityappi*, and, "she maketh herself gasp" (bewaileth herself), *tityappeach*. Similar words, but what a contrast! The latter because of the former, and both her own acts, caused by herself! She refused to yield her soul, her life, to her Maker, her Husband, her Redeemer; she must yield it to murderers, who sought her life while posing as lovers. Therefore her weary soul is yielded to murderers. On this note ends the dirge of the Lord over His unfaithful spouse.

71

CHAPTER 5

3. Inescapable Destruction Brought On by the Lack of Faith

A. The universal lack of faith and godliness thwarts God's promise of forgiveness, vv. 1-9

1 Traverse the streets of Jerusalem, and look, and see, and search her squares, if you can find a man, any one doing what is right, diligently seeking faith, and I will forgive her.

2 Even if they say: As the LORD liveth! surely they swear falsely.

3 O LORD, are not Thine eyes directed towards faith? Thou hast stricken them, and they did not writhe; Thou hast destroyed them, and they refused to accept the punishment; they have made their faces harder than a rock, they re-

4 fuse to turn. I said: These are the lower classes! They are foolish; they do not know the way of the LORD, the judgment of their God.

5 I will go to the upper classes, and I will speak to them, for they know the way of the LORD, the rights of their God. Alas, all of them to-gether break the yoke, tear the

6 bonds. Therefore the lion of the forest will smite them, and the wolf of the desert will ruin them; a leopard is lying in wait for their cities, all that go out of them will be torn to pieces; for many are their rebellions, without number

7 their apostasies. In view of this, how can I pardon you? Your children have forsaken Me and swear by non-gods. I have fed them, but they keep on committing adultery and assembling by troops in harlot

8 houses. They are as well-fed stallions roaming about, every one neighs after his neighbor's wife.

9 Shall I not punish them for these things? is the oracle of the LORD; and shall I not take vengeance upon a nation which is like this?

Vv. 1-3. "Run ye to and fro," go up and down and down and up the "streets," avenues, lanes, and alleys of the city. "And see now," observe carefully, "and know," come to knowledge by experience. "And seek," search, "in the broad places thereof," the large open spaces or areas of which larger cities had a number, particularly at the city gates (cp. ch. 1:15). Here one was sure to find people at any time of day. "Executeth judgment," rather, to establish "judgment," what is right in God's sight, what God has established as the norm to be followed (cp. ch. 23:5), that norm which He Himself had laid down in His holy Word, His Law and His Gospel.

"That seeketh the truth," אֱמוּנָה. The word is derived from אמן, to be firm, steadfast, unwavering. The etymological meaning is still apparent in the first passage in which the term occurs, Ex. 17:12: "His [Moses'] hands were אֱמוּנָה," firmness, steadiness, being supported, steadied, by Aaron and Hur. As an ethical concept, the Hebrew term *emunah* is used to describe the unwavering firmness, the unchangeable faithfulness of the Lord in fulfilling His Word, His threats, His promises. In Deut. 32:4 God Himself interprets His faithfulness, and there each of

72

the seven statements concerning His *emunah* supplements the others, and all of them may be summed up in any one of these terms. In this sense the term is very frequently used in the Psalms, usually linked up with such terms as mercy (Ps. 36: 5; 89: 1, 2, 24), loving-kindness (Ps. 88: 11; 89: 33, 49), salvation (Ps. 40: 10), righteousness (Ps. 96: 13; 119: 138; 143: 1), where the added "faithfulness" designates the unalterableness and steadfastness of the quality named in connection with it.

It is used quite frequently to denote the faithfulness of man, man's faithful performance of his duties (so 1 Chron. 9: 22, 26, 31; 2 Chron. 31: 15, 18), where the phrase "in their set office" is to be translated "because of their faithfulness." Most commentators attribute this sense to the term wherever it occurs in Jeremiah.

There is, however, another usage of the term *emunah* as predicated of man. Hab. 2: 4 Gesenius-Buhl translates: "the faithful holding fast to God and His Word." There can be no reasonable doubt as to the correctness of this translation, and there ought to be no doubt as to the nature of the Word of God to which the righteous man holds fast in a firm and steadfast grip. Hab. 2: 3 speaks of a vision, a prophecy, for the fulfillment of which the people are to wait, which is to be the object of their unwearied hope and unfaltering faith (v. 4), since it would surely be fulfilled in its appointed time, toward which it was even now hastening. "The prophet is speaking of a vision that tarries, but that will surely come at last. Thus it is not the righteous man's truthfulness, reliability, uprightness, virtues that he may have, which may waver, but his faith. The prideful Chaldean disregards God and His promise, and thus is lost; the righteous man trusts, believes, and thereby lives." (Lenski, *Romans*, p. 90.)

To deny that the only correct translation of Hab. 2: 4 is "faith," and not "faithfulness," i. e., faithful performance of one's duty, is to deny not only the correctness of Paul's translation of this term Rom. 1: 17; it would undermine his entire argument for the doctrine of justification, not by any works of man, but solely through faith in the vicarious atonement effected by Christ Jesus. He would base his argument for this thesis on a Scripture passage which in fact teaches the exact opposite: Salvation by faithful performance of one's duty. The Holy Spirit speaking through Paul certainly knew what He meant by *emunah* when He spoke Hab. 2: 4 through His prophet (cp. 1 Peter 1: 10-11).

Text and context demands the translation of *emunah* as "faith" also in Jer. 5:1, 3. Israel's failure to "execute judgment" consisted not merely in an occasional lack of faithfulness, nor merely in transgressions multiplied and backslidings repeated time and again. Their sin is far more deep-seated, far worse. The Lord describes it as a refusal to "return," to return to Him in the manner just outlined by Him in the preceding chapters. They refused to regard Him as the Fountain of living waters (ch. 2:13), refused to accept His gracious invitation (ch. 3:1), refused to thoroughly break up their fallow ground (ch. 4:3), refused to circumcise themselves to the Lord and take away the foreskin of their hearts (ch. 4:4); they refused to wash their hearts from wickedness (ch. 4:14); they refused to return to the Lord with a humble confession of their sins and disobedience (ch. 3:25), yet in the firm trust that in spite of their shame and confusion (ch. 3:25) there was salvation for them in the Lord God of Israel (ch. 3:25). They refused to believe not only the threats of God's Law, belying Him by saying: Evil shall not come upon us (ch. 5:12), refusing to receive correction (ch. 5:3); forsaking Him and swearing by non-gods (ch. 5:7), and when they said: The Lord liveth, by swearing falsely (ch. 5:2). They belied the Lord also by refusing to say Yea and Amen to His Gospel promises, by making their faces harder than a rock against His gracious invitations to return to Him as to their God and Lord of mercy and grace. Not only the foolish, ignorant masses, but in even greater measure the men of education, the men of rank, the upper classes — all refused to know, to love, to follow the way and the judgment of their God. As they said No! to the demands of the Law, so they shouted out their No! to the Gospel invitations. Their sin was unbelief, lack of faith, a state of hardening their hearts against their Creator and Redeemer.

In contradistinction to this universal lack of faith, this general refusal to regard faith as being the one factor of greatest importance, or as being a factor at all in one's life, it was just this faith for which the Lord looked and upon which He directed His eyes (cp. ch. 9:24). And the history of God's people proved that it was not so much the faithfulness of the people in serving God which God regarded, but their faith in the promise of a Redeemer who would save them in spite of their many acts of unfaithfulness. It was faith in the promise of the coming Messiah and Savior that the Lord counted to Abraham, the forefather of Israel, as righteousness (Gen. 15:6). And God caused this fact to be recorded in Holy Writ as an example of what He regarded as righteousness and what all men were to seek, to strive after, if they desired to be accounted righteous. And it was this faith, this firm adherence to God's Gospel promise, which the ancient heroes of faith sought and held fast as their most glorious possession. So Eve (Gen. 4:1), and Lamech (Gen. 5:29), and Jacob on his deathbed (Gen. 49:18), and David (2 Sam. 7:18-29), and the believers in general (Ps. 14:7). Compare also Hebrews 11. Text and context demand the translation "faith," not "faithful performance of one's duties." Naturally the latter is not ruled out as a factor in the believer's life. But it is faith which regenerates and enables the believer to walk in the way of God's Law. Emphasizing faith as the all-important factor in a believer's life, we do not "make void the Law of God through faith. God forbid! Yea, we establish the Law!" (Rom. 3:31.)

So highly the Lord esteems faith that He is ready to go even farther than Abraham dared to ask Him to go in that remarkable plea for Sodom (Gen. 18:22-33). Abraham stopped at ten; the Lord is willing to forgive the city if anyone is found that seeks faith. What a height of grace and long-suffering and loving-kindness, and what a depth of depravity and unbelief must the all-seeing eyes of the Lord have beheld in that city He had chosen to place His name there, that He could challenge the people to find one who would seek to establish His judgment, His norm, and strive after faith to be the ruling factor in this city! This refusal to regard faith as the one thing needful was the source of all their other sins and their persistence in sin in spite of all chastisements and punishments of God (v. 3 b).

V. 4. "Poor," the poverty-stricken masses (Jer. 39:10), oppressed and downtrodden, who have seen only the seamy side of life, whose hardships have hardened their hearts in unbelief.

V. 5. The great men, wealthy and cultured, were even worse; altogether yoke breakers. Their idea of freedom was lawlessness, license to do as they pleased, freedom from every restraint imposed by man or the Lord.

V. 6. "Lion," collective singular for plural. "Evenings," עֲרָבוֹת, not evenings, but, lowlands, plains, the haunts of wolves and jackals. "Leopard," the "striped one," the panther, lying in wait (same word as "hasten," be wakeful, watch, ch. 1:12) for the unwary traveler. The land will be full of wild beasts (cp. Ezek. 14:15, 21; Lev. 26:6, promise, v. 22, threat; Deut. 32:24; 2 Kings 17:25ff.). No need, therefore, to regard the three beasts as symbols of the enemy armies.

75

V. 7. How shall I, how can I forgive? Their unbelief makes forgiveness impossible. They have rejected Me and swear by false gods!

Vv. 8-9. Their unbelief is manifested by their wickedness. They roam about like well-fed stallions, each one lusting for his neighbor's wife, only one example of their atrocious wickedness. The very nature of His covenant with them compels Him to take the course He is about to take. While they broke the covenant, He will keep it (Deut. 28:15-68).

B. Unbelief will not frustrate God's threat, vv. 10-19

10 Ascend her terraces and destroy, but do not make a full end! Shear off her tendrils, for they are not
11 the LORD'S own. For the house of Israel and the house of Judah have treacherously broken faith with Me,
12 is the oracle of the LORD. They have denied the LORD and keep on saying: "It is not He!" And: "Evil will not come to us; neither will we
13 see sword and famine; and prophets are as wind, and the word is not in them. Thus shall it happen
14 to them." Therefore thus says the LORD, the God of Hosts: "Because you have spoken this word, behold, I have made My words in your mouth as fire and this people as firewood, and it shall consume
15 them. Behold, I am about to bring against you a nation from afar, O house of Israel, is the oracle of the LORD, a powerful nation this, an ancient nation this, whose language you do not know and whose speech you do not understand.
16 Their quiver is like an open grave,
17 all of them are men of valor. He will eat your harvest and your bread. They will eat your sons and your daughters; he will eat your flocks and herds; he will eat your vines and your fig trees; he will beat down your fortified cities, on which you have placed your confidence,
18 with the sword. And yet in these days, it is the oracle of the LORD. I will not make a complete end
19 of you. And when you shall say: On what account does the LORD, our God, do all this to us? then you shall say to them: Just as you have forsaken Me and have served alien gods in your land, so you shall serve strangers in a land not yours.

V. 10. Jerusalem is compared to a vineyard soon to be destroyed (cp. Is. 5:1ff.; Jer. 2:21). The Lord calls upon the enemies to scale the vineyard walls and to destroy, remove, her "battlements," rather, branches, tendrils, which the Lord disowns because they are wild, degenerate shoots (Jer. 2:21), unfruitful, worthless. The vineyard is forsaken by its Owner and turned over to marauding bands of robbers. Yet they are not to destroy the vineyard completely, they are to remove only the dead and unfruitful branches. The vine itself is to remain alive. The oncoming destruction was not to be the final rejection.

V. 11. Treachery, Judah's sin (ch. 3:7-12), is here, like ch. 3:20, attributed to both kingdoms.

Vv. 12-13. "Belied," denied (Joshua 24:27; Is. 59:13). "Not He!" He, the Covenant God, who has adopted us as His own, cannot and will not turn against His people! That is misrepresenting the unchanging Lord! "Prophets become wind!" The prophets speaking against us and boasting that they are instruments of רוּחַ (wind, spirit, Spirit), are nothing but רוּחַ, wind, "windbags." "And the word," or as it may be translated: "He who speaks," is not in them. They speak their own mind. "Thus," as they threaten us, "shall it be unto them." "This passage reveals the shocking hardihood, skepticism, and ripened depravity of the people" (Cowles).

V. 14. "The LORD, the God of Hosts." Jehovah, the Covenant God of Israel, is at the same time "the LORD, the God of Hosts," whose scepter rules all nations. Majestically He answers the slanderous charge the people made against His prophets and vindicates them as His messengers. The first words are directed to the scoffers. Then He turns away from them to address His faithful messenger. "Behold! I am about to make My words in thy mouth a fire and these people fagots, kindling wood, and it shall eat them." That despised prophet is acknowledged by the Lord as His spokesman, whose word is God's word and, though spoken by a human mouth, will lose nothing of its power.

V. 15. The destruction is fast approaching. God is sending a nation whose manpower is as unlimited as its natural resources are inexhaustible. "An ancient nation," dating back to the very dawn of history (Gen. 10:10). Their language will be unintelligible to the Jews, they will not be able to understand their demands and for that very reason be treated by a merciless enemy as disobedient, rebellious people, maltreated, tortured, killed.

Vv. 16-17. The destruction is complete. Their quiver, the singular is collective; "an open sepulcher"; as the open grave gapes for its victims (Prov. 30:16), so the quiver of the bowmen gapes relentlessly for ever more victims (cp. Hab. 2:5). The bowmen with their huge bows, used not only for killing, but also for shooting firebrands into the city, formed one of the chief divisions of the ancient armies. Their insatiable hunger for plunder and robbery and murder will spare neither the necessities of life, nor their sons and daughters, nor their flocks and herds, nor the luscious fruits, nor their cities on whose strong fortifications they had placed their trust instead of confiding in their Lord. All that they cherished will be taken from them.

V. 18. The destruction is not yet final. Into the darkness of human

77

cruelty and divine darkness there shines a gleam of hope. The exile for Judah shall not be a complete and final rejection (cp. v. 10). The same prophet who is God's messenger of wrath is also His spokesman of grace.

V. 19. Instead of recognizing their own sins as the cause of God's judgment, they ask in querulous tones: Why does God do this to us? God tells them that since they have served foreign gods in God's land, they shall serve foreigners in a foreign land.

C. Judah's guilt the sole cause of her ruin, vv. 20-31

20 Announce this to the house of Jacob, and publish it in Judah, 21 saying: Hear this, O foolish people and without understanding. You have eyes and see not, you have 22 ears and hear not. Will you not fear Me, is the oracle of the LORD, or will you not tremble before Me, who has placed sand as a boundary for the sea, as an everlasting decree, and it shall not pass over it? Though its waves toss themselves, they shall not succeed, and though they roar, they shall not pass 23 over it. But this people has a revolting and rebellious mind; they 24 revolt and go away. Neither do they say in their heart: Let us fear the LORD, our God, who gives us rain, the early and the latter rain, in His time, and has preserved for us the appointed weeks of the 25 harvest. Your iniquities have prevented them, and your sins keep 26 the blessings from you. For wicked men are found among My people. Every one lies in wait, crouching as a fowler; they set their traps; 27 men they catch. As a basket that is full of birds, so their houses are filled with fraud. Therefore they 28 become great and rich. They are fat; they are sleek; they also surpass the deeds of the wicked. They do not plead the cause, the cause of the orphan, to carry it to success; and the cause of the poor they do 29 not judge. Shall I not punish because of all these things? is the oracle of the LORD, or shall My soul not avenge itself upon a nation 30 such as this? A horrible and appalling thing is happening in the 31 land: The prophets prophesy falsehoods, and the priests rule at their side; and My people love to have it so! And what shall you do at the end?

Vv. 20-21. The Lord addresses not only the prophet, but all that still have the welfare of God's kingdom at heart, to testify against the sins that the people, blind to God's judgments and deaf to His warnings, foolishly continue to heap up as a huge mass of guilt.

Vv. 22-23. What folly not to stand in holy awe before the almighty and all-wise God! Tiny grains of sand, so small as to be symbolic of weakness, so light that every gust of wind can pick them up and whirl them away, are used by the Lord to establish an impassable barrier to the sea. While the wild waves of the ocean must obey their Creator, this people has a revolting and rebellious heart. On "revolting and rebellious" cp. Deut. 21:18, 20, where this sin is described as a capital crime, to be punished by stoning. Such a revolting and rebellious heart directs the ways of the people. They have "revolted," and they "keep going" on their self-chosen ways of stubborn revolt.

V. 24. The wickedness and folly of their disobedience is manifested also in their ingratitude. Only one item is mentioned, the providing of their daily food. The God of the Covenant manifested His faithfulness by giving them (the participle denotes what is characteristic) rain showers, both the early rains, from the middle of October to the middle of December, so essential to soften the ground parched and hardened by the long rainless, hot summer season, and without which the seed could not sprout and grow, and the "latter rain" (cp. ch. 3:3). As the Lord kept His covenant with the rain (cp. Job 28:26; 38:25-28, 34-38) in His appointed time, so also He "reserveth," faithfully observes and keeps the appointed weeks (weeks of decrees = decreed weeks) of harvest "for us." The great Lord of nature places Himself in the position of a servant to His people.

V. 25. The Covenant God is not only the Giver of good gifts, He can also withhold His gifts if His people do not live in accordance with the stipulations of this covenant (cp. Deut. 28:15-68). Since they have become guilty of sins and iniquities, the Lord in fulfillment of the covenant withheld His blessings by sending unseasonable weather, heavy rains, parching droughts, destructive mildew, or blight, voracious locusts. These withholdings of His blessings proved that God was still watching over His covenant, which they were constantly disregarding.

V. 26. "For among My people" are found, are manifest, publicly known, wicked men, ungodly. "Among" My people, not of them! "They lay wait," as the crouching of snarers. They carefully plan and go to great trouble to carry out their wicked schemes. They try to keep in hiding. They secretly set their traps and snares to catch not birds or beasts, they are out to catch men! And they meet with success.

V. 27. "As a cage is full of birds." Commentators are undecided on the exact meaning. Some render: As a basket is full of birds placed into it by the successful trapper, others, a basket used to trap birds. We prefer the latter rendering. The LXX translates snare. In Ecclus. 11:30 Jesus Sirach speaks of a decoy partridge in a "basket," a word occurring also Deut. 26:2, 4; 2 Kings 10:7; Jer. 6:9, translated "basket." This decoy partridge, placed into a basket for the purpose of luring others into the basket trap is used as an illustration of the heart of the proud man. Evidently the LXX knew of the use of basket traps or trap baskets for catching birds. Jeremiah, the close observer, uses these baskets gradually being filled with birds as an illustration of the houses and business places of the wicked, where one employee or partner after the other is lured into the wicked schemes, until the whole house is filled with deceit and fraud. And as a result of their shrewd schemes they become great, leaders, and grow richer and richer.

V. 28. "They are waxen fat, they shine," they ooze prosperity; their circumference grows with their increasing riches; and so does their wickedness. "They overpass the deeds of the wicked"; no atrocity too heinous, no crime too abominable, as long as it serves their purpose. Inconsiderate of the rights of the fatherless and needy, they have only one interest, their own gain (cp. Amos 2: 6-8; 8: 4-6).

V. 29. See v. 9.

Vv. 30-31. "A wonderful," literally, astonishing, stunning, horrifying. "Horrible," שַׁעֲרוּרָה, derived from a stem denoting filthiness, dirt, rottenness, occurs only Hos. 6: 10; Jer. 18: 13; 23: 14; 29: 17. In our passage it describes the rotten wickedness of the prophets, the priests, and the people. The prophets are deceivers. The priests ruled, led the people, "by their means," literally, "at their hands," side by side with the prophets, marching shoulder to shoulder, hand in hand with them in their horrible deception of the people, fostering a superficial religion, false security based on perfunctory performance of ritualistic forms. Their deceit was filthiness, akin to the rottenness of Sodom, in God's view; nor did it exempt them from the holy wrath and just judgment of the Supreme Judge. "And My people love to have it so." The people who despised and blasphemously ridiculed the true prophets and their divine oracles, loved these prophets who satisfied their ears, itching for just such promises of Peace! Peace! "And what will ye do in the end of it?" What will a man that has rejected God, and His Law, and His Gospel, and His Redeemer, do in the end, when death comes, when he stands before the Judgment Throne? (Rom. 6: 21; James 1: 15.)

CHAPTER 6

4. Irrevocable Judgment!

A. Exhortation to flee from Jerusalem, vv. 1-8

1 Flee, O children of Benjamin, out of Jerusalem! In Tekoah blow the trumpet! At Beth-Hakkerem raise a signpost! For evil arises from the 2 north and complete ruin! I destroy the beautiful and delicate one, the 3 daughter of Zion. Against her shall come shepherds and their flocks; they pitch their tents round about her; each one pastures his plot. 4 Prepare war against her! Up! Let us attack her at noon! Woe unto us, for the day declines, and the shadows of evening are length- 5 ening! Up! Let us attack her at 6 night and destroy her palaces. For thus says the LORD of Hosts: Cut down trees, and raise ramparts against Jerusalem. For she is a city doomed to punishment. Nothing but oppression is within her! 7 As a fountain causes its water to bubble forth, so she bubbles forth her wickedness; violence and oppression are heard in her. Always before Me are sickness and wounds! 8 Take warning, O Jerusalem, lest My soul be removed from you, lest I make you desolate, an uninhabited land.

Grammatical Notes

V. 2. "I have likened . . . woman." דָּמָה in the sense of "likened to" would require the addition of ל or אֶל. Another root דמה, construed with accusative, has the undisputed meaning "to destroy, to annihilate." (Cp. Hos. 4:5 and the passive Niphal, Hos. 4:6; 10:15; Is. 15:1; Zeph. 1:11; Jer. 47:5.) Volz regards that as too strong an expression, but does not give any reason. God uses still stronger language concerning Jerusa-lem's fate (2 Kings 21:12-14; Jer. 7:20; 9:11, 15-22; etc.).

V. 3. "In his place," אֶת יָדוֹ = what is in his hand, what he has taken, or what has been assigned to him, his patch, area, plot.

"Feed," pasture, here in sense of pasturing clean, till nothing is left, cp. Ezek. 34:18; Micah 5:5 (A. V., v. 6); Jer. 2:16.

V. 1. "O ye children . . . Jerusalem." The prophet, being a Benjamite, is particularly interested in the welfare of his fellow tribesmen. In ch. 4: 6 the people were urged to flee to Jerusalem. Now even this strong city is no longer a safe refuge place. Trumpet blasts from Tekoah (= trumpet) were to call the people to assemble there in their flight to the wilderness of southwestern Judah. "Sign of fire," the word denotes any signal post, not necessarily a fiery beacon. *Beth-haccerem,* probably "Frank Mountain," a square-shaped hill east of Bethlehem. (Stanley, *Sinai and Palestine,* p. 231.)

V. 2. "I have likened," rather, "I will destroy" (same word as Hos. 4: 5, 6; 10: 15; Is. 15: 1). "Comely," lovely; "delicate," fondled, petted. The Lord loved His bride, showered her with bridal gifts, Deut. 32: 9-14; but Israel repaid her Spouse with basest ingratitude (cp. Deut. 32:15), and now the Lord prepares to fulfill His threat (Deut. 32:19-25). "Daughter," a great honor bestowed on Israel. "Zion," the hill chosen by the Lord as His earthly abode; and in this home Judah was not only a slave, a guest, but a beloved, lovely, pet daughter! This Judah, God will destroy!

V. 3. The enemy is compared to shepherds pitching their tents round about Jerusalem. As sheep crop the pasture close till nothing but the bare soil remains, so the enemies will "depasture," devastate, the land to the point of exhaustion.

Vv. 4-5. "Prepare," literally, "sanctify," "consecrate." Before beginning a campaign or a battle, the Israelites offered sacrifices (1 Sam. 7:9; 13:9), an inspirational address was delivered either by a priest (Deut. 20:2) or an officer (1 Chron. 20:22), and then the battle cry was shouted (1 Sam. 17:52; Is. 42:13; Jer. 50:42). Other nations had similar customs. As soon as these preparations were finished, the soldiers, like a pack of hungry wolves, hastened to their bloody work. We hear their eager shouts as they urge each other to the greatest possible hurry and exertion. Let us go up at noon! Usually the scorching midday hours were given to relaxation and rest. Not here! Noontime passes, the afternoon hours pass by, and still they have not reached their goal. And still they go on. The lengthening evening shadows announce the coming of the night. Instead of cooling their ardor, they incite them only to greater exertion. Let us go by night! As they did not permit the scorching noonday sun to stop their march, so throughout the darkness of the night the tramp of the soldiers, the hoofbeats of the horses, the rattling of the chariots go ceaselessly on! "Destroy her palaces!" Plunder, arson, rape, murder, devastation, and ruin alone will satisfy their implacable hatred, their ruthless passions.

V. 6. Though they know it not, they are merely the instruments of the Covenant God of Israel, who is the Lord of the nations, who through them carries out His threat of destruction (v. 2). It is He who from His throne on high issues His commands. "Hew ye down trees." Assyrian and Babylonian kings boast of the many trees they felled to be used for battering rams and catapults and other engines of war, or to help furnish the material for the "mounts," the sloping siege mounds, built up by "casting" or pouring out basketfuls of earth, until "every head was bald and every shoulder peeled" by the heavy loads carried on head and shoulders (Ezek. 29:18). The mounds sloped upward until they reached half the height of the city wall. From the towers erected on the top of the mound heavy stones were hurled against the wall, or firebrands thrown into the city, or arrows shot at the defenders on the walls (cp. Hab. 1:10; 2 Sam. 20:15; Is. 37:33). The hills, denuded of their trees, the valleys, of their orchards and vineyards, are left bare and barren. The symbols of life and vigor (Ps. 37:35; 92:12) became by the judgment of the Lord of Life the instruments of death and destruction, because when He had set before them life and death, and blessing and cursing, in order that they might choose life (Deut. 30:19-20), they had deliberately chosen death by rejecting God and His Word of life and becoming a city doomed to punishment, because there was "wholly oppression within her."

V. 7. "As a fountain . . . wickedness." "Casteth out," bubbles forth, wells forth, from a stem denoting the welling up of a spring. Sennacherib boasted: "I dug," i.e., I caused to flow, to well up, "and drank water" (2 Kings 19:24; Is. 37:25). Jerusalem is so thoroughly wicked that her wickedness wells up constantly in all she does. "Violence," insolent injustice, and "spoil," robbery, oppression, are openly and boastfully committed without fear of man or God. "Grief," sickness, "wounds," physical agony, and heartaches caused by their cruelty.

V. 8. God had sufficient reason to annihilate so wicked and ungrateful a nation. Yet once more He urges Jerusalem to turn from her wickedness, assuring her that she will not be punished if only she accept His instruction. That is the sure way of escape, and the only way! Else My soul will depart from you. And as if convinced that even this last appeal will be futile, He now foretells the complete destruction of the land.

B. Judah shall be gleaned thoroughly, vv. 9-15

9 Thus says the LORD of Hosts: Glean the remnant of Israel thoroughly like a vine. Keep on like a grape gatherer passing your hand 10 back and forth to the baskets. To whom shall I speak and give warning that they may hear? Behold, their ears are uncircumcised, and they cannot give heed. Behold, the Word of the LORD has become a reproach to them; they take no 11 pleasure in it. I am filled with the wrath of Jehovah; I am weary of holding it back! Pour it out upon the children in the street and also on the gatherings of young men. For husband and wife shall be taken prisoners, the old man to- 12 gether with him of full days. And their houses shall be turned over to others together with fields and wives, for I shall stretch out my hand against the inhabitants of the land, is the oracle of the LORD. 13 For from their least to their greatest every one is out for unrighteous gain, and from prophet to priest 14 every one practices deceit. And

they heal the wound of My people carelessly, saying, Peace! Peace! 15 and there is no peace! They shall be put to shame, for they commit abominations without the least shame. They no longer know how to blush. Therefore they shall fall with those that fall. When I shall punish them, they shall stumble, says the LORD.

V. 9. The enemy shall thoroughly glean what still remains of My once glorious people of Israel. "Turn back . . . baskets," the ever-repeated, incessant turning one's hand from vine to basket, from basket to vine, until the last grape is picked off the vine and it stands destitute of fruit. We think of the repeated deportations and slayings of the Jews that had survived the long siege (Jer. 39: 5-10; 41:1-10; 42:19-22; 52:15, 24-30).

V. 10. "To whom shall I speak . . . hear?" For the first time the prophet voices his discouragement, complains of the difficulty and hopelessness of his task. As he contemplates the wickedness of his people, it assumes ever greater proportions. "Their ear is uncircumcised," because they refuse to permit the Lord to open their ears by His Word and Spirit. They have arrived at the stage that they cannot hearken, because by divine judgment their ears are made heavy (Is. 6:9f.), dulled, deafened. The Word of the Covenant God is not a delight to them; it is an object of their reproach and ridicule, suitable perhaps for children and imbeciles, but not to their adult taste, to their enlightened understanding, their superior learning. To preach to such people seems too hopeless, too ungrateful a task. Why continue?

V. 11. The prophet at once silences the complaint of his flesh. "I am full of the fury." (Cp. Ezek. 2:8; 3:3; Jer. 15:16; and notes on Jer. 1:2.) Success or no success, his duty was to preach God's wrath to all the wicked. And since this wrath filled him, it would be far too wearisome and impossible a task to "hold in," to refuse to publicly preach it. In self-exhortation he cries out: Pour out, as you have done, so continue to pour out God's wrath on this wicked nation, on the children abroad, playing on the streets, wicked offspring of wicked parents; on the assembly of young men together, on the gatherings of the adolescent youth, where under the influence of gang leaders they plan their sinful doings; on husband and wife, mature people, maturing also in their enmity against God and His Word; on the aged, whose hoar head is not a crown of glory found in the way of righteousness, but who have grown old in the love and service of sin and self; and on them that are "full of days," tottering to the grave, whose only regret is that they can no longer enjoy the pleasures of sin and the flesh. Pour out on all the fury of God's wrath!

V. 12. Houses, fields, wives — a climax of increasing value. All that is near and dear to them is taken away from them. The hand of the Lord, once stretched out to deliver them from their enemies (Ex. 3:20; Deut. 7:19), now is stretched out against them to deliver them to their enemies.

Vv. 13-14. Young and old are given to covetousness, that root of every evil, and evil only. Even the prophets and priests seek only the applause and good will and favor and gifts of the people and for that reason "heal slightly the hurt of the daughter of My people." Slightly, as if it were a mere trifle, they apply soothing, balmy words of "Peace! Peace! All is well! God cannot forsake His people," while the hurt is not a slight matter, but a matter of life and death, a breaking down of morality that threatens their very existence as God's people, while they themselves are totally blind to their real condition. And this dangerous state is due largely to the flattering, soft-soaping, self-seeking priests and prophets.

V. 15. Unashamed, they proceed in their wicked ways to their ruin. The visitations of the Lord, which might have served their purpose to be corrective chastisements, became by their own foolish wickedness dire punishments. "They shall fall!"

C. Look for the ancient paths, and walk on them, vv. 16-21

16 Thus says the LORD: Stand in the ways, and see, and inquire for the ancient paths, where the good way is, and walk on it, and find rest for your souls. But they keep on saying: We will not walk on it! 17 And I have set watchmen over you. Hearken to the sound of the trumpet! And they say: We will 18 not hearken! Therefore hear, O nations! O congregation! Realize 19 what is in them! Hear, O earth! Behold, I am bringing evil upon this people, the fruit of their plannings; for they paid no attention to My words, and as for My Law, 20 they rejected it. Why should incense from Sheba be brought to Me, and sweet cane from a land afar off? Your burnt offerings are not pleasing to Me, and your bloody 21 offerings do not satisfy Me! Therefore thus says the LORD: Behold, I am placing stumbling blocks before this people, and fathers and sons together shall stumble against them, the neighbor and his friend shall perish.

Vv. 16-17. "Stand ye in the ways. . . ." Once more the Lord in truly divine patience, far more enduring than that of human beings, seeks to check their headlong rush to their everlasting perdition by flashing a signal of warning. Stand! Halt! "Ask for the old paths!"

Since here these "old" paths are to be sought by men who are walking on paths that lead to destruction, the "old" paths are such as have in olden times led men to salvation. They are the ways on which the people of God walked in the days before the Flood, which were chosen by the patriarchs, by men of whom God Himself testified that He was pleased with them (Gen. 4:4; 5:24; 6:8-9; 12:9; Job 1:8; 2:3; 42:7-8), because they believed in His promises and led a godly life (Gen. 4:1; 5:29; 15:6; 49:18; Job 19:25-27). Therefore this way is called "the good way," not because "antiquity gives a presumption of rightness" (*Pulpit Commentary*), but because it is the way God Himself has chosen for the good, the welfare, the salvation of mankind.

"Ye shall find rest for your souls." Only in the assurance that the promised Messiah would comfort them in their work and toil on the accursed earth (Gen. 5:29); that the Righteous Servant, stricken, smitten, and afflicted for their transgression laid on Him that they might have peace (Is. 53:4-6); only in this assurance would they find rest for their souls (cp. Matt. 11:28). What a gracious invitation extended by the God of holiness to wicked apostates! And oh! the black ingratitude with which this plea was met! They said, they kept on saying (imperfect): "We will not walk!" All the continued efforts of the Lord to woo and win them back to the way of good by setting watchmen over them (v. 17), warning them against the impending danger, met with the same stubborn reply: We will not hearken! Cp. Matt. 23:37.

Vv. 18-19. "Therefore hear, ye nations!" The Lord calls upon all nations to hear and "know," apply to themselves the lesson He is about to teach in the punishment of His people. "Congregation" is the term usually applied to the Israelites in assembly; but it is also used of other gatherings (cp. Ps. 7:7; 22:16; Num. 16:5, 6, 11, 16; Judg. 14:8, a swarm of bees). The Lord addresses the nations as an "assembly," a "congregation," perhaps in order to indicate that no longer He regards the people of Judah as His congregation. (Cp. Acts 13:46; 18:5-6.)

"What is among them." These words have been translated and interpreted in many different ways. It seems best to translate: "what is in them." The nations shall hear and realize what is in the people who call themselves God's chosen people, yet refuse to do His will; a people in whose heart dwells such ingratitude as is rarely, if ever, found among the Gentile nations. (Cp. Jer. 2:9-13.) The whole earth shall hear of the horrible judgment to be executed by the Lord as "the fruit," the direct result of their rejection of God's Law. The Jews, scattered throughout the nations, became the advertisers of their own sin and guilt. (Cp. Deut. 28:37; 29:24-28; 1 Kings 9:7-9; Jer. 19:8; 22:8.)

V. 20. "To what purpose . . . unto Me." "Incense," here the finest of its kind, the white incense imported from distant Sheba, in the extreme southeastern boundary of the Arabian peninsula, some 1,400 to 1,500 miles south of Jerusalem; it was used as an ingredient of the holy incense to be used in the Temple only (Ex. 30:34). "Sweet cane," an ingredient of the holy anointing oil (Ex. 30:23), was most likely the Acorus Calamus, the *kanu tabu* of the Assyrians. It came "from a far country," most likely India. The Children of Israel went to great trouble and expense to provide the exact ingredients prescribed by the Lord and offered large quantities of incense every day. Yet the Lord bluntly tells them that their incense and all their sacrifices are unacceptable to Him, that they are to no purpose, a useless waste of time and money and energy. These words have been construed as a protest against every sacrifice. Volz, e. g., in commenting on this passage is quite positive in stating that Jeremiah opposes not only the incense offering as a cultic innovation, but every form of sacrifice (*Der Prophet Jeremias*, pp. 81f., 103). Did Volz overlook the pronoun "your" before "burnt offerings" and "sacrifices"? The prophet is speaking to a rebellious, wicked, impenitent people. Moreover, the same prophet approves these sacrifices (Jer. 17:26; 27:21-22; 33:10-11, 18). R. Payne Smith writes: "It is remarkable that this rejection of ritual observances is made by the two prophets Isaiah and Jeremiah, who chiefly assisted the two pious kings Hezekiah and Josiah in restoring the Temple service. God rejects not the ceremonial service, but the substitution of it for personal holiness and morality. If it be the expression of love and piety present in the heart, it is the beauty of holiness; if it take the place of love and duty, it is an abomination. On the views of the prophets, see 1 Sam. 15:22; Is. 1:11; Micah 6:7-8; etc." (*The Bible Commentary*, V, p. 365.) True love and piety, of course, was possible only when faith in the promised Messiah dwelt in the heart of the sacrificer. Else there is lacking that inward relation to God which the Lord at the very first sacrifice recorded described as essential and whose lack made both the sacrificer and his sacrifice unacceptable to God (Gen. 4:3-7). Cowles makes a very proper application: "It would be only like the common human nature of our age if the Jews at Jeremiah's time gave the more to God in costly spices, as they gave him less of the true homage of their hearts. By a sort of compromise of their own, men are often fain to make up in the outer what they choose to lack of the inner." (Cowles, p. 70.)

V. 21. Because of the hypocritical worship of this disobedient people the Lord will cause their utter ruin.

D. The enemy from the north is approaching to punish the sinful people, vv. 22-26

22 Thus says the LORD: Behold a people is coming from the North-land, and a great nation is stirring 23 from the ends of the earth. They bear bow and javelin. Merciless are they and have no pity. Their voices roar like the sea; on horses they ride, equipped as a man for war against you, O daughter of Zion. 24 As we hear the report of them, our hands lose their strength. Anguish has overwhelmed us, pain like that 25 of a woman in childbirth. Do not go out into the field! Do not walk on the road! For there is the sword of the enemy, terror round about! 26 O daughter of My people, gird yourself in sackcloth, and wallow in the dust. Cry out in mourning as for an only son, a bitter wailing; for suddenly shall the destroyer come upon us.

Vv. 22-23. The enemy, already foretold to Jeremiah (ch. 1:14) and announced by him (ch. 4:6; 5:15), now is coming with his allies and vassals from the farthest corners of the world, well armed with bows and javelins, a cruel and heartless enemy. The noise of the countless soldiers and horsemen and chariots is like the roaring of the sea. And fully equipped for a war of total destruction, they come — to whom? "Against thee, O daughter of Zion!" Zion, the dwelling place of the Lord, from which He has departed (Ezek. 11:21-23), because the daughter of Zion, the once beloved child of the Lord, has played the harlot and refuses to give up her wicked ways! We can imagine how Jeremiah's heart ached when he penned these words!

Vv. 24-25 describe the panic and despair of the people as they hear of the approach of the enemy. The very rumor of the cruelties and atrocities committed by the relentless hosts deprives them of their strength, robs them of every vestige of courage, completely enervates them. Anguish grips them, agony like that of a woman in travail. No one is safe, neither field nor road offer possibility of flight or refuge. Everywhere the enemy and his sword! Terror round about!

V. 26. Daughter! My people! The brokenhearted prophet tells his people, whom he still loves as a father loves his daughter, that since they refuse to weep the tears of sincere repentance, they will have to shed the bitter, anguished tears of hopeless despair, clothe themselves in sackcloth and wallow in ashes, because swift and in-

escapable destruction will come "upon us." The prophet is part of
his people, feeling their destruction as his own.

E. The prophet has assayed his people and found them worthless silver, vv. 27-30

27 A tower I have made you among
My people, a fortified city! And
you shall learn to know and then
28 assay their way. They all are rebellious revolters, slandermongers,
brass and iron; all of them, cor-
29 rupters they are! The bellows
blow; from their fire comes forth
lead! In vain the smelter has
smelted, and the wicked are not
30 separated! Reprobate silver they
call them, for Jehovah rejects them.

Grammatical Notes

V. 27 presents difficulties that can
hardly be solved to the satisfaction of
all. The chief difficulty lies in the
translation of בָּחוֹן and מִבְצָר, the first
and last word of the first clause of
v. 27. A. V. translates the first "tower,"
and the second "fortress." LXX translates בָּחוֹן δοκιμαστήν, a term designating a Greek official whose duty it
was to examine and approve candi-
dates for citizenship or certain offices.
LXX evidently read עַמִּי מִבְחָר instead of
the present text, added me, and translated: "I have set you a prover (ex-
aminer) among the people approved,
and you shall know Me from My proving of their way"; Lucian, "among My
enclosed people"; Symmachus, "among
My besieged people"; Aquila and Theo-
dotion, "among strong nations"; Targum reads בָּחוּר, "I have made you a
chosen one among My people, in a
strong, fortified city"; Vulgate, "I have
placed you as a sturdy prover among
My people, and you shall know and
prove their way."

On the translation of בָּחוֹן as prover,
smelter, practically all modern interpreters are agreed. For this translation they have the almost universal
testimony of the ancient translators
(except the Targum) and the fact that
the verb בחן, which occurs twenty-six
times, always means to prove, to test.
They vary in the interpretation of מִבְצָר

This word occurs some thirty-five times
and invariably designates something
well fortified, inaccessible. The verbal
stem means to be inaccessible, unap-
proachable, impossible to accomplish
(Gen. 11: 6; Job 42: 2; Is. 22: 10; Jer.
51: 53, only four times). The substan-
tive means something inaccessible, well
fortified, "fenced city" (Jer. 1: 18, etc.).
Luther has adopted this meaning in his
translation, connecting it with "My
people," "I have placed you as a smelter
among My people, which is so hard"
(as to be inaccessible to instruction).
Others connect מִבְצָר with בֶּצֶר, gold ore
(only Job 22: 24f.), and בְּצֻר, gold ore
(Job 36: 19), and translate: I have
placed you a prover among My people,
the gold, or ore. Or the word is pointed
מִבְצָר, without gold; there is no "gold"
among My people. These interpretations seem rather farfetched. Kittel
suggests מְבַצֵּר, "smelter," but the verb
is never used in this sense. Kautzsch
deletes the word as superfluous. Volz
deletes all the names of metals as
marginal notes that crept into the text
later by mistake. Keil translates:
I have placed you as a prover among
My people, as a fortified city, and refers
to Jer. 1: 18. This interpretation and
Luther's do no violence to the text.
And since the prophet is told in v. 27b
to prove the people, בָּחוֹן in v. 27a may
mean "prover." However, the render-

ing of A. V. is not impossible and would also fit well into the context. We must remember that the word *bachon* occurs only here. Similar words, בָּחוּן (only Is. 23:13) and בַּחַן (only Is. 32:14), are translated "towers" universally. בָּחוֹן, occurring only in Jer. 6:27, may be a third form of this word, and its correct translation may be that of A. V., "tower." Then v. 27 a would serve as a reminder and a renewed guarantee of God's promise of ch. 1:18, where both the verb "set thee," "made thee," and the noun, "fenced city," "fortress," occur. "Let neither the apparent uselessness of your efforts (ch. 6:10 ff.) nor the coming destruction (ch. 6:16-26) discourage you! Remember, I have placed you in this nation and at this time a tower and a fortress! Be not dismayed!" The "tower," would be a fourth symbol of strength and endurance added to the three named ch. 1:18, one of which is repeated here to remind Jeremiah of God's promise. V. 27 a would then introduce vv. 27 b-29, the admonition to prove or test God's people and the announcement of the dire result of such a proving. We per-

sonally prefer the translation of A. V., but leave the whole matter to the decision of the reader.

V. 29. נָחַר may be Niphal of חרר, to burn, the bellows are burnt, scorched; or it may be Qal, to snort, of which root no other verb form occurs but two nouns denoting the snorting of a horse (Jer. 8:16; Job 39:20). Either translation is acceptable. מַפֻּחַ, from נפח, to blow, the bellows, is masculine, singular. מאשתם, the K'tib, must be read מֵאֵשָׁתָם, "from their fire," and presupposes a noun, אֵשֶׁה, fire, which does not occur elsewhere, but is formed quite normally from אֵשׁ, masculine, fire. The Q'ri, which requires the translation "from the fire is consumed," מֵאֵשׁ תַּם, if connected with the preceding "bellows," would be translated: "The bellows snort, from the fire it is consumed. Lead!" The despairing cry of the smelter, who looked for precious metal and found lead. If connected with the following "lead," "from the fire is consumed (the) lead" would connect the feminine "lead" with a masculine predicate, תַּם, a construction not at all unusual.

V. 27. On "tower" and "fortress" see Grammatical Notes. "Try" or "test," originally used of the testing of ore or metals, metaphorically applied to the testing of people. From the usage of the word we gather that it denotes not merely the assaying of ore in order to ascertain its ingredients and their proportions. It implies also the method and the purpose of such assaying, both of which are definitely described in Holy Scripture. There are four passages which speak of the method employed in "testing." All four speak of testing by smelting in a refining pot, or crucible, the furnace (Prov. 17:3; cp. 27:21), hence by means of fire (Zech. 13:9; Jer. 9:7; and the context, Jer. 6:29). In all these passages the smelting of ore by means of fire in a furnace or crucible is also applied to the testing of men in the fire or furnace of trials and tribulations. Nor are we left in doubt as to the purpose of the testing, the smelting. It is to refine, to purify the metal, to free it from the adhering dross. In ancient times lead was sometimes used as a flux to promote the fusing of the minerals, the lead and dross going to the bottom, the pure silver being left at the top. In like manner the purpose of God in testing people by means of adversities and sufferings is to cleanse, to purify them of the dross and impurity of sin, of unbelief, of evil habits, and renew them in righteousness and true holiness. For this purpose Jeremiah was appointed by the Lord. He was to get to know the people and their wickedness by his own experience (that is the meaning of "know" here, as in Jer. 5:1), and as a result of this knowledge (note the strong *waw* before "try") he was to "test" them. By preaching to them the Law of God in its fullest implications, its inexorable demands, its threats of destruction, death, and damnation for all transgressors, and by proclaiming the Gospel of the coming Messiah, the Lord our Righteousness, he was to purify, to renew the wicked nation, to cause it to return to God, to be re-established as the Lord's own. At the same time he was to separate from this holy nation all those who would refuse to accept His Word, reject the Law of the Lord of unalterable justice and righteousness, and despise the Gospel of the Lord of unchanging mercy and grace. Jeremiah finds no silver or gold; only worthless dross remains, to be cast away. That was to be the experience of Jeremiah as tester of the nation. Their unblushing wickedness and point-blank refusal to obey God's Word had been described in the preceding sections and is once more summarized in v. 28.

V. 28. "Grievous revolters," incurably rebellious, constantly rising in opposition and mutiny to all authority, divine or human. "Walking with slanders," on the way of slander (cp. Lev. 19:16; Prov. 11:13; 20:19). Unfaithful to God and unfaithful to man; backsliders and backstabbers. "Brass and iron," as hard and intractable as brass and iron (Is. 48:4). On the relative value of brass and iron as compared with that of gold and silver, see Is. 60:17; Ezek. 22:18. All of them are corrupters. This term, without an object (as in Gen. 6:12; Zeph. 3:7), is used in the sense of "dealing corruptly." The participles "walking" and "dealing" denote a characteristic, continuous state. All that they do is corrupt. Their very life and being: corruption!

As such utterly corrupt people, Jeremiah learned to know his people by his own sad experiences, and still it was his duty to prove them and their way, to endeavor to bring them back to the way of righteousness. Yet it was a hopeless job. *All* are corrupt, rotten to the core.

V. 29. "The bellows are burned," or snort, blow furiously; "the lead is consumed of the fire." The meaning is clear, no matter which translation is adopted. The smelter makes every effort to find precious metal. But "the founder melteth in vain." In vain he "smelts a smelting," is assiduously concerned to smelt successfully. The material he is assaying makes success impossible. In spite of all efforts the wicked are not "plucked away," cut off, separated, like dross from silver, for there is no silver in that ore! There are no righteous from which the wicked could be separated! All are corrupt! The whole nation is wicked!

V. 30. "Reprobate silver shall men call them," because the prophet's assaying, smelting them, preaching to them, was in vain. God loathed them, was disgusted with them, rejected them. Henceforth they shall be known to all people and called by them "Reprobate Silver." Once they had been silver (cp. Deut. 5: 27-29), but their silver became dross (Is. 1: 22); not merely second- or third-grade silver, but absolutely worthless, a loathing to the Lord. As they had rejected their God, so their God now has rejected them.

IV. Which Way to Salvation? Ch. 7—10

CHAPTER 7

1. External Ritualism Without Sincere Repentance Leads to Destruction, Ch. 7:1—8:3

A. The Temple cannot protect a wicked nation, vv. 1-15

1 The word which came to Jeremiah
2 from the LORD, saying: Stand at the gate of the house of the LORD and proclaim there this word, saying: Hear the word of the LORD, all Judah, you who enter by these
3 gates to worship the Lord. Thus says the LORD of Hosts, the God of Israel: Amend your ways and your works, and I will let you
4 dwell in this place. For your own sake, do not trust in deceitful words, such as, the Temple of Jehovah, the Temple of Jehovah, the
5 Temple of Jehovah are these! For if you properly amend your ways and your work, if you diligently establish justice in your mutual
6 dealings, if you do not oppress strangers, orphans and widows, nor shed innocent blood in this place, nor follow after other gods, to your
7 own harm, then I will let you dwell in this place, in the land which I have given to your fathers for-
8 ever and ever. Behold, you are trusting in deceitful words that
9 cannot do you any good. What? You steal, murder, commit adultery, swear falsely, and offer sacrifices to Baal, and run after other gods
10 which you do not know, and then you come and stand before Me in this house upon which My name has been called, and say: We are safe! with no other purpose than to commit all these abominations?
11 Has this house upon which My name has been called become a den of gangsters in your eyes? I also, behold, I have observed, is the
12 oracle of the LORD. Go to My place which was at Shiloh, where I formerly established My name, and see what I have done to it because of the wickedness of My
13 people Israel. And now, because you are doing all these deeds, is the oracle of the LORD, and I spoke to you early and late, and you did not hear, I cried to you, and you
14 did not answer, I will do to the house upon which My name is named, in which you trust, and to this place which I have given to you and to your fathers, just as
15 I have done to Shiloh. And I will cast you from My face as I have cast off all your brethren, all the seed of Ephraim.

V. 1. This "Temple Speech" is usually identified with that of ch. 26, dated in the beginning of Jehoiakim's reign. The reasons advanced for this identification do not seem convincing. 1) The same demand for a change of conduct. Yet that was the subject and purpose of all the preaching of Jeremiah. 2) The same occasion, a festival. Yet these festivals gave an opportunity to preach to all the people and were quite generally used by the prophets. 3) The same place. Yet Jeremiah and others spoke in the gates and courts of the Temple, cp. ch. 19:14; 35:2, 4; 36:5-10; also 28:1, 5. 4) In ch. 26 only the main thoughts of ch. 7 are repeated. That does not prove identity! 5) The reference to Shiloh. Why should not Shiloh have been repeatedly mentioned as a warning example of the folly of relying on external possession of God's house? A warning like this was not only possible, but quite to be expected in the days of Josiah, when the Lord announced His readiness to fulfill all the threats contained in the rediscovered Book of the Law (2 Kings 22:16-20). One of these threats referred to the overturning of Jerusalem "as Sodom and Gomorrah" (Deut. 29:23), involving the destruction of the Temple. Linking up with Huldah's message, Jeremiah may have reminded the Jews of the destruction of the Tabernacle at Shiloh as a warning against misplaced trust in the Temple. In ch. 7 there is not the slightest indication of opposition. That also would fit well into the time of Josiah's reform.

V. 2. The gate from which Jeremiah was to address the people was probably not one of the outer gates leading into the people's court, but one leading from the latter to the inner or priests' court, and offered a vantage point to the speaker. "All of Judah" justifies the dating of this speech on one of the three great festivals, when all males were obliged to come to the Temple (Lev. 23:1-44; Deut. 16:1-17).

V. 3. "Amend," cause to be good. "Ways," the underlying principles and directives of their "doings," their conduct. Their principles and actions are not good, not in accordance with His will revealed to them. Continuance in their present course will lead them ever farther away from God and forfeit their right to dwell in God's land. As the God of unchanging grace He is willing to let them continue to live in His land, but as the God of unalterable holiness He must insist on a complete rehabilitation, a fundamental change of their principles and actions.

V. 4. The thrice-repeated boast of the lying prophets reminds one of the frenzied shouting of the Ephesians (Acts 19:28). The Ephesians made the creation of man's ideas their object of trust, the Jews a man-made house of wood and stone, essentially the same idolatry. The Temple and its cult were indeed divine institutions; yet the blessings of the Covenant were guaranteed to Israel only as long as they were sincerely faithful to the God of the Covenant, while a reliance on the outward cult and the Temple without the inner fear and loving trust of God was sure to bring ruin to the people (Deuteronomy 28).

94

Vv. 5-7 are a conditional sentence, vv. 5-6 forming the protasis, if — if —; v. 7, the apodosis, then —. Vv. 5-6 the Lord briefly summarizes the Covenant Law, stating first the people's duties toward their fellow men, then their obligations to the Lord. "Thoroughly execute," rather, "establish judgment," that "judgment," that norm, governing the relation of man to his fellow men as laid down in God's holy Covenant Law and summarized Lev. 19:18. Instead of this loving consideration of the neighbor, Judah had become guilty of transgressions ranging from social injustice in the form of oppression of the stranger, the widow, and the orphan, to the willful shedding of innocent blood, judicial and other murders (cp. 2 Kings 21:16; 24:4; Jer. 2:34; 19:4; 22:3,17; 26:15,23). And the cause of this widespread lack of love and loyalty toward their fellow men was their failure to remain faithful to their Covenant God, their "walking after other gods" (v. 6 b), to their "hurt," their own harm, for idolatry leads deeper and deeper into sin and its dire consequences.

V. 7. Forever and ever. עוֹלָם denotes a period of time, the beginning and end of which, or either of the two, is not known, or cannot be known, or is non-existent; hence a period of time of indefinite but long duration, either in the past or in the future; which duration may be without beginning and without end, everlasting, or only of long duration, the extent of which may or may not be known to man.

Vv. 8-11 the prophet shows up the astonishing wickedness of Judah. The people make the fulfillment of God's sincere offer impossible by their habit of trusting (participle) in the words of deceit, which by their very nature cannot ever profit them. In astonishment at the wickedness of His people the Lord asks two questions, which He Himself answers: the first, vv. 9-10, the second, v. 11a; God's answer follows v. 11b. God sets before them their brazen shamelessness. While they are committing these atrocities, they come into the presence of that God whose every Commandment they have broken, stand in the dwelling of the God of unchanging justice and righteousness, and having gone through their rites, they say: We are delivered, now we are safe, we are God's own! And all that not for the purpose of changing their ways, but to keep on doing all these abominations!

What? Do you regard this house, My house, as a den of robbers, a meeting place of gangsters? Have I and My name and My house sunk so low in your eyes? Then listen! Also I have eyes to see, not

95

blinded eyes like yours, but eyes like flames of fire (Rev. 1:14; Ps. 139:1-4; 90:8; Heb. 4:13). I see! I observe! says He who is I AM THAT I AM.

Vv. 12-15 the divine Landlord serves His notice of eviction. The Lord asks Judah to go up to Shiloh and observe what had happened to the city where after the forty years of wilderness wanderings and several years of warfare the Tabernacle of God had finally found a permanent resting place (Joshua 18:1). There it had stood throughout the centuries of the Judges (1 Sam. 1:3) and had harbored the Ark of the Covenant until the death of Eli (1 Sam. 4:10-22). In Jeremiah's time it was a heap of ruins. We are not told when Shiloh was destroyed. Modern excavations made at Seilun, built on the site of Shiloh (cp. Judg. 21:19), during the years 1922—1931, "reveal no evidence that there was ever a Canaanite settlement at Shiloh; the Hebrews appear to have founded the settlement after their conquest of Palestine. . . . As the potsherds bear witness to no settlement here from about 1050 B. C. till about 300 B. C., the archaeological soundings confirm the text of the Bible" (Barton, *Archaeology and the Bible,* Sixth Ed., p. 134f.). It may be that the Philistines, after defeating the Israelites at Mizpah, destroyed Shiloh completely. That would agree with the fact that no potsherds were found dating after "about 1050 B. C.," Eli's death being dated at some time between 1100 and 1000 B. C. The same Lord who saw the wickedness of Israel, His people, and because of this wickedness destroyed the city of Shiloh (v. 14), the sanctuary (v. 12), and about a century before Jeremiah the whole seed of Ephraim (v. 15), sees also Judah's works equaling Israel's wickedness and surpassing it (v. 13; ch. 3:11) in spite of the oft-repeated and eager pleas of the Lord (v. 13). He is now ready to cast all of Judah out of His sight as He cast out all the seed of Ephraim.

Placing one's trust in the possession of orthodoxy received by tradition from the fathers, or in the correctness of ritualistic forms, or in the prayers one speaks, or in the services attended, or in the offerings given, is in God's sight a form of idolatry, no matter whether committed in Judah or in America, by Jews or pagans or Lutherans, and is the same abomination to the Lord in the twentieth century after Christ that it was in 600 B. C., and will meet with the same judgment that came upon Israel and Judah.

B. Neither prophetic intercession nor multiplication of sacrifices will save an apostate nation, vv. 16-28

16 And you, do not pray for this people, nor offer any entreaty or supplication in their behalf, nor plead with Me, for I do not intend
17 to hear you. Have you not seen what they are doing in Judah's cities and in the streets of Jeru-
18 salem? The children are gathering fagots, and the fathers are kindling the fire, and the women are kneading the dough to make cakes for the Queen of Heaven, and they pour out drink offerings to other gods in order to provoke Me to
19 anger. Are they provoking Me, is the oracle of the LORD, and not rather themselves to their own con-
20 fusion? Therefore thus says the Lord Jehovah: Behold, My anger and My furor shall be poured out upon this place, upon man and upon beast and upon the trees of the field and upon the product of the earth, and it shall burn un-
21 quenchably. Thus says the LORD of Hosts, the God of Israel: Add your burnt offering to the bloody
22 offerings, and eat flesh! For I did not speak to your fathers and did not command them on the day I brought them out of the land of Egypt, for the sake of burnt offer-
23 ing and sacrifice. But I did give them this command: Obey My voice, and I will be your God, and you shall be My people and walk in all My ways that I have commanded you so that it may be well
24 with you. And they did not hear nor incline their ears, but walked in the counsels and in the hardness of their wicked heart; and they went backward and not forward.
25 From the day on which your fathers went out of the land of Egypt to this day I sent to them all My servants, the prophets, daily,
26 early and late. And they did not hear Me, nor did they incline their ear. They stiffened their necks; they did more evil than their
27 fathers. Even if you tell them all these words, they will not hear you! If you preach, there will be
28 no response! Therefore you shall say to them: This is the nation which will not hear the voice of the LORD, their God, and will not accept instruction. Gone is faith, cut off from their mouths!

Grammatical Notes

V. 18. "Queen of Heaven." מְלֶכֶת is perhaps a distorted pointing, to replace the original מַלְכַּת, queen. The Masoretes pointed the word to read מְלֶאכֶת, "work" of heaven, i. e., the starry host of heaven; so LXX στρατιά, here, but βασιλίσσα Jer. 44:17-19, 25 (LXX 51: 17-19, 25), "queen."

V. 16. The prophet, so fervently loving his people, is deprived by God's prohibition of what was by divine grant one of the most precious privileges of the prophets, that of intercession for his people (cp. Gen. 18: 22-32; 20: 7; Ex. 32: 11—34: 10; Num. 14: 13-20; 1 Sam. 7: 5-9). He is told: "Pray not thou for this people," do not intercede for them (Gen. 20: 7; Deut. 9: 20; 1 Sam. 7: 5), "neither lift up cry," loud, vehement, fervent prayer (Ps. 17: 1; 88: 2; Jer. 11: 14; 14: 12), "nor prayer," תְּפִלָּה, invocation of God as the Judge, pleading with Him as the Advocate for the people (cp. 1 Kings 8: 38; Ps. 4: 1-3;

80: 4ff.; 88: 2a and context). "Make intercession," make appointment for the purpose of fervent entreaty (cp. Ruth 1: 16). In no wise is Jeremiah to utter either in words or thoughts any plea for Israel, "for I will not hear thee," I am not one that makes it a practice of hearing (participle) you in a prayer for these people.

V. 17. The Lord appeals to His prophet's sense of justice and judgment. What he sees will convince him that God's prohibition of intercession is fully justified by the facts.

V. 18. Jewish homes, where the Lord's name was to be loved and honored and trusted (cp. Gen. 18: 19; Deut. 6: 6-9; Joshua 24: 15b), had become exactly like the homes of the heathen, the whole family, father, mother, children, eagerly devoting their time and energy to the service, not of the Lord of heaven and earth, but to a deity far more pleasing to them, the Queen of Heaven. Mothers will often exercise a wholesome, Christian influence on the children of the home, even if the father is an unbeliever; rarely will the Christian father's influence outweigh the wicked influence of a godless mother. And if both father and mother deliberately and assiduously teach their wicked ways to their offspring, there is little, if any, chance of the child growing up to be a child of God.

"Queen of Heaven." This term is found also ch. 44: 17-19, 25. See Grammatical Notes. The Queen of Heaven is evidently to be identified with Astarte (Ashtarte), or Ashtoreth, a Semitic goddess, the Ishtar of the Babylonian-Assyrian cult; the Mother Goddess, the consort of Bel-Marduk, the goddess of the star Venus, who was worshiped in the Babylonian-Assyrian religion as the queen of heaven, or as the queen of heaven and stars. The cult of the Queen of Heaven, or the Mother Goddess, was an ancient custom extending throughout the Orient in various forms and under various names, but of the same nature. We meet with it throughout the centuries of antiquity. "Her primary, although not exclusive, province was physical fertility in man and beast. . . . She was the goddess of sensuous love and the patroness of generative and growing life. . . . Like Ishtar, Ashtarte had a number of men and women ministrants, who were described as consecrated persons, *Qedeshah, Qadesh.*" (Kittel, *The Religion of the People of Israel*, p. 25.) Cp. Gen. 38: 21; Deut. 23: 18; 1 Kings 14: 24; 15: 12; 22: 46; etc. In Babylonia and Cyprus all women before marriage were obliged to prostitute themselves to strangers at the sanctuary of Ishtar, or Astarte. Herodotus calls her Mylitta and identifies her with Aphrodite. Her. I, 199. Ishtar was also regarded as the goddess of war and the chase, similar to Diana; in some countries she was regarded as the lunar deity.

Excavations in Palestine everywhere have brought to light a mass of Astarte statuettes of various types. (Babylonian, Egyptian, ancient Cyprian, and native Canaanite types; at Gezer also plaques of Astarte. See Barton, *Archaeology,* Plate 69, Fig. 214.) Excavations in the ancient Canaanite city of Taanach (Joshua 12:21) in the valley of Esdraelon produced no statues of Baal, but many of Astarte, all nineteen of one peculiar type, a crowned head, a neckband, hands folded on the breast, a girdle, ankle bracelets, hair braided, a type different from all others so far found. (Koenig, *Theol. A. T.,* p. 92, Note 1.)

According to Duncan, "Terra-cotta figures of an undraped female deity are a feature of every excavation. These are regarded as figurines of the mother Goddess, Astarte, and the earliest examples date from at least 2000 B. C., some being regarded as earlier. . . . These figures are doubtless the teraphim, or household gods, of the O. T., referred to in Genesis XXXI. 30, 34, and elsewhere, as well as the images of the Queen of Heaven, whose worship is defended by the women in Jeremiah XLIV. 15-19." (Duncan, *Digging Up Biblical History,* II, p. 80.)

The prophet also mentions the "cakes" baked by the mothers. כַּוָּנִים, most likely the Hebrew form of the Assyrian *kamanu*, baked food, perhaps in the form of images of the goddess, like Christmas cookies in the shape of Santa Claus, etc. These cakes were offered at the altar of the Queen and were eaten by the family assembled at the worship of the Mother Goddess (cp. Hos. 3:1, "flagons of wines," rather, raisin cakes, offered and eaten at the idol meals). Volz compares the moon- or crescent-shaped cakes which the Athenians baked for Artemis, and quotes a hymn in honor of Ishtar, the Queen of Heaven, represented by the star Venus: "O Ishtar, I prepared for you a pure oblation of milk and cake and salted toast; I placed a flagon for you. Hear me, and be gracious to me!" (Sellin, *Kommentar zum Alten Testament, Jeremiah,* p. 100.) Jeremiah also names libations offered to the Queen and other gods here and ch. 44:17.

"That they may provoke Me." This is the first time this word occurs in Jeremiah; also v. 19; ch. 8:19; 11:17; 25:6-7; 32:29-30, 32; 44:3, 8. It is derived from a root signifying to be annoyed, vexed, angry, out of sorts, unhappy. Piel and Hiphil causative. So Peninnah made Hannah "unhappy," "provoked her" (1 Sam. 1:6, Piel; v. 7, Hiphil). Sanballat was vexed, became angry (Neh. 3:33 — A. V., 4:1),

Qal; the wicked is grieved, vexed (Ps. 112:10), Qal; violently disturbed. Man has sorrow (Eccl. 5:17), Qal; "be angry" (Eccl. 7:9). In Jeremiah, God uses this term to express the thought that sin calls forth His anger, provokes His wrath (ch. 8:19; 25:6; 32:30). No less than six times He charges Judah with committing sin for the purpose of vexing, provoking Him (ch. 7:18; 11:17; 25:7; 32:29, 32; 44:3). The Jews knew that their idolatry would call forth God's holy wrath. Beginning with the First Commandment at Mount Sinai and continuing throughout the Old Testament Covenant, the Lord had constantly designated idolatry as apostasy and rebellion against the Covenant God, a fundamental breach of the covenant relation. If in spite of these ever-repeated prohibitions and warnings the Jews still persisted in following strange gods, then one cannot escape the conclusion that they did it for the purpose of provoking the Lord Jehovah to anger. In fact, the people themselves openly declared that they preferred the worship of idols to that of Jehovah (cp. ch. 2:25, 31; 3:13; 6:16-17; 7:23-28; 18:12; 44:15-19). Their idolatry was a deliberate, purposeful disavowal of Jehovah, an open declaration of rebellion in order to cause grief, vexation, unhappiness to the Covenant God.

V. 19. In answer to their avowed purpose to provoke the Lord, He asks: Do they provoke Me to anger? Evidently the question is to be answered in the negative, They do not provoke Me! How can God say that in view of His repeated statements that sin does provoke Him to anger? He says this in order to correct the wrong conception of the Jews concerning God and His wrath against sinners. Human conceptions of God are and remain impure. Cp. what God has said Is. 40:18, 25; 46:5; 44:6-9. Yet man continues to shape his deity more or less in the pattern of humanity. His gods are man-made gods, made in man's own image, after his own likeness, with like passions, like emotions, like weaknesses. Man is irritated, rendered unhappy, if anyone dares to run counter to his wish and will. And therefore man hopes to disturb God's peace of mind, make Him feel unhappy, miserable, wretched, by willful transgressions of His commandment. Man forgets that God is the everlasting I AM THAT I AM; that there are no conflicts in God; that as little as His love of sinners (John 3:16) is affected by His wrath and hatred against sinners (Ps. 5:5-6), and His anger against the sinner by His long-suffering, so little is His everlasting bliss affected by the sins of man. He is ever the Lord, I AM THAT I AM, as unchanging in His beatitude, His heavenly happiness, as He is unchanging in His grace and unalterable in His wrath. The sins of man will not deprive God of His happiness, nor even disturb it. But it will seriously vex them, be to them what they hoped it would be to Jehovah, a source of vexation, misery, anguish.

V. 20. They will be swept away with all they have by the anger and fury of the Holy One (Deut. 32:20-25).

Vv. 21-22. Liberal critics have used this passage and ch. 8:8 to prove their theory that the laws pertaining to sacrifices and the cult were not part of the original Mosaic legislation, but were added to the Torah by the lying pen of later scribes. According to these critics, the prophets were unrelenting enemies of the cult as such with its sacrifices and rituals. Jeremiah, they say, here states definitely that God in His Sinai Covenant did not command burnt offerings or any other kind of sacrifice; that observing the Temple cult was not only a mistake, not merely without value, but actually harmful and sinful. (Volz, *Jeremias,* pp. 89, 104, 105.)

Jeremiah's words lend not the least support to this theory. In the first place, the phrase employed here by Jeremiah, "concerning burnt offerings or sacrifices," does not compel us to take "concerning" in the sense of legislating "about" or "on" sacrifices. The expression עַל־דִּבְרֵי occurs Deut. 4:21; 2 Sam. 18:5; 2 Kings 22:13; Ps. 7:1; Jer. 7:22; 14:1. In the very first passage listed, only the translation of the A. V., "for your sakes," Luther, "um eures Tuns willen," expresses the sense of the Hebrew phrase used here. In four of the remaining passages the phrase evidently was chosen in order to express the active interest or concern involving either the speaker or the person spoken of, or addressed. So 2 Sam. 18:5, David's concern for Absalom caused him to give charges to all his captains; 2 Kings 22:13, the Lord was enquired "concerning" the book, because of, on account of, the book, in anxious concern about it. Ps. 7:1 (A. V., superscription), "concerning," not "about," but because of them, deeply concerned about them; Jer. 14:1, "concerning the dearth," because of, on account of. Hence Jer. 7:22 need not be translated, "I have never legislated concerning, about, on, burnt offerings, sacrifices"; but the usage of the word not only permits, but strongly favors the translation: "I have not legislated in the interest of, out of concern for, sacrifices; that was not My chief or only concern." Cp. *The Five Books of Moses,* O. A. Allis, p. 168ff.

This latter translation is demanded by the fact that, in the second place, Jeremiah, far from opposing every form of cult, in fact sup-

101

ported Josiah's reform, which included the re-establishment of the ancient cult of the Passover (2 Chron. 35:1-9). Cp. Dean Smith's comment on Jer. 6:20, quoted p. 87.

In the third place, if Jeremiah had actually opposed the cult as sinful and illegal, it would be passing strange that he was not once charged with opposing the cult by the priests, the staunchest defenders of the Temple cult and the most vehement enemies of Jeremiah. It was not the cult that Jeremiah opposed, but the abuse of the cult, the substitution of externalism and ritualism, the *opus operatum,* for the fear and love and trust of God. He condemns the sacrifices not of believing children of God, but of wicked, determined apostates, who regarded the cult as a panacea for all evils, a charter for their wickedness (vv. 8-11, 17-18).

In scathing irony He tells them to heap their burnt offerings upon their other sacrifices, hecatombs upon hecatombs (v. 21). That will not quench the fire of His furious wrath (v. 20). "Eat flesh!" Gorge yourselves with meat! The sacrificial meals (Lev. 7:14-19; Deut. 12:5-12; 14:22-27; 27:7) seemed more attractive to them and gained greater attention than the real purpose of the sacrifice, just as did the "love feasts" connected with the Lord's Supper in the apostle's time (1 Cor. 11:20-22), and as in our day the turkey dinner takes the place of the true Thanksgiving and true Christmas spirit. Hence there is no reason why these words of the prophet should be construed as a protest against the Temple cult. The Lord emphasizes that in this legislation He was not deeply and anxiously concerned about receiving offerings. His chief concern was to have an obedient people willing to fulfill all His Commandments.

Vv. 23-24. "But this thing I commanded." The first word the Covenant God spoke to His people from Mount Sinai was a demand to obey His words (Ex. 19:5), and the very first promise Israel had made was the solemn vow Ex. 19:8. The ever-repeated refusal of obedience was the sin of Israel which thousands of rams could not atone for and which made their sacrifices an abomination to the Lord.

Vv. 25-28. No matter who spoke to them, they refused to listen; because "truth," faith (see ch. 5:1ff.), is perished. There is no "Yea" to God's commands, since there is no more "Amen" to God's promises. Their mouth may utter prayers, but they are faithless prayers, mere babblings, because faith is cut off from their mouths, since it was no longer in their heart.

C. Wicked Judah is rejected by God, ch. 7:29—8:3

29 Cut off your hair and throw it away! Raise a dirge on the bare hills! For the LORD has rejected and forsaken the generation of His 30 wrath. For the children of Judah have done wickedness in My sight, is the oracle of the LORD. They have erected abominations in the house upon which My name has been called, in order to defile it. 31 And they have built the high places of Topheth in the Valley of Ben-Hinnom, to burn their sons and daughters in the fire, which I never commanded, nor has it entered My 32 mind. Therefore, behold, days are coming, is the oracle of the LORD, that they shall no longer call it Topheth and Valley of Ben-Hinnom, but "valley of slaughter," and they shall bury in Topheth until 33 there is no more place. And the carcasses of this people shall be food for the birds of heaven and the beasts of the field, nor shall there be anyone to frighten them 34 away. And I shall silence in the cities of Judah and on the streets of Jerusalem the voice of joy and the voice of gladness, the voice of the bridegroom and the voice of the bride; for the land shall be 8:1 desolate. At this time, is the oracle of the LORD, they shall remove the bones of the kings of Judah, and the bones of their princes, and the bones of the priests, and the bones of the prophets, and the bones of the inhabitants of Jerusalem from 2 their graves, and they shall spread them out before the sun and the moon and all the host of heaven, which they had loved, and which they had served, and which they had followed, and which they had sought, and which they had worshiped. They shall neither be gathered nor buried, they shall become 3 dung upon the land. And death shall be chosen rather than life by all the remnant remaining of this wicked generation in all the places whither I have dispersed them, is the oracle of the LORD of Hosts.

Grammatical Notes

V. 29. "Hair" here רֶזַנ, from a stem denoting to separate, consecrate; the noun = separation, consecration. It is used to designate the long, unshorn hair of the Nazarites (Num. 6:1-21), male or female, one of the symbols of their consecration to the Lord.

V. 29. "Cut off thine hair!" All the suffixes are feminine. Judah-Jerusalem, so often called the virgin or bride of the Lord, is addressed. Whereas the hair of the undefiled Nazarite was offered and burned when the days of his vow were fulfilled (Num. 6:13-18), the Nazarite in whose presence a person had died was regarded as defiled and had to cut his hair, which could not then be offered to the Lord (vv. 9-12), but was to be thrown away. To this custom the prophet here refers. The virgin of Judah is told to cut off her hair and cast it away. She is no longer the virgin consecrated to the Lord. She has defiled herself by becoming a vile harlot, spiritually and physically, by her unfaithfulness to her Bridegroom, running after her paramours, seeking the favor of Gentile nations and their idols in preference to the Lord. You have no right to pose as the consecrated bride of the

103

Lord. Cut off your hair! Cast it away! Stand bald and ugly, an object of ridicule and contempt to your lovers. "Take up a lamentation on the high places," the bare dunes and hills defiled by your idolatry, for rejected has the Lord and cast away the generation of His wrath! No longer is He the loving Protector of His people. He is the offended, avenging Judge pouring out the vials of His wrath. Why? A third atrocity is named: they have changed My house into an idols' temple.

V. 30. The children of Judah, no longer His children, have brought His anger upon themselves by their wickedness committed before the very presence of the Covenant God. They have placed their idols into My holy house (cp. Ahaz, 2 Kings 16:10-18; Manasseh, ch. 21: 4-7), defiling it.

V. 31. Another horrible wickedness is charged against Judah, the sacrifice of their children to Moloch by burning them at the high places of Topheth. The meaning of this name is uncertain. Many modern interpreters follow W. Rob. Smith, who connects the word with the Aramaic t'fala, hearth, fireplace. Others, on the basis of Job 17:6, derive it from חוף, "to spit," a root which does not occur in Hebrew literature, but in the related dialects, Ethiopian, Egyptian, Coptic. A. V. translates Job 17:6 "tabret," evidently unsuitable; LXX, γέλως, laughter, mockery. The parallelism demands a word denoting ridicule, contempt. No greater contempt can be imagined than spitting upon a man. The beautiful valley had become a disgraceful object of contempt to the Lord and His faithful few. Isaiah graphically describes a תָּפְתֶּה prepared for the king of Assyria (Is. 30:33). (Koenig, Das Buch Jesaias, p. 278, translates: "a topheth arrangement.") Isaiah saw a deep and wide pit surrounding an altar upon and round about which is piled a huge mass of wood, while fire and brimstone burn furiously, devouring the king of Assyria and his mighty army. Such clear passages as Jer. 7:31; 19:5; Ezek. 16:20-21 leave no doubt that the Jews actually had adopted the horrible custom of the Canaanites and burnt their children as a sacrifice to Moloch (2 Kings 23:10), to Baal (Jer. 19:5). Whether this mode of sacrifice is to be identified with the rite of making the children to pass through the fire (Lev. 18:21; Deut. 18:10; 2 Kings 17:17; etc.), or whether the latter phrase merely designates a lustration, carrying them or causing them to walk between two rows of fire, or waving them in the fire in order to cleanse and sanctify them, cannot be definitely determined.

Vv. 32-33. These names symbolize the history of the valley:

Topheth, reminiscent of the detestable form of idolatry practiced there, which shall be eradicated in the time coming; Ben-Hinnom, reminiscent of the original beauty of this parklike valley. It shall be called the "valley of slaughter," because it will be a vast cemetery of people slaughtered by the triple sword of war and famine and pestilence, and even this vast cemetery will be insufficient to offer burial places to all that are slain. Large numbers of corpses will be devoured by birds of prey and wild beasts, whom no one will drive away. Thus will the Holy One defile the land consecrated by His people to the abominable worship of idols.

V. 34. Since the whole city had become a Topheth by its idol worship (ch. 19:12; 32:35), Jerusalem also shall meet the fate of Topheth (cp. ch. 19:3-15). The Lord, the Covenant God, whose sabbaths they have desecrated, will cause a sabbath, הַשְׁבַּתִּי, a day of rest, the cessation of all joy and rejoicing, the cessation of the joyful conversation of loving bridal couples. For the entire land will be a vast desert (cp. 2 Chron. 36:21).

CHAPTER 8

V. 1. "In that time," connects ch. 8:1-3 with the preceding chapter. Even death and burial and decomposition will not prevent the shameful maltreatment of their bodies. Vv. 1 and 2 are built with great skill. Five times the bones of five groups are mentioned, and five times the sins of which every one of the groups became guilty. The first pentad is followed by a triad of the idols worshiped by the five groups; the second, by a triad of the shameful penalties to be inflicted on them (cp. Deut. 28:26). On star worship cp. 2 Kings 21:3, 5; 23:4, and notes on Jer. 7:18. The bones of kings and princes, of priests and prophets, will be treated no better than the bones of the people they ruled. All alike dead, all alike desecrated! And their gods? The sun, and the moon, and the stars, whom they loved, and served, and followed, and eagerly sought, and faithfully worshiped? Sun, moon, and stars, all of them "look down with utter indifference upon the wretched doom of their former worshipers!" (Cowles.) And man? their fellow humans? "None so poor to do them reverence!" None stoops to gather them; none labors to bury them; dung they are upon the face of the earth, a gruesome portent of the eternal shame awaiting them on the Last Day (Is. 66:24; Mark 9:44, 46, 48). The fulfillment of this prophecy is renewed time and again throughout the centuries. The greed of grave robbers, the excavations of the builders, the missiles of warfare, the plow and hoe of peasant and gardener, the archaeologist's spade, all continue unwittingly in the fulfillment of this word of the eternal Lord.

V. 3. "And death shall be chosen. . . ." They had rejected God and His Word, they had refused to choose life offered by Him (Deut. 30:19-20). Now their life — a godless, joyless, hopeless life — is a burden to them, not worth living. They prefer death! Alas, they have not yet experienced, and refuse to know and believe, what death means without God, although the Lord had told them clearly enough (Deut. 29:20; 32:22; Ps. 73:18-20; Prov. 11:7). What fools to leave God, to prefer a godless death to godless life, while they might have had a life of blessing, a blessed death, a life of everlasting blessing and happiness!

2. Judah's Stubborn Apostasy Is the Sure Way to National Ruin
Vv. 4-23

A. Its unreasonable stubbornness, vv. 4-12

4 And you shall say to them: Thus says the LORD: If men fall, will they not rise? If they turn away,
5 will they not turn back? Why, then, does this apostate people, Jerusalem, the everlasting turncoat, persist in their deceit, refuse to re-
6 turn? I paid close attention and listened; they kept on speaking what was not right; not a man repented of his wickedness, so as to say: What have I done? Every one turned to his course as a horse
7 rushing into battle. Even the stork in the heavens knows her seasons, and the turtle dove and the swallow and the crane observe the time appointed for their coming. But My people do not know the ordinance
8 of the LORD! How can you say: We are wise! And the Law of the LORD is with us!? Surely! Behold, unto deceit the deceitful pen of the
9 scribe has labored! Wise men shall be put to shame, they shall be confused, and so they shall be taken. Behold, they have rejected the Word of the Lord, and what kind
10 of wisdom have they? Therefore I will give their wives to others and their fields to conquerors, for from the least to the greatest everyone is out for gain; prophet as well as priest, all of them practice deceit.
11 And they heal the hurt of the daughter of My people carelessly, saying: Peace! Peace! while there
12 is no peace. They were put to shame, for they commit abominations, yet they do not feel at all ashamed; nor do they know how to blush. Therefore they shall fall among the fallen; in the time of their visitation they shall stumble, says the LORD.

Grammatical Notes

V. 7. The A. V. and the Masoretic text list four classes of migratory birds: 1) the stork, חֲסִידָה, the pious one, so named because of its tender care for its young ones; 2) the "turtle," the turtle dove, whose gentle cooing was wel- comed as a harbinger of spring (cp. Cant. 2:12); 3) the "crane," סוּס, or as Q'ri points, סִיס; the LXX renders it "swallow." Some interpreters think that the swift is here intended; 4) the "swallow," עָגוּר, is an unknown bird, the

LXX have simply transcribed the word, ἀγροῦ, which, however, may be the genitive of ἀγρός, acre, field. The Targum and Syrian translate "crane." Many interpreters regard the last two words as the name of one bird, but are not able to define עָגוּר, the root of which occurs in no other form.

V. 8. "Made he," עָשָׂה, without object, in sense of labor, work (cp. Gen. 30: 30, "provide," A. V.; Ruth 2: 19; Prov. 31: 13).

A new section (vv. 4-23) begins, introducing another effort to induce the people to return to the Lord, pointing out the unnaturalness and unreasonableness of their refusal to repent (vv. 4-12) and the penalty of such refusal (vv. 13-23).

V. 4. "Shall they fall. . . ." We see a man as he begins to fall, and from that very moment making desperate efforts to regain a firm stand, and continuing his efforts even after he has fallen. That is the natural reaction, just as natural as the return of a man to his home from which he has set out. The application of v. 4a is left to the reader. It is the same that the Lord makes of v. 4b in v. 5 in a play on words of which Jeremiah is so fond.

V. 5. Why, then, has this people, Jerusalem, turned a perpetual turning? Why do they cling with all their strength to deceit, to the idols, nonentities, frauds, deceiving all who put their trust in them? (Ps. 115: 4-8; Jer. 10: 1-15.) Why do they refuse to turn away from these idols and to return to eternal realities, to Him who is Life and gives life? How unreasonable!

V. 6. The Lord listens attentively (cp. Ps. 11: 4; 14: 2-3), but He hears not a word that would be in order in such a situation. Not a word of repentance, of sorrow for their sins. Eagerly, impatiently they all hurry to their idols, as the horse rushes headlong into battle. We need but watch the crowds struggling to get into the temples of amusement, there to offer their money and their time to the idols of this world (1 John 2: 16-17), and we shall see one of the modern forms of ancient idolatry and deception.

V. 7. On stork, turtle, crane, swallow, see Grammatical Notes. The underlying idea is clear, even if we do not know which migratory birds are meant. Even the birds, irrational creatures, know their appointed time and return to their homes, which they have left. Instinctively, unhesitatingly they obey the norm fixed for them by the Creator; they travel hundreds and thousands of miles, because that is their Maker's will. Unbelieving, impenitent Jerusalem has sunk below the level of these lower creatures.

V. 8. The term scribe, סֹפֵר, occurs fifty-four times in the Old

107

Testament. Four times it is translated "writer" (Judg. 5:14; Ps. 45:1; Ezek. 9:2, 3), fifty times "scribe." In most of these passages, scribes are officials at the royal court, secretaries of the king, writing his letters, managing his finances (cp. 2 Kings 12:10; etc.). Others were military officers, attending to, e. g., the mustering of troops (Judg. 5:14; Jer. 52:25). In 1 Chron. 2:55 "families of scribes" are named in the genealogical list of Judah, yet there is no indication as to the exact nature of their work, nor of the time at which they lived. A class or order of scribes is mentioned 2 Chron. 34:13, where we have the record of "an order of scribes, forming a distinct division of the Levitical body" (*Bible Commentary*, ad loc.), instituted by Josiah in the reform inaugurated in his eighteenth year, 622. But again we are not informed of the exact nature of their duties.

Ezra, living in post-Exilic times, is called "a ready scribe in the Law of Moses" (Ezra 7:6). The nature of his work is outlined vv. 10-11. In v. 12 he is addressed as a "scribe." Here the term is used as an official title designating a profession, whose members devoted their lifetime to the copying, preservation, editing, study, and teaching of Holy Scripture.

There is no reason why we may not assume that already in Jeremiah's time and prior to it the same functions were carried out by the "scribes," and a number of considerations may be cited in proof of this assumption. 1) In Josiah's time (2 Chron. 34:13) "scribes," writers, were selected from the Levites, the official teachers of the people (Lev. 10:8-11; Deut. 33:8-10; 2 Chron. 15:3; 17:8). Quite evidently they were to make their teaching material available also in written form. 2) The prophets put their messages down in writing to preserve them for the future, and for this purpose some of them employed scribes (Jer. 36:1ff.; 45:1). 3) The "men of Hezekiah" collected a series of Solomonic proverbs (Prov. 25:1) in order to preserve this teaching material dating back to Solomon. It would be strange, to say the least, if the teaching scribes of the tribe of Levi would not have been equally concerned about the copying and preservation of the Torah, the Bible as it gradually came into existence (cp. Deut. 31:9-12, 19, 24-27; Joshua 24:26).

As there were not only true prophets, but false prophets in great number, pious priests and ungodly priests, good kings and wicked kings, so there were also faithful, God-fearing scribes and lying, deceitful scribes, siding in with the ungodly leaders, priests, prophets, and kings.

Against such wicked scribes (whose exact duties we may not be able to define) were directed the scathing words of God's spokesman. The deceitful scribes, blind and lying leaders of the blind, had succeeded in changing the Law of the Lord, His holy Word, into a lie, into deceit. How is that possible? We need only think of the many "keys to Scripture" offered in our day by Eddyites, Russellites, Jehovah's Witnesses. The lying pen of the scribes worked unto deception, unto lies, not only six hundred years before Christ, it is still doing its insidious work. How can they do it? asks God in astonishment and at once pronounces His judgment.

V. 9. Such wise men will stand ashamed, caught in the web of their own lies. That true wisdom (Ps. 111:10; 2 Cor. 10:4) which gives heavenly joy and hope to the humble believer (Rom. 5:1-3), this wisdom they have rejected, and what kind of wisdom remains? The present conditions in the world, the result of a wisdom mocking the Word of God and regarding as outmoded His Law as well as His Gospel, teach the truth of this word of the unchanging I AM THAT I AM.

Vv. 10-12. See ch. 6:12-15. Such repetitions are part of Jeremiah's style. Cp. ch. 7:31-33 and 19:5-7; 10:12-16 and 51:15-19; 15:13-14 and 17:3-4; 16:14-15 and 23:7-8; etc.

B. The horror of inevitable ruin, vv. 13-17

13 I have thoroughly gleaned them, is the oracle of the LORD. Yet, no grapes on the vine and no figs on the fig tree! The leaves are withered, and I have appointed for them 14 such as overrun them. Why are we sitting so quietly? Let us get together and go to the fortified cities, and there let us meet our doom. For the LORD, our God, has decreed annihilation for us, and He causes us to drink poison water, for we have sinned against Jehovah! 15 We hope for peace, and there is nothing good; and for a time of 16 recovery, and behold, terror! From Dan is heard the snorting of his horses. The whole land trembles at the sound of the neighing of his stallions. And they shall come and shall consume the land and all that is in it, the cities and their inhabit- 17 ants. For behold, I am sending against you venomous serpents against which there is no conjurer, and they shall bite you! is the oracle of the LORD.

Grammatical Notes

V. 13. Surely consume, אָסֹף אֲסִיפֵם. The abs. inf. of אָסַף, to gather, take away, and the Hiphil of סוּף, to make an end of, destroy. Two verbs of different roots joined to intensify the idea of destruction (cp. Zeph. 1:2).

Pass away. עָבָרוּם. A clause as the object of a verb is sometimes added without a relative pronoun or conjunction (cp. Ps. 50:21; Judg. 9:48; Is. 48:8; Hos. 7:2). I have appointed for them: they overrun them, i. e., such as overrun them. (G.-K. 157a.)

109

V. 13. The Lord will completely destroy them. The garden the Lord had planted and so tenderly cared for has disappointed His expectations. There are neither grapes nor figs. Even the leaves are dried and shriveled, the trees and vines dying. Therefore He will appoint to them multitudes passing over them, overwhelming them like a destructive flood (cp. Is. 8:7; Dan. 11:10).

Vv. 14-17. The prophet hears the despairing wail of an impenitent, hopeless people as they see judgment approaching like an overwhelming flood. The people in northern Israel are the first to realize the danger. For what purpose are we continuing to sit here idle, doing nothing? On this sense of "sit" see Judg. 5:16,17; Is. 30:7. Why expose ourselves to the cruelties and brutalities of the savage hordes? Why wait until they come to ravish our wives and daughters, to lead us captive into exile and slavery? Rather let us go to the fortified cities where there is at least a slight hope of finding shelter and safety. And if this hope fails, far better to be silenced in death by famine or pestilence than to fall into the hands of a cruel, pitiless enemy. For the Lord, our God, has put us to silence, has made us drink bitter, poisonous water because of our sins. Now they remember the Lord. Now they think of their sins. (V. 14.) But theirs is the repentance of Cain (Gen. 4:13-14), of Judas (Matt. 27:3-5), the sorrow of the world (2 Cor. 7:10b). Willingly had they listened to the lies of their false prophets. Now they grumblingly complain: We waited for peace, and nothing good has come. (V. 15.) How can God do that to us? Already the snorting of the war horses is heard. On they come, in seemingly endless masses. The land is consumed, its products gulped down by the insatiable hosts, its cities licked clean, its inhabitants swallowed up. Ruin, terror, desolation, horror everywhere! (V. 16.) The Lord explains why such devastation is possible in the land He called His own. He Himself has turned against His people. The warring hosts are only the instruments of His judgments. They are the serpents, the "cockatrices," basilisks, venomous snakes, against whom the skill and cunning of the conjurer is useless. There is no possibility of escape; "they shall bite you!" The Piel describes the eagerness with which they sink their death-dealing fangs deep, deep into the flesh of their helpless victims. (V. 17.)

C. The prophet's commiseration with his people, vv. 18-23

18 Oh, my Comfort against sorrow! My heart is faint in me! Behold, I hear the cry of the daughter of my people from the land afar off, Is the LORD no more in Zion? Or is there no more king in her? Why

have you vexed Me with your images, with the vain idols of foreign lands? The harvest is past, 20 the summer has ended, and we? — 21 we are not delivered! Because of the hurt of the daughter of my people I am hurt, I mourn; horror 22 has taken hold of me! Is there no balm in Gilead? no physician there? Why does not healing come to the daughter of my people? 23 (A. V., 9:1) Oh, that my head were waters and my eyes a fount of tears! Then I would bewail day and night the slain of the daughter of my people!

Grammatical Notes

V. 18. מַבְלִיגִית, only here. The root, to beam, occurs only in Hiphil (Amos 5:9), to cause to beam or shine upon; intr. to beam with joy (Ps. 39:14; Job 9:27; 10:20). The noun is the participle with feminine ending, that which causes one to beam with joy = comfort, consolation, or transitively, exhilaration, joy. Gesenius-Buhl defines it: *Erheiterung*. Since the Hebrew word is a regularly formed participial noun form, we do not change the text, which far from being meaningless (Volz), affords us a glimpse into the soul life of the prophet.

V. 18. "When I would comfort myself . . . ," rather, O my Comfort, or Joy, upon, or against sorrow! Unlike the grumbling despair of his fellow men, the prophet flees to the loving heart of his God, his Comforter and Joy (cp. Ps. 73:23-26). He is sure that there he can find exhilaration, cheer, and consolation. He needs it. "My heart is faint in me," literally, upon me my heart is sick. His heart is deeply wounded because he must see the misery of his people which he cannot heal.

Vv. 19-20. He hears in spirit the lamentations of the captives in distant Babylon, far from the land of their God. It seems to them that the taunting mockery of the heathen (Ezek. 36:20b) is a reality. They feel so utterly forsaken! Is it possible that God has rejected Zion? Has He lost His regal power? And Jeremiah hears God telling them what he, the prophet, had told them time and again: "Why have they provoked Me to anger with their graven images and with strange vanities, foreign nonentities?" Instead of pleading for mercy, the impenitent people only continue in their despairing wail of hopeless frustration: "The harvest is past, the summer is ended, and we are not saved!" The cold, icy winter of abject despondency holds them in its icy grip.

Vv. 21-22. This unbelief and despair of the people cause even deeper anguish to the prophet than the sorrows of the exile. That is the "hurt," the smashing blow, which might be the deathblow to many of his fellow Jews, whom he still loves as a father loves his daughter, and this "hurt" hurts him. "I am black," in deepest

111

mourning; astonishment, horror hath taken hold of me! In deepest anguish he cries out, v. 22: "Is there no balm in Gilead?" Gilead, on the east side of the River Jordan, stretched some ninety miles from near the southern shore of the Sea of Galilee southward to the Arnon River flowing into the Dead Sea about halfway between its northern and southern shores. Gilead's northern portion was heavily wooded and was well known for its balm, a resinous exudation from the terebinth, or turpentine tree, and the mastic, or pistachio tree, a small evergreen of western Asia. This resin was used in the preparation of healing ointments and was one of the chief articles of export, widely known and eagerly sought. It is used here in the general sense of medicine. "Is there no physician there?" "In the land of balm the use of it was best understood" (Naegelsbach). Neither healing nor healer is to be found for his people. "Then," rather, "for," states the reason for the negation. "The health," אֲרֻכָה, is the new flesh growing over, coming up and covering, the wound. There is no healing because the Lord Himself uses the scourge upon His people, who are no longer His own. Only if they do what they have refused to do in spite of all His pleas, only if they turn in sincere repentance to their Lord, will the Lord, their Physician (Ex. 15:26), heal them (Deut. 30:1-6).

V. 23 (A. V., 9:1). "Fountain," מְקוֹר, denotes a reservoir fed by perennial springs. The prophet wishes that his head might be an inexhaustible body of water, feeding the fountain of his eyes with a never-ceasing supply of water, so that day and night he might weep, give expression to his anguish at seeing the wholesale slaughter of his people. They are still *his* people, whom he loves as a father loves his only daughter, and their sorrow and anguish is his own.

Yet the prophet does not permit himself to be overcome by his personal feelings. The ruin of his people is the well-deserved penalty for their sins, sent by the Lord of everlasting justice and righteousness. This thought is brought out in ch. 9.

CHAPTER 9

3. The Folly of Deceitfulness and Sin Service
Vv. 1-21 (A. V., Vv. 2-22)

A. Judah's deceit, vv. 1-8

1 (A. V., v. 2) Oh, that I had in the desert a travelers' inn that I might leave my people and go away from them! For they all are adulterers, a band of traitors!

2 (A. V., v. 3) They bend their tongue as their bow for deceit; they do not rule in the land in the interest of truth, for they proceed from wickedness to wickedness, and

Me they do not know, says the LORD.

3 (A. V., v. 4) Let everyone be on his guard against his friend, and do not trust any brother; for every brother is deceitful as Jacob, every friend is a slandermonger.

4 (A. V., v. 5) Everyone deceives his neighbor, and truth they never speak. They accustom their tongue to speak lies; they tire themselves in committing crookedness.

5 (A. V., v. 6) You are living in the midst of deceit; in deceit they refuse to know Me, says the LORD.

6 (A. V., v. 7) Therefore thus says the LORD: Behold, I must smelt them and test them, for what else can I do in view of the daughter of My people?

7 (A. V., v. 8) Their tongue is a sharp arrow, it speaks deceit; with his mouth he continually speaks fair to his neighbor, and in his mind he seeks to trap him.

8 (A. V., v. 9) Shall I not punish them for these things? says the LORD, or shall I not avenge Myself upon a nation such as this?

Grammatical Notes

V.6. "Shall I do," עֲשֹׂה, in the sense of act, proceed, see Jer. 14:7; Lam. 1:21; Ezek. 31:11.

"For the daughter," מִפְּנֵי, "in view of the fact" that she is the daughter. Cp. Gen. 41:31; Jer. 23:9; 51:64.

V. 1 (A. V., v. 2). "Oh, that I had." Who will give to me, "in the wilderness," the lonely desert (Deut. 32:10; Jer. 2:2, 6, 24; 14:6; 17:6), "a lodging place of wayfaring men," a humble night lodging where an occasional traveler might stop for a night's rest or pause for a refreshment and then hurry on? He calls Judah "my people," because they were no longer worthy to be called the people of the Lord (cp. Ex. 32:7). "Adulterers." The spiritual adultery rebuked in ch. 2:20; 3:8-9 manifested itself in gross immoralities at the sanctuaries of Baal and other idols and on other occasions. (Cp. Jer. 5:7-8; 13:27; 23:10, 14.) "An assembly," עֲצֶרֶת, denotes the festival gatherings particularly on the seventh day of the Festival of Unleavened Bread (Deut. 16:8), the eighth day of the Festival of Tabernacles (Lev. 23:36; Num. 29:35; Neh. 8:18; 2 Chron. 7:9), on a day of repentance (Joel 1:14; cp. Is. 1:13; Amos 5:21), of Baal worship (2 Kings 10:20). Even when they gathered for their divinely appointed festivals, their assemblies were those of hypocrites, deceivers, traitors (cp. Jer. 3:7, 10-11), an abomination to the Lord, a loathing to the prophet. To be obliged to preach to such people, daily to come in contact with such nauseating filth — what a task! Gladly would he have dwelt in solitude (on cohortative see G.-K., 108f.) rather than among such people. Had he followed his inclinations, he might have become the patron saint of monasticism. But his life motto was: Not my will, but Thine, O God, be done! Not in solitude was he to bewail the fate of his nation nor give himself up to indignation over their wickedness. He was sent to preach, to speak, and speak to people, and to priests, and prophets, and kings, whether that agreed with or grated on his personal feelings; irrespective of success or non-success. In the strength of His God (ch. 1: 8, 17-19) the prophet continued his difficult work.

V. 2 (A. V., v. 3). They used their tongues as their bows for deceit in order to hurl the deadly arrows of deception. They use flattering speech or menacing words, whichever suits their deceitful purpose best (cp. v. 7; A. V., v. 8). "They are not valiant for the truth," rather, "not strong in faith" (cp. ch. 5: 1), they "go all out" from evil to evil; evil their starting point, evil their goal. Every rung on their ladder of success is evil, treachery, deviltry. The real cause of their wickedness is their lack of faith, the saving and sanctifying knowledge of the Lord (cp. ch. 9: 23-24).

V. 3 (A. V., v. 4). Even the intimacy of kinship and friendship is shamefully abused if that suits the wicked designs of the deceiver. "Utterly supplant," עָקוֹב יַעְקֹב, an allusion to Jacob's shameful deceit (Genesis 27, particularly v. 36). The verb means to take by the heel (Gen. 25: 26; Hos. 12: 3), to follow the heel for the purpose of trapping, to deceive. The abs. inf. intensifies the ever-repeated defrauding of the brother. In this respect they all were true offspring of their father Jacob at his worst, before he became Israel (Gen. 32: 24-30). "Walk with slanders" (cp. Jer. 6: 28).

Vv. 4-5 (A. V., vv. 5-6). The prophet cannot find words enough to describe adequately the universal treachery, their refusal to speak the truth, their habitual lies (cp. Ps. 36: 3-4). And God agrees with the prophet in pronouncing Judah treacherous. Their refusal to know the Lord (v. 3) is not due to ignorance; it is directly traceable to their treachery. Their own interests outweigh the considerations for God's will (cp. Ps. 2: 1-3), they shut the Lord out of their lives deliberately and purposively. Yet they deceive themselves. They cannot shut out Jehovah.

V. 6 (A. V., v. 7). On "smelt" cp. ch. 6: 29; on "try," or "test," ch. 6: 27 b. God is not yet ready to reject forever His people. He will, humanly speaking, make another effort to cleanse them from the dross by casting them into the furnace of tribulation. "For how shall I do," proceed, act? See Grammatical Notes. "For the daughter of My people," in view of the fact that she is the daughter, as dear to Me as an only daughter. "Of My people" is the appositional genitive, explaining "daughter," His chosen people, Ex. 19:5-6. Cp. Hos. 11:7-9; Jer. 31:20.

Vv. 7-8 (A. V., vv. 8-9). A nation that requites such loving-kindness as He had shown Judah with such wickedness and treachery cannot remain unpunished (Amos 2:9—3:2). Yet the ultimate purpose of His punishment is not the utter destruction of His people, but their purification, as silver is purified by fire (v. 7). What unmerited grace!

B. Wormwood and gall for the sinner! Vv. 9-15

9 (A. V., v. 10) For the mountains I lift up a weeping and sighing, and for the pastures of the steppe a dirge; for they are parched so that no man passes over them, and no more does one hear the lowing of the cattle. The birds of the air as well as the cattle have disappeared, are gone!

10 (A. V., v. 11) I will make Jerusalem heaps of stones, the lair of jackals; and the cities of Judah will I make desolate, without an inhabitant!

11 (A. V., v. 12) Who is the wise man that will understand this and to whom the LORD speaks, that he may tell why the land is destroyed, parched as the steppe, so that no one passes through it?

12 (A. V., v. 13) The LORD says:

Because they have forsaken My Law, which I set before them, and they did not obey My voice and did not walk according to it,

13 (A. V., v. 14) but have walked in the stubbornness of their heart and have followed the Baalim, to which their fathers accustomed them.

14 (A. V., v. 15) Therefore thus says the LORD of Hosts, the God of Israel: Behold, I will cause them, this very people, to eat wormwood and will cause them to drink poisoned water.

15 (A. V., v. 16) And I will scatter them among nations which neither they nor their fathers have known, and after them will I send the sword until I have annihilated them.

Vv. 9-10 (A. V., vv. 10-11). His judgment will come not only upon His people, but on the land which they have defiled, for which He mourns, since it is the innocent victim suffering for the sins of man (cp. Rom. 8:19-22). On the pity of the Lord for His creation cp. Jonah 4:11. "Dragons," rather, jackals (Jer. 10:22; 14:6; Is. 13:22; etc.).

V. 11 (A. V., v. 12). They lack that wisdom and understanding required to realize the true cause of the terrible desolation that shall come upon Judah, because such wisdom is acquired only by listening attentively to the words and declarations of the Lord, which they had refused to do (ch. 7:24-28).

Vv. 12-15 (A. V., vv. 13-16). Once more the Lord reveals the true cause and the extent of their ruin.

115

C. The death song, vv. 16-21

16 (A. V., v. 17) Thus says the LORD of Hosts: Get a clear conception of the actual situation! And call the wailing women so that they shall come, and send to the wise women that they shall come.

17 (A. V., v. 18) Let them come hurriedly and lift up a wailing over us, and our eyes shall flow with tears and our eyelashes stream with water.

18 (A. V., v. 19) For the voice of lamentation is heard from Zion: Woe! We are destroyed! We are put to great shame, for we have left our land, for they have torn down our dwellings!

19 (A. V., v. 20) Therefore hear, O women, the words of the LORD, and let your ears receive the word of His mouth; and teach your daughters a lament, and each one a dirge to her neighbor!

20 (A. V., v. 21) Death has climbed up through our windows! It has come into our palaces; it has cut off the children from the street, the young people from the market places.

21 (A. V., v. 22) Say: Thus saith the LORD: There shall fall the carcasses of men as dung upon the field, and as sheaves behind the harvester, and there is none to gather them.

Vv. 16-17 (A. V., vv. 17-18). Consider ye, cause yourselves to understand, to distinguish from other visitations, what will happen to you. The death of your nation is at hand! Call the mourning women that they may come, and send to wise women that understand their business of weeping and raising the emotions of the mourners to the highest pitch. The repeated "that they may come" indicates the urgency with which the call to these women is to be voiced. "And they shall hurry and raise a wailing over us," as was the custom when a person had died (cp. ch. 16: 4; 22: 18; Mark 5: 38), in which wailing all the nation will join, weeping bitterly.

Vv. 18-19 (A. V., vv. 19-20). The two "for," vv. 18 and 19, state the reason for this universal dirge. The nation is devastated, in deepest ignominy; they must leave their land; their homes are torn down; the death knell of Judah has been tolled. Therefore the women, the wives and mothers, who had been so fanatic in their service of strange gods and goddesses (ch. 7: 18; cp. ch. 44: 15-19), who had refused to listen to God's voice calling them to repentance, must now hear Judah's death sentence out of the mouth of the Lord, which they are to teach their daughters and one another (the sons and husbands having been slain in battle) in the form of one of the most gruesome descriptions of the inescapable power of the King of Terrors.

V. 20 (A. V., v. 21). Having fled from the enemy to the safety of their homes, they see Death climbing through the windows to carry off his victims. The palaces and mansions of the rich offer as little protection as the huts and hovels of the poor; Death enters them, as

116

he stalks through the streets and broad places (cp. ch. 5:1) to slay the children and young men.

V. 21 (A. V., v. 22). As in springtime the peasant scatters heaps of fertilizer over the field till the ground is covered with them, so the Prince of Terrors scatters the corpses of the slain as dung upon the earth; and as in autumn the harvester hastens to cut the grain and in his hurry leaves handful upon handful to rot upon the field, so the Grim Reaper unmercifully cuts down men and women and children and lets them lie where they fall, food for the dogs and wild beasts that roam undisturbed through the fields. Death rules everywhere, in the homes and in the streets, in the crowded city and in the open country. Judah bewails her children, for they are no more!

---

4. Wisdom unto Salvation, Ch. 9:22 (A. V., V. 23) to 10:25

A. Glorying in the knowledge of the Lord, ch. 9:22-25

22 (A. V., v. 23) Thus says the LORD: Let not a wise man glory in his wisdom, and let not the mighty man glory in his might, and let not the rich man glory in his riches.
23 (A. V., v. 24) But he that glories, let him glory in this, that he understands and knows Me, that I am the LORD, creating loving-kindness, judgment, and righteousness in the land, for I find pleasure in these things, says the LORD.

24 (A. V., v. 25) Behold, days are coming, says the LORD, and I will punish all who, though circumcised, are really uncircumcised.
25 (A. V., v. 26) Egypt, and Judah, and Edom, and the children of Ammon, and Moab, and all who have their temples shaved, that live in the steppe; for all nations are uncircumcised, and all the house of Israel is uncircumcised in heart.

Grammatical Notes

V. 24 (A. V., v. 25). "Circumcised with the uncircumcised."

מוּל is part. pass. Qal of מול, to circumcise; cp. Joshua 5:5, plural. "With the uncircumcised," בְּעָרְלָה, the ב essentiae of the older grammarians, designating the form, or manner, or character, in which a person or object appears, circumcision in the manner of uncircumcision; circumcised in the flesh but not in spirit; not in obedience to God's command. It cannot be translated "uncircumcised in or on the foreskin," for the verb is always construed with the accusative, both of the person and of the foreskin, never with בְּ, "on the foreskin."

V. 25 (A. V., v. 26). "In the utmost corners," literally, shaved at the side, the temples. Arabian and Syrian youths on reaching the age of puberty cut off the hair at the temples and consecrated them to their deity (Herodotus III, 8; Jer. 25:23; 49:32). This rite was prohibited to the Jews (Lev. 19:27; Deut. 14:1).

Vv. 22-23 (A. V., vv. 23-24). To the prophet standing heartbroken in the midst of ruin and devastation and death, the Lord turns with words of divine consolation and strength in one of the comparatively few promises scattered like fragrant flowers throughout the scenes of heart-rending woe and misery, promises the sweeter because of their rarity. Pointing out briefly the vanity and folly of boasting in one's own wisdom and power and riches as exemplified in Judah's downfall, the Lord shows the only really satisfying and worth-while object of glory: the knowledge of Him, the Lord.

Wisdom, power, riches — that is the trinity in which man glories. Wisdom, superior knowledge, that was the glittering bauble dangled before the eyes of Eve by the shrewd Deceiver, and which caused her downfall (Gen. 3:5-6). Riches and power are to this day the sole glory of many who can call them their own and the object of envy to those who do not possess them. They seemed to Satan some of the strongest weapons to fell the God-Man (Matt. 4:8-9). Yet human wisdom, human power, material riches, are vanity, as one of the richest and wisest and most powerful of men had experienced to his sorrow (Eccl. 1:2ff.). To Judah the trust in this trinity had brought ruin, devastation, death. The only way to escape like disaster is to cast aside all reliance on man's wisdom, all hope in one's own power, all trust in one's own riches, and to make the one object of one's glory the knowledge and understanding of the Lord. "Understand" הַשְׂכֵּל = to have correct insight into the nature of an object and to act in keeping with such proper understanding; to conduct oneself wisely, to deal prudently. "Know," here also *nosse cum affectu et effectu*. While in *haskel* the intellect and will is stressed, in *yada'*, intellect, emotion, and will are included. The two terms combined express all the powers and faculties of the mind being focused on, and motivated and directed by, the Lord at all times. And the supreme object of man's glory is to understand and know Jehovah, that He, Jehovah, "exercises," עָשָׂה, rather, creates, establishes, loving-kindness, judgment, and right-eousness on the earth, and that He delights in these things. Here it is the characteristic participle describing His nature as manifested in His dealings with man. What incomprehensible mercy and loving-kindness to give to a clod of earth not merely the beauty of perfect manhood, but to breathe into this body the breath of life, to endue it with a rational soul, and to implant in this soul the image of His own righteousness; to grant to man the lordship over God's creation and close and intimate communion with his Maker! What unfathomable loving-kindness in His dealing with man after his fall, in promising a Deliverer; in His plan, conceived from eternity, of redemption, justification, sanctification of mankind; in establishing the norm of His Gospel, the forgiveness of sin, and the promise of the resurrection of the body and of everlasting life! That is the loving-kindness established on earth in His Kingdom of Grace, which makes possible in this world of sin and iniquity such conditions as described in Ps. 85: 8-13; Jer. 31: 33-34; Ezek. 36: 26-32; Luke 1: 68-75; Phil. 2: 12-15; 3: 3-14; Titus 2: 11-14. In the New Testament as well as in the Old, he that glorieth, let him glory in the Lord, 1 Cor. 1: 30-31.

Vv. 24-25 (A. V., vv. 25-26). Three classes of people are distinguished with respect to circumcision. 1) Judah, the house of Israel, the Covenant nation, to whom by divine command circumcision was given as the sign of the Covenant (Gen. 17:10) and as a seal of the righteousness of faith (Rom. 4:11). 2) A second class are those nations which practiced circumcision without divine command. Five nations are named: Egypt, Edom, Ammon, Moab, and all that are in the utmost corners. See Grammatical Notes above. It is possible and quite plausible that among the five nations circumcision was practiced. Jerome states that they still practiced it in his time. For Egypt we have the older testimony of Herodotus II, 36, 104; Josephus states that the Arabian tribes were circumcised after the thirteenth year because Ishmael was circumcised at that age. *Ant.* I, 12. 2. For Moab, Ammon, and Edom we have no records. 3) A third class are "all nations" (of course with the exception of Judah and the five nations named above) which are uncircumcised.

In one respect, however, Israel is like the other nations, circumcised or uncircumcised: like them, it is uncircumcised in heart. It lacks that circumcision of which the outer circumcision was a symbol, the circumcision of the heart (Deut. 10:16; 30:6; Jer. 4:4; Rom. 2: 25-29), and therefore is as little immune against God's wrath as the other nations. In our day we might apply this lesson to such baptized church members as do not live in accordance with God's Word and will. They are no better than the unchurched (whether the latter are baptized or unbaptized), who do not obey God's will. All of them are subject to God's wrath and punishment.

CHAPTER 10

B. Idols or Jehovah, which will you choose?

a. The folly of idolatry, vv. 1-5

1 Hear the word which the LORD speaks to you, O house of Israel!
2 Thus says the LORD: Do not become accustomed to the ways of the Gentiles, and do not be dismayed at the signs of heaven, for the Gen-
3 tiles are dismayed at them. For the customs of the peoples are vanity; for it is a tree from the forest which one has cut down, which the hands of the carpenter have made
4 with the ax. With silver and with

gold he adorns it, with nails and hammers they fasten them so that
5 it will not move. They are like a pillar in the cucumber field. They do not speak. They must be carried, for they cannot walk. Do not be afraid of them, for they can do no harm, neither can they benefit in any way.

Vv. 1-2. Judah had been charged with uncircumcision of the heart (ch. 9:24-25). Now the Lord warns them not to learn the "ways," the conduct, especially the moral and religious ways, of the heathen (cp. Gen. 6:12; Prov. 3:17; Jer. 12:16). "Learn," to accustom oneself by practice and exercise. The Lord has in mind not merely an occasional lapse of an individual. The situation in Judah was far worse. They had practiced idolatry so long that it had become second nature to them (cp. Jer. 2:10-28; 7:17-18; 11:13; 2 Kings 16:10-18; 21:2-11). Even Josiah's reform did not succeed in eradicating it (2 Kings 23:26 f.). If Judah would continue in this course, every line of demarcation between God's chosen people and the Gentile world would soon be erased, and they would sink down to the level of pagandom, not only in the inner uncircumcision and blindness of their hearts (ch. 9:25), but just as surely in the outer manifestation of their heathendom, the superstitions and idolatries and abominations of the Gentiles.

In order to halt, if possible, this downward course, the Lord in bitter irony ridicules the foolishness and futility of idolatry.

Vv. 3-4. The "customs" of the heathen, their firmly established rituals of worship are "vain," vapor, spindrift, serving only to befog the people. Their idols are wood, cut down by the ax of men, dead timber, and dead wood they remain, no matter how gorgeously they are ornamented. The men who worship them must come to their aid with hammer and nail to fasten the image to its support, lest it totter and fall. (Cp. Is. 41:7ff.)

V. 5. "Upright," rather, "of turned work," "like one of those stiff, inelegant pillars, something like a palm tree, which may be seen in oriental architecture" (*Bible Commentary*). Others translate: "like a pillar, or scarecrow, in a cucumber field." They cannot utter one command nor voice a single word of comfort; nor can they come to anyone's aid. Why fear them or trust in them?

b. *The Lord, the living God and King, preserves His heritage forever, vv. 6-16*

6 Where can we find one like Thee, O LORD? Great art Thou, and
7 great is Thy name in power! Who would not fear Thee, O King of the nations? This surely is Thy due! For among all the wise men of the Gentiles and in all their kingdoms
8 there is none like Thee! They are

altogether stupid and foolish; the instruction of idol vanities is wood! 9 Beaten silver is brought from Tarshish and gold from Uphaz. They are the work of a carpenter, the handiwork of the goldsmith; blue and red purple is their clothing, all 10 of it the work of wise men. But the LORD is God! Truly, He is the living God and the eternal King! At His wrath the earth trembles, and the Gentiles cannot bear His 11 fury! Thus shall ye say to them: The gods that have not made the heavens and the earth, they shall perish from the earth and beneath 12 the heavens. He who made the earth by His strength and established the world by His wisdom has also by His understanding spread 13 out the heavens. When He utters His voice, there is the noise of waters in the sky; and He causes clouds to arise from the ends of the earth. He creates lightnings for rain and brings forth the wind from its chambers. Stupid is every man, 14 without knowledge! Every refiner is put to shame by his image, for his castings are frauds, and there 15 is no breath in them. Vanity they are, ridiculous work! In the time of their punishment they will per- 16 ish! The Portion of Jacob is not like these! For He it is that forms all things, and Israel is the tribe of His possession. The LORD of Hosts is His name!

Grammatical Notes

V. 11. Volz calls attention to the fact that the last half of v. 11, b, is the first half of the verse, a, read backwards with the necessary grammatical changes.

a: 1) *elahaya* 2) *di shemayah* 3) *w'arkah* 4) *lo 'abadu*
b: 8) *elleh* 7) *umin t'chat shemayah* 6) *me'ar'ah* 5) *ye'abadu*

"The usual form of the demonstrative pronoun 'they, these,' in Aramaic is אִלֵּין, but also אֵלֶּה occurs in Aramaic (cp. Ezra. 5:15); in Nabatean inscriptions and in the Assuan Papyri, see Strack, *Gramm. d. Bibl. Aram.*, 5 Aufl., 6d." (Volz, *Der Prophet Jeremias*, p. 122.)

V. 6. "Forasmuch," rather, "whence." The heathen gods are taken from the forest wood, but whence is there one like the Lord? No human mind could possibly conceive God. He owes His origin to no one, for He is in fact I AM THAT I AM, great, too great for human comprehension, as His name, His revelation and manifestation of Himself, is great, powerful, too great for man's feeble understanding.

V. 7. God's supreme majesty as manifested in His government of the world demands that all mankind fear Him; stand in holy, adoring awe before their Creator and Ruler. Such fear appertains to Him, becomes Him, is His due (cp. Is. 6:3; Rev. 4:8-11). No one can equal His wisdom (Is. 40:18, 25, 28; Rom. 16:27).

V. 8. The wise among men are brutishly foolish (Rom. 1:21-22), and since the idols of these men are the product of the wisdom of men, they are no less brutish and foolish than their makers, as the stories related about the heathen gods amply testify. "The stock is a doctrine of vanities," rather: The doctrine, or instruction, of these

121

vanities, these idols, is wood, no better than the material they are made of, dead lumber, lifeless, insipid, a fraud.

V. 9. "Tarshish" is Tartessus in Spain, known for its silver mines. Uphaz has not been identified. Since Tartessus is in the extreme West, Uphaz may be the name of a gold-producing country in the extreme East. The Targum and Syrian change it to Ophir. The embellishment of the images by means of precious metals brought from afar, and costly garments, does not make the gods any wiser or stronger; they still remain the handiwork of men.

V. 10. From these vanities the prophet turns his gaze upward to the Lord, who alone deserves the name *Elohim,* the Strong. His alone is life, His only, eternity. He rules the elements and the nations.

V. 11 (see Grammatical Notes) ties up with v. 10, contrasting the idols of the Gentiles with the true God. It is impossible to decide whether this proverb, written in the Aramaic idiom and introduced by the Aramaic formula "So shall you say to them," was composed by Jeremiah or was a popular proverb of which Jeremiah reminded his readers and which they might use in answer to the taunts of the heathen enemies. Most modern interpreters regard it as a gloss or marginal note which accidentally found its way into the text, interrupting the connection. Yet it does not interrupt the context. It links up with v. 10, and v. 12 links up with it. Keil correctly states that it has not the nature of a gloss and that a copyist would not have placed an Aramaic gloss into a Hebrew text accidentally or purposely. Moreover, it is found in all the ancient versions.

Vv. 12-15 link up closely with v. 11, contrasting the omnipotence of the Creator with the impotence of man-made idols (v. 11). The Lord proves His unlimited power, wisdom, and understanding by creating, preserving, and ruling the universe (Gen. 1: 1-30; Deut. 32: 8; Acts 17: 26; Is. 40: 26-28; Ps. 147: 4-9). Man betrays only his ignorance and stupidity by worshiping his own handiwork, placing his trust on frauds, doomed to become the laughingstock of future generations and to perish like their makers. Who still fears Marduk and Baal and the thousand and one gods and goddesses of antiquity whose very names are forgotten?

V. 16. "The Portion of Jacob," He who has given Himself to His people as their Portion, their very own (cp. Ps. 73: 26; 119: 57; 142: 5). The "rod" or tribe of His inheritance, chosen by the Lord as His heirs. He is what His name implies, the Lord of Hosts, the unchanging, eternal Ruler of heaven and earth, the Covenant God of His Church.

c. Forsaking the Lord brings ruin and disaster, vv. 17-22

17 Take up your bundle from the ground, you that are living in a
18 state of siege! For thus says the LORD: Behold, this time I am hurling forth the inhabitants of the land, and I shall distress them in order that they may be found.
19 Woe is me because of my ruin! Incurable is my wound! And I say: Alas, this is my ailment, and I must
20 bear it! My tent is destroyed, and all tent cords are broken! My children have gone away from me and are no more! There is no one that erects my tent and stretches my
21 curtains. For the shepherds are stupid and do not seek the LORD, therefore they have no understanding, and the flock is scattered.
22 Hark! A rumor! Lo, it comes! A great commotion from the Northland, to make the cities of Judah desolate, the lair of jackals.

Vv. 17-18. Judah has forsaken this Lord and therefore is now told to get ready for exile. Gather up thy "wares," כִּנְעָה. This word, occurring only here, may have been chosen because it is derived from the same stem as Canaan. The Canaanites were great tradesmen. And commercialism had become the besetting sin of Judah; money dictated their policies. "Inhabitant of the 'fortress,'" the Hebrew word means both "fortress" and "siege," "distress." The fortified city a city of distress, of siege! And this siege will end in destruction. Other sieges were lifted by the Lord's aid. "This once," this time He Himself is the enemy of Judah. He will hurl them out of the land they have defiled, as a stone is hurled from the sling. "That they may find." Jerome read the passive, יִמָּצְאוּ, for יִמְצְאוּ, and they shall be found, i. e., none shall escape. This is a better rendering than many others suggested.

Vv. 19-22. The prophet laments the smashing destruction of the nation; humbles himself under the mighty hand of God (v. 19), recognizing the justice of His judgment (v. 21), severe as it is (vv. 20, 22). Bruit (v. 22), report, rumor. In spirit he already hears the dread report of the approach of the enemy.

d. Plea for true knowledge of the Lord and deliverance from judgment, vv. 23-25

23 I know, O LORD, that man's way is not his own, and that man as he walks cannot direct his steps.
24 Chastise me, O LORD, only in judgment, not in Thy anger, that
25 I may not be annihilated! Pour Thy wrath upon the Gentiles that will not know Thee, and on those tribes that do not call upon Thy name, for they consume Jacob and consume him and finish him and make desolate his dwelling place.

V. 23. Neither אָדָם, the lowly, earthborn creature, nor אִישׁ, the man of strength, the noble man, can determine his own ways, nor even, though he is walking, direct his steps. Human wisdom, human

123

strength, human resources, are no more than human, fleeting, mortal, in spite of all their pomp and self-glorification. No man can lift the veil that hangs over the future, over tomorrow, over the next step. Man may propose, it is God who disposes, who rules the world as He has determined. Despairing of his own wisdom and strength, the prophet leaves the future to God, has only one plea.

V. 24. "Chastise me, O LORD" of everlasting grace and mercy (Ex. 34:5-7a), train, teach me, and if necessary, chastise me. I need Thy training, I have deserved Thy chastisement, but if Thou must punish Thy wayward child, then do it "with judgment," according to the norm Thou hast established as the Lord of unchanging grace. Chastise me as Thy child. "Not in Thine anger, lest Thou bring me to nothing," make me a small, insignificant people, no longer the nation of Thy choice, a kingdom of priests, a peculiar treasure unto Thee above all people (Ex. 19:5-6). The prophet, speaking as the representative of his people, is willing to endure all that God intends to do in chastising them, so long as He will not reject them utterly. This plea was heard by the Lord. In the Exile a new generation grew up that feared and loved and trusted in the Lord their God.

V. 25. Jeremiah firmly trusts that the Lord will not finally and forever reject His people, that even the Exile will be merely a chastisement for the training of the people. At the same time he knows that the enemies have in mind the complete annihilation of Judah as a nation. Such a destruction would seem to make the fulfillment of God's promise of a Redeemer impossible. Therefore the prophet asks God to frustrate the plans of His and His people's enemies. This is not the prayer of a nationalistic Jew against the detested *Goyim;* it is a prayer that God might destroy them before they could accomplish their wicked intention to destroy God's people.

V. Covenant, Conspiracy, Condemnation, Ch. 11—13

CHAPTER 11

1. The Lord's Covenant to Be Obeyed by Judah, Vv. 1-8

1 The word which came to Jeremiah
2 from the LORD. Hear the words of this covenant, and speak to the men of Judah and to the inhabitants of
3 Jerusalem. And thou shalt say to them: Thus says the LORD, the God of Israel: Cursed be the man who will not obey the words of
4 this covenant which I have commanded to their fathers on the day that I brought them out of the land of Egypt, the iron furnace, and said: Obey My voice, and do just as I have commanded you, and you shall be My people, and I will be
5 your God, in confirmation of the oath which I have sworn to your fathers, to give to them a land flowing with milk and honey as it is this day. And I answered and said:
6 Amen, O LORD! And the LORD said to me: Proclaim all these words in the cities of Judah and on the streets of Jerusalem, saying: Obey the words of this covenant,
7 and do them! For I solemnly testified to your fathers on the day that I brought them out of the land of Egypt, and to this day, and have testified early and late: Obey My
8 words! And they did not obey and did not incline their ears, but every man walked in the hardness of their heart. Therefore I shall bring upon them all the words of this covenant which I commanded them to keep, but which they did not keep.

Vv. 1-2. Six times the word "hear" is used in this brief message, always in the sense of obey. Obedience is the basic and ever-repeated demand of the Lord of the Covenant (Ex. 19:5; 1 Sam. 15:22; Ps. 50: 7-23; Mal. 4:4). A second command, closely connected with the first, is the command to speak, added to the first by the perfect with strong ן; describing the speaking as implicitly contained in, and naturally flowing from, the first command. Hear, in order that you speak! or, Hear, and then you will speak! (Cp. Ps. 116:10; 2 Cor. 4:13; Acts 4:20.) This command is addressed to all people. The Lord institutes here an "Each One Reach One" movement. Hear, obey, believe! and then: Go and tell! Everyone is to be reached, the city people as well as the small-town people and the rural population. All are to hear, all are to tell the words of this covenant.

Vv. 3-5. The Lord has a special spokesman (ch. 1:5), who has a special commission to proclaim the word of God so that the people may hear and become speakers of God's word. He is to utter first a curse against all those who had refused and would continue to refuse to obey God's command. Then he is to remind them of God's promise of spiritual (v. 4b) and material (v. 5) blessings in order that the Lord may carry out His oath in the days of Jeremiah's generation as

125

He had fulfilled it in the days of their fathers. Amen, O Lord! the prophet cries out. He is ready to do what the Lord commands him.

To which covenant does the Lord refer here? Certainly not, as many modern critics assert, to the so-called Deuteronomic Covenant, based on a newly found book hitherto unknown, the product of some pious scribe living in the eighth century B. C., or of the promoters of a centralized sanctuary, ca. 625. The Author of the covenant referred to in this chapter describes it as the covenant which He made with the fathers of Israel at the time of their deliverance out of Egypt (v. 4). In v. 4b there is a direct reference to Ex. 19: 5-9; 29: 45; Lev. 20: 24, 26; 26: 12; Deut. 7: 6; 29: 13; while v. 5 takes us back to the days of Moses' call (Ex. 2: 24; 3: 6-17) and his farewell address (Deut. 6: 3, 10; 7: 6-8; etc.). Josiah's reformation was based on the Book of the Law of the Lord by the hand of Moses (2 Chron. 34: 14). The covenant made by King Josiah and the people in the eighteenth year of his reign was merely a reaffirmation on their part to remain loyal to the Sinaitic Covenant established with the fathers by the Lord.

Vv. 6-8. Jeremiah may have hoped that Josiah's reform would be successful. The Lord knows Jeremiah's preaching will meet with no better success than He Himself had experienced during the past centuries. God had faithfully kept His covenant with His people, yet they despised His goodness and hardened themselves against His severity. Now God, who still remains true to His covenant, "will bring upon them all the words of this covenant," will fulfill His threat that the land will spue them out if they had defiled it (Lev. 18: 28; 20: 22; Deut. 29: 28).

---

2. Judah's Conspiracy Against the Lord Will Ruin the Nation
Vv. 9-17

9 Then the LORD said to me: A conspiracy is found among the men of Judah and the inhabitants of Jeru-
10 salem. They have turned back to the iniquities of their first fathers, who refused to listen to My words; they run after other gods to serve them. The house of Israel and the house of Judah have broken My covenant, which I have established
11 with their fathers. Therefore thus says the LORD: Behold, I am bringing evil upon you from which you cannot escape. When they cry unto Me, I shall not listen to them.
12 And the cities of Judah and the inhabitants of Jerusalem shall go and cry to their gods to which they are offering sacrifices, and they will not at all be able to help them
13 in the time of their evil. For as numerous as your cities are your gods, O Judah; and as numerous as the streets of Jerusalem are the altars you have erected to the shameful thing, altars to offer sacri-
14 fice to Baal. And you! — do not intercede for this people, and do

not lift up supplication and prayer on their behalf, for I will not listen at the time they call to Me in their 15 troubles. What right has My loved one in My house? she who is committing treachery? Will vows and holy flesh remove your evil? Then 16 you might rejoice! Jehovah has called you a green olive tree, beautiful with well-formed fruit! Amidst the crashing of thunder the LORD has set fire to it, and they 17 have broken its branches. The LORD of Hosts, who has planted you, has spoken evil against you, because of the wickedness of the house of Israel and the house of Judah that they have committed to their own harm in order to provoke Me, by burning incense to Baal.

Grammatical Notes

V. 15. The present M. T. form presents great difficulties. "Beloved" is masc. construed as fem., "her doings." LXX and Syrian read fem. יְדִידִי. On the basis of twenty-five Mss., LXX, and Syr., Kittel suggests to read עָשְׂתָה instead of עֲשׂוֹתָה.

"Lewdness," the A. V. evidently regarded מְזִמָּה as a synonym of זִמָּה, which cannot be proved. It means plan, device, particularly evil schemes, machinations. The ending תָה, originally the accusative of direction or intention, is quite frequently used as a fuller form for the fem., particularly in poetic speech. Cp. Ex. 15:16; Ps. 3:3; 63:8; cet. G.-K. 90g. — "With many," הָרַבִּים, "the many," has not found a satisfactory explanation. LXX evidently read הַנְּדָרִים, εὐχαί, vows. Vulgate: adipes = fats, reading חֲבָלִים; others suggest הָרֻנִּים, from רנן, to cry, wail (Lam. 2:19), "wailings." — "Passed over," to be read as Hiphil. "When thou doest evil," read with LXX, ancient Latin, Vulg., רָעָה מֵעָלָיִך, evil from her.

V. 9. Judah and Jerusalem have lost every right to be blessed and protected by the Lord of the Covenant. Their conspiracy is no longer a matter of secret planning. It is "found," it is manifest, it has broken out in open revolt and has spread far and wide.

V. 10. As the fathers rebelled (Exodus 32 ff.; Num. 14:1-45; 16: 1 ff.), so their children are covenant breakers.

Vv. 11-12. They have pursued evil constantly; now evil shall continually pursue them. They refuse to hear Me; and I shall refuse to hear them. All they look for is help, and help they shall not obtain, not from their gods, for they have not the power, nor from Me, for I no longer have the will and inclination to help. Duped and betrayed by their gods, forsaken and rejected by the Lord of the Covenant which they have conspired to break — all that remains for them is the time of their trouble, from which there is no escape in time or eternity.

V. 13 proves the correctness of God's charge of open conspiracy (cp. ch. 2:28). There was not a city that had not adopted its special tutelary deity; not a street in Jerusalem where altars had not been erected to that shameful thing, Baal (cp. ch. 3:24).

V. 14. (Cp. ch. 7:16.) Can starker tragedy be imagined than that the same Lord, who has commanded us to pray and promised to hear us, forbids His prophet to pray for the nation God had chosen as His own peculiar people; and tells His spokesman that if he should nevertheless intercede for his people, the Lord will not hear him? Nor will He hear His people even though they should cry to Him because of the evils coming upon them!

V. 15. Jedidiah, "Jehovah's beloved one," had been the honorable name given to Solomon by his teacher Nathan (2 Sam. 12:25). Like Solomon, Judah-Jerusalem had been the Lord's beloved (Ps. 78:68f.; 87:2; Jer. 12:7). But Judah had no longer the right and privilege to dwell in the Lord's house. In justified indignation the Lord asks: What has My beloved to do in My house? He accuses her that she commits treachery, harbors evil devices, is guilty of machinations. Yet neither her vows (or supplications) nor holy flesh, that is, sacrifices (Hag. 2:12), will remove her "evil" (רעה denotes both sin and punishments), though she would certainly rejoice if that were possible! Not God's will and Word, but their own selfish, sinful interests were the norm of their lives!

V. 16. Once more the thoughts of the Lord revert to the days of Israel's youthful devotion, her bridal love (Jer. 2:2). He regarded her then as a green olive tree. "Those who see olive trees for the first time are occasionally disappointed by the dusty color of their foliage; but those who are familiar with them find an inexpressible charm in the rippling changes of their slender gray-green leaves" (Wm. Smith, *Dictionary of the Bible*, p. 473f.). It is not, however, the beauty of the foliage that the Lord admires, but the beauty of the fruit produced by Israel in loving service of her Bridegroom. Literally, beautiful as to fruit of form. Her beauty consisted in the well-formed fruit she brought forth, not sickly, worm-eaten olives, unfit for the oil press, or furnishing a very poor grade of oil, but perfect fruit, things of beauty in every respect. The oil of which the olive is the source is a symbol of the Holy Spirit and His gifts (Ps. 45:7; Acts 10:38). So the Church of God and its individual members became by the grace of God the source of spiritual life and blessing to their fellow men, their words and deeds testifying to the life-changing power of their God and Savior. On the symbol cp. Zech. 4:1-14; on the idea, John 7:38-39.

Such an olive tree bearing well-formed olives, Judah by the grace of God had been in the days of her youth, thoroughly furnished unto all good works. Yet now the same Lord must destroy this tree. "With the noise of a great tumult," amidst the crashing of thunder and tempest (הֲמוּלָה occurs only here and Ezek. 1:24), the Lord sets fire to the olive tree, "and its branches are broken," literally, and they broke its branches, the enemies at God's command had stripped the tree of its unfruitful branches, so that it was fit only for firewood, to be consumed by the fire of God's fury. Why?

V. 17. The Lord once again dins into the ears of the stubborn people the real cause of their evil: Because they had forsaken the Lord, who had planted them, and worshiped Baal! Therefore the Lord, the God of the Covenant, now carries into effect the evils long ago pronounced against them.

3. Conspiracy Against Jeremiah and Its Punishment, Vv. 18-23

18 The LORD informed me, and I came to know it. Then Thou causedst me to realize their doings.
19 And I was like a pet lamb, brought to slaughter. I did not know that they planned schemes against me: "Let us slay the tree with its fruits and cut him off from the land of the living, and his name shall never
20 again be remembered." O LORD of Hosts, Thou righteous Judge, testing kidneys and heart, I shall see Thy revenge upon them, for I have laid my cause before Thee!

21 Therefore thus says the LORD regarding the men of Anathoth, that seek your soul, saying: Prophesy not in the name of the LORD, then
22 you will not die by our hands. For thus saith the LORD of Hosts, Behold, I will punish you! Their young men shall die by the sword; their sons and their daughters shall
23 die by famine. No remnant shall be left to them! For I will bring evil upon the men of Anathoth in their year of visitation!

V. 18. Note the repeated statement that the prophet came to a realization of the wicked plot against him only by information and revelation of the Lord.

V. 19. He was, indeed, like a pet lamb, unsuspectingly trusting his fellow citizens, unable to realize that they were actually harboring plans of leading him to slaughter (cp. on this expression Is. 53:7; Jeremiah a type of the Messiah). Their plan was to "destroy the tree with the fruit thereof," literally, "in his bread," a proverbial expression denoting complete destruction. Since he was unmarried, ch. 16:2, the bread, or food produced by the tree, refers not to children, but to his whole life's work, which they hoped to nullify. Once he is gone, his very memory will be forgotten.

129

V. 20. Such personal hatred against the spokesman of the Lord, whose Word was anything but bread of life to them, was particularly puzzling and irksome to him. He turns to the Covenant God, the Lord of Hosts, the righteous Judge, the Searcher of kidneys and heart, of emotions and mind, who knows the faithfulness of His servant as well as the treachery of the opponents, and in full reliance on His justice confidently states his conviction: I shall see Thy vengeance upon them! Literally, from them; the vengeance of God becomes manifest from their punishment.

Vv. 21-23. His confidence in the Lord will not be disappointed. In due time his spiteful opponents will meet with the fate they had planned against him.

CHAPTER 12

4. The Prophet's Complaint, Vv. 1-4

1 Righteous art Thou, O LORD, when I plead with Thee. Yet I will speak with Thee on matters of judgment. Why is the way of the ungodly successful? Why do all that practice treachery live peace-
2 fully? Thou hast planted them, and they have taken root; they grow up, and they also bring fruit! Near art Thou to their mouths, and far away
3 from their inner life. Yet Thou, O LORD, knowest me, Thou hast observed me, and so Thou hast tested my heart with Thee. Cut them off as sheep ready for slaugh-ter, and set them apart for the day
4 of slaying. How long shall the land mourn and the vegetation of the whole field wither? Because of the wickedness of its inhabitants cattle and birds are clean gone. For they say: He will not see our end!

V. 1. This chapter offers to us a glimpse into the heart of the prophet and reveals another of the many fightings within that disturbed the peace of his mind and might become a serious menace to the faithful performance of his office. He had entrusted his case to the Lord (ch. 11:20), but it seems to him that the Lord is rather tardy in prosecuting his suit, in calling the enemies into judgment. And once more he approaches his Lord to discuss this matter with Him. It is the same question which had agitated David (Psalm 37) and seriously perturbed Asaph (Psalm 73), the age-old question: Wherefore doth the way of the wicked prosper, while the righteous must suffer? At the very outset he professes his firm conviction that God is righteous, one who is right, correct, whose every action is in full keeping with the norm of justice and righteousness. "Yet" he would like to talk with God of His "judgments," here the visible manifestations of His righteousness in His dealings with man, in shaping the lives and fortunes of mankind. Right here God's ways and judgments seem at times to run directly counter to His promises to His children and His threats to the wicked. Why do people who "treacherously commit treachery," whose whole life is spent in an effort to devise new and more effective methods of deceiving people, why "are they happy," at rest, secure from danger and misfortune?

V. 2. They have sent their roots deep into the soil, are firmly established trees. The perfects "planted," "taken root," denote these acts as accomplished facts. "They grow." The imperfect "grow," denotes progressive growth, pictures them as they plan new schemes and undertake new projects, gradually spreading their business and their influence wider and wider, while the ultimate result of every individual effort and of all of them combined is effectively summed up in the perfect denoting the completed state: "they have brought forth fruit," have met with success. And all that although they are wicked men, treacherous deceivers! Why hast Thou planted them, why granted them success? The prophet has in mind not Gentiles, but members of his own people, who constantly use God's name. Hearing them speak, one should think that they were close to God, united with Him in mutual friendship and love. Yet their knowledge of God goes no farther than their mouth, it has not penetrated to their "reins," the seat of feelings, emotions, affections. Their knowledge is not a living knowledge. It is a matter of the intellect, the mind, the mouth. And such hypocrites, such wicked deceivers are granted continued blessings and success!

V. 3. "But Thou, O LORD, knowest me." "Know" here denotes "to know by experience, observation, reflexion" (cp. Gen. 15:8; Ex. 7:17; Ezek. 6:7, 13). "Thou hast seen me," observed me; the imperfect denotes progressive duration. And the result of this long continued observation is stated by the perfect with the strong ׀, "Thou hast tested my heart with Thee." Mine is a heart tested by Thee, the Searcher of hearts (Jer. 17:10), as being with Thee. Why dost Thou permit them to endanger my life and my life's work (ch. 11:18-23)? Tear them out whom Thou hast planted! Tear them out like a flock for "the day of slaughter," and (cp. Zeph. 1:7 ff.) "prepare," "sanctify them, set them apart, "to slaughter," since they refuse to be sanctified for Thy service. (Here the root meaning of קדש, "to be separated," appears quite clearly.) Jeremiah knows very well what he would do if he were the judge. And impetuously he tells God to make His

131

messenger's idea of justice the standard to be adopted by the Eternal I Am That I Am in His passing judgment upon His creatures.

V. 4. The prophet motivates his plea by pointing out some of the dire consequences of the wickedness of these hypocrites. Hos. 2: 21-22 the earth is represented as pleading with the heavens and with God to hear the pleas of Israel for corn and wine and oil. In our passage the earth is mourning because the wrath of God prevents her from producing the foodstuffs she would like to produce. Beasts and birds are consumed. Because the wicked persist in their wickedness and their rejection of the Word of the Lord's prophet, therefore the whole creation must suffer and groan and travail in pain (cp. Rom. 8: 22), while the real malefactors grow fat and flourish, so that, flushed with their success and secure in their riches, they sneeringly exclaim: He (either the prophet, or the third person is indefinite, "anyone") shall not see our end. Who cares for the predictions of a prophet whose prophecies of doom have never been fulfilled? — Jeremiah has presented his case and awaits the Lord's answer. This answer is not what the prophet had expected.

5. God's Answer, Vv. 5-17

A. Your present trials are only the forerunners of still greater heartaches, vv. 5-6

5 If you have raced with foot racers and they have made you weary, how will you run a race with the horses? And if you make a peaceful land your trust, what will you do in the canebrakes of Jordan?

6 For even your brothers and the house of your father, even they have treacherous plans against you; even they are raising a hue and cry after you. Do not trust them when they speak friendly to you.

V. 5. Instead of explaining His actions, instead of promising His prophet brighter and better days, God tells Jeremiah that the conditions which seem unbearable to the prophet are but a feeble foretaste of far bitterer experiences. His present grief is as little to be compared with the horrors to come as a foot race with men is to be compared with a race with horses. If the former will weary him, how can he hope for success in the latter! And if his is the character of a man that will make a land of peace his sole basis of trust and hope, what will he do, how will he fare in the "pride of Jordan," in the canebrakes of the riverbanks, infested by wild animals (Jer. 49: 19; 50: 44; Zech. 11: 3) and by robber bands? Days are coming in comparison with which his present troubles will appear as days of peace. Precious little comfort for the harassed prophet! He must prepare for still greater hardships and heartaches if he is to remain a faithful servant of the Lord, if he is to stand as an iron pillar and walls of brass against his enemies, cp. ch. 1:18.

V. 6. The Lord mentions one such heartache in store for the prophet. Not only his fellow citizens of Anathoth, no, even his brethren, even his father's house, his own flesh and blood, will act treacherously against him, even they will cry a full measure, raise a hue and cry against him, as one cries in pursuit of a thief or murderer. Even their kind words, their flatteries, are merely a cloak to cover their murderous schemes. What a dire prospect for the loving prophet to be betrayed by the very people who are nearest and dearest to him!

B. God's judgment upon the wicked conspirators, vv. 7-13

7 I have forsaken My house; I have left My heritage; I have given the beloved of My soul into the hands 8 of her enemies. My heritage has become unto Me as a lion in the forest; it has raised its voice against 9 Me, therefore I hate it. Has My heritage become unto Me as a many-colored bird of prey? Are birds of prey gathered round about against her? Go, gather all the beasts of the field, bring them to 10 devour! Many shepherds have destroyed My vineyard; they have trodden under foot My portion; they have made My precious por- 11 tion a desolate waste. They have made it desolate; it mourns before Me desolate; desolate is all the land; for there is none that took 12 it to heart! Against all bare hills in the steppe destroyers have come; for the sword of the LORD devours the Lord's own, from one end of the land to the other, so that there is 13 no safety for anyone. They have sowed wheat and have harvested thorns; they have labored to exhaustion and have no profit! They are disappointed by their harvest because of the anger of the LORD.

Grammatical Notes

V. 9. "Speckled," צָבוּעַ, usually derived from צבע, not occurring in Biblical Hebrew, but in related dialects, "to color," cp. צֶבַע, colored garment of many hues (Judg. 5:30).

V. 9. "Bird," עַיִט, a bird of prey (Gen. 15:11; Is. 18:6; 46:11; Ezek. 39:4; Job 28:7); the stem עיט means to rush, fall upon.

Vv. 7-8. God forsakes "My house" (Ex. 29:45-46; Num. 35:34), "My heritage" (Deut. 4:20; 9:26, 29; Is. 19:25); "the dearly beloved of My soul" (cp. ch. 11:15), to whom He was attached in love such as only God is capable of (cp. John 3:16; Jer. 31:3), because it has "roared" against the Lord as a wild beast, a lion in the forest. Their declaration of independence from God was actually pronouncing their own death warrant (Deut. 32:35; Heb. 10:30f.).

V. 9. "Speckled bird," see Grammatical Notes above. A gaudily colored bird of prey appears in a flock of other birds of prey, which attack him, displume and mutilate him. Those nations with which the highly favored and beautified Jewish nation mingled against God's will, shall now pluck it to pieces. From near and far the enemies come. God Himself calls them and all the beasts of the field to join in the kill.

Vv. 10-12. The spiritual leaders, instead of cultivating the garden of God, have by their neglect reduced God's vineyard to desolation, for spiritual decay led to national destruction.

V. 13. In bitter irony the Lord describes the disappointing result of their labor. All their strength, their labors, their time and money — like wheat, precious gifts of God — were squandered in vain efforts to gain the favor of the world rulers contrary to God's will, only to be horribly disappointed! Instead of the expected "wheat," power and prestige, they harvest "thorns," humiliation, ruin, devastation, death. The Lord, whom they rejected, now rejects them.

C. God's purposes in His world government, vv. 14-17

14 Thus says the LORD concerning all my wicked neighbors that lay their hands on the heritage which I have given as a heritage to my people, Israel: Behold, I am uprooting them from their land and will uproot the house of Judah from 15 their midst. Yet after I have uprooted them, I will again have compassion with them and will bring them back everyone to his heritage 16 and everyone to his land. And if they thoroughly learn the ways of My people, to swear by My name: "As the LORD liveth!" as they have taught My people to swear by Baal, then they shall be built among My 17 people. But if they will not obey, I will uproot such a nation, uproot and destroy it.

Grammatical Notes

V. 17. "Uproot and destroy," uproot, נָתוֹשׁ, the absolute infinitive, "an uprooting," denotes thorough and complete eradication. "Destroy" may be either the absolute infinitive, "a destroying," or the first person singular Piel of אבד, אֲאַבֵּד, with elision of the first א, cp. G.-K. 23c. 68k.

V. 14. God is the Ruler of the world and even in His punitive judgments has the eternal welfare of mankind at heart. Judah's land is Jehovah's land (Lev. 25:23; 2 Chron. 7:20; Jer. 2:7; 16:18), and therefore Judah's neighbors are Jehovah's neighbors. What a wealth of practical application comes to our mind as we apply this truth to our own homes and possessions! Wicked neighbors, Edom, Moab, Ammon, Philistines, etc., had time and again encroached upon the land given by the Lord of all the earth (Ex. 19:5; Deut. 32:8-14) to Israel (see Jer. 49:1; Ps. 80:12-13). For this violation of Israel's rights and the Lord's will they will be rooted out of their own lands, a reference to the Babylonian custom of deporting subjugated people into other sections of their vast empire. That will be God's judgment upon the wicked people. Yet wicked Judah shall not escape God's judgment. The Covenant God of unchanging justice will uproot and pluck them out of the midst of the surrounding nations, will fulfill His threat for defilement of His land (Lev. 18:24-30). The way of the wicked, be they Gentiles or Jews, shall not always prosper, as Jeremiah had complained. In His own time and manner God will judge in righteousness. Be patient and wait for His Day!

Vv. 15-17. Yet even His righteous judgments upon Gentiles as well as Jews have as their final purpose the salvation of both. Having punished according to His unalterable justice, the Lord of never-ceasing, unlimited grace and mercy will again have pity upon the displaced people and will bring them back to their homeland. A marvelous prediction of the changed policy introduced by Cyrus, as evidenced by his edict. (Barton, *Archaeology*, p. 483.) Mighty King Cyrus (read his many titles in his edict) the instrument in God's hand to carry out God's will (Ezra 1:2-4)! And this political change, this change of statesmanship, this return of deported nations to their homeland, was to teach them the all-important lesson, the only saving truth, that Jehovah is the true Ruler of the world, the God of justice and mercy, of judgment and forgiveness, of death and of life. Turn to him and live! To swear by a deity is to acknowledge that deity as the one to be accepted and trusted and worshiped and served. Learning His ways, accepting His grace and His promised Savior, making His Word the standard of one's living, will exalt a nation, will cause that nation to be built up in the midst of God's people, acknowledged by the Lord as His own, whether Jew or Gentile. That is another part of God's answer to the complaint of His prophet. Even among the wicked Jews and Gentiles and their posterity the Lord has His chosen children, and for their sakes He is long-suffering, not willing that any should perish, but that all should come to repentance.

Yet if any nation or individual will not hear, that nation and that individual shall be plucked up, destroyed in everlasting perdition (Mark 16:16).

Jeremiah and all children of God, impatient with His mysterious and unfathomable ways, have no reason to quarrel with Him, to judge Him by their feeble sense. God is His own Interpreter, and He will make both His justice and His grace plain in His own time.

CHAPTER 13

6. Two Symbols of God's Impending Judgment, Vv. 1-14

A. The spoiled girdle, vv. 1-11

1 Thus said the LORD to me: Go and buy for yourself a linen girdle, and put it on your loins, and do
2 not put it into water. I bought the girdle according to the word of the LORD and put it on my loins.
3 Then the word of the LORD came to me the second time, saying:
4 Take the girdle which you have bought and which is on your loins, and arise, go to the Euphrates, and hide it there in a crevice of the
5 rock. Then I went and hid it on the Euphrates as the LORD had
6 commanded me. And it came to pass after many days had passed that the LORD said to me: Rise and go to the Euphrates, and take the girdle away from there which
7 I told you to hide there. So I went to the Euphrates and dug and re-moved the girdle from the place where I had hid it; and, behold, the girdle was spoiled, altogether
8 unusable. Then the word of the
9 LORD came to me saying: Thus says the LORD: Like this I will spoil the pride of Judah and the
10 great pride of Jerusalem. This wicked people who refuse to listen to My words, but walk in the hardness of their heart and follow other gods to serve them and to worship them, shall be like this
11 girdle, unfit for anything. For as a girdle clings to the loins of a person, so I caused the whole house of Israel and the whole house of Judah to cling to Me, is the oracle of the LORD, to be unto Me a people and a name and a praise, but they did not obey!

Grammatical Notes

V. 1. "A linen girdle." אֵזוֹר, girdle, occurs besides this chapter (eight times) only six times more (2 Kings 1:8, Elijah's leather girdle; Is. 5:27; Ezek. 23:15, the warrior's girdle; Job 12:18, "fetter"; Is. 11:5, twice, of Messiah's truth and faithfulness closely attached and clinging inseparably to Him). The term is never used to denote the priestly girdle, which is called אַבְנֵט. The אֵזוֹר is the girdle commonly worn by the Jews, fastened tightly around the loins so that it clung to them (cp. v. 11) and could serve its purpose to hold up the long, loose upper garment while walking or working.

V. 1. Three times the Lord speaks of the procurement and attaching of the girdle, in vv. 1, 2, 4; because both acts are symbolical, as explained v. 11. The girdle was not to be put in water, not to be washed, but worn by the prophet until it had become filthy.

Vv. 2-5. The prophet obeys the Lord and after some time is told by the Lord to take the girdle to the River Euphrates and hide it there by burying it in a cleft of a rock. (Cp. v. 7; and on this meaning of "hide" see, e. g., Gen. 35:4; Ex. 2:12; Joshua 7:21f.) The prophet obeys, sets out on the long journey to the Euphrates and back to his home.

Vv. 6-7. After a long time he receives the command again to go to the Euphrates and to remove the girdle from its hiding place. Jeremiah obeys and finds the girdle decayed, no longer usable for anything.

It has seemed inconceivable to a number of interpreters that Jeremiah actually made the two long journeys to the Euphrates and back. Some point to the fact that the name Euphrates has the word "river" attached to it twelve out of the fifteen times it occurs, not reckoning this passage. Yet the very fact that there are three passages, seven with our chapter, in which the simple term Phrath denotes the Euphrates (Gen. 2:14; Jer. 51:63; 2 Chron. 35:20), invalidates this argument and renders unnecessary such attempts to change the word to read "Perez," a gap, denoting any gap chosen by the prophet, or "Ephrath," the ancient name of Bethlehem (Gen. 35:19), or the modern Wadi Farah, near Anathoth. Some interpreters regard the narrative not as an actual experience, but either as a vision or as a dialog between the Lord and His prophet cast in the form of a parable by the latter. "The parable is narrated as an actual experience, but it would be wrong to interpret it literally because of its plastic language. To the vivid imagination of the Oriental the parable becomes an actual experience, cp. 2 Sam. 12:1ff." (Volz, *Jeremias*, p. 149.) What does that make of the prophet? Certainly as truthful and clear-minded a man as Jeremiah was would know the difference between a parable and an actual occurrence and would not narrate a parable as a personal experience which never occurred! The whole matter is presented as an actual command by the Lord actually carried out by the prophet as a symbolic action which the Lord Himself interprets to His prophet. As such we accept it.

Vv. 8-9. "After this manner will I mar, destroy, the pride of Judah." "Pride," highness, majesty, self-exaltation, haughtiness. Judah was guilty of pride. Jerusalem even more so; her pride was great.

V. 10 describes this pride and its folly. It was pride, evil, wicked pride, self-exaltation, that caused them to reject God's Word as the norm of their lives and, instead, to choose the imagination of their heart as the standard of their actions; a heart that is deceitful above all things and desperately wicked (Jer. 17:9). It was pride, as foolish as it was wicked, that caused them to cast away their God as a man casts away the trinkets of his childhood, once cherished so highly, now regarded as outmoded and out of date, and to choose, instead, strange gods, to serve those who could not help them, to worship them

137

who could not even hear their prayers. It was dangerous pride, because on account of this pride they would become as Jeremiah's dirty girdle, a good-for-nothing people, losing all their glory God in His loving grace had given them.

V. 11. The girdle cleaving, clinging to the loins of a man symbolizes the affectionate cleaving of Israel and Judah to the Lord as their Husband; cp. cleave, the same word, Gen. 2:24. This loyal attachment was not initiated by Israel, represented by the girdle. As Jeremiah procured and put on the belt, so the Lord procured Israel for Himself by redeeming them out of the slavery in Egypt. He it was also that caused the Israelites to cleave to Him in true love (cp. Deut. 7:6-8; 9:4-6; Phil. 2:13). The purpose for which the Lord had procured Israel and attached it to Himself was that they might be to Him a people, a name, i. e., a people through whose godlike life of love, of holiness, the holy name of God was to be made known to all the world and praised and glorified among all the nations (Deut. 4:6-8; 1 Kings 8:41-43; Ps. 102:14-22; 145:4-7, 10-12; Is. 43:21). Alas, Israel "would not hear," and therefore will be rejected.

B. The broken bottles, vv. 12-14

12 And you shall say this word to them: Thus says the LORD, the God of Israel: Every crock shall be filled with wine. Then they shall say to you: Do we not know very well that every crock shall be filled 13 with wine? Then you shall say to them: Thus says the LORD: Behold, I am about to fill all the inhabitants of this land, and the kings that sit on David's throne, and the priests, and the prophets, and all the inhabitants of Jeru- 14 salem, with drunkenness. And I will dash them against one another, and fathers and children together, is the oracle of the LORD; I will not pity, and will not spare, and will have no compassion, but destroy them.

Vv. 12-14. Because of Judah's incorrigible wickedness the prophet now is commanded to foretell their destruction in a manner that is sure to attract their attention and to drive home the lesson intended. Every "bottle" shall be filled with wine! The Hebrew term may mean the skins of animals prepared to serve as containers of liquids, or it may mean earthen jars or vessels used for the same purpose (cp. John 2:6ff.; Is. 30:14; Jer. 48:12). We hear the people ridicule the prophet: What marvelous wisdom! What an amazing privilege to be a prophet in order to tell people what every child knows! The prophet's answer ought to have shocked them — if they still could be shocked — into seeing the impending danger. The manner in which he keys their expectation is also highly effective. He tells them that the Lord is getting ready to "fill" them; then he names five classes of people, and finally the astounding revelation like a clap of thunder, one word: drunkenness! a well-known symbol of irrationality and helplessness. They have rejected God, the Fount of wisdom, and therefore God will deprive them of wisdom, so that they will make the most senseless blunders, adopt the most foolish policies, become blind and deaf to all warning voices. Each one poses proudly as the savior of his country only to be ridiculed and pilloried by others whose plans are just as ineffectual. Like drunken men they quarrel and fight among themselves, the rulers against the people, the people against their government, priest against priest, and prophet against prophet, parent against child, and child against parent. So the Lord will dash them one against another, until the nation goes down in ruin, chaos, death, destruction. The Lord whom they discarded now discards them. The Lord of infinite grace and long-suffering loving-kindness shows no more pity, no more compassion, no more mercy. His wrath, burning into deepest hell, has but one purpose in view: destruction! He remains the Lord of the Covenant, whose threats will be carried out (Ex. 20:5; Deut. 28:15-68). In leaving God, the nation adopted by the Lord as His own has committed suicide.

7. A Last Plea, Vv. 15-17

15 Hear and give ear, do not exalt yourself, for the LORD speaks!
16 Give glory to the LORD, your God, before He causes darkness and before your feet begin to stumble on the dusky mountains, and while you hope for light, He turn it into shadow of death and make it dense
17 darkness. And if you will not obey, my soul shall weep in secret because of your pride, and I will cry bitterly, and my eye will flow with tears, for the LORD's flock has been deported.

V. 15. Overwhelmed by the message which by divine command he proclaimed to his people, the prophet does all in his power to avert this horrible judgment. Once more he pleads with them to do what so long they have stubbornly refused to do: Hear! Give ear! Do not be proud, lifted up with haughty pride. Your self-exaltation, your high opinion of your own wisdom, your own riches, your Temple, your sacrifices, is the surest way to destruction. The Lord Himself, the great I AM THAT I AM, the God of the Covenant, is addressing you. Listen to Him! Obey Him! Follow Him!

V. 16. Give to the Lord, your God, glory by choosing Him as your Leader in these critical times. The road you are traveling is not an easy one. It is like traveling over precipitous mountains, where even in broad daylight dangers lurk at every step. Take the Lord as your Guide and Protector lest He withdraw the sunshine of His grace and cause you to be enveloped by darkness, so that your feet will stumble in the ever-increasing dusk of twilight. And while you hope for the light of day to return, He will turn the light into the shadow of death and leave you without the comfort of His sure rod and safe staff. And gradually, instead of the dawn hoped for, He will place round you densest darkness (cp. Is. 8:20-22). Harsh words, indeed, but words issuing from a loving heart bursting with desire to save his people from the dreadful doom awaiting them!

V. 17. While unrelentingly exposing their sin, unceasingly rebuking their wickedness, the stern prophet, proclaiming judgment and destruction upon a godless nation, yet in the secrecy of his home, alone with his God, weeps bitter tears welling forth from the depth of his soul, tears of anguish because their foolish pride keeps them from hearing and obeying the Lord's message, tears of deepest sorrow and compassion, because the Lord's flock is dragged into captivity. (Cp. ch. 8:23; A. V., 9:1.)

---

8. A Final Threat, Vv. 18-27

18 Tell the king and the queen-mother: Sit down in lowest depths! For the ornament of your head, your glorious crown, shall come
19 down! The cities of the Southland are blockaded, and there is none to raise the siege. All of Judah is
20 exiled, everyone is exiled. Lift up your eyes and see them coming from the north. Where is the flock given to you? Your glorious flock?
21 What will you say when He shall place those over you as poison hemlock whom you have trained to be friends to you? Will not pains grip you as a travailing woman?
22 And if you shall say in your heart: Why does this happen to me? Because of your great iniquity your skirts will be stripped off,
23 your heels bastinadoed. Can the Ethiopian change his skin, or the leopard his spots? Then also you shall be able to do good, you that
24 are so used to do evil! And I will scatter you as stubble flies away
25 before the desert wind. This is your lot, your apportioned measure from Me, is the oracle of the LORD. Because you have forgotten Me and
26 have trusted in lies, I also will lift up your skirts over your face, and
27 your shame shall be seen. Your adulteries and neighings, the lewdness of your harlotry upon the hills in the open field I have seen, your abominations! Woe to you, O Jerusalem! You will not be clean even after how long a time!

Grammatical Notes

V. 21. "Chief." ראש has a twofold sense, "head, chief," and "a poison plant." Evidently the prophet intends a play on words, one of his frequent figures of speech.

140

V. 18. "Queen," the Hebrew term denotes the ruling queen, a term used for the king's wife (1 Kings 11:19) and for his mother (2 Kings 10:13; 2 Chron. 15:16; Jer. 29:2). Jehoiachin's mother is mentioned besides his wives among those deported (2 Kings 24:15). King and queen refused to humble themselves before God in true repentance. Therefore God will humble them and make them sit down in lowest depths. Their "principalities," rather, "that which is on the head"; the added attribute explains this term: "the crown of your glory." The royal crown was the object of their glory. They forgot the Giver for the gift and shall lose both gift and Giver.

V. 19. "The south," the Negeb, will be shut up, surrounded by enemies, shut up in a cage like a bird, as Sennacherib boasted of Jerusalem. (Cp. Barton, *Archaeology and the Bible*, p. 471.) While Hezekiah was delivered, there is no such hope in store for Judah.

V. 20. Already the prophet sees the enemy approaching from the north. What will become of the king's beautiful flock, once a royal priesthood, God's peculiar treasure (Ex. 19:5-6; cp. Jer. 2:2-3)?

V. 21. "Punish," rather, "appoint"; the object is expressed in an exclamatory sentence: "and you had trained them as your friends." (On this sense of "friends" cp. Micah 7:5; Ps. 55:14; Prov. 16:28; 17:9; Jer. 3:4.) These God has appointed as "chief"; the word also means poison (Deut. 29:17; 32:33; Amos 6:12; Jer. 8:14; 9:15; 23:15; Lam. 3:19). Their self-chosen friends and allies will be appointed to them by the Lord as heads, as poison! Then indeed sorrow, anguish, will overwhelm them, a sorrow unto death (2 Cor. 7:10b; cp. Jer. 4:31).

V. 22. Theirs is the sorrow of impenitence: Why must I suffer these horrors? God answers them. Their great, shameless wickedness deserves severe, shameful penalties, their nakedness shall be uncovered, the bastinado applied to their heels; "made bare" = treated with violence, whipped with a rod. The impudent, shameless harlot receives the harlot's penalty (cp. Hos. 2:10). Judah shall be deprived of all she gloried in.

V. 23. As little as the Ethiopian can change his skin, or a leopard his spots, so little can Judah change her sinful nature. Instead of being disciples of the Lord, taught by the divine Teacher (Is. 54:13), they are taught, trained, accustomed to evil deeds, disciples of wickedness, willing slaves of sin (cp. Rom. 6:19-20). And this sin is not merely an acquired habit, which they might give up at any time they chose to do so. They can relinquish their sinful nature as little as the Ethiopian can rid himself of his skin or the leopard erase his spots.

Ever since Adam's fall all children of Adam are, like their father, sinful, every imagination of the thoughts of their hearts being only evil continually (Gen. 6:5; 8:21; Jer. 17:9; Rom. 5:19; Eph. 2:1-2). To make man willing to yield himself to God and his members as instruments of righteousness unto God is a miracle even greater than changing an Ethiopian's skin and a leopard's spots, a miracle possible only to the almighty grace of the Lord Jehovah (Jer. 31:18, 20, 31-34; 33:8).

Vv. 24-25. Impenitent Judah will be scattered by the Lord as stubble before the wind, because, forgetting God, who had revealed Himself to them (Deut. 4:32-38), they placed their trust in lies and deceits.

V. 26 repeats the penalty of v. 22 b.

V. 27. Judah persists in her spiritual harlotry and physical immoralities despite all efforts of the Lord to cleanse her. She steadfastly prefers her filth to the purity He offers to her, a hardened, incurably wicked harlot.

VI. God's Determination to Punish Judah, Ch. 14—17

CHAPTER 14

1. No Intercession Permitted, Ch. 14:1—15:9

A. The occasion of this revelation, a severe drought, vv. 1-6

1 What came as Jehovah's word to Jeremiah with regard to the
2 drought. Judah sorrows; her gates languish, in mourning are bowed down to the ground; and the cry
3 of Jerusalem goes up. The mighty ones send their servants for water; they go to the watering places, but they find no water. They return, their vessels empty. Disappointed, dejected, they cover their heads.
4 On account of the ground which is dismayed — for there is no rain in the land — the peasants are bewil-
5 dered, veil their heads. For even the doe in the field gives birth and forsakes (her kid), for there is no
6 grass. And the wild asses stand on the bare hills, gasp for air like jackals. Hollow are their eyes, for there is no grass.

V. 1. "The dearth"; the plural occurs again ch. 17:8. It may be the intensive plural, the great drought, or it may designate a series of droughts. From ancient times Palestine suffered from droughts and famine (Gen. 12:10; 26:1; 42:1-2; Ruth 1:1; 2 Sam. 21:1; 1 Kings 8:37; Deut. 11:10-17; 28:23-24).

Vv. 2-3. Nation-wide suffering and lamentation, in the city and in the country, in field and forest and steppe (vv. 2-6). The climax: mourning, languishing, sitting in dirty clothes, blackened from the dust they heaped on themselves (2 Sam. 13:19; 21:10; Job 2:12; Lam. 2:10). "Gates" are personified, pictured as bemoaning the absence of the people that used to gather there. "Little ones" (v. 3), the servants. "To the waters," rather "for" water. "Pits," artificial reservoirs, cisterns, tanks (cp. 2 Kings 3:16, "ditches"). Cover one's head, a sign of deep grief (2 Sam. 15:30; 19:4). A picture true to life, see 1 Kings 18:5-6.

V. 4. "Chapt," rather, dismayed, a personification. How can I produce food, fulfill my purpose (Gen. 1:11), since there is no rain? Plowmen, tillers, farmers, disappointed, grieve.

Vv. 5-6. Hind, wild ass; two animals, as different in their appearance as in their character, represent the suffering animal world. How fierce the drought, when even the tenderhearted doe, that emblem of motherly affection, is forced to abandon her young because of lack of food; and the scrubby, shaggy wild ass, inured to the hardships of the desert, dies of hunger and thirst. The dry wind it sniffs to detect the slightest trace of moisture which might lead it to water, only sucks up like a greedy vampire what little moisture is left in that walking skeleton. "Dragons," rather, jackals, characterized by their wide-open, wolflike jaws.

B. Jeremiah's first intercession is rejected, vv. 7-12

7 If our sins testify against us, O LORD, act for the sake of Thy name! For many are our apostasies, against Thee have we sinned.
8 O Thou Hope of Israel! Its Savior in time of distress! Why hast Thou become as a stranger in the land and as a wanderer who turns aside
9 for a night's lodging? Why hast Thou become as a man taken unawares, as a strong man that cannot save? Yet Thou art in our midst as the LORD, and Thy name has been called upon us! Do not
10 pass us by! Thus says the LORD to this people: Thus do they love to rove! They do not restrain their feet! And the Lord takes no pleasure in them! Now He remembers their iniquity and punishes their
11 sins! Then the LORD said to me: Do not intercede for the good of
12 this people! When they fast, I will not hear their lament; and when they offer burnt offerings and meat offerings, I have no pleasure in them; for by the sword and by famine and by pestilence I will annihilate them.

V. 7. "Iniquities," crimes, perversions, guilt, bear witness against the people as together with the prophet they stand before the judgment throne of God. The prophet has no excuse to offer. There is only sin and guilt. Yet he calls the Judge "Jehovah," the Covenant God, and in unconditional surrender he cries out, Do! Act! (cp. ch. 18:23; 39:12), adding, however, "for Thy name's sake!" Jehovah is not only the God of unalterable justice, He is the God of unchanging grace. So He has revealed His name (Ex. 34:5-7). Why should He be gracious? "For our backslidings, apostasies, are many, we have sinned," etc. Apostasies and sins innumerable make up the history of Israel. Therefore act, O Lord, in accordance with Thy name! Frank acknowledgment of the guilt, yet firm and confident trust in God's mercy and grace. That is the prayer of faith (Heb. 11:1), a prayer that faith alone can speak.

Vv. 8-9. "Hope of Israel." Hope here denotes tense, yet patient and confident waiting, not easily disappointed. In spite of the terrible drought the Lord is still the object of the prophet's hope and trust. "Savior," a term applied to the Judges (Judg. 3:9, 15; Neh. 9:27); to King Jehoahaz of Israel (2 Kings 13:5, 25); to the saviors promised in Obad. 21; to God for the first time in 2 Sam. 22:3; then, Ps. 106:21; eight times in Isaiah (19:20; 43:3, 11; 45:15, 21; 49:26; 63:8); Hos.

13:4. A study of these passages will give us the proper understanding of this marvelous name.

This Lord seems to have lost interest in His people and His land. "Stranger," a non-citizen; "a wayfaring man," a non-resident traveler, using the land only as a place to pitch his tent while passing through. "A man astonied" (only here); surprised, having lost one's presence of mind. "Yet." It seems impossible that the Lord should have forgotten Judah. He is the unchanging Lord; He is still in their midst; they are called by His name. His name has been called and is daily being called and placed upon them (Num. 6:24-27). To this Lord the prophet appeals: Leave us not!

Vv. 10-12. The Lord refuses to hear Jeremiah's plea. "Thus," so, have the people wandered. In the manner of a human speaker He waves His hand back and forth in order to characterize the wanderings of His people from one idol to another. Such people the Lord cannot and will not accept. Nor shall the prophet intercede any longer, v. 11. Nor will the Lord regard their fasting and sacrifices, but will consume them by sword, famine, pestilence (ch. 21:7, 9; 24:10; 27:8, 13). Exile is added ch. 15:2-3.

C. Jeremiah's second plea is rejected, vv. 13-18

13 And I said: Ah! Lord LORD! Behold, their prophets are telling them: You shall not see a sword, and you shall not suffer hunger, for I am giving you assured peace
14 in this place. And the LORD said to me: The prophets prophesy deceit in My name. I have not sent them, and I have not spoken to them. Visions of deceit, and divinations, and nonentities, and frauds conceived by their own mind these men are prophesying to you.
15 Therefore thus says the LORD concerning the prophets that prophesy in My name, although I have not sent them, and that are saying: "Sword and famine shall not come upon this land!" By the sword and the famine shall these prophets perish. And the people to whom they are prophesying shall be cast into the streets of Jerusalem because of the famine and the sword, and there will be none to bury
16 them, themselves and their wives and their sons and their daughters, and I shall pour out upon them their wickedness. Now tell them
17 this word: My eyes overflow with tears night and day, and they will not cease, for a severe blow has smitten the virgin daughter of my people, a very grievous wound.
18 When I go out into the field, behold, the sword! and when I come into the city, behold, people famished with hunger! For even the prophets and the priests will go roving about in a land they do not know.

Vv. 13-16. The prophet makes another plea. He blames the prophets for the prevailing wickedness. The Lord tells him that while the prophets are responsible and will be called to account, the people are no less guilty because they have believed the silly lies of the false prophets. "Divination," prophecy in the manner of heathen conjurers (Deut. 18:10; 2 Kings 17:17; Ezek. 13:6).

Vv. 17-18. In the form of a dirge the prophet is charged to foretell some of the harrowing details of the coming judgment. "Go about," used of herdsmen and tradesmen traversing the land (Gen. 23:16; 37:28; 34:10, 21; 42:34; Ezek. 27:36; 38:13). All labor and business and every profession shall be carried on no longer in their homeland, but in a land they know not.

D. Jeremiah's third attempt meets with absolute refusal, ch. 14:19—15:9

19 Hast Thou altogether rejected Judah? Or does Thy soul loathe Zion? Why hast Thou smitten us and there is no healing for us? We hope for peace, and there is no welfare; and for a time of healing, 20 and, behold, horror! We acknowledge, O LORD, our ungodliness, the guilt of our fathers, for we have 21 sinned against Thee! For Thy name's sake, do not loathe us! Do not disgrace the throne of Thy glory! Remember and do not break 22 Thy covenant with us! Is there any among the vain idols of the Gentiles that can send rain? And can the heavens give showers? Art not Thou He, O LORD, our God? And we hope in Thee, for Thou hast made all of this!

Vv. 19-22. Still the prophet continues his plea with increased fervency. It seems impossible that the Lord of unchanging grace should have loathed and rejected Zion. While the Jews have become covenant breakers, he pleads with the Lord not to break His covenant and thus disgrace His throne of glory (Jer. 17:12). Compare Moses' pleas, Ex. 32:11-12; Num. 14:13-16. If He, the only God, the Creator, the only Hope of Israel, will not help, there is no help possible.

CHAPTER 15

1 Then the LORD said to me: If Moses and Samuel would stand before Me, I have no affection toward this people. Drive them away from 2 Me, let them go away! And if they say to you: Where shall we go? then say unto them: Thus says the Lord: Those that are appointed for death, to death; and those that are appointed for the sword, to the sword; and those that are appointed for the famine, to the famine; those that are appointed for the exile, to 3 the exile! And I have assigned against them four kinds, the sword to slay, and the dogs to drag, and the birds of the sky and the beasts of the field to devour and destroy. 4 I will give them for perturbation to every kingdom of the earth because of Manasseh, the son of Hezekiah, the king of Judah, because of 5 what he did in Jerusalem. For who shall have compassion upon you, O Jerusalem? And who shall mourn for you? And who shall turn out of his way to seek what may serve for your welfare? You 6 yourself have cast Me down, is the oracle of the LORD; you have gone

backward, and I shall stretch forth My hand against you and destroy 7 you! I am tired of pitying! And I will winnow them with a winnowing fork in the gates of the land. I will deprive My people of children and will destroy it; because they do not turn from their 8 ways. Their widows have become for Me more numerous than sand of the sea. I will bring against them, against the mother of young men, a destroyer at high noon. Suddenly I will cause distress and 9 horror to fall upon her. Exhausted is she who bore seven; her soul gasps; her sun goes down while it is still day; she is bewildered and dejected. And what is left of them I will give to the sword before their enemies, is the oracle of the LORD.

Grammatical Notes

V. 4. "To be removed," לְזַוֲעָה. This form occurs six times, but only once (Is. 28:19) the points read זַעֲוָה; in Jer. 15:4; 24:9; 29:18; 34:17; 2 Chron. 29:8 it is pointed זַעֲוָה, which demands the reading זְוָעָה, a form which occurs Deut. 28:25; Ezek. 23:46. The word is generally derived from זוע, of which the Qal occurs twice in the sense of moving back and forth, quake, tremble (cp. Aramaic זַוְעָא, earthquake), with fear (Esther 5:9); from old age (Koh. 12:3); Pilpel occurs Hab. 2:7, "vex," to cause to tremble. A. V. translates the noun "vexation" (Is. 28:19), "to trouble" (2 Chron. 29:8); in all the other passages "to be removed." Delitzsch translates the basic passage, Deut. 28:5: "a moving back and forth," and interprets: "A ball for all the kingdoms to play with (Schultz)." Most interpreters translate: "an object of terror, trembling, horror to"; Ges.-Buhl offers "Beunruhigung, Misshandlung," troubling, maltreatment. Naegelsbach suggests the possibility of taking the word in the sense of "being a commotion," stirring up the people, and regards לְרַעָה as the result of this stirring up. "Why should not the prophet wish to say that the Jews should not merely be given up to destruction, but should be the cause of destruction to others also? Has not the Jewish people, sighing under the curse, even to the most recent times, developed the bad elements of its native peculiarity in many ways to the destruction of the nations among whom it has been driven?" (Lange-Schaff, Jeremiah, p. 220.) Since the term in ch. 24:9; 29:18; 34:17 is closely connected with other sufferings inflicted by divine judgment upon Israel by their enemies, we prefer to take it in the sense adopted by Delitzsch and Gesenius, perturbation, persecution, ill treatment. We regard Deut. 28:65–67 as the best explanation of this term, occurring for the first time in v. 25 of the same chapter (A. V., "removed into"; Luther, "zerstreut werden," scattered). Therefore we translate: I will give them, surrender them, to all kingdoms of the earth for perturbation.

V. 9. "Given up the ghost." נָפַח never has this meaning, always "to blow," Gen. 2:7; Is. 54:16; Jer. 1:13; here with נֶפֶשׁ = to gasp, languish.

V. 1. Any attempt on the part of Jeremiah to change the Lord's determination is hopeless. Even if Moses and Samuel, the two greatest prophets in the history of Israel (Ps. 99:6), stood before Jehovah, they could not change His mind. (On the supplications of these two men cp. Ex. 32:7—34:11; Num. 14:1–39; 1 Sam. 7:3–12; 12:14–25). God's spokesman is to send them away from God's gracious presence, and away they shall go! In addition to the prohibition of intercession the prophet now receives the charge to forbid his people to approach the throne of God in prayer. His task becomes ever more heart-breaking. "My mind," My soul. God's feelings and affections are no longer directed toward Judah, but against her. To be detested by God's soul, to be sent away from His face, means death and destruction in time and eternity.

Vv. 2-4 bring out in harrowing detail the doom of what was once God's own people: death, sword, famine, exile (cp. ch. 14:12)! By divine decree none shall escape! Those appointed to death shall not have the honor of a decent burial, shall be torn and devoured by beasts and birds (v. 3). Those appointed to exile are appointed "to be removed." On this term see Grammatical Notes above.

Vv. 5-7. "Who shall go aside . . . ," leave his work, or leisure, to inquire after your welfare? Not a sign of pity will Judah experience from their enemies. Nor will God pity them. So often have they forsaken God after His repeated re-acceptance of His people that He is now weary "with repenting," rather, "with having compassion." Now He will stretch forth His hand for their destruction (v. 6). "Fan" = winnow. After threshing, the grain, preferably on a moderately windy day (Jer. 13:24), was cast into the air by means of a winnowing fork, so that the wind carried away the chaff, while the grain fell to the winnowing floor. Here the gates of the city are compared to such winnowing floors, because the Lord will scatter the people in exile. The wind of His judgment will carry them like chaff out of His cities and His land into foreign countries (cp. Is. 41:16; Jer. 49:32, 36). He will bereave them of children, either by death (Deut. 32:25; Lam. 1:20) or by barrenness (Hos. 9:14-17), so that the nation will be destroyed.

Vv. 8-9. Wives will be deprived of their husbands (v. 8a); mothers of their sons, warriors and young, strong men. The mother of seven shall mourn, "hath given up the ghost," rather, "her soul gasps in agony" (the Hebrew term never means to expire), as she sees her sons slain by the enemy who suddenly, unexpectedly, attacked at noonday, while usually the armies rested at noon because of the intense heat. Her sun has gone down, henceforth life is dark and dreary for her, "ashamed and confounded," all her hopes have been blasted, her expectations shattered.

2. God Comforts, Warns, and Strengthens His Sorrowing, Despondent Prophet, Ch. 15:10-21

10 Woe unto me, O my mother, because you have born me, a man of controversy and a man of contention for all the land. I have not lent, nor have men lent to me, yet
11 all curse me. The LORD said: Surely, your deliverance shall be for good. I will cause the enemy to come to you to petition you in the time of trouble and in the time
12 of distress. Shall iron break the northern iron and the bronze?
13 I will give your wealth and your treasures as spoils, without price, and that because of all your sins,
14 and in all your boundaries. And I will enslave you to your enemy in a land you do not know. For a fire is kindled in My anger; it will
15 burn against you! Thou knowest, O LORD! Remember me, and visit me and avenge me on my persecutors. Do not take me away by deferring Thine anger; consider that for Thy sake I am bearing
16 shame! Thy words were found, and I ate them. And Thy words were unto me the joy and rejoicing

of my heart; for Thy name has been called upon me, O LORD, God
17 of Hosts! I did not sit in the assembly of merrymakers, so that I might rejoice; by Thy will I sat lonely; for Thou hadst filled me
18 with indignation. Why is my pain unceasing and my wound incurable, refusing to be healed? Thou hast surely become unto me as a
19 liar, as waters that fail. Therefore thus says the LORD: If you turn and I shall turn you, you will continue to stand before Me. And if you cause the precious to come forth from the vile, you shall be as My mouth. Let them return to you; but you, do not turn away to
20 them! And I will make you toward this people as a brazen wall impregnable. They will war against you and will not overpower you. For with you I am, to save you and to deliver you, is the oracle of the
21 LORD. And I will deliver you from the hands of the wicked and will redeem you from the hand of the violent.

Grammatical Notes

V. 11. "Thy remnant." The Masoretic text presents difficulties. The K'tib demands the reading שְׁרוֹתְךָ or שָׁרוֹתְךָ, Q'ri שָׁרִיתְךָ. Kittel lists nine different variants found in various manuscripts; prefers the LXX reading יְכֵן for אָמַר, and suggests to read שֵׁרַתִּיךָ, Piel of שׁרת, to serve, to minister. Volz adopts these suggestions and translates: "Verily, LORD, I served Thee!" The Hebrew form may be derived from שׁרה, loosen, deliver; שׁרר, to be firm; שׁרת, to minister; and it may be infinitive with suffix, or first person singular with suffix. Still others see here a defective writing of שְׁאֵרִית, your "remnant."

V. 14. "Make thee to pass," twenty-

seven Mss. read הַעֲבַדְתִּי, enslave you, instead of הַעֲבַרְתִּי.

V. 17. "Mockers." Piel of שׂחק is never used in this sense; it denotes jesting, making merry, laughing.

V. 19 consists of two conditional sentences introduced by "if." "Thou shalt stand," "thou shalt be," etc.; are universally regarded as apodoses, as two promises. The first אִם is followed by two verbs connected by ו, the second אִם by one verb. Views differ as to the translation of the verbs following the first אִם. Some interpreters, LXX, Vulgate, Luther, Rothstein (Kautzsch, *Die Heilige Schrift des Alten Testaments*), and others translate as the A. V.: *"Then*

149

will I bring thee again"; and all of them add an "and" before "you stall stand," although this clause has no conjunction. Others, e. g., Naegelsbach, Ball (*Expositor's Bible*, Sellin), translate: "I will cause thee" again "to stand before Me." But the Hiphil of שוב does not occur elsewhere in this sense. — There is a third possibility: to regard the apodosis of the first conditional sentence as beginning with "You shall stand" and to take וַאֲשִׁיבְךָ in the sense of "and I will turn thee." On this sense of הֵשִׁיב, cause to return, bring back, see 2 Sam. 15: 8, 25; Jer. 37:20 (physical return); Ps. 80:4, 8, 20 (A. V., vv. 3, 7, 19); Jer. 23:22; 31:17; Lam. 5:21. Two conditions are named: Jeremiah must turn, God must cause him to turn, then Jeremiah will again stand before God. This interpretation adds no "and" and takes אָשִׁיב in its usual sense.

"If," אִם with imperfect presents the condition as being possibly or probably fulfilled in the present or future.

V. 10. The repeated absolute refusal of the Lord to grant the fervent prayer of His prophet almost breaks Jeremiah's heart. Overcome by anguish, he becomes dissatisfied with his calling and his life. He would rather not have been born than to be a man of "strife," lawsuit, and "contention," judging, to all the land. Constantly to accuse, judge, condemn, his own people had become an odious business to him who loved peace and quiet. He had not been an exacting, penny-squeezing Shylock, requiring his pound of flesh; nor was he a debtor refusing to pay or hating his hardhearted creditor. Yet all curse him as if he were the peace disturber, the self-elected critic and judge. Cp. Acts 16:20-24; 19:26; 21:28; 1 Cor. 4:9-13.

V. 11. See Grammatical Notes. Aquila, Targum, Vulgate translate "thy remnant"; Symmachus, "you will remain, survive"; Naegelsbach, "I have oppressed you for your good"; others, "I have loosed, delivered you, etc." Either of the latter two seems to be preferable to the others. "Entreat thee well," literally, "cause to meet you for some purpose," here that of supplication, pleading. In the day of trouble they will come to him for advice or to ask for an oracle. On the fulfillment of this promise compare ch. 21:1-2; 37:3, 17; 38:14; 42:1-7. God assures him that his enemies, now cursing him, will acknowledge him as God's prophet.

V. 12. "The northern iron," iron from the north, a symbol of the Babylonian empire, compared to "steel," rather "brass," or "bronze," a mixture of copper and tin. The alloy of copper and zinc, the modern brass, was unknown to the ancients, as well as steel. Babylon is like bronze, the strongest metal known to the ancients (ch. 1:18); common iron cannot break it. Human power is unable to defeat the mighty power sent by the Lord to destroy Judah.

V. 13. "Substance," strength, power, both military and political. I will give your power and riches as spoils without asking any money. This shows God's contempt for the things Judah was proud of. "In all thy borders," boundaries, territory, not a particle of which shall be spared.

V. 14. "Make thee to pass." 27 Mss. read: "I will enslave," and 8 Mss., LXX, Syrian, Itala, add "you" (cp. ch. 17:4), which may be the correct reading. Vv. 12-14 were addressed to Judah, but spoken to Jeremiah in order to show him that Judah's ruin was irrevocably determined.

Vv. 15-16. Jeremiah submits to God's judgment. Who am I that I should dare to oppose Thy determination? He appeals to God to remember and protect him against his enemies. "Visit," supervise, watch over. "Revenge me of," punish them with a view to my deliverance. If God continues His long-suffering toward the enemies, Jeremiah fears that God would "take him away," abandon him to an early death. He points out his willingness to suffer "rebuke," reproach, calumny, for God's sake. "Found," v. 16, used here of something that came to the finder without any exertion or even expectation (cp. Matt. 13:44-46). He found God's words, when the Lord put them into his mouth (Jer. 1:7). To eat these words, to make them his own, his life's element, the constant food for his own spiritual life as well as the sum total of all his utterances, became in ever greater degree his desire (Ezek. 2:9—3:10; 1 Tim. 4:14-16). He had learned to regard God's Word as the joy and rejoicing of his heart, his intellect, his emotions, his will. And the reason for this joy was that from this Word he had learned that the name of the Lord God of Hosts was called upon him (see Num. 6:22-27 and his call into the prophetic office, Jer. 1:4-19).

V. 17. In obedience to God's demand (ch. 16:1-9), he had led a life of solitude. "Mockers," the particular form of this word is never used in this sense, but always in the sense of "make merry," "laugh," "rejoice." And the very content of his preaching had made him unpopular. He had preached chiefly "indignation," the wrath and judgment of God, and had done that in spite of the rebellious thoughts of his own heart, against his own feelings.

Yet now his feelings suddenly change.

V. 18. Again the question haunts him, Why? Cp. ch. 12:1ff.; 14:8-9, 19. While at that time he had not understood why God should forsake Israel, so now it seems to him that God had forgotten His servant, who had been preaching only what God had told him and whose reward was only hatred and persecution. Why may I not see the least success? Why must I constantly preach damnation, while I would much rather like to preach peace and salvation to the people I love, my own people? Why is my pain, my anguish ceaseless? The term for "pain," כְּאֵב, occurs only six times and invariably denotes agonizing, extreme pain (Job 2:13; 16:6; Ps. 39:3-4, A. V., 2-3; Is. 17:11; 65:14). His wound, the blow he has suffered, is incurable, refuses to be healed.

Overwhelmed with grief, he plunges from the high pinnacle of joy and rejoicing (v. 16) into the deepest depth of gloom and despair. He charges God with having altogether become unto him as a "liar," the word occurring only here and Micah 1:14; "as waters that fail," like a brook that runs dry in summer, that lacks water when water is needed most; the opposite of the perennial stream (Amos 5:24; cp. Job 6:15-18). That is the language of unbelief! Here Jeremiah's flesh speaks, that flesh which is enmity against God (Rom. 8:7). The fact that the flesh happens to be that of a believing child of God does not make it one whit better than the flesh of the unbeliever. David's flesh made him an adulterer and murderer; Peter's, a renegade; Jeremiah's flesh made him a blasphemer. To charge the God of the Amen (Is. 65:16) with being a liar, to accuse the Fountain of Life (Ps. 36:9) and Living Waters (Jer. 2:13) with being like waters that fail, untrustworthy, that is blasphemy, whether spoken by wicked men (Ps. 10:4-13; 73:11) or by the flesh of God's own prophet. The fact that his patience was sorely tested until it reached the breaking point does not excuse him. He broke down because his trust in God was fast disintegrating, so that Satan was successful in seducing this chosen vessel of God into doubt, unbelief, despair, blasphemy.

V. 19. The Lord does not at once reject Jeremiah. He speaks to His prophet. As the Lord of unchanging justice He is not a respecter of persons. Importunate Moses (Ex. 32:32) is rebuked (v. 33); doubting Moses punished severely (Num. 20:7-12); David, the man after God's own heart (1 Sam. 13:14; 2 Sam. 7:8-16), is told 2 Sam. 12:7-12. Jeremiah, the prophet so highly honored (Jer. 1:5-10), doubting God's wisdom and love, is told that he must repent or be dismissed from his office. "If you turn." In order to remain God's spokesman, he must repent, turn from the way of doubt and mistrust. That is an indispensable condition! And that is a condition which Jeremiah cannot fulfill by his own strength, even though he is still a child of God. The Lord adds: "and (if) I turn you." See Grammatical Notes.

The Lord teaches His prophet two truths of essential importance: that repentance is necessary, and that God must work this repentance. "If," see Grammatical Notes. And in order to bring about the fulfillment of this needed turning, the Lord promises him to restore to him the great honor of being the Lord's prophet. "Thou shalt stand before Me." As His highly honored servant, to be one of the Lord's chief officers (cp. 1 Kings 12:6, Solomon's ministers; Jer. 52:12, commander in chief; 1 Kings 17:1; 2 Kings 3:14, prophet), to go wherever he was sent (Jer. 1:7), to speak whatever he was commanded (ch. 1:9). But only if he would turn back to God with all his heart, in a manner which could be wrought only by the almighty grace of God. Jeremiah learned his lesson; he learned to pray, and taught others to pray: "Turn Thou me, and I shall be turned, for Thou art the LORD, my God" (Jer. 31:18; Lam. 5:21).

"If thou take forth the precious from the vile." Luther translates: "If thou teachest the godly to come forth from the ungodly people." He evidently connected "vile" with "they" of the following verse. Yet Jeremiah had always been faithful in warning the wicked. Just because of his faithfulness in this unpleasant task he was hated and persecuted. He had been faithful to God's command, and God seemed to him unfaithful to His promise. It is this unbelief and despondency that God reproves. There was still the precious gold of faith and trust hidden in the treasure house of Jeremiah's heart, else he would not have turned to his God in his agony and poured out his heart to the Searcher of hearts. Yet the vile, base refuse of doubt and despair was beginning to mingle with the precious ore. Out with that vile stuff! "Take forth," literally, "cause to come out," separate that precious treasure, your faith and trust in Me, which I have implanted in your heart, from the vile dross of distrust! Then shall you be as My mouth, My spokesman. Then only, but then surely shall you remain My prophet. Your lamentations and accusations are not becoming one whom I have honored to be My spokesman.

"Let them return. . . ." Naegelsbach, Cheyne, and others render: "They shall return," the enemies. So well will the Lord provide for His servant that the enemies will turn to him, cease their enmity, and accept his warning. Yet the A. V. rendering is preferable. Very few turned to Jeremiah during his lifetime. Only in exile did they begin to turn to the Lord. What the Lord means to say is that if there is any turning to do, let them do it by turning to you, and do not you turn to them. Moffatt translates very suitably: Let other men come over to your side, but go not over to join them!

V. 20. The Lord has not answered the prophet's question, Why? (V. 18.) Yet He applies healing balm to the prophet's heart by repeating the promise spoken years ago (ch. 1:18-19). Yet, while on the day of his call the last word was: "I will deliver thee," now He ends with: "the oracle of Jehovah!" How could you and why should you ever doubt or mistrust the grace and power and loving-kindness of the God of the Covenant, I AM THAT I AM?

V. 21. God applies this word spoken years before to the prophet's present situation. I will fulfill My word! I will deliver you (same word as ch. 1:19) out of the hand of the wicked and redeem, buy back, save, you out of the hand of the terrible. No matter how fierce their hatred, how great their power, I am greater than they. And even if you have fallen into their hands and there seems no possibility of escape, I, Jehovah, will save you. For fulfillment see ch. 26:7-24; 36:19-26; 37:11-21; 38:1-28; 39:11-14; 40:1-6.

We are thankful for this chapter, which, like ch. 12 and 20, so clearly reveals to us the doubts and fears and disappointments which harassed the prophet and at times brought him to the brink of despair. This man had been told not to show any sign of fear before his enemies, and not once did he break down before them, not once voice before his fellow men any doubt of God's grace and mercy, His justice and holiness, His power and His wisdom. That does not mean that he never doubted, never was dissatisfied. No, in order to stand up and speak (ch. 1:17), he had to gird his loins, and one of the necessary preparations for his lifework was to fight down his worst enemy, his own flesh and blood, which was always inclined to doubt God and His Word, to charge God with lack of power or lack of willingness to keep His promise. Yet he fought this battle in solitude, alone with his God, to whom he poured out all his fears and disappointments and despairs, before whom he broke down completely, revealing to us the absolute truth of His word ch. 17:9. And his faithful God was with him in these dark, dismal hours, warned him, comforted him, strengthened him, revealing to us bottomless depths of divine justice and mercy. And from these battles with his flesh, from these controversies with his God, he rose by the grace and in the power of his God more than a conqueror; facing undauntedly and fearlessly the wicked kings, the lying prophets, the treacherous courtiers, the howling mobs; not a weeping prophet, not a sob sister, but a man's man, God's man, the one real man in an age of cruelty and cowardice and belly service and egotism. And as a man of God he penned not only his victories, his accomplishments, his bravery. With equal candor and rare truthfulness he painted himself, as he was, his doubts, his human weakness, his sins. We thank him for his manlike honesty and seek to learn the lesson for which these words also are penned, for our admonition and warning (1 Cor. 10:11-13) and our comfort (Rom. 15:4).

CHAPTER 16

3. The Prophet Is to Symbolize by His Solitary, Joyless Life the Hopeless Sorrow of the Impending Judgment, Vv. 1-9

1.2 And the word of the LORD came to me, saying: You shall not take a wife, nor shall you have sons or 3 daughters in this place. For thus says the LORD regarding the sons and the daughters that are born in this place and regarding their mothers who gave birth to them and their fathers who begot them 4 in this land: They shall die painful deaths. They shall not be lamented nor buried. They shall be as dung on the ground and shall perish by sword and by famine; and their bodies shall be food for the birds of the sky and the beasts of the 5 earth. For thus says the LORD: Do not enter the house of mourning, nor go to lament or bemoan them, for I have taken away My peace from this people, is the oracle of the LORD, My loving-kindness 6 and compassion. And they shall die, both great and small, in this land. They shall not be buried; none shall lament for them, nor gash himself, nor cut off his hair 7 for them. None shall break the bread of mourning for them, to comfort them for the dead. None shall give them the cup of consolation to drink for one's father and 8 for one's mother. You shall not go into the house of feasting, to sit 9 with them, to eat and to drink. For thus says the LORD of Hosts, the God of Israel: Behold! In this city, before their eyes, and in their days I will silence the sound of joy and the sound of rejoicing, the voice of the bride and the voice of the bridegroom.

V. 1ff. The Lord had expressed His readiness to retain His repentant prophet in His service and to give him strength to endure all hardships and overcome all temptations so inseparably connected with the high office to which he had been called. The prophet had complained of his loneliness, of the perpetual pain and anguish he suffered in preaching only judgment and destruction to a stiff-necked and unyielding people. The Lord does not relieve the prophet of this heavy burden. His sorrows and trials are to continue, to be aggravated rather than removed. Three injunctions, each one tending to increase the loneliness and lonesomeness of the prophet, were laid upon him. He was to refrain from marriage (v. 2), to refrain from mourning and pitying his people (v. 5), to refrain from rejoicing with them (v. 8). In ever-increasing measure his was to be a lonely and lonesome

155

life. The man with the tender heart yearning for companionship and love, and overflowing with pity and compassion, ever ready to rejoice with those who rejoiced, to weep with those who wept (Rom. 12:15), was to lead a life devoid of joy, bereft of fellowship, deprived even of the liberty to show his sympathy with his suffering people.

This divine injunction seems like a flat denial of his unspoken plea to be relieved of his loneliness, a downright refusal to even listen to the complaint of His harassed prophet. Yet it is fully consistent with the terms laid down in the first call to Jeremiah (ch. 1: 5-19), and which the Lord had just now briefly and summarily repeated (ch. 15: 19-21). The Lord had from the very outset promised him not a life of ease and happiness and visible success, but He had very clearly and definitely spoken of the duty to root out, and pull down, and to destroy, and to throw down, and only then to build and to plant. And the Lord had just as clearly foretold the ensuing enmity, the hardships and heartaches the prophet would experience. But he had promised twenty years before that He would be with His messenger, comfort and strengthen and deliver him, and He now has reiterated this promise. Now the Lord expects His ambassador to trust the word of his Creator and Redeemer that all would be well with him. In such unflinching trust he is to shoulder the burdens and hardships incidental to his high calling, and not become disheartened because so little of the joy and happiness one might expect of so glorious an office would fall to his lot. The one essential duty of the Lord's messenger is faithfulness in performing his work, loyalty to the Word and will of the Lord of Hosts. He was to preach by word and by acts what God demanded of him to proclaim. As his message, so his life was to be a preachment and a prophecy of judgments to come.

These judgments were to be proclaimed to the people by the symbolical act commanded to, and performed by, the prophet. The prohibition to marry was to teach the people that the time was approaching when the voice of the bridegroom and bride would no longer be heard (v. 9), for there would be no more marriages contracted. The prophet's refusal to join in festive celebrations was to forecast the days when no longer there would be anyone to rejoice and be merry (v. 9). His refusal to sympathize with the mourners foretold a time when so many would die of "grievous deaths" by sword and famine and pestilence (v. 4), that the survivors would become so accustomed to seeing people die as to lose the faculty of mourning over the loss. They would be satisfied that there was one less to feed, or glad to see them die rather than continue in a living death. So calloused would the people become as to neglect even the least expression of mourning, whether permitted (vv. 5, 6a, 7) or forbidden (v. 6b), even for the nearest and dearest relatives, father and mother (v. 7); that they would leave the dead bodies unburied, regarded at all times as the greatest shame and disgrace (vv. 4, 6). And all this because the Lord, whose spokesman the prophet was also in these symbolic acts, had taken away His peace from His people, even His loving-kindness and mercies (v. 5). What a dreadful judgment! Far worse than the most dreadful war and bloodshed! Forsaken of God — the helpless, hopeless captives of Satan!

Already the black thunderclouds of God's judgment were gathering, already death and hell were sharpening their scythes to reap their grim harvest, already the dread outrunners of the Prince of Terrors, war, famine, pestilence (ch. 15:2) were beginning to go forth on their errand of destruction. This was not a time for joy and merriment! This, above all others, was the time for sorrow and tears of sincere repentance (ch. 3:2-25).

Vv. 4-7. A number of Jewish customs at the death and burial of a relative or friend are named. "Lament," three times; "bemoan," to shake the head in sorrow or sympathy (ch. 18:16), perhaps including violent sobbing, shaking the whole body (ch. 15:5; 22:10, 18; 31:18; cp. 2 Sam. 1:17-27; 3:31-39; 18:33; Matt. 9:23; Mark 5:38). "Cut themselves," as did the prophets of Baal (1 Kings 18:28), and "making themselves bald," shaving the beard or part of the head, were pagan customs, forbidden to Israel (Lev. 19:27; Deut. 14:1), but practiced by them (Jer. 41:5). "Tear themselves," rather, "break bread" (Is. 58:7). After the burial the friends of the mourners prepared a meal for them, cp. "cup of consolation." This meal may be meant by the term *beth marzeach,* "house of mourning," v. 5, occurring only here and Amos 6:7, the meal being accompanied by wailing and lamentations (cp. Ezek. 24:17, 22; Deut. 26:14; Hos. 9:4).

V. 8. "House of feasting," literally, drinking, a festive meal (Judg. 14:10, 12, 17; Gen. 40:20; Is. 5:12). "House of feasting" occurs also Eccl. 7:2; Esther 7:8. This "house of drinking" was not a tavern, or saloon, but in contrast to "house of mourning" a house in which a festive company had gathered for a banquet. To use v. 8 as a prohibition of entering a tavern would involve a like prohibition of participating in any joyous or sorrowful assembly. Jeremiah was forbidden to enter either house only for the specific reasons stated vv. 5, 9.

4. Merciless Rejection and Merciful Re-acceptance, Vv. 10-15

10 And when you announce all these words to this people and they will say to you: Why does the LORD speak all this great evil against us? What is our guilt? And what is the sin we have committed against the 11 LORD, our God? Then shall you say to them: Because your fathers have forsaken Me, is the oracle of the LORD, and have followed other gods and have served them and have worshiped them, but Me they have forsaken and My Law they 12 did not keep. And you — you have done greater wickedness than your fathers, and you are walking each according to the hardness of his evil heart, and intentionally do not 13 listen to Me. Therefore I hurl you out of this land into a land neither you nor your fathers have known, and there you will serve other gods day and night, because I will grant 14 you no more grace. Therefore, behold, days are coming, is the oracle of the LORD, when they shall no more say: "As the Lord liveth, who has brought the Chil-15 dren of Israel out of Egypt!" But "As the LORD liveth, who has brought the Children of Israel out of the Northland and from all the countries to which He had driven them." And I shall bring them back to their land which I have given to their fathers.

V. 10. This refusal of the prophet to associate with his people, this self-ostracism, as we might call it, so conflicting with social custom and so contrary to prophetic usage, was a mystery to the people. Foreseeing their resentment to the message and behavior of His servant, the Lord instructs His servant how to answer their surly questions betraying their self-righteousness and blindness. The history of Israel from Horeb onward was that of ever-repeated apostasy (v. 11), the present generation exceeding their fathers' wickedness (v. 12). As the apostate fathers could not enter the Land of Promise because of their disloyalty, so the disloyal sons could not remain in the land of God, whom they had disowned. In a land unknown to them and their fathers they would serve idols to their hearts' content, for there He would no longer be gracious to them, but turn them over to the imaginations, the hardness, of their own heart. Many of the exiled Jews were paganized in Babylon, as were the Jews going down to Egypt against the Lord's will (Jer. 44:15-27).

Vv. 14-15. This is to be a complete deportation of the Jews, so complete that in future years only such children of Israel would live in the Promised Land as had been brought again into the land from those foreign countries into which the Jewish nation of Jeremiah's time would be scattered.

While these words serve to confirm the threat of a nation-wide deportation, they at the same time promise a restoration. As ch. 15: 19-21 was spoken for the purpose of comforting the prophet in his loneliness with the assurance of God's continued presence and deliverance, so ch. 16:14-15 served to console the prophet, heartbroken over the ruin and destruction about to be visited upon his beloved people, by the assurance that the Exile would not be the final end of his nation, that again God would have compassion upon them in His own time and restore them to their land. This promise was not a new one. God merely reminded the prophet of what he had told him ch. 3:18-19. Even during the Babylonian Exile God had not yet completely and finally rejected Judah as His own people (cp. Ezek. 11: 14-21; Jer. 29:1-14). That was to take place only after their final rejection of the Messiah (cp. Matt. 23:37-38; 1 Thess. 2:15-16).

5. Punishment Before Re-acceptance, Vv. 16-18

16 Behold, I am sending for many fishers, is the oracle of the LORD, and they shall fish for them, and after them I will send for many hunters to hunt them from every mountain, and from every hill, and 17 from every cleft of the rocks. For Mine eyes are upon their ways, they are not hidden before Me, and their guilt is not concealed from Mine 18 eyes. First I will recompense their guilt and their sins twofold, because they have profaned My land by filling My heritage with the carcasses of their abominable gods and their horrible idols.

Vv. 16-17. Many of the older interpreters refer these verses to the conversion of the Jews. But the prophet speaks here of men being dragged forth from their hiding places into which they had fled (v. 16), and of a fishing which is in the nature of a penalty for their iniquity constantly before the Lord (v. 17). After the brief comforting assurance (vv. 14-15) the Lord continues to describe the thoroughness of the depopulation. The enemy will do a thorough job of mopping up.

V. 18. "First." Forestalling any plea on the part of Jeremiah to spare the horrors of the ruin of the land to His people, the Lord states very emphatically that first, before there is any hope of the land's being repopulated by Jews, He will recompense their guilt twofold. During the 800 years of Judah's possession of the land the Lord had frequently punished them by sending war, famine, epidemics, and other plagues; yet they had been permitted to remain in their homeland. Now, in addition to the horrors of war, a second judgment would come, exile. They had defiled God's chosen land with the carcasses of their "detestable things," frequently used as a term for idols (Jer. 4:1; 7:30; etc.), and their "abominations" (Deut. 7:26; 2 Kings 16:3, etc.). "Carcass," the singular is collective, the word indicating not only the lifelessness of idols, but their unclean, defiling character (Lev. 11:24-40; 26:30). Now the Lord would fulfill His threat Lev. 18:25-28.

159

6. Jeremiah's Trustful Prayer and God's Assurance that Judah Will Also Be Brought Back to the Saving Knowledge of the Lord
Vv. 19-21

19 O LORD, my Strength and my Fortress and my Refuge in the day of distress! To Thee the Gentiles shall come from the ends of the earth and shall say: Only deception have our fathers inherited, vain superstitions,
20 which are good for nothing. Shall a man make gods for himself? Such
21 gods are not gods! Therefore, this time I will teach them! I will teach them My hand and My power, and they shall understand that My name is LORD.

Grammatical Notes

V. 21. "I will teach," מוֹדִיעָם, the participle denotes a characteristic trait; the imperfect, אוֹדִיעָם, the progressive stages of His teaching; the perfect, with strong ו, וְיָדְעוּ, their knowledge as an accomplished result of His instruction.

V. 19. Like the Syrophoenician woman (Mark 7: 27-28), Jeremiah clings with the strong arms of faith to the promises hidden among so many refusals and regains his balance, his confidence and joy in Jehovah, whose mercy after all is as enduring as His justice. "My Fortress," used of objects in which one could trust because of their inherent strength, so of God Ps. 27: 1; 28: 8. Comforted by God's promise (v. 15), he flees to the Lord, his "Fortress" and "Refuge," defensively, and his "Strength," offensively. He is ready to do what the Lord demands, since even in the day of distress the Lord will be with him.

God's promise (vv. 14-15) had also reminded him of the promised restoration of Israel (ch. 3: 14-19) and the conversion of the Gentiles (ch. 3: 17). With the eyes of faith he sees the fulfillment of this glorious prophecy; Gentiles coming from the ends of the earth confessing the vanity of their idols, the unprofitableness of serving gods who are lies, and the folly of worshiping man-made gods (v. 20).

V. 21. The Lord speaks. "Therefore," because I am the Lord of justice and grace. "I will cause," etc. See Grammatical Notes. In the Exile they would learn that the righteous God in His punishment is no respecter of persons; that His powerful hand could protect and bless them even in a foreign country (Jer. 29: 5-7; Ezek. 11: 16); that His grace was unchanging (the sending of Daniel and Ezekiel to the exiles). So they would gradually and in ever-increasing measure learn that knowledge which alone is worthy of glorying; that His name, His essence, is Jehovah (Jer. 9: 23-24). These are words of comfort to the heartbroken prophet (ch. 14: 8-9, 18-22; 15: 10, 18) and to the repentant Jews in the Exile.

CHAPTER 17

7. Sin Deceives and Destroys. Faith in the Lord Gives Life and Salvation

A. Judah's deep-seated and manifest idolatry and its punishment, vv.1-4

1 Judah's sin is written with an iron stylus, with a diamond point; it is engraved upon the table of their heart and upon the horns of their 2 altars, even as their children remember their altars and their Asherahs beside the green trees on 3 the high hills. O My mountain in the field! Your wealth, all your treasures I will give for a spoil, your high places in all your bound- 4 aries, because of your sin. And you shall lose your hold on your inheritance which I have given to you, and I will make you serve your enemy in a land which you do not know, for you have kindled My wrath, which shall burn forever.

V. 1. "Pen," a stylus; "point of a diamond," a diamond set in iron; "graven," deeply cut, so as to last a long time. The ancient inscriptions on stones and mountains (Moabite stone, Hammurabi stele, Behistun, etc., cp. Job 19:24) defy the ravages of time. So the sin of Judah is written indelibly, for all times, in the table of their heart. The Searcher of the heart (Jer. 17:10) reads there the declaration of their independence from the rule of the Lord, from His Law and His Gospel. "On the horns of your altars" (Ex. 27:2; 29:12; 30:1-3, 10). Judah's altars were to declare Judah's humble and repentant plea for forgiveness through the blood of the promised Redeemer, and their love and loyalty to this God of grace. Instead, there was sin engraved on their altars, the brazen altar and the altar of incense in the Temple. For the sacrifices at these altars were offered by an impenitent, impious, yet self-righteous people and therefore were displeasing, abhorrent to God. The plural may also include the idol altars, the great number of which (ch. 2:28; 11:13) proclaimed the great wickedness, the widespread idolatry of the people.

V. 2. "Whilst their children remember," literally, "according to the remembering." The only manner in which the children remembered the worship of their fathers is that of a hypocritical or an idolatrous worship. They saw the wicked life, they saw the idolatrous worship throughout the land (Jer. 2:28; 7:17-18) and even in the Temple (2 Kings 21:2-5; Ezek. 8:8-16).

Vv. 3-4. Cp. 15:13-14. "O My mountain in the field." There is no need to connect these words with v. 2 (so Targum, Syrian, Jerome, and many modern interpreters). In the form of a vocative they are the object of the following verb, "give." "Field" does not neces-

161

sarily mean a level field, but the open country in contrast to the city (Gen. 2:20; 2 Sam. 17:8; Ezek. 20:46; M. T. 21:2), compare "the rock of the plain," plateau, *mishor,* either level or hilly (Jer. 21:13), which expression, like "mountain in the field," refers to Jerusalem, particularly to Mount Zion, rising abruptly out of the surrounding valleys. "Discontinue" (v. 4), to throw away (2 Kings 9:33), to release, abandon (Ex. 23:11; Deut. 15:1, 2). "Even thyself" = for thy sake, because of your sins, you will have to abandon all I gave you. God punishes the neglect of the stewardship duties He requires of His people. "You have kindled," in ch. 15:14 "is kindled." They themselves have caused the fiery wrath which consumes them. Another intensifying change is "forever," instead of "upon you" (ch. 15:14).

B. The roots of wickedness and destruction, vv. 5-11

a. The lack of trust in God, vv. 5-8

5 Thus says Jehovah: Cursed is the man who trusts in man and makes flesh his strength and whose heart 6 departs from the LORD. He shall be as a lonely tree in the wilderness, and he shall not see when good comes; he shall dwell in parched lands in the wilderness, in 7 an uninhabited salt steppe. Blessed is the man who trusts in the LORD 8 and whose trust is the LORD. He shall be as a tree planted at waters, which sends out its root to the stream, and he will not fear when heat comes. His leaves will remain green, and in the drought he will not be anxious, nor will he cease to bring fruit.

Vv. 5-6. Cursed is the "man," גֶּבֶר, man as male, the strong; that trusteth in "man," אָדָם, man as made out of dust and returning to dust (Gen. 3:19; 18:27b; 1 Cor. 15:47-48). "Flesh," here used of that which is perishable, sinful, weak, mortal, in contrast to God (Gen. 6:3; Job 10:4; Ps. 56:4; Is. 31:3; 2 Chron. 32:8). The imperfects "trusteth" and "departeth" describe the actions as progressing from the first beginning to their final consummation. "Heart." God demands not merely outward acts, but the heart, the very seat of life (Deut. 4:9; 5:29; 6:5-6). "Heath," v. 6, a word occurring only here and Ps. 102:17; derived from a root meaning naked, destitute. Ps. 102:17 the reference is to a person; here usually regarded as the tamarisk (LXX, Targum, Vulgate) or the juniper; others, "a destitute person." The sense remains unchanged. In contrast to "tree" (v. 8), "tamarisk," or "juniper," seems preferable here. The unbeliever does not even see, recognize, the good things when they are offered to him in the Gospel. In the midst of riches, of honor, of influence, he is like a desert plant barely subsisting in the dry desert, cp. Eph. 2:11-12. All he has will pass away, and all that remains for him is the solitary, parched, salty wilderness of eternal despair and damnation. Cursed indeed!

Vv. 7-8. Cp. Ps. 1:3; 52:8. "River," literally, a perennial stream. This man receives nourishment from waters that never fail (Jer. 2:13; Ps. 36:9). He will not fear the heat of trial and tribulation, for he learns from the Word of God its purpose and blessing. By the gracious strength of the Lord his leaves will not shrivel, and even the hottest year of drought, long continued trials, will not leave him void of fruit, but bring his fertility in good works to even greater perfection (Rom. 5:3-5; Heb. 12:9-11).

---

b. The wicked, deceitful heart of man, vv. 9-11

9 The heart is treacherous above all things, and incurable. Who can 10 understand it? I, the LORD, am a searcher of the heart and a tester of the kidneys, in order to reward everyone according to his ways, according to the fruit of his actions.

11 Like a partridge that broods but does not hatch, so is he that gets wealth, and not by rightful means; in the midst of his days he must forsake it and in his end appear a fool.

Vv. 9-10. The "heart" in Hebrew thought is the center and fountainhead of life in its every form and phase (Prov. 4:23). This heart is "deceitful," literally, following the heel, dogging one's footsteps for the purpose of betraying him. Compare "Jacob" Gen. 25:26; 27:35-36, the name derived from the same root word. In point of deceitfulness, treachery, the human heart exceeds all things. And the greatest deception it has conceived is the lie of the natural goodness of man's heart. On this fallacy all efforts of man at self-reform and national reform are based. This treacherous lie is the greatest obstacle to a humble return to God. "Desperately wicked," a very apt translation of the Hebrew word, literally, "incurable," occurring eight times Is. 17:11; Jer. 15:18; 17:9, 16; 30:12, 15; Job 34:6; Micah 1:9. The verb occurs once (2 Sam. 12:15). Desperately wicked! See Gen. 6:5; 8:21; Matt. 15:19. "Who can know it?" Just because of its inherent incurable treachery no man can fully fathom the depths of the depravity of man's heart. The Lord is not speaking here of particularly wicked degenerates. He describes the human heart, the life seat of every human being. And the diagnosis of the Searcher of man's heart, the greatest Psychologist, is: Incurably wicked! This Searcher of the heart is also the Judge!

V. 11. For our warning He presents an example of this treachery

163

and of the fatal folly of trusting in anything but the Lord. "The partridge," the "caller," cp. the imitative name "bobwhite" for the American quail. The A. V., agreeing with Luther, offers the only correct rendering of this verse, and agrees fully with the application made of this fact. The prophet speaks here primarily not of the sinfulness of hoarding riches, but of its folly and the disappointment in store for the hoarder. "Shall leave them in the midst of his day," cp. Ps. 37: 9; 49: 6-13; 73: 18-20; Luke 12: 16-21.

C. Jeremiah's trustful prayer for salvation and deliverance from his enemies
vv. 12-18

12 O throne of glory, exalted from beginning, the place of our sanc-
13 tuary! O Hope of Israel, the LORD! All that forsake Thee shall be put to shame. They that depart from Me shall be written in the ground; for they have forsaken the LORD,
14 the Fountain of living water. Heal me, O LORD, and I shall be healed! Save me, and I shall be saved!
15 For Thou art my Praise. Behold, they are saying to me: Where is the word of the LORD? Let it

16 come! And I myself did not refuse to be a shepherd, following Thee; nor did I long for the fatal day. Thou knowest! Whatever issued from my lips was manifest to Thee.
17 Be not a terror to me! Thou art my
18 Refuge in the day of evil. Let my persecutors be put to shame, but let me not be put to shame; let them be abashed, and let not me be abashed. Bring upon them the day of evil, and destroy them with twofold destruction!

V. 12. From man's folly and wickedness, from the contemplation of man's heart, the prophet turns in fervent adoration and trusting prayer to the Lord, his God. "A glorious high throne," etc. The accents demand three different phrases, three sets of vocatives. Mount Zion is addressed in contrast to the high places and altars of idols, as the third phrase clearly states. On Mount Zion, in the Most Holy Place, the glorious throne of God was established, God throning between the cherubim on the Ark of the Covenant (Ex. 25: 22; Num. 7: 89; 1 Sam. 4: 4; etc.). Jerusalem was called the throne of glory Jer. 3: 17; 14: 21; Ezek. 43: 7. "Exalted from beginning," not only because God had determined to choose this city as His dwelling place (Ex. 15: 17; Ps. 132: 13-14), but because there Melchizedek, the only royal priest mentioned in the Bible, had ruled as the type of Christ (Genesis 14; Psalm 110; Hebrews 5—10). "The place of our sanctuary," given to the chosen nation, uniquely planned by the Lord, built according to His specifications (1 Chron. 28: 11-19; cp. Ex. 25: 9, 40; 26: 30; etc.). Here was the worship prescribed by Jehovah; here was forgiveness of sin through the blood of sacrificial animals typifying and foreshadowing the sacrifice of Christ; here was God dwelling among His people. What black ingratitude to forsake these privileges and choose, instead, idolatry!

V. 13. While v. 12 was an exclamation of intense loyalty to Jerusalem similar to Ps. 137:5-6, v. 13 is a confession of faithful trust in the Lord, the only Hope of Israel (Jer. 14:8), without whom there is no salvation. "Depart from me," the prophet is speaking in full assurance that he is the Lord's spokesman (ch. 1:7-10). Departing from the prophet is departure from the Lord, for the prophet's word is the Lord's word (Luke 10:16). "Written in the earth," in the ground (John 8:8). Such writing would soon be obliterated, their names forgotten (Ps. 1:4; 37:34-38; 73:17-20). What folly to forsake the Fountain of living waters and follow vanities! To this Fountain the prophet turns with a plea for healing and life.

Vv. 14-15. Jeremiah knows by experience the truth of v. 10. He knows that whatever there is of loyalty and obedience in him, he owes to the Lord's gracious help, and if he is to remain faithful, the Lord must heal and save. The Lord alone is the object of his praise. He keenly feels the need of the Lord's healing and saving hand. The constant contempt with which his message is received is a constant temptation to become disloyal. Everywhere he hears sneering remarks: Where is the word of the Lord? Let it come. For so many years you have been threatening dire punishments, and where are they? To you applies Deut. 18:22! Even the terrible drought had not impressed the people. There may have been some who openly denied the power of Jehovah to carry out His threats.

Vv. 16-18. Turning to the Lord, he calls attention to his loyalty in preaching God's Word (v. 16), then pleads for a speedy fulfillment of this Word (vv. 17-18).

Three items prove his loyalty: 1) He did not hasten, hurry away, from being the Lord's prophet, but, overcoming his own hesitancy, he willingly became a "pastor," a shepherd; "after Thee," following God's footsteps, walking in the paths He had chosen, clinging to His Word (ch. 1:7; 25:3). 2) "Desired the woeful day." The Hithpael is causative-reflexive, he did not cause his own wishes to move him to action, to stir him up, to whip up his desire to have his people ruined. He threatened judgments because God had given him this message. 3) He calls upon God as a witness of his own sincerity in the execution of God's command. "Thou knowest!" Here are three characteristics of a true preacher and pastor: obedience to God's call and command, refraining from venting one's own spite, sincerity in doing the work of the ministry (1 Cor. 4:1-5; 2 Cor. 4:2-5; 1 Thess. 2:3-6).

Vv. 17-18. "Be not a terror to me," literally, consternation, abashment. Jeremiah asks God to fulfill His promise given ch. 1:17; not to make him abashed, confounded, by retarding the fulfillment of His threat. He does this in full assurance that he need not fear "the evil day," for the Lord is his sure Refuge Place. Therefore God should cause the sneering enemies (v. 15) to be abashed and put to shame by speedily sending the day of His judgments, rather than permit His faithful messenger to be put to further shame and disgrace by his opponents.

---

8. Observe the Sabbath of the Lord! Vv. 19-27

A. Prove your obedient trust in the Lord by keeping the Sabbath, vv. 19-23

19 Thus said the LORD to me: Go and stand in the gate of the sons of the people by which the kings of Judah pass in and out, and in 20 all the gates of Jerusalem. And say to them: Hear the word of the LORD, O kings of Judah, and all Judah, and all inhabitants of Jerusalem that enter by these gates. 21 Thus says the LORD: Take heed for yourselves, and do not carry any burden on the Sabbath day, to bring it through the gates of Jerusalem. 22 And do not bring out a burden from your homes on the Sabbath day, nor do any work; but sanctify the Sabbath day, as I have commanded your fathers. 23 Yet they did not listen and did not incline their ears, but stiffened their necks neither to hear nor to accept instruction.

Vv. 19-23. Jeremiah had stressed the absolute necessity of placing one's trust in the Lord alone. Such trust is not a mere theoretical matter. The religion of the Lord is not mere speculative theology; it is eminently practical throughout. The people are to manifest their trust by their works. Faith and works are correlatives (Eph. 2:1, 10; James 1:18; 2:17-20). One of the ways whereby Judah was to prove its trust in God was the sanctification of the Sabbath day. The Lord had promised to bless their labor abundantly (Deut. 28:1-14) so that they could well afford to set aside one day for the study of God's Word, trusting Him to fulfill His promise. The Jews lacked this trust, as became evident by their disregard of the Sabbath law (v. 23). "Burdens," sales goods from near and far were brought into the city by caravans, tradesmen, farmers, or left the city on the Sabbath just as on any other day.

This commission (v. 19 ff.) addressed to kings and people alike, in all the gates, given widespread publication, would certainly not increase the popularity of the prophet, cp. Neh. 13:15-21, yet faithfully he did his duty.

B. Then I will continue to prosper you, vv. 24-27

24 And when you obediently hear Me, is the LORD's oracle, not to carry a burden through the gates of this city on the Sabbath day and to sanctify the Sabbath day by not 25 doing any work, then there shall pass through the gates of this city, kings and rulers sitting on the throne of David and riding in chariots and on horses, they and their rulers, the men of Judah, and the inhabitants of Jerusalem; and this city shall be inhabited forever. 26 And there shall come from the cities of Judah, and from the environments of Jerusalem, and from the land of Benjamin, and from the lowlands, and from the hill country, and from the Southland, such as bring burnt offerings and bloody sacrifices and meat offerings and incense, and bring thankofferings to 27 the house of Jehovah. But if you do not obey Me in point of sanctifying the Sabbath day and not carrying any burden while going through the gates of Jerusalem on the Sabbath day, then I will kindle a fire in her gates, and it shall consume the palaces of Jerusalem and shall not be quenched.

Vv. 24-27. Hallowing the Sabbath day would not impoverish the people or their rulers. The city would regain its earlier glory and prosperity.

While Jeremiah sternly denounced externalism and legalism, he just as sternly opposed any and all disobedience to God's laws, ceremonial as well as moral.

"From the plain" (v. 26), translated "valley" (ch. 32:44), "vale" (ch. 33:13). The *Shephelah,* the lowlands between the Judean Mountains and the Mediterranean Sea, together with the foothills of the hill country; others confine the term to the foothills.

VII. God Is the Sovereign Ruler, Ch. 18—21

In His hands the nations of the earth are like clay in the potter's hand (ch. 18). He can smash Judah as easily as a man can smash a bottle (ch. 19). He delivers wicked Pashur and Judah into the hands of the king of Babylon (ch. 20). He foretells His judgments against the king, the nation, and the royal dynasty (ch. 21).

1. The Symbol of the Clay and the Potter

CHAPTER 18

A. The symbol, vv. 1-10

1. 2 The word which came to Jeremiah from the LORD: Arise, and go down to the potter's house, and there I will reveal to you My words. 3 So I went down to the potter's house and saw him busy at work 4 on the wheels. And the vessel which he was forming from the clay was spoiled in the hand of the potter, and he again formed it into another vessel, whatever the potter 6 saw fit to make. And the word of the LORD came to me: Can I not deal with you, O house of Israel, as this potter? is the oracle of the LORD. Behold, as the clay in the hand of the potter, so are you in 7 My hand, O house of Israel! At one moment I speak concerning a nation and a kingdom to uproot and to tear down and to destroy it. 8 And if this nation repent of its wickedness, on account of which I have threatened it, then I will repent of the evil which I thought 9 to do to it. And at another moment I speak concerning a nation and a kingdom to build and to plant it. 10 And if it does what is evil in My view, will not listen to My voice, I will repent of the good that I have spoken to benefit it.

Vv. 1-3. By divine direction the prophet goes to a potter's workshop, perhaps in the southern parts of the city, where claypits have been found. Here the Lord intends to give to His prophet an important revelation and a message of vital significance to His people. The potter was just preparing to begin his day's work on the wheels, the stones or disks, fastened to a wooden rod placed into a hole in the ground. The lower disk was worked by the foot, thus setting in motion the upper disk, on which the potter worked the clay and shaped it into whatever vessel he chose to make. "After shaping the clay into a conelike form, he placed his thumb into the top of it, opened a hole in the center which he constantly widened by pressing the edges of the revolving cone between his hands. As it enlarged and became thinner, he gave it whatever shape he pleased." (Thomson, *The Land and the Book,* p. 520, quoted in *Pulpit Commentary, in loc.*)

V. 4. The vessel in the hands of the potter was marred in the making. We are not told the cause. That is not the point of the lesson.

The real point is that the potter can do as he pleases with the clay on which he works; discard it after an accident, or finish the marred vessel, or make an entirely new vessel out of the clay, one like the former one or one altogether different, exactly as seems good and right to him. The clay in his hand is in his power.

Vv. 5-6. The Lord's interpretation. All nations, including Judah, are in the power of the Lord, who shapes their history according to His will.

Vv. 7-10. Application to the nations. The Lord is able to destroy a wicked nation and able to prosper it upon repentance. We think of Nineveh (Jonah 3:4-10). He can build a nation, and destroy it if it does evil. Prosperous Sodom and Gomorrah (Gen. 13:10) were destroyed (Gen. 19:24-25); the Amorites (Amos 2:9-10); Assyria (Nahum 1—3); other nations (Jer. 46-51). Yet the Lord, though the absolute Ruler of the nations, is not an arbitrary God, ruled by sudden whims or fancies. He remains the God of unchanging justice (Ex. 20:5-6).

B. The application to Judah, vv. 11-17

11 And now speak to the men of Judah and to the inhabitants of Jerusalem: Thus says the LORD: Behold, I am forming evil against you and devising a plan against you. Let everyone turn from his wicked way and amend your ways and 12 works. But they say: It is hopeless! For we will walk according to our plans, and we will act everyone according to the hardness of his 13 heart. Therefore thus says the Lord: Go, inquire among the nations whether anyone has ever heard anything like this? A horrible thing has the virgin of Israel 14 committed! Does the snow of Lebanon forsake the rock of the field? Or do foreign, cold, gushing waters 15 fail? Yet My people have forgotten Me; they sacrifice to vanities, which caused them to stumble on their ways, the paths of old, to walk on 16 the paths of an ungraded way, with the result that they will make their land desolate, an everlasting derision; everyone passing through it will be astonished and will shake 17 his head. Like the east wind I will scatter them before the enemy; their backs, and not their faces, will I see on the day of their distress.

Vv. 11-12. This truth is applied to Judah as a solemn warning and a final call to repentance. Judah stubbornly rejects this plea. They will not hear!

Vv. 13-14. Israel's horrible sin of rejecting its God is unheard of among the heathen nations (v. 13). It is unnatural! (V. 14.) Look at snow-capped Lebanon, the "rock" rising out of the "field," the plains. The snow will not leave the mountain even in the hottest summer. Neither are the foreign (because not belonging to Israel), ice-cold, gushing waters ever "uprooted" so that they cease to flow. Even the foreign waters, irrational creation, do not fail in their divinely appointed duty to serve their Maker. Judah, God's own, not a foreign nation, has sunk not only below the Gentiles despised by her; she has sunk beneath the irrational creatures!

V. 15. What a contrast! Jehovah and nothingness! Yet His people were bringing their offerings to vanity and had forgotten the Lord. And they seduced others to stumble in their ways, chosen for them by Jehovah, "ancient" paths, everlasting in their nature and their goal, and to walk in ways not "cast up," ungraded, altogether unfit for leading anyone to God and His heaven.

Vv. 16-17. The result of their wickedness is to make their land the object of derisive, malevolent mockery, astonishment at their wicked folly, and wagging of heads in scornful sneer. The Lord Himself will prove the truth of v. 6. "Scatter them" (cp. ch. 13:24). Because they had turned their back to Him (ch. 2:27), He will do the same to them. He will no longer bless them (Num. 6:25-26), but reject them.

C. The people's reaction and the prophet's prayer, vv. 18-23

18 Then they said: Come, let us plan a plot against Jeremiah; for instruction is not beginning to depart from the priest, nor counsel from the wise man, nor word from the prophet. Come, let us slay him with the tongue, and let us not pay 19 attention to his words! Pay heed to me, O LORD, and hear the voice 20 of my adversaries! Shall good be rewarded with evil? For they are digging a pit for my soul! Remember that I stood before Thee to intercede for their welfare, to turn 21 Thy furor from them. Therefore give their sons to famine, and pour them out upon the power of the sword! Let their women become bereft of children and widows, and their men be murdered by death, their young men slain by the sword 22 in battle. From their houses may howling be heard, for suddenly a troop shall come upon them; because they dug a pit to trap me and 23 laid snares for my feet. And Thou, O LORD, knowest all their counsel against me to kill me. Do not pardon their guilt, and do not blot out their sin before Thee. Let them be prostrated before Thee! In the time of Thy anger deal with them!

V. 18 proves the truth of God's Word, v. 12. The leaders of the people plot against the Lord's prophet, seek to undermine his influence. They boast of having God's priests, etc., privileges once enjoyed, but now forfeited by their wickedness. Why listen to that prophet of doom, everlastingly finding fault? Let us slay him with the tongue, expose him as the deceiver and dangerous fellow he is! They will not shrink from slanderous, lying accusations (cp. ch. 9:3-8) in order to rouse the people against him. One of the false charges was the non-fulfillment of his prophecies, a mortal crime (Deut. 18:20-22), cp. Jer. 17:15; 20:7-8. "Let us not give heed" reveals their stubbornness and, like the whistling of a boy passing the graveyard, betrays their fear that after all these threats will be fulfilled (cp. Matt. 27:62ff.; Acts 5:28; 7:54,57; 9:5).

Vv. 19-23. We do not know how this plot came to the prophet's knowledge. It opened to him an abyss of human depravity, for which even he, who knew so well the human heart (ch. 17:9), was not prepared. He is deeply perturbed by the ingratitude of his people, for whom he had pleaded (ch. 14—16; cp. 7:16; 11:14), and wept (ch. 9:1). He knew the cause of their hatred, his faithfulness to God's command (ch. 1:7,17). To this Lord he turns and pours out his troubled heart. The enemies will not heed him, therefore he pleads with God to give heed to him and avenge the blasphemies directed not only against the Lord's messenger, but against the Lord Himself. The prophet had always been faithful to his people and to his God. Now let God be faithful to His word and fulfill those threats (ch. 4:6-31; 9:17-22; 14:15-18; 15:2-9) which His loyal messenger proclaimed so boldly even against his personal feelings. The prayer of the prophet not to forgive the iniquity of these self-hardened people merely re-echoes the Lord's refusal to forgive (ch. 7:16; 14:10,12; 15:1,6; 16:5b). Compare the Lord's curse, Matt. 23:13-36; Paul's, 1 Cor. 16:22; Gal. 1:8-9; John's word, 1 John 5:16b.

2. The Symbol of the Broken Bottle. Ch. 19—20

CHAPTER 19

A. The proclamation of God's curse upon wicked Judah, vv. 1-9

1 Thus said the LORD: Go and procure a potter's earthen bottle, and of the elders of the people and of
2 the elders of the priests, and go out to the Valley of Ben Hinnom, which is before the gate of the potter.
3 And thou shalt speak: Hear the word of the LORD, ye kings of Judah, and inhabitants of Jerusalem. Thus speaks the LORD of Hosts, the God of Israel: Behold, I will bring evil upon this place, so that the ears of everyone that
4 hears it shall tingle. Because they have left Me and have made this an alien place by offering sacrifices in it to other gods which they and their fathers and the kings of Judah did not know; and they have filled this place with blood of innocents.
5 They have built the high places of Baal to burn their sons in the fire as sacrifices to Baal, which I have not commanded, and not said, and which did not enter My mind.
6 Therefore, behold, days are coming, is the oracle of the LORD, that no longer shall this place be called the Topheth and the Valley of Ben Hinnom, but the valley of slaughter.

7 And I will pour out the counsel of Judah and Jerusalem in this place, and I will cause them to fall by the sword before their enemies and by the hand of those who seek their lives, and I will give their carcasses as food to the birds of the air and 8 to the beasts of the earth. And I will make this city desolate and a hissing; all passing by her shall be astonished and shall hiss because of all the smiting she has suffered. 9 And I will make them eat the flesh of their sons and their daughters, and one will eat another's flesh in the siege and distress with which their enemies and those who seek their lives shall distress them.

Grammatical Notes

V. 2. "The east gate," חֶרֶס = sun, Judg. 14:18; Job 9:7. K'tib חַרְסוּת, Q'ri חַרְסִית, potter's clay, or potsherd.

Chapters 19 and 20 are closely connected, as ch. 20:1 proves. No date is given, but we are quite safe in placing events of these chapters in the early years of King Jehoiakim. The situation presented ch. 20: 1-2 could not have occurred during the reign of Josiah. No Temple guard would have dared to imprison Jeremiah as long as this pious king and friend of Jeremiah occupied the throne. Josiah died 609. After the fourth year of Jehoiakim, 605 B. C., Jeremiah was in hiding (cp. ch. 36:26). There is no record of any public activity of the prophet during Jehoiakim's rule (609—597) after the latter's fourth year. In the beginning of Jehoiakim's reign the arrest and deliverance of Jeremiah occurred (ch. 26). The events of ch. 19 and 20 may have happened a short while later. The protectors of the prophet may not have been present or the arrest carried out so swiftly and secretly that they could not come to his rescue. The influence of these friends may have caused his early release.

Ch. 19 and 20:1-6 form the background for the outbreak of deepest and conflicting emotions recorded ch. 20:7-18. Ch. 21, although chronologically much later, is attached to these two chapters in order to show that the prophet was not rejected, but continued to speak God's Word in spite of his own personal feelings in obedience to God's command (ch. 1:4-10). Since this was the general theme of the first part of the book (ch. 1—24), ch. 19, 20, and 21 were closely connected, though chronologically separated by years.

V. 1. "A potter's earthen bottle." The Hebrew term is derived from a root denoting "to gurgle, guggle," the guggling heard at emptying the bottle. It may have been one of the long-stemmed jars flaring out toward the bottom. Isaiah's threat (Is. 30:14) was now to be brought home to the people by this symbolic act in a far more impressive manner than by an oral threat.

172

Jeremiah was also told to get some of the elders of the people (cp. Ex. 3:16; 12:21; 1 Kings 20:7; etc.) and elders of the priests (cp. 2 Kings 19:2), perhaps identical with the "chief of priests" mentioned 2 Chron. 36:14, occupying positions of honor because of their age or rank. In solemn procession the prophet, carrying the bottle, and the representatives of the priesthood and of the civic power marched through the streets of Jerusalem, attracting wide attention. Soon multitudes of people gathered and followed the dignitaries, anxious to ascertain the purpose of this strange procession.

Vv. 2-3. "The east gate," margin "sun gate," cp. Judg. 14:18; Job 9:7, see Grammatical Notes. The Targum identifies it with the Dung Gate, at the southwest part of the city wall; Gesenius-Buhl translates "Potter's or Potsherd Gate"; LXX transliterates *charsith*. It may have been a small gate, otherwise unknown, through which the rubbish of the city was conveyed to the dumping ground in the Valley of Hinnom. Kings and people are addressed, all equally guilty. "Ears shall tingle," used in connection with threats of especially severe judgments (1 Sam. 3:11, Eli; 2 Kings 21:12, Manasseh).

Vv. 4-5. In an effective climax the sins are listed. The basic sin, "forsaking the Lord," led to ever greater vices. 1) "Estranged this place," made God's city and land a heathen land by introducing foreign cults unknown to the fathers; 2) bloody murders of all that opposed their idolatry or otherwise seemed objectionable (cp. ch. 2:34; 7:6; 22:3, 17; 2 Kings 21:16); 3) high places for Baalim and human sacrifices (cp. ch. 7:31).

Vv. 6-9. On v. 6 see ch. 7:32. God "makes void," literally, pours out (cp. v. 1), the counsel of the Jews, their sinful folly of seeking alliances with heathen nations from whom they hoped to derive greater benefits than from the Lord. In unnatural suppression of parental affection they had burnt their own children to Baal. Now their own bodies will be slain and lie unburied, food for birds and beasts. On v. 7 see Jer. 7:33; 16:4; on v. 8 see ch. 18:16. In abject selfishness they will cast away the last shred of parental love and kill and eat their own children (Deut. 28:53-54; 2 Kings 6:28ff.; Lam. 4:10).

B. The breaking of the bottle and its meaning, vv. 10-13

10 Then you shall break the flask before the eyes of the men accompanying you, and then shall you
11 speak to them: Thus says the LORD of Hosts, like this: I will break this people and this city, as he has broken the potter's flask, which can no more be repaired. And in Topheth shall they be buried till there be no more room

12 for burials. Thus will I do to this place, is the oracle of the LORD, and to its inhabitants, as to change
13 this city into a Topheth. The houses of Jerusalem and the houses of the kings of Judah shall be unclean like Topheth, even all the houses on whose roofs they offered sacrifices to all the host of heaven and poured libations to other gods.

Vv. 10-13. Now the crash of the bottle hurled on the rocky ground by the spokesman of the Lord resounds in the ears of the assembly as the confirmative Amen to this terrible curse of the just and holy God, which Jeremiah repeats.

C. Jeremiah repeats his message in the Temple, vv. 14-15

14 And Jeremiah came from Topheth, whither the LORD had sent him to prophesy, and stood in the court of the LORD's house and spoke to all
15 the people: Thus says the LORD of Hosts, the God of Israel: Behold, I am about to bring upon this city and upon all her cities all the evil which I have spoken against her, for they have stiffened their necks and will not hear My words.

So overwhelmed were the elders and the people by the words and act of Jeremiah that not one dared to interrupt him, not one raised a hand against him. But the prophet's mission was not yet finished. Boldly, courageously he returns from Hinnom, the place of idolatry, to the Temple, the house of the Lord, and there repeats his message to the throng of people assembled there. It is useless to speculate whether v. 15 is merely a summary of his words or whether he was interrupted at once after he had spoken v. 15. He had the courage to go where the Lord sent him and to speak whatever the Lord commanded him.

CHAPTER 20

D. Jeremiah is put in the stocks and pronounces God's judgment upon Pashur
vv. 1-6

1 And Pashur, the son of Immer, the priest, who was the chief overseer in the house of the LORD, heard Jeremiah prophesy these things.
2 Then Pashur beat Jeremiah the prophet and placed him in the stocks at the upper Gate of Benjamin of the house of the LORD.
3 The next morning Pashur released Jeremiah from the stocks, and Jeremiah said to him: The LORD calls your name not Pashur, but "Terror
4 Round About." For thus says the LORD: Behold, I am about to make you a terror to yourself and to all your friends, so that they shall fall by the sword of their enemies, and your eyes shall see it. And I will give all Judah into the hand of the king of Babel; and he shall deport them to Babel and slay them with
5 the sword. And I will give away all the wealth of this city and all her gain and all she holds precious;

and all the treasures of the kings of Judah I am giving into the hands of their enemies. They shall plunder them and take them and will 6 bring them to Babel. And you, Pashur, and all who live in your house shall go into captivity, and you shall come to Babel, and there you shall die, and there you shall be buried, you and all that love you, to whom you have prophesied falsely.

V. 1. "Chief governor," the chief of the Temple watch, ranking next to the high priest (cp. Jer. 29:25-26 with 52:24). His duty was to see that no unauthorized person entered the Temple, that no disturbance or nuisance was committed within the sacred courts. Probably identical with the "captain of the Temple" (Acts 4:1; 5:24, 26).

V. 2. "Jeremiah the prophet." This title does not occur in ch. 1—19. Its occurrence from now on does not prove difference of authorship or redactional additions and changes. As Keil observes (p. 231, footnote), the official title is used only when the official character of Jeremiah is to be emphasized.

In misplaced zeal Pashur treated Jeremiah as a disturber of the peace, had him scourged (Deut. 25:3; 2 Cor. 11:24), and placed in the stocks, a painful and shameful penalty (Job 13:27; 33:11; Jer. 29:26; Acts 16:24). "The high Gate of Benjamin," most likely identical with the "higher gate" of Ezek. 9:2, built by Jotham (2 Kings 15:35), a wide gate most frequently used by the people, leading from the Temple court upward toward the city. It must not be confused with the Gate of Benjamin in the city wall (Jer. 37:13; 38:7). At this gate the prophet was exposed to the sneers and curses of the people, who hated this prophet of doom.

Vv. 3-6. After his release, Jeremiah in holy indignation utters a curse similar to that of ch. 19:3-11, applying to an individual what was said of all people. "Terror round about," one surrounded by horror on all sides and who becomes an object of horror and fear to himself and others. The horrible details are enumerated vv. 4-6. And all the time his conscience will cry out: Pashur, terror round about! And all the time his friends will point at him the accusing finger: Pashur, Horror! For your horrible rebellion we must go through these horrors! Pashur, Horror All Around!

The prophecy was fulfilled most likely at the deportation of Jehoiachin, 597, as shortly after this event Zephaniah is addressed as the chief supervisor of the Temple (ch. 29:25-26). It may have occurred in an earlier deportation mentioned Dan. 1:1-3, the third year of Jehoiakim, 606.

175

E. Jeremiah's dissatisfied lament, joyous trust, and deepest despondency, vv. 7-18

a. The lament, vv. 7-10

7 Thou hast allured me, O LORD, and I was lured; Thou hast been too strong for me and hast overwhelmed me. I am a laughingstock all the day, everyone mocks me.
8 For as often as I speak, I must cry "Violence!" and "Oppression!" must I shout. Surely, the Word of the LORD has become unto me shame and derision all day long. When
9 I said: I will no longer remember Him and will not speak any more in His name, there was in my heart as a burning fire shut up in my bones. I am worn out trying to bear it. I cannot put up with it
10 any longer. For I hear many whisper: "Terror round about! Denounce him! Let us denounce him!" Every one of my intimate friends was anxiously watching for a misstep on my part: Perhaps he will be deceived so that we may overcome him and take our revenge on him.

Vv. 7-10. Pashur's shrewd plan to break down the courage of the prophet by means of physical torment and mental and spiritual anguish had not failed altogether. While dealing with the people and with Pashur, Jeremiah had remained an iron pillar and walls of brass. But in the solitude of his home a reaction sets in. Alone with his God, he breaks down completely. Forgotten was that great honor bestowed upon him to be an ambassador of the Most High, a spokesman of the Lord of Lords. His office appeared to him as an intolerable burden. Forgotten was God's word that He was also called to build and to plant (ch. 1:10), forgotten the marvelous Gospel promises he had already uttered. He remembered only the fearful denunciations and curses He had been obliged to pronounce against his people, whom he loved. He is disgusted with his office, dissatisfied with his God, who had called him into this office. He charges God with having deceived him. This charge is without foundation, for God had very definitely foretold trials against which it would be necessary to stand like an iron pillar and brazen walls (ch. 1:18), and had promised to be with him. Jeremiah's flesh is speaking here, chafing under the constant opposition and derision of God's Law and curse. And when because of this derisive rejection of his preaching the prophet resolved to put it out of his memory and to discontinue its proclamation, then this Word became in him as a fire burning in his bones, so that he could no longer endure that inner conflict raging in his soul. On the one hand, there was the prospect of continually reaping the hateful ridicule and scornful rejection of his message if he continued in its proclamation. There was, on the other hand, his sense of duty, his prophetic obligation, his willingness to obey the Lord, and above all the Lord's Word that burnt in his heart as a fire, threatening to consume the very marrow of his bones (cp. Heb. 4:12-13). So the battle raged on till he was utterly wearied, at the end of his strength (v. 10). For whenever he was ready to continue his preaching, he heard round about the sneering cavils of the multitudes. "Terror round about? We do not see it! Let him bring it on if he can!" And "Denounce him!" and "We will denounce him!" His constant denunciations of our leaders stamp him a dangerous person, a public enemy. Away with him! Even his "familiars," men of his welfare, men who greet him with the familiar greeting of friendship, Peace be with you! even they are anxiously watching (participle characterizing) for his downfall. "Perhaps he can be deceived, seduced to make a mistake, so that we can overcome him, can catch him, trap him, and satisfy our vengeance!"

---

b. Jeremiah's joyous trust, vv. 11-13

11 But the LORD is with me as a powerful warrior. Therefore my persecutors shall stumble. They shall be thoroughly put to shame — for they have not acted wisely — to eternal shame which shall not be 12 forgotten. O LORD of Hosts, who testest the righteous, who observest the reins and the heart, I shall see Thy vengeance on them, for to Thee have I entrusted my cause. 13 Sing to the LORD! Praise the LORD! For He has delivered the soul of the destitute from the wicked.

God uses the very perfidy of the enemies to restore peace and quiet to his wearied, heartbroken prophet. "We will overcome him!" So he hears them cry. And that word reminds him of the word the Lord had spoken to him on the day of his call, when He had told the prophet that his enemies would fight against him and not overcome him: For I am with thee, saith the Lord, to deliver thee! This word of promise lifts him out of the slough of despondency. If all the world is against me, yet the Lord is with me (ch. 1:8, 19; 15:20). His God had promised to deliver him out of the hands of the terrible ones (ch. 15:21). And this God is with him, a Strong One, mighty to help him, a "Terrible One" to his enemies, consuming the enemies of the prophet as He, the Deliverer of Israel, had consumed Pharaoh's host in the Red Sea (Ex. 14:19-20, 24-25). The prophet's enemies shall "stumble," fall, and not prevail, be utterly dismayed, for they have no insight, theirs will be eternal, unforgettable shame! The lessons taught by the Lord on former occasions, the gracious promises received years ago flash back into the prophet's memory and enable

177

him to issue forth from the wearying battle raging in his soul a victor, victor through the power of God's Word. Committing his cause to the Lord (v. 12), he voices his grateful trust in the Covenant God (v. 13).

---

c. Deepest despondency, vv. 14-18

14 Cursed be the day on which I was born! The day on which my mother bore me, let it be unblessed!
15 Cursed be the man who brought the good news to my father: A son is born to you! and made him ex-
16 ceedingly glad! Let this man be as the cities which God mercilessly overturned, and may he hear shouting in the morning and alarm
17 at noontime, because he did not kill me from the womb so that for me my mother had been my grave, and her womb had forever re-
18 mained pregnant. Oh, why did I come forth from the womb to see trouble and heartache, and my days end in shame?

V. 14. The human heart is deceitful above all things and desperately wicked. Who can know it? (Jer. 17:9.) And the prophet remained human, intensely human, and experienced the truth of his own statement. From the summit of joyous trust that heart plunges suddenly, unexpectedly, unexplainably, into the deepest abyss of black despair. There is a complete blackout of God's love and grace and mercy! He sees only his misery, his destitution, sees only the howling mob, the rabble, the evildoers, the wicked men in high places, mocking, sneering, seeking his life, tormenting his soul with their blasphemous accusations. And the Lord, who was so close at his side a moment ago, seems now so far, so dreadfully far away! Jeremiah breaks forth in one of the most violent outbursts of dissatisfaction and denunciation of the ways of the Lord ever uttered by human tongue. He curses the very day on which he was born, and as if that were not sufficient, he wishes this day to remain forever destitute of praise and blessing.

Vv. 15-18. He curses the man who brought the tidings of the birth of a man-child as good news to his father, and as if that were not enough, he invokes upon this man the inexorable judgment of Sodom and Gomorrah. May he never be at peace! May he hear in the morning "the cry," the anguished shrieks of terror uttered by the inhabitants of a city as in hopeless despair they see the victorious enemy scale the walls. May he hear the "shouting," the triumphant war cry, the bellowing shouts of the bloodthirsty, lecherous soldiers as they go from house to house to plunder and rape and put to the sword whomsoever they find. Rather than joyfully run to my father with the news of the birth of a son, why did he not slay me before I was born? Why was I permitted to see the light of day? Why, O Lord, did I come forth from the womb to see nothing but labor and sorrow, toil and trouble, and that my days should be consumed with shame, dishonor, disgrace? Why, O Lord, why?

With this cry of utter hopelessness and despair this chapter ends. We are not told what the Lord answered to this horrible execration uttered by His messenger. Neither are we told that the Lord intervened directly as He did on former occasions, or just what means He used to restore and comfort His servant. While the prophet's wail of bitter disappointment and dissatisfaction with God and his dreadful curse still rings in our ears, he drops the curtain. He has given us not merely a brief glimpse, but a long look into the depths of deceitfulness and wickedness and rebellion, of depravity of the human heart, that heart which by nature even the child of God still carries in his bosom and which remains our heart to our dying day.

Two questions arise: Was it right for the prophet to curse the day of his birth? and: How is it possible that such a curse could follow immediately after the joyous confidence of v. 13? Luther, the man who had gone through similar trials, writes: *"Ergo qui damnant impatientiam hanc et monent de patientia, die sind nur theologii speculativi. Kompt yhr auch in die practiken, tunc videbitis. Huiusmodi historiae sunt valde magnae. Non est de eis speculative disputandum."* (Weimar, *Tischreden,* I, No. 228, p. 96 f.) "Therefore those who condemn this impatience and call attention to [the need of] patience, are mere speculative [theoretical] theologians. If you will meet with actual experiences of practical life, you will understand. Stories such as this one are too great than that we should dispute about them in a merely theoretical fashion."

Cowles compares the experience of Jeremiah with that of Elijah. "As to its striking dissimilarity to vv. 11-13, the thing to be said is this: It comes of the frailties of human nature that Christian experience should have very dissimilar phases; that frail flesh, weak nerves, and little faith have moments for asserting their terrible sway, not of right, but of fact; and that it is simple historic truth to give utterance to their impressions and voices. Jeremiah and Elijah had seasons of being strong in the Lord, and also seasons of being sadly weak in the Lord, or rather weak through not being just then very much in the Lord, but rather in the flesh, and under the control of a prostrate nervous system." (Cowles, *Jeremiah,* p. 167.)

We agree with Luther and Cowles. There is no need to regard vv. 14-18 as a misplaced fragment, nor to place an interval between vv. 13 and 14 and to regard the two spiritual conflicts (vv. 7-13 and vv. 14-18) as having occurred at different times. Any Christian that knows Satan's tactics in tempting God's children, knows from his own experience that Satan will not always cease the fight after he has once been beaten back, but that the inveterate foe may return immediately with still greater ferocity in order to attack the Christian rejoicing in his victory and less ready or altogether unprepared for such a second attack. He is and remains the past master in tempting mankind, the seducer of a thousand wiles.

The Lord of the Covenant did not reject His servant. Nowhere in the life of Jeremiah does the grace and long-suffering of God with His erring children appear in fuller measure and in a more glorious light than here. And there are few passages in the Bible where the contrast between the believer's sinfulness and God's magnanimous, magnificent grace is brought out in sharper lines than here. And in recording these facts Jeremiah again shows his masterful pen, his powerful skill in using every means at his command to magnify the grace of his Lord Jehovah, the God of the Covenant.

With the storm still raging with full fury in Jeremiah's soul, his mouth still overflowing with bloodcurdling curses and maledictions, chapter 20 ends. The very next verse, originally not separated from the maledictions by a chapter division, introduces the same prophet speaking the word committed to him by the same Lord to the delegates sent to the prophet by Zedekiah some ten or fifteen years later. The God of infinite loving-kindness and unlimited patience overlooked this outburst of Jeremiah's flesh, did not deal with him after his sins nor reward him according to his iniquity. He applies to His prophet His own promise: I will forgive their iniquity and will remember their sin no more! (Jer. 31:34.)

CHAPTER 21

3. Jeremiah, Retained by the Lord as His Prophet, Continues His Faithful Service to the End

A. Zedekiah's request for an oracle, vv. 1-2

1 The word which came to Jeremiah from the LORD when King Zedekiah had sent to him Pashur, the son of Malchiah, and Zephaniah, the 2 son of Maaseiah, the priest: Please ask the LORD on our behalf; for Nebuchadrezzar, the king of Babylon, is advancing against us. Perhaps the Lord will deal with us according to all His miraculous power, so that he will withdraw from us.

The time is 588 B. C. Pharaoh Hophra (588—569), the Apries of Herodotus, the energetic son of Psammetich II, had ascended the throne of Egypt and at once renewed the ancient Egyptian claims on the southwestern portion of the Babylonian empire. In a campaign of vast dimensions he sought to regain Palestine and Phoenicia in the hope of gradually establishing Egypt as the sovereign world power. Misled by his promises, or yielding to his threats, prodded on by the fanatic war party in Jerusalem, who hoped to regain independence from Babylon, weak, vacillating Zedekiah rebelled against Nebuchadnezzar. The Chaldean king immediately proceeded to end once for all these irritating disturbances. One fortified city after the other had fallen before the powerful enemy. Terrified at the result of his breach of faith with Babylon, Zedekiah turns to Jeremiah. The lonely prophet, maligned as a calamity howler, persecuted as a traitor (ch. 26), now is the last resort of the depairing king, the man honored by a royal delegation pleading with Jeremiah to obtain for them an oracle from Jehovah. The two men are named. Pashur, the son of Malchiah, who is named (ch. 38:1) as one of the four princes who later accused Jeremiah of treasonable activities, represents the civic authority, while the priesthood is represented by Zephaniah, the son of Maaseiah (cp. ch. 29:25; 37:3; 52:24). Gods promise to His prophet (ch. 15:11b) was being fulfilled. This plea, however, was not the humble petition of penitent sinners, confessing their wickedness and imploring God's grace. Not a word is said of repentance, of desire for forgiveness. Jeremiah is asked to procure an oracle. They hope that God will deal with them according to all His wondrous works, manifested so often in the history of Israel.

B. A threefold oracle of Jehovah, vv. 3-14

In answer to the arrogant request for an oracle, the Lord gives not one oracle only, but three in one, the first to Zedekiah, the second to the people, the third to the royal house of David.

---

a. The oracle to the king: Defeat and death! Vv. 3-7

3. 4 And Jeremiah said to them: Thus shall you say to Zedekiah: Thus says the LORD, the God of Israel: Behold, I am about to turn back the weapons of war which are in your hands, with which you are fighting the king of Babel and the Chaldeans attacking you without the wall, and I will assemble them 5 into the midst of this city. And I Myself will fight against you with an outstretched hand and a strong arm, and in anger and in wrath and 6 in great fury. And I will smite the inhabitants of this city, both man and beast; they shall die in 7 a great pestilence. And afterwards, is the oracle of the LORD, I will

give Zedekiah, king of Judah, and his servants, and the people, and those who are left in the city from the pestilence, and from the sword, and from the famine, into the hand of Nebuchadrezzar, the king of Babylon, and into the hand of their enemies, and into the hand of them that seek their lives, and he shall smite them with the edge of the sword. He will have no mercy upon them, have no pity, have no compassion.

The Captain of the host of the Lord is no longer for Judah and against her adversaries (Joshua 5:13-14). While He is still the Lord of wondrous works, He will now do a work "which, whosoever heareth, his ears shall tingle" (ch. 19:3). He Himself, the Lord, mighty in battle, stands at the head of the Babylonian invaders. He will turn back the weapons of Judah and the men carrying them, fighting against the approaching hosts in the vain hope of defeating them before they reach the city. He will, after the ignominious defeat of Judah, lead the hostile bands into the city. He will send a pestilence, an epidemic into the city. Those who are left after famine and pestilence and sword have reaped their bloody harvest, He will deliver to King Nebuchadnezzar and their cruel enemies to be slain without pity and without mercy. Has the Lord lost His saving power? No! But His outstretched hand and strong arm, which had so often fought for His people (Deut. 26:8), now fights against them in anger and in fury and in great wrath.

b. To the people: Unconditional surrender the only way of escape! Vv. 8-10

8 And to this people say: Thus says the LORD: Behold, I am placing before you the way of life and the 9 way of death. He that stays in this city shall die by sword and by famine and by pestilence, and he that goes out and surrenders to the Chaldeans attacking you shall live, and his life shall be as a spoils to 10 him. For I have set my face against this city for evil and not for good, is the oracle of the LORD. Into the hand of the king of Babel shall it be given, and he shall burn it with fire.

Disobedience to the Lord's Word is, as always, the way of death. The stubborn resistance of the fanatic warmongering defenders of liberty and independence was, in fact, a suicidal policy and would result in death, either by the sword or by famine or by pestilence. Obedient submission to the Word and will of the Lord, even if that will runs counter to our own, is as always the way of life. Everyone that would leave the doomed city and surrender to the enemy would save his life. For the face of the God of unending holiness and unchanging justice is set against the city, which shall be captured by the enemy and burnt with fire, reduced to dust and ashes.

c. To the royal house: Change your ways or perish! Vv. 11-14

11 And to the royal house of Judah say: Hear the word of the LORD!
12 O house of David, so says the LORD: Judge lawfully every morning, and deliver the oppressed from the hand of the oppressor, lest My fury go forth like fire and burn unquenchably because of the wickedness of your actions. Behold,
13 I am against you that dwell in the valley on the rock of the plain, is the oracle of the LORD, you who say: Who shall come down against us? And who shall come against
14 our homes? And I shall punish you in accordance with the fruit of your actions, is the oracle of the LORD. I will kindle a fire in her forest, and it shall consume all her environments.

As the Lord had pointed out to the people the way of life and of death, in order that they might choose life (Deut. 30:19), so the royal house is shown a last opportunity to avert disaster from themselves and the city. Two things are necessary: First, a change of their policy of tolerating and thus encouraging oppression and social injustice, which change involved the establishment and maintenance of impartial justice and righteousness. Secondly, a cessation of their insane pride in privileges and favors promised by the Lord to His people and the royal dynasty (1 Kings 9:4-5), but long ago forfeited by their wickedness; and a cessation of their paradoxical trust in the saving power of the Lord, whom they had turned against themselves by their unbelief and disobedience, which called down upon themselves His consuming wrath.

On "valley, the rock of the plain," v. 13, see Jer. 17:3, p. 161 f.

VIII. The Wicked Leaders and the True Shepherd, Ch. 22—24

CHAPTER 22

1. Against the Wicked Kings

A. General warning against injustice and oppression, vv. 1-9

1 Thus said the LORD: Go down to the house of the king of Judah, and
2 there speak this word: Say: Hear the word of the LORD, O king of Judah, sitting upon the throne of David, you and your servants and your people passing through these
3 gates. Thus says the LORD: Establish judgment and justice, and deliver the suppressed from the power of the oppressor, and do not harass nor violate the stranger, the orphan, and the widow, nor shed innocent
4 blood in this place. For if you shall faithfully fulfill this charge, then through the gates of this house shall come kings sitting as David's seed on his throne, riding on chariots and on horses, he and his servants
5 and his people. And if you do not obey these words, I swear by Myself, is the oracle of the LORD, that this house shall become a deso-
6 lation. For thus says the LORD concerning the house of the king of Judah: A Gilead are you unto Me, the head of Lebanon! Surely I will make you a desert, as un-
7 inhabited cities. I will also appoint destroyers against you, men and their weapons, and they shall cut down the choicest of your cedars
8 and throw them into the fire. And many nations will pass by this city and say to each other: Why did the LORD deal with this great city in
9 this manner? And they shall say: Because they forsook the covenant of the LORD, their God, and worshiped other gods and served them.

Vv. 1-5. Like Nathan (2 Sam. 12:1 ff.), Jeremiah was sent to address the king personally. Subduing all fears and misgivings, Jeremiah obeys. Judah's kings were not like David, men after God's own heart (1 Sam. 13:14), nor did they follow his example in repenting of their wickedness (Psalm 51). The prophet is to direct his words also to the state officials and the people at large, who were not less guilty, though they still worshiped at the Temple.

"Execute," establish judgment, see Jer. 5:1; 23:5. Judah was a church state, and its kings were responsible for the spiritual and material welfare of their people (Deut. 17:18, 20). It was their duty to enforce the moral, civic, and ceremonial legislation of God's commonwealth, particularly, to establish social justice. — To this day the public administration of civic righteousness and justice by government and citizens is one of the fundamentals of civic welfare and prosperity (Prov. 14:34).

Vv. 6-9. Gilead, the land of fertile pastures and stately forests, and Lebanon, covered with cedars and capped with everlasting snow, were symbols of that beauty, that majestic power and permanence which the Lord had in mind for His people if they would keep His

Commandments (Deuteronomy 7; 28:1-14). Apostasy from the Lord, disobedience to His Word, would be punished severely (Deut. 28:15ff.). The Lord is ready to carry out His threats (v. 7). On vv. 8-9 cp. Deut. 29:24-28; 1 Kings 9:8-9; Jer. 40:3.

B. Special prophecies, vv. 10-30

a. Concerning Jehoahaz, vv. 10-12

10 Do not weep for the dead one, and do not bewail him! Weep bitterly for the one going away, for he will no more return nor see the land of
11 his birth. For thus says the LORD concerning Shallum, the son of Josiah, king of Judah, who ruled instead of his father, Josiah, and has gone away from this place: He
12 will no more return! For in the place to which they deported him, there shall he die, and this land he shall see no more!

Vv. 10-12. After the general admonition (vv. 1-9) follow special messages to individual kings. V. 10 refers to Josiah's early death (2 Kings 23:29; 2 Chron. 35:20-25) and was spoken shortly after his burial. Shallum is to be identified with Jehoahaz (2 Kings 23:30-34), since he was the only one to rule in the stead of his father and was carried away never to return. Jehoiakim, who reigned "in the room" of Josiah, was not deported (2 Kings 23:34; 24:6; Jer. 22:18f.), while Jehoiachin, who was deported never to return (2 Kings 24:8-12), reigned in the stead of Jehoiakim (2 Kings 24:6). Jehoahaz was to be lamented rather than Josiah, whose seemingly premature death delivered him from the horrors of the years to come. Cp. Is. 57:1-2.

b. Against Jehoiakim, whose wickedness shall bring God's curse upon himself and the land, vv. 13-23

13 Woe to him that builds his house by unrighteousness and his upper rooms by injustice, that makes his neighbor to slave for nothing and
14 does not give him his wage; that says: I will build me a house of great size, its upper rooms to be airy; and cuts windows for it and panels it with cedarwood and paints
15 it with red ochre. Shall you reign because you are rivaling others with cedar houses? Did not your father eat and drink and establish judgment and righteousness? Then
16 he flourished! He judged the cause of the poor and needy. Then he flourished. Is not this the true knowledge of Me? is the oracle of
17 the LORD. But your eyes and your heart are directed only to your own gain and to shed innocent blood and to practice oppression and extor-
18 tion! Therefore thus says the LORD concerning Jehoiakim, the son of Josiah, king of Judah: They shall not lament him: Ah, brother! Ah, sister! They shall not lament him: Ah, Lord! Ah, his honor!
19 With the burial of an ass shall he be buried, dragged, and cast out beyond the gates of Jerusalem.
20 Ascend Lebanon and cry, and lift up your voice in Bashan, and cry from Abarim! For all your friends

185

21 are extinct! I have spoken to you in your good times. You said: I will not hear! This has been your manner from your youth, for you did 22 not listen to My voice. Wind is shepherding all your shepherds, and your friends are going into cap-

tivity. Yes, then you shall be ashamed and perplexed because of 23 all your evil deeds. You that dwell in Lebanon and make your nest in cedars, how shall you sigh when pains come to you, anguish as of a travailing woman!

Vv. 13-19 are addressed to Jehoiakim (v. 18). In a few lines Jeremiah here presents the picture of a wicked, selfish, vainglorious, cruel, covetous ruler; a man lacking every virtue sought in a king, yet immensely proud of his achievements. Dissatisfied with the palace occupied by his fathers, and aping the great builder kings of Assyria and Babylon, he enlarged, modernized, beautified the royal edifices. New stories, spacious halls, high ceilings, cedar panelings on walls and ceilings, immense windows, gaudy decorations in glaring vermilion. So he, the puny prince, hoped to rival the magnificent structures erected by the rulers of Egypt and Babylon. In bitter, biting irony the prophet asks him: Will that make you a king, if you "close" yourself (v. 15), if you seek to rival or outdo these kings by your cedar buildings? In one respect he did equal them, in cruel suppression and exploitation of his subjects (v. 13). His father "ate and drank," was not an ascetic, enjoyed the material blessings God granted him without oppressing the people. He established justice and righteousness and fared well. Note the contrast between Josiah's justice and righteousness (v. 15) and Jehoiakim's unrighteousness and wrong (v. 13). "Was not this to know Me?" The knowledge of the Lord is not merely an intellectual matter, it is to trust the Lord, to love Him, to obey His Law, to serve one's fellow men, within one's allotted sphere of duty. Because of Jehoiakim's flagrant wickedness (v. 17) he shall meet with an especially shameful end (vv. 18-19). The fulfillment of this threat, repeated ch. 36: 30, is nowhere recorded. The remark that he slept with his fathers (2 Kings 24: 6) does not conflict with a literal fulfillment, for the same expression is used (1 Kings 22: 40) of wicked King Ahab's shameful death (1 Kings 21: 19; 22: 30-38). (The Hebrew text reads: "and harlots washed him." A. V. is untenable.)

Vv. 20-23. Like shepherd, like flock, alike in guilt (cp. Jer. 5: 1; 26: 8-9), alike in punishment. They are to ascend to the tops of the highest mountains, Lebanon in the north, Bashan northwest, "the passages," = Abarim, a mountain range southeast, east of the Dead Sea. Their lament shall rise to the very clouds, for their sins rose high as the heaven, and their judgments from on high shall overwhelm them. Alone they shall stand in their misery, their "lovers" are destroyed, according to v. 22 their civic and spiritual leaders, regarded as lovers by the people because they did not, like the true prophets, constantly threaten, but pleased the people by crying "Peace! Peace!" (Cp. ch. 5:30-31.) The wind shall eat up, rather pasture, the shepherds; the stormwind of God's judgment shall sweep them away into exile. "Lebanon" (v. 23), here, Jerusalem with its royal palace and the mansions of the rich built of cedarwood from Lebanon (1 Kings 7:2; 10:17, 21).

---

c. Against Jehoiachin, vv. 24-30

24 As I live, is the oracle of the LORD, even if Coniah, the son of Jehoiakim, the king of Judah, were a signet ring on My right hand, I will
25 tear him off! And I shall surrender you to the hand of those that are seeking your life and to the hand of those of whom you are afraid, into the hand of Nebuchadrezzar, king of Babylon, and into the hand
26 of the Chaldeans. And I shall hurl you and your mother, who has born you, into another land in which you were not born, and there you shall
27 die. And into the land into which they desire to return, they shall not
28 return. Is this man Coniah so despised and broken a vessel, a vessel that pleases no one? Why has he and his seed been cast out and hurled away into a land which they
29 do not know? O land, land, land!
30 Hear the word of the LORD! Thus says the LORD: Write this man down as childless; as a man who shall have no success in his days, for he shall not succeed in having one of his sons sit on the throne of David, or rule again in Judah!

Grammatical Notes

V. 24. Coniah, כָּנְיָהוּ, occurring also v. 28 and ch. 37:1, which is the shorter form of Jeconiah, יְכָנְיָה, 1 Chron. 3:16, 17; Jer. 27:20; 28:4; 29:2; Esther 2:6; כָּנְיָהוּ Jer. 24:1. The form כָּנְיָהוּ was perhaps his original name and therefore appears in his genealogy. He is also named Jehoiachin, יְהוֹיָכִין, 2 Kings 24:6ff.; 2 Chron. 36:8f.; Jer. 52:31; or יוֹיָכִין, Ezek. 1:2, A. V.: Jehoiachin. The five forms have the same meaning: Jehovah will firmly establish; a beautiful name, yet dishonored by its bearer.

Vv. 24-30. Against Jehoiachin, here called Coniah. See Grammatical Notes. On the character of Jehoiachin cp. 2 Kings 24:9; Ezek. 19:5-9 (for "desolate palaces," v. 7, read with M. T. "widows"). A young, lecherous prince, ruled by his passions, entirely unfit to be the ruler of God's people. "Signet ring," used for sealing important documents, very highly valued and guarded against possible loss. Even if Jehoiachin had been so valuable an instrument, God would have rejected him (vv. 24-27). The interrogative sentence (v. 28) is to be answered in the affirmative. Sometimes the Hebrew asks a ques-

187

tion to indicate that the fact stated in the question is well known and generally accepted. We might translate: Surely this man is, etc. (Cp. Gen. 3:11; 27:36; 29:15; Deut. 11:30; Micah 3:1; etc.) G.-K. 150e. Jeremiah elsewhere employs the repeated question to state an unnatural, incomprehensible fact (ch. 8:4f.; 8:22; 14:19). The threefold "Earth!" (v. 29) is intended to rouse all the earth to listen to the announcement of his tragic fate. He is to die "childless," not absolutely (cp. 1 Chron. 3:16f.), but without an heir to the throne of David (v. 30). And this despised, broken "idol" (v. 28), rather, "vessel," "something formed," was by the Lord's inscrutable counsel to be one of the ancestors of King Messiah, the Righteous Branch of David, the Lord Our Righteousness (ch. 23:5; Matt. 1:11-12). Surely, the Lord of Hosts is wonderful in counsel and excellent in working (Is. 28:29).

CHAPTER 23

2. The Righteous Branch, the Lord Our Righteousness, Vv. 1-8

1 Woe unto the shepherds that destroy and scatter the flock of My pasture! is the oracle of the LORD.
2 Therefore thus says the LORD, the God of Israel, concerning the shepherds that tend My people: You have scattered My flock and dispersed them, you did not watch over them. Behold, I am watching over you to punish you for your wicked deeds, is the oracle of the
3 LORD. And I Myself shall gather the remnant of My flock out of all the countries whither I have scattered them, and I will bring them back to their fold, and they shall
4 be fruitful and increase. And I will appoint shepherds over them, and they shall pasture them, and they shall no longer fear nor be dismayed, nor shall they be sought,
5 is the oracle of the LORD. Behold, days are coming, is the oracle of the LORD, when I will raise up unto David a Righteous Sprout, and He shall rule as a King and do wisely and establish judgment and
6 righteousness in the land. In His days Judah shall be saved, and Israel shall dwell in safety, and this is His name which one shall call Him: the LORD Our Righteousness!
7 Therefore, behold, days are coming, is the oracle of the LORD, when they no more shall say: "As the LORD liveth, who brought the Children of Israel out of Egypt,"
8 but: "As the LORD liveth, who brought up and led the seed of the house of Israel out of the land of the north and out of all the countries whither I had scattered them, and they dwell in their own land.

Grammatical Notes

V. 5. "Branch." The other terms referred to as denoting lowliness are חֹטֶר, "rod," twig; נֵצֶר, "branch" (Is. 11:1); יוֹנֵק, "tender plant," sucker, young twig; and שֹׁרֶשׁ, "root" (Is. 53:2). "Righteous," צַדִּיק = right, correct, without fault, flawless.

"Judgment and justice." The Hebrew word *mishpat*, rendered "judgment" here, is used in various senses: the act of judging, Lev. 19:15; Jer. 39:5; 51:9; — the place of judgment, Job 14:3; 22:4; Ps. 143:2; — the sentence, Ps. 36:7 (A. V., v. 6); Jer. 12:1; especially punitive, Jer. 1:16; 4:12; — the object of judgment, the case, lawsuit, Num. 27:5; — what judges = the norm, God's Law, Ex. 21:1; Ps. 119:7, 13, 20; human law, Amos 5:7; Micah 3:9; custom, usage, 1 Kings 18:28; Ezek. 11:12; — the right that a person or object has or ought to have, 1 Kings 8:49; Jer. 30:18; 49:12; or his duty, Jer. 32:7; — the manner of appearance or activity, Ex. 26:30; Judg. 13:12 (order); 2 Kings 1:7, While in all these senses the idea of judging preponderates, "justice," righteousness, zedek, zedakah, in all its various shades of meaning always stresses the idea of right: that which is right, correct, Gen. 18:19; Lev. 19:36; Jer. 9:23; — the right thing as spoken = truth, Prov. 12:17; 16:13; Is. 45:19, — the righteousness as established, — norm, Prov. 8:15; Is. 26:9-10; — righteousness as observed in obeying, or administering, the norm, Prov. 10:2; 31:9; Is. 56:1; Jer. 22:15; — God's righteousness in rewarding good and punishing evil, 2 Chron. 12:5-6; Neh. 9:33 ff.; Ps. 129:4; Lam. 1:18; Dan. 9:7, 14.

In Israel, God had established a norm (mishpat), determining what was right and correct (mishpat), and according to which judgment (mishpat) was pronounced by the judge (shophet) before whom one was called into judgment (mishpat). A person who lived up to the requirements of the norm was a righteous man (zaddik), possessed of righteousness (zedek, zedakah) which was acknowledged as such in the judgment (mishpat), was declared righteous (hizdik).

While an Israelite in a civic lawsuit might be declared righteous according to the civic norm, before God it is impossible to be justified, or declared righteous, on the basis of one's own righteousness, Ps. 130:3; 143:2; Is. 6:5; 64:6. Yet throughout the Old Testament we learn of a righteousness which man does not acquire for himself by his correct living, which is rather accounted or imputed to the believer by the Lord, Gen. 15:6; Ps. 32:2. It is the righteousness procured by the promised Redeemer, the Woman's Seed, Gen. 3:15; see Exposition, p. 191.

Vv. 1-4. The shepherds, the leaders of the people (cp. ch. 3:15), had neglected their duty and by their wickedness had caused the scattering of the flock in fulfillment of God's threat (Deut. 28:15 ff.). "Visit," watch over them. Now the chief Shepherd, the Overseer of the flock, will depose them from office. He Himself will gather the remnant (cp. Is. 10:20-22; Rom. 9:27), the believing remnant according to the election of grace (Rom. 11:5-6), and will bring them back to their folds, the covenant relations with the Great Shepherd, where they will multiply (ch. 3:16). He will give to them leaders who are worthy of the name shepherd, not mere hirelings. They shall be free from fear and anguish; see notes on ch. 23:6. "Lacking" = sought. None shall be sought, for none have strayed away, "they shall not turn away from Me" (ch. 3:19. Cp. Rom. 8:30-39).

V. 5. "Behold!" A noteworthy event is being announced. "The days come," a common expression for the Messianic era, see Jer. 31: 27-34, quoted Heb. 8:8-12;10:16-17. This message is "an oracle of the LORD," the Covenant God, the God of the Amen (Is. 65:16; Rev.

3:14), who will keep His word (2 Cor. 1:20). This oracle points back to the promise given to David (2 Sam. 7:3-5, 11-16, cp. 1 Chron. 17: 1-15). The promised Woman's Seed (Gen. 3:15), the Seed of Abraham (Gen. 22:18), was to be an offspring of David, a true human being, in order to be our substitute (Isaiah 53; Gal. 4:4-5; Phil. 2:6-8; Heb. 2: 9-18; 4:15; 5:7-9).

This Seed of David is called a "Branch." *"Zemach,"* the Hebrew term, never denotes a twig, an individual branch of a tree, but a growth, a sprout that grows directly out of the ground or directly from a root, forming a new or a second plant or tree (Gen. 19:25; Ps. 65:10, "springing"; Is. 61:11; Ezek. 16:7; 17:9-10; Hos. 8:7). All branches, leaves, fruits, are only products of the *Zemach.* Though a son of David (2 Sam. 7:12; 1 Chron. 17:11), this Branch will not be a mere branch in the family tree of David. He will be established as a fresh growth, springing up from the seemingly dead root of the house of David, growing up by the power of the omnipotent Lord into a new tree, a family tree with innumerable branches and leaves, a *Zemach.*

This term is one of the proper names of the Messiah (Is. 4:2; Zech. 3:8; 6:12). It denotes not so much His lowliness (for which different terms are used; see Grammatical Notes), but the fact that in Him the royal dynasty of David was to gain its greatest glory.

"A Righteous Branch." All other descendants of David had to confess with him Ps. 51:5, and plead Ps. 143:2. This Branch is righteous; as already the Lord had called Him "the Righteous One, My Servant" (Is. 53:11), because He was sinless (Is. 53:9; cp. Matt. 3:17; 17:5; John 8:46; 1 Pet. 1:19; 2:22; 1 John 3:5; Heb. 7:26). This was not merely an acquired righteousness. God raised Him as a Righteous Branch. Righteousness is His very essence, His nature and being. He is born as "that Holy Thing" (Luke 1:35). Therefore He could bear our sin (Isaiah 53; John 1:29; 2 Cor. 5:21), fulfill the Law perfectly (Matt. 3:15; Gal. 4:4), and become our perfect Savior and Example.

"And a King shall reign." He shall reign, a King; not merely as a subordinate king, or a king among His peers. He is *Zemach,* a living, life-producing, and preserving Person, and as such a King He rules. His kingdom partakes of the nature of this King, is like Him a living, life-producing kingdom. His royal glory shall never know decay, will never perish. (Dan. 2:44; 7:14; Luke 1:33; Eph. 1:20-23; Phil. 2:9-11; Rev. 5:5-14). He rules right royally!

"And prosper." The Hebrew term denotes rather the necessary prerequisites for a successful activity, to have insight, act with intelligent understanding. The King knows fully the will of the Lord, since He Himself is Jehovah (v. 6); cp. John 1:18; 3:12-13. He is not only willing (Ps. 40:6-8), but able (Is. 9:6-7; 52:13-15; 53:10-12) to carry out God's plan of salvation to successful completion. He knows also the plans of His enemies and how to foil and utterly defeat their schemes (Matt. 4:1-11; 26:1-5, 45; 27:62-66; John 2:24-25; 12:7; 14:30).

"Execute judgment and justice." "Execute" in connection with "judgment" or "judgment and justice (righteousness)" occurs seven times in Jeremiah (ch. 5:1; 7:5; 9:24, "exercise"; 22:3, 15; 23:5; 33:15). In every one of these passages the translation "establish" is the proper rendering demanded by the context. Jer. 5:2-5; 7:6-9; 22:3b, 9, 13-17 speak of a state of injustice and disorder to be replaced by the establishment of proper norms and living. Jer. 7:3, 5; 22:3-17 demand a thorough amending of their ways and doings, establishing a new order. In like manner the expression is used Ps. 99:4 in parallelism with ‎כּוּן, establish. And in Gen. 18:19; 2 Sam. 8:15 (1 Chron. 18:14); 1 Kings 10:9 (2 Chron. 9:8); Ezek. 18:8ff. "establish" is evidently the intended sense. In our passage Jeremiah does not mean to merely repeat what he had said a moment before, that the King is to be personally righteous in all His actions. He adds a new thought. As a king or ruler He is to make, create, establish a new norm, a new righteousness, because of which He shall be called "Our Righteousness," sinful man's righteousness. That is not a righteousness of the Law: "Do this, and you shall live. Fail to do it, and you shall die!" Nor is it to be a lawless righteousness, calling wrong right, and sin righteousness. It is a norm that is established by the righteous King, and a righteousness that this righteous King, whose righteousness is that of Jehovah, acknowledges as an all-sufficient righteousness. It is the righteousness which the Seed of David, who is the Woman's Seed of Gen. 3:15, procures for mankind by bruising Satan's head. As the Servant of the Lord He bore the sins of man (Is. 53:11), which the Lord laid on Him (v. 6) who had done no wrong (v. 9) and who suffered all the penalties man had deserved (vv. 5-6). By His vicarious, substitutionary fulfillment of all the demands of the mandatory and punitive justice of God He became "Our Righteousness," establishing this righteousness as the norm to be followed in His kingdom. Since this righteousness was procured and established by Him whom God calls "Jehovah Our Righteousness," it is a righteousness not only promised in the Old Testament, but as the righteousness procured

191

by Jehovah it is as timeless as the Lord, retroactive (Heb. 9: 15); it was offered to man after the first sin (Gen. 3: 15), accepted by them (Gen. 4: 1), by Lamech (Gen. 5: 29); it was counted as righteousness to believing Abraham (Gen. 15: 6); it became the hope and trust and joy of all believers in the Old Testament (Heb. 11: 1-40); it was the basis of all blessings, spiritual and material, temporal and eternal, granted in the Old Covenant. It is that vicarious righteousness on account of which the Righteous Servant throughout the ages justifies many (Is. 53: 12), makes them righteous by declaring them righteous, children of God, heirs of salvation for the sake of the salvation He has procured. For this reason "righteousness" is so frequently linked up with "salvation" (cp. Ps. 71: 15; 132: 9, 16; Is. 45: 8; 51: 5-6, 8; 56: 1; 59: 16-17; Zech. 9: 9; etc.).

V. 6. "In His days Judah shall be saved, and Israel shall dwell safely." The two expressions combined present the full picture, the first describing the deliverance, the second the ensuing freedom from fear and danger and want enjoyed by Judah and Israel once more united under one King (Hos. 1: 11; Is. 11: 13). Deliverance and safety here are spiritual blessings. Israel and Judah never regained their political independence. They were ruled by foreign nations, the Persians, Alexander, the Seleucidae and Ptolemies, the Idumaean Herod, the Romans. Particularly the last three centuries of their national life were centuries of constant war and cruel oppression. Yet during all the troublous times the true Israel (Rom. 2: 28-29; Deut. 10: 16; 30: 6), the "remnant," enjoyed that spiritual peace and liberty flowing from the righteousness procured for them by the Righteous Branch, the gift of God for Christ's sake to all believers (Num. 6: 24-26; Is. 9: 6; 26: 3-4; 57: 15-21; Luke 1: 68-79; 2: 29-30; Rom. 5: 1ff.).

Grammatical Notes

V. 6. "And this is His name whereby He shall be called, the LORD Our Righteousness." We have taken for granted the correctness of the translation adopted by A. V. and Luther, who do not follow the LXX, Yozedek, nor the Vulgate, *Dominus iustus noster;* Our righteous Lord, or, The Lord, our righteous One. A close study of the passage will prove the correctness of the rendering adopted by Luther and the A. V.

On יִקְרְאוֹ, instead of the more usual form of יִקְרָאֵהוּ, cp. the similar formations יִרְדְּפוּ (Hos. 8: 3), תִּלְכְּדוֹ (Ps. 35: 8), also Eccl. 4: 12; Ex. 22: 29. G.-K. 60 d. The וֹ may have been chosen instead of אֵהוּ for rhythmical reasons. Note also the two Maqqephs, or "connectors," placed between אֲשֶׁר and יִקְרְאוֹ, and between זֶה and שְׁמוֹ, connecting each pair of words so closely that with regard to tone and punctuation they are regarded as one and have but one accent on the ultimate (G.-K. 16a). Read *wezeshshemo* and *asheryiqreo*. The effect of this pointing is to emphasize the pronoun *o*, His, Him. The two clauses "This is His name" and "Whereby one shall call Him" are connected by the conjunctive accent (*Merkha*) under שְׁמוֹ. The distinctive accent (*Tiphcha*) under יִקְרְאוֹ separates this clause from the following sentence. The *Tiphcha* is frequently used as a minor separator, and in short sentences it often takes the place of the major separator *Athnach* (G.-K. 15f. 5). This pointing indicates that the Masora did not intend "Jehovah" to be the subject of יִקְרְאוֹ: "Jehovah calls Him," but a predicate accusative, the second object to "call," stating the name by which one is to call the Branch. By the conjunctive *Merkha* under Jehovah, connecting it with צִדְקֵנוּ, the intention to separate "Jehovah" from the preceding יִקְרְאוֹ is intensified and "Jehovah" designated as the name of the Branch. And by placing the dividing line (*Paseq*, divider) after "Jehovah," the Masora evidently indicated that צִדְקֵנוּ is not to be regarded as the predicate of Jehovah, "Jehovah is our righteousness," but as a second name, "Our Righteousness," "Jehovah" denoting the deity of the Branch, "Our Righteousness" His work. Compare on this use of the *Paseq* Ex. 17:15 (Jehovah! *Nissi!*); Gen. 22:11 (Abraham! Abraham!); Gen. 22:14 (Jehovah! He shall provide!); Ezek. 48:35 (the Lord! At this place!).

The Masoretic pointing therefore clearly indicates that it intended this passage to be understood in the sense of A. V., "The LORD Our Righteousness," and of Luther, "Der HERR, der unsere Gerechtigkeit ist." This punctuation represents the traditional interpretation of the ancient Synagog. It is remarkable that the Masoretes retained this reading even though the Christian Church used this passage as one of the prooftexts for the deity of Jesus of Nazareth.

This interpretation is found in the Talmud. In the tract *Baba Bathra* we read that Samuel B. Nahmeni said in the name of R. Johanan (200—279): "The following three will be named with the name of the Holy One, blessed be He: the Upright, as said above (Is. 43:7): 'Everyone that is called by My name'; — The Messiah, as it is written (Jer. 23:6): 'And this is His name whereby He shall be called: The Lord Our Righteousness'; — and Jerusalem, as it is written (Ezek. 48:35); 'And the name of that city shall be from that day: The Lord is there.'" (Rodkinson, *The Babylonian Talmud*, Vol. XIII, p. 212.)

The *Midrash Tehillim*, Commentary on Psalms, 200—500 A. D., says on Ps. 21:1: "God calls King Messiah by His own name. But what is His name? Answer: Jehovah is a man of war (Ex. 15:3)." And concerning Messiah we read: "*Yahwe* Our Righteousness. And this is His name," etc. (Jer. 23:6).

Midrash Mishle, Commentary on Proverbs, 200—500 A. D., has the following: "R. Hunna (ca. 212—297) said: Eight names are given to the Messiah, which are: Yinnon (Ps. 72:17, sprout), Shiloh, David, Menachem (Comforter; cp. Lam. 1:16), Jehovah, Justitia nostra, Zemach, Elias."

Echa Rabbathi, 200—500 (Lamentations in Large Commentary on Pentateuch and five scrolls), on Lam. 1:16: "What is the name of Messiah? R. Abba Ben Cahana (200—300 A. D.) has said: Jehovah is His name, and this is proved by 'This is His name' (Jer. 23:6)." (Schoettgen, *Horae Hebraeicae*, p. 200; Calov, Ad Jer. 23:6, p. 427 A).

On the other hand, there are many Jewish interpreters who disagree with the authorities just cited.

The Targum paraphrases: "And this is His name whereby He shall be called: Our righteousness shall come to us from the face of the Lord because of our reverence." Quoted by Hengstenberg, *Christologie*, III, 558. Calov, Ad Jer., p. 427 B.

The LXX translates: "And this (is) His name, which the Lord shall call Him: Iosedek."

"Rabbi Saadi Gaon (892—942), as quoted by Aben Ezra, and Menasse ben Israel translate: This is His name that Jehovah shall call Him." Keil,

ad Jer. 23:6. Keil adds: "This translation is rejected by most Jews as conflicting with the accents." Calov, on the other hand, quotes Saadi Gaon on Dan. 7:13: "Behold with the clouds of heaven one like the Son of Man. This is Messiah, our Righteousness."

Dav. Kimchi (1160—1240): "The Israelites call Messiah by this name, *Jehovah Zidkenu*, because in His times the righteousness of God will be firm and stabile for us and shall never withdraw." (Schoettgen, *Horae Hebr.*, p. 4. 200.)

In the history of the interpretation of this passage we may distinguish three classes:

1. The Messiah here is directly called Jehovah Our Righteousness.

2. The name ascribed to the Branch is a symbolical name in analogy to Zedekiah, or to such symbolical names as Jehovah-yireh etc. (Gen. 16:14; 22:14; 33:20; 35:7; Ex. 17:15; Judg. 6:24), which prove that Jer. 23:6 is a symbolic name in the form of a sentence stating no more than that Jehovah is our righteousness, and that this passage cannot be used as a prooftext for the deity of the Messiah.

3. The name is applied not to Messiah, but is a symbolical name ascribed to Jerusalem, or Israel-Judah, as proved by Jer. 33:16.

Leaving the refutation of interpretation three to the discussion of Jer. 33:14-16, we shall now show that a study of the passages listed under 2 above will disprove the claim that Jer. 23:6 is formed in analogy to these passages.

a. "Zedekiah" is not "most perfectly analogous" to *Jehovah Zidkenu*, as Hengstenberg (*Christologie des Alten Testaments*, Vol. III, p. 560) asserts. Zedekiah is a composite noun, quite the common formation of Jewish proper names. *Jehovah Zidkenu* is a name composed of two separate nouns. *Jehovah Nissi*, the Lord, my banner, Ex. 17:15, is an analogous formation.

b. In Gen. 16:14, etc., an inanimate object, which none of the persons involved would ever have intended to identify with Jehovah, is given a name which briefly describes the nature and meaning of the event narrated in the preceding context. In Jer. 23:6 a name is given not to an inanimate object, but to a human being, and one who was well known to be more than a human being, the promised

Messiah, whom Eve had recognized as the Lord (Gen. 4:1); and Hagar (Gen. 16:13; cp. v. 7-11, "Angel of the LORD"); and David (2 Sam. 7:19; Ps. 45:6-7); whom God had acknowledged as His Son (Ps. 2:7-12), as Immanuel (Is. 7:14), as the Mighty God, the Everlasting Father (Is. 9:6-7); to whom He had said: Sit Thou at My right hand (Ps. 110:1).

c. In Jer. 23:6 it is not a human being who speaks, as in the passages listed under 2. It is Jehovah, who has said Is. 42:8. Jehovah now states clearly that the name of the Branch shall be Jehovah. Jehovah speaks realities!

d. We must not overlook the unusual manner in which this name is introduced. The Lord does not merely say: His name is or shall be (e. g., Gen. 17:5b; Ezek. 48:35), nor: Call Him (Gen. 16:14; 33:20; 35:7; Judg. 6:24), nor: Call His name (Gen. 16:11, 13; 21:3; 22:14; Ex. 17:15), nor: This shall He be called (Jer. 33:16). He uses a phraseology unique in the entire Old Testament, occurring only here. "And this (is) His name which one shall call Him." That is not idle redundancy. Two facts of greatest importance are stressed. The first one: "This (is) His name. Name, as used here by the Lord, is not a mere label or tag, but designates the very nature, the essence and being of the Branch. And secondly, He expresses His will that mankind should know this *Zemach* and acknowledge Him and call Him by that name, given to Him by the Lord God of Hosts, which describes to us His inmost essence, as Jehovah Himself knows and understands it. God is not satisfied if one merely calls His Messiah a man, or the Branch of David, or the Righteous One, or the Wise and Understanding One, or the King and Ruler, or the Executor of Judgment and Justice, or the Establisher of a new world order, or the Prince of Peace and Security. No, though He is all that, and all that in the highest possible sense, far excelling the sense in which these terms are usually understood in our day, the Christ of God is far more than that. And He would not be the Christ of God and could not be the Savior of the world if He were not far more than what men usually connect with these terms. *This* is His name, which I, the Lord, give to Him, and which one shall call Him, Lord, Jehovah, I Am That I Am. The Messiah our Savior is, with the Holy Ghost, Most High in the glory of God the Father, God of God, Light of Light, Very God of Very God, being of one substance with the Father.

On "our righteousness" see remarks on "righteous" pp. 189—192.

Vv. 7-8. The promise of deliverance out of the Babylonian cap-

195

tivity overshadowing the deliverance out of Egypt (ch. 16:14-15) is repeated here and linked by "therefore" to the promise of the coming of the Branch as to its underlying cause. Only for the sake of the vicarious atonement to be effected by the promised Messiah did God graciously grant to His Old Testament people another opportunity to dwell in Palestine as in the Promised Land and as God's own people. And after the final rejection of Judah as a nation (1 Thess. 2:15-16), for the sake of this Branch individual Jews and Israelites will be received into God's kingdom, even though they will not return to Canaan, since this land has lost its symbolical significance. Now the Christian Church is the true homeland of all believers on earth (Heb. 12:22ff.; Gal. 4:21-31; 6:15-16).

3. Against the Prophets, Vv. 9-40

A. The wickedness of the prophets, vv. 9-15

9 Against the prophets. My heart is broken within me; all my bones tremble; I am like a drunken man and as a strong man overpowered by wine, in the presence of the LORD and in view of the words 10 of His holiness. For the land is full of adulterers. For the earth mourns because of a curse, and because of a curse the pastures of the steppe are dried up. Their course is wickedness, and their 11 power is crookedness. For the prophets as well as the priests are defiled, and even in My house I have found their wickedness, is 12 the oracle of the LORD. Therefore their way shall become for them as slippery places in dense darkness. They shall be pushed forward and fall on it. For I shall bring evil upon them in the year of their reckoning, is the oracle of the 13 LORD. In the prophets of Samaria I observed insipid folly; they prophesied by Baal and led My people 14 Israel astray. But in the prophets of Jerusalem I observe horrible sins, adultery and fraudulent dealing. They strengthen the hands of evildoers, so that no one turns away from his evil deeds. They all are to Me as Sodom, and her inhabitants are as Gomorrah! 15 Therefore thus says the LORD of Hosts concerning the prophets: Behold, I will feed them with wormwood and give them poison water to drink. For from the prophets of Jerusalem ungodliness has spread out over all the land.

V. 9. The "prophets" are not the prophets of Baal (1 Kings 16:31; 18:19-29; Jer. 2:8), from whom they are distinguished (vv. 13, 27); nor the "sons of the prophets," organized into schools by Samuel (1 Sam. 10:10-11; 19:18-24; 1 Kings 18:4, 13; 20:35-43; 2 Kings 2:3-18; 9:1-13; Amos 7:14), for these are always described as true prophets of the Lord. The prophets opposed here by Jeremiah were such as purported to speak in the name of the Lord but were disowned by Him. Already Moses had warned against them (Deut. 13:1-3;

18:20-22). We meet them in the time of Ahab, ca. 900—850 (1 Kings 22:5-12), opposing the true prophets (vv. 7-9, 13-28). They were very numerous in Jeremiah's time, antagonistic to him, but popular (Jer. 5:30f.; 14:13-18; 26:7-16; 28:1-17; 29:20-32; 37:18-21). "My heart is broken." This phrase denotes a heart crushed and terrified by God's judgment and filled with hatred of sin (Ps. 34:18 [M. T. 19]; Ps. 51:17 [19]). The heart broken by reproach (Ps. 69:20 [21]) is not only sorrowful, but filled with indignation and holy wrath against His adversaries (Ps. 69:21-28). Jeremiah's heart is filled with indignation against prophets that dishonor the Lord and His holy Word by placing their word on a level with God's, palming off the dreams of their deceitful and wicked heart as the oracles of the God of truth. It breaks his heart with sorrow to see his people deceived and led into ruin by these wicked men who promise them peace and prosperity. Such wickedness and the resultant judgments agitate him so violently that his very bones tremble and he loses self-control, like a man overcome by wine, as he sees the Lord preparing the very judgments He has threatened and which these prophets and the deceived people sneeringly refuse to believe.

Vv. 10-12. Adultery, physical and spiritual, is rampant. "Swearing," rather, "curse"; the curse pronounced, e. g., Lev. 26:14ff.; Deut. 28:15ff., is being fulfilled; the land mourns (Jer. 14:1ff.). "Course," what they run after, is wickedness; their "force," strength, is used for doing what is not "right," "straight." Not only the masses are guilty, the spiritual leaders are leaders in wickedness, polluting even the Temple by their idolatry (ch. 32:34; Ezek. 8:5-6) and hypocrisy, while the prophets concur in lulling the people into false security (v. 11). Their way, the way they chose, will be a slippery, dangerous one, on which they will have to walk in the darkness of sin and unbelief. No light of God's Word will illumine their path. Unmercifully they will be driven on by Satan to their ruin, for God has rejected them, will bring on the year, the long time, of punishment (v. 12); cp. ch. 13:16, p. 140.

Vv. 13-14. "Folly." The root idea is "unsalted, tasteless" (Job 6:6; cp. Lam. 2:14; Job 1:22; 24:12), foolishly sinful. The prophets of Baal in the Northern Kingdom were guilty of foolish superstitions, silly auguries, not only foolish, but sinful and offensive to God. But they at least were honest; they prophesied by Baal, not by the Lord. These deceivers of Israel were regarded as particularly wicked people by the Jews. Yet in the Lord's eye the prophets of Judah were far more wicked (cp. ch. 3:6-11). While professing to be the Lord's prophets, they were guilty of a "horrible thing" (v. 14). The Hebrew term occurs only five times (Hos. 6:10; Jer. 5:30; 18:13; 23:14; 29:17), denoting extreme wickedness. The prophets were adulterers. Experience teaches that moral offenses occur frequently among fanatic prophets and preachers (cp. Jer. 29:23). "Walk in lies," which had become second nature to them; leaders in, and seducers to, wickedness, until Judah had become a second Sodom.

V. 15. "Wormwood," *Artemisia absinthium,* very bitter, used as a vermifuge. "Gall," a poison plant, perhaps poison hemlock (Deut. 29:18), of quick growth (Hos. 10:4), bitter (Ps. 69:21); used of bitter, poisonous grapes (Deut. 32:32), of poison of serpents (Deut. 32:33; Job 20:16). Like preachers, like people! Seducer and seduced shall perish.

B. The false prophets have not stood in God's council, nor do they follow God's Word, vv. 16-22

16 Thus says the LORD of Hosts: Do not listen to the words of the prophets that prophesy to you. They are deceiving you. They speak the vision of their own heart, not from the mouth of the LORD.
17 They say continually to those that despise Me: "The LORD has spoken: 'You shall have peace!'" and to everyone walking in the hardness of his heart they say: "No harm shall come to you!"
18 For who has stood in the council of the LORD to see and hear His Word? Who has paid attention to
19 His Word and heard it? Behold the LORD's stormwind! Fury is gone forth, and a whirlwind, hurling itself against the heads of the
20 wicked. The wrath of the LORD will not turn back until it has accomplished and carried out the plans of His heart. In the end of the days you shall fully under-
21 stand it. I have not sent the prophets, yet they ran! I did not speak
22 to them, yet they prophesied! If they had stood in My council, then they would have announced My Word to the people and would have turned them from their wicked way and from their wicked deeds.

V. 16. "Make you vain," fill you with vanity, wind, lies, befog you. "Heart," the seat of life, intellect, emotion, will, all is evil (Jer. 17:9); they speak the sinful thoughts, the selfish desires, the vain hopes of their own mind; and not "out of the mouth of the LORD" (cp. ch. 1:7, 9; 5:14).

V. 17. An example of their sinful vanity. See Jer. 5:12-13; 6:14; 14:13. "They say still," the participle with the absolute infinitive intensifies the ceaseless flow of words, whereby they seek to cover up their windy vanities and to impress and overwhelm their victims.

V. 18. There are only two possibilities to ascertain the will of God, either to stand in the council of God and there to "perceive," to see, and hear God's Word; or to "mark," pay close attention to

His Word as revealed in Scripture and thus to hear it. Neither method has been followed by the false prophets. Else they would not be promising peace to those that despise God.

Vv. 19-20. Already the judgments of God are approaching like a whirlwind, to be fully understood in the New Testament era, the latter days, when Israel's rejection will become fully manifest (1 Thess. 2:16).

Vv. 21-22. They "run," hurry with unbecoming eagerness to assume the prophetic office, without My sanction! How unlike God's prophets! (Ex. 3:11; 4:1 ff.; Amos 7:14-15; Is. 6:1-8; Jer. 1:1-15.) Their message proves that I have not sent them.

C. God's omnipresence and its implications with reference to the prophetic office
vv. 23-32

23 Am I a God at hand, is the oracle of the LORD, and not a God afar
24 off? Can anyone hide himself in secret places so that I cannot see him? is the oracle of the LORD. Do not I fill the heavens and the earth? is the oracle of the LORD.
25 I have heard what the prophets say that prophesy falsehood in My name, saying: I have dreamt!
26 I have dreamt! How long will they carry on? Do these prophets imagine — who prophesy falsehood and are prophets of the delusions
27 of their heart — do they plan to make My people forget My name by their dreams which they relate to each other, as their fathers have forgotten My name because of
28 Baal? The prophet who has received a dream should narrate a dream, but he that has received My Word should speak My Word truthfully. What has chaff in common with wheat? is the oracle of
29 the LORD. Is not My Word like fire, is the oracle of the LORD, and like a hammer that shatters the
30 rock? Therefore, behold, I am against the prophets, is the oracle of the LORD, that steal My Word
31 from one another. Behold, I am against the prophets, is the oracle of the LORD, that take their tongue
32 and oracle oracles. Behold I am against the prophets of lying dreams, is the oracle of the LORD, that narrate them and seduce My people by their deceptions and their haughty boastings; although I have not sent them, nor have I commanded them, nor will they be of any benefit whatever to this people, is the oracle of the LORD!

V. 23. Am I a God "at hand"? God is not like the gods of the heathen, a local god, confined to his shrine, his temple, whom one can approach at will, whose plans one can learn by approaching him and gaining his favor; a god whose knowledge is as limited as his sovereignty, who sees and knows only what is before him, who has no world-wide perspective, but is a provincial deity. He is rather a God afar off, dwelling where no man can approach Him; His vision and knowledge embrace all things happening in the world, past, present, and future (Ps. 33:13-15; 139:1-6). He is One that filleth heaven and earth, omnipresent, closer to every being than the skin is to our flesh, as far remote at the same time as the most distant star; and He is that because He is Jehovah. Three times He calls attention to this name (cp. Ex. 3:14). He is "I Am," unlimited by space and time, absolutely self-determining, subject to no one's beck and call, responsible to no authority, of unlimited power and wisdom, the one and only Jehovah.

The implications of this remarkable self-revelation are as varied as are the possibilities of its application. The Lord Himself makes several applications with regard to the false prophets, leaving others to the readers of this remarkable passage.

1. V. 24. Being the Lord afar off, filling heaven and earth, no hiding place can offer concealment from the Lord nor grant to the false prophets secrecy and security from His presence (Ps. 139:7-12; Amos 9:1-4).

2. V. 25. Being so close to everyone as to fill his very heart and mind, He also knows man's inmost secrets (Ps. 139:1-6). He knows the origin of their prophecy. God hears the lying prophets exclaim in boasting self-conceit: I have dreamed! as if that mere statement proved them to be prophets of the Lord. While God at times used dreams to reveal His will (Gen. 20:3; 31:24; 37:5; Matt. 1:20; 2:12, 13, 19, 22), yet the mere dreaming of a dream is not a revelation of God, nor is every dreamer a prophet. "The dream is farthest withdrawn from the control of other men. Nothing is easier than to say: Last night I dreamed this or that! Who can refute it? These prophets made an immoderate and questionable use of dreams." (Naegelsbach.) And the fact that these dreamers permitted what God had forbidden stamped their dreams as products of their own heart and the dreamers as false prophets (Deut. 13:1-3).

3. Vv. 26-27. A third application: God is able to read the malevolent purpose of the false prophets to deceive God's people. — The Lord asks two questions. One is a brief question of impatience, How long? (V. 26a.) The second extends through vv. 26-27 and is introduced by an interrogative, v. 26b, which is repeated at the beginning of v. 27. How true to life is this picture of false prophets peddling their dreams, their fantastic ideas, their delusions, from door to door with a zeal worthy of a better cause. If only preachers of the truth and Christians in general worked with equal eagerness to spread the saving truth! "As their fathers have forgotten" etc. False doctrine is as dangerous as idolatry. Every error, if accepted as God's word,

will lead man away from the truth as revealed in Holy Writ; and the more subtile the error is, the more difficult will be its detection; and the more cunningly and convincingly it is presented, the greater will be the danger of seduction. What a shameful, brazen wickedness in the presence of the omniscient God to palm off one's dreams as God's revelation, one's lying deceits as God's saving truth. How long shall God stand by and permit such shameful deceit?

4. Vv. 28-29. A fourth application. Since I am the omnipresent God, let every prophet be honest and faithful in preaching My Word. — God, who knows the heart of man, demands that man be honest. If a prophet has had a dream which he would like to tell his neighbors, let him be honest enough to say: I am telling you a dream of my own. And if a prophet has My Word, let him speak My Word faithfully, literally, as truth, just as it has been given to him, without alteration, without changing its sense in the least. How dare man mingle the chaff of his own dreams into the pure wheat of the Word of the omnipresent, omniscient Lord Jehovah in order to find more ready and willing hearers! And let every preacher of My Word, and everyone professing to be a spokesman of the Lord, guard against adding his own views and opinions to My Word! Is not My Word as a fire consuming all sinners and surely him also that dares to mingle into My Word the chaff of his own wisdom? Is not My Word like a hammer that breaks in pieces, smashes, crushes, all false teachers?

5. A fifth application (vv. 30-32): God will not tolerate false prophets, but will punish them. In order to show the justice of His intolerance and punishment, the Lord names three characteristics of false prophets which merit His severest penalties.

V. 30. They steal God's words. Whatever divine truth they preached, they did not obtain, as they claim, by divine inspiration. They stole this truth, "a man from his neighbor," from someone else, either directly from a true prophet, or from some other false prophet who also had stolen it, or from any other person. They are dishonest in claiming to be God's messengers, while He had not sent them, and they were dishonest in the purpose for which they used what truth they preached. Their purpose was to cover up their lies and errors by these truths, which served as a sugar-coating for their poisonous errors. "Unmixed falsehood betrays itself too easily and is insipid. But falsehood mingled with truth is powerful error, and the beauty of truth serves to embellish and cover the ugliness of error." (Naegelsbach.)

V. 31. A second characteristic. They "use," literally, "take," their tongues. The true prophet spoke an oracle of the Lord only when the Lord put His words into the mouth or on the tongue of the prophet (Jer. 1: 7, 9; 2 Sam. 7: 1-5; Amos 2: 11; 3: 8). The false prophets fairly thirsted for an opportunity to gush forth their own wisdom or folly and had the audacity to palm off as an oracle of Jehovah what was frequently silly twaddle, tongue gymnastics.

V. 32. A third characteristic. They prophesy *false* dreams, opinions, judgments, principles, which not only lack wisdom, but are downright lies, falsehoods, deceptions; which they keep on telling, repeating, and thereby cause God's people to err by their lies, and by their "lightness," their empty, vacuous talk, satisfying only their craving to hear themselves talk. Talk they will, tell lies they will, even though they lead their followers into error and destruction. Three times the Lord, omnipresent, omnipotent, omniscient, tells them, I am against you! What a contrast to Jer. 1: 8, 19!

D. Do not use the name and Word of God in vain! Vv. 33-40

33 And if this people or a prophet or a priest asks you: What is the burden of the LORD? then you shall tell them: You are the burden! And I will cast you off! is
34 the oracle of the LORD. And the prophet and the priest and the people which will say: Burden (*massa*) of the LORD, I will punish
35 this man and his house. So shall everyone say to his neighbor and everyone to his brother: What has the LORD answered? and what
36 has the LORD said? "Burden of the LORD" you shall no more mention, for His Word shall become for everyone the burden; for ye have perverted the Word of the living God, the LORD of Hosts,
37 our God. Thus shall you say to the prophet: What has the LORD answered, and what has the LORD
38 said? And if you say "Burden of the LORD," then thus says the LORD: Because you say this word, "Burden of the LORD," while I sent to you, saying: Do not say
39 "Burden of the LORD," Therefore behold! I will absolutely forget you and will cast you and the city which I have given to you and your
40 fathers, from Me; and I will place upon you eternal shame and eternal dishonor which shall not be forgotten.

Grammatical Notes

V. 33. "What burden?" אֶת־מַה־מַשָּׂא. LXX, ancient Latin, and Vulgate divide the unpointed text to read אַתֶּם הַמַּשָּׂא. You are the burden! The combination אֶת־מַה־מַשָּׂא is unusual, and the translation of Keil: "With reference to your question, What burden? I will unload you," is rather unwieldy. The LXX reading is more effective, less unwieldy, and the sense is unchanged.

V. 39. "Utterly forget," וְנָשִׁיתִי אֹשׁ, a play on מַשָּׂא, which a number of Hebrew manuscripts and ancient versions needlessly change to וְנָשָׂאתִי אֹשׁ, "I will take you up" and cast you down.

V. 33. To the denouncement of false prophets is added a prohibition of the mocking, blasphemous use of the term *"massa"* for
the divine prophecies. The Hebrew word *massa* has a double meaning.
It is derived from a root "to lift up," the noun denoting "burden."
The verb is often used in connection with "voice" in the sense of
lifting up one's voice, uttering words. So Gen. 27:38; Is. 24:14; etc.;
without "voice" in the sense of "speak," Num. 14:1; Is. 3:7; 42:2;
Ex. 20:7; etc. Hence the noun *massa,* usually translated "burden" in
the A. V., Luther: *Last,* was used in the sense of prophecy, including
prophecies of evil (Is. 13:1; 15:1; etc.), and of both good and evil
(Mal. 1:1; Hab. 1:1; etc.).

Jeremiah's public prophecies addressed to an impenitent people,
hardening their hearts against God's Law and God's Gospel, naturally
were preponderatingly prophecies of condemnation, though personally
he would far rather have changed the character of his message
(cp. 15:10; 20:8-9).

He spoke of burdens indeed, the burdens of guilt piled up by
the people and the burdens of penalties to follow in the wake of this
massive guilt. Sneeringly the people and their leaders privately and
publicly asked the prophet while meeting him on the street or in
the Temple: "What is the burden today? Have you thought up a new
burden for us?" And when they gathered together, they asked one
another: "Have you heard Jeremiah's latest burden? What new
burden has this calamity howler for us?" "Thou shalt then say unto
them: What burden?" Rather, "You are the burden." (See Grammatical Notes above.) "I will even forsake you," uproot, eradicate
them by having them deported.

Vv. 34-35. Because of this shameful abuse the term "massa"
shall no longer be used, neither by prophets, priests, nor people.
God threatens severe penalties for the use of this word. Rather should
they say: "What hath the Lord answered" in response to our request
for an oracle, or "spoken" as a revelation of His will?

V. 36. Another reason is added for the prohibition of the term
"massa": "Every man's word shall be his burden" (cp. Matt. 12:36-37).
If the Lord forbids to use a certain word, the use of this word will
become for that man a burden dragging him down to hell, unless
he finds forgiveness. "Ye have perverted etc." They were heaping
their insults not only on an innocent fellow man, nor only on a prophet
who had faithfully performed his office for a quarter century, a man
of God, divinely appointed and honored as God's messenger to Israel

and to all nations. The Lord charges them with perverting, twisting His Word, making God's terminology the butt of their jokes, blasphemously disparaging "the words of the living God, of the LORD of Hosts, our God."

Vv. 38-40. Since they would persist in their disdain of God and His Word, the Lord in scornful irony plays upon the same word "massa," with which they had made merry. "I will utterly forget you." (See Grammatical Notes.) "And I will cast you out of My presence, away from My face, My countenance." On the sense of "face" here compare Num. 6: 25-26. As you have reproached and put to shame My words, so will I bring upon you everlasting, perpetual reproach which shall not be forgotten, unforgotten by Me, unforgettable to you.

CHAPTER 24

4. The Symbol of the Two Baskets of Figs

A. The basket of good figs, vv. 1-7

1 The LORD caused me to see, and, behold, two baskets of figs placed in front of the Temple of the LORD (after Nebuchadrezzar, the king of Babylon, had deported Jehoiachin, the son of Jehoiakim, the king of Judah, and the princes of Judah and the craftsmen and the carpenters from Jerusalem and brought 2 them to Babylon). The one basket contained very good figs, as the early figs; the other, very bad figs, which were so bad that they could 3 not be eaten. And the LORD said to me: What are you seeing, Jeremiah? Then I said: Figs; the good figs very good, the bad figs very bad, which are so bad that they 4 cannot be eaten. And the word of the LORD came to me, saying: 5 Thus says the LORD, the God of Israel: Like these good figs, so will I regard with favor the exiles of Judah, whom I have sent out of this place into the land of the 6 Chaldeans. And I will direct Mine eyes upon them for good, and I will bring them back into this land and build them, and not tear them down; I will plant them, and not 7 root them out. And I will give to them a heart to know Me, that I am the LORD. They shall be a people unto Me, and I will be their God, for they shall return to Me with all their heart.

Grammatical Notes

V. 1. "Were set" מוּעָדִים, Part. Hophal of יָעַד, to determine, appoint (cp. 2 Sam. 20:5; Jer. 47:7; Ex. 21:8, 9). The Hiphil occurs three times, always in the sense of calling into court, arraigning (Job 9:19; Jer. 49:19; 50:44), appoint Me the time = arraign Me. The Hophal occurs again Ezek. 21:16 (MT 21:21), "thy face is set," appointed, ordered, by the Lord. In this sense the word is used here.

V. 2. "Figs," תְּאֵנָה, "sycomore," שִׁקְמָה (1 Kings 10:27; Is. 9:9; Amos 7:14).

V. 1. On the historical background of this chapter see p. 3 f. Shortly after the deportation of Jehoiachin, here called Jeconiah,

Jeremiah was granted a remarkable vision by the Lord, who sees things not as man sees them (1 Sam. 16:7), a vision of divine comfort to the prophet and the exiles, of divine warning to the people remaining in Judah and Jerusalem. "The LORD showed me," caused me to observe, an expression quite frequently used to indicate the divine origin of the vision (cp. Ex. 25:9; Zech. 1:20; 3:1; Amos 7:1, 4,7). This vision has no connection with the custom of offering the first fruits to the Lord (Deut. 26:1ff.). No Jew would have dared to offer a basket of such rotten figs, nor would the priests have permitted such a basket to remain standing before the Temple, here called "palace" in the original text (cp. Jer. 7:4; 50:28; 51:11; Is. 6:1; etc.). It is the royal dwelling place of the King and Judge of all the world, the Searcher of hearts (Jer. 17:9-10). The vision does not refer to the figs as gifts of the people; the figs rather are symbols of the people (vv. 5-10). The two baskets of figs "were set" (see Grammatical Notes), appointed, cited, arraigned, before His judgment seat to receive their verdict. The symbol recedes into the background, the prophet sees the people symbolized by the baskets arraigned in God's court.

V. 2. The figs in the one basket were very good, like the early figs ripening in June, regarded as a delicacy (cp. Is. 28:4, "hasty," i. e., early, "fruit"; Micah 7:1). The figs in the other basket were very bad, which could not be eaten, literally, which are not eaten, which do not, or no longer, serve their purpose, to delight and nourish, so bad, so spoiled were they, fit only to be thrown away. Some commentators think here of the fruit of the sycomore, or mulberry-fig tree, "which unless they are punctured while they ripen contain an acrid juice which renders them uneatable" (*Bible Commentary, in loc.*). Yet the latter is always called sycomore, never fig, see Grammatical Notes.

Vv. 3-5. Three times in this important matter the information is designated as coming from the Lord (vv. 3, 4, 5). First He asks His prophet: What seest thou? (Cp. Jer. 1:11,13; Amos 8:2.) The vision was not a product of the prophet's mind, a mere psychological phenomenon. It came to him by divine revelation. The prophet sees only the two baskets and their contents. The Lord must interpret these symbols, and does so. "Like these good figs, so will I acknowledge them that are carried away. . . ." Acknowledge, look at closely, recognize on the basis of close observation (Gen. 27:23; Job 4:16); to acknowledge, regard favorably (Deut. 21:17; 33:9; Is. 63:16).

Judged by outward appearance, the Jews still dwelling in Jerusalem were God's favorites (cp. Ezek. 11:15), while the Jews in Babylon were exiles, sent there by the Lord Himself (v. 5) because of their sins and iniquities. Yet these castaways the Lord regards as "these good figs." In these He takes delight as a man rejoices over the first figs of the season. This high regard He had shown even when He caused them to be deported; He had done that "for their good," to spare them the horrors of the last siege and destruction of Jerusalem.

V. 6. In Babylon, the foreign country, they are not removed from His gracious presence and protection. Throughout the Exile He sets His eyes upon them for good. The perfect denotes the completed action extending throughout the duration of their captivity (cp. Ezek. 11:16). In his own time He will lead them back to their homeland and build and plant them there, give them a firmly established home.

V. 7. The best gift of all and the basic gift for the material blessings of v. 6 is the renewal of their heart. Lovingly they shall know Him as the Lord, the God of the Covenant, who keeps His promises as He had carried out His threats; and so they shall be His people, and He will be their God. Why? They shall return to Him with their whole heart, they shall dedicate their whole life to Him in faith and trust and love. Not by their own power, but because He will give them a heart to know Him; He will create in them the seat and source of a new life that consists in the knowledge of their Covenant God. For them, indeed, the Exile was to be a source of unending good, of richest divine blessing.

B. The basket of bad figs, vv. 8-10

8 But like the bad figs, which are so bad that they cannot be eaten, surely, says the LORD, so will I make Zedekiah and his princes and the remnant of Jerusalem, both those who remain in this land and 9 those who live in Egypt. I will give them for perturbation to every kingdom of the earth, a shame and a proverb, a byword and a curse in all the places to which I have 10 driven them. And I will send the sword and famine and pestilence among them, until they are annihilated from the land which I gave to them and to their fathers.

Grammatical Notes

V. 8. As the evil figs — so will I give. ותן‎, to give, place, establish, make, render, with ל‎, to render similar to, like something in a certain respect (Gen. 42:30, in his charge and treatment of them; Ruth 4:11, with reference to building the house of Israel; 1 Kings 10:27, with regard to their number). In our text, with regard to their nature and their fate.

V. 8. "Surely," כי‎ is used here as an affirmative (cp. Lam. 3:22; Ps. 118:10, 11, 12), surely, certainly.

V. 8. "And like the evil figs which are not eaten because they are so evil, so will I make Zedekiah. . . ." Since rulers as well as people persist in being and doing evil in spite of the long-continued pleading of the Lord and His prophets, the Lord will make them like the evil figs shown to Jeremiah. He will progressively render them more like these figs, gradually harden them in their enmity against the Lord. On the path they have chosen and will not give up, He will lead them deeper and deeper into sin and depravity. Compare the hardening of Pharaoh (Exodus 6—14) and the thrice-repeated "gave" Rom. 1:24, 26, 28. That is the curse of sin. That is God's penalty for the sinner who persistently closes his eyes and ears and heart against God's Word. And as evil figs are thrown away, so God will reject His apostate, depraved people.

V. 9. He will cast them out of His holy land, either by scattering them among the heathen kingdoms or by surrendering them to the three furies: sword, famine, epidemics. Thus will this evil generation, the rotten figs, be completely removed from the land graciously given to them and to their fathers by the God of the Covenant.

As the impartial Judge He makes no distinction. King Zedekiah and his court as well as the people, those dwelling in Jerusalem as well as those who, in contempt of the land to which God had brought them out of the land of bondage (Ex. 12:42; Deut. 5:15; Is. 30:1-2; Jer. 2:6, 18), had made, or would make, Egypt their dwelling place (Jer. 42:1-22). In ch. 42:15-18 Jeremiah repeats the threat of ch. 24:10, and in ch. 42:10-12 he promises to those that would remain in Judah the same blessings promised ch. 24:6 to the exiles at Babylon.

And even in exile their punishment will not cease. In contrast to their fellow Jews at Babylon, whom they despised, yet upon whom the eye of the Lord shall be for good, they will meet the fate of rotten figs, of evil people. God will "deliver them to be removed." (See Grammatical Notes on ch. 15:4.) In all the kingdoms, no matter to which distant land the Lord will send them, He will cause them to live in constant trembling fear of their enemies, to suffer evils and maltreatments of every kind, to be exposed to the gibes and jokes, and ridicule, and slanders, and maledictions, and desecrations of the people. And the cause of the persecutions and enmities they had to endure was not their faith and loyalty to their Lord and Messiah (cf. Matt. 5:10-11), but their rejection of their Covenant God and His promise. Instead of being blessed by the nations (Deut. 4:6-8), they became the accursed people.

207

IX. The Faithful Preacher, Ch. 25

CHAPTER 25

1. During the Past Twenty-Three Years, Vv. 1-7

1 The word which came to Jeremiah concerning all the people of Judah, in the fourth year of Jehoiakim, the son of Josiah, king of Judah — this is the first year of Nebuchad-
2 rezzar, king of Babylon — which Jeremiah the prophet spoke concerning all the people of Judah and all the inhabitants of Jerusalem,
3 saying: From the thirteenth year of Josiah, the son of Amon, king of Judah, up to this day, for these twenty-three years the word of the LORD came to me, and I spoke to you at all times diligently. Yet you
4 did not hear. And the LORD sent to you all His servants, the proph-
ets, at all times; yet you did not hear nor did you incline your ears
5 to hear. They said: Let everyone turn from his wicked way and from the wickedness of your works, and you shall live in this land which the LORD has given to you and to your fathers from everlasting to
6 everlasting. Do not follow other gods to serve them and to worship them, and do not provoke Me to anger by the work of your hands,
7 and I will not harm you. But you did not listen to Me, is the oracle of the LORD, in order to provoke Me to anger by the work of your hands for your own harm.

Vv. 1-2. The fourth year of Jehoiakim was an important year. (Cp. p. 12 f.) The battle of Carchemish, making Babylon the mistress of Western Asia, the death of Nabopolassar, and the ascent of Nebuchadrezzar to the throne, all were epochal events, of life-and-death importance also to Judah and Jerusalem. Once more the Lord sounded the voice of warning, pleaded with His people to read and consider the handwriting on the wall, to return to their loving Husband in repentant trust and loving service before He would cast them out of His land into captivity in a foreign country. Though He knew that even this call to return to Him would remain unheeded, His love to His people constrains Him to make another effort, and His faithful prophet is ready to continue his thankless office of being God's spokesman (v. 2).

V. 3. In a survey of the twenty-three years of his activity since his call in the thirteenth year of King Josiah, the prophet points out his unflagging zeal ("rising early and speaking") in proclaiming to the people of Judah and Jerusalem the Word of the Lord as it came to him. And loyally he performed his divine duty, although throughout the twenty-three years he met only with a universal refusal to hear and obey his message.

V. 4. This disobedience was the more reprehensible because he was not the only messenger the Lord sent to His people. Untiringly the Lord kept on sending His prophets and wearied not, although

208

He saw all His efforts to bring His people to repentance remain as unsuccessful as Jeremiah's eager labors. The people would not hear Jeremiah, nor the prophets, nor the Lord. Five times this disobedience is mentioned vv. 3-8.

Vv. 5-7. "They said" introduces the contents of the message the prophets proclaimed by divine command: "Turn from your evil ways, and you shall dwell in the Land of Promise." Two imperatives: Turn! Live! the second being the strongest incentive to obey the first. Yet neither imperative, that of the unfailing promise of the Lord of unending mercy as little as that of the just demand of the Lord of unchanging holiness, evoked obedience, though both were the living and life-giving Word of the Lord of life. Just as little success greeted the added admonition not to serve other gods nor to provoke the Lord to anger by their idolatrous conduct, and the promise that then no harm would come to them, while disobedience would result in their own hurt.

2. His Faithfulness in Continuing His Thankless Duty, Vv. 8-38

A. Judah and the neighboring countries under Babylon's rule for seventy years until Babylon's fall, vv. 8-14

8 Therefore thus says the LORD of Hosts: Because you have not listened to My Word, Behold, I am 9 about to send for and take all the tribes of the North, is the oracle of the LORD, and also Nebuchadrezzar, the king of Babylon, My servant, and I will bring them against this land and against its inhabitants and against all these nations round about, and they shall annihilate them and make them a horror and a mockery and an everlasting ruin. And I will re- 10 move out of their midst the voice of joy and the voice of rejoicing, the voice of the bridegroom and the voice of the bride, the voice of the hand mill and the light of the 11 lamp. And this whole land shall be waste and desolate, and these nations shall serve the king of 12 Babylon seventy years. But when the seventy years are completed, I will punish the king of Babylon and that nation, is the oracle of the LORD, for their guilt, and also the land of the Chaldees, and I will 13 make it desolate forever. So will I bring upon that land all My words which I have spoken against it, all that is written in this book which Jeremiah prophesied con- 14 cerning all nations. For they also shall become servants to many nations and great kings, and I will recompense them according to their deeds and the work of their hands.

Vv. 8-11. Since Judah refuses, the Lord pronounces His judgment upon His rebellious people. The enemy from the North so often mentioned during the preceding twenty-three years is now definitely named for the first time (ch. 21: 2, 7; 24: 1 were spoken in the time of Zedekiah). It is Nebuchadnezzar, the king of Babylon. He is God's servant through whom the Lord will carry out His punishment of an apostate people, a destruction so complete that not only every sound of joy and rejoicing will be silenced, but every activity stopped. No more would the grinding noise of the hand mill be heard, the routine work of the women preparing the flour for the daily bread. No more would be seen the light of the candle, the lamp in which olive oil fed the wick to give light in the darkness. There would be no more bridegrooms to rejoice over their bride, no more families to feed, no more homes to be illumined. The whole land would be devastation and destruction, a dead country, where the silence of death ruled far and wide, while the former inhabitants would be captives in the land of their enemies in far-off Babylon! There they would live not days, or months, or only a few years, but seventy long years, until most of them would be buried in foreign soil. That is the just punishment for a rebellious people refusing to hear the Lord.

Vv. 12-14. Yet this Lord is still the God of the Covenant and still the Lord of nations, the Ruler of the world. After seventy years the Lord will recompense the king of Babylon and his people for their guilt and will make their land a perpetual desolation. And He will do that in accordance with all the words He had spoken to His people, as they were written in the book of prophecies by His servant Jeremiah, whom He had appointed a prophet over the nations (ch. 1:10) and whose word would be fulfilled to the letter, both threats and promises.

The Lord of the Covenant, who must fulfill the threats of the covenant because of the wickedness of His people and because He is the God of unchanging holiness and justice, still remains the Lord of unfailing mercy and loving-kindness and therefore provides the necessary means to keep His children from despair and to nourish and preserve their faith even in the sorrowful days of the Exile.

V. 14. "Serve themselves of," enslave Babylon, cause Babylon to serve them, and thus will proud and cruel Babylon be recompensed for its enslavement of the nations.

B. Jeremiah makes the nations drink the cup of God's fury, vv. 15-29

15 For thus the LORD God of Israel said to me: Take this cup of wine, of fury, from My hand, and make all the nations to which I am send-
16 ing you, drink it. And they shall drink and stagger and rave because of the sword which I am sending 17 into their midst. And I took the cup from the hand of the LORD, and I made all the nations to which 18 the LORD sent me, drink it; Jerusalem, and the cities of Judah, and their kings and their princes, to make them waste and desolate, an

19 object of hisses and curses, as it is on this day; to Pharaoh, the king of Egypt, and to his servants and

20 his princes and all his people, and to all the mingled people, and to all the kings of the land of Uz, and all the kings of the land of the Philistines, and Ascalon, and Gazah, and Ekron, and the remnant of

21 Ashdod, to Edom, and to Moab, and

22 to the children of Ammon, and to all the kings of Tyrus, and to all the kings of Sidon, and to all the kings of the islands which are

23 beyond the sea, and to Dedan, and to Tema, and to Buz, and to all

24 that cut short the hair, and to all the kings of Arabia, and all the kings of the mingled people that

25 dwell in the desert, and to all the kings of Zimri, and to all the kings of Elam, and to all the kings of the

26 Medes, and to all the kings of the North, near and far, the one and the other, and to all the kingdoms of the world which are on the earth; and King Sheshach shall

27 drink after them. And you shall say to them: Thus says the LORD of Hosts, the God of Israel: Drink and become drunk, and vomit, and fall, and do not rise again from the sword which I am sending among

28 you. And if they refuse to take the cup from your hand to drink, then you shall say to them: Thus says the LORD of Hosts: You will have

29 to drink, drink! For, behold, I am beginning to destroy the city which is called by My name, and shall you go altogether unpunished? You shall not remain unpunished! For I am calling the sword upon all the inhabitants of the earth, is the oracle of the LORD!

Grammatical Notes

V. 15. "This wine cup of fury." Fury, חֵמָה, is explanatory apposition to wine. הַזֹּאת, this, refers to כּוֹס, fem., or to "fury." Drink "it," אֹתוֹ, refers to יַיִן, masc.

V. 26. "Sheshach" is the cipher writing called *atbash*, in which the letters of the Hebrew alphabet were written out in one line, and in another line under the first were written in reverse order, so that ת was written under א, ש under ב, ר under ג etc.

V. 15. "Drinking the cup of God's wrath," is a figure frequently employed by the prophets (e. g., Is. 51:17, 22; Ezek. 23:31-34; Hab. 2:16; Ps. 60:5 [A. V., v. 3]; Jer. 49:12; 51:7; etc.). The cup contains not wine, but wrath; and this wrath the prophet is to offer to the people by proclaiming it to them (cp. v. 27, "say unto them"; v. 30, "prophesy unto them"). The word of the prophet being God's word caused them to drink, to suffer God's wrath, even as the word of the judge causes the criminal's punishment. There is as little need to think of a literal wine cup here as, e. g., in Is. 51:17, 21, 22.

V. 16. Like a drunken man reeling on to his fall and ruin, so the nations weakened by their vices are given over by divine justice to madness and infatuation, reel on with tottering steps toward destruction. *Quem Deus vult perdere, prius dementat.*

V. 17. The prophet carries out God's command by proclaiming the message of God's wrath and impending doom to the nations.

V. 18. The judgment begins at Jerusalem and all the cities of Judah, the people of God (cp. 1 Peter 4:17), because they had been granted greater grace than any other nation (Luke 12:47-48). In fact, the judgment upon Jerusalem had already begun. In the preceding year, the third of Jehoiakim, Nebuchadnezzar had taken Jerusalem and deported a number of Jews and some of the Temple vessels to Babylon (Dan. 1:1-4). That was the beginning of the destruction that was to overtake wicked Jerusalem and make the land an object of horror, derision, and cursing to the surrounding nations. So it was already "this day," in the fourth year of Jehoiakim.

In vv. 19-26 the countries are named which were to drink the cup of God's wrath. The list begins with Egypt, the southernmost country, and "the mingled people." This term occurs for the first time Ex.12:38, "the mixed multitudes" living in Egypt, many of whom joined the Israelites at the Exodus (cp. Num. 11:4; also Ezek. 30:5), in connection with Egypt. It may mean people who were living in Egypt without having acquired citizenship, colonists, or traders, or hired soldiers. The term occurs also v. 24 in connection with Arabia, and ch. 50:37 speaks of the mingled people in Babylon. "The land of Uz," most probably the homeland of Job (Job 1:1). Lam. 4:21 speaks of Edomites dwelling in Uz, hence Uz may have bordered on Edom either to the east or, as many interpreters assume, to the west, extending to the eastern boundary of Egypt, since it is mentioned here between Egypt and Philistia. No such kingdom appears in the historical records, however. One of the five large cities of Philistia is not mentioned, Gath, probably because it had lost its importance. "The remnant of Ashdod," which had fallen after a thirty-nine year siege by Psammetich I of Egypt, ruling from 663 to 609 (cp. Herodotus, 2, 157). The city later recovered from this destruction (cp. Neh. 13:23). Now follow three kingdoms east of Jordan: Edom the southernmost, Moab, and Ammon in the north. The two powerful Phoenician cities of Tyre and Sidon and their many colonies on the coasts of the Mediterranean as far as Tartessus in Spain likewise will have to drink the cup of God's furious but righteous wrath. From the extreme West the prophet turns to the East: Dedan (cp. Gen. 10:7; Is. 21:13, 14; Jer. 49:8); Tema, Ishmaelite (Gen. 25:15); Buz (Gen. 22:21; Job 32:2); three tribes of northern Arabia. "All that are in the utmost corners," rather, "all that clip the corner" of their hair (cp. ch. 9:26). "All the kings of Arabia" and "of the mingled people," the sheiks of the many Beduin tribes dwelling in the desert country east and southeast of populated Transjordania. "Zimri" (v. 25), missing in LXX, an unknown people, perhaps neighbors to the two powerful nations next named. The name has been connected with Zimran, a son of Abraham (Gen. 25:2). Elam, on the eastern and northern coasts of the Persian Gulf, south of Media, a Semitic people (Gen. 10:22), whose king Chedor-Laomer is named as the leader of the campaign against the kings of the Valley of Siddim (Gen. 14:5), remained a powerful nation until its defeat by Ashurbanipal (668—626) and after the fall of Nineveh (612) was absorbed by Media and later by Persia. Its capital was Shushan (Neh. 1:1; Esth. 2:8). The Medes, or Madai, were Japhetites (Gen. 10:2), a powerful nation east of Assyria, north of Elam, for many centuries the opponent of Assyria, sometimes defeated, sometimes victorious, finally revolted against Assyria, destroyed Nineveh (612), divided the mighty empire with Babylon, Nebuchadnezzar taking the southern half, Cyaxares, the powerful king of Media, the northern section and extending the boundaries of Media to the River Halys, the eastern boundary of the Lydian empire. Under Cyrus (558—529), Media was merged with Persia into the Medo-Persian world power finally destroyed by Alexander the Great.

V. 26. All the kings of the world, powerful rulers as well as puny sheiks, nations great and small, famed or forgotten, peoples dwelling in populous cities and countries, or on distant shores of the sea, or in the wilderness of the desert, Shemites, Japhetites, Canaanites, all without exception and distinction shall drink the cup of destruction which Jeremiah the prophet at the command of the Lord gives to the individual kings and nations. "And the king of Sheshach shall drink after them." On Sheshach see Grammatical Notes. This form occurs also Jer. 51:41. Whether the name has a symbolic meaning, "humiliation," from a root, "to bow down," and why it was used, we can no longer decide. Certainly the reason to choose this designation was not fear to divulge the name of Babel (cp. v. 12).

Vv. 27-28. The destruction shall be a total one (v. 27), and inescapable. In spite of their refusal they shall certainly drink, for it is not man, but the Lord of Hosts who gives the cup of His wrath to these nations, and against Him there is no resistance.

V. 29. In evidence of the irresistibility of His judgment He points to Jerusalem. He is already beginning to bring evil upon the city upon which His name is called, which is still His city, in which there are still people who know and serve Him. And if His judgments are being poured out upon this city, shall the heathen nations "go unpunished"? literally, to be free from guilt and therefore free from

213

punishment. They are not guiltless, therefore they shall not and cannot escape the judgment of the just Judge, who is even now calling for the sword upon all the inhabitants of the earth, all of whom are guilty (cp. Ps. 14:2-3).

C. The universality and the horror of God's judgment upon the nations
vv. 30-38

30 And you yourself shall prophesy to them all these words and shall say to them: The LORD roars from on high and shouts from the dwelling of His holiness; He roars aloud against His pasture; He shouts as vintagers shout loud against all the
31 inhabitants of the earth. The noise reaches to the end of the earth, for the LORD has instituted a lawsuit against the nations; He sits in judgment on all nations; the wicked He delivers to the sword, is the oracle
32 of the LORD. Thus says the LORD of Hosts: Behold, evil goes forth from nation to nation, and a great tempest is rising from the ends of
33 the earth. And those who are slain by the LORD on that day shall extend from one end of the earth to the other end. Unmourned, un-gathered, unburied, they shall be
34 dung on the earth. Howl, you shepherds, and cry aloud! and wallow in the dust, you leaders of the flock! For fulfilled are your days for slaughter and your dispersions, and you shall fall down like a
35 precious vessel. And refuge shall vanish from the shepherds, and escape from the leaders of the flock.
36 Hark! the cry of the shepherds and the howling of the leaders of the flock, for the LORD is destroy-
37 ing their pasture. Devastation has come to the peaceful pastures from the furor of the LORD's anger.
38 Like a young lion He has left His covert, for their land has become desolate because of the furor of the Destroyer, because of the furor of His anger.

Grammatical Notes

V. 34. "For the days of your slaughter . . . accomplished." מָלְאוּ יָמִים is, as far as I can see, never used to denote the future fulfillment or coming of days, but always the ending of days of a certain activity; so Gen. 25:24; 29:21; 50:3; Lev. 8:33; Num. 6:5; 2 Sam. 7:12; Is. 40:2; Jer. 25:12; Lam. 4:18. Nor is it necessary to translate the active inf. לִטְבֹחַ, to slaughter, as a passive, to be slaughtered: "The days in which you shall be slaughtered, are now fulfilled, have now come." The correct translation is, Your days to, or "for," slaughter are fulfilled. The days in which you slaughtered are now ended!

V. 34. "Your dispersions," תְּפוֹצוֹתִיכֶם; the pointing presents difficulties. The Masoretes evidently regarded it as a verbal form; and Hitzig, Naegelsbach, Keil, and others have regarded it as Tiphil, reading תְּפִיצוֹתִיכֶם. LXX omits the word, Volz changes the text, since "the form is impossible." There is no need of omission nor of radical change. Gesenius-Buhl lists תְּפוֹצָה and defines it "Dispersion, diaspora." The only change needed is pointing the first וֹ as וּ. It is the plural form with preformative תְ, used quite frequently to denote acts or abstract nouns; תְּבוּאַת אָרֶץ, what the earth brings forth, תְּנוּפָה the moving (of the hands) to and fro. G.-K., par. 85 r. This suits the context. פוּץ = scatter, disperse. "Your days of slaughter and your dispersions (of people) are fulfilled, have ended."

V. 30. The prophet is exhorted to continue his prophecy of judgment, whether the nations hear or rebel. The Lord quotes Amos 1:2, but very significantly He does not name Jerusalem and Zion as the place from which His roaring issues, because here He is dealing with the Gentile nations in His kingdom of power, while Jerusalem and Zion symbolized chiefly His kingdom of grace. Moreover, Jerusalem and Zion have also become objects of His wrath, against whom He begins to roar (vv. 18, 29), and from which He is ready to withdraw His gracious presence (cp. Ezek. 11:23; Jer. 14:11-12; 15:1-2; 16:5b). From His throne on high, He, the exalted Lord, who is at the same time the Holy One, hating sin, the inveterate enemy of iniquity, who is not a respecter of persons, roars in His wrath against His "own habitation," literally, His sheepfold. The faithful Shepherd has turned into a roaring lion because of the wickedness of His flock. And as the treaders in the winepress shout aloud while treading down the grapes, so He will raise the triumphant cry of the victor over all the inhabitants of the earth lying at His feet, a conquered, vanquished host.

V. 31. Like a whirlwind He will sweep over the whole earth in global war and bloodshed.

Vv. 32-33 describe vividly the whirlwind of God's wrath as it spreads from nation to nation, until the whole earth from one end to the other is a vast necropolis in which the unburied and unlamented corpses lie like dung upon the ground.

V. 34. While often the "shepherds," the leaders of a nation, escape the sufferings of the common people, in this judgment the shepherds shall perish with their flocks. For the days of their cruel slaughtering, butchering of other nations (cp. Hab. 1:13-17; 2:8, 10, 12), are fulfilled, ended, as are also their "dispersions," their cruel custom of deporting entire nations, scattering them throughout their vast empire. Your days of glory are past, and you shall fall like a precious vessel. No matter how beautiful and costly a vessel may be, if it falls to the ground, it is broken in bits like the commonest piece of houseware. Even the glory of Babylon was not immune against a destruction which equaled its glory in its completeness.

V. 35. Every means of escape is cut off.

Vv. 36-38. Their proud boastings and imperious commands are suddenly changed to shrieks of despair and howls of mortification, for the Lord has destroyed their pastures from which they grew rich, and devastated the fields to which they owed their welfare and prosperity. Like a lion He has left His lair. Their land is devastation "from the fierceness of the oppressor," rather "from the devastating fury." Some twenty manuscripts, LXX, Latin, Targum, read *chereb*, sword, the destroying sword, the same phrase as found Jer. 46:16; 50:16. The sense is not changed by the variant.

Ch. 25 is a fitting conclusion to the First Main Division of Part One. It presents Jeremiah as the faithful spokesman of God proclaiming in selfless submission to His Lord whatever he is told to preach. Suppressing his personal feelings, he had for twenty-three years preached God's judgment against apostate Judah (vv. 1-8). He is ready to remain chiefly a preacher of condemnation, though he would far rather have preached the life-giving Gospel of God's grace. Vv. 8-38 sum up the message he is by divine command to proclaim in the future, and we hear no word of protest or dissatisfaction with his thankless profession during the remainder of the book.

SECTION TWO

The Prophet's Faithfulness in Spite of Opposition and Persecution

Chapters 26—36

X. Opposition at Home, Ch. 26—28

CHAPTER 26

1. Opposition by the People, the Priests, the Prophets, and the King

A. At God's command Jeremiah publicly foretells the destruction of the city and the Temple, vv. 1-7

1 In the beginning of the rule of Jehoiakim, the son of Josiah, the king of Judah, came this word from 2 the LORD: Thus says the LORD: Stand in the court of the house of the LORD, and speak to all the cities of Judah that come to worship in the house of the LORD all the words that I have commanded you to speak to them; do not omit 3 a word. Perhaps they will hear and turn each from his evil way so that I may repent of the evil which I am planning to bring upon them because of the wickedness of 4 their deeds. You shall say to them: Thus says the LORD: If you will not obey Me by walking in My Law, which I have placed before 5 you, and by obeying the words of My servants, the prophets, which I am sending to you with unceasing concern — although you have not obeyed — then I will make this house like Shiloh, and this very city I will make a curse to all the 7 nations of the earth. The priests and the prophets and all the people heard Jeremiah speaking these words in the house of the LORD.

Vv. 1-2. Pious King Josiah had died; Jehoahaz had ruled only three months, and now wicked Jehoiakim sat on the throne of David. On his character cp. 2 Kings 23:37; 2 Chron. 36:5-8, and particularly Jer. 22:13-19; see pp. 3, 186. During the early years of Jehoiakim's reign the Lord commanded His prophet to go to the court of the Temple and there preach to the Jews assembled from all the cities of Judah (cp. ch. 7:2). The Lord's command reminds the prophet of his first commission (ch. 1:7). The Lord particularly warns him not to diminish a single word, the only time this warning is recorded. The Lord knows that this errand would be an especially dangerous one. The protection of pious Josiah was no longer available; he would feel for the first time the full force of public persecution. At such a time Jeremiah might be tempted to omit or tone down some of the sternest condemnations. Hence the warning. The mouth of the prophet in spite of opposition from without was to remain the obedient and willing instrument of the Lord in time of persecution that it had by God's grace remained during the twenty years of Josiah's rule in spite of his own doubts and inclinations (ch. 1:9).

217

V. 3. Strong, harsh language was necessary in order to halt the downward course the nation had been pursuing with far greater fervor than they had devoted to the Lord's cause and to their own salvation. These words, however, stern and uncompromising as they were, had the building up, and planting of, the people in view: "if so be that they will hearken," etc. On the possibility of escaping the penalties threatened, cp. v. 19; ch. 18:7-8; 36:3; Jonah 3:8-9. That is not a "change" in God, but the accomplishment of His original purpose to work repentance and faith in the heart of the wicked. God's word of salvation is at the same time a cleansing and a destroying fire (Is. 6: 1-13; 55:7-11; Jer. 23:29; Mark 16:15-16; John 6:60-71; 12:44-48; 2 Cor. 2:14-16; Heb. 4:12-13).

Vv. 4-7. The prophet is told to repeat what he had already on a previous occasion proclaimed to the people (cp. ch. 7:12-15). Whether the words recorded ch. 26:4-6 were the only ones commanded him, or were a digest of a longer address along the lines of ch. 7:2-15, or were all he was permitted to speak before the riot broke out, we cannot tell. The Biblical record states that the vast audience listened until he had spoken every word the Lord had commanded him to speak, whether that was a lengthy sermon or the brief remarks recorded. The Lord had tested His prophet, and the prophet had passed the test. He had seen the scowling faces, the clenched fists, the threatening gestures, but, undaunted, he had not suppressed a word he had been told to speak. And the Lord, according to His promise (ch. 1:8), had been with him, had restrained the hatred of the enemies until he had finished his allotted task.

B. Jeremiah is arrested and sentenced to death, vv. 8-11

8 And as soon as Jeremiah had finished speaking all that the LORD had commanded to speak to all the people, the priests and the prophets and all the people arrested him, telling him: You must surely die!

9 Why do you prophesy in the name of the LORD, saying: This house shall be as Shiloh, and this city shall be waste, uninhabited? And all the people were assembled against Jeremiah in the house of 10 the LORD. When the princes of Judah heard of these matters, they went up from the king's house to the house of the LORD and sat down in the entry of the New Gate

11 of the LORD. Then the priests and the prophets addressed the princes and all the people, saying: We demand death penalty for this man! For he has prophesied against this city as you have heard with your ears!

Vv. 8-9. Jeremiah needed this encouragement, for now suddenly the storm broke in full fury. The people resented the words of the prophet. Urged on by the fanatic priests and false prophets (cp. Matt.

26:59; 27:20, 39-44; John 11:47-57), their spiritual leaders, they charged him with having spoken words worthy of death. Undoubtedly Jeremiah would have met with the fate of Stephen (Acts 7:54-60), had not the Lord come to the aid of His loyal servant (cp. Jer. 1:17-19). Jeremiah's time had not yet come. His work was not yet completed. His sufferings and persecutions had only begun. He was to become a still greater hero of faith and loyalty than he had been under the protecting aegis of Josiah. He was to overcome not only doubts, and fears, and dissatisfactions, and disappointments, and despondencies within, but stand like a strong fortress, etc. (ch. 1:18), the fiercest attacks in the form of opposition, hatred, persecution, imprisonment. In the strength of the Lord, his Righteousness, he was to come forth from every trial more than a conqueror.

Vv. 10-11. The noise of the tumult was heard in the royal palace, where the princes (see p. 32 f.) were assembled. Hurrying to the Temple, their very arrival seems to have quieted the people, and the princes sat down in the entrance of the New Gate to institute a legal and orderly investigation. The New Gate is usually identified with the gate leading to the inner, or priests', court (ch. 36:10), which was built by Jotham (2 Kings 15:35). Here the priests and prophets advance their charges before the princes and the people, who formed the highest tribunal (cp. v. 16). They demand "judgment of death for this man!" A threat such as pronounced against the Lord's house by this man is blasphemy, a mortal crime! (Cp. Ex. 20:7; Lev. 24:16; Acts 6:11-14.)

C. Jeremiah's defense, vv. 12-15

12 And Jeremiah said to all the princes and to all the people: The LORD has sent me to prophesy against this city and against this house in the terms which you have
13 heard. And now amend your ways and your works, and listen to the voice of the LORD, your God, and the LORD will repent of the evil that He has spoken against you.
14 As for me, behold! I am in your hands! Do with me what seems
15 good and right in your eyes. Only know for certain that if you are going to kill me, you are surely bringing innocent blood upon yourselves and upon this city and upon its inhabitants. For truly the LORD has sent me to you to proclaim all these words in your hearing.

V. 12. Jeremiah is given an opportunity to defend himself. He addresses the princes and the people in a masterpiece of brevity and convincing argumentation. He does not retract nor even apologize for a single word. His defense is: "Jehovah has sent me to prophesy

219

against the city!" From the court of men he appeals to the court of Jehovah. And he was too well known to all as a prophet of the Lord to admit of any possibility of refuting his claim. For the past twenty years he had been publicly acknowledged as God's spokesman (cp. Jer. 25:1ff., spoken three years later). Will you be found even to fight against God? (Acts 5:39.)

V. 13. This appeal to the Highest Tribunal is followed up by a fervent appeal to all present to repent and obey their Lord, then the evil threatened would be recalled (cp. 18:7-8).

Vv. 14-15. As far as his own person is concerned, they may do as they please. He is ready to die. Yet to sentence him to death would be murder, and his blood would be avenged upon the judges, the city, the people, by the Lord, who had sent him.

D. Jeremiah's deliverance in spite of Jehoiakim's bitter hatred of God's prophets
vv. 16-24

16 Then the princes and all the people said to the priests and to the prophets: This man is not guilty of death, because he has spoken to us in the name of the LORD, our 17 God. Then some of the elders of the land arose and addressed the whole assembly of the people: 18 Micah, the Morashthite, was prophesying in the days of Hezekiah, the king of Judah, and said to all the people of Judah: Thus says the LORD of Hosts: Zion shall be plowed, and Jerusalem be ruins, and the Mountain of the House 19 a high place in a forest. Did Hezekiah and all Judah think of killing him? Did he not fear the LORD and implore the Lord, so that the LORD repented of the evil He had spoken against them? And we are ready to commit so great a wicked- 20 ness against our souls! There also was a man prophesying in the name of the LORD, Uriah, the son of Shemaiah, from Kirjath-Jearim, and he prophesied against this city and against this land, just as Jere- 21 miah had done. And King Jehoiakim and all his military officers and all the princes heard his words, and the king sought to put him to death. When Uriah heard this, he was afraid and fled and went to 22 Egypt. But King Jehoiakim sent men to Egypt, Elnathan, the son of Akbor, and men with him to Egypt, 23 who brought Uriah out of Egypt and brought him to King Jehoiakim; and he slew him with the sword and threw his body on the 24 graves of the common people. But the influence of Ahikam, the son of Shaphan, protected Jeremiah, so that he was not surrendered to the people for execution.

Grammatical Notes

V. 16. "Then rose up." The strong ו does not indicate that the elders spoke only after the prophet had been acquitted. Very frequently it expresses "concomitant occurrence," or the narrator "in describing a series of transactions will hasten at once to state briefly the issue of the whole, and afterwards, as though forgetting that he had anticipated, proceed to annex the particulars by the strong ו" (Driver, *Hebrew Tenses*, p. 99 f.). Driver quotes Ex. 2:10; Gen. 27:24 ff., not subsequent to "so he blessed him," v. 23 b; Gen. 37:6; 42:20 ff.; 45:21-24, and other passages.

V. 16. The calm nobility of the prophet, his confident trust in the Lord, his willingness to die rather than change the Lord's Word, deeply impressed not only the princes, but also the people no longer incited by the fanatic priests. They refuse to pass sentence upon a man who had done no more than to speak to them in the name of the Lord, their God.

Vv. 17-19. This impression had been strengthened (see Grammatical Notes) by the elders, who pointed out the action of Hezekiah, the renowned king, on a similar occasion, when Micah had uttered a like prophecy against Zion and the Temple. The elders are not to be identified with the princes, but were men who by virtue of primogeniture and because of their age and experience occupied a position of honor and respect among the people (cp. Ex. 3:16, 18; 12:21; 2 Kings 6:32; 10:1; 23:2; etc.), without being officials in the strict sense of the term. In the orderly court proceedings under the leadership of the princes, these men had an opportunity to give their opinion and advice, which they did not have while the priests had inflamed the people to blind fanaticism. — The quotation from Micah is in literal agreement with Micah 3:12. One hundred years later than Micah had spoken, these elders were able to quote verbatim the text that has come down to us. A remarkable testimony for the general accuracy of the copies current among the people and handed down through the centuries!

Vv. 20-24. The murder of Uriah, the Lord's prophet, by King Jehoiakim.

While the prophet was acquitted, his opponents, smarting under their failure to get rid of Jeremiah, continued to conspire against the prophet, watched his every move, and wherever an opportunity offered sought to disparage and stigmatize the faithful ambassador of Jehovah (cp. notes on ch. 20, particularly vv. 2, 10). Jehoiakim's position toward the Lord's prophets is illustrated by his persecution of Uriah, a contemporary of Jeremiah, who, like Jeremiah, prophesied against Jerusalem and Judah. When he heard that Jehoiakim sought to put him to death, he fled to Egypt; that was not sinful cowardice, but in full keeping with the later words of Christ (Matt. 10:23). Cp. the example of Elijah (1 Kings 17:1-5; 19:1-8), Jeremiah (ch. 36:19, 26), Jesus (Matt. 2:13-23; Luke 4:28-30; John 8:59), Paul (Acts 9:23f.). Jehoiakim sent messengers to Egypt, asking the Pharaoh for a writ of extradition, and had the prophet put to death. The only reason why Jeremiah escaped death under the rule of wicked Jehoiakim was

God's promise ch. 1:19. God's instrument in this case was Ahikam, the son of Shaphan, the latter having held the office of secretary of state under King Josiah (2 Kings 22:8). Ahikam was one of the high officials whom Josiah sent to Huldah the prophetess after the finding of the Book of the Law (2 Kings 22:14) and is there named immediately after Hilkiah the high priest as the first of the civic officials. His son was Gedaliah, whom Nebuchadnezzar later appointed as governor of Judah after the destruction of Jerusalem (Jer. 40:5). The influence of God-fearing and courageous Ahikam, who boldly took sides with Jeremiah, was so great that neither the king nor the bloodthirsty priests and false prophets could carry out their wicked schemes to put Jeremiah out of the way. It may have been Ahikam whom the Lord used to hide Jeremiah and Baruch when Jehoiakim sought to slay them (Jer. 36:19, 26).

---

2. Opposition by False Prophets in Jerusalem, Ch. 27—28

CHAPTER 27

A. At a gathering of foreign ambassadors at Jerusalem, Jeremiah urges submission to the Babylonian

a. Addressing the foreign ambassadors, vv. 1-11

1 In the beginning of the rule of Jehoiakim, the son of Josiah, the king of Judah, came this word to Jeremiah from the LORD, saying:

2 Thus said the LORD to me: Make fetters and yokes for yourself, and

3 place them on your neck. And send them to the king of Edom, and to the king of Moab, and to the king of the children of Ammon, and to the king of Tyre, and to the king of Sidon, through the ambassadors that have come to Jerusalem,

4 to Zedekiah, king of Judah. And command them to say to their lords: Thus says the LORD of Hosts, the God of Israel: Thus shall

5 ye say to your lords: I have made the earth, with the men and beasts which are on the earth, by My great power and My outstretched arm, and I have given it to whom it seemed proper in Mine eyes.

6 And now I give all these countries into the hand of Nebuchadnezzar, the king of Babylon, My servant; and also the animals of the field have I given to him to serve him.

7 And all nations shall serve him, and his son, until also the time of his country shall come; and many nations and great kings shall en-

8 slave him. And the nation and the kingdom which will not serve Nebuchadnezzar, king of Babylon, and will not yield its neck to the yoke of the king of Babylon, I will punish that nation with the sword and with famine and with pestilence, is the oracle of the LORD, until I have completely put them

9 into his power. And you, do not listen to your prophets, and to your soothsayers, and to your dreamers, nor to your diviners, nor to your sorcerers who are saying to you: You will not serve the king of

10 Babylon, for they are prophesying lies to you in order to remove you far from your land, and I would have to drive you away, and you

11 would perish. But the nation which

places its neck into the yoke of
the king of Babel and serves him,
I will permit to live quietly in its

country, is the oracle of the LORD,
and till it and dwell in it.

Grammatical Notes

V. 1. "In the beginning of the rule of
Jehoiakim." Evidently "Jehoiakim" is
a copyist's error for Zedekiah, cp. vv.
3, 12, and the fact that the yoke which
Jeremiah wore by divine command
(ch. 27:2) was broken by Hananiah

(ch. 28:10) "in the same year" (ch. 28:1)
in which Jeremiah was told to wear
the yoke and send yokes to the neighboring kings (ch. 27:3), and this "same
year" is definitely stated to be the
fourth year of Zedekiah (ch. 28:1).

Vv. 1-3. Jeremiah emphasizes that all his words and actions are
carried out in obedience to God's command. The Lord tells him to
prepare "bonds," cords, ropes, with which the two parts of the
"yokes" were fastened together, and place the yoke about his neck.
Wearing this yoke (cp. ch. 28:10), he was to enter the hall where
ambassadors from five of the surrounding kingdoms were assembled.
While the purpose of the meeting is not stated, it is evident from
the prophetic warning directed by God's command to the foreign
ambassadors (vv. 4-11), to Zedekiah (vv. 12-15), and to the priests
and people at large (vv. 16-22).

Vv. 4-5. The message to the ambassadors. Jehovah, the Covenant
God of the small kingdom of Judah, is the almighty Creator of all
the earth, and of every living being, and therefore can and does give
the rule of His earth to whomsoever He pleases. The God of creation
is the God of history. The dynasties ruling in the various epochs of
history are appointees, commissioners, stewards of Jehovah, His
"servants" (v. 6). Jehovah demands obedience to His appointees
from all nations. Rebellion against them is rebellion against the Lord
of creation.

Vv. 6-7. At the present time the appointee of Jehovah is Nebuchadnezzar. To him God has given power over all countries and all
their resources down to the beasts of the field. He and his son and his
son's son shall rule, three generations, Nebuchadnezzar, Evil-Merodach
(2 Kings 25:27; Jer. 52:31), and Belshazzar (Dan. 5:2), Nebuchadnezzar's grandson, his father Nabonidus having married a daughter
of Nebuchadnezzar. Cp. *Concordia Theological Monthly*, III, 1932,
p. 215; R. D. Wilson, *Studies in the Book of Daniel*, I, p. 124 ff. Then
also the divinely appointed time of his removal from power shall come,
and mighty nations and great kings shall subjugate the Babylonian
Empire.

V. 8. Refusal of obedience to Nebuchadnezzar will be ruinous

223

to the rebels. For the Lord Himself will punish through His servant with the sword of a human king and the resulting famine and pestilence, until Jehovah has consumed them by the hand of the Babylonian. Behind the rulers of the world and their schemes, behind the wars and famines and epidemics, due to natural causes, stands Jehovah. He is Imperator Summus, the Lord, our Covenant God, the Lord Our Righteousness!

Vv. 9-11. The nations should not listen to their prophets, nor to their "diviners," prophesying from the position of arrows cast to the ground, nor to their "dreamers," their "enchanters," interpreting various signs, their "sorcerers," conjurers; five classes of prognosticators, one as deceptive as the other. "To remove you," for the purpose of, the Hebrew term designating ironically a purpose directly opposite to that intended. If they follow their lying prophets, all their plotting will serve no other purpose than to cause that very ruin they are hoping to escape, while the nations that submit to God's will and surrender to Nebuchadnezzar, shall remain in peaceful possession of their land.

---

b. Addressing Zedekiah, vv. 12-15

12 And to Zedekiah, the king of Judah, you shall speak in like manner, saying: Place your necks under the yoke of the king of Babylon, and serve him and his 13 people, and you shall live. Why will you die, you and your people, by the sword and by famine and by pestilence as the LORD has said concerning the nation which will not serve the king of Babylon?

14 And do not listen to the words of the prophets who say to you: You shall not serve the king of Babylon! for they are prophesying lies 15 to you. For I have not sent them, is the oracle of the LORD, and they prophesy falsely in My name, so that I would have to drive you away and you would perish, you and the prophets prophesying to you.

Vv. 12-15. The appeal to Zedekiah and his advisers, cp. the plurals "your necks," etc. Jeremiah here stresses the utter futility of the attempt to shake off the yoke of Babylon and the disastrous consequences of such a rebellion for king and people. It would be national suicide, as they learned to their sorrow a few years later. Why refuse to do the Lord's will? Why die by sword and famine and pestilence, while they might live in peace and prosperity if only they would surrender to Nebuchadnezzar? The prophets of Judah are no better than the prophets of the heathen nations (cp. vv. 9-10). They are not sent by the Lord; they speak lies; they do not benefit the people, but will lead the nation to destruction. Do not obey them, but obey the Lord!

c. Addressing the priests and the people, vv. 16-22

16 And to the priests and to this whole people you shall say: Thus says the LORD: Do not listen to the words of the prophets that prophesy to you, saying: The vessels of the house of the LORD shall be returned from Babel in a short time now; for they are
17 prophesying falsely to you. Do not listen to them! Serve the king of Babylon, and live! Why shall this
18 city be laid waste? If these men are prophets, and if the word of the LORD is with them, then let them plead with the LORD of Hosts that the vessels remaining in the house of the LORD and in the house of the king of Judah and in Jerusalem may not be brought to
19 Babylon. For thus says the LORD of Hosts concerning the pillars and the laver and the bases and concerning the rest of the vessels re-
20 maining in this city, which Nebuchadnezzar, the king of Babylon, did not take when he deported Jeconiah, the son of Jehoiakim, the king of Judah, from Jerusalem to Babylon, and all the noblemen of
21 Judah and Jerusalem. Thus says the LORD of Hosts, the God of Israel, concerning the vessels remaining in the house of the LORD and in the house of the king and
22 in Jerusalem: To Babylon they shall be brought, and there they shall be until the day when I will visit you, it is the oracle of the LORD, and I will bring them back and return them to this place.

Vv. 16-22. The appeal to priests and people. They had been promised a speedy return of the Temple vessels (cp. ch. 28:2-3). Again the warning: Believe them not! They are lying prophets! Why should this city, including the Temple, be laid waste? If these prophets were prophets of the Lord, they would rather pray that the vessels still remaining in the Temple, in the palace, in the homes, be not carried away to Babylon. And in order to impress this fact the more deeply in the minds of priests and people, to warn them, to call them to repentance, the prophet twice foretells the complete removal of all valuables in Temple and city to Babylon. At Babylon they shall remain until the day of the Lord's gracious visitation. Then He will bring them back and restore them to this place, the Temple. This promise implies the restoration of the city and the Temple, but in the Lord's time and by His gracious power. With this ray of hope the prophet ends his message to the priests and people. For its fulfillment see Ezra 1—8.

CHAPTER 28

B. Hananiah vehemently opposes Jeremiah

a. He prophesies a return of the exiles within two years, vv. 1-4

1 In the same year, in the beginning of the rule of Zedekiah, the king of Judah, in the fourth year, in the fifth month, Hananiah, the son of Azur, the prophet from Gibeon, said to me in the house of the LORD in the presence of the
2 priests and all the people: Thus

says the LORD of Hosts, the God of Israel: I have broken the yoke 3 of the king of Babylon. Within two years I shall bring back to this place all the vessels of the house of the LORD which Nebuchadnezzar, the king of Babel, took from this place and brought to 4 Babylon. And Jeconiah, the son of Jehoiakim, the king of Judah, and all the exiles of Judah that went to Babylon I shall bring back to this place, is the oracle of the LORD, for I have broken the yoke of the king of Babylon.

In ch. 26:7-8, 11, false prophets had been named among the fanatic opponents of Jeremiah seeking his death. Ch. 27 tells of the continued opposition of these men against the Lord and His prophets during the reign of Zedekiah. In the present chapter Jeremiah singles out one of the ringleaders of his bitter adversaries, Hananiah ben Azur of Gibeon, a priestly city in the tribe of Benjamin (Joshua 9:3ff.; 21:17), the modern El Jib, about eight miles northwest of Jerusalem. Perhaps on some Sabbath or festival day when the Temple court was crowded with people, Jeremiah also came to the Temple, wearing the symbol of subjection to Nebuchadnezzar (ch. 27:2-8). The sight of the prophet roused Hananiah's resentment. Approaching Jeremiah, he told him in the hearing of priests and people as an oracle of the Lord of Hosts, the God of Israel: I have broken the yoke of the king of Babylon. The perfect denotes the accomplished fact. Continuing, he foretold the return to Jerusalem within two years of all the Temple utensils now at Babylon, of King Zedekiah, and of all the exiles. "I will break" (v. 4) = I am in the act of breaking. We can imagine the enthusiasm bordering on fanaticism that swept through the vast audience, the thunderous applause, the joyous shouts that echoed through the spacious court at this oracle so positively and so publicly proclaimed as the very word of the Lord of Hosts.

b. Jeremiah's response, vv. 5-9

5 Then said Jeremiah the prophet to Hananiah the prophet, in the presence of the priests and in the presence of all the people standing in 6 the house of the LORD, and Jeremiah the prophet said: Amen! May the LORD do thus! May the LORD establish your words which you have prophesied, to return the vessels of the house of the LORD and all the exiles from Babylon to this 7 place! Hear, however, this word which I am ready to speak in your hearing and in the hearing of all 8 the people: The prophets who were before me and before you from ancient times and who prophesied concerning many countries and concerning great kingdoms, spoke of war and of evil and of pestilence. 9 The prophet who prophesied of peace was recognized as a prophet whom the LORD had truly sent only when the word of the prophet was fulfilled.

Vv. 5-9. The prophet's answer. Does Jeremiah remain silent? Does he try to escape? Does he regard the present time as inopportune? Why expose yourself to the fury of these fanatics? Wait until the people have come to their senses! It was not an easy task to face his opponent. Note the emphasis placed on the fact that he spoke (vv. 5-7). Like an iron pillar he stands alone in that howling mob and speaks, speaks boldly, courageously, but wisely. He does not thunder forth the Law. He does not break out in violent denunciation of the false prophet. No! "Amen!" he says. Let this be most certainly true. So may the Lord do! May the Lord establish thy word! That was not spoken in irony, in bitter mockery. No, these words were the sincere, heartfelt prayer of a man who had time and again pleaded for his beloved people, at home and in exile, prayed for the preservation of the nation, the city, the Temple (cp. ch. 8:18—9:1; 14:7-9); even after the Lord had forbidden him to pray (ch. 14:11-12; cp. 14:17-22). The noble prophet is not afraid to confess that his inmost desires and most fervent prayers are directed toward a speedy end of the Babylonian Exile. Yet dearly as he loves his country and his people, there is One to whom he is attached in even greater love and loyalty: Jehovah, the God of the covenant so shamefully and so persistently broken by his people. As Jehovah's spokesman he turns to the self-appointed prophet: "Only listen to this word which I myself am about to speak in your hearing and in the hearing of all the people. From time immemorial the prophets before me and before you have prophesied against many countries and great kings of war and evil and pestilence." Jeremiah, of course, has in mind only the true prophets of Jehovah. Every one of them prophesied evil against the nations because of their wickedness. And since Judah and Israel were guilty of like wickedness, the prophets pronounced God's judgment upon them also. In doing this they were repeating the threats of the God of the Covenant clearly stated by Him at the establishment of His covenant with Israel (Ex. 20:5-7, and in greater detail Deut. 28:15—29:29). Jehoiachin's deportation was the penalty of the Covenant God upon His wicked people, a harbinger of still greater evils to come, if Judah would persist in breaking God's covenant.

V. 9. "Of peace." The word is used here not in the sense of salvation, but according to the context of that civic peace, that national well-being, that political deliverance out of the exile, which Hananiah had promised to Judah. The unalterable condition of such a return from exile had been stated in unmistakable language by the Lord of the Covenant (Deut. 30:1-5): a return to the Lord and obedience to His Word with all their heart and all their soul. Of this change of heart, the essential prerequisite of a return out of exile (cp. Ezra 1:6), Hananiah had said nothing, nor was there the slightest evidence of such a change on the part of the nation.

c. Hananiah breaks the yoke worn by Jeremiah, who prophesies the early death of Hananiah, vv. 10-17

10 Then Hananiah the prophet took the yoke from Jeremiah's neck and 11 broke it. And Hananiah said in the presence of all the people: Thus says the LORD: Like this I break the yoke of Nebuchadnezzar, the king of Babylon, within two years from the necks of all nations. Then Jeremiah the prophet went on his 12 way. And the word of the LORD came to Jeremiah, after Hananiah the prophet had broken the yoke 13 off Jeremiah's neck, saying: Go and tell Hananiah: Thus says the LORD: A wooden yoke have you broken, now make an iron yoke 14 in its stead. For thus says the LORD of Hosts, the God of Israel: I have placed an iron yoke on the necks of all these nations to serve Nebuchadnezzar, the king of Babylon, and they will serve him. Also the beasts of the field I have given 15 to him. And Jeremiah the prophet said to Hananiah the prophet: Now hear, Hananiah! The LORD has not sent you, and you have seduced this people to put their trust in 16 a falsehood. Therefore thus says the LORD: Behold, I shall send you away from the earth. This year you shall die! For your words are rebellion against the LORD! 17 And Hananiah the prophet died that year in the seventh month.

Vv. 10-11. Unable to answer the prophet's quiet and convincing argument, Hananiah resorts to violence. In fanatic passion he vents his wrath on the yoke so hateful to him, tears it off the prophet's neck and smashes it to bits. And for the third time he cries out: "Thus says the LORD," etc., adding as a climax, "from the neck of all nations." The prophet submits to this indignity. He had an argument in answer to Hananiah's words, but to his violence he made no answer whatever. He suffered in silence, leaving it to the Lord to vindicate His prophet.

Vv. 12-17. God's judgment upon Hananiah. The Lord did not disappoint His faithful servant. He sends Jeremiah back to Hananiah with the message: A wooden yoke have you broken, and you have made instead of it an iron yoke. By his brazen-faced assertion that he was the Lord's prophet, by his smashing of the yoke which Jeremiah wore by divine command, he had caused the people to believe his lie (v. 15), to harden their hearts in unbelief, and thus to increase the severity of their punishment. He had made the wooden yoke an iron yoke for them. Compare the increase in the severity of Zedekiah's punishment because of his stubborn refusal to surrender to Nebuchadnezzar (Jer. 38:17-23). And now the Lord publicly disavows Hananiah, who had called himself a prophet of the Lord. "The LORD hath not sent thee!" (v. 15.) You are a lying prophet, leading the people into ruin. Therefore "I will cast thee from off the face of the earth" (v. 16), rather, I will send thee (the same word used v. 15) away from the earth. "This year thou shalt die, because thou hast spoken revolt, rebellion, against the Lord" (same phrase as Deut. 13:5), who has made Nebuchadnezzar the ruler of the world. Rebellion against the Lord's appointee is rebellion against the Lord. "So Hananiah the prophet died" only two months later (v. 17; cp. v. 1). He is called "Hananiah the prophet" because that was his official title. He was a prophet not by the will and call of God, but was by his own choice a member of a profession that had usurped the name and honor which the Lord gave to those only whom He had prepared and ordained prophets (ch. 1:5). This self-styled prophet was revealed to be what Jeremiah had called him, a teacher of lies (v. 15) and of rebellion against the Lord (v. 16), guilty of a capital crime, while Jeremiah stood acknowledged by the Lord as His chosen spokesman.

XI. Opposition of the False Prophets at Babylon, Ch. 29

CHAPTER 29

1. Introductory Remarks, Vv. 1-3

1 These are the words of the letter which Jeremiah the prophet sent from Jerusalem to the elders remaining among the exiles and to the priests and to the prophets and to all the people which Nebuchadnezzar had deported from Jerusa-
2 lem to Babylon (after Jeconiah, the king, and the queen mother, the officers, the princes of Judah and Jerusalem, and the craftsmen and carpenters had left Jerusalem),
3 through Elasah, the son of Shaphan, and Gemariah, the son of Hilkiah, whom Zedekiah, the king of Judah, had sent to Babylon to Nebuchadnezzar, the king of Babylon:

V. 1. The letter was addressed to "the residue of the elders," a number of whom may have succumbed to the hardships of the long journey or perished during the siege; to the priests, the prophets, the civic and spiritual leaders, and to all the people deported by Nebuchadnezzar, when he deposed Jehoiachin after his brief reign of three months (2 Kings 24: 8-16) and deported him and the "queen" (the term may mean the king's wife, 1 Kings 11: 19, or his mother, 1 Kings 15: 13; cp. 2 Kings 24: 12), his "eunuchs," here as in ch. 38: 7; 41: 16; 52: 15, most likely not castrates, but higher officials at court or in the army. The eunuch * (Gen. 39: 1) Potiphar was married. 2 Kings 18: 17; Jer. 39: 3, 13 speak of a "chief eunuch," Dan. 1: 7: 11, 18 of a "prince of eunuchs." "Assyrian sculptures present some of the higher officials as beardless, while the king and the highest honoraries are bearded. The Targum still knows the correct meaning (Jer. 29: 2; 34: 19; 41: 16, *rabrabi*, 'mighty men'; ch. 38: 7, *geber rab*, 'mighty man')." (Volz, *Jeremias*, p. 320, note n.) On "princes" cp. Jer. 1: 18, p. 32 f.; "carpenters," craftsmen, workers in stone, wood, or metal; "smiths," doubtful, either locksmith or goldsmith. The total number of exiles is stated as 10,000 (2 Kings 24: 14), but perhaps the 7,000 "men of might" and 1,000 craftsmen and smiths (v. 16) have to be added. The better class of people, socially and morally, were deported, leaving only the lower class, the rabble, who took over the homes and positions of the exiles. See Jer. 24: 1, referring to this deportation, where the deported people are compared to good figs, Zedekiah and the Jews remaining in Judah and Egypt, to

---

* A. V. calls Potiphar an officer, although the Hebrew term is *saris*, which is translated 13 times "chamberlain," 12 times "officer," 17 times "eunuch." The latter may have been the original sense, but since many of the eunuchs became high officials, the term acquired the secondary sense of high official.

evil figs; cp. also Ezek. 11:1-25, spoken in the sixth year of Jehoiachin's captivity (Ezek. 8:1) and explaining the difference (ch. 11:16-21).

Whether all the exiles were settled at the "river of Chebar" (Ezek. 1:1), "Tel-Abib" (Ezek. 3:15), now identified with a canal passing by Nippur, southeast of Babylon, or whether this was only one of a number of settlements, we do not know. At the time of Zerubbabel, ca. 536, the Jews were scattered throughout the vast empire (Ezra 1:1-4), and Ezra mentions a colony of Levites at Casiphia, north of Babylon (Ezra 8:15-20). While captives in a foreign land, the Jews were granted a great measure of liberty. They were permitted to form colonies, to retain religious and civic institutions (cp. Ezek. 8:1), elders (Dan. 3:28-29); they had prophets, Ezekiel and Daniel (Jer. 29:8-9); some of the Jews occupied responsible positions (Dan. 1:3-4, 19; 2:48-49; 3:30). There was no iron curtain drawn between them and their homeland; they were permitted to correspond freely (ch. 29:1, 24, 25, 31). In fact, many grew so prosperous and became so devoted to their new home that they remained in Babylon even after Cyrus had given them permission to return and had encouraged them to rebuild the Temple (Ezra 1:1ff.).

V. 3. Jeremiah's letter was entrusted to an embassy sent by Zedekiah. We are not informed of the purpose of this embassy. It may have carried a tribute from Zedekiah to the Babylonian king in gratitude for the royal crown bestowed upon him, and at the same time may once more have pledged a vassal's loyalty to his liege lord in order to allay any suspicions possibly harbored by the sovereign ruler.

The two men chosen for this embassy were selected from the priesthood and the aristocracy. Both Elasah and Gemariah were noblemen in the best sense of the word. Elasah was the son of Shaphan, the secretary of state under Josiah (2 Kings 22:8-14). Like his father and his brother, Ahikam (2 Kings 22:12; Jer. 26:24), Elasah was loyal to God, loyal to Jeremiah and his directions, loyal therefore also to Nebuchadnezzar, the sovereign ruler appointed by the Lord (Jer. 27:4-14). Ahikam's son, Gedaliah, later was appointed governor of the colony of Jews left in Judah because of his loyalty to Nebuchadnezzar (Jer. 40:5). Gemariah was the son of Hilkiah the high priest, who took so active a part in Josiah's reform (2 Kings 22:2; 2 Chronicles 34 and 35). The families of Hilkiah and Shaphan are living evidence that even among a corrupt priesthood and a venal government the Lord has believing, faithful servants, shining lights among a perverse generation.

The fact that the time when the letter was written is so definitely described almost compels us to date the letter shortly after the arrival of the exiles at Babylon. The exiles were chafing under the indignity of deportation, far away from their country and Temple, strangers in a foreign land, captives of a Gentile nation (cp. Ezek. 11:15-16). False prophets and soothsayers kept on crying: Peace, peace! Your exile cannot last long! Cp. Hananiah a few years later (ch. 28:2-4, 10-11). These dangerous agitators succeeded in adding fuel to the fire of discontent. The exiles refused to settle down in quiet submission to God's will; they hoped for some miracle to happen, for some revolutionary movement to be started which they could join and after Babylon's defeat return to their own country, the land of the Lord. In order to stop this dangerous propaganda and to cut off every hope of a speedy return, Jeremiah sends this letter to his fellow men whom he still regards as part of his flock and loves with the tenderness of a faithful shepherd's heart.

2. Admonition to Submit Peacefully and Patiently to the Babylonian Government, Vv. 4-7

4 Thus says the LORD of Hosts, the God of Israel, to all the exiles whom I have deported from Jerusalem to Babylon: Build houses, and live in them! And plant gardens, and eat of their fruit. 6 Take wives, and beget sons and daughters, and take wives for your sons, and give your daughters to husbands, and let them beget sons and daughters that you may increase there and not diminish. 7 And seek the welfare of the city to which I have deported you, and pray for it to the LORD; for in the welfare of the city you shall fare well.

V. 4. Whether spoken or written, the prophetic message is the Word of God. This God is the Lord of Hosts, the almighty Ruler of all nations (Ex. 19:5), the God of Israel, whether they are dwelling in the land He calls His own (Lev. 25:23) or in the land of the enemy, whether Israel is free and independent or a vassal, captive nation. His power and His love extend far beyond the boundaries of His land (Gen. 46:3-4; 48:5, 9; 50:24; Ex. 2:23-25). It was Nebuchadnezzar who had deported the Jews (v. 1), yet here the Lord tells them: "I have caused them to be carried away from Jerusalem to Babylon." Even if the way of His people goes into exile and captivity prepared for them by an enemy nation, they go not without the Lord's knowledge and will. He permits defeat and national ruin for wise and salutary reasons. And always He is and remains, also in times of adversity, the same God of justice and grace, the same Covenant God of His people that He was in days of progress, prosperity, and peace.

V. 5. It will not be a brief captivity. They are to build houses, not tents or shacks, but permanent homes in which they may dwell, settle down, live for a long period of time. They are to provide their own food by tilling the soil, planting gardens, eating the products of their own labor, not relying for their living on other men, their government, their friends, not becoming a nation of paupers, but retaining as much of their personal independence as possible, even after having lost their national freedom.

V. 6. Here in the foreign country they are to establish homes in which the fear of God rules supreme, homes upon which rests the favor of God, even as it rested upon such homes in the Land of Promise (Deut. 5:32-33; 6:5-9, 17-18). Such homes are at all times the safest and surest foundation of any commonwealth. They are to practice no race suicide, but live in accord with God's creation ordinance (Gen. 1:28) and establish in the midst of a heathen nation a commonwealth of God-fearing servants of the Lord, a powerful, indisputable evidence of the life-changing, sanctifying influence of the Word of Jehovah.

V. 7. Not only by their example, but by actively seeking the welfare of their community they were to become a salt of the earth. This is the country into which I have placed you for seventy years. Use your social, civic, political influence wherever it is possible to give it at least the semblance of a model community. "Pray to the LORD for your country." It is part of His vast kingdom of power. He, the Lord of the whole earth, will hear your prayer and in answer to your intercession grant His blessings to your new homeland, and you will share in these blessings. While the Lord often spares a city or a country, or blesses it for the sake of His elect (Gen. 18:23-32; Is. 65:8; Jer. 5:1; Ezek. 22:30), the believers also enjoy the peace and security and prosperity of the commonwealth for which their prayers ascend to the throne of the Most High. While vv. 4-7 are positive statements: Submit in true humility to God's will; make Babylon your homeland; be loyal subjects of your government; pray for your country — the next section is negative, a prohibition.

---

3. Warning Against False Prophets Promising a Speedy Return
Vv. 8-10

8 For thus says the LORD of Hosts, the God of Israel: Let not the prophets which are in your midst and the soothsayers beguile you, 9 and do not listen to your dreams which you have caused to be dreamed. For they prophesy deceitfully to you in My name.

I have not sent them, is the oracle of the LORD. For thus says the LORD: As soon as seventy years have been ended for Babylon, I will visit you and fulfill for you My gracious promise to return you to this place.

Grammatical Notes

V. 10. "As soon as," 'פְּ = according to, in keeping with (cp. Gen. 47:12; Ex. 12:4); here, in accordance with the fulfillment of the seventy years allotted to Babylon.

Vv. 8-10. As in Jerusalem (ch. 28), so in Babylon false prophets promised a speedy return to Judah. The people hoped and wished for an early return to their homeland; this wish was father of their dreams. Knowing this, the false prophets, whose chief aim was to please the people, proclaimed the dreams of the people as oracles of the Lord revealed to them in their dreams. These dreams of the prophets, if real, were caused by the dreams of the people and not by divine revelation, hence were, like all their prophecies, lies, deception. Once more, therefore, the Lord's prophet tells them that the Lord, who alone shapes the history of the world, would not end their exile until the seventy years of Babylon's rule were ended (Jer. 25:11, spoken in the fourth year of Jehoiakim, 605). Then immediately the Lord's promise would be fulfilled, but not before.

---

4. The Exile a Salutary Chastisement, Vv. 11-14

11 For I, I know the thoughts which I am thinking toward you, is the oracle of the LORD, thoughts of good and not of evil, to give you 12 a future and hope! Then shall you call Me and proceed to pray to Me, 13 and I will listen to you! Then shall you seek Me, and you shall find Me, if you shall seek Me with 14 all your heart. And I shall be found of you, is the oracle of the LORD. I will turn your captivity, and I will gather you out of all nations and from all places into which I have scattered you, is the oracle of the LORD, and I will bring you back to the place from which I have deported you.

Vv. 11-14. He, the everlasting I Am That I Am, never does anything inconsiderately. His actions are not the whims and caprices of a despot; they are well-considered plans, eternally conceived, never forgotten, invariably carried out in due time. And He is the Covenant God of unchanging grace. His plans concerning His people are always thoughts of good, of blessing. Even if He is obliged to use the rod, it is the rod not of wrath, but the Father's rod of chastisement for their temporal and eternal welfare. There is not a single item of evil in His plans for His people, neither in their

234

motive, nor in their conception, nor in their revelation, nor in their consummation. All is good, all is blessing. His purpose is to give them an "expected end"; literally, an end and hope. "End" is often used of the outcome, the issue (Prov. 5:4; 16:25; 23:18; Is. 46:10), also of a happy ending (Job 8:7; Prov. 23:18, "end"; Prov. 24:14, "reward"). In the latter two passages both words, end and hope, expectation, are used synonymously. The phrase "end of days" is a well-known term for the Messianic era, on which all the hopes of Israel were centered (Gen. 49:18; 1 Sam. 2:10; Ps. 14:7; Mal. 3:1). This promise of Messianic salvation, however, was inseparably linked up with the Holy Land (Is. 2:3; Micah 4:2; Is. 8:20—9:7), particularly since Bethlehem had been designated as the birthplace of Messiah (Micah 5:2). Although, therefore, they were at present exiles in a foreign land, although also the rest of the nation would be deported and the land left desolate (vv. 16-19), yet the Lord had planned in eternity and promised to His people through Moses that He would bring back His people to the Land of Promise, the land of Messiah's birth, the land from which the news of salvation would be spread throughout the world. This return would be possible only after they had humbled themselves and in sincere repentance would return to the Lord (Deut. 30:1-5). As in the desert, so in Babylon the old rebellious generation would die, and a new nation be created by the Lord's omnipotent grace (Deut. 30:6); they would call upon the Lord, and He would hear their prayer and bring them back to the land from which they were deported (vv. 12-14). Vv. 12-13 are a renewal of God's ancient promise (Deut. 4:29-30), and v. 14 is a résumé of Deut. 30:3-5. What a powerful motive not to listen to the false prophets and their lying promises, but patiently, humbly, believingly to wait for the consummation of the plans conceived by their Covenant God! In the exile the people will be restored to God, and God will restore the exiles to His and their land.

---

5. The False Prophets will be Punished, Vv. 15-23

15 When you say: The LORD has raised up prophets for us in Baby-
16 lon! Surely, thus says the LORD to the king that is sitting on the throne of David and to all the people dwelling in this city, your brethren who have not gone forth
17 with you to exile, thus says the LORD of Hosts: Behold, I am sending among you the sword and famine and pestilence, and I will make them like vile figs which are so bad that they cannot be eaten.
18 And I will pursue them with the sword, and with famine, and with pestilence, and will give them for perturbation to all kingdoms of the earth, and a curse, and a consterna-

tion, and horror, and shame among all nations among whom I have 19 scattered them, in retaliation for their failure to listen to My Word, is the oracle of the LORD, because I have sent to them My servants, the prophets, early and late, and you did not listen, is the oracle of 20 the LORD. And you! Hear the Word of the LORD, all you exiles whom I have sent from Jerusalem 21 to Babylon! Thus says the LORD of Hosts, the God of Israel, to Achab, the son of Kolaiah, and to Zedekiah, the son of Maaseiah, that have falsely prophesied to you in My name: Behold, I will give them into the hand of Nebuchadrezzar, the king of Babylon, and he shall 22 slay them before your eyes. And from their fate all the exiles of Judah which are in Babylon shall take a curse: The LORD make you like Zedekiah and like Achab, whom the king of Babel roasted 23 in the fire. Because they practiced wicked folly in Israel and committed adultery with their neighbors' wives, and they have spoken deceitful things in My name which I had not commanded them; I know it and am a witness of it, is the oracle of the LORD.

V. 15. The prophet hears the exiles arguing: "Why, we have prophets here also, in Babylon, much closer to the royal court, far better able to understand the actual situation, and they tell us that everything points to a speedy return!" Jeremiah cuts short their argument. No matter how many prophets you may have, and no matter how often and how enthusiastically and positively they promise an early end of the exile, the deciding factor is not what the prophets say, but what God says. And the Lord, instead of promising a speedy return, speaks only of a deportation of the remaining Jews and the complete destruction of the city. Jeremiah repeats in almost identical words what he had told them time and again and what he continued to tell the inhabitants of Judah and Jerusalem. On vv. 16-19 cp. ch. 21: 4-14; 24:8-10; 25:8-11; 27:1-22; 34:2-3. These threats became stark realities within a few years after this letter was written, as pictured by Jeremiah, an eyewitness, in Lamentations 1 and 2. Instead of hoping for and desiring a speedy return to Jerusalem, the exiles had every reason to thank God that they were spared the horrors of the last days of Jerusalem. Surely, God had thoughts of good concerning them, and not of evil! Trust Him and listen not to the false prophets speaking lies and deceit.

There is another reason why they should not permit themselves to be deluded by men calling themselves prophets.

Vv. 21-23. The Lord singles out two prophets who were guilty of practicing adultery, a sin with which Jeremiah charges the false prophets at Jerusalem in general (ch. 23:14). The Lord will turn these villains over to the civil authorities. The Hammurabi Code imposed the death penalty upon adulterers, who were to be bound and thrown into the fire. Whether Nebuchadnezzar was the first to impose death by fire as the penalty for this crime, we do not know. On being burnt alive cp. Dan. 3:6ff.; 2 Macc. 7:3ff. Their death shall cause another form of curse to become current (v. 22). The Lord declares that they have committed "villainy," "folly," used here in the sense of extreme wickedness, mortal sin (cp. Joshua 7:15, Achan's theft; Gen. 34:7; Deut. 22:21; Judg. 20:6, fornication and adultery). God regards them doubly worthy of a shameful, accursed death, because of their adultery (Deut. 22:20-24) and because of their prophesying lies in His name (Deut. 13:10). I have known it, and I testify against them! Let not men of this nature deceive you. It would be wickedness and folly to follow their lying deceit rather than the Word of the living God spoken by His servant Jeremiah.

6. Shemaiah Demands that the Temple Authorities Call a Halt to Jeremiah's Agitations, Vv. 24-28

24 To Shemaiah of Nehelam say the
25 following: Thus says the LORD of Hosts, the God of Israel: Because you have sent letters in your name to all the people in Jerusalem and to Zephaniah, the son of Maaseiah, the priest, and to all the priests,
26 saying: The LORD has appointed you priest in the stead of Jehoiadah the priest, to be overseers in the house of the LORD over every madman who plays the prophet and to place him into stocks and
27 the collar. Now, why did you not rebuke Jeremiah of Anathoth, who
28 is prophesying to you? For therefore he has sent a letter to us in Babylon saying: It will be of long duration! Build houses, and live in them; plant gardens, and eat their fruits.

Vv. 24-28. Reaction toward Jeremiah's letter was not altogether favorable. One instance is singled out. Shemaiah the Nehelamite, otherwise unknown, sent letters to the people, the priests, and in particular to Zephaniah, the "second priest" (ch. 52:24; cp. 21:1; 37:3), ranking next to the high priest (2 Kings 23:4; 25:18). Shemaiah objected (v. 28) to Jeremiah's statement (Jer. 29:5-10). He asks Zephaniah to follow the example of Jehoiada, one of the renowned high priests, who had been the leader in eradicating Baal worship by slaying the idolatrous prophets and wicked Athaliah, who had tried to make Baal worship the official religion of Judah (2 Kings 11:1-20). Shemaiah places Jeremiah on the level with these frenzied, "mad," self-styled, and self-deluded prophets and demands that Zephaniah become a second Jehoiada in his zeal for the Lord. For that very

237

purpose the Lord had placed him into the priesthood, in the place of Jehoiada the priest. Zephaniah evidently was not moved by this flattery. He seems to have been friendly inclined to Jeremiah and showed the letter to the prophet.

---

7. The Lord Rebukes Shemaiah, Vv. 29-32

29 Zephaniah the priest read this letter aloud in the hearing of Jere-
30 miah the prophet. Then came the word of the LORD to Jeremiah,
31 saying: Send to all the exiles, saying: Thus says the LORD concerning Shemaiah of Nehelam: Because Shemaiah prophesied to you while I did not send him, and he has caused you to trust a lie,
32 therefore thus says the LORD: Behold, I am going to punish Shemaiah of Nehelam and his seed. Not one shall he have living among this people, nor shall he behold the good fortune which I shall grant My people, is the oracle of the LORD, for he has spoken revolt against the LORD.

Vv. 29-32. The Lord again fulfills His promise of ch. 1:8, 19; 15:20. No harm came to Jeremiah, while the exiles were to be notified that Shemaiah and his family would die in Babylon, because he had taught rebellion. Not Jeremiah, but Shemaiah is the rebel against Jehovah.

XII. The Book of Consolation, Ch. 30—33

CHAPTER 30—31:1

1. Triumphant Song of Israel's Salvation

A. God's command to write this prophecy, vv. 1-3

1 The word which came to Jeremiah 2 from the LORD, saying: Thus says the LORD, the God of Israel: Write for yourself in a book all the things 3 which I speak. For, behold, days are coming, is the word of the LORD, that I will turn the captivity of My people Israel and Judah, says the LORD, and I will bring them back to the land which I have given to their fathers, and they shall possess it.

Vv. 1-3. The prophecy recorded in ch. 30—33 was by divine command to be written in a book, not, however, to be read or proclaimed in public assembly like the collection of prophecies referred to in ch. 36:1-6. Jeremiah was told to write this book for himself, "write thee" (v. 1), for his personal comfort and that of such as were, like him, looking for just this comfort. It is the promise of the complete destruction of Babylon; of the return of God's people, reunited Israel and Judah, out of the exile and the rebuilding of cities and palaces (ch. 30:3-20), the coming of Messiah (ch. 30:21), and the establishment of His Kingdom of Grace and Peace, in which Israel and Judah and the Gentiles will be united into one holy Church (ch. 30:22 to 32:44).

Calov in *Biblia Illustrata* makes the following appropriate remarks in connection with this chapter. After stating that "David" (ch. 30:9) is the Messiah and so is recognized by the ancient Jewish Church, he proceeds: "While Christian interpreters agree that this prophecy refers to the Messiah, they disagree as to the time and to the nature of the promised delivery." He rejects the reference to the spiritual deliverance in the Messianic era as well as that to the Last Day and the final Judgment and deliverance, because neither interpretation does justice to text and context. "One thing is certain: that the prophet speaks of the Babylonian Captivity and its sorrows. Neither can it be denied that a deliverance out of this captivity is promised, since the prophet threatens destruction to all nations among which the Israelites had been scattered, while he promises grace and deliverance to Israel and comforts his people with this consolation. Intermingled with these promises of material blessings are promises of spiritual gifts and blessings. Naturally one and the same prophecy does not speak in the literal sense of the type (the deliverance from the Babylonian Captivity) and in a mystical sense of the antitype (a spiritual deliverance). That would be contrary to sound hermeneutics. While the prophets often connect both material and spiritual promises, they make a distinction between the two classes. What they posit as spiritual blessings must be understood of spiritual matters only, and what they describe as material gifts must be restricted to these. Otherwise blessings separate and distinct from each other would be confused. If, therefore, a deliverance out of the exile and a homecoming to Canaan is promised — and we do not deny that here — then we must say that the purpose of this return is here stated, namely, that they are to serve God and their King Messiah, whom God would at some future time raise up in accordance with His promise (Jer. 23: 5-6) and to whose service David also had exhorted the people (Ps. 2: 12). For Messiah is to be served by believers not only in the New Testament, but at all times (Heb. 13: 8)." (Calov, *Biblia Illustrata,* on Jer. 30: 10.)

B. Israel's deliverance through judgment over the nations, vv. 4-11

4 These are the words which the LORD speaks concerning Israel 5 and concerning Judah. For thus says the LORD: We have heard the voice of horror; fear and no 6 peace! Ask, and see! Did ever a male give birth? Why, then, do I see every strong man with his hands on his loins as a woman in childbirth, and all faces have 7 turned deathly pale? Woe! for great is that day and none like it. This is a time of distress for Jacob, but he will be delivered from it! 8 And on this day, is the oracle of the LORD of Hosts, I will break his yoke from off his neck, and his fetters will I tear off; and strangers 9 shall no more enslave him; but they shall serve the LORD, their God, and David, their King, whom 10 I will raise up for them. Fear not, My servant Jacob, is the oracle of the LORD, and do not be dismayed, O Israel; for, behold, I am ready to deliver you from afar and your seed from the land of their exile, and Jacob shall return and rest and live in peace, with no one dis- 11 turbing him. For I am with you, is the oracle of the LORD, to deliver you; for I will make a full end of all nations among whom I have scattered you. But I will not make a full end of you. Yet I will chastise you according to judgment, and I do not regard you as innocent.

Vv. 4-11. The days preceding the return shall be days of fear and agony, the death throes of the mighty Babylonian world empire. For Babylon the great day will come, the like of which it had not experienced in all the centuries of its existence, the final judgment day, the *dies irae,* when even the strongest men will tremble with fear, their faces turn, take on that ashen-gray pallor characteristic of deathly fright. (Cp. Dan. 5: 1-7, 22-30.) This day of judgment for

Babylon is for Israel also "the time of Jacob's trouble." Israel (vv. 2, 4, 10) is the honorable name, the man who conquered God (Gen. 32:28). Jacob, "deceiver" (vv. 7, 10, 18), the one looking only to his own profit (Gen. 25:29-34; 27:12-24, 35-36), sinful, weak Jacob. Israel-Jacob was exposed to the ravages of warfare, the hardships accompanying Babylon's destruction, just as the Church of God will be affected by the woes preceding the final Day of Judgment (Jer. 25:29; 49:12; Ezek. 9:6; 1 Pet. 4:17). But there is a great difference between Babylon, the mighty ruler, and Jacob, the despised exile. Babylon is to be destroyed, Jacob is to be saved! (Cp. Luke 21: 28-31; 2 Thess. 1:4-10.) The yoke of the Assyrian-Babylonian captivity would be removed from Israel's neck, and once more would they be able to worship and serve in their homeland the Lord, their God, and David, their King, great David's greater Son, the Messiah (cp. Hos. 3:4-5; Ezek. 34:23-24; 37:24-28). Long before His coming the Messiah, Jesus Christ, yesterday, today, forever, was worshiped (Heb. 13:8). Therefore they should not be terrified at the horrors of these days, because the Lord will be with them to deliver them (cp. Jer. 1:8-9).

C. This deliverance is an act of pure grace, vv. 12-17

12 For thus says the LORD: Incurable is your wound, fatal your affliction.

13 There is none to plead your cause or bandage you; there are no healing medicines for your recovery.

14 All your lovers have forgotten you and no longer care for you; for I have struck you down with a hostile blow, with heartless punishment, because your guilt is so great, your sins so innumerable.

15 Why are you crying over your affliction, that your wound is incurable? It is because of the multitude of your iniquities, because your sins are great, that I have

16 done these things to you! Therefore all that consume you shall be consumed! And all your oppressors, all of them, shall go into exile! They that plunder you shall be plundered, and all that despoil

17 you I shall make a spoil! For I will bring recovery to you and heal you of your wounds, is the oracle of the LORD, for they called you the rejected one: Zion, for whom no one cares!

Vv. 12-17. The exile and its humiliation, together with the horrors preceding the destruction of Babylon, were indeed a severe chastisement for the Jews, but a well-deserved one, because of the enormous guilt piled up by their innumerable sins. There was no one to plead for them (v. 13); their own iniquities condemned them (v. 14); the Lord Himself had treated them like an enemy (v. 14). Yet since there is no healing medicine (v. 13), the Lord Himself, the God of the Covenant, whose mercy is everlasting, will turn against their oppressors and will heal their wounds (cp. Isaiah 59). "Restore health," literally, cause new flesh to grow over the wound. He will prove that the sneering charge of the enemies that Israel is a forsaken outcast is false (v. 17b; cp. Ezek. 36:20-24).

D. Restoration of Israel and destruction of the enemies, ch. 30:18—31:1

18 Thus says the LORD: Behold, I shall turn the captivity of the tents of Jacob, and I will have compassion on their dwelling place. Cities shall be built on their hills, and palaces shall be inhabited in 19 keeping with their rank. Then songs of thanksgiving shall issue out of them and the sound of laughing voices. I will increase them, and they shall not diminish. I shall honor them, and they shall 20 not be despised. Their children shall be as of old, and his congregation shall stand firm before Me, and I will punish all their op-21 pressors. And his Glorious One shall be one out of their midst, and his Ruler shall come forth out of its midst. And I will permit Him to approach, and He shall come near to Me. For who is He that will pledge his life to come near to Me? is the oracle of the 22 LORD. And you shall be My people, and I Myself will be your 23 God. Behold, a tempest of the LORD! Fury goes forth! A whirlwind! It will hurl itself upon the 24 heads of the ungodly. The fury of the LORD's anger will not turn away till it has accomplished its purpose and till it has carried out the thoughts of His heart. In the end of days you shall under-31:1 stand it. At that time, is the oracle of the LORD, I will be the God of all the tribes of Israel, and they shall be My people.

Grammatical Notes

V. 18. "The city shall be builded," etc. "City" and "palace" without article do not refer to Jerusalem and the royal palace, or the Temple, but are collective singulars, every city and palace, or cities, palaces.

"Upon their own heap." Hebrew *tel*. Cities were usually built on hills. Rubbish accumulated, houses were destroyed by fire, or torn down, or demolished in times of war. On this rubbish heap the new city was built, and so layer after layer was added to increase the height of the *tel* and to preserve much material valuable to the archaeologist.

"Remain," *yesheb*, in sense of "be inhabited," cp. Joel 4:20; Is. 13:20; Jer. 17:6, 25; Ezek. 26:20.

"After the manner thereof," *al mishpato* = in suitable, proper manner.

Vv. 18-22. The waste cities and ruined homes will be rebuilt; joy and rejoicing will be heard throughout the land; the nation will increase and again be a glorious congregation before the Lord. And now the Glorious One, the Noble One, will arise out of their midst, the Ruler prophesied Micah 5:2, the Messiah, who will as the representative of His people and their Priest be permitted to approach the Lord and who will draw nigh to Him, a privilege granted to only a few chosen people (cp. Ex. 19:22, 24; 20:21; 24:1-2), "for who else is there that would stake his heart to come close to Me?" (Cp. Ex. 33:20; 1 Tim. 6:16; Ps. 130:3; 40:6-8; Heb. 7:22-28; 9:12; 10:5-14.)

The ancient Jewish rabbis recognized this as a Messianic prophecy. From this passage they took one of the ten names of the Messiah, Addir, Noble One, Prince. — The Midrash Tehillim on Psalm 21: "Rabbi Berachiah said in the name of R. Samuel: One Scripture says: And He came to the Ancient of Days, and they brought Him before Him (Dan. 7:13). And another Scripture says: And I shall cause Him to draw near, and He shall approach unto Me (Jer. 30:21). And, behold, in what manner! Angels brought Him into their midst; God, however, extended His hand and brought Him to Himself." Targum: "And He shall raise up Himself from among them as their King, and as their Messiah from among them He shall reveal Himself." — And once again there shall be a people who are indeed God's people, and whose God the Lord is in truth (v. 22). God accepts people, sinful men, as His own people! Can greater privilege be imagined? God gives Himself to His people! What gift more glorious can human mind conceive?

Vv. 23-24. The same words formerly applied to the false prophets (ch. 23:19-20) are now applied to the Gentile enemies, particularly wicked Babylon, which shall fall victim to the furious wrath of the Lord in a manner which shall be fully understood only in the latter days, the days of the New Testament. While Babylon was for several centuries a large and important city, so that Alexander the Great had planned to make it his royal city, it is now a mere heap of ruins.

"In the latter days," literally, in the end of days. The end is in Biblical language the opposite of the beginning. Deut. 11:12: "The eyes of the LORD, thy God, are always upon it [the Land of Promise], from the beginning of the year even unto the end of the year." The phrase "from the beginning to the end" designates the year in its entirety. The time intervening between beginning and end is not especially designated, but included in the phrase. Compare the phrase, so common in Kings, "The rest of the acts of King David, first and last, are they not written . . ." (1 Chron. 29:29; cf. 2 Chron. 9:29; 12:15; 16:11; 20:34; etc.), which does not mean that *only* the first and last acts are recorded, but includes the intervening events. Cf. also the phrase "I am the First and the Last" (Is. 41:4; 44:6; 48:12).

There are only two periods of time according to the Old Testament viewpoint: first and last. What is not included in "the first,"

243

is comprehended in "the last days," and vice versa. The history of God's kingdom on earth is therefore divided into two halves, the first and the last days; the Old and the New Covenant.

Ch. 31:1. Since the phrase "Thus saith the LORD" (ch. 31:2) introduces a new paragraph (see ch. 30:2, 5, 12, 18; 31:7; etc.), we regard ch. 31:1 as the conclusion of ch. 30. It repeats the glorious promise of ch. 30:22. The phrase "At the same time" refers to "the latter days" of ch. 30:24. Note the frequent references to the "latter days" or the New Testament era in ch. 30, 31, 33. Besides these two we find: "days are coming" (ch. 31:27, 38), "the days come" (ch. 33:14), "in those days" (ch. 31:29; 33:16), with "and at that time" added (ch. 33:15), "after those (these) days" (ch. 31:33). Jer. 31: 31-34 is quoted as referring to the New Testament in Heb. 8:8-12; 10:15-18; Jer. 31:15 in Matt. 2:17-18.

Who are "all the families of Israel" (ch. 31:1)? This question is answered by the Lord Himself in ch. 31:7, where He limits His people, the families of Israel, whose God He will be, to the "remnant of Israel." On this term compare Is. 1:9; 10:20-22; Micah 2:12; 4:6-7; etc., and Rom. 9:22-30; 11:1-6; and on "Israel" of the New Testament, Rom. 2:28-29; Gal. 6:15-16. Hence throughout ch. 30—33 "Israel," "Ephraim," "Judah," etc., refer to the true Israel, the Church of God, the elect remnant composed of the believing Jews and such Gentiles as joined the Church of God through faith in the promised Messiah, who appeared in Jesus Christ. In the "latter days" this Israel is composed chiefly of believing Gentiles. The promise of a physical return to Canaan (ch. 30:4-20) ended with the abrogation of the Old Covenant and is no longer part of God's covenant with His people in the latter days.

CHAPTER 31:2 ff.

2. Behold, I Make All Things New

A. A new union established between God and His Church, vv. 2-8

2 Thus says the LORD: The people that escaped from the sword have found grace in the desert! Let Israel go to dwell peacefully!
3 From afar the LORD appeared to me. I have loved you with everlasting love, therefore I have drawn you to Me in loving-kindness.
4 Again will I build you, and you shall be built, O Virgin Israel! Again will you adorn yourself with timbrels and go out in the dance 5 of those who rejoice. Again will you plant vineyards on the hills of Samaria, the planters will plant 6 and enjoy the fruit. For a day shall come when the watchmen cry on the Mount of Ephraim: Arise! Let us go up to Zion, to the LORD, 7 our God! For thus says the LORD:

Shout joyfully for Jacob! Rejoice over the Head of the nations! Proclaim! Praise! Say: LORD, save Thy people, the remnant of 8 Israel! Behold, I will bring them out of the Northland, and I will gather them from the ends of the earth! Among them the blind and the lame, the pregnant woman and the woman in childbirth, together. As a large congregation shall they return here.

Grammatical Notes

V. 2. "I went to cause him to rest." הָלוֹךְ הָלוֹךְ לְהַרְגִּיעוֹ, the abs. inf. may take the place of any verbal form. It may be cohortative, "I will go"; or perfect, "I went," as A. V. renders it; or Jussive, "Let Israel go!" So in Lev. 6:7; Num. 6:5; Ex. 30:36. רגע = to rest; Hiphil either causative (Jer. 50:34) or intransitive (Deut. 28:65; Is. 34:14), be in rest, dwell safely. The latter sense is preferable here, connected with Jussive, "Let Israel go to his rest."

V. 2. "Left of the sword," refers not to the deliverance out of Egypt, but to those who escaped the sword of the Babylonians and were captives in Babylon, "the wilderness," as compared with God's own land. In Babylon the exiles "found grace." Through the efforts of Jeremiah, Ezekiel, and Daniel the nucleus of a new nation was formed, willing to serve the Lord, and David, their King (ch. 30:9). "When I went," see Grammatical Notes. It is a command: Let Israel go to rest peacefully! The people that found grace are the true Israel and shall dwell safely in God's land, His holy Church, the Jerusalem of Jer. 3:17.

V. 3. "Of old," rather "from afar," the usual sense of this phrase. Israel and Judah had gone far away from God, had forsaken Him (ch. 2:13, 17, 19, etc.) days without number (ch. 1:16), and God had cast them out of His sight (ch. 7:15; 15:1). Yet these Israelites, scattered far and wide, who had found grace in the wilderness, now joyously acknowledge the grace of the Lord, who loved them with an everlasting love and therefore had drawn them to Himself in loving-kindness. The rendering "drawn," adopted by A. V. and Luther, is the correct one. The marginal reading adopted by many interpreters, "extended to thee," would require the dative; while the accusative with "draw" is frequently used in the sense of drawing toward oneself, or out of; so Gen. 37:28; Deut. 21:3; Judg. 4:7; Is: 5:18; Jer. 38:13; Hos. 11:4. Then "therefore" adds a result, instead of a mere repetition. On the thought cp. Hos. 2:19-23.

Vv. 4-5. The "virgin" who had done a very horrible thing (ch. 18: 13, 15) is still the object of God's love, a chaste and pure virgin, as in the days of old (Jer. 2:2-3; cp. 2 Cor. 11:2; Rev. 14:4). Why? The answer, ch. 31:34. Forgiveness! To her He promises restoration to

245

glory and joy. "Plant vines . . . Samaria," which from 722 B. C. was populated by a semipagan people (1 Kings 17:22-41). Even this country, like Galilee of the nations (Is. 9:1), shall revert to God's people; not as a physical possession, but by conversion (v. 6; cp. Is. 2:3; Micah 4:2). To go to Zion in Old Testament prophecy is to join the Christian Church (Is. 2:3b; 18:7; Heb. 12:22ff.). The New Testament records the fulfillment of this prophecy: 1) The frequent visits of Christ in Galilee (Matt. 4:12-17); Galilee was the scene of His greatest activity and of innumerable miracles. 2) The nobleman of Capernaum coming to Cana in Galilee (John 4:43-46). 3) The Samaritan woman and the city of Sychar (John 4:1-42; cp. vv. 20-22, salvation is of the Jews!). 4) Jesus' charge Acts 1:8 ("in Samaria"). 5) Samaria accepts the Gospel (Acts 8:5-17). 6) Cornelius, the Gentile, stationed at Caesarea in Samaria (Acts 10:1ff.).

V. 7. The Church is addressed. "Shout among," to shout for joy, exult "for" = "because of." "The Chief of the nations" does not refer to Israel, as some interpreters hold, pointing to Deut. 26:19, where, however, not "chief," "head," but "high," is used. The Head of the Gentiles is the Messiah, the Noble One (ch. 30:21), David the King (ch. 30:9), Jehovah Our Righteousness (ch. 23:6). The Church is to rejoice in its Savior, proclaim Him, and pray for the growth and preservation of the remnant, the Church of God's elect (Is. 10:20-21).

V. 8. The prayer of the Church is answered by the Lord. He will bring His chosen people from Babylon and Assyria and the farthest points of the earth to spiritual Zion, His Church, by sending preachers of the Gospel (Acts 1:8). "With them," rather, among them the blind and the lame, etc., such as could never by their own reason or strength believe in Jesus Christ or come to Him and His Church. Yet for the Lord no obstacle is too great, and no life condition makes it impossible for Him to bring His elect to faith and salvation, Is. 40:29-31; Ezek. 34:13-16; Matt. 19:24-26.

A great "company," rather, "congregation," shall return hither, to Jerusalem. "Congregation" is the term constantly used of Israel after leaving Egypt as an organized community, the congregation, the assembly, the church of Israel. (Ex. 12:6; 16:3; Lev. 4:13-14, 21, etc.). A new congregation has been formed, the congregation of the Israel of the New Testament, Jews and Gentiles becoming one in Christ (Eph. 2:11-22; Acts 15:7-17). This cannot refer to the returning exiles, who were no great company. Ezra 2:64; cp. 2 Sam. 24:9.

B. A new relationship: Fatherhood of God based on redemption, vv. 9-11

9 They will come with weeping, and in their supplications I will lead them; I will bring them to streams of water by a straight way on which they shall not stumble, for I am Israel's Father, and Ephraim 10 is My first-born son. Hear the Word of the LORD, O nations, and publish it in the islands afar off! Say: He that scattered Israel has gathered him and keeps him as a 11 shepherd his flock. For the LORD has ransomed Jacob and redeemed him from the power of him that is stronger than he.

Grammatical Notes

V. 11. "Redeemed," פָּדָה, by paying the ransom price (Ex. 13:13, 15; 34:20); "ransomed" גָּאַל, by obligation of kinship (Lev. 25:25 f., 48 f.; Num. 35:12, 19 ff.; Ruth 2:20; 3:9; 4:1, 8, 14).

V. 9. With tears of repentance and joy, with prayers and supplications, shall they come, led by the Lord and receiving from Him grace for grace in response to their pleadings. The Lord will remove all obstacles in their way to their eternal home, so that they shall not stumble, lame and blind and feeble and ill though they are. He will lead them by the rivers of water, the never-ceasing streams of His Gospel (cp. Ps. 23:2; Ezek. 34:13).

For God is the Father of Israel, and Ephraim is His first-born. In Ex. 4:22 God had spoken this of Israel in bondage of Egypt and on this account demanded Pharaoh to set God's son free (Ex. 4:23). In like manner the infernal Pharaoh, Satan, will not be able to hold the sons of God in captivity. Because the elect of God are God's own sons, therefore God will see to it that they are brought to His Zion, His Church on earth, His Kingdom of Grace on earth and of Glory in heaven.

Vv. 10-11. The nations, all the Gentiles, are told to hear the Word of the Lord, accept His Gospel with a believing heart, and then to publish it in the "isles," the coast lands, afar off. No distance shall be too great, no journey too perilous to bring the glad tidings to Israel that the Lord is willing to bring them back to His fold, His Church. Mission work among the Jews is the glorious privilege and solemn duty of Gentiles, once aliens, now fellow citizens of the saints by the grace of God, due to the fact that Jews brought to them the saving Gospel. "Jacob," God's Israel (Gal. 6:16), shall be brought to salvation, for the Lord has "ransomed" him from captivity and "redeemed" (see Grammatical Notes) him from slavery, so that he is delivered out of the hand and power of him who is stronger than he, from whose dread rule he could not deliver himself (cp. Luke 11: 21-22; Heb. 2:14-15).

C. New and everlasting joy, vv. 12-14

12 And they shall come and shout for joy on the height of Zion, and they shall stream to the goodness of the LORD, for corn, and new wine, and oil, and for the young of the flock and herd. Their soul shall be as a watered garden, and they shall 13 sorrow no more. Then shall the virgin rejoice in the dance and young men and old men together. I will turn their sorrow to joy, and I will comfort them after their 14 anguish. I will satisfy the soul of the priests with fat, and My people will be satiated with My goodness, is the oracle of the LORD.

Vv. 12-14. Since the Gentiles are proclaiming a divine redemption wrought by the Lord Himself (ch. 23:6), their preaching is not in vain. Jews and Gentiles shall "flow together," shall stream to Zion, to the goodness of the Lord (cp. ch. 3:17), and there obtain wheat, the bread of life, and wine, the Gospel, and the oil of the Holy Spirit, and the young of the flock and of the herd, many other gifts of divine grace. No more sorrow for them! Again a proof for the spirituality of the deliverance and blessings here described; a joy which the new man of the child of God continually enjoys, even though the Christian is harassed by fightings without and fears within (2 Cor. 7:5; Rom. 5:1ff.); a foretaste of the heavenly peace and joy (Is. 35:10). Men and women, young and old (v. 13), priests, the spiritual leaders, and people (v. 14), all together rejoice and are satisfied and grow and flourish spiritually, no matter what their material and physical condition may be.

D. New comfort in sorrow, vv. 15-17

15 Thus says the LORD: Hark! Lamentation is heard on the height! Bitter weeping! Rachel is weeping for her children and refuses to be comforted for her chil-16 dren, for they are no more! Thus says the LORD: Restrain your voice from weeping and your eyes from tears. For there is a reward for your labor, is the oracle of the Lord, and they shall return from 17 the land of the enemy. There is hope for your future, is the oracle of the LORD, and your children shall return to their homeland.

V. 15. The joyous picture suddenly, abruptly, changes into one of bitter woe. Rachel, the ancestress of the tribe of Benjamin, died near Bethlehem-Ephrath (Gen. 35:18-19), and was buried there. The pillar marking her grave was situated at Zelzah in the border of Benjamin, the exact site of which is unknown (1 Sam. 10:2). Bethlehem-Ephrath was allotted by Joshua to the tribe of Judah (Judg 17: 7-8; Ruth 1:1-2; Micah 5:2). The boundary line between the two tribes ran through the Valley of Hinnom (Joshua 18:16), Jerusalem belonging to Benjamin (Joshua 18:28). Ramah is one of the cities allotted to Benjamin (Joshua 18:25), about five miles north of Jerusalem.

Rachel, the tribal mother of Benjamin, is still living in her descendants. Bitterly she weeps for her children, because they are not, they are dead (Gen. 42:36). Her weeping is heard in Ramah. That does not necessarily imply that Ramah is close to Bethlehem, or that the grave of Rachel was near Ramah, or that the tragedy causing her weeping actually occurred in Ramah. Her weeping was heard there; the tragedy may have occurred elsewhere.

What lamentation has the prophet in mind? Opinions differ. Most commentators refer it to the lamentations of the mothers in Israel when the northern tribes were deported to Assyria, 722 B. C. Rachel is regarded as the tribal mother of the northern tribes, and she is told that her children would return. Others interpret this lament as symbolizing the great catastrophe of 586 and the deportation of the Jews to Babylon.

Neither of these interpretations in their various forms does justice to the text and context.

1. Nowhere does Scripture call Rachel the tribal mother of northern Israel. She was the mother of Joseph and Benjamin and through the former, of Ephraim and Manasseh, three tribes; while Leah was the ancestress of five tribes; Bilhah, Rachel's maid, of two; and Zilpah, Leah's maid, of two (Gen. 29:31—30:25; 35:16-18). Benjamin, Rachel's son, was always part of the kingdom of Judah, Leah's son, while northern Israel had four ancestral mothers.

2. Why should the people exiled in 722 be regarded as "children" of Rachel, and the mothers of the exiled people as Mother Rachel? The deportation of 722 was a total depopulation of the northern territory, mothers and children being transplanted to Assyrian provinces, while Israel was populated by foreign nations (2 Kings 17).

3. Nowhere are we told that in 586 there was a special lamentation at Ramah. Jer. 40:1, adduced as proof for this assertion, simply states that Jeremiah was released at Ramah. The lamentation of 586 began at Jerusalem and continued to Babylon.

4. Nowhere is Ramah designated as the site of Rachel's tomb. Some commentators are so positive in their identification of the two that they stamp "which is Bethlehem" in Gen. 35:19 as a later interpolation.

5. The Masoretic text points "in Ramah" not as a proper noun, but as a common noun, "on the height." Accordingly the Sinaitic

249

and Alexandrian codices of the LXX, Aquila, the Vulgate, the Targum, translate "on the height." In Matt. 2:18 the Vulgate has "in Rama," while Luther translates in both instances "on the height," *auf der Hoehe, auf dem Gebirge.* — The Greek New Testament followed the reading of the Vatican Code. — If we translate "heights," Ramah is left completely out of the picture. If we translate "Ramah," this city may be named because Herod may have named it in his decree to slay the infants of Bethlehem and the surrounding country, or because the weeping was heard as far as Ramah. Rachel is introduced as bewailing her children because her tomb was located at Bethlehem, where the infants were to be slain.

These reasons are sufficient in themselves to discredit the interpretation referring this passage to one of the deportations of either the Northern or the Southern Kingdom. There remains another reason which is definitely decisive against these theories. In the New Testament this passage is definitely stated to have found its fulfillment in Herod's murdering the infants of Bethlehem, Matt. 2:17-18. Keil's farfetched explanation of the typical character of this prophecy may suffice as an example of the futility of the "typical" interpretation. "The typology presupposes a causal connection between the two events. The annihilation of Israel is a type of the murder of the children at Bethlehem in so far as the sin which caused the deportation of Israel was basic for the fact that Herod, the Edomite, became the king of the Jews, who planned to annihilate the true King and Savior of Israel in order to safeguard his own rule."

But does not the context of Jer. 31:17-18 speak of the dispersion and extermination of Israel? What has the murder of the infants by Herod to do with this deportation? Must we not assume either that Matthew was mistaken in regarding Herod's atrocious deed a fulfillment of Jeremiah's prophecy or that he viewed the destruction of Israel or Judah as a type of the murder of the innocents? No! Certainly not. The entire context of ch. 31, beginning ch. 30:20 and continuing to ch. 33:26, is Messianic. The four chapters speak of the approach of the Lord's salvation, of the coming of Messiah to reestablish the Kingdom of David in the form of a new covenant, of which forgiveness of sins is to be the foundation (ch. 31:31-34); a kingdom in which every weary and sorrowful soul shall be fully comforted (vv. 12-14, 25). As an example of this comfort the Lord introduces the consolation to be extended to mothers who had suffered great loss for the sake of Christ, the cruel murder of their infant sons. For in close connection with the tragedy and the resultant sorrowful weeping of heartbroken Rachel, described in v. 15, we read words of sweetest comfort in vv. 16-17. These little babes murdered for Christ's sake, the first martyrs, are not lost to their mothers nor to the kingdom of Israel, the Church. God tells them that their work shall be rewarded. What they have done, their labor in bearing children, shall not be in vain. Their children are not annihilated. They still are members of His covenant nation. They shall come again from the land of the enemy, the enemy of the New Testament Church, death (cp. 1 Cor. 15: 25-26). "There is hope in thine end," for thy end. "Hope for" always indicates the one for whose welfare there is hope; and "end" here means either "future," as in ch. 29: 11, or as it is used in several passages, "your posterity," offspring (cp. Ps. 37: 38; 109: 13; Dan. 11: 4). In both translations the hope of resurrection is expressed. So they shall come to their "own land," the new heaven and earth, of which the Promised Land, Canaan, was a pledge and guarantee (Heb. 11: 14-16). The true Israelites regarded themselves merely as sojourners and pilgrims in the land of Canaan (Gen. 17: 8; 23: 4; Ps. 39: 12).

E. New and God-pleasing sorrow for sin, vv. 18-19

18 I clearly hear Ephraim lament: Thou hast chastened me, and I was chastened as an untrained calf. Turn Thou me, and I shall be turned, for Thou art the LORD, my

19 God! For after I have turned, I repent; and after I was brought to knowledge, I smite my thigh, I am ashamed, I was dismayed, for I bore the shame of my youth.

Vv. 18-19. The lament of Ephraim, the true Israel, the Church of God, is heard. The believers deplore the tardy acceptance of the Lord's instructions. They were like a calf that would not submit to the yoke. They craved freedom, the license to sin, rather than the easy and blessed yoke of obedient love of God. Only through bitter chastisement were they brought to self-despair. Repentant Ephraim, the converted remnant, now turns to the Lord with the sincere request: Turn Thou me, and I shall be turned. So only a converted person can speak. Prayer is the fruit of faith, a proof of conversion (Acts 9: 11). All efforts of the sinner to convert himself are in vain, and all efforts of the converted child of God to remain a Christian by his own efforts are useless. It is God who must turn the sinner from sin and Satan to God, and it is the Lord who must continually turn the converted sinner away from the path of sin to the way of faith and obedience. Conversion and preservation in faith are the work of the Lord (Phil. 2: 13; 2 Cor. 8: 16). "I smote upon my thigh."

251

This is the godly sorrow of which only a believer is capable; a sorrow caused by the recognition of God's unfathomable love and the black wickedness of a life spent in enmity against this God (Ezek. 36: 31; Jer. 3: 22-25; 2 Cor. 7: 8-11). "I was ashamed," rather, I am ashamed. The memory of past sins drives the blush of shame to the Christian's face; "confounds," abashes, humiliates, crushes him to the ground before the majesty of his God. And yet he confidently prays this very God, to whom he dares not to lift up his eyes: God, be merciful! Turn me, and I shall be turned!

F. New blessings and new faithfulness, vv. 20-28

20 Is Ephraim My precious son? Or is he My darling child? For as often as I speak against him, I still hold him in loving memory! Therefore My heart yearns for him; My full compassion goes out to him, 21 is the oracle of the LORD. Raise waymarks for yourself! Erect guideposts! Set your mind upon the highway, the way you have walked! Return, O Virgin Israel! 22 Return to these your cities! How long will you hesitate, you apostate daughter? For the LORD creates something new in the land: Woman 23 shall surround man. Thus says the LORD of Hosts, the God of Israel: Once more will they speak this word in the land of Judah and in its cities, when I shall turn their captivity: May the LORD bless 24 you, O habitation of salvation, O mount of holiness! And Judah and all her cities will dwell there, plowmen and those that go out 25 with the flock. For I will satisfy the weary soul, and every lan- 26 guishing soul will I fill. At this I awoke and looked up, and my 27 sleep was pleasant to me. Behold, days are coming, is the oracle of the LORD, when I will sow the house of Israel and the house of Judah with the seed of men and 28 with the seed of cattle. And it shall be, as I watched over them for the purpose of uprooting, and tearing down, and throwing down and destroying, and doing evil, so will I watch over them for the purpose of building and planting, is the oracle of the LORD.

V. 20. Ephraim certainly was not worthy of God's love. He had by no means been a dear son, a child in whom the parent could take delight. Yet as often as God speaks of him, He remembers him, cannot forget him, His "bowels," womb, the seat of pity, His heart yearns for him. He must have pity on him. God Himself, humanly speaking, is surprised at His own sympathy and mercy for wicked sinners. This pity moves Him to call Ephraim, the apostate (Jer. 3: 12, 14, 22), back to His home.

V. 21. "Waymarks," stone markers (Ezek. 39: 15). "High heaps," rather, high poles or beacons, pointing out the way to Zion. Pay close attention to the "highway," a leveled way (cp. "highway," Is. 35: 8, same root), prepared by the Lord in contrast to their self-chosen ways of sin and idolatry (ch. 2: 18, 20, 23, 33; 3: 13). Israel had walked on God's highway of holiness in the days of her youth (ch. 2: 2), but had left it. "Virgin," see v. 4. She is invited to return to "these thy cities," the bridal gift of her divine Bridegroom.

V. 22. "Go about," roam, Hithpael is causative, reflexive. Her roaming was caused by her own willful purpose. "Daughter," God still loves her. He is ready to receive her and adds a remarkable promise in order to induce her to return. The Lord of infinite power and grace will create an entirely new thing. "A woman shall compass a man." "Woman," נְקֵבָה, denotes woman as woman, as the female sex, as the weaker vessel (1 Peter 3: 7), the helpmeet for man (Gen. 2: 18); cp. also Gen. 1: 27, "male and female." "Man," גֶּבֶר, strong, virile, powerful. The anarthrous construction, man, woman, stresses the qualitative force of the terms, man as man, woman as woman. "Compass," here in the sense of faithful "surrounding," loving adherence, clinging to an object. Cp. Deut. 32: 10 (led him about, "compassed" him); Ps. 26: 6; 32: 7, 10. David "compasses" the altar, is faithfully attached to it; God's mercy clings, remains loyal to the believer. The virgin Israel is a feeble woman, but will "surround" Him, who is a mighty Man, Jehovah, her Righteousness, and cling to Him as the ivy surrounds and clings to the oak, receiving its support from the strong tree, so that it will fall to the ground only if the tree falls. The imperfect describes the ever-renewed surrounding, embracing ever closer Him without whom she could not live or exist. That is something new on earth, altogether and essentially different from the nature of the Old Testament nation of Israel. And that is a creation of the Lord, the Covenant God, who brings to perfection this loyalty of the Church to the Lord characterizing the New Testament Covenant and only foreshadowed by the people of the Old Covenant; many, if not most of them, did not "surround" Jehovah, but roamed continually away from Him. How God will create this state of unfailing loyalty is told vv. 31-34, after describing still more fully the blessedness of the New Testament Church.

Vv. 23-25 are directed to Judah. But it is the Lord of Hosts, the God of Israel, that addresses Judah. What was said concerning Israel and Ephraim vv. 1-22 concerns Judah also. Hence both are named side by side in vv. 27 and 31, and in vv. 36 and 37 the seed of Israel, the whole seed of Israel, is named. That expression points back to Jer. 31: 1, "all the families of Israel," called in v. 7 "the people of God," the remnant of Israel. Jewish Judah and paganized Israel have become one nation (cp. Jer. 3: 18; Hos. 1: 11; Ezek. 37: 21-22), addressed once by the one, then by the other name.

253

V. 23. In the language of the Old Covenant the prophet pictures the glory of the Church of God of all times. The Church recognizes gratefully the blessings God has bestowed upon it in making it a dwelling place of salvation, of righteousness (see Jer. 23: 6), the mountain of holiness, sanctification. Justification and sanctification are the two chief gifts of God to His Church. Spiritual peace and increase shall be granted to it (v. 24), and every weary, sorrowful, languishing soul shall be comforted and fully satisfied (v. 25). Cp. Matt. 11: 28.

V. 26. Hearing this marvelous promise, the prophet awoke from his sleep and "saw," here in sense of recognizing, realizing (cp. 1 Sam. 12: 17; Jer. 2: 19; etc.). The imperf. denotes progressive action, he began to realize in ever-increasing measure that his sleep had been indeed a sweet one, since he had received a message of hope and comfort without the slightest threat or condemnation, the only one of this nature on record in his book.

There can be no reasonable doubt that this revelation was granted to Jeremiah while asleep, though this is the only instance on record that Jeremiah received revelations in sleep. We know that not only Nebuchadnezzar had received a remarkable revelation in the form of a dream (Dan. 2: 1, 5, 28-29), which later was granted to Daniel in a night vision (v. 19; cp. also Dan. 4: 2-7). Daniel also received the vision of the four kingdoms in the form of a dream (Dan. 7: 1-2, 7, 13). There is no valid reason why God should not have been able to reveal His plans to Jeremiah in his sleep. Such a "dream" or vision was essentially different from the dreams of the prophets (Jer. 23: 25), for they prophesied without God's commission (ch. 23: 21), the visions of their own heart (vv. 16, 26), in order to cause the people to err and forget Jehovah's name (vv. 27, 32), while Jeremiah's prophecies, whether revealed to Him while asleep or awake, had a different origin, a different content, a different purpose. Whether he received the continuation of this revelation while awake or after he had again gone to sleep, we cannot tell, nor does it matter. The marvelous content is not changed by the manner of reception.

Commentators (Bugenhagen, Calov, and others) read v. 26 as a continuation of God's speech. That seems impossible, for then God would have been sleeping while restoring the fortunes of His people (vv. 23-25), awakening only because, or after, He had accomplished all that.

Vv. 27-28. The Lord presents Himself as the Sower of seed from which men and cattle shall issue. Cities and country (ch. 4: 7, 25;

14:15-18; 33:10,12) shall again teem with human and animal life (cp. Zech. 2:4). "Watch," same word as ch. 1:12. As the Lord had been alert to uproot, so He will be eager to build, to plant, to bless with spiritual and material gifts.

G. New understanding of the wickedness and evil consequences of sin, vv. 29-30

29 In those days they shall no more say: The fathers have eaten the sour grapes, and the teeth of the children have been set on edge.

30 But everyone shall die for his own iniquity; he that eats sour grapes shall have his teeth set on edge.

Vv. 29-30. Misinterpreting such passages as Ex. 20:5; 15:4; etc., the Jews had used the proverb v. 29, charging God with injustice and cruelty for the punishment of children, who ought not to be accountable for their father's sin. A conscientious self-examination would have revealed to them that this was merely the hypocritical excuse of self-righteous sinners, who excelled their father in wickedness. In the New Covenant the absolute justice of God will be fully acknowledged, and every child of God will recognize and acknowledge that the primary cause of every punishment and chastisement lies in man's own deceitful, desperately wicked heart (ch. 17:10), in his own iniquity.

H. The new covenant, vv. 31-40

a. Its spirituality, vv. 31-34

31 Behold, days are coming, is the oracle of the LORD, when I will make a new covenant with the house of Israel and the house of
32 Judah. Not like the covenant which I made with their fathers on the day that I took hold of their hand to lead them out of the land of Egypt, which My covenant they broke, although I was married to them, is the oracle of the LORD.
33 For this is the covenant which I shall make with the house of Israel after those days, is the oracle of the LORD: I will give My Law within them and will write it upon their heart; and I will be their God,
34 and they shall be My people. And no longer shall one teach his neighbor and his brother, saying: "Learn to know the LORD," for all of them will know me, both small and great, is the oracle of the LORD, for I will forgive their guilt, and their sins I will remember no more.

V. 31. This New Covenant is made with reunited Judah and Israel, joined by the Gentiles (Jer. 3:16-19; Hos. 1:10-11; Rom. 9:25f.; 1 Peter 2:10), who will then form the one holy Christian Church (John 10:16; 11:52). It is described negatively (v. 32) and positively (vv. 33-34).

255

V. 32. Dissimilarities. 1) The Old Covenant made with "the fathers," the descendants of Israel. "To bring them," etc. Its establishment included all the events narrated from Exodus 3 to Num. 10:11, from the call of Moses to the dedication of the Tabernacle (Ex. 40: 1-38; Num. 10:12). It comprised all Israelites, believers and unbelievers, that had been delivered out of Egypt. Its laws regulated the entire religious, political, social, and home life of every citizen of the commonwealth of Israel, an unbearable yoke (Acts 15:10) of bondage (Gal. 5:1)!

2) This covenant "they brake" almost as soon as it was established (Exodus 32), again and again (Numbers 14; 16; Jer. 7:25-28; Ps. 95: 8-11; Acts 7:51-53). They broke it "although I was an Husband to them." The LXX, quoted Heb. 8:9, translates: "I regarded them not," but the Hebrew verb בָּעַל is never used in this sense. The Lord accepted the whole nation as a nation into marital relation (Ex. 19:1ff.) under condition of obedience. In spite of this undeserved love they became unfaithful to their heavenly Bridegroom.

Vv. 33-34. The nature of the New Covenant. God Himself will put His Law, the norm of the New Covenant, into their inmost parts, so that this teaching will permeate their entire being. The Hebrew perfect "I put" designates this placing as an accomplished fact. What this Law is we shall learn later. The manner in which it is placed into the inmost parts is next described. "I will write it in their hearts," the seat and fountainhead of their life and all their activities. The Hebrew imperfect "I will write" denotes progressive duration. We see God as He is writing. Since this writing is the very essence of the covenant, it never ceases, but throughout the duration of the covenant He is continually writing it afresh into the heart so that it will not be forgotten. This writing goes on in the heart of every member of the covenant without exception, *their* inward parts," *their* hearts," so that I will be the God of every one of them, "their God," "and they," all of them, "shall be My people not in name only, but in deed and truth. The membership of this covenant consists exclusively of such as have the Law of God within themselves, written there by the Lord Himself.

V. 34. "They shall teach no more . . . brother." The repetition of "neighbor" and "brother" is to impress on the reader that these terms are not to be used in the general sense of "one another," forbidding therefore the teaching of neighbors and brethren in general. He denies the need of a certain instruction to be given to such as are "neighbors," fellow citizens with the saints, and "brethren" in the household of God (Eph. 2: 19). There is no need of ever-repeated teaching (the Hebrew imperfect is progressive) the fellow Christian, "Know the Lord!" To know the Lord is saving faith (Jer. 9: 24; John 17: 3; Gal. 4: 8-9), the basic and indispensable essential of membership in God's New Covenant. A Christian certainly need not to be told to become a Christian, to come to the knowledge of the Lord. He *has* come to this knowledge, he is a Christian. "For," as the Lord continues, "they," the members of this New Covenant, shall all know Me, from the least of them to the greatest, young and old, the humblest and the most renowned, the baptized infants (Matt. 28: 19; Gal. 3: 26-27; Titus 3: 5), standing at the threshold of life, and aged Simeons, at the end of the journey (Luke 2: 29f.), all of them shall know the Lord. "For I will forgive . . . no more." There is no work of man, no self-acquired holiness as a condition for entering this covenant. The New Covenant has a sacrifice which alone can procure what the ever-repeated sacrifices of the Old Covenant typified and foreshadowed, the perfect sacrifice of the Woman's Seed, the Suffering Servant, the Righteous Branch, the Lord Our Righteousness. The Hebrew imperfects "I will forgive, not remember" denote the ever-repeated forgiveness, "richly and daily," and the daily blotting out from God's memory of the sins we daily commit. Cp. Micah 7: 18-19 and Jer. 50: 20 on the thoroughness of God's pardon and forgiveness. This Gospel of forgiveness, justifying, sanctifying, preserving unto the end, is the "Law," the teaching put into the innermost life by being written in the hearts of all members of the covenant by the Lord.

These are the factors distinguishing the New Covenant from the Sinai Covenant. The Sinai Covenant demanded perfect obedience, the New Covenant offers forgiveness of sin. The Old Covenant was written on tables of stone, the New Covenant into the heart of the members. The Old Covenant embraced all the physical descendants of Israel, the New Covenant all those that know the Lord, Jews and Gentiles, but only believers. The forgiveness of sins in the Old Testament was a forgiveness by means of types to be fulfilled and hopes to be realized. The New Covenant has the body and the reality.

---

b. *Its permanence, vv. 35-37*

35 Thus says the LORD, who has given the sun as a light for the day, the ordinances of the moon and stars as a light for the night, who stirs up the sea, and its waves roar, the LORD of Hosts is His 36 name: When these ordinances shall be removed before Me, is the oracle of the LORD, then also the seed of Israel shall cease to be a

nation before Me for all times.
37 Thus says the LORD: If the heavens above can be measured and the foundations of the earth below are searched out, then will I also reject the whole seed of Israel for all they have done, is the oracle of the LORD.

Vv. 35-37. God's faithfulness in keeping His ordinances in the realm of nature is here made the visible pledge of like faithfulness in His keeping His covenant promises. For six thousand years He has sent sun, moon, and stars on their daily course. For the same time there has not been one day on which the waves of the sea have ceased their constant ebb and flow. And until the end of time the same Lord will fulfill His gracious promise, His ordinance, that there shall be a seed of Israel as His people for all times. And only when man will be able to measure the heavens above and fathom the foundations of the earth, and that will never occur, only then He will reject the whole seed of Israel for their sins. At all times to the end of the world there will be children of Israel according to the flesh who are Israelites in spirit also, the true Israel among the Israel in name only. Though blindness in part has befallen Israel, though this part may be the great majority, it is only a part. There always will be some Jews who together with Gentiles will praise the Lord Jesus as their Messiah and Redeemer. After all, Israel is the tree, the Gentiles are the branches grafted into the root stock of Israel. Rom. 11:1-26. Yet this very promise of God (v. 37) implies the warning that while not all of Israel will be rejected, those who persist in their unbelief will meet with final rejection. (Cp. Rom. 11:20-23.)

c. Its perfect holiness, vv. 38-40

38 Behold, days are coming, says the LORD, when the city of the LORD shall be built from the Tower of Hananeel to the Gate of the Corner.
39 And the measuring line shall go out still farther, straight forward to the hill of Gareb and turn toward Goath. And the entire valley of the carcasses and of the ashes and all the fields till the brook Kidron, to the corner of the Horse Gate on the east shall be holy unto the LORD. It shall no more be uprooted nor destroyed forever!

Grammatical Notes

V. 40. "The fields," הַשְּׁרֵמוֹת, occurs only here. LXX transliterates, ἀσαρημωθ; either derived from a root occurring in cognate dialects, denoting gully, ravine, or a copyist's error for הַשְּׁדֵמוֹת, the fields (Deut. 32:32; Hab. 3:17). "Many Mss., Q'ri, Aquila, read הַשְּׁדֵמוֹת" (Kittel, Bibl. Hebr.).

Vv. 38-40. "Tower of Hananeel," at the northeast corner of the city, near the Sheep Gate (Neh. 3:1; 12:39; Zech. 14:10); "Gate of the Corner," at the northwest corner (2 Kings 14:13; 2 Chron. 26:9; Zech. 14:10); "Horse Gate" (v. 40) at the east side near the Temple (Neh. 3:28; 2 Chron. 23:15). Gareb and Goath, or Goah, are unknown. Gareb = scabies, itch (Lev. 21:20; 22:22; Deut. 28:27), a mild form of leprosy, rendering the affected person unclean. Goath occurs only here. "Over against" (v. 39) indicates neither geographical direction nor distance. "The valley . . . ashes" (v. 40), evidently the Valley of Hinnom, defiled by Josiah (2 Kings 23:10; cp. Jer. 7:32-33; 19:11-13). "Dead bodies," unburied carcasses (Is. 14:19; 66:24; Jer. 33:5; 41:9; etc.); "ashes," the ashes of the offal of the sacrifices, burnt without the camp (Lev. 4:11-12; 7:17,19); others, the ashes of the sacrificial fats burnt on the altar (Lev. 1:16; 6:10; etc.). "The fields" (v. 40). Cp. Grammatical Notes. The underlying idea of this passage (vv. 38-40) is not the enlargement of Jerusalem, but its complete sanctification. Even the areas formerly unclean "shall be holy unto the Lord." This is the Jerusalem of Jer. 3:17; the *Una Sancta* (Eph. 1: 3-7; 1 Cor. 1:2; Eph. 5:25-27; Heb. 12:22-24), and in its final consummation, the heavenly Jerusalem (Revelation 21; 22; particularly 21:2, 27).

CHAPTER 32

3. The Symbolical Purchase of Hanameel's Field by Jeremiah

A. Time and circumstances of the command, vv. 1-5

1 The word which came to Jeremiah from the LORD in the tenth year of Zedekiah, the king of Judah. (This was the eighteenth year of 2 Nebuchadrezzar.) At that time the armies of the king of Babylon were besieging Jerusalem, and Jeremiah the prophet was imprisoned in the Court of the Guard in the palace 3 of the king of Judah, because Zedekiah, the king of Judah, had imprisoned him, saying: Why do you prophesy: Thus says the LORD: Behold, I am giving this city into the hand of the king of Babylon, 4 and he shall take it; and Zedekiah, the king of Judah, shall not escape the hand of the Chaldeans, for he shall certainly be given into the hand of the king of Babel and shall speak to him mouth to mouth and 5 shall see him eye to eye. And to Babylon shall Zedekiah be sent, and there he shall remain until I visit him, is the oracle of the LORD. Your war against the Chaldeans shall be void of success!

Since both the time and the circumstances caused the prophet to air his misgivings before the Lord (vv. 16-25), they are given here in detail. The tenth year of Zedekiah synchronizes with the eighteenth year of Nebuchadnezzar. The siege of Jerusalem, begun in the ninth year of Zedekiah (ch. 52:4; 2 Kings 25:1f.), had to be raised tempo-

259

rarily on the approach of Pharaoh-Necho's Egyptian army (ch. 37: 3-5). During this breathing spell the shameful breach of covenant, narrated ch. 34: 8-22, had occurred. Jeremiah took the opportunity afforded by the raising of the siege to go to Anathoth for the purpose of dividing an inheritance. While passing through the city gate, he was arrested and imprisoned (ch. 37: 11-21).

V. 3. "Zedekiah" does not contradict "princes" (ch. 37: 15), since Zedekiah did nothing to stop the imprisonment, but turned the prophet over to his enemies (ch. 38: 5). On vv. 4-5 see ch. 34: 2-3.

B. The purchase of the field, vv. 6-15

6 Jeremiah said: The word of the
7 LORD came to me, saying: Behold, Hanameel, the son of Shallum, your uncle, is coming to you, saying: Buy my field which is at Anathoth, for you have the redeemer's right
8 to buy it. And Hanameel, the son of my uncle, came to me in accordance with the word of the LORD into the Court of the Guard and said to me: Buy my field which is at Anathoth in the land of Benjamin, for you have the right of possession, and yours is the right of redemption. Buy it for yourself! Then I realized that this was the
9 word of the LORD. So I bought the field at Anathoth from Hanameel, my uncle's son, and weighed out unto him the silver, seventeen
10 shekels of silver. Then I signed the deed and sealed it and summoned witnesses and weighed the
11 silver in a scale. And I took the sealed purchase deed, as it is customary and lawful, and the open
12 copy, and took the purchase deed to Baruch, the son of Neriah, the son of Machaseiah, in the presence of Hanameel, my uncle, and in the presence of the witnesses who had signed the purchase deed in the presence of all Jews seated in the Court of the Guard. Then I commissioned Baruch in their presence,
14 saying: Thus says the LORD of Hosts, the God of Israel: Take these deeds, this purchase deed, both the sealed one and this open copy, and seal them in a potter's vessel, that they may last for many
15 days. For thus says the LORD of Hosts, the God of Israel: In this land, houses and fields and vineyards shall again be bought.

Vv. 7 and 12 Hanameel is called Jeremiah's uncle, דֹּד; in vv. 8 and 9, his uncle's son. Either the word "son" was omitted by the copyist, or the term "uncle" is used in a wider sense, a close relative.

In the dark days of impending disaster, Jeremiah received a divine command and promise which seemed like mockery to him. The command was to obey the request of his cousin Hanameel that Jeremiah make use of his right and duty as nearest of kin to purchase the field of Hanameel situated in Jeremiah's native city, Anathoth (cp. Lev. 25: 8-55). While the members of the tribe of Levi had no special tribal territory assigned to them, the priests were allotted thirteen cities

(Joshua 21:19), the Levites forty-eight (Joshua 21:41; Num. 35:2-9). Hence they owned real estate which, however, could be sold only to a fellow Levite and bought only by a Levite (Lev. 25:32-34). The reasons for the sale (poverty? removal?) and for the seemingly small sum are not stated, and it is useless to speculate on them. What really is of importance is the fact that a legal sale and a legal purchase of real estate was made at this particular time by divine command. Solemnly and with careful attention to all legal details the sale is concluded and the deed executed in the customary manner. The price is agreed upon, and the pieces of silver are carefully weighed, seventeen shekels. In the Maccabean era a shekel was worth about sixty-two cents of our money; its value in Jeremiah's time is unknown.

V. 10f. On the legal execution of sales deeds, Volz has some interesting notes: "Extra-Biblical parallels fully clarify the custom referred to here of writing duplicate deeds as well as that of tying up and sealing them. Cp. Fischer, *Z. A. W.*, 1911, pp. 136—142. In Elefantina, Greek duplicate deeds dating from the fourth century B. C. have been found. The identical text was written on one sheet in duplicate; between the two texts there was always left an empty space of 2 to 3 cm. [¾ to one inch]. The papyri were folded, tied, and sealed in the following manner: The papyrus sheet was divided crosswise in the center of the empty space by a sharp cut extending to the center of the sheet; the entire width of the upper half of the sheet was rolled up, this roll dented in the center and folded together. Narrow papyrus bands were drawn through three holes, securely fastening the folded roll, and on these bands the seals were affixed. Then the lower half of the papyrus sheet was folded, the folded sheet rolled up, and this roll was finally turned under the sealed roll, so that the open roll hung loosely on the sealed roll. In other instances a simpler method of rolling was found. There was no cut between the two deeds. The two sheets were rolled up in their entire width toward the vacant space in the center, then tied by papyrus bands drawn through holes punched in the vacant space. The papyri found in Elefantina were found preserved in an earthen vessel. The discoverer reported that, apart from minor impairment, the papyri were found in the same state in which they had been placed into the vessel. The Babylonians observed the same custom of duplicate deeds in using their clay tablets. The deed was inscribed on a clay tablet and the seal impressed upon it. After this clay tablet had been baked, it was enveloped by another layer of clay on which the same writing and

261

seal were placed and then baked." (Volz, *Jeremias,* Sellin's *Kommentar zum Alten Testament,* p. 306 f.)

The sales deed is executed according to prevailing custom in duplicate copies, one open for examination at any time, the other sealed for purpose of verification (vv. 10-11). The witnesses subscribe the deed which is handed to Baruch, a scribe, Jeremiah's secretary, who is told to put the deed into an earthen vessel, most likely the manner customary to preserve or hide writings and documents. This whole transaction was to be symbolical. "Houses and fields and vineyards shall be possessed again in this land" (v. 15).

C. Jeremiah's prayer, vv. 16-25

16 After I had given the purchase deed to Baruch, the son of Neriah, I prayed to the LORD, saying:
17 Ah, Lord LORD! Behold, Thou hast made heaven and earth by Thy great power and Thy outstretched arm. Nothing is too wonderful for Thee!
18 Thou showest loving-kindness for thousands and avengest the inquity of the fathers upon the bosom of their children after them. Thou art the great and powerful God, whose name is the
19 LORD of Hosts, great in counsel and mighty in deed, whose eyes are open upon all the ways of the children of men to give to everyone according to his ways and accord-
20 ing to the fruit of his works. Thou hast performed signs and miracles in the land of Egypt to this day and in Israel and among mankind, and hast made Thyself a name, as
21 is evident this day. Thou hast led Thy people Israel out of the land of Egypt, with signs and miracles, and with a strong hand and with an outstretched arm and by great
22 terror, and hast given to them this land, which Thou hast sworn to their fathers to give to them, a land
23 flowing with milk and honey. But when they came and took possession of it, they did not listen to Thy voice, neither did they walk in Thy Law; they did nothing of all Thou hadst commanded them to do, and Thou hast brought all
24 this evil upon them. Behold, the siege mounds have approached the city to take it, and the city is given into the hands of the Chaldeans fighting against it by sword, by famine, and by pestilence. Thy threat is being carried out! And
25 behold, Thou art observing it! And still, O Lord LORD, Thou hast told me: Buy the field for yourself for money, and summon witnesses! while the city is given into the hand of the Chaldeans!

Vv. 16-25. Jeremiah's prayer. While the prophet had faithfully obeyed the Lord's command, had even revealed the symbolical purpose of the entire transaction, this divine promise seems to him utterly incongruous with the present circumstances and God's constantly repeated threats of the complete desolation of the land. Once more, as in ch. 12, 15, and 20, he pours out his doubts and misgivings to his Lord, this time not because he cannot understand God's judgments, but because God's gracious promise surpasses his comprehension. In one of the most beautiful prayers recorded in the Bible the prophet praises the Lord's absolute omnipotence as evidenced in the creation of the world (v. 17), His grace and justice (v. 18), His wise, mighty, and just providence (v. 19), as proved by His miracles performed in Egypt and to this day in Israel and among all mankind (v. 20). He remembers God's unmerited grace in delivering Israel out of Egypt and giving to His people the Land of Promise (vv. 21-22), and acknowledges that the shameful ingratitude and disobedience of the Chosen People has fully deserved the evils Judah is now suffering (v. 23). And now he reveals the problem that worries him. God's word and command is a riddle to the prophet (vv. 24-25).

D. God's answer, vv. 26-44

a. The almighty and just Lord delivers His apostate people to their enemies
vv. 26-35

26 Then the word of the LORD came
27 to Jeremiah, saying: Behold, I am the LORD, the God of all flesh! Is there anything too wonderful
28 for Me? Therefore thus says the LORD: Behold, I am giving this city into the hand of the Chaldeans and into the hand of Nebuchadrezzar, the king of Babylon, and
29 he shall take it! And the Chaldeans battling against this city shall come and set on fire this city and burn it and the houses on the roofs of which they sacrificed to Baal and offered drink offerings to other gods in order to provoke Me to
30 anger. For the children of Israel and the children of Judah from their youth have been doing only what was evil before Me. For the children of Israel have only been provoking Me to anger by the works of their hands, is the oracle
31 of the LORD. For this city has roused My anger and My wrath from the day they built it to this day, to the point of putting it away
32 before Me, because of all the evil which the children of Israel and of Judah did to provoke Me to anger, these, their kings, their princes, their priests, and their prophets, the men of Judah and the inhabit-
33 ants of Jerusalem. They turn their back to Me, and not their face. I taught them with unflagging zeal, and no one listened to
34 accept instruction. They placed their detestable things into the house upon which My name is
35 called to defile it. They built the high places of Baal which are in the Valley of the Son of Hinnom to offer up their sons and their daughters to Moloch, which I did not command them, nor did it enter my mind that they should do these abominations to make Judah sin.

Vv. 26-35. The Lord takes up the three main points of Jeremiah's prayer and answers them. 1) V. 27. Jeremiah had confessed his faith in God's omnipotence (v. 17). The Lord declares Himself to be Elohim, the strong, powerful Creator and Ruler "of all flesh."

(Cp. Num. 16: 22; 27: 16.) Before Him man is "flesh," a weak, sinful, mortal being. Neither the bitterest hatred of the strongest of His enemies nor the doubts and misgivings of His perplexed and puzzled child can nullify the plans and purposes of the omnipotent God. As if in astonishment at the prophet's unbelief in the very truth he had confessed (v. 17), God asks v. 27: Why do you not draw the proper conclusion from your conviction and trust Me that I can do whatever I promise?

2) Vv. 28-35. Jeremiah has confessed that Israel had deserved the judgments of God by its rebellion against their Redeemer. He knew that God was powerful enough to keep His threats (vv. 20-23). God confirms this truth also. As the Lord of the Covenant He fulfills His threats, although the Jews had not believed that God would or could reject His people. Why, then, does Jeremiah doubt that God can fulfill His promises even if that seems impossible to the prophet?

3) And now God proceeds to answer the doubting question asked by the prophet (vv. 24-25) by repeating that selfsame promise, vv. 36-44.

---

b. The almighty and gracious Lord will again restore His penitent people to the Land of Promise, vv. 36-44

36 And now, therefore, thus says the LORD, the God of Israel, concerning this city, of which you say, It is given into the hand of the king of Babylon by sword and by
37 hunger and by pestilence: Behold, I will gather them from all the countries into which I have scattered them in My anger, in My wrath, and in My great fury, and I will bring them back to this place and will make them dwell in
38 safety. And they shall be My people, and I will be their God.
39 And I will give them one heart and one way, to fear Me forever, for the welfare of themselves and
40 their children after them. And I will make an everlasting covenant with them, that I will not turn away from them as far as My blessing them is concerned, and I will give My fear into their hearts that they shall not turn aside from
41 Me. I will take delight in doing good to them, and I will plant them in this land securely with all My
42 heart and all My soul. For thus says the LORD: Just as I have brought upon this people all this great trouble, so I shall be bringing upon them all the good which
43 I have promised them. And fields shall be bought in this land of which you say that it is waste, without man or beast, given into
44 the hands of the Chaldeans. Fields shall they buy for money, and deeds shall be written and sealed and witnesses summoned in the land of Benjamin and in the environments of Jerusalem, and in the cities of Judah, and in the cities of the hill country, and in the cities of the Shephelah, and in the cities of the Southland. For I will restore their fortune, is the oracle of the LORD.

Vv. 36-38. "Now, therefore" resumes the argument begun v. 27.
As the omnipotent Lord is able to execute the judgments threatened
in His covenant, so even the complete destruction of the city and the
deportation of the people will not frustrate His covenant promises.
Once more He tells His prophet that they will be carried out to the
letter. V. 37 recalls the promise of the Mosaic covenant (Deut. 30: 1-5);
v. 38 the covenant promise of Ex. 19: 5-6, repeated Ex. 25: 8; 29: 45-46;
etc. But did not God stipulate the condition of repenting return to
the Lord before the people would be permitted to return to their
homeland (Deut. 30: 2)? The Lord of omnipotent grace will attend
to that also. What is impossible to man, He will do.

V. 39. He will give them "one heart." Their heart will no longer
be divided between the Lord and idols. And "one way," no longer
will they scatter their ways, running from one idol to another (Jer.
3: 13; cp. 2: 5, 11, 13, 18-25). "Heart" denotes the inner disposition;
"way," the outer expression. Their entire conduct will manifest that
they "fear" the Lord, that in their heart rules that love and childlike
confidence toward their Covenant God that stands in holy awe of
Him and fears nothing more than to do that great wickedness and sin
against Him. "Forever," all days, all their lifetime, this fear will fill
their hearts and direct their ways, and this fear will redound not only
to their own, but to their children's good. They will follow the example of their ancestor and spiritual father Abraham (Gen. 18: 19;
cp. Deut. 6: 1-9). Again, this is exactly what He promised in His covenant (Deut. 30: 6). The salvation of man from beginning to end, his
conversion, his sanctification, his preservation, is God's work.

V. 40. I will make with you an everlasting covenant. That is
the covenant with His elect, which stands fast to all eternity; a covenant in which God will not turn away "from after them" (M. T.) to
do them good, showering down upon them His gifts, pursuing them
with His blessings. And I will give My fear into their hearts. Constantly and ever anew will He generate that fear, that loving, trusting
awe, that is all He requires of man (Deut. 10: 12). And the result is
that on their part there will be no departing from Him. And again
that is not their own, but God's work, the grace and loving-kindness
of the Covenant God.

V. 41. While sinful, rebellious Judah was a source of grief and
anger to the holy Lord, the Lord now will rejoice over His people,
whom He has made, and not they themselves, to be His people
(Ps. 100: 3), and He will evidence His joy by gladly doing them good.

Cp. the covenant promise Deut. 28: 63; 30: 9; also Is. 62: 5; Zeph. 3: 17. And since the Sinaitic covenant is still in force with its specific promise of possession of the land of Canaan, He will, in keeping with His covenant promise, gladly and wholeheartedly again plant into the land He promised the people He converted. The Lord, who has no pleasure in the death of the wicked (Ezek. 33: 11), far rather and far more willingly keeps His promises than He must carry out His threats.

Vv. 42-44. Divine logic to convince Jeremiah: As God has done the one, He can and will do the other. And so will come to pass what Jeremiah had thought impossible. (On "valley," v. 44, cp. ch. 17: 26.)

As God does not apologize for His judgments nor even explain them, so He does not go to great lengths to prove the possibility of His unfathomable grace and mercy. He simply repeats what Jeremiah already had been told: He is I AM THAT I AM (Ex. 3: 14), who will be gracious to whom He will be gracious (Ex. 33: 19). Only believe! Trust Me, that I know why I do what I do as I do it, and that I am the Lord of unchanging justice and never-ending grace, even if you cannot fathom My ways and judgments.

CHAPTER 33

4. The Future Glory of the True Israel, the Church of God

A. The return of repentant Israel to the Land of Promise and the material and spiritual blessings granted to them, vv. 1-13

1 The word of the LORD came to Jeremiah a second time while he was imprisoned in the Court of the
2 Guard, saying: Thus says the LORD, who is the Creator of it, the LORD, the Former of it, so that it stands firm, LORD is His
3 name: Call to Me, and I will answer you! And I will reveal to you great and impenetrable mat-
4 ters, which you do not know. For thus says the LORD, the God of Israel, concerning the houses of this city and the houses of the kings of Judah which have been torn down (as a means of protection) against the ramparts and
5 against the swords, while men are coming to battle against the Chaldeans and to fill them with car-

casses of men whom I have slain in My anger and in My wrath, and because I have hidden My face from this city on account of all
6 their wickedness. Behold, I am bringing to her recuperation and healing, and I will heal them, and I will lay open for them an abun-
7 dance of peace and truth; and I will turn the captivity of Judah and the captivity of Israel, and I will build them as in the begin-
8 ning; and I will cleanse them from all their iniquity which they have sinned against Me, and I will forgive all their iniquities which they have sinned against Me and whereby they have rebelled against
9 Me. And it shall be to Me a joyful name, a praise and glory for all the

266

nations of the earth, who shall hear of all the good that I am doing to them, and they shall fear and tremble because of all the good and all the salvation which 10 I shall create for it. Thus says the LORD: In this place of which you say: It is desolate without men and without beasts, in the cities of Judah, and in the streets of Jerusalem, which are waste without men and without inhabitants and without beasts, there shall again be 11 heard the sound of joy and the sound of gladness, the voice of the bride and the voice of the bridegroom, the voice of those saying: Give thanks to the LORD of Hosts, for the LORD is good, for His mercy endures forever; while they are bringing their thankofferings to the house of the LORD. For I will turn the captivity of the land as in the beginning, says the 12 LORD. Thus says the LORD of Hosts: In this place which is desolate, without men and without beasts, and in all cities there will again be the homesteads of shep-13 herds shepherding a flock. In the cities of the hill country, in the cities of the lowlands, and in the cities of the Southland, and in the land of Benjamin, and in the environments of Jerusalem, and in the cities of Judah, flocks shall again pass under the hands of those who count them, says the LORD.

Vv. 1-2. "The second time," shortly after he had received the comforting revelation ch. 32. "Court of the prison," see ch. 32:2. The command "Call unto Me!" is addressed not to Jeremiah, but to the nation. "To reassure the sinking faith of the few believers, these reiterated promises are given here in the very jaws of national ruin." Cowles. "The Maker thereof," of the acts about to be revealed, which He devises in order to carry them out, "establish" them. In the very name Jehovah is implied the fulfillment of His predictions.

V. 3. In answer to the prayer, to which the Lord encourages His people, He will tell them great and "mighty," rather, hidden things, unknown to them, not experienced by them, the complete destruction (vv. 4-5) and restoration of the city and country (vv. 6-13).

Vv. 4-5. "Thrown down," torn down. "By the mounts," rather, against the "mounts," the bulwarks erected by the enemy and the battering rams and other siege machinery. "Sword," in general, all manual weapons. In defense against these, houses were torn down (Is. 22:10), and the stones and lumber so obtained were used to repair the breached walls. Therefore the Lord vividly presents the houses as coming to battle against the enemy (v. 5), but only "to fill the city with dead men"; for the Lord has turned His face against the city because of its wickedness, and every effort to repel the enemy will only serve to increase the horrible butchery (ch. 21:1-10; 38:2).

Vv. 6-8. "Health" here denotes the healthy flesh growing over a wound. The Lord will restore "it," the city, "them," the nation (Ex. 15:26), will graciously reveal, manifest to them, peace and truth, true, reliable peace and welfare that no enemy can take from them (cp. John 14:27; Phil. 4:7). This peace is founded on the free and full forgiveness of all their iniquities, their guilt, be that caused by sinning, missing the mark (*chata*), or by transgressing, revolting against the Lord (v. 8). Because of this free pardon He will permit them to return to their homeland and will restore their former prosperity (v. 7).

V. 9. This gracious restoration of His covenant nation to their former glory will be a joyful "name," a revelation of His power and grace, because all nations shall hear of His goodness and stand in reverent awe and adoring astonishment at this marvelous manifestation of the omnipotent grace of Jehovah.

Vv. 10-13. The curse of God, repeated three times (ch. 7:34; 16:9; 25:10-11), shall be lifted. Joy and rejoicing, peace and prosperity, shall be restored to city and country. "The hands of him that telleth them." The shepherds counted the sheep as they passed out of the fold in the morning, and again as they passed into it in the evening. On "vale" (v. 13), the "Shephelah," cp. ch. 17:26.

B. The glory of the New Testament Church, vv. 14-26

a. The spiritual body of the Messiah, vv. 14-16

14 Behold, days are coming, is the oracle of the LORD, when I will fulfill the good word which I have spoken to the house of Israel and 15 to the house of Judah: In those days and at that time I will cause a righteous branch to sprout up for David, and it shall establish judgment and righteousness on the 16 earth. In those days Judah will be saved and Jerusalem dwell in safety; and this is what one shall call her: The LORD Our Righteousness.

Vv. 14-16. At first reading this promise seems to be merely a repetition of ch. 23:5-6. Yet there are several omissions and changes, some of them of great significance, which stamp this prophetic utterance as differing from ch. 23:5-6.

1. Jer. 23:5 we read: "Behold, the days come"; Jer. 33:14: "In those days and at that time," referring to the time when the Lord shall have fulfilled His promise to send the Messiah (v. 14).

2. Jeremiah 23 we read: "I will raise"; Jeremiah 33: "I will cause a branch to sprout"; the perfect there denotes an accomplished fact; the imperfect here a repeated act.

3. There we read: "a Righteous Branch; here: "a branch of righteousness." These terms may be synonymous, but may just as well be chosen to denote a distinction.

4. The clause "A King shall reign and prosper," is omitted here.

5. Judah and Israel are named there, here Judah and Jerusalem.

In v. 14, "and" before "to the house of Judah" is the specifying "and," to be translated "namely," "in particular." Cp. Gen. 3:16, particularly thy conception; 1 Sam. 17:40, even (Hebrew, and = namely) in a scrip; Ps. 18:1, particularly from Saul; Is. 2:1, in particular, Jerusalem; Zech. 9:9, namely, upon a foal; etc. See G.-K. 154a, note 1b.

6. There we read: "This is His name whereby," etc. Here: "And this is what one shall call," etc. Why the significant omission of "name," designating His very nature as He reveals it?

7. There we read: "His name," one shall call Him; here, one shall call "her," i. e., Judah-Jerusalem.

This last fact forces upon us the conclusion that ch. 33:15-16 is not a mere repetition of ch. 23:5-6, but that these are two separate and distinct prophecies, ch. 23:5-6 speaking of Messiah, the Christ, ch. 33:14-15, of Judah and Jerusalem "in those days and at that time," i. e., the Church of God in the era of the Messiah, the New Testament Church of God.

1. The Christian Church came into existence only after Messiah had come.

2. The raising up of the Branch was a unique fact, complete in the coming of Christ, hence the perfect is used in the Hebrew text; the Church is constantly sprouting to the end of time, hence the imperfect.

3. The Messiah is the Righteous Branch, personally righteous in divine perfection; the Church is "a sprout of righteousness," because her righteousness is an imputed righteousness, and even her personal righteousness is accounted perfect righteousness only because of Christ's vicarious perfection.

4. In the Christian Church, Christ alone rules as a King; therefore this clause is omitted in ch. 33:15.

5. The Church is Christ's instrument through which He will establish "judgment," His norm, the Gospel, and "righteousness," procured by Him, and offered, conveyed, and sealed to mankind by this Gospel.

269

6. Jerusalem is named ch. 33:16b, instead of Israel, ch. 23:6, because Jerusalem is the Holy City, the dwelling place of God; and Judah-Jerusalem shall be called Jehovah Our Righteousness only because of the presence of Jehovah Our Righteousness in Jerusalem, the city of God.

Now the question arises: By what right may the Church be called Jehovah Our Righteousness? We answer that no one really has the right to ask this question, since God, who is responsible to no one, has clearly stated here that the Church shall be called Jehovah Our Righteousness. Nor is this an isolated case.

In the Old Testament, God's name, the Lord's name, was named upon the Tabernacle and the Temple (Jer. 7:10, 11, 12, 14, 30; 32:34; 34:15; 1 Kings 8:43; 2 Chron. 6:33); upon the city of Jerusalem (Jer. 25:29; Dan. 9:18, 19); the people of Israel (2 Chron. 7:14; Is. 4:1; 63:19; Jer. 14:9); upon the converted Gentiles (Amos 9:12); upon Jeremiah (Jer. 15:16). In all these passages the expression "on which is called My name" is used, not: "This is His name whereby He shall be called" (Jer. 23:6). In Is. 43:7 "called by My name" is used. In Num. 6:27 the priests are told that "they lay Jehovah's name upon Israel" when pronouncing the Aaronic blessing upon them. Jehovah's name was placed upon them, the people were to be known as Jehovah's people, the city as Jehovah's city, the Temple as Jehovah's house. In Is. 62:2 God promised to give to the New Testament Jerusalem, to His Church, a new name. What this new name is we learn from the New Testament, which clearly connects the new name to be given to the redeemed in heaven with Jer. 23:5-6 and 33:15-16. Only the Son of God knows His own name, His own essence and being. Yet this name shall be written on the foreheads of the blessed in heaven (Rev. 22:3-4). To wear the name on the forehead is to be publicly acknowledged as that which the name implies. This is a name incomprehensible to all except the recipients of the white stone on which it is written (Rev. 2:17), for it is the name of Christ's God, of the city of Christ's God, Christ's *new* name, the name He bears since His exaltation (Rev. 3:12). We have here a clear reference to Jer. 23:6 and 33:16; Christ's name is Jehovah (cp. Ex. 3:2, 4, 14; 23:20, 21; Phil. 2:9-11; Rev. 3:12); and that is the new name which Christ will write upon all believers in heaven, publicly acknowledging them as His own by writing His name (Jer. 23:6) and the name of Jerusalem (Jer. 33:16), Jehovah Our Righteousness, on their foreheads; the same name whereby He had called her while she still dwelt on earth.

This is in full keeping with such passages in the New Testament where the Church is called the body of Christ (1 Cor. 12:27; Eph. 1: 22-23; 4:12; 5:28-32; Col. 1:24), or where Christ is called the Head of the Church (Eph. 4:15-16; 5:23; Col. 1:18; 2:19). Paul goes so far as to directly call the Church, Christ (1 Cor. 12:12; cp. 2 Peter 1:3-4, "partakers of the divine nature").

The Church being the bride, the wife of the heavenly Bridegroom, is called by His name, just as the wife is called by the name of her husband, having been received into a family and given a name which was not hers by birth.

This does not mean that the Church will be essentially Jehovah, equal to God. Note the significant omission of "This is His name." She shall be called, one shall give her the name Jehovah, because she is Christ's, Jehovah's, spouse, one with Him in mystical union (cp. John 17:20-23).

The Church is "Our Righteousness" because only through the Church do we obtain the righteousness of Christ by means of the Gospel the Church preaches. If Christ is Our Righteousness, then the Church, one with Christ, is Our Righteousness. *Extra Christum nulla salus* (Acts 4:12), *extra ecclesiam nulla salus* (Eph. 2:19-22; 1 Cor. 12:12-13). No salvation without Christ; no salvation without the Church.

---

b. An everlasting royal priesthood, vv. 17-26

17 For thus says the LORD: David shall never lack a man to sit on the throne of the house of Israel.
18 And the Levitical priests shall never lack a man before Me to sacrifice burnt offerings and to offer up meat offerings and to bring
19 bloody sacrifices. And the word of the LORD came to Jeremiah,
20 saying: Thus says the LORD: If you can break My covenant of the day and My covenant of the night, so that days and nights shall no
21 longer come in their season, then also My covenant with David, My servant, will be broken, so that no more a son of his shall be ruling upon his throne; and with the Levites, the priests, who serve Me.
22 As the host of heaven cannot be numbered and the sand of the sea

cannot be measured, so I will multiply the seed of David, My servant, and the Levites serving
23 Me. And the word of the LORD
24 came to Jeremiah, saying: Have you not perceived what these people are saying: "The LORD has rejected the two families whom He chose," and that they regard My people as being unworthy to be
25 a nation in their estimation? Thus says the LORD: If My covenant with day and night shall vanish, and if I no longer uphold the ordi-
26 nances of heaven and earth, then also I will reject the seed of Jacob and David, My servant, and no longer take from their seed rulers over the seed of Abraham, Isaac, and Jacob. For I will turn their captivity and have mercy on them.

271

V. 17. "Shall never want," etc. (Cp. 1 Kings 2:4; 8:25; 9:5; 2 Chron. 6:16; 7:18; Jer. 35:19.) This expression does not promise perpetuity to the political throne of Judah (cp. Hos. 3:4; Jer. 22:30). But when there shall be "a throne of the house of Israel," a descendant of David shall sit on it. The Herodian dynasty was never acknowledged by the Lord as sitting on the throne of Israel. They were enemies of God's true Israel. When God's "kingdom of Israel" was again established, there sat on the throne an offspring of David as King of Israel (Luke 1:32-33; John 18:36; Eph. 1:20-23; Rev. 17:14).

V. 18. Also the priests and Levites shall not lack a man "before the Lord." On this phrase cp. Ex. 29:42; Lev. 10:3, 19; 16:1, 13. This prophecy also is fulfilled in Jesus Christ, who united in His person the two offices (Psalm 110; Zech. 6:12-13), who "did sacrifice continually" (Heb. 7:22-25; 9:11-12; 10:11-13).

Vv. 19-21. "My covenant of the day," "of the night"; "day" and "night" are appositions to "My covenant"; they constitute God's covenant in their unchanging alternation. "Season," the appointed time, fixed by the Lord (Gen. 9:9ff.). Man cannot change this covenant, and God will not as long as the earth endures. Just as immovable and unchangeable is God's covenant with David and Levi (v. 21).

V. 22. This covenant shall be fulfilled not only in the coming of Christ as King and Priest. The seed of David, the Lord's servant, and the Levites functioning before Him shall be innumerable (cp. Gen. 15:5). Israel's royalty and priesthood (Ex. 19:6) was by representation, the tribe of Levi representing the priesthood; the house of David, the royalty. In the time of Messiah all subjects of this priestly King are priests and kings (1 Peter 2:9; Rev. 1:6; 5:9-10), the unique glory of God's Israel in the New Covenant.

Vv. 23-26. In answer to the unbelieving Jews who charged God with having cast off His people and broken His covenant, the Lord solemnly reiterates the immutability of His covenant with the true seed of Abraham (cp. Rom. 11:1-2a).

Yet there is a slight alteration or, rather, an addition to His promises of vv. 18, 21. In this nation of kings and priests, He will establish special "rulers." The fulfillment is found in the New Testament Scriptures. In Matt. 19:28; Luke 22:28-30 the Lord gives special promises to His twelve apostles, who shall rule with Him in heaven, in eternity. But already in time and here on earth the apostles and evangelists are the rulers of the Church, the infallible leaders and guides in all matters of doctrine and life, whose writings, given by inspiration of God, are normative for the Church of all times. In like manner all pastors are called rulers, or leaders (Heb. 13:7, 17), overseers, bishops (Acts 20:28; 1 Peter 5:2-3; 1 Tim. 3:1; Titus 1:7). Compare the "diversities of gifts, of administrations, of operations" (1 Cor. 12:4-6), including clergy and laity; the helps (deacons having charge of sick) and governments (helmsman, steersman, shipmaster, gubernator) of 1 Cor. 12:28. See also Eph. 4:11-13. All the offices which are needed in the Christian Church for the perfecting of saints, for the work of the ministry, for the edifying of the Church, for the establishment and maintenance of good order and discipline, are gifts of Christ, the Priest-King, to His New Testament Church of priests and kings in fulfillment of this promise.

XIII. Obedience Versus Disobedience, Ch. 34—36

CHAPTER 34

1. The Shameful Breach of a Solemn Covenant

A. The shameful breach, vv. 1-11

1 The word which came to Jeremiah from the LORD, when Nebuchadnezzar, king of Babylon, and his whole army and all the kingdoms of the countries subject to his powerful rule and all the people were fighting against Jerusalem 2 and all her cities, saying: Thus says the LORD, the God of Israel: Go and speak to Zedekiah, king of Judah, and tell him: Thus says the LORD: Behold, I am giving this city into the hand of the king of Babylon, and he shall burn it with 3 fire. And you yourself shall not escape from his hand, for you certainly shall be captured and given into his hand, and your eyes shall see the king of Babylon eye to eye, and you shall speak to him mouth to mouth, and you shall go to 4 Babylon. Yet hear the word of the LORD, Zedekiah, king of Judah! Thus says the LORD regarding you: You shall not die by the 5 sword. Peacefully shall you die, and they shall burn spices at your funeral, as they burnt spices at the funeral of your fathers, the former kings, which were before you; and they shall lament for you: Alas, Lord! For I have spoken the word! 6 is the oracle of the LORD. And Jeremiah the prophet spoke all these words to Zedekiah, king of 7 Judah at Jerusalem, while the army of the king of Babylon was fighting against Jerusalem and against all the remaining cities of Judah, against Lachish and against Azekah, for these were the only fortified cities which were left 8 among the cities of Judah. The word which came to Jeremiah from the LORD, after King Zedekiah had made a covenant with all the people which were at Jerusalem, in the form of an emancipation, 9 to proclaim to them, that everyone was to release his Hebrew bondservant, and everyone his Hebrew bondmaid, so that no Jew should hold his fellow Jew in slavery. 10 And all princes and all the people that had entered into the covenant had been willing that each one was to set free his bondservant or his bondmaid, so that they should no longer enslave them, and they had 11 set them free willingly. Yet afterward they had changed their mind and had brought back the bondservants and bondmaids whom they had set free and had forced them again to be their bondservants and bondmaids.

V. 1. Ch. 33 had ended on a joyous note, the assurance of deliverance from the Babylonian captivity and of a glorious future far exceeding their greatest past glory. In glaring contrast to the future stands the present reality. Jerusalem is engaged in a death struggle with mighty Babylon, and the end is fast approaching. Already all the fortified cities have been taken, only Jerusalem, Lachish, and Azekah remaining unoccupied by the enemy. The city of Lachish has been definitely identified with Tell ed Duweir, 20—25 miles southwest of Jerusalem. Excavations have shown that Lachish was twice destroyed within a few years, corresponding to Nebuchadnezzar's campaigns 598 (Jehoiachin) and 587 (Zedekiah). In the debris of this latter destruction a clay seal was found with the inscription "The property of Gedaliah, who is over the house." This may point to Gedaliah, the governor appointed by Nebuchadnezzar (Jer. 40: 5-6; 41: 2). On "over the house," denoting a high official, see 2 Kings 18: 18; Is. 22: 15-21. In 1935 eighteen ostraca were found in this last layer, in 1940 three more. They record the correspondence between Hoshaiah, who was doing outpost duty, and his superior, Yaosh, a high commanding officer at Lachish. Several times a prophet is mentioned. In one of the letters Hoshaiah refers to a letter of Tobiah, which came to Shallum, son of Jaddua, "through the prophet," warning Shallum to beware. Another letter speaks of letters of the king and the princes (*sarim*), which Yaosh had sent to Hoshaiah for careful reading in order to convince him that "the words of the prophet are not good, but to weaken your hands and to slacken the hands of the men." This is the same charge raised in almost identical words by the princes (*sarim*) against Jeremiah (ch. 38: 4). Here the word "prophet" is almost illegible, and Albright suggests to read "princes." Yet it is hardly credible that this charge should be raised against the princes. They did their utmost to encourage continued resistance. In Letter XVI the name of the prophet was mentioned, but unfortunately only the last letters, YHU, remain intact. In Letter XVII the letters RMYHU are plainly readable. Hoshaiah defends himself against the suspicion of siding with the prophet and assures Yaosh of his loyalty to the king. One can hardly escape the conclusion that the prophet spoken of here is Jeremiah. At any rate, the same tenseness, excitement, suspicion, fear, is vividly presented here that Jeremiah pictures in his account of the months preceding the end of Judah-Jerusalem. Hoshaiah is a name occurring in Jer. 42: 1; 43: 2 as the name of the father of two of the leaders of the people opposing Jeremiah. See W. F. Albright in *Bulletin of the American Schools of Oriental Research*, No. 70, pp. 11—17; 80, pp. 11—13; 82, pp. 20 ff.; Burrows, *What Mean These Stones?* §§ 52, 81, 170.

Azekah, about midway between Lachish and Jerusalem according to Joshua 10: 10; 15: 35; 1 Sam. 17: 1, is supposed to be the modern Tell Zekariah some distance west of Bethlehem, where an important citadel was uncovered 1898—1900. Both cities were strong fortifications to protect Jerusalem against attacks from the south and southwest, from Philistia, Egypt, and Arabian tribes. Nebuchadnezzar, like Sennacherib, planned to take these cities before attacking Jerusalem in order to cut off supplies and prevent Egypt from using these fortifications as bases of attack against the Babylonian forces.

Already in his letter to the captives in Babylon, written shortly after their deportation 597, Jeremiah had foretold the destruction of Jerusalem and the exile of its people for a period of seventy years (ch. 29:10). In the early years of Zedekiah's rule he had told the assembled ambassadors and Zedekiah that the only escape from complete destruction was unconditional surrender to the Babylonian king (ch. 27—28). The fanatic people refused to believe the prophet (cp. ch. 28; 29:25-32); they would not read the handwriting on the wall. Once more the Lord of grace and long-suffering sent His messenger to the king, for the purpose of urging him to surrender rather than needlessly to sacrifice the lives of his subjects.

Vv. 2-3. For the first time the king is told that Jerusalem would be burnt with fire. Zedekiah would not escape capture, he would with his eyes behold the king, speak with him mouth to mouth, and be deported to Babylon. Ezekiel's prophecy seems to contradict this word (Ezek. 12:6, 12-13), yet both were fulfilled to the letter (Jer. 52:9-11).

Vv. 4-5. In order to induce Zedekiah to surrender, before it would be too late, the prophet assures him that he would be treated with due honor, both in life and death. "Burnings of thy fathers," of course, does not refer to cremation of the corpse on a funeral pyre, but to the burning of spices at royal funerals (2 Chron. 16:14; 21:19). This is not an idle promise, rashly spoken. It is a word spoken by the Covenant God, the God of Amen (Is. 65:16, "truth" = Amen).

Zedekiah's reaction to this warning was, as usual, negative. Nothing is said of any willingness to obey God's will to surrender to Nebuchadnezzar. It rather seems that his proposal to liberate the slaves was another compromise between obedience and downright refusal. He hopes to mollify the Lord and obtain God's deliverance by a plan of his own which on the face of it might seem to be a repetition of Josiah's reform, the re-establishment of an ancient, long-neglected law of God.

V. 8. According to ancient Babylonian custom a bankrupt debtor was permitted to sell his wife, sons, or daughters, as bondslaves to the creditor, the slaves to be released after three years (*Hammurabi Code*, par. 117). Israel had adopted a similar custom, permitting also the man to sell his own person. This custom was regulated by special legislation (Ex. 21:2-11; Deut. 15:12-18), which ordered the release of such bondslaves after six years of service unless they preferred to remain in this state (Ex. 21:5f.; Deut. 15:16f.). As poverty increased in Israel, many an Israelite was forced to sell himself and his family in order to insure at least a living. Yet the bondmasters kept them in involuntary servitude far beyond the legally stipulated limit. Zedekiah's plan was to abolish this abuse. At his initiative all the people by a solemn covenant (vv. 18-19) agreed to liberate every Hebrew slave serving them. "Liberty" is employed (Lev. 25:10) to denote the manumission of all Hebrew bondslaves after they had served six years, or in the year of jubilee (every fiftieth year), if this should fall before the completion of the six years of service (Lev. 25:39-41). What caused the people to obey the demand of their king, we do not know. Some may have obeyed in order to show their love and fear of their Lord; others in deference to the king; or because they hoped that as freedmen the former slaves would become more active and willing defenders of the city; or they were glad no longer to be required to feed so many mouths.

V. 11. The sudden re-establishment of slavery after the army of Nebuchadnezzar had temporarily raised the siege (see v. 22), would seem to justify the thought that the whole procedure was a hypocritical farce. The king and the vast majority of the people evidently were motivated only by the hope of gaining the deliverance of the city as a reward for their obedience to God's Law. When that purpose seemed to have been accomplished, when the enemy had been obliged to march against the powerful army of the Egyptians, when the gates were opened and the people were permitted to go and come as they pleased (Jer. 37:11-13), then their obedience no longer was deemed necessary, then they annulled their covenant and forced their brethren back into slavery.

B. The dreadful consequences of the breach of their covenant, vv. 12-22

12 Then came the word of the LORD to Jeremiah from the LORD, say-
13 ing: Thus says the LORD, the God of Israel: I made a covenant with your fathers on the day that I brought them out of the land of Egypt, from the house of slaves,
14 saying: At the end of seven years every one of you shall release his fellow Hebrew, whom you have bought for yourself. When he has served you six years, you shall release him from your service. But your fathers did not obey Me and did not incline their ears to Me.
15 But now you had turned and had done what was right in My sight, by proclaiming to one another liberty, and you had made a covenant before Me in the house upon which My name has been called. Yet now you have turned again and profaned My name, and every one of you has taken back his bondservant and bondmaid, whom you had liberated, so that they could

do as they pleased, and have forced them again to become your bond-

17 servants and maids. Therefore thus says the LORD: You have not obeyed Me in proclaiming a release to your brothers and your neighbors. Behold, I am proclaiming a release for you to the sword, to pestilence, to famine, and I will make you objects of maltreatment for all the kingdoms of the earth!

18 I will also make those men who transgressed My covenant, who did not fulfill the words of the covenant which they made before Me, as the calf which they cut in two, and between whose parts they

19 passed (the princes of Judah and the princes of Jerusalem, the eunuchs and the priests and all the people of the land who passed be-

20 tween the pieces of the calf); and I will give them into the hand of their enemies and into the hand of those that seek their life; and their carcasses shall be food for the birds of the air and the beasts of

21 the earth. And Zedekiah, king of Judah, and his princes I will give into the hand of their enemies and into the hand of those that seek their life and into the hand of the army of the king of Babylon which

22 has gone away from you. Behold, I am issuing a command, is the oracle of the LORD, and I will bring them back to this city, and they shall fight against it and take it and burn it with fire; and the cities of Judah I will make an uninhabited waste.

Grammatical Notes

V. 18. The verb וְנָתַתִּי at the beginning of v. 18 is to be connected with הָעֵגֶל, as the second object, the first being "the men that . . ."; "I will give, deliver, appoint, the men that have trans- gressed . . . as, or like the calf which," etc. Others suggest to read כָּעֵגֶל.

V. 19 is an apposition to "the men" of v. 18.

Vv. 12-15. The Lord reminds His people of their long-standing neglect of His law of manumission. He acknowledges the outer act, which in a few isolated cases may have been the fruit of a sincere repentance, as doing what was right, as a turning away from their usual course of violating His Law. Even mere civic righteousness is approved and rewarded by the Lord (cp. 1 Sam. 15: 30-31; 1 Kings 21: 27-29; Prov. 14: 34). The Lord, however, expects more than mere outward obedience; He demands a better fulfillment (Deut. 6: 5). Such love was lacking completely in this entire manumission, else they would not have renounced it.

Vv. 16-22. In a scathing rebuke the Lord denounces their shameful hypocrisy. Instead of re-establishing the ancient covenant law of manumission, they are covenant breakers. They have broken their covenant with their brethren, although they made it before the Lord in the house called by His name. It is a breach of covenant, which is at the same time a pollution of God's name (v. 16), a desecration of His Temple, a contemptuous flaunting of His glorious Presence.

V. 17. As long as they had been God's obedient people, they were

holiness to Him, and He had avenged all wrongs done to them
(Jer. 2:3). They had become a stubbornly apostate nation, and therefore the Lord in bitter irony proclaims "liberty" for them, liberty from
the covenant which they regarded as an unbearable yoke of slavery,
freedom from the Lord's protection, who turned them over to that
fourfold alliance of evils, sword, pestilence, famine, and exile. The
covenant they broke was not merely an agreement between man and
man, it was the Lord's covenant which they transgressed (v. 18).
Their transgression appears the more wicked, their hypocrisy the
more shameful in view of the particularly elaborate and solemn rites
observed by them in making this covenant, to which the Lord calls
special attention, "cutting the calf in twain and passing between the
parts thereof." (Cp. Gen. 15:10.) There is good reason to believe
that dividing of the bodies of animals or birds, laying the halves
opposite each other, and then passing between the halves in confirmation of a covenant was an ancient custom. This is proved by the
phrase "cut a covenant," for "make a covenant," which occurs in
various ancient languages; Hebrew, *karath b'rith;* Greek, ὅρκια τέμνειν;
Latin, *foedus ferire.* Ephraem Syrus (d. ca. 380 A. D.), commenting
on Gen. 15:10, writes that this rite was customary among the Chaldeans and that therefore God observed it in making His covenant with
Abram, the Chaldean. Koenig (*Commentary on Genesis*) remarks
that the same custom was observed when Matilu of Northern Syria
obligated himself to Assurnirari of Assyria. From our passage it is
evident that the custom was still being observed in the days of
Jeremiah. According to some authorities the division of the animals
symbolizes the two parties making the covenant, while their passing
between the rows signifies their uniting in the covenant. The Lord
through Jeremiah gives a different and a more suitable interpretation. He will make the men that had passed between the rows like
the calf which they had cut in two, that is, they will be slain, and
their corpses will be devoured by wild animals and birds of prey.
Hence Volz correctly defines the rite as involving a self-malediction
in case of a breach of the covenant. Although all the princes of Judah
and Jerusalem (cp. p. 32 f.), the "eunuchs," the higher officials of the
state (cp. ch. 29:2; 38:7; 41:16), the priests, the "people of the land,"
not merely the rural population, but all people in distinction to the
clergy and nobility, entered into this solemn covenant, they broke it
almost as soon as it was made. Such treachery and hypocrisy God
will punish without respect of persons; they will either be slain or
deported by the same army which now had raised the siege. For the

Babylonian king and his forces are but the instruments of the Lord, who has turned against His treacherous people. They are fulfilling God's prophecy spoken more than forty years before, at Jeremiah's call. God's mills grind slowly, but surely and crushingly!

CHAPTER 35

2. The Fidelity of the Rechabites and the Faithlessness of the Jews

A. The Fidelity of the Rechabites, vv. 1-11

1 The word which came to Jeremiah from the LORD in the days of Jehoiakim, the son of Josiah, king 2 of Judah, saying: Go to the house of the Rechabites, and speak to them and bring them to the house of the LORD to one of the chambers, and offer them wine to drink. 3 So I took Jaazaniah, the son of Jeremiah, the son of Chabazziniah, and his brothers and all his sons, and all the house of the Rechabites, 4 and I brought them to the house of the LORD into the chamber of the sons of Hanan, the son of Igdaliah, the man of God, which was next to the chamber of the princes, which is above the chamber of Maaseiah, the son of Shallum, the keeper of the threshold. 5 And I placed bowls full of wine and cups before the sons of the house of Rechabites and told them: 6 Drink wine! And they said: We never drink wine, for Jonadab, the son of Rechab, our father, has commanded us, saying: Do not drink wine, you nor your children 7 forever! Neither shall you build houses, nor sow seed, nor plant or own vineyards, but you shall dwell in tents all your days, that you may live long in the land in which you 8 happen to live. And we obey the voice of Jehonadab, the son of Rechab, our father, in all he has commanded us, not to drink wine all our days, neither we, nor our wives, nor our sons, nor our 9 daughters. Nor do we build houses for us to live in, and we own no 10 vineyards, nor fields, nor seed. But we live in tents, and obey and do according to all that our father 11 Jonadab has commanded us. But when Nebuchadrezzar, the king of Babylon, came up into the land, we said: Come, let us go to Jerusalem before the army of the Chaldeans and the army of Syrians. And so we are staying in Jerusalem.

V. 2. The house, or family (cp. v. 5), "sons," of the Rechabites, whose father, or founder, was Hemath, a Kenite (1 Chron. 2: 55). The Kenites were a Midianite tribe. Hobab, Moses' brother-in-law, a Midianite (Num. 10: 29), is called a Kenite (Judg. 1: 16). He accompanied Moses on the journey through the wilderness as a guide (Num. 10: 29-32). His descendants lived among the Israelites, some in the Desert of Judah (Judg. 1: 16; 1 Sam. 27: 10; 30: 29), some in Naphthali in the north (Judg. 4: 11, 17 ff.). In the time of Saul, Kenites were living among the Amalekites south of Judah (1 Sam. 15: 6). Wherever Kenites are mentioned in the history of Israel, they appear as loyal associates of Israel and staunch adherents of Jehovah

(cp. Judg. 4:11, 17-23; 5:24-31; 2 Kings 10:15-28). Jonadab, or Jehonadab (v. 8, M. T.), the son and successor of Rechab, had commanded
the Rechabites and their descendants not to drink wine, nor to build
houses, nor sow seed, nor own or plant vineyards, but to dwell in
tents (Jer. 35:6-7). Diodorus Siculus, a Greek historian, a contemporary of Julius Caesar and Augustus, writes of similar laws adopted
by the Nabataeans, nomadic Arabs, who occupied the territories of
Edom and Moab about 400 B. C.: "They have a law not to sow grain,
nor to plant any fruit-bearing plant, nor to use wine, nor to build
houses." The purpose of this law, Diodorus says, was the preservation
of their liberty and independence against foreign rulers. This love of
freedom may have been an even more potent reason for Jonadab's
rules than the dangers connected with overindulgence in strong drink
and the fear of the seductive influence of large cities. They were not
the forerunners of modern prohibitionists. We hear of no propaganda
for their customs. Respect for their ancestor, love of independence,
and a wholesome desire to keep their minds clear and their bodies
sound (cp. v. 7b) may have been the motives for their continued strict
observance of their laws prescribed by their ancestor more than
250 years before. It might serve as an interesting sidelight, that the
Nabataeans lost their liberty when they began to lead a life of luxury
and indulgence.

When the armies of the Chaldeans and Syrians overran the whole
land of Israel, these Rechabites left their camps in the wilderness,
which no longer seemed safe against marauding attacks of the powerful enemy, and sought security behind the strong and seemingly
impregnable walls of Jerusalem. But even in the city they observed
the customs received by tradition from their father.

Vv. 3-4. Jeremiah receives the divine command to bring all the
Rechabites, young and old, into the Lord's house, "into the chamber
of the sons of Hanan." "Chamber" = a large or small room or hall,
particularly a room in the Temple used as a storage place for utensils,
provisions, for offices of the officials, for dwelling places for the
servants, etc. (Cp. Jer. 36:10, 12, 20; 1 Chron. 23:28; 28:12; 2 Chron.
31:11ff.; after the Exile, Ezra 8:28, 29; Neh. 10:38-40.) Jaazaniah
undoubtedly was the leader of the tribe. Hanan is here called "a man
of God," an honorable title of the prophets (Deut. 33:1; 1 Sam. 9:6-8;
1 Kings 12:22; 13:1; 17:18). His "chamber," or cell, or office, was
next to that of the "princes" (cp. Jer. 1:18), whose chamber was
above that of the "doorkeeper," keeper of the sill, the supervisor over
the three doorkeepers (2 Kings 25:18; Jer. 52:24), whose duty it was

to keep order in general and to see that no unworthy person entered the Temple. These doorkeepers seem to have ranked next to the high priest and his representative (cp. 2 Kings 25:18; Jer. 52:24). Maaseiah may be identical with the father of Zephaniah, the second high priest (Jer. 21:1; 29:25; 37:3; 52:24).

V. 5. At the command of the Lord, Jeremiah placed "pots of wine," large bowls, from which the cups were filled, before the Rechabites, together with drinking cups, and told them: Drink wine! As the Lord had told Satan to test Job, knowing that Job would not yield to the temptation, so here He commands Jeremiah to test the Rechabites, knowing that they would refuse and thus present a shaming example of obedience to disobedient Judah.

Vv. 6-11. At once they answer that in view of their ancestor's command they had not drunk wine, and would not drink it, but obey as in the past they had obeyed, and do as in the past they had done, according to all that Jonadab, their father, had commanded. Only the urgent need of saving themselves from the enemy had compelled them to come to Jerusalem.

B. The application to the Jews, vv. 12-15

12 Then the word of the LORD came
13 to Jeremiah, saying: Thus says the LORD of Hosts, the God of Israel: Go and say to the men of Judah and the inhabitants of Jerusalem: Will you not learn the lesson of obedience to My word? is the
14 oracle of the LORD. The words of Jehonadab, the son of Rechab, which he commanded to his sons that they drink no wine, are being rigidly obeyed. They do not drink wine to this day, for they obey the command of their father! But 15 I have spoken to you time and again, and you have not listened to Me! And I have been sending all My servants, the prophets, to you, zealously and unceasingly saying: Let everyone turn from his evil way and amend his actions, and do not run after other gods to serve them; then ye shall live in the land which I have given to you and to your fathers. But you did not incline your ears and did not listen to Me.

Vv. 12-14. For 250 years the Rechabites had obeyed the command of a human father and refused to disobey him even when they were tempted, although his command was merely a matter of human judgment. The God of Israel, the Lord of Hosts, had for centuries spoken earnestly and untiringly to His people. They did not listen to Him.

V. 15. He had sent prophet upon prophet who urged them to obey their God, who had promised them divine blessings. They had refused to listen to them.

C. The punishment of the Jews and the reward of the Rechabites, vv. 16-19

16 Because the sons of Jehonadab, the son of Rechab, rigidly observed the command given to them by their father, and these people have
17 not obeyed Me, therefore, thus says the LORD God of Hosts, the God of Israel: Behold, I am bringing upon Judah and upon all the inhabitants of Jerusalem all the evils that I have spoken concerning them, because I have spoken to them and they did not hear, and I called repeatedly to them and
18 they did not answer. And to the house of the Rechabites Jeremiah said: Thus says the LORD of Hosts, the God of Israel. Because you have obeyed the command of Jehonadab, your father, and have observed all his commandments and have done according to all
19 that he has commanded you, therefore thus says the LORD of Hosts, the God of Israel: Jonadab, the son of Rechab, shall not want a man standing before Me forever.

Vv. 16-17. The Lord will now reward Judah according to her disobedience, bring upon her all the evil threatened for so long.

Vv. 18-19. The Lord rewards the unwavering obedience and loyalty of the Rechabites to their father by the promise that Jonadab should not want a man to stand before the Lord forever. While this phrase usually designates the special liturgical services of the priests and Levites (Deut. 10:8; 18:5, 7; 1 Kings 8:11; 2 Chron. 29:11; Ps. 134:1; 135:2), yet it is already used of the worship of the patriarchs (Gen. 19:27), of Moses' and Samuel's intercession (Jer. 15:1), and of the people appearing in worship before the Lord (ch. 7:10). Hence the Lord did not promise that they would become Levites or priests, but that there shall always be obedient servants of the Lord among the descendants of Jonadab. The fact that certain tribes in Arabia claim to be descendants of the Rechabites (Keil, *Bible Commentary;* Volz, and others) cannot be adduced in proof of the fulfillment of this promise, neither the rather obscure passage 1 Chron. 2:55, for not all descendants of Hemath (the grandfather of Jonadab?) were descendants of Jonadab, to whom this promise was given. There can be no doubt that the Lord fulfilled His promise, but how He did it, we have no way of ascertaining.

CHAPTER 36

3. The Nation's Wickedness Culminates in the Burning of Jeremiah's Scroll

A. By divine command Jeremiah's prophecies are written in a book, vv. 1-8

1 In the fourth year of Jehoiakim, the son of Josiah, king of Judah, this word came to Jeremiah from
2 the LORD: Take unto yourself a book scroll, and write on it all the
words that I have spoken to you concerning Israel and concerning Judah and concerning all the nations from the day that I spoke to you in the days of Josiah to this

3 very day. Perhaps when the house of Judah will hear of all the evil which I am planning to do to them, they will turn each from his evil way, and then I would pardon 4 their iniquity and their sin. So Jeremiah called Baruch, the son of Neriah, and Baruch at the dictation of Jeremiah wrote on a book scroll all the words of the Lord that He 5 had spoken to him. And Jeremiah commanded Baruch, saying: I am prevented from going to the house 6 of the LORD. Now you go, and read from the scroll, which you have written at my dictation, the words of the LORD in the hearing of the people in the house of the Lord on the day of fasting, and read them also in the hearing of all Judah that come from their cities. 7 Perhaps they will humbly present their supplication to the LORD, and everyone will turn from his evil way. For great is the anger and the fury which the LORD has spoken concerning this people. 8 And Baruch, the son of Neriah, did all that Jeremiah had commanded him for the purpose of reading from the book the words of the LORD in the house of the LORD.

Vv. 1-3. On the critical fourth year of Jehoiakim compare p. 12 f. In this fourth year Jeremiah had called the attention of the people to his unceasing proclamation of God's Word throughout the twenty-three years of his prophetic activity and to the ever-increasing disobedience toward his divine message on the part of the people (ch. 25:1). Now the Lord makes another attempt to lead His people to repentance. He tells Jeremiah to put down in writing all the words of the Lord which had been spoken to him in the past. None of the people had heard all of these words. Some of them may never have heard the prophet. Whether they had heard him often, or would hear him for the first time, the cumulative effect of hearing at one reading all the horrors confronting them, escape from which was possible only by early and sincere repentance, might induce them to return to the Lord.

Vv. 4-8. At once Jeremiah calls his secretary, Baruch (cp. ch. 32:12), and dictates to him, while faithful Baruch writes out all the words on a book roll, or scroll, a long sheet of leather parchment or papyrus. Evidently Baruch used papyrus; else the king would have found a different way of destroying the roll than by burning it. The stench of burning leather would have been almost intolerable. The writing on these scrolls was done in the form of columns of prescribed width and height, called "doors" because of their resemblance to small doors. The sheet was then rolled on a stick, sometimes on two sticks, and unrolled while being read. Baruch wrote with ink (v. 18), most likely prepared from lampblack mixed with water and perhaps the juice from the gallnut. The "pen" was a reed sharpened with a penknife (v. 23), always carried by the scribe. "The writing desk of a scribe of the Persian period was found in Egypt a few years ago.

It consists of two boards hinged together and was doubtless held on the scribe's knee as he wrote. In one of the boards there is a little cup to hold ink, some of which actually remains in a solidified state. There is also a groove for the reeds used as pens. A few Aramaic characters are legible, showing the language used by the scribe and indicating that he wrote memoranda, or perhaps tried out his pens, on the desk itself. Pictures of scribes using such desks, or perhaps tablets of similar form, appear on an Assyrian relief of the seventh century and on the Bar-Rekub stele of Zendjirli" [in northern Syria]. (*What Mean These Stones?* by Millar Burrows, pp. 184—185.)

For some unstated reason, Jeremiah was "shut up," restrained from going to the Temple (cp. 1 Kings 18:44; Neh. 6:10; Job 4:2 on this sense of the word). He was not held captive, for then the princes could not have urged him to escape (v. 19). He delegates Baruch to read to the people and expresses his fervent hope that the Lord's purpose (v. 3) might be accomplished (v. 7). "Reading in the book" (v. 8), rather, "for the purpose of reading." Having finished the book, the two waited for an appropriate opportunity to read it to the people.

B. Baruch reads the scroll in the Temple and before the princes, vv. 9-19

9 In the fifth year of Jehoiakim, the son of Josiah, king of Judah, in the ninth month, a fast before the LORD was proclaimed for all the people in Jerusalem and all the people that came from the cities of Judah.

10 Then Baruch read in the hearing of all people from the book the words of Jeremiah in the house of the LORD in the chamber of Gemariah, the son of Shaphan, the secretary, which was in the upper court at the entrance to the new gate of the

11 house of the LORD. When Micaiah, the son of Gemariah, the son of Shaphan, heard all these words of

12 the Lord from the book, he went down into the king's house, to the chamber of the secretary, and, behold, there sat all the princes, Elishama, the secretary, and Delaiah, the son of Shemaiah, and Elnathan, the son of Akbor, and Gemariah, the son of Shaphan, and Zedekiah, the son of Hananiah,

13 and all the princes. So Micaiah reported to them all the words he had heard Baruch read from the

book in the hearing of the people.

14 Then all the princes sent Jehudi, the son of Netaniah, the son of Shelemiah, the son of Kushi, to Baruch and told him: Take the scroll from which you have read in the hearing of the people into your hand, and come to us. And Baruch, the son of Neriah, took the scroll into his hand and went to

15 them. And they told him: Sit down and read it in our hearing. And Baruch read it in their hearing.

16 And when they had heard all the words, they turned in fright to one another and said to Baruch: We will surely report this whole matter

17 to the king. Then they asked Baruch: Pray, inform us, how did you write all these things at his

18 dictation? Then Baruch told them: From his mouth he dictated to me all these words, and I kept on

19 writing in the book with ink. And the princes said to Baruch: Go and hide, you and Jeremiah, and let no one know where you are!

V. 9. This opportunity (v. 8) came when "they," the proper authorities, proclaimed a fast day for the ninth month of the fifth year of Jehoiakim. The prophet may have waited for almost a year before having his book read. Yet it seems more plausible to adopt the suggestion of Volz, that since the regnal years began in the fall of the year (hence Jehoiakim's fourth year extended from October, 604, to October, 603), while the lunar years began in spring (extending from March-April, 604, to March-April, 603), the ninth month of the lunar year, 604, December, fell into the fifth regnal year of Jehoiakim, extending from October, 604, to October, 603.

No reason is stated for the proclamation of a fast day. The Talmud, Taanit I, 5, prescribes: "If the first day of Kisleu (December) has arrived and rain has not yet fallen, the council appoints fast days for the entire congregation." On the horrors of drought, cp. Jer. 14:1ff. No matter what the occasion for the fast day may have been, this was an opportune moment for reading Jeremiah's book.

V. 10. Baruch read the scroll in the chamber, or office, of Gemariah, the son of Shaphan, one of the secretaries and, like his father, Shaphan, and his brother, Ahikam (Jer. 26:24), a stanch friend and supporter of Jeremiah. (He is not to be identified with Gemariah of ch. 29:3.) This office was located "in the higher court, at the entry of the new gate." The higher court, into which this gate led, was the priest's court lying higher than the court of the people. The location of the new gate is uncertain. Probably it is to be identified with the high, or upper, gate of Benjamin (ch. 20:2), built comparatively late, in the time of Jotham (2 Kings 15:35), and still retaining the name "new gate." One of the doors of the office evidently led into the people's court. From this vantage point, overlooking the assembly, Baruch read the scroll. So suitable to the occasion were the contents of the book, and so overwhelming was the impression made by these words, that the assembly listened with rapt attention to all the words of the Lord read to them from the book.

Vv. 11-13. A specially interested listener was Michaiah, the son of Gemariah; and when Baruch had finished, he decided that the princes, who were assembled for a business session in the office of Elishama, must have an opportunity to hear this remarkable book.

Vv. 14-18. The princes at once summoned Baruch to appear before them with the scroll, received him respectfully and cordially, and asked him to sit down to read to them. They also were deeply impressed. "Were afraid, both one and other." Consciousness of their

286

own shortcomings, fear of the threatened judgment mingled with worrying forebodings of Jehoiakim's reaction towards this bold step taken by the prophet and his faithful secretary. They were convinced that it was their duty to report at once to the king. Before doing so, they inquired as to the exact manner of writing. "All these words" at, from, the mouth of Jeremiah. Honest, straightforward Baruch can tell them no more than that Jeremiah "with his mouth," out of his mouth, "pronounced," spoke loudly and distinctly while dictating, the only time this term is used in this sense of dictation. There was no danger of misunderstanding any one of his words. He spoke "all these words." "And I wrote," was writing, the participle describes continued action; "all these words," I added nothing. All I did was to write on the scroll with ink what Jeremiah dictated to me. From v. 1 we learn that the Lord Himself told the prophet to write the scroll. To this writing also applies what applied to all his prophecies: the Lord gave His words into the mouth of Jeremiah (ch. 1:9). Jeremiah's mouth spoke in dictation. Baruch wrote what Jeremiah spoke as the Word of the Lord. The princes now urged Baruch that he and Jeremiah hide at once and reveal to no one their place of refuge.

C. Jehoiakim burns the scroll, vv. 20-26

20 After they had deposited the scroll in the chamber of Elishama, the secretary, they came to the king into the court, and they reported the whole matter in the hearing of
21 the king. The king sent Jehudi to get the scroll, and he got it from the chamber of Elishama, the secretary; and Jehudi read it in the hearing of the king and in the hearing of all the princes
22 standing before the king. Now the king sat in the winter house in the ninth month, and there was a fire burning on the brazier before him.
23 When Jehudi had read three or four columns, he cut it with a pen-knife and hurled it into the fire in the brazier until the entire scroll was consumed in the fire in the
24 brazier. But neither the king nor any of his servants who had heard all these words were alarmed, nor
25 did they rend their clothes. Although also Elnathan, and Delaiah, and Gemariah pleaded with the king not to burn the scroll, he did
26 not listen to them. Then the king commanded Jerahmeel, the son of the king, and Sheraiah, the son of Azriel, and Shelemiah, the son of Abdeel, to arrest Baruch, the secretary, and Jeremiah the prophet. But the LORD kept them hidden.

V. 20. After depositing the scroll for safekeeping in the office of Elishama, the princes went out to the court of the royal palace, where the king presided at a judicial session in order to report the whole matter to him. After Jehudi, who is not further identified, was sent to get the scroll, he was ordered to read it to the king, who sat on

287

his throne, while before him stood, besides the princes named v. 12, other princes. Because of the cool weather in the month of December the king sat in the winter apartment of the palace close to a brazier filled with live coal. The chill of the season did not cool the hot temper of the king. When Jehudi had read three or four columns, the king jumped up from his throne, tore the book out of Jehudi's hands, cut it to pieces with a penknife, and threw the pieces into the fire until the entire roll was consumed. That it was the king and not Jehudi who burned the scroll, is stated clearly vv. 25, 27, 28, 32, four times.

Vv. 24-26. So calloused were the king and his ministers that not a sign of sorrow or fear was in evidence while the terrible denouncement and dreadful curse spoken by the Covenant God were being read. Not one rent his clothes in bitter penitential anguish. In spite of the pleas of Elnathan, Delaiah, and Gemariah, the king persisted in burning the scroll until not a shred remained. Not satisfied with the destruction of the scroll, Jehoiakim gave orders to imprison Jeremiah and Baruch, in the hope of silencing these intrepid servants of the Lord as he had silenced Urijah (ch. 26:20ff.). His plan failed because the Lord is greater than man.

D. Jehoiakim's blasphemous challenge is met by God's command to Jeremiah to rewrite the scroll and the repetition of God's curse upon king and people, vv. 27-32

27 The word of the LORD came to Jeremiah after the king had burnt the scroll and the words which Baruch had written at the dictation 28 of Jeremiah: Take another scroll, and write on it all the original words which were on the first scroll, which Jehoiakim, king of 29 Judah, burnt; and concerning Jehoiakim, king of Judah, say: Thus says the LORD: You have burnt this scroll, saying: Why have you written: The king of Babel will certainly come and destroy this land and will exterminate from it 30 man and beast? Therefore, thus says the LORD concerning Jehoiakim, king of Judah: He shall have no one sitting on the throne of David, and his dead body shall be cast out to the heat during the day 31 and to frost at night. And I will punish him and his seed and his servants for their iniquity, and I will bring upon them and upon the inhabitants of Jerusalem and the men of Judah all the evil that I have spoken concerning them; 32 and they would not listen. So Jeremiah took another scroll and gave it to Baruch, the son of Neriah, the secretary, and at the dictation of Jeremiah he wrote all the words of the book which Jehoiakim, king of Judah, had burnt with fire, and besides there were added to them many words of the same kind.

The scroll was burnt, and Jeremiah was in hiding. Jehoiakim had apparently succeeded in silencing him, but that did not change the curse pronounced against Judah and the royal house. The Lord tells Jeremiah to have the book rewritten, and He repeats the curse on king and people: You have exalted yourselves above Jehovah, you shall be humbled into the dust. (On v. 30, cp. ch. 22:19.)

Jeremiah obeys, and there were added many similar prophecies to those written on the scroll and burned by Jehoiakim. Just how much of our present book was contained in the original scroll, and how much of the contents of these two scrolls is found in our present book, is impossible to say, just as impossible as to know what became of the second scroll. We have the Book of Jeremiah, the book that God has preserved for all generations. Let us heed Christ's admonition Luke 16:29. The Bible may be burned; the witnesses of God's Word may be killed or exiled; in spite of the opposition and enmity of puny mortals the Word of God liveth and abideth forever!

Complete Destruction!
Chapters 37—45

XIV. Last Days of Jerusalem, Ch. 37—39

1. Jeremiah's Warning to Zedekiah, His Arrest and Imprisonment
Ch. 37—38

CHAPTER 37
A. Zedekiah interviews the prophet, vv. 1-10

1 And Zedekiah, the son of Josiah, began his royal rule in place of Coniah, the son of Jehoiakim, whom Nebuchadrezzar, king of Babylon, had made king of Judah. And 2 neither he nor his servants nor the people of the land obeyed the words of the LORD which He spoke through Jeremiah the 3 prophet. And King Zedekiah sent Jehucal, the son of Shelemiah, and Zephaniah, the son of Maaseiah, the priest, to Jeremiah the prophet, saying: Pray, intercede in our behalf with the LORD, our God. 4 And Jeremiah moved about freely among the people; they had not yet placed him in the prison house. 5 Pharaoh's army had gone out from Egypt, and the Chaldeans besieging Jerusalem had heard the report and had raised the siege of Jeru-

6 salem. Then the word of the LORD came to Jeremiah the prophet, 7 saying: Thus says the LORD, the God of Israel: Thus shall ye say to the king of Judah, who has sent you to me to ask me: Behold, Pharaoh's army, that is coming forth for your aid, will return to 8 its land, Egypt. And the Chaldeans shall again fight against the city, will capture it, and burn it with 9 fire. Thus says the LORD: Do not deceive yourselves by thinking that the Chaldeans certainly are going to leave us; for they shall not leave. 10 For if you should defeat the whole army of the Chaldeans fighting against you and there would be left among them only mortally wounded men, yet they would arise, everyone in his tent, and burn this city with fire.

Vv. 1-2. A period of eighteen years intervenes between ch. 36 and 37. The complete destruction of Jerusalem, foretold at Jeremiah's call (ch. 1:11-16), was rapidly approaching. Zedekiah, placed on the throne by Nebuchadnezzar in 597, was not as aggressively wicked as Jehoiakim, his brother, had been. Yet, instead of trying to re-establish the fear of God in his kingdom, he disobeyed God's Word and Law, as spoken "by," by the hand, through the instrumentality of, Jeremiah (cp. 2 Kings 24:19; 2 Chron. 36:12). He was a weak, vacillating character, hesitating to do what he knew to be right, stubbornly proceeding on his self-chosen paths of compromising. "He drifted and drifted, and at last was smashed to fragments on the rocks, as all men are who do not keep a strong hand on the helm and a steady eye on the compass." (Maclaren, *Exp. of Holy Scriptures,* Jeremiah, p. 359.) With him, and largely by his fault, the nation perished.

Vv. 3-5. Nebuchadnezzar had besieged the city, ch. 32:1-2; but the siege had been temporarily raised when Pharaoh Hophra had begun his relief expedition. During this breathing spell the king sent a delegation to Jeremiah, asking him to intercede for king and people: Jehucal, most likely to be identified with Jucal (ch. 38:1), a bitter enemy of the prophet; and Zephaniah (ch. 21:1-2), the deputy ("second") high priest (ch. 52:24), one of the gatekeepers in the Temple (ch. 29:26), who seems to have been kindly disposed to the prophet (ch. 29:24-32); both men of high standing.

Vv. 6-10. The Lord, who had repeatedly forbidden His prophet to pray for the people (ch. 7:16; 11:14; 14:11), announces the failure of Pharaoh's expedition and the capture and burning of Jerusalem, and warns the people against self-deception. Even a weakened army would be victorious over Jerusalem because Jerusalem's doom was determined by the Lord of justice.

B. Jeremiah's arrest, vv. 11-15

11 It came to pass when the army of the Chaldeans had raised the siege of Jerusalem because of the army 12 of Pharaoh, that Jeremiah went out from Jerusalem to go into the land of Benjamin to settle an inheritance 13 case there among the people. And as he was in the Gate of Benjamin, there was the chief of the watch, and his name was Irijah, the son of Shelemiah, the son of Hananiah; and he arrested Jeremiah the prophet, saying: You are deserting 14 to the Chaldeans. And Jeremiah said: A lie! I am not deserting to the Chaldeans. But he would not listen to him. And Irijah arrested Jeremiah and brought him to the 15 princes. The princes were angry with Jeremiah and whipped him and put him into the prison house, in the house of Jonathan, the secretary, for they had made this the prison.

Vv. 11-12. "To separate himself thence." The Hebrew term never means "to separate," but to divide, to share, used of land (Joshua 14:5; 18:2); inheritances (Prov. 17:2), spoils (Prov. 16:19). The Hiphil is causative, to institute a sharing, or apportionment. The object is not named. It could not be Hanameel's field (ch. 32), since that was not to be apportioned, but bought. "In the midst of the people" is to be connected not with "went forth," but with the division, which was to be made in public assembly. The departure of the Babylonian army gave an opportunity to call a public, official meeting.

Vv. 13-15. While passing through the city gate, Jeremiah was arrested by the captain of the guard on a charge as false as it was foolish. If Jeremiah had intended to desert to the Babylonians, he could not have chosen a more inopportune time. The Babylonians were gone! In spite of Jeremiah's protest, he is delivered to the princes (p. 32 f.). They heap indignities upon him (v. 15). Unbelief is intolerant of God's truth and the preachers of this truth, for it hates both.

C. Zedekiah's secret interview with Jeremiah and change of Jeremiah's prison
vv. 16-21

16 When Jeremiah went into the house of the dungeon, namely, the
17 vault, and Jeremiah sat there, then King Zedekiah sent to him and got him. And the king asked him secretly and said: Is there a word from the LORD? Jeremiah said: Yes. And he said: Into the hands of the king of Babel you will be
18 given! And Jeremiah said to King Zedekiah: What have I sinned against you and against your servants and against this people that you have put me into prison?
19 And where are your prophets who prophesy to you, saying: The king of Babylon will not come up against
20 you and against the city? Now pray, hear, my lord the king: May my plea find favor with you, and do not return me into the house of Jonathan, the secretary, that I may
21 not die there. And King Zedekiah ordered that Jeremiah be held captive in the Court of the Guard and to give him a loaf of bread every day from Bakers' Street, until all the bread in the city had been consumed. And Jeremiah remained in the Court of the Guard.

V. 16. Zedekiah interviews Jeremiah. Jonathan's house evidently offered an access to the "cabins," the series of subterranean vaults, caverns, cisterns, tunnels, with which the soft limestone underlying the city is honeycombed. (See Duncan, *Digging Up Biblical History*, II, pp. 199—215, and pp. 19—28 on cisterns and their use.) These vaults and cisterns were used for the imprisonment of dangerous criminals, serving the purpose at times of the oubliettes of medieval times. In this dark, unventilated cistern house the spokesman of God was confined many days. Unbelief, constantly demanding toleration and charity, is unbelievably intolerant and cruel against opposition.

Vv. 17-19. One day Zedekiah had Jeremiah secretly brought to the royal palace. "Is there a word of the LORD?" he asks. Unbelief makes cowards of men, victims of an evil conscience. The king fears to approach God, but hopes to get good news from the prophet. He completely misread the character of Jeremiah. Seemingly so soft and yielding, Jeremiah once more proves himself an iron pillar. "There is!" he says. "Into the power of the king of Babylon shall you be given!" What remarkable courage, particularly under the prevailing circumstances! And now the subject becomes the judge of the weak king. "What wrong have I done," where have I failed to do my full duty towards you, your officials, and this people, "that you," and that includes the king, who did not dare to oppose the enemies of Jeremiah, "have imprisoned me?" Unbelief is unreasonable in its hate of the prophets of truth! And just as foolish in following their own prophets of peace and prosperity (v. 19).

Vv. 20-21. In answer to Jeremiah's humble plea he is transferred to a more favorable prison. The prophet as the spokesman of God has spoken. Now speaks the subject to the king in due humility. Please hear, my lord the king! Let my petition fall before your face, your presence. In casting his petition at the feet of the king, he humbles himself into the dust even though he insists on less than his legal right. The prophets, like the apostles, were not self-appointed martyrs. They made use of the means at hand to save their life, their safety and convenience. Jeremiah was ready to go wherever the Lord would send him, even into prison and into death; but he was equally determined to be sure that the Lord was sending him. He did not insist on being released out of prison. He left that to the king. Yet he asks for humane treatment, a better prison, where he would not be sure to die. Zedekiah did not set him free. He may have feared to rouse the hatred and opposition of his courtiers to himself and to Jeremiah, who, unguarded, would fall an easy prey to the machinations of his enemies. The weak king, ruled by the princes, took what he regarded as the safest course to guard the prophet and himself. "The court of the prison," rather, the Court of the Guard, the palace guard in distinction from the king's personal guard. "Bakers' Street," the various tradesmen seem to have had special streets either chosen by them or assigned to them (cp. 1 Kings 20:34). While still a prisoner, the prophet enjoyed not only a comparative safety from the vicious hatred of his opponents, but freedom of movement (cp. Paul, Acts 28: 16, 30f.) and contact with the people. Courageously he continued to fulfill his mission to his people (ch. 38:1ff.).

CHAPTER 38

D. Jeremiah is accused of treason and thrown into a cistern, vv. 1-6

1 And Shephatiah, the son of Mattan, and Gedaliah, the son of Pashur, and Jucal, the son of Shelemiah, and Pashur, the son of Malchiah, heard the words that Jeremiah had spoken unto all the 2 people, saying: Thus says the LORD: Everyone remaining in the city shall die with the sword and from famine and from pestilence, and everyone who goes out to the Chaldeans shall live. His life shall

be to him spoils, and he shall live.
3 Thus says the LORD: Certainly this city will be given into the hand of the army of the king of Babylon, 4 and he shall take it. Then the princes said to the king: Certainly this man should die! For in this manner he is slackening the hands of the soldiers remaining in this city and the hands of all the people by saying to them words such as these! For this man is no longer seeking the welfare of this people, 5 but rather their evil. And King Zedekiah said: Behold, he is in your hands, for the king can do 6 nothing against you. And they took Jeremiah and cast him into the cistern of Malchiah, the son of the king, which was in the Court of the Guard, and they let Jeremiah down with ropes, and there was no water in the cistern but mud, and Jeremiah was immersed in the mud.

Vv. 1-4. Evidently the end was fast approaching. "Men of war that remain" (v. 4) proves that many, if not most, of the soldiers had been killed or had deserted. Jeremiah saw clearly that the Lord's threat would be fulfilled shortly and in love toward his people sought to save them from the triple divine nemesis of sword and famine and pestilence by urging speedy and unconditional surrender. Undoubtedly large numbers would have been willing to surrender. But the fanatical warmongers cowed the people by threats and false promises, being blinded by their unbelief against the overt facts. Rather let all perish than surrender! They sought to silence the only true friend the people had by charging him with lack of patriotism, dangerous speeches, and treasonable acts, and demanded his death. Unbelief ever is fanatical in its intolerance of the truth and resorts to false charges and despicable lies in order to get rid of the prophets of God's truth.

V. 5. Here we see brazen wickedness meeting weak-kneed vacillation, and, as always, vacillation losing out (cp. Matt. 27:11-26). Silencing his conscience, Zedekiah betrays Jeremiah in order to keep the good will of these murderers. Behold, he is in your hands! What can the king do against you? What a cowardly shifting of responsibility and blame! What a disgraceful surrender of his power, shameful betrayal of duty, degrading confession of his own weakness, and ineptitude for his high office! Unbelief makes cowards of men!

V. 6. With the royal consent they hurry him off to his doom. "Dungeon" = cistern. "The son of Hammelech," rather, "the son of the king" (cp. ch. 36:26), one of the royal family, not necessarily a son of Zedekiah. The cistern was located in the Court of the Guard, where Jeremiah had been kept confined (ch. 37:21). So deep was the pit that they had to let him down with ropes. While there was no water in the cistern, its bottom was covered with a deep layer of mud, into which the unfortunate prophet sank. There they left him! Men that had gone so far would hardly go to the trouble of providing him with food. While they were not guilty of shedding blood (cp. Gen. 37:18-27), they had succeeded in effectually silencing him. He was to be a forgotten man! If he be God's prophet, let God take care of him! Unbelief makes man cruel, worse than the cruelty of a beast, the refined cruelty of a hypocrite.

The faithful prophet of the Lord was doomed to die a lingering, horrible death in a dark, evil-smelling pit. Was this to be the end? God had not forgotten His servant and in a remarkable manner foils the plan of the enemies and fulfills again His promise of ch. 1:19.

E. Jeremiah is rescued by Ebedmelech, vv. 7-13

7 And Ebedmelech, the Ethiopian, one of the eunuchs and one of the royal household, heard that they had put Jeremiah into the cistern. Now the king was sitting in the 8 Gate of Benjamin. Then Ebedmelech went out from the gatehouse of the king and spoke to the 9 king, saying: My lord, the king, these men are doing wickedly in all that they have been doing to Jeremiah the prophet, because they have cast him into the cistern, and he will die under it for hunger, and there is no bread any more in 10 the city. And the king commanded Ebedmelech, the Ethiopian, saying: Take with you from here thirty men and pull Jeremiah the prophet out of the cistern before he die. 11 And Ebedmelech took the men with him and came to the house of the king, to the lower chamber, and took from there worn-out clothes and tattered clothes and let them down to Jeremiah into the cistern 12 with ropes. And Ebedmelech, the Ethiopian, said to Jeremiah: Place these old and tattered clothes under your armpits under the 13 ropes. And Jeremiah did so. And they drew Jeremiah out by means of the ropes and brought him up out of the cistern. So Jeremiah remained in the Court of the Guard.

Vv. 7-13. The Lord has forgotten neither His prophet nor His promise. Jeremiah's dungeon was not to become a death chamber. The Lord uses a foreigner, an Ethiopian slave, a eunuch, excluded from the congregation of Israel by divine law (Deut. 23:1). He happened to be stationed in the royal palace and there heard of Jeremiah's imprisonment. What he heard, filled him with intense pity for the old man, whom he had often seen and heard and whose word had touched and changed his heart. With a courage that put to shame the cowardice of the king, he hurried out of the palace to the Gate of Benjamin, where the king was seated to speak justice and judgment. The Nubian slave becomes the advocate of God's prophet. Humbly ("My lord, the king"), yet courageously, he declares that the enemies of Jeremiah had been guilty of wickedness in proceeding

295

against Jeremiah from their first charge to the final culmination of their evil scheme. He pleads for his rescue before he dies of hunger. The conscience-stricken king grasps this opportunity, hoping to silence the accusing voice of conscience and to be relieved of the gnawing sense of guilt. In order to guard against any possible interference on the part of the opponents, Zedekiah tells Ebedmelech to take thirty men as his aids. Before the enemies have time to stop the rescue, Ebedmelech hurries back to the Court of the Guard. Jeremiah shows his appreciation of Ebedmelech's kindness by describing at length the sympathetic consideration and the skillful manner in which the rescue was effected (vv. 11-13). The Lord's appreciation is narrated ch. 39: 15-18. Already in the Old Testament the Lord had His chosen children not only in Israel, but among the Gentiles.

F. Zedekiah's last consultation with Jeremiah, vv. 14-28

14 And King Zedekiah sent and brought Jeremiah the prophet into his presence, into the third entrance in the house of the LORD, and the king said to Jeremiah: I am going to ask you a thing; do not keep anything from me.

15 And Jeremiah said to Zedekiah: If I will reveal to you, will you not surely kill me? And if I advise you, you will not listen to me.

16 And King Zedekiah swore to Jeremiah secretly, saying: As the LORD liveth, who has created for us this soul, I shall not kill you nor give you into the hands of these men who are seeking your life. And Jeremiah said to Zedekiah: Thus says the LORD, the God of Hosts, the God of Israel: If you will go forth to the princes of the king of Babylon, then you shall live, and the city shall not be burned with fire. You shall live,

18 you and your house. But if you do not go forth to the princes of the king of Babylon, then this city will be given into the hand of the Chaldeans, and they shall burn it with fire, and you shall not escape

19 from their hands. Then King Zedekiah said to Jeremiah: I am afraid of the Jews who have gone over to the Chaldeans, lest I be

20 handed over to them and they vent their spite on me. Then Jeremiah said: They shall not surrender you. Pray, listen to the voice of the LORD as I have been telling it to you. Then it shall be well with you, and your life shall be spared.

21 But if you refuse to surrender, this is the word which the LORD has

22 revealed to me: Behold, all the women who are left over in the house of the king of Judah shall go forth to the princes of the king of Babylon and shall say: Your good friends have deluded you and overwhelmed you. Your feet are stuck in the mud — they have

23 turned their backs to you! All your wives and your sons shall be brought out to the Chaldeans, and you shall not escape from their hands, for by the hand of the king of Babylon will you be taken captive, and your city will be burnt

24 with fire. Then Zedekiah said to Jeremiah: Let no man know of this conversation, then you shall

25 not die. And if the princes will hear that I have spoken with you and will come to you and say to you: Now report to us what you have spoken to the king, do not conceal it from us, and we will not kill you, and what has the

26 king spoken to you? Then say to them: I brought my petition before the king that I might not be returned into the house of Jonathan to die there. And all the
27 princes came to Jeremiah and asked him, and he reported in keeping with all these words which the king had commanded him, and they desisted from him, for the conversation had not been over-
28 heard. So Jeremiah remained in the Court of the Guard until the day that Jerusalem was captured.

Vv. 14-28. Zedekiah evidently hoped that Jeremiah, in gratitude for the royal permission to release him, would be willing to give him a favorable answer to his anxious inquiry as to the future policy. He completely misunderstands the prophet and his mission. Jeremiah prepares him for an answer which may so enrage the king that he will be ready to kill him rather than follow his advice. The king vows a solemn oath that he neither will kill him nor permit his opponents to harm him (v. 16). The prophet repeats (vv. 17-18) what he had said before: Surrender! That is the only way to save yourself and the city. Cowardly Zedekiah fears the ridicule of the Jews who had deserted to the Babylonians, but Jeremiah assures him that he would not be surrendered to them, while stubborn refusal to follow the prophet's advice would not save him nor his family from captivity and would place the blame for the destruction and burning of the city directly on his shoulders (v. 22). Nor would he escape the ridicule he so feared that he would rather see the city destroyed. The women still remaining in the palace would make him the butt of their taunt song (v. 22), ridiculing his weak and vacillating policy in following his alleged friends who urged him on to a hopeless struggle and would leave him sticking helpless in the mud. Again Zedekiah proves his weakness toward doing good and his stubbornness in following his self-chosen way toward evil by dismissing the prophet with the request to keep this interview secret. If the princes would hear of it and ask him to reveal to them the subject of their conversation, he should tell them that he had asked the king not to return him to Jonathan's house. Jeremiah obeyed the king. He did not tell them a falsehood, for the petition as formulated v. 26 was certainly implied in vv. 15-16. He did not tell them the whole truth, for that was neither necessary, nor did they have a right to demand such information, and he would have broken his promise to his ruler and betrayed what was revealed to him as the spiritual adviser, the pastor, of the king.

"He was there when Jerusalem was taken" (v. 28b). The M. T. cannot be translated as the A. V. reads. "It came to pass when Jerusalem was about to be taken" is the protasis of ch. 40:1.

297

CHAPTER 39

2. The Destruction of Jerusalem and Zedekiah's Deportation
Ch. 38:28b—39:10

Ch. 38:28b When Jerusalem was about
Ch. 39:1 to be captured in the ninth
year of Zedekiah, king of Judah,
in the tenth month, Nebuchadrezzar, king of Babylon, and all his
army advanced against Jerusalem
2 and besieged it. In the eleventh
year of Zedekiah in the fourth
month on the ninth day of the
3 month the city was breached, and
all the officials of the king of Babylon came and sat down in the
middle gate, even Nergal-sharezer,
Samgar, Nebo-sar-sechim, the rab-
saris, Nergal-sharezer, the rab-mag,
with all the rest of the officials of
4 the king of Babylon. And when
Zedekiah, king of Judah, and all
the men of war saw them, they fled
and left the city by night by way
of the king's garden by the gate
5 between the walls. And they went
out on the way to the Arabah.
Then the army of the Chaldeans
pursued them and overtook Zedekiah in the fields of Jericho and
took him and brought him to Nebuchadrezzar, king of Babylon, to
Riblah in the land of Hamath. And
there he pronounced judgment
6 against him. And the king of
Babylon slew the sons of Zedekiah
at Riblah in his sight. The king of
Babel also slew all the noblemen
7 of Judah. And he put out the
eyes of Zedekiah and bound him
with brass chains to bring him to
8 Babylon. The Chaldeans burnt the
house of the king and the houses
of the people and tore down the
9 walls of Jerusalem. And the rest
of the people that were left in the
city, and the deserters that had
gone over to him, and the rest of
the people that were left over,
Nebuzaradan, the commander of
the guard, deported to Babylon.
10 Nebuzaradan, the commander of
the guard, left a number of the
common people, who had nothing,
in the land of Judah and at the
same time gave them vineyards and
fields.

Grammatical Notes

Ch. 38:28b. "And he was there when
Jerusalem was taken"; the M. T. has
separated this clause from ch. 38:28a by
ם and from ch. 39:1 by פ, both letters
indicating new paragraphs. Others
connect the clause with ch. 39:3 and
regard ch. 39:1-2 as a parenthesis. That
seems to be a very awkward construction. Driver says: "The perfect is employed to indicate actions the accomplishment of which lies indeed in the
future, but is regarded as dependent
upon such an unalterable determination of the will that it may be spoken
of as having actually taken place." He
lists among other passages Ruth 4:3,
מָכְרָה, lit., has sold = has resolved to
sell; Gen. 23:11, 13, 15, 18; Ps. 20:7
(A. V., v. 6), the Lord saveth (perfect) = is sure to save. (Driver, Hebrew Tenses, p. 20f., par. 13.) Applying this rule here will obviate the
awkward parenthesis and the supposi-
tion of a corrupted text. Therefore we
have translated as above, regarding
ch. 38:2b as the protasis, ch. 39:1 as
the apodosis: "When Jerusalem by
divine determination was to be taken,
then," etc. Ch. 39 narrates the fall of
Jerusalem (vv. 1-3), Zedekiah's flight,
capture, and punishment (vv. 4-7), the
destruction of the city (v. 8), the deportation of all survivors of the siege
with the exception of a few of the

poorer class who were to form a new colony (vv. 9-10). Vv. 11-14 briefly report what happened to Jeremiah; and finally the divine message to be announced to Ebedmelech (ch. 38:7-13) is added. The arrangement of the material is logical rather than strictly chronological.

The names listed v. 3 as compared with those of v. 13 present difficulties. Many interpreters regard the two lists as originally having been identical and the present "confused" form as due to copyists' errors. The text of the LXX is entirely unreliable, since vv. 4-13 are missing, and the names v. 3 are corrupted: "Marganasar, and Samagoth, and Nabusachar, and Nabusaris, and Nagargasnaser, Rabamath." It is not necessary to substitute Nebu-

saradan (cp. v. 13) for the first Nergal-sharezer (v. 3). In a list found by Koldewey in Babylon, this latter name appears among the officials of Accad as governor of Sinmagir. "Samgar" of our text has practically the same consonants, the n being assimilated to the following m. Samgar is either the name of Nergal-sharezer's province or of another official. "Nebo" is to be connected with Sar-sechim, Nebo-sar-sechim, a second officer, designated as a *rab-saris*, the chief eunuch (a term used for various high officials, cf. Grammatical Notes on Jer. 29:2). The last official is another Nergal-sharezer, designated as the *rab-mag*, Assyrian *rab-mugi*, the meaning of which is uncertain. Cp. M. Burrows, *What Mean These Stones?* P. 43 f.

Vv. 1-3. After his decisive defeat of Pharaoh Hophra, which made Jerusalem's fall only a question of time, Nebuchadnezzar evidently had gone to Riblah, almost 200 miles north of Jerusalem. At this strategic observation post he had established his headquarters. The final conquest of Jerusalem was left to his generals (cp. ch. 38:17-18, "princes"), of whom Nebuzaradan was chief. He is called captain of the guard (ch. 39:9, 10, 11), literally, chief of the cooks, or butchers (cp. 1 Sam. 9:23-24), because the bodyguard had to supervise the preparation of the royal food, a position of highest trust (cp. Gen. 39:1; 40:1-2). As such Nebuzaradan "served" the king (Jer. 52:12), literally, stood before him, was in closest personal contact with him. At his orders the three officers named v. 3 took up their position "in the middle gate," most likely the gate of the wall separating the new city from the old. They were to establish a semblance of order in the city, to line up the captives, etc.

Vv. 4-10. Cowardly Zedekiah with the remnant of the army sought to escape under cover of night. The exact position of "the two walls" is unknown, the "king's garden" on the southeastern slope, near the junction of the Hinnom and Kidron Valleys. He was captured, his army scattered. At Riblah, Nebuchadnezzar ordered the slaying of the royal children and all the nobles before the eyes of Zedekiah and then had him blinded. So were fulfilled the seemingly contradictory prophecies Ezek. 12:13; 17:16; and Jer. 32:5; 34:3. Nebuchadnezzar decided once for all to end any possibility of further rebellion and at the same time prevent Jerusalem from becoming an Egyptian stronghold, a thorn in his side. Therefore he ordered the burning of the city and the deportation of the remaining people with a few exceptions. Nebuzaradan returned to carry out these orders four weeks after the capture of the city.

3. Nebuzaradan Commits Jeremiah to the Protection of Gedaliah
Vv. 11-14

11 And Nebuchadrezzar, the king of Babel, had issued orders regarding Jeremiah to Nebuzaradan, the com-
12 mander of the guard, saying: Take him, and keep your eyes on him, and do not do him any harm. But
13 do with him as he tells you. And Nebuzaradan, the commander of the guard, gave orders, and Nebu-shasban, the *rab-saris,* and Nergal-sharezer, the *rab-mag,* and all the
14 king of Babylon's officials sent and took Jeremiah from the Court of the Guard and committed him to Gedaliah, the son of Ahikam, the son of Shaphan, to bring him to his home. So he stayed among the people.

Vv. 11-14. With regard to Jeremiah the king gave special orders that the chief of the bodyguard make it his personal business to "look well to him," to set or keep his eyes on him (an expression occurring only here, ch. 40:4, and Gen. 44:21), so that no harm would come to the prophet. A very necessary charge, as events proved. After a consultation with the other leaders for the purpose of preventing any possible harm to Jeremiah by conflicting orders or ignorance of the royal decree, they had Jeremiah transferred from the Court of the Guard (ch. 38:28) and committed him to Gedaliah, whom the king had appointed as governor of the colony to be established (ch. 40:5). Gedaliah took him to "the home," the governor's mansion. At last Jeremiah was at liberty and mingled freely with the people, urging them not to despair, comforting, strengthening them. The heathen king honors his political friend far more than the Jews did their loving, divinely appointed prophet. How often has that been repeated in the history of the Church!

Evidently while mingling with the people, Jeremiah was picked up by Babylonian soldiers under orders to fetter the Jews, who did not know him nor the royal command, was bound and deported with the other captives to Ramah (ch. 40:1). Nebuchadnezzar's order, therefore, remained unobeyed without any fault of Nebuzaradan or Gedaliah.

4. Ebedmelech Blessed by the Lord, Vv. 15-18

15 When Jeremiah was imprisoned in the Court of the Guard, the word of the LORD came to him, saying:
16 Go and tell Ebedmelech, the Ethiopian: Thus says the LORD of Hosts, the God of Israel: Behold, I am ready to fulfill My words concerning this city for evil and not for good. And they shall be fulfilled before your eyes on that 17 day. But I will deliver you on that day, is the oracle of the LORD, and you will not be given into the power of the men of whom you 18 are afraid. For I will certainly let you escape, and you will not fall by the sword, and your life shall be as spoils to you, for you have trusted in Me, is the oracle of the LORD.

Vv. 15-18. The Lord provides not only for His chosen spokesman, as He had promised (ch. 1:8, 19), He thinks with like loving care for one who was not the protégé of a mighty ruler, but a poor, unknown, friendless slave, harassed with dread fear as to his future. Ebedmelech (cp. ch. 38:6-13) had given more than a cup of water (Mark 9:41) to the prophet, and in keeping with His promises (Ps. 37:40; 41:2; 97:10) the Lord was with him also in his hour of need. The prophet, still in the Court of the Guard, was commissioned by the Lord to relieve this servant of the Lord of his fears by assuring him that he would neither be slain nor fall into the hands of the enemy, "because thou hast put thy trust in Me!" The Searcher of hearts saw that the wellspring of that daring rescue was not merely natural pity, but true faith in the Lord of justice and mercy. Through faith he had delivered Jeremiah, through faith he would be delivered from harm.

XV. Dawn and Night, Ch. 40—44

CHAPTER 40

5. Captive Jeremiah, Set Free at Ramah, Joins Gedaliah, Vv. 1-6

1 The word which came to Jeremiah from the LORD after Nebuzaradan, commander of the bodyguard, had released him at Ramah, where he had found him bound with chains among all the exiles from Jerusalem and Judah that were being 2 deported to Babylon. Now the commander of the guard took Jeremiah and said to him: The LORD, your God, announced this calamity 3 concerning this place. And the LORD has certainly fulfilled what He spoke, for you have sinned against the LORD and did not listen to His voice, and so this 4 thing has come upon you. And now, behold, I have released you today from your chains, which were on your hands, and if you are willing to come to Babylon with me, come, and I will keep my eye upon you; but if you are not willing to come with me to Babylon, forget about it! See, the whole land is before you. You may go wherever it seems good and proper 5 to you. (And as he still did not turn away:) You may go to Gedaliah, the son of Ahikam, the son of Shaphan, whom the king of Babylon has appointed over the cities of Judah, and stay with him among the people, or go any place that seems proper to you. Then the captain of the guard gave him an allowance and a gift and re- 6 leased him. So Jeremiah went to Gedaliah, the son of Ahikam, to Mizpah and stayed with him among the people remaining in the land.

V. 1. "The word" includes the revelations given at various times during the critical period pictured ch. 40—44, just as ch. 1:1-3 the singular includes all the revelations from Jeremiah's call to the fall of Jerusalem (ch. 1:4 to ch. 39). Even in the turbulent times following the destruction of Jerusalem the Lord revealed Himself to His prophet, and Jeremiah remained the counselor of the remnant left in the land, advising them not merely as a shrewd statesman, but as the spokesman of the Lord. Men had mocked him, had imprisoned him, had sought to kill him, had fettered him, but the Lord had fulfilled His promise (ch. 1:8, 17-19; 15:19-21). Another test was in store for the aged prophet. At the command of Nebuchadnezzar he had been liberated from prison, but in the general confusion he had been taken captive by Babylonian soldiers, who naturally did not know him, had been bound with chains and sent to Ramah with other captives. Had the Lord forgotten him after all? No! Whether Gedaliah instituted a search, or Nebuzaradan, remembering his charge (ch. 39:12), or both, we cannot tell. At Ramah the mistake was discovered, and Jeremiah at once was released. The Lord had not forsaken him! He had strengthened the faith and trust of His prophet for still severer tests awaiting him.

302

Vv. 2-3. Commentators have regarded these words of Nebuzaradan as a later insertion by a "pious" reader, since a heathen could not possibly have spoken in this manner. Yet that is not impossible. Even the heathen Nebuzaradan may have been overwhelmed by the manner in which the prophecies of Jeremiah had been fulfilled to the letter. Even if Jehovah seemed to him a tribal deity inferior to his own gods, yet He was the God ruling in the land of Israel and had predicted through His prophet the destruction of the city against the hopes and expectations of the fanatic Jews. The word of the prophet, rejected by his own nation, had deeply impressed this great and powerful man. What an encouragement for Jeremiah to keep on proclaiming this word, to continue as a prophet unto the nations (ch. 1:5)! On the language of the Babylonian general, cp., e. g., the edicts of Cyrus (Ezra 1:3-4, and Barton, *Archaeology and the Bible,* 6th ed., p. 484), of Darius (Ezra 6:1-12), of Huram of Tyrus (2 Chron. 2:11-12), Necho's message to Josiah (2 Chron. 35:21), Rabshakeh's boast (2 Kings 18:25), also the permission of the Assyrian king and its motivation (2 Kings 17:24-28).

V. 4. Nebuzaradan treated Jeremiah with utmost respect. Strange, the heathen honors the prophet, whom he regards as a political friend, as his equal, as a man worthy of honor, while Jeremiah's fellow Jews had heaped on the venerable prophet all the shame and dishonor they could think of, though he had spent his lifetime in untiring efforts to seek their temporal and eternal welfare and salvation. Shameful ingratitude! Yet how often must faithful pastors accept that as their only reward from men who call themselves Christians!

Nebuzaradan permits the prophet to choose his own course of action. He offers Jeremiah his personal patronage and protection, if he should care to go to Babylon. Or he may go wherever he wishes. Yet if he should choose to remain in his homeland, Nebuzaradan advises him to join Gedaliah, the newly appointed governor of Judah.

We cannot doubt that the prophet would have been highly honored and richly rewarded had he chosen to go with Nebuzaradan to Babylon. The very fact that Nebuchadnezzar had given orders to let Jeremiah make his own choice free and unhampered, proves the high esteem in which he was held by the mighty ruler of the Babylonian Empire. But Jeremiah had no desire for earthly glory and material rewards. His place was with the remnant of his people, was with Gedaliah. There was work to do that he alone could do. And where God placed him, where God had plainly chosen for him a field of activity, there he in his old age was as willing to go as he had been in his youth, on the day of his call, when God had told him: Thou shalt go wherever I send you (ch. 1:7).

6. The Founding of a New Colony, Vv. 7-12

7 And when all the leaders of the military forces which were afield, they and their men, heard that the king of Babylon had appointed Gedaliah, the son of Ahikam, over the land and that he had committed to him the men, women, and children of the poor of the land, those that were not deported to 8 Babylon, they came to Gedaliah at Mizpah: Ishmael, the son of Nethaniah, and Johanan and Jonathan, the sons of Kareach, and Seraiah, the son of Tanchumet, and the sons of Ephai of Netophah, and Jezaniah, the son of the Maachathite, to- 9 gether with their men. And Gedaliah, the son of Ahikam, the son of Shaphan, assured them and their men under oath, saying: Do not fear to serve the Chaldeans. Settle down in the land, and serve the king of Babel, and you will fare 10 well. And I, see, I am going to reside in Mizpah to represent you before the Chaldeans who may come to us, and you may gather wine and summer fruits and oil and store them in your vessels and remain in your cities which you have 11 taken. Likewise, all the Jews who were in Moab and among the children of Ammon and in Edom and in all the countries heard that the king of Babylon had left a remnant of Judah, and that he had placed Gedaliah, the son of Ahikam, the son of Shaphan, over 12 them. So all the Jews returned from all the places to which they were scattered and came into the land of Judah to Gedaliah at Mizpah and gathered very much wine and summer fruit.

V. 7. Jerusalem, the populated and beautiful city (Lam. 1:1, 6), had been reduced to a heap of ashes. So often had it rebelled against Nebuchadnezzar, so often had it proved a serious obstacle in carrying out his ambitious military plans, so often had he been forced to subdue it at great costs of men and money, that he had determined for once and all to remove this thorn in his flesh. A strong and well-fortified Jerusalem would have remained a continual menace to Babylon's world power, a springboard for future attempts by the Jews, who were constantly being prodded by Egypt, to revolt against the hated Eastern sovereign and to help their next-door neighbor to defeat the ambitious plans of their inveterate rival.

Nebuchadnezzar had moved the seat of government to Mizpah, some miles north of Jerusalem. Its exact site has not yet been definitely determined. Various suggestions have been made: El Bire, ten miles north of Jerusalem; Nebi Samwil, six miles northwest; Tell el Nasbi, seven miles north of Jerusalem.

While Jerusalem was completely destroyed, it was not Nebuchadnezzar's plan to leave the whole land desolate. For future possible campaigns against Egypt it would be advantageous to have cultivated land available which could furnish at least part of the provisions needed for his huge armies. As governor he did not appoint a Babylonian, probably because he did not want to arouse the resentment of the remaining Jews. Neither did he appoint a descendant of the house of David. Most of the members of the royal family had been slain, and to appoint a descendant of the Davidic dynasty might have aroused the hopes of the colonists and the exiles in Babylon for a speedy restoration of the royal house of David and might have strengthened any thoughts of revolution and rebellion that might still burn in the breasts of the Jews like a spark under ashes to blaze forth suddenly with renewed fury at any time. Nebuchadnezzar made a very wise choice in appointing Gedaliah, the son of Ahikam. Gedaliah belonged to a God-fearing, influential family, which, like Jeremiah, submitted to God's will and regarded Nebuchadnezzar as their divinely appointed ruler, since both Jehoiachim and Zedekiah had sworn allegiance to the Babylonian sovereign (2 Kings 24: 1, 17, 20). Gedaliah's father, Ahikam, had protected Jeremiah against the false accusations of lying priests and a fanatic mob (Jer. 26: 24). His grandfather, Shaphan, had been secretary of state under Josiah (2 Kings 22: 8). In choosing Gedaliah, Nebuchadnezzar proved himself an eminent statesman. His plan was to rebuild Judah into a flourishing, self-supporting Jewish commonwealth under Babylonian sovereignty and supervision, but enjoying home rule to a great extent and complete freedom in industry and commerce, and particularly in religion. He knew that a satisfied people, having an opportunity to make a decent living, would be more willing to remain loyal to Babylon and at the same time to resist Egyptian efforts to annex Judah or to foment rebellion against Babylon among the Jews, than if he would deprive them of all their liberties and reduce them to a state of virtual slavery. One cannot catch birds by throwing clubs and brickbats at them. Some modern statesmen might learn a lesson from ancient Nebuchadnezzar.

The wisdom of Nebuchadnezzar's choice of Gedaliah became evident at once. Scattered throughout the land were small commandos, military bands, that had escaped capture or annihilation by the Babylonian armies. Ishmael, the son of Nethaniah, who later turned traitor; two brothers, Johanan and Jonathan, sons of Kareach; Seraiah, the son of Tanhumeth; the sons of Ephai of Netophah, a village mentioned Ezra 2: 22; Jezaniah, the son of the Maachathite (cp. ch. 42: 1) — seven or more military leaders, together with their men came to

Gedaliah, who gave them the assurance, affirming it with a solemn oath, that they had no reason to fear to enter into the service of the Chaldeans. He urged them to live quietly and orderly in the land (on this meaning of "dwell" cp. Lev. 12: 4; 2 Kings 14: 10; Hos. 3: 3), commit no act of insubordination, and promised them a life of peace and security. In order to encourage them to willing obedience, he called their attention to his own example. He would remain at Mizpah as the resident representative of Nebuchadnezzar, and he would deal with the Chaldean officials sent from time to time to receive reports on the progress made and to deliver the imperial mandates. They would not have to meet with these men, he would attend to all the duties incumbent upon the governor. As he was willing to do his duty to the new sovereign, so they should cheerfully submit to the changed circumstances and make the best of them. They still had time to gather ample stores for the coming winter season. Do not let the blessing go to waste that God has offered to you as an evidence of His loving-kindness. And then dwell in quietness and contentment in the cities of which you shall have taken possession (cp. ch. 39: 10; and on Gedaliah's advice, ch. 29: 5-7).

All the Jews who had fled into the neighboring countries now returned to Judah and, after having reaped an abundant harvest, settled down in their homeland. Well might they have been grateful that the Lord of the Covenant had provided so amply for them even during the dreadful months of war and bloodshed.

7. Murder of Gedaliah, Ch. 40:13—41:9

A. The plot revealed to Gedaliah, ch. 40:13-16

13 Then Johanan, the son of Kareach, and all the leaders of the military forces which were afield came to
14 Gedaliah to Mizpah and said to him: Do you know at all that Baalis, the king of the Ammonites, has sent Ishmael, the son of Nethaniah, to take your life? But Gedaliah, the son of Ahikam, did not
15 believe them. And Johanan, the son of Kareach, said to Gedaliah secretly at Mizpah: I will go and slay Ishmael, the son of Nethaniah, and no one shall know it. Why should he slay you, and all Jews gathered around you be scattered and the remainder of Judah perish?
16 And Gedaliah, the son of Ahikam, said to Johanan, the son of Kareach: You shall not do this, for you have spoken a lie against Ishmael.

Vv. 13-16. The dark clouds of war and its horrors were gradually receding, and the sunshine of peace and quiet and security seemed to have returned, but already new storm clouds were gathering. Envy and ambition began to raise their ugly heads. Baalis, the Ammonite king, who had hoped that Judah would fall an easy prey to his hunger for more territory, was sorely disappointed when Gedaliah was appointed governor and a stable, firm government was about to be established. And there was Ishmael, one of the military leaders that had joined Gedaliah, who was equally disappointed that he had not been Nebuchadnezzar's choice. He became the willing tool of Baalis, ready to slay Gedaliah in the hope that the Ammonite king would appoint him governor of the colony. Selfish ambition, envy, the green-eyed monster, shrinking not even from murder and rebellion, were ready to destroy the puny state. Somehow word of these treacherous plans came to Johanan, one of the military leaders loyal to Gedaliah. At once he warned the governor. But honest Gedaliah was unwilling to believe the report. Such treachery seemed impossible to the man of integrity and truthfulness. Johanan knew that the removal of Gedaliah would spell disaster and ruin for the little colony. He was convinced of the truth of the report and offered to take upon himself the responsibility of slaying this public enemy. Yet Gedaliah refused to believe that Ishmael could harbor such devilish schemes and forbade Johanan to carry out his intention.

CHAPTER 41
B. The treacherous murder of Gedaliah and other Jews, vv. 1-9

1 In the seventh month, Ishmael, the son of Nethaniah, the son of Elishama, of royal seed, and with him the royal princes, ten men, came to Gedaliah, the son of Ahikam, to Mizpah, and they ate bread together there at Mizpah. 2 Then Ishmael, the son of Nethaniah, and the ten men that were with him arose and slew Gedaliah, the son of Ahikam, the son of Shaphan, with the sword and killed him, whom the king of Babylon had appointed 3 over the land. And Ishmael slew all the Jews that were with him, with Gedaliah, in Mizpah, and the Chaldean soldiers that were found 4 there. On the second day after the murder of Gedaliah, while it was 5 still not known to anyone, came from Shechem, from Shiloh, and from Samaria, eighty men, with their beards shaven and their clothes torn and their bodies gashed, carrying offerings and incense to bring them to the house 6 of the LORD. So Ishmael, the son of Nethaniah, went out from Mizpah to meet them, walking, and weeping all the way. When he met them, he said to them: Come to Gedaliah, the son of Ahikam. 7 When they had come into the center of the city, Ishmael, the son of Nethaniah, and the men accompanying him slew them and cast them 8 into a cistern. But there happened to be ten men among them who said to Ishmael: Do not kill us, for we have stores of wheat and barley and oil and honey in the field. So he stopped and did not kill them together with the others. 9 The cistern, into which Ishmael threw all the dead bodies of the men whom he had slain besides Gedaliah, is the one which King Asa had made as a protective means against Baasha, the king of Israel. This cistern, Ishmael, the son of Nethaniah, filled with the slain.

Vv. 1-3. Only two months after the destruction of the city, Ishmael came to Mizpah with a small band of picked assassins. Unsuspecting Gedaliah invited the captain and his men to a meal. In flagrant violation of the sacred relations of hospitality, Ishmael and his band of cutthroats suddenly slew Gedaliah and in the ensuing panic succeeded in murdering all the Jews present in the banquet hall, and even the Chaldean bodyguard.

Vv. 4-9. On the very next day, before the rumor of Gedaliah's assassination had spread, eighty men from Shechem, Shiloh, and Samaria came down to bring their offerings to the ruined Temple at Jerusalem. The names of the three cities are not given in geographic order; perhaps, as Keil suggests, the majority of men came from Shechem, which therefore is named first. Evidently these eighty men were pious Israelites living in the territory of the former Northern Kingdom, but coming to Jerusalem for the appointed festivals. Treacherous Ishmael, weeping crocodile tears, lured them into the city by his promise that there they would be welcomed by Gedaliah. The unsuspecting men followed him, and, with the aid of his ten assassins, Ishmael murdered these innocent people and threw their corpses into an old cistern, constructed centuries before for storage of water by King Asa, when he fortified Mizpah against a possible attack by Baasha (1 Kings 15: 22; 2 Chron. 16: 6). "Because of Gedaliah" = at the side of Gedaliah's corpse, which also had been thrown into this cistern, now filled to capacity by the seventy murdered men. Evidently the report that Baalis intended the ruin of the remnant in Judah (ch. 40: 15) was true, and Ishmael's murder of these men was motivated by this wicked design of Baalis.

Ten of the eighty men were spared, because they offered to turn over to Ishmael their stores of wheat, barley, oil, and honey which they had hidden in the field. Most likely, these "treasures" were stored away in underground cisterns on their fields. It was customary to store the threshed grain and other products in such dry, cool, and almost airtight cisterns, the tops of which were covered with plaster and earth in order to hide them from robbers or marauding soldiers. Such supplies were needed at a time of general scarcity, and the bribe seemed sufficient to Ishmael to spare the lives of these ten men.

---

8. Ishmael Defeated and His Captives Freed, Vv. 10-16

10 Then Ishmael took captive all the rest of the people at Mizpah, the king's daughters and all the people remaining at Mizpah, over whom Nebuzaradan, the commander of the guard, had appointed Gedaliah,

and marched on to cross over to
11 the Ammonites. But when Johanan, the son of Kareach, and all
the commanders of the military
forces who were with him heard of
all the atrocities which Ishmael, the
son of Nethania, had committed,
12 they took all their men and set out
to fight against Ishmael, the son of
Nethaniah, overtaking him at the
13 great waters at Gibeon. So when
all the people that were with Ishmael saw Johanan, the son of
Kareach, and all the military commanders with him, they rejoiced.
14 And all the people which Ishmael
had carried captive from Mizpah
turned and went back to Johanan,
15 the son of Kareach. But Ishmael,
the son of Nethaniah, with eight
men escaped from Johanan and
16 went to the Ammonites. So Johanan, the son of Kareach, and all
the military commanders who
were with him took all the rest of
the people (whom Ishmael, the son
of Nethaniah, had carried captive
from Mizpah after he had slain
Gedaliah, the son of Ahikam),
men, soldiers, and women, and
children, and eunuchs, whom he
had brought back from Gibeon.

After the wholesale murder of the Israelites, Ishmael and his
gangsters took captive the entire population of Mizpah, including "the
daughters of the king," the princesses, whom Nebuchadnezzar had
permitted to remain in their homeland (another generous gesture
to gain the good will of the Jews), and started out on their way back
to Ammon. A dozen energetic gangsters, well armed, may easily hold
several hundreds of unarmed men and women and children in panicky
fear by threatening to kill everyone who would dare to show the
least sign of resistance.

When Johanan and the other military leaders finally heard of
this daring raid, they immediately set out in pursuit of the robbers
and murderers. At Gibeon, some miles north of Jerusalem, they
overtook the slowly moving company of captives, who rejoiced at the
sight of possible deliverance, while Ishmael and eight of his men
succeeded in escaping to Ammon. Evidently two had been slain by
the deliverers. The leaders who had caused this horrible tragedy
went scot-free as far as the records go.

9. Contrary to God's Will and Jeremiah's Advice the Jews Flee to Egypt, Ch. 41:17—44:30

A. Fearing the wrath of Nebuchadnezzar, the Jews plan to seek refuge in Egypt ch. 41:17-18

17 And they went and stayed at the
inn of Chimham, which is near
Bethlehem, to go on to journey to
18 Egypt. For they were afraid of the
Chaldeans, because Ishmael, the
son of Nethaniah, had slain Gedaliah, the son of Ahikam, whom the
king of Babylon had appointed over
the land.

309

Unnerved by the horrible occurrences of the last days, Johanan and the remaining military leaders, together with the colonists, dreaded to return to Mizpah, the scene of such atrocious crimes. The curse of God surely must rest upon such a city, and above all they feared the wrath of Nebuchadnezzar; his representative, the governor appointed by him, was cruelly murdered; the Chaldean officers assassinated. That was an act of overt rebellion, an insult to the mighty world emperor that could not remain unpunished. Though the Jews were not guilty, yet they would surely feel the avenging wrath of the Chaldeans, since the guilty ones had succeeded in escaping. Moved by these fears, to a great extent ungrounded, they by-passed Mizpah and went directly south as far as Bethlehem to the inn of Chimham. Chimham is named as the son of Barzillai (2 Sam. 19:37), who had brought refreshments to David when he fled from his son Absalom, and he may have built this as a resting place for travelers. Here the Jews stopped for the night, worn out completely after the exciting events of the day. Their utter confusion and helplessness brings out in sharp contrast the marvelous leadership of Gedaliah. As long as Gedaliah lived, all seemed well. Civilians as well as military men had unbounded confidence in him. They trusted Gedaliah to a far greater extent than they had ever trusted and believed the prophet, the spokesman of God. Their sudden dejection and despair proved that after all they had not turned to the Lord with all their heart; that to them still applied the word of the prophet, Jer. 17: 5-6.

CHAPTER 42

B. The Jews ask Jeremiah to intercede for them, vv. 1-6

1 Then all the military leaders, Johanan, the son of Kareach, and Jezaniah, the son of Hoshaiah, and all the people from the least to the greatest, approached Jeremiah the 2 prophet and said to him: May our petition find favor with you, to intercede for us with the LORD, your God, in behalf of this entire remnant; for there are only a few remaining from a multitude as you 3 may see with your own eyes; that the LORD, your God, may show us the way on which we are to walk 4 and what we are to do. And Jeremiah the prophet said to them: I have heard! Behold, I am ready to intercede with the LORD, your God, according to your words. And whatever the LORD shall answer you, I will report to you; I will not 5 withhold a word from you. So they said to Jeremiah: May the LORD be a true and trustworthy Witness against us if we do not act in full accordance with every word that the LORD, your God, may send to 6 you concerning us. Whether it be favorable or unfavorable, we will obey the voice of the LORD, our God, to whom we are sending you, in order that it may be well with us, because we have obeyed the voice of the LORD, our God.

Vv. 1-6. Perhaps the very next morning the leaders, together with the people, assembled before Jeremiah in order to receive an oracle from the Lord. A vast assembly. We see the women weeping bitter tears of despair, and little children crying and, like their mothers, stretching forth their hands in an appeal to the prophet; the men anxiously watching Jeremiah, as he listens to the well-worded plea of the leaders to intercede with God, to look with pity on the small remnant left of a large nation. Jeremiah, who loved his people to the last, promised at once to fulfill their request. Knowing, however, that they have come only to hear good news, he tells them in straightforward manner that whatever thing the Lord would answer he would declare to them, keeping nothing back from them. With a solemn oath they promise to obey the word of the Lord as transmitted to them by the prophet.

C. The Lord tells them to remain in their homeland, where they would prosper, while they would perish in Egypt, vv. 7-22

7 After ten days the word of the
8 LORD came to Jeremiah. So he called Johanan, the son of Kareah, and all the military leaders who were with him, and all the people
9 from the least to the greatest, and said to them: Thus says the LORD, the God of Israel, to whom you have sent me to present your peti-
10 tion before Him: If you will settle down in this land, then I will build you and not tear you down, I will plant you and not uproot you, for I repent of the evil that
11 I have done to you. Do not be afraid of the king of Babylon, of whom you are afraid! Do not be afraid of him, is the oracle of the Lord, for I am with you to save you and to deliver you from his
12 hand! I will have pity upon you, and he will have pity upon you and will restore you to your land. But
13 if you are going to say: We will not stay in this land; if you refuse to obey the voice of the LORD,
14 your God, and say: No! We shall go to the land of Egypt, where we shall see no war and will not hear the sound of the trumpet nor hunger for bread, and there will
15 we settle, then hear now the word of the LORD, O remnant of Judah: Thus says the LORD of Hosts, the God of Israel: If you firmly set your mind to go to Egypt and go
16 to settle there, then the sword of which you are afraid shall overtake you there, in the land of Egypt; and the famine, which you are dreading, will dog your footsteps there in Egypt, and there you
17 will die! And all men who have set their minds upon going to Egypt in order to settle there shall die by sword, by famine, and by pestilence, and none shall remain or escape from the evil which I am going to bring upon you.
18 For thus says the LORD of Hosts, the God of Israel: As My anger and fury has been poured out on the inhabitants of Jerusalem, so shall My fury be poured out on you if you go to Egypt, and you shall become a curse, objects of maltreatment, a desecration, and a reproach, and you shall never again
19 see this place! The LORD has spoken concerning you, O remnant of Judah: Do not go to Egypt! And be certain of this, that I have

20 testified against you today! For you are leading astray at the cost of your lives if, after sending me to the LORD, your God, telling me: Intercede for us with the LORD, our God, and report to us exactly everything the LORD, our God, has
21 spoken, and we shall do it; and if, after I have reported to you today, you will not obey the voice of the LORD, your God, in regard to anything that He has sent me to tell
22 you, Now be certain of this, that you shall die by the sword, by famine, and by pestilence in the place where you desire to go and settle there.

Grammatical Notes

V. 20. "Ye dissembled in your hearts," rather, "you are leading astray at the cost (or risk) of your own lives. בְּ pretii. The object is omitted as in Is. 3:12; 30:28. In fact, they were leading themselves and others astray. There is no reason to follow the LXX, who read הֲרֵעֹתֶם, you have done evil against = you have harmed, or wronged, yourselves, instead of "dissembled" = led astray.

Vv. 7-22. The people and Jeremiah are put to a severe test. Ten days elapse before the word of the Lord comes to Jeremiah. Immediately Jeremiah summons the leaders and the people and tells them the either-or which the Lord had proposed. Either they will remain in Judah, and then God will bless them, protect them, and save them from the hand of Nebuchadnezzar (vv. 9-12), or they will insist upon going to Egypt against God's will, in the vain hope of finding peace and plenty there (v. 14), and then all that they hope to escape shall overtake them. They shall perish by sword and famine and pestilence, and shall see this place no more (vv. 13-18). Jeremiah now pleads with them not to go into Egypt; but as he watches the expressions of the people, he can readily see their answer. It is a positive No. He charges them with duplicity and self-deception. They had sent him to Jehovah for information. In response to his prayer the Lord had revealed His plans. The prophet in turn had told them, and, instead of keeping their promise, they refused to obey a single word the Lord had told them. This disobedience had sealed their own death warrant. Their unbelief will not change the word of the Lord. "Now, therefore, know certainly that ye shall die by the sword, by the famine, and by the pestilence in the place whither ye desire to go" (v. 22).

CHAPTER 43

D. Ignoring Jeremiah's warning, the Jews flee to Egypt, vv. 1-7

1 When Jeremiah had finished speaking to all the people all the words of the LORD, their God, even all these words for which the LORD, their God, had sent him to them,
2 then Azariah, the son of Hoshaiah,

and Johanan, the son of Kareach, and all the defiant men said to Jeremiah: You are telling a lie! The LORD, our God, has not sent you to us to say: Do not go to the land of Egypt to settle there, 3 but Baruch, the son of Neriah, is inciting you against us in order to deliver us into the hands of the Chaldeans, that they might slay us 4 or lead us captive to Babylon. So Johanan, the son of Kareach, and all the military leaders and all the people did not obey the voice of the LORD to remain in the land 5 of Judah. But Johanan, the son of Kareach, and all the military leaders took all the remnant of Judah that had returned from all the nations, among which they had been scattered, in order to settle in the land 6 of Judah, men and women and children and the king's daughters and every person whom Nebuzaradan, the commander of the guard, had left with Gedaliah, the son of Ahikam, the son of Shaphan, and Jeremiah the prophet, and 7 Baruch, the son of Neriah, and they went into the land of Egypt; for they did not obey the voice of the LORD. So they came to Tahpanhes.

Vv. 1-7. Jeremiah's charge that the Jews did not obey his word was justified. Hardly had he finished his plea when opposition arose. Azariah, most likely a brother of Jezaniah (ch. 42:1), seemed to have been especially vehement in his demand for the exodus to Egypt and was now the chief spokesman. Together with them were "proud men," insolent, arrogant bullies, loudmouthed ruffians that invariably get to the front in times of trouble and assume the leadership. They did not try to answer Jeremiah's arguments. They simply challenged his veracity. It is the old trick of Satan: "Hath God said?" They charged him with deliberately deceiving the people, posing as God's spokesman, while it was Baruch who had told him to give this advice. They also charged him with treasonably intending to deliver them into the hands of the Chaldeans. They feared man rather than God. They trusted in their leaders rather than in the power of the Lord. Hurriedly, as if they already felt the grasp of Nebuchadnezzar, they started out under the leadership of Johanan on their long and tedious journey to Egypt, taking Jeremiah and Baruch with them. The word of Jeremiah, spoken eleven years before (Jer. 24:8-10), was now being fulfilled. For a while it had seemed as though God might have applied His rule of Jer. 18:8: "If that nation, against whom I have pronounced, turn from their evil, I will repent of the evil that I thought to do unto them." But by their obstinate disobedience the Jews themselves caused the fulfillment of the dreadful threat of complete destruction. They were marching into the jaws of death, which they hoped to escape by following their own desires.

E. Symbolic prophecy of Egypt's subjugation by Nebuchadnezzar, vv. 8-13

8 Then came the word of the LORD to Jeremiah at Tahpanhes, saying: 9 Take large stones in your hand, and embed them in mortar in the brick pavement at the gateway of the house of Pharaoh in Tahpanhes, in the sight of the Jewish men, 10 and say to them: Thus says the LORD of Hosts, the God of Israel: Behold, I am sending Nebuchadrezzar, the king of Babylon, whom I have selected as My servant, and I shall place his throne upon these stones which I have embedded, and he shall spread his canopy over 11 them. And he shall come and smite the land of Egypt; such as are appointed for death, to death; as are appointed for exile, to exile; as are appointed for the sword, to the 12 sword. He shall kindle fire in the houses of the gods of Egypt and shall burn them and carry them away captive; and he shall wrap himself in the land of Egypt as a shepherd wraps himself in his cloak, and shall go out of it unmolested. He shall also break the 13 images at Beth Shemesh, which is in the land of Egypt, and the houses of the gods of Egypt shall he burn with fire.

It was not Israel in the true sense of the word that was now returning to Egypt to make that land of their former bondage their homeland. To the true Israelites God had promised: "Ye shall henceforth return no more that way" (Deut. 17:16). To impenitent Israel God had threatened: "The Lord shall bring thee into Egypt again with ships, by the way whereof I spake unto thee: Thou shalt see it no more again; and there ye shall be sold unto your enemies for bondmen and bondwomen, and no man shall buy you" (Deut. 28:68). As an apostate, impenitent nation, the Jews went down to Egypt against God's will, without His blessing. God will send Nebuchadnezzar, His servant, and he shall smite Egypt, and there, together with the Egyptians, the Jews will fall by the sword of Nebuchadnezzar, which would have done them no harm had they remained in Canaan in obedience to the Lord. As a token of the fulfillment of this threat the Lord commanded Jeremiah to take great stones and "hide them," place them deep and firm into mortar or cement in the brick "kiln," most likely the brick pavement at the entrance of Pharaoh's palace at Tahpanhes, one of the capital cities of Egypt. Upon these very stones which Jeremiah had embedded in this pavement, Nebuchadnezzar, whom you have sought to escape, will establish his throne and here spread his royal tent. "He shall array himself with the land of Egypt as a shepherd putteth on his garment." With unusual ease he shall conquer all of Egypt, destroy the houses of their gods, and then the Jews shall meet their fate, which they had hoped to escape by going down into Egypt. Note that Nebuchadnezzar here is called God's servant. God Himself will set Nebuchadnezzar on the throne, above the stones which God through the instrumentality of Jeremiah had embedded in the pavement. Mighty Nebuchadnezzar, a puppet in God's hand, and Jeremiah, God's representative. Of the two servants of God, Jeremiah, the prophet despised and rejected by his people, is by far the greater and more honorable. This prophecy was fulfilled in 568, when Nebuchadnezzar came to Egypt and proceeded as far south as Syene, the modern Assuan, about 500 miles from the Mediterranean Sea. According to Josephus, who dates this campaign somewhat earlier, all the Jews living in Egypt were then deported to Babylon.

CHAPTER 44

F. The Jews publicly renounce Jehovah and renew their pledge of loyalty to the Queen of Heaven, vv. 1-19

1 The word which came to Jeremiah concerning all the Jews living in the land of Egypt, that lived in Migdol and in Tahpanhes and in Memphis and in the land of 2 Pathros: Thus says the LORD of Hosts, the God of Israel: You have seen all the evil that I brought upon Jerusalem and upon all the cities of Judah, and, behold, they are ruins and uninhabited today 3 because of the evil which they have done to provoke Me by going to sacrifice and to serve other gods which they knew not, neither they 4 nor you nor your fathers. I sent to you all My servants, the prophets, sent them at all times, saying: Ah, do not do this abominable 5 thing, which I hate! But they did not obey, nor did they incline their ears to turn away from their wickedness, no longer to sacrifice to 6 other gods. So My fury and My anger was poured out, and it kept burning in the cities of Judah and the streets of Jerusalem, and they became a ruin and waste, as they 7 are this day. Now, thus says the LORD, the God of Hosts, the God of Israel: Why are you endangering your lives by your persistent evildoing, cutting yourselves off from among Judah, men and women, infants and sucklings, so that there will not remain even a remnant for

8 you, by provoking Me with the works of your hands, sacrificing to other gods in the land of Egypt, where you have gone to settle, in order to cut yourselves off and to become a desecration and a reproach among all nations of the 9 earth? Have you forgotten the wicked deeds of your fathers, and the wicked deeds of the kings of Judah, and the wicked deeds of their wives, and your wicked deeds, and the wicked deeds of your wives, which they did in the land of Judah and in the streets of Jeru- 10 salem? To this day they have not humbled themselves, nor do they fear nor walk in My Law and My ordinances, which I have set before you and before your fathers. 11 Therefore thus says the LORD of Hosts, the God of Israel: Behold, I am setting My face against you for evil and to cut off all Judah. 12 And I shall take away the remainder of Judah, which have set their faces to go to the land of Egypt to settle there, so that all shall be exterminated in the land of Egypt; they shall fall by the sword, by famine be exterminated; from the least to the greatest they shall die by sword and famine; and they shall be a curse, a horror, 13 a desecration, and a reproach! And I will punish those living in the

land of Egypt, as I have punished Jerusalem, by sword, by famine,
14 and by pestilence. There will be no escape nor deliverance for those remaining of Judah who came to settle there in the land of Egypt, so that they might return to the land of Judah, to which they long to return to live there; for they shall not return, except some es-
15 caped ones. Then all the men that knew that their wives were in the habit of sacrificing to other gods, and all the women standing there, a great assembly, all the people that lived in the land of Egypt and in Pathros, answered Jeremiah, say-
16 ing: As for the word which you have spoken to us in the name of the LORD, we are not going to
17 listen to you! But we are certainly going to carry out every word that has proceeded from our mouth: to bring sacrifices to the Queen of Heaven and to offer libations to her exactly as we have done, we, our fathers, our kings, and our princes in the cities of Judah and in the streets of Jerusalem. Then we were satisfied with bread, and we prospered and saw no trouble.
18 But from the moment that we ceased to bring sacrifices to the Queen of Heaven and to pour libations to her, we lack everything, and we die by sword and famine.
19 And when we were bringing sacrifices to the Queen of Heaven and poured libations to her, was it without the approval of our men that we made cakes for her and baked them in a form and poured libations to her?

Vv. 1-14. Jeremiah makes a last appeal to the apostate people. Not all Jews had settled at Tahpanhes (ch. 43:7-8). There was a colony at Migdol, a city near the northeastern boundary of Egypt, about twelve miles south of Pelusium. Others had gone farther south, to Noph, Memphis, about 125 miles south of the Mediterranean Sea, still others had gone as far as Pathros, the Egyptian Pa-ta-ris, "Land of the South," Southern, or Upper Egypt, extending southward from ancient Memphis. From all these places Jews had gathered, perhaps at Tahpanhes, where Jeremiah seems to have remained, to celebrate a great festival (cp. vv. 15, 20), not, however, in honor of the Lord, but in honor of a heathen deity, the Queen of Heaven, who was worshiped under various names by all the Oriental countries from Assyria to Egypt, as the goddess of the star Venus or of the moon. Jeremiah is told by the Lord to address another call to repentance to these apostate Jews. Even though they have gone to Egypt against His will, He is still the Covenant God, seeking to save that which was lost, calling His wayward people to repentance. Again it is His prophet, called into office more than forty years ago, who is sent, and again Jeremiah goes where he is sent (ch. 1:7). Jeremiah had been sent to kings and priests and prophets and courageously had faced them. Now he is sent to the miserable remains of his people and must drink to the very dregs the bitter cup of heartache and disappointment. He sees his lifework thwarted, his life's purpose frustrated, his life's hopes dashed to the ground. He had lived and labored and hoped and prayed in vain! After his forty-three years of strenuous, tearful efforts his people had deliberately left the land of Jehovah and the worship of Jehovah and had chosen, instead — the Queen of Heaven! To these people he was to go, to them he was to bring a message of the Lord!

Still he does not complain. He does not resign from office nor refuse to go on. Loyally and faithfully he does what the Lord had told him on the day of his call and what he had done for more than four decades: he goes where the Lord sends him. And trustingly he clings to the promise of the Lord, the fulfillment of which he had so often experienced: I will be with thee to deliver thee! Noble Jeremiah! The tenderhearted, inexperienced, timid youth had become by the Lord's power a fenced city, an iron pillar, a brazen wall, and one of the greatest heroes of all ages. He goes to that fanatic rabble, those shrieking women, those treacherous men, and tells them once more the oracles of God. Manfully, unafraid, in never-flinching loyalty to his God, he faces that festival assembly and tells them: Hear ye the word of the Lord! And they listen! Listen to him though he tells them bitter truths. Judah and Jerusalem destroyed! (V. 2.) Why? In punishment for their wicked idolatry (v. 3). Although the Lord had sent large numbers of prophets (v. 4), the Jews had refused to change their ways (v. 5), and as a result God poured forth His wrath, Jerusalem is wasted, desolate (v. 6). Why, then, do they persist in committing national suicide by continuing their idolatry and remaining stubbornly impenitent? (Vv. 7-10.) Therefore none shall return, but such as shall "escape" (v. 14, end), be delivered by divine grace; cp. on this sense of "escape" Is. 66: 19; Jer. 50: 28; 51: 50; and the noun, Gen. 45: 7; Is. 4: 2; Joel 3: 5; Obadiah 17. Only those whom the Lord delivers, who accept the deliverance offered by the Lord, shall return. Gospel in the midst of the sternest preaching of the Law, for the Lord of the Covenant is a stern Judge and a merciful Deliverer (cp. Mark 16: 16; John 3: 18, 36).

Vv. 15-19. The Jews openly disavow Jehovah and choose the Queen of Heaven. Both men and women declare that they will not follow the word spoken by Jeremiah in the name of the Lord. They do not deny that the Lord spoke by Jeremiah, but they deny obedience to this Lord. They will do "whatsoever thing goeth forth out of our own mouth" (v. 17). They declare their independence. No longer will they worship a god who does not keep his promises, who only demands, but never gives. The Queen of Heaven rewarded their

317

worship by giving them food aplenty and peace and prosperity (v. 17). But since they ceased to offer sacrifices to her, they see nothing but war and famine (v. 18). And, add the women: Do not think that we acted contrary to the will of our husbands. As good wives we asked for and received their full consent and co-operation (v. 19).

G. The Lord renounces His people and foretells their destruction and the salvation of a small remnant, vv. 20-30

20 Then said Jeremiah to all the people, both men and women, to all the people that had given him 21 this answer: Those sacrifices you offered in the cities of Judah and in the streets of Jerusalem, you and your fathers, your kings and your princes, and the common people — does not the LORD remember them, and are they not 22 rankling in His mind, so that He could no longer bear your wicked deeds, the abominations you committed, so that your land became a desolation and a horror and a curse, devoid of people, as it is 23 this day? Because you offered idolatrous sacrifices, and because you sinned against the LORD and did not obey the voice of the LORD and did not walk in His Law and in His ordinances and in His testimonies, therefore this present evil 24 has come to you. Then Jeremiah said to all the people and to the women: Hear the word of the LORD, all Judah, which is in the 25 land of Egypt. Thus says the LORD of Hosts, the God of Israel, saying: You and your wives, your mouth has pledged, and your hands have carried out, your vow: "We certainly will pay our vows which we have vowed, to offer incense to the Queen of Heaven and to pour libations to her." By all means fulfill your vows, and carry out your 26 pledges to the finish! Therefore hear the word of the LORD, all Judah living in the land of Egypt: Behold! I have sworn by My great name, says the LORD, My name shall no more be uttered by the mouth of any person of Judah in all the land of Egypt, so as to say: 27 As the Lord LORD liveth! Behold, I am watching over them for evil and not for good, and every man of Judah who is in the land of Egypt shall be exterminated by the sword and by famine, until they are completely annihilated. But such as 28 have escaped from the sword, a few mortals, shall return from the land of Egypt to the land of Judah, and all the rest of Judah that went to the land of Egypt to settle there shall know whose word shall be 29 fulfilled, Mine or theirs! And this shall be a sign for you, is the oracle of the LORD, that I am going to punish you in this place, in order that you may know that I will fully establish My word of doom for 30 you. Thus says the LORD: I am giving Pharaoh Hophra into the hand of his enemies and into the hands of those that seek his life, as I have given Zedekiah, the king of Judah, into the hand of Nebuchadrezzar, the king of Babylon, his enemy, who sought his life.

Vv. 20-30. Once more the prophet tells them that the cause of their misfortune was their faithlessness to their Covenant God (vv. 21-23).

While they will serve their idols with greater loyalty than they ever devoted to the service of Jehovah, these idols will not be able to avert the evils which the Covenant God of Israel will send to His faithless, covenant-breaking people. The more loyally they will serve their idols, the more horrible will be the judgments of the Lord, whom they disowned.

And once more a Gospel message! (V. 28.) That is the last appeal of the faithful prophet to his wicked people, an appeal directed to each individual: Will you not wish to be one of that small number? Oh, turn to the Lord before it is too late, before you will perish as the king of Egypt will perish! Hophra, the king in whom you trust that he will protect you against Nebuchadnezzar, will be delivered by Me into the hands of the Babylonian, even as I delivered Zedekiah, who trusted in Hophra and rebelled against Nebuchadnezzar, into the hands of those who sought his life.

XVI. The Lord Comforts Baruch

CHAPTER 45

1 The word which Jeremiah the prophet spoke to Baruch, the son of Neriah, when he was writing these words into a book at the dictation of Jeremiah in the fourth year of Jehoiakim, the son of 2 Josiah, the king of Judah: Thus says the LORD, the God of Israel, 3 concerning you, Baruch: You say: Ah! Woe is me! For the LORD has added grief to my wound! I am becoming weary of my sighing, and 4 I have not found rest! Thus shall you say to him: Thus says the LORD: Behold, what I have built I am tearing down, what I have planted I am uprooting. And this 5 means the whole earth! And you! You are seeking for yourself great things! Do not seek them, for, behold, I am going to bring evil upon all flesh, is the oracle of the LORD. But your life I will give to you as a spoils wherever you shall go!

For the third time the fourth year of Jehoiakim is mentioned (cp. ch. 25:1; 36:1). On the historical importance of this year see p. 12 f.

In this year Jeremiah had been commanded to put down in writing all the prophecies he had spoken from the day of his call, 627, to the present day, 605. The prophet employed his secretary, Baruch, the son of Neriah, for this task and dictated to him all the words the Lord had spoken to His prophet during these two decades (ch. 36: 2-4). The effect of writing so long a series of charges against Judah and Jerusalem, charges of the most serious nature, charges of wickedness, of apostasy, of disobedience, of abominations heaped upon abominations, sins which called forth constantly renewed threats of war and famine and destruction and rejection, was depressing to Baruch, and this depression grew to despondency, since the occasional promises of peace and salvation were to be fulfilled only in the distant future. Baruch realized with ever-greater clarity that during his lifetime he could look only for hardships, persecution, shame, poverty, destitution. This prospect did not please him. Bitterly he lamented, because the Lord was adding grief to grief, and sorrow to sorrow, until life began to appear altogether intolerable. He sighed and cried until he was utterly wearied and worn out. Try as he might, he could find no rest, could not regain his quiet and confident trust in the Lord. Always the disturbing question came back: Why? Why must I go through all these harrowing experiences? Why cannot I enjoy at least some peace and happiness?

As the Lord came to the aid of His disturbed, despairing prophet (ch. 12: 5-17; 15:11-14, 19-21), so He, the Lord of the Covenant, sends

320

His spokesman to tired, weary Baruch. He does not promise him immunity from the woes of the times, as little as he had promised that to Jeremiah. He has a different way, a way often seeming strange and incomprehensible to us, yet a better way, of comforting and strengthening His weary servants. He reminds Baruch that it is the Lord, I AM THAT I AM, the God of the Covenant, that is still ruling the world. What His power had built and planted, He was now about to break down and root out; even the whole earth. Not only Judah, but the entire world would go through catastrophic changes during the next decades.

V. 5. Under these circumstances, in so universal a calamity, do you seek great things, peace, security, prosperity, an undisturbed life? Says Calov: "It is characteristic of human weakness to let one's imagination dream of great things for oneself in times of universal calamities" (*Biblia Illustrata, in loc.*). While all the world is going through catastrophic upheavals, we hope to escape ruin, to remain unharmed, enjoy peace and quietude, and often cry like spoiled children because some convenience, some comfort, or even some seeming necessity is no longer available. The Lord warns Baruch against this trend of human nature. "Seek them not! For behold, I bring evil upon all flesh." "Flesh" = all mankind, particularly as it is mortal, sinful mankind. (Cp. Gen. 6:3,13; Ps. 56:4ff.; 78:38f.; Is. 31:3.) Because of the universal sinfulness of all flesh, including also the children of God as sinful beings, the judgments of God come upon all flesh. (Cp. 1 Peter 4:17-18; Jer. 10:24; 30:10-11; 46:28.) "I will bring evil." God still remains the Ruler, who carries out His plans no matter how chaotic, how utterly planless world conditions seem to us. And He, the God of infinite power, of inflexible justice, remains at all times the God of unchanging grace and loving-kindness. He promises Baruch that He will preserve his life. While He takes, He gives. While Baruch must look for evil days, while the Lord speaks of "all places whither thou goest"; while Baruch will be a fugitive, without an abiding home, yet "thy life will I give unto thee . . . in all places." The Lord tells Baruch that he must learn to appreciate the things which he, as we all do, had taken for granted and, no matter how great his loss, to be thankful for every gift the Lord permitted him to keep. If that gift is no more than bare life, it is a precious gift, a life created by divine power (Job 10:9-12; Ps. 139:14-16), redeemed from destruction by divine grace (Ps. 103:4), protected by divine loving-kindness (Ps. 91:1-16; Matt. 10:29-31), the vestibule to eternal bliss (Gen. 49:18; Ps. 73:23-24; Is. 25:8; 26:19).

If God had given us no more than such a life, an eternity would not suffice to express our gratitude.

Six times the Lord emphasizes what He has done and will do in the life of nations and of individuals. "I have built; I break down; I have planted; I will pluck up; I will bring evil upon all flesh; I will give unto you your life for a prey." The Lord Jehovah rules supreme indeed! No matter how violent and extensive the political, economical, social, or religious revolutions and upheavals may be, the throne of Jehovah remains unmoved, unaffected by the convulsions that smash human thrones and shatter earthly kingdoms. This Jehovah is your Lord, Baruch! He will provide for you! Let His presence and grace be sufficient to you. In Him seek and find peace and rest by quietly submitting to His will. That is God's lesson to Baruch and to believers at all times (1 Peter 4: 6, 7, 12, 19).

This chapter is a fitting conclusion to the third main division of Part One, which describes the complete destruction of Jerusalem and the Jewish commonwealth, affecting not only the wicked apostates, but the children of God as well.

Part II

The Prophecies Against the Nations
Chapters 46—52

The Prophecies Against the Nations

The LXX has changed the order of sequence, listing the nations as follows: Elam, Egypt, Babylon, Philistia, Edom, Ammon, Kedar-Hazor, Damascus, Moab. We can see no reason for changing the order followed in the Hebrew Bible.

For analysis, see p. 14 f.

I. The Prophecy Against Egypt, Ch. 46

CHAPTER 46

1. Introduction, Vv. 1-2

1 What came as the word of the LORD to Jeremiah the prophet
2 against the nations? Concerning Egypt. Against the army of Pharaoh-Necho, king of Egypt, which was at the River Euphrates at Carchemish, which Nebuchadrezzar, king of Babylon, defeated in the fourth year of Jehoiachim, the son of Josiah, king of Judah.

V. 2. As Nahum had been privileged in a remarkable vision to foresee and foretell the unexpected and complete downfall of Nineveh (612), so Jeremiah is granted a prophetic review of the equally unexpected catastrophic defeat of Egypt at Carchemish (605) and Nebuchadnezzar's conquest of Egypt (568). His prophecy is divided by a second heading (v. 13) into two sections, vv. 3-12 and vv. 13-26. An appendix is added, vv. 27-28, words of comfort for Judah.

2. The Disastrous Defeat of Egypt at Carchemish, Vv. 3-12

3 Prepare buckler and shield! March
4 onward to battle! Saddle the horses, and mount them, O horsemen, and stand ready, helmeted! Polish your spears; put on your
5 coats of mail! Why do I behold these men dismayed? They retreat to the rear, and their strong men are crushed, and headlong they flee; and not do they turn! Terror
6 round about, saith Jehovah. No escape for the swift! No getaway for the strong! In the north beside the River Euphrates they
7 stumble, and they fall! Who is this like the Nile rising up? Like the great streams rushing onward
8 their floods? It's Egypt like the Nile rising up, and like great streams rushing onward their floods. And he says: I will rise, I will cover the land, destroy both
9 cities and dwellers therein. Run along, O ye steeds! Rush swiftly, O chariots! Cush and Put, that carry the shield, and Ludim, that
10 carry and bend the bow! Yet this day is for the Lord Jehovah of Hosts a day of vengeance, to avenge Himself upon His enemies. The sword shall eat and be sated and be drunk with blood, for a bloody sacrifice it is for the Lord Jehovah of Hosts in the Northland
11 on the River Euphrates. Go up to Gilead, and get balsam, O virgin daughter of Egypt! In vain you shall multiply remedies! No heal-

325

12 ing for you! The nations shall hear of your shame, and your wailing shall fill the earth. For warrior stumbled against warrior, both of them together have fallen.

This section consists of two parallel poems, Egypt's defeat in spite of careful preparation (vv. 3-6) and huge numbers (vv. 7-12).

A. Egypt's defeat in spite of careful preparation, vv. 3-6

Vv. 3-4. The army's readiness for battle. "Buckler," the small round shield; "shield," the large shield covering the entire body, often carried by the shield-bearer. "Horseman," the Hebrew term is used for both "horse" and "rider"; here, probably, "horses." Prance, ye horses, or, Mount, ye horsemen! (Cp. 1 Sam. 8: 11; Is. 21: 7-9; Hab. 1: 8.) "Brigandines," the armor, or "coat of mail," an armor of chains, or rings, or scales, worn by a brigand, a member of a brigade or troop. The army is ready and confident of victory.

Vv. 5-6. Suddenly the picture changes. Defeat, panic, flight. Pashur's doom becomes Egypt's (Jer. 20: 3, 10; also ch. 6: 25; 49: 29). "Saith the LORD," answers the wherefore (v. 5a). It is His judgment: inescapable defeat. In headlong flight they stumble exhausted, or over the slain, or one against the other.

B. Huge numbers, vv. 7-12

Vv. 7-8. Bloody slaughter and political ruin in spite of vast numbers. The prophet sees the hosts rolling onward like the mighty Nile in flood time. "Flood," the Nile. "Rivers," the arms and canals of the Nile and its delta (Ex. 7: 19; 8: 5; Is. 19: 8).

V. 9. "Ethiopians," A. V., Ethiopia, Hebrew, Cush, is the Nile Valley south of Egypt, including Nubia and Ethiopia. The Cushites, a Hamitic nation (Gen. 10: 6-8), a warlike people (2 Kings 19: 9; 2 Chron. 12: 2f.; 14: 9f.), had conquered and ruled Egypt from 712 to 661, until the Assyrian king, Esar-Haddon, defeated them and made Egypt an Assyrian province. Psammetik I, 663—610, regained independence for Egypt. The "Libyans," A. V., the Hebrew Put, are identified by the LXX and Josephus with the Libyans dwelling west of northern Egypt. A better identification seems to be that with the Egyptian Punt, the ancient name of what is now Somaliland, extending south from the Gulf of Aden along the Indian Ocean, opposite the southwestern tip of Arabia. "Lydians," Lud, identified by some with the powerful Semitic nation of Lydia in the upper Euphrates and Tigris territory (cp. Gen. 10: 22; 1 Chron. 1: 17), but more generally with some North African tribe, otherwise unknown descendants of

Ham (Gen. 10:13). All three nations furnished mercenaries to Egypt; Lud and Put also to Tyre (Ezek. 27:10). Mercenaries from distant countries, serving as light and heavy-armed soldiers, shield-bearers, bowmen, chariot drivers, cover the earth as far as the eye can see. Who can withstand so vast a host? The victory is as good as won, Egypt's world supremacy an assured fact! Man proposes, God disposes.

V. 10. "For," here in sense of "but," "yet," introducing a glaring contrast. It is not man's preparation and great numbers that decide the battle. It is the Lord Jehovah, who rules the world and the history of mankind. "The Lord's day" designates that day which the Lord has reserved for His punishment of the wicked and deliverance of His people.

The Egyptians are called the Lord's adversaries. They had unmercifully oppressed the Israelites, to whom they owed the preservation of their country (Genesis 41; 47; Exodus 1); had hardened themselves against the Lord (Exodus 5—14); had warred against Jerusalem (1 Kings 14:25f.); had come to the aid of the tottering Assyrian Empire, the archenemy of Israel, when Necho hoped to wrest the supremacy of Western Asia from Babylon; had slain Josiah; had deposed and deported Jehoahaz; had finally dug the grave of the Jewish commonwealth by goading Zedekiah to his ill-fated rebellion against Nebuchadnezzar.

V. 11. Gilead, see ch. 8:22; v. 12b, "stumble," cp. v. 6.

3. Conquest of Egypt, Vv. 13-26

13 The word that the LORD spoke to Jeremiah the prophet with regard to the coming of Nebuchadrezzar, king of Babylon, to smite
14 the land of Egypt. Declare it in Egypt, and tell it in Migdol, and publish it in Memphis and in Tahpanhes! Say: Stand and get ready! For the sword shall devour round
15 about you! Why has your strong one been swept away? He did not stand fast because the LORD has
16 thrown him down. He caused many to stumble, and one fell against another. They said: Up, and let us return to our people, to the land of our birth, before the
17 deadly sword. There they shall cry out: Pharaoh, king of Egypt, the Big Noise, has let his appointed
18 time pass by. As I live, is the oracle of the King whose name is the LORD of Hosts, like Tabor among the mountains, and Carmel
19 by the sea, shall he come. Prepare your baggage for exile, Daughter of Egypt, sitting at rest, for Memphis shall become desolate,
20 an uninhabited waste. A very beautiful heifer is Egypt. A gadfly from the north, it comes, it comes!
21 Even her mercenaries within her are like calves of the stall; even they have turned and fled together. They did not stand still, for their day of doom had come upon them and the day of their visitation.
22 Her din passes away like a serpent! For they shall advance in force and come against her with axes

23 like fellers of trees. They shall cut down her forest, is the oracle of the LORD, for it cannot be searched out, for they are more in number
24 than locusts, innumerable. The daughter of Egypt is put to shame, surrendered to the people of the
25 north. The LORD of Hosts, the God of Israel, says: Behold, I will punish Amon of Thebes, and Phar-

aoh, and Egypt, and her gods, and her kings, and Pharaoh, and all
26 who trust in him. And I will surrender them to those that seek their lives, and to Nebuchadrezzar, king of Babylon, and to his servants. But afterward she shall dwell as in the days of old, is the oracle of the LORD.

Grammatical Notes

V. 15. "Your valiant men," אַבִּירֶיךָ = strong, valiant, courageous, used of leaders, men of importance, soldiers (Judg. 5:22; 1 Sam. 21:8; Job 24:22; 34:20; Lam. 1:15), of strong animals, the horse (Jer. 8:16; 47:3; 50:11), the bull (Ps. 22:12; Is. 34:7). Sixty-five Mss., LXX, Vulgate, read אַבִּירְךָ, singular with pausal suffix. This, together with the fact that the two verb forms (swept away, stood) and the suffix of "drive" are singular, seems to warrant that a reference to Apis, the sacred bull of Egypt, representing the highest deity, is intended. If the plural אַבִּירֶיךָ is the correct reading, it may be the majestic plural, like *elohim*. "Drive," הדף = to push, overthrow.

V. 20. "Destruction," קֶרֶץ from קרץ to pinch, sting.

V. 14. Migdol, on the northeast boundary of Egypt. Noph = Memphis. Tahpanhes, cp. Jer. 2:16; 43:7-9. To these cities the Jews had fled (ch. 44:1ff.). There they also shall perish in the ruin of Egypt (cp. ch. 42—44).

V. 15. See Grammatical Notes. On "drive," to overthrow, cp. the overthrow of Dagon (1 Sam. 5:1-12).

V. 16. "Fall" (cp. vv. 6, 12) here refers to the mercenaries (v. 21) or other settlers returning to their native countries.

V. 17. "A noise." Egypt had at all times been a braggart, and always strong in breaking promises (Is. 30:7). "Passed the time appointed" by the Lord's command to surrender to Babylon (ch. 25: 14-19).

V. 18. Tabor and Carmel overtowering the landscape are emblems of the overpowering conqueror, Nebuchadnezzar, the Lord's instrument.

V. 20. "Very fair," well fed, sleek, beautiful. Egypt had enjoyed wealth, luxury. Now comes "destruction," see Grammatical Notes. Aquila and Symmachus, "a stinger"; Chrysostom, "gadfly, an insect that stings oxen and drives them to madness."

V. 21. Also their "hired men," the mercenaries, well paid and fed, leave her in the lurch. Herodotus states that hirelings from Asia

Minor, Charrans and Ionians, whom Hophra had taken into his pay to the number of thirty thousand men, were settled by him "in the midst" of Egypt in the fertile lands above Bubastis in the Delta country. (Herodotus 2, 152. 163.) These hirelings, having gotten what they could out of Egypt and reading the handwriting on the wall, hastily fled into their homeland.

V. 22. "The voice thereof," her voice, refers to Egypt. "Voice" denotes any sound, the human voice, the rustling of leaves, the noise of a city (1 Kings 1: 41), of a multitude of people (Is. 13: 4), of battle (Ex. 32: 17). The noise of busy Egypt, in city and country, shall depart as the snake, disturbed in its haunts, silently flees (cp. Is. 29: 4).

V. 23. The glory of Egypt, its wealth, culture, its architecture, its military prowess, is likened to a forest which the axmen, the Babylonian armies, fell unmercifully. "It cannot be searched" refers to the innumerable host of destroyers, compared to huge swarms of locusts.

Vv. 24-26. Egypt will be given into the hands of the people of the north. The Lord of Hosts, Israel's Covenant God, will punish "the multitude of No," rather, "Amon of Thebes," the sun god, for centuries the chief god of the Egyptian pantheon, identified with Zeus by the Greeks. (Herodotus 2, 32.) "The kings," the officials of royal blood. "Afterward it shall be inhabited," etc. On this meaning of "inhabit" compare ch. 17: 6; 50: 39; Is. 13: 20. This refers to the Messianic times. Compare "afterward," ch. 49: 6, alternating with "and in the end of days," ch. 48: 47; 49: 39. Egypt was for centuries a stronghold of the Christian Church.

4. Comfort for Judah, Vv. 27-28

27 And fear not, My servant Jacob, and be not dismayed, O Israel! For, behold, I will deliver you from afar, and your seed from the land of their exile. Jacob shall return and rest and live in peace, and no 28 one shall disturb him. Fear not, My servant Jacob, is the oracle of the LORD, for I am with you. For I will make a full end of all nations whither I have scattered you. But I will not make a full end of you. Yet I will chastise you according to judgment, and I do not regard you as innocent.

Vv. 27-28. See ch. 30: 10-11.

II. The Prophecy Concerning the Philistines

CHAPTER 47

1 What came as the word of the LORD to Jeremiah the prophet concerning the Philistines, before
2 Pharaoh had captured Gaza. Thus says the LORD: Behold, waters are arising in the north, and they shall become a rushing stream overflowing the land and all that is in it; and men shall shriek, and all the inhabitants of the land shall
3 howl at the noise of the stamping of the feet of their warhorses, the rattling of their chariots, the rumbling of the wheels. The fathers will not turn to the aid of the children, for their hands are power-
4 less because of the day that comes to destroy all the Philistines in order to cut off every remaining aid for Tyre and Sidon. For the LORD is the Destroyer of the Philistines, the remnant of the isle
5 of Caphtor. Baldness has come upon Gaza, Ashkelon is ruined! The remainder of their valleys, how long will you slash yourselves?
6 Woe! O sword of the LORD, how long will you not rest? Return to your sheath! Rest and be quiet!
7 How can it rest, while the LORD has commissioned it against Ashkelon and the coast of the sea? There He has appointed it!

V. 1. (Introduction.) Once more the prophet very definitely designates the prophecy as to its content and its form as "the word of Jehovah" (cp. ch. 14: 1; 46: 1; 49: 34; G.-K. 138e, Note 1), and, like ch. 46: 1; 49: 34, he adds the honorary title "the prophet" to his name. He is merely the spokesman of the Lord (ch. 1: 7, 9). The prophecy is directed against Philistia and follows immediately after that concerning Egypt, because this country adjoined Egypt, and perhaps also because the Philistines were descendants of Mizraim (Gen. 10: 13-14), a son of Ham (ibid., v. 6). V. 4 the island of Caphtor is named as the original homeland. On the basis of Zeph. 2: 5; Ezek. 25: 16; and such passages as 1 Sam. 30: 14; 2 Sam. 8: 18; etc., Caphtor has been identified with Crete. Others identify it with the coastal Nile Delta. The ancient versions mistook it for Cappadocia. According to Gen. 10: 14, "Casluhim (out of whom came Philistim) and Caphtorim," the Philistines may have been descendants of the Casluhim or have dwelt with them in Egypt and then emigrated with the Caphtorim to Crete (Amos 9: 7). They had already in the time of Abraham (Gen. 21: 32, 34; 26: 1-18) settled in the fertile coastland of Western Jordanland, which derived its name "Palestine" from the Philistians. They were a constant thorn in the side of Israel (cp. Ezek. 25: 15-17).

This prophecy was spoken before Pharaoh captured Gaza. We do not know which Pharaoh is meant nor when Gaza was taken. Herodotus (II, 159) narrates that Pharaoh Necho, after defeating the Syrians at Magdolos, had captured Cadytis, a large city of Syria.

Magdolos is regarded as Herodotus' spelling of Megiddo, and Cadytis as his version of Gaza. But it is highly improbable that Necho returned after the defeat of Josiah at Megiddo to besiege and take Gaza. And the equation of Gaza and Cadytis is still less probable. It is far more reasonable to regard Cadytis as the Greek equivalent of Kadesh, Assyrian Kadshu, an important city just north of Riblah on the trade and military road to Carchemish, and that Herodotus' note has no reference to Gaza.

The prophecy may be divided into two parts: vv. 2-4 and vv. 5-7.

1. The Invasion of Philistia by an Enemy from the North, Vv. 2-4

Vv. 2-3a. Like a flash flood which changes the trickling waters of a shallow river bed into a torrential stream, carrying ruin and death along its course, so suddenly, swiftly, the devastating armies of Babylon coming from the far north shall like a deluge overflow Philistia in its entirety, its cities, its inhabitants. The prophet hears the agonized shrieks, the howls of despair; hears the noise of stamping hoofs, the rattling of the chariots, the rumblings of the wheels, as the enemy speeds onward in his victorious *Blitzkrieg* (vv. 2b-3a).

Vv. 3b-4. So unnerving is the panic created by the sudden onrush of the enemy that the terror-stricken parents are unable to help their children. Their hands are numb, for the day of ruin has come for Philistia, in order to cut off from Tyre and Sidon any and every refugee that might help Phoenicia in its warfare against the mighty conqueror. Unable to obtain any more mercenaries from Philistia, the proud, rich commercial cities (cp. Ezek. 27:1-25) shall be humiliated (Ezek. 26:1-21; 27:26-36).

2. The Result of the Invasion, Vv. 5-7

V. 5. Gaza and Ashkelon were the two chief cities of Philistia. (Cp. Jer. 25:20; Amos 1:6-8; Zeph. 2:4, 7.) Gaza shall become bald, a sign of shame and humiliation (Jer. 7:29; 16:6; 48:37; Micah 1:16). (Cp. Acts 8:26.) Ashkelon is "cut off," ruined (Is. 6:5); "their valley," the fertile lowlands or plains surrounding the cities, which were built on mounds. עֵמֶק does not necessarily mean a deep valley; it is used as a designation of the Plain of Jezreel (Joshua 17:16; Judg. 5:15; Hos. 1:5) and of the plains of Philistia (Judg. 1:19, 34). Hence there is no need of adopting the reading of the LXX "Anakim," particularly since it is hardly probable that Anakim still dwelt in Philistia. Already in Joshua's time only a few remained (Joshua 11:22), and they are never mentioned in the later books. "How long wilt thou cut thyself," slash yourself in order to rouse the pity of your gods? (Cp. 1 Kings 18:28.) This question of the prophet intends to point out both the helplessness of their man-made idols and the folly and futility of self-mutilation to avert the impending ruin.

V. 6. The prophet's question is answered by a counterquestion: O sword of Jehovah, how long will you not rest? to which is added the plea: Return to your scabbard! Be quiet, and rest! As in the time of Samuel the Philistines feared and trembled at the presence of the Ark of Covenant (1 Sam. 4:5-8); as after experiencing the mighty power of Jehovah (1 Sam. 5:1-12) they hoped to be delivered from His wrath by offering presents to Jehovah and returning His Ark, so the Philistines here hope to escape Jehovah's judgment by pleading with Him to desist from punishing them. In both instances they regard Jehovah as a tribal god who temporarily has gained the supremacy over their gods. Their plea is directed to the sword of the Lord. They are interested only in deliverance from punishment. There is not the least sign of sincere sorrow for their rejection of Jehovah, nor of trusting faith in Him, nor of willing submission to His will. Therefore the prophet, as spokesman of Jehovah, must reject their plea.

V. 7. How can the sword be quiet, since the Lord has given a charge against Ashkelon and the whole seashore, all of Philistia? There, against the whole nation, has He appointed it! First make your peace with Jehovah, the Lord of Lords, and then submit to His will, and accept what He sends to you.

Ezekiel repeats the threat of Philistia's ruination (Ezek. 25:15-17), and so does Zechariah after the Exile (Zech. 9:5-6), but the latter adds a Messianic promise (v. 7), fulfilled in the New Testament, when Philistia was conquered for God's kingdom by the Gospel (Acts 8:40; 9:32-43).

III. The Prophecy Against Moab

CHAPTER 48

The Moabites, descendants of Lot (Gen. 19:37), spread from Zoar (Gen. 19:30) southward to Edom, northward across the River Arnon to some distance beyond the northern shore of the Dead Sea along the Jordan River, expelling the Emim (Deut. 2:9-11). Cp. "the fields of Moab" (Num. 22:1; 33:48-50; Joshua 13:32). Israel had by divine command by-passed Moab on their journey to Canaan, but had conquered the trans-Jordan kingdom of Sihon. This roused the fear and enmity of the Moabites, who hired Balak to curse Israel (Numbers 22—24). This enmity continued with occasional interruptions (cp. 1 Sam. 22:3-4) for centuries (Judg. 3:12-30; 1 Sam. 14:47; 2 Sam. 8:2; 2 Kings 3:4-5; 2 Kings 3:6-27; 2 Chron. 20:1ff.; 2 Kings 13:20). After the deportation of the northern and eastern tribes of Israel, 734—722, the Moabites regained their former territory north of the Arnon.

Against this hereditary enemy of Israel, Jeremiah directs a lengthy prophecy of judgment, ending with the promise of salvation in New Testament times. Already Balaam (Num. 24:17) and later Isaiah (ch. 15:1-7; 16:6-12; 25:10-12) and Amos (ch. 2:1-3) had pronounced God's judgment upon proud Moab. Jeremiah skillfully weaves these prophecies into his own, sometimes quoting them verbatim, but usually adapting them to his specific purpose. We may divide the chapter into seven parts.

---

1. The Destruction of Moab's National Life, Vv. 1-8

1 Concerning Moab. Thus says the LORD of Hosts, the God of Israel: Woe to Nebo, for it is destroyed! Dismayed, captured is Kiriathaim! Dismayed is the fortress and stupe-
2 fied. Gone is the glory of Moab! In Heshbon they planned evil against her: Come, let us cut her off from being a nation! Madmen, also you shall be silenced! The
3 sword shall follow after you! Hark! a cry from Horonaim! "Great de-
4 struction and ruin!" Moab is shattered! One hears the shrieking of
5 their little ones. On the ascent to Luhith they ascend with weeping! On the descent of Horonaim one hears distressed bewailings of the
6 ruin. Flee! Save your lives! Even if you are like a destitute man in
7 the desert! Surely, because you put your trust in your own works and in your wealth, you also shall be taken. Chemosh shall go into exile, his priests and princes to-
8 gether with him. And the destroyer will come upon every city, and no city shall escape. The valley shall perish and the plain be laid waste, as the LORD has said.

Grammatical Notes

V. 2. "Madmen, be cut down," מַדְמֵן תִּדֹּמִּי, דמם, to be stunned into silence, as a stone, Ex. 15:16; Lam. 2:10; cease from every activity, Ps. 4:5; Jer. 47:6. Niphal, to be silenced. Here a play on words.

333

Vv. 1-2 name cities in the northern section of Moab, formerly occupied by Israel, for the enemy, though not named in this prophecy, comes from the north. Nebo Kiriathaim, "the double city." Madmen (perhaps a variant of Medebah, here used to make an effective play on words: "O silent one, you shall be silenced!"), all lie around Mount Nebo, which was named in honor of the Semitic deity Nabu (Is. 46:1). Woe upon all of them! In Heshbon (Num. 21:26), now occupied by the Ammonites (Jer. 49:3), just north of the boundary of Moab, the enemies are assembled to plan the conquest of Moab, which is stupefied at the rapid advance of the victorious conquerors. Dismay, destruction, the silence of death, rule the once so noisy city.

Vv. 3-5. Luhith and Horonaim (double cave) are unknown. Wailings are heard far and wide. Up the hills and down the hills terrified men, excited women, shrieking children, hurry panic-stricken to reach the southern desert lands.

Vv. 7-8. Moab's pride and trust in its accomplishments and its riches shall be humbled. The land and its god, Chemosh, shall go into exile.

2. Moab's Destruction will Be as Sudden as It Is Complete, Vv. 9-15

9 Give wings to Moab, for flying he shall go out, and his cities will become waste, without an inhabi-
10 tant in them. Cursed be he that doeth the work of the LORD slothfully, and cursed any one withholding his sword from blood.
11 From his youth Moab was quiet and resting on his lees; he was not poured from vessel to vessel, nor did he go into exile; therefore his taste stayed in him, and his aroma
12 was not changed. Therefore, behold, days are coming, is the oracle of the LORD, that I will send him tilters, and they shall tilt him and empty his vessels and dash to
13 pieces their flagons. Then shall Moab be ashamed of Chemosh, as the house of Israel was ashamed of
14 Bethel, their trust. How can you say: We are strong men, powerful
15 men of war? Ruined is Moab, and one scales her cities; the choicest of her young men go down to slaughter, is the oracle of the King, LORD of Hosts is His name.

Vv. 9-10. Moab would have to have wings in order to escape the coming destruction (cp. v. 28), which will be complete devastation. This is "the work of the LORD" (v. 10) which He has committed to human destroyers. His curse is pronounced upon everyone failing to do thoroughly and immediately the task allotted to him by the Lord. While v. 10 applies here to a specific task, it teaches a general truth applicable to any work the Lord demands.

Vv. 11-13. Chiefly because of its geographic situation (the Dead

Sea on the west, the desert on the east) and the mountainous character of its territory, Moab had in the past been comparatively undisturbed in its national life and customs. Their racial, national, and social character had remained practically unchanged by foreign influences. They were proud of their ancient culture, proud of their mighty god, Chemosh, to whom they attributed their national wealth and strength. Moab had never, like so many of the surrounding nations, "been emptied from vessel to vessel," had never been deported from its native land. Therefore its taste and flavor had remained unimpaired, unchanged. It had settled on its lees. In ancient times the new wine was permitted to settle on its lees, the sediment, until it had acquired the highest degree of flavor and strength. Then it was carefully poured off the lees into new vessels of skins or earthenware. Moab's pride of race and culture, its inveterate jealousy and hatred of Israel, remained unaltered through the centuries. They will shortly be changed completely. "Wanderers," i. e., tilters, who tilt the wine vessels in order to drain the clear wine off the lees, will come. And these tilters will go about their work recklessly. They will pour Moab out and smash the vessels; they will cause a complete change in the national and political life of the nation. Moab will be deported and sold into slavery; their age-long trust in Chemosh will be rudely shattered. They will realize the helplessness, the nonentity of their god, as Israel, the northern tribes, had realized the utter folly of their Bethel-worship when the Assyrians defeated and deported them. Their calves had miserably deceived them (Hos. 8:5-7).

Vv. 14-15. Also their pride in their military strength will be doomed to horrible disappointment. "Shattered is Moab." The enemy scales the walls of the cities, usually built on hills, hence goes up, ascends; while the flow of Moab's youth descends to slaughter, to be slain in battle. The full title of Jehovah emphasizes the certainty of fulfillment.

---

3. Moab's Glory is About to be Turned to Shame, Vv. 16-25

16 Closely approaching is the destruction of Moab, and its evil is in a
17 great hurry! Mourn for him, all his neighbors; and all that know his name, say: How utterly broken is the staff of strength, the rod of
18 beauty! Get down from your glory! Sit in thirst, inhabitant of Bath-Dibon! For the destroyer of Moab is coming up against you; he will
19 ruin your fortifications! Stand on the way and watch, inhabitant of Aroer! Ask the fleeing man and the escaping woman: What has
20 happened? Moab is put to shame, for it is dismayed! Howl and shriek! Proclaim in Arnon that
21 Moab is destroyed! And judgment

has come upon the land of the plain, on Holon, on Jahazah, on
22 Mephaath, and on Dibon, and on
23 Nebo, and on Beth-Diblathaim, and on Kiriathaim, and on Beth-Gamul,
24 and on Beth-Meon, and on Kerioth, and on Bozrah, and on all the cities of the land of Moab, far and near.
25 The horn of Moab is cut off, and his arm is broken, is the oracle of the LORD.

Vv. 16-17. The end is near, prophesied by Balaam 800 years before (Num. 24:17), repeated by Amos (ch. 2:1-3) and Isaiah (ch. 15—16) centuries later. The ruin of Moab is now rapidly approaching. Most of the present generation will live to see it. In sincere sympathy with ravaged Moab the prophet calls upon all neighboring countries to bewail the ruin of once-glorious Moab, and upon all that have learned to know her name and fame to take up a dirge for the fallen kingdom, because broken is the staff of her power, the rod of her splendor.

V. 18. Addressing Dibon (cp. Num. 32:3-4; Joshua 13:9), the royal city of Mesha (2 Kings 3:4-5), the prophet as spokesman of the Eternal Judge pronounces judgment. He commands Dibon as the representative of the entire nation to descend from her glory and sit or dwell in thirst; not only in dust, where refreshment might be brought, but in thirst shall she dwell, with no one to cool her parched tongue (Luke 16:24). "Daughter" symbolizes the population. Once more complete destruction is foretold. Like a death knell this word resounds throughout the prophecy.

V. 19. Aroer, the modern Aroir, where extensive ruins are found on a high, steep hill projecting from the slope of the wide gorge of the Ammon Valley, over 1,900 feet deep. The inhabitants of Aroer (the destitute) are told to stand "by the way," the ancient King's Highway (Num. 20:17-19), an age-old trade and military route leading from the Gulf of Akabah to Damascus, a distance of 300 miles. It was used most likely by the kings of Genesis 14 in their campaign against Sodom and Gomorrah. (Cp. Glueck, *The Other Side of the Jordan,* pp. 15—16.) This highway passed through Aroer and Dibon. The inhabitants of Aroer see a strange procession coming along this highway from the north. Straining their eyes, they see fugitives, men and women, young and old, rich and poor, coming to seek refuge in these uninviting surroundings. In astonishment they ask: What happened? The fugitives evidently arrived before the report of the disaster could reach Aroer. Jeremiah gives the answer.

Vv. 20-25. He tells the fugitives and inhabitants of Aroer to spread the sad news of Moab's destruction and the judgment of God that is coming upon all the land. On Jahazah (v. 21) cp. Is. 15:4; on Dibon, v. 18; on Nebo, v. 1; on Bethmeon, Ezek. 25:9; on Bozrah, probably Bezer, Deut. 4:43. The location of most of these cities is uncertain. Probably all lay between Medeba and Dibon.

4. Moab's Pride and Fall, Vv. 26-35

26 Make him drunk — for he has exalted himself against the LORD — so that he shall splash in his vomit, and he also shall be a laughingstock!
27 And was not Israel to you a laughingstock? Was he found among thieves so that you shook your head as often as you spoke of him?
28 Leave the city, and live in the rock, O inhabitants of Moab, and be like the dove that builds her nest on the other side of the mouth of the abyss.
29 We have heard of the pride of Moab; he is excessively proud; of his self-exaltation, his pride, his haughtiness, his high-flying spirit.
30 I, I know, is the oracle of the LORD, his hot temper. His prattlings are falsehoods, falsehood
31 his deeds. Therefore will I howl because of Moab, because of all of Moab will I shriek, because of the men of Kir-Heres will I sigh.
32 A bitterer weeping than that of Jazer will I weep for you, O vine of Sibmah. Your branches ran over to the sea, they reached till the sea of Jazer. The destroyer has fallen upon your summer fruit and your
33 vintage. Joy and rejoicing will be removed from the garden land and from the land of Moab. I have stopped the wine from the wine vats; no one treads with shouting;
34 shouting is no shouting! From the cry of Heshbon they raise their voice till Elealeh, till Jahaz; from Zoar till Horonaim, Eglath; for also the waters of Nimrim have become
35 waste places. For I will make an end of Moab, says the LORD, of them that go up to the high places and that sacrifice to their gods.

V. 26. God commands that Moab be made drunken, deprived of his reason. Whom God would destroy, He first deprives of reason. Like a drunken man, Moab shall reel and totter and finally fall down flat into his vomit, into the filth and shame that he has brought upon himself by his haughty self-exaltation against the Lord. Reason, pride, culture, strength, character, all his glory, gone! He shall be made the laughingstock of all surrounding nations.

V. 27. "Eye for eye, tooth for tooth" (Deut. 19:21). Had not Israel been the laughingstock of Moab? Did they not shake their heads whenever they spoke of Israel as if he had been a thief caught in the act of stealing? Now Moab will be ridiculed by all nations.

V. 28. Moab will have to seek refuge in the most inaccessible places, in the caves and clefts of the mountains, like the wild pigeon seeks its nesting place "in the sides of the hole's mouth," rather, on the other side of the mouth of the opening. As one chases a fleeing pigeon, suddenly there opens before him a yawning abyss, and on the opposite side of this yawning mouth, high up on the inaccessible rock, is the nest, where the pigeon finds refuge. The meaning, of course, is that of v. 9.

Vv. 29-30. Castigates the haughty pride of Moab.

V. 31. On vv. 31-33 cp. Is. 16: 7-10. The prophet expresses once more his sincere sympathy with Moab, Kir-heres, the chief fortification of southern Moab, called Kir Moab (Is. 15: 1; cp. 2 Kings 3: 25f.), the modern El Kerak, still a city of some importance.

V. 32. Jazer wept bitterly over its ruined vineyards; but deeper is the prophet's sorrow that God's blessing, evidenced in the rich grape harvests of Sibma, whose rank grapevines reached to the very shore of the Dead Sea and to the Sea of Jazer (site unknown), was so ruthlessly trampled down and destroyed by the enemy, together with the summer fruits. Jazer lay eight to ten miles west of Rabbah-Ammon, Sibma close to Heshbon, according to Jerome.

V. 33. "Shouting is no shouting." The shouting that is heard is no more the joyous shouting of the grape treaders, but the terrifying shouting of warriors. The Hebrew word denotes both kinds of shouting.

V. 34. From Heshbon in the north to Elealeh, about two miles south, then on to Jahaz, from Zoar on the Dead Sea to Horonaim in the north, cries of woe are heard, "as a heifer of three years old." Perhaps a proper name, Eglat-Shelishiah, though no such city is known.

V. 35. Since the whole land is depopulated, idolatry will cease.

---

5. Dirge over Moab, Vv. 36-38

36 Therefore my heart sighs as the flute for Moab, and my heart sighs as the flute for Kir-heres, because the wealth he acquired is perished.
37 For every head is bald, every beard is shorn, on all hands are gashes 38 and on the loins sackcloth. On all the roofs of Moab and in all its squares there is mourning, for I have broken Moab as a vessel in which I am not pleased, is the oracle of the LORD.

Vv. 36-37. Another expression of sympathetic sorrow (cp. Is. 16: 11). For Isaiah's "harp," Jeremiah substitutes "pipes," flutes, used at funerals (Matt. 9: 23). "Riches," what remains, what is over and above the needs; savings, riches, abundance, all is lost! Wherever he looks, he sees the signs of sorrow, hair cut off, beards shaved (cp. Job 1:20; Jer. 41:5); cuttings on their hands (Lev. 19:28; Jer. 16:6); sackcloth about the loins (2 Sam. 3:31; 1 Kings 21:27).

V. 38. On every roof and in every open square, formerly resounding with laughter and merriment, all is lamentation, because the Lord has smashed Moab like a vessel no longer pleasing to Him.

6. Inescapable Destruction, Vv. 39-46

39 How great a dismay! They howl! Ashamed does Moab turn her back! Moab is a laughingstock and a terror to all round about them!
40 For thus says the LORD: Behold, as the eagle he soars and spreads
41 his wings over Moab! Cities are captured and strongholds taken, and the heart of the strong men of Moab on this day shall be like the heart of a woman in travail.
42 Moab is destroyed so that it is no longer a people, for it exalted itself
43 against the LORD. Panic and pitfall and trap for you, O inhabitant of Moab, is the oracle of the LORD.
44 He that escapes from the panic falls into the pit; and he that clambers out of the pit is caught in the trap; for I am bringing upon you, upon Moab, the year of their punishment, is the oracle of the
45 LORD. In the shadow of Heshbon stand the fugitives without strength! For fire comes forth from Heshbon, and flames from the midst of Sihon, and it devours the side of Moab and the skull of the
46 sons of tumult. Woe to you, Moab! The people of Chemosh is perished! For your sons are brought into exile and your daughters into captivity!

Grammatical Notes

V. 45. "Because of the force," מִכֹּחַ. The מִן is *min privativum*, "without" force, or strength, power. (Cp. Gen. 27:39; 2 Sam. 1:22; Jer. 15:19; Ezek. 32:15; etc.)

Vv. 39-42. Complete, horrible destruction.

Vv. 43-44. Inescapable destruction! Jeremiah quotes Is. 24:17-18. *Pachad wapachath wapach.* Panic, and the pit, and the trap!

Vv. 45-46. "Shadow" is a symbol and a synonym of protection, defense, refuge. Compare "shadow of one's wing" (Ps. 17:8; 36:8; A. V., v. 7; etc.), so without "wings" (Ps. 91:1; 121:5; Lam. 4:20; Eccl. 7:12, twice). Once more Heshbon is mentioned. The prophet returns at the end of his prophecy to its beginning (v. 2). There he spoke of the plan agreed upon by the enemies, here the final effect of this plan. Moab evidently had relied on Heshbon and the Ammonites for help against the enemy, and some fugitives may have fled to the strongly fortified city. Yet even under the protection of Heshbon they stand powerless; fleeing, instead of conquering. Why? The Lord answers: "But," rather "for," "fire shall go forth from Heshbon," etc. (Cp. Num. 21:28.) This ancient proverb finds a new application. "Corner," here not merely the edge of the beard, the

339

singeing of which would be a very minor calamity, but the side of
the body. "And the crown," etc., the skull. There is not much life
left in anyone whose side and skull, the seat of the brain, have been
consumed by fire. "Tumultuous ones," children of noise, tumult. The
Moabites are so called because of their noisy and boastful opposition
against the Lord and His people. "The people of Chemosh," placed
their man-made idol above the eternal, almighty I AM THAT I AM.
This brought inescapable death and destruction to the national life
of Moab. The fulfillment of this prophecy began five years after the
destruction of Jerusalem, when the Babylonian king after his expedition against Coelosyria subjugated the Ammonites and Moabites.
(Josephus, *Antiq.*, X, 97.)

7. Promise of Salvation, V. 47

47 And I will turn the captivity of   the oracle of the LORD. Thus far
    Moab in the end of the days, is   is the judgment concerning Moab.

The Lord of infinite grace and mercy will bring back the captivity of Moab "in the latter days," the New Testament era. While
Moab's national existence has ceased forever, descendants of Moab
also are among the elect of God, and He knows where and how to
find these individuals chosen by Him to be heirs of eternal life.

IV. The Prophecy Concerning the Ammonites, Vv. 1-6

CHAPTER 49

1 Concerning the Ammonites. Thus says the LORD: Are sons lacking to Israel? Or are heirs lacking to him? Why does Malcam possess Gad and his people dwell in his 2 cities? Therefore, behold, days are coming, is the oracle of the LORD, when I will cause a battle cry to be heard against Rabbah of the Ammonites, and it shall become a desolate hill; her daughters shall be burnt by fire, and Israel shall possess its possessors, says the 3 LORD. Howl, O Heshbon, for Ai is destroyed! Shriek, O daughters of Rabbah! Gird yourselves with sackcloth! Mourn and rush about among the hedges! For Malcom is going into exile, his priests to- 4 gether with his princes. Why do you boast of your valleys? Your valley overflows, O apostate daughter, you that trust in your riches: 5 Who shall attack me? Behold, I am ready to bring terror to you, is the oracle of the Lord LORD of Hosts, round about you, and you will be driven out, everyone headlong, and there will be none to assemble 6 the fugitives. And after this I will turn the captivity of the Ammon- ites, is the oracle of the LORD.

V. 1. Jeremiah refers to the gradual infiltration and subjugation of Israel's territory, the fertile trans-Jordan plain, the tribal possession of Gad (Num. 21:21-31; 32:1-39), which occurred during the Syrian-Ephraimite war, 740—732, and the period following the deportations of the northern tribes to Assyria by Pul, 734, and Shalmaneser and Sargon, 722. On Ammon's cruelty see Amos 1:13; on their jealousy and perfidy, Jer. 40:14.

"Their king." The same word occurs v. 3 with the added "his priests and his princes." The LXX in both instances translates "Melchol," i. e., Milcom (1 Kings 11:5, 33), the god of the Ammonites, called Molech (1 Kings 11:7; Lev. 18:21; etc.). The LXX is followed by all ancient versions and a number of commentators. The god of the Ammonites represents the people just as Chemosh (ch. 48:7) the Moabites. Others take "Malkam" in both instances in the double sense of "their king" and "their King," their god. Ch. 48:7 decides in favor of Molech, whose worship became the dominant worship of the former land of Gad. Why have Molech and his people "inherited," taken possession of, Israel's land, as if Israel no longer had any sons or heirs?

V. 2. Such theft of land belonging to God's people will be avenged by the Lord of the Covenant. Rabbah, the capital city of Ammon, shall become a desolate heap, a "tel" of desolation. On "tel" cp. ch. 30:18, Grammatical Notes. "Her daughters," the capital city is the "mother" of the other cities.

341

V. 3. Heshbon (ch. 48: 45), in Moses' time the royal city of the Amorites (Num. 21: 26), later taken over by Ammon. "Ai," unknown. "Hedges," stone walls around fields, vineyards (Nah. 3: 17; Ps. 89: 40), and sheepfolds (Num. 32: 16, 24, 36; Zeph. 2: 6). In their flight the people sought hiding places behind these walls. Together with their god and his priests and princes they will go into exile.

V. 4. Ammon had many fertile valleys, particularly the valley of Jabbok, which enriched not only Rabbah, situated on one of its tributaries, but the entire country. Rabbah, later the important city of Philadelphia, a member of the Decapolis, the modern Aman, is surrounded by a large number of ruins, silent evidences of the ancient culture of this territory. Instead of turning to Jehovah, they boasted of their riches, their "flowing" valley (cp. Ex. 3: 8, 17; Num. 13: 27; etc.), regarded themselves as invincible.

V. 5. On the fulfillment of this prophecy see Jer. 48: 46. On v. 6 see ch. 48: 47.

V. The Prophecy Concerning Edom, Vv. 7-22

1. Edom's Doom Is Inescapable, Vv. 7-13

7 Is wisdom no more in Edom? Has counsel perished from the sages?
8 Has their wisdom vanished? Flee! Turn! Hide yourselves, O inhabitants of Dedan! For I will bring Edom's doom upon him, his time
9 of punishment. If grape gatherers came to you, they would leave no gleanings behind. If robbers came by night, they would destroy till
10 they were satisfied. So I will strip Esau bare, I will uncover his hiding places, so that he shall not be able to hide himself. Destroyed is his seed and his brethren and his neighbors; and he is no more!
11 Forsake your orphans! I will keep them alive! Let your widows trust
12 in Me! For thus says the LORD: Behold, they who are under no judgment to drink it must certainly drink, and you, being what you are, shall you be entirely exempt? You shall not be exempt! You shall
13 drink, drink! For by Myself have I sworn, is the oracle of the LORD, Bozrah shall become a horror, a reproach, a waste, and a curse, and all her cities shall become everlasting wastes.

V. 7. "Edom." From the Gulf of Akabah, an arm of the Red Sea on the east side of the Sinaitic peninsula, separating it from Arabia, Edom stretched northward a hundred miles to the River Zered, the boundary river between Edom and Moab, flowing into the southern tip of the Dead Sea. Eastward was the boundless Arabian desert; westward, the Arabah, that deep depression through which the Jordan flows and which reaches its greatest depth at the outlet of the Jordan into the Dead Sea, 1,275 feet below sea level. South of the Dead Sea the terrain gradually ascends until, some fifty miles south, about twenty miles west of Petra, it has risen to 288 feet above sea level, while Petra towers 3,805 feet above sea level. Edom was an exceedingly mountainous country, originally settled by the Horim, cave dwellers, the descendants of Hori (*hor,* cave), whose tribal ancestor was Seir (Gen. 14: 6; 36: 20-22), for whom the land was called Seir (Gen. 32: 3; 36: 8, 9). Edom expelled the Horim (Deut. 2: 12, 22). Edom owed its prominence among the nations to its ancient iron and copper mines and to its control of the main trade route from Akabah to Damascus, the King's Highway (Num. 20: 17, 19). Esau's jealousy and bitter hatred of his brother (Genesis 27), of which he repented later (Gen. 33: 1-16), was unfortunately inherited by his descendants (cp. Num. 20: 14-21; 1 Kings 11: 14-25; 2 Chron. 20: 10-24; 2 Kings 8: 20-22; 14: 7).

Teman was the first-born grandson of Esau (Gen. 36: 11, 15). The name denotes either the entire country or, as here, a city or

343

province in the southern part of Edom. Teman was noted for its wisdom (cp. Obadiah 8; Job 4:1). Yet their wisdom has perished. Before God destroys a nation, He usually takes away their wisdom and understanding (cp. ch. 48:26; Is. 3:1-8; 19:11-14; 29:13-16). Rom. 1:22 holds true in the sphere of politics and statesmanship as well as in that of religion.

V. 8. Dedan was a grandson of Abraham and Keturah (Gen. 25: 1-3), related to the Midianites and dwelling south of Edom (cp. Ezek. 25:13). Dedan evidently carried on an extended commerce with the surrounding nations (cp. Is. 21:13f., "caravans"). They are to "dwell deep," to retire into the deepest depths of the vast desert south and east, for only there would they be safe from the overwhelming flood that would pour out over Edom. The God of grace gives fair warning.

Vv. 9-10. Obadiah had used the same comparison to describe Esau's cruel greed (Obadiah 5—6). Now "eye for eye" (Deut. 19:21; Mark 4:24). Unsparingly the enemy will impoverish Edom. The Lord Himself will uncover their secret retreats so that there will be no possibility of escaping complete ruin. "His seed," his descendants; "his brethren," the Semitic nations surrounding him; "his neighbors," nations not related to Edom dwelling in the neighborhood, will be destroyed. "He himself is not," his national existence shall cease. His children and wives become helpless orphans and widows, having no one to provide for them. Yet one Provider there is. Unexpectedly, in the midst of the most horrible threats we read a marvelously beautiful promise.

V. 11. Your children, whom you by My decree must leave orphans, will I keep alive! Your widows, let them trust in Me! Only Jehovah, the God of unchanging justice and unalterable mercy, can speak words of this order. What a gracious, potent plea to Esau to turn to Jehovah with all his heart and soul, while there is still time!

V. 12. Cp. ch. 25:29.

V. 13. Bozrah, "the inaccessible," chief city of northern Edom (Gen. 36:33; Amos 1:12; Is. 34:6; 63:1f.), the modern El-Buseireh. It was built on a hill of solid rock, its strong and lofty walls seemingly growing out of the native stone. Judging from the references to vintagers (v. 9; Obadiah 5; cp. Is. 63:1-3), vineyards may have covered the fertile hills and dales of northern Edom. Yet, neither its strength nor the fertility of its soil shall save it from sharing the fate of all cities of Edom.

2. The Horror and Cause of Edom's Judgment, Vv. 14-18

14 I have heard a message from the LORD, and an ambassador is sent to the nations: Gather together, and come against her, and rise up 15 to the battle! For, behold, I make you small among the nations and 16 despised among men. The terror you inspired has deceived you, the pride of your heart! You who dwell in the clefts of the rocks, who cling to the height of the hill! Though you build your nest as high as an eagle, I will bring you down from there! is the oracle of 17 the LORD. Edom shall become a horror! Everyone that passes by her shall be horrified and shall hiss 18 at all her wounds. As in the overthrow of Sodom and Gomorrah and the neighboring cities, is the oracle of the LORD, no man shall dwell there, no son of man shall sojourn there.

Vv. 14-15. The Lord is represented as sending His ambassador to the nations, calling them to attack Edom. He guides the counsels of the nations. Without their own knowledge, and often against their own inclination, they carry out His plans. The Lord's purpose is to humble proud and cruel Edom (v. 15); therefore He gives success to the enemy. Cp. Obadiah 1.

Vv. 16-18. Amos and Obadiah charge Edom with unnatural, pitiless hatred (Amos 1:11; Obadiah 10—14); Jeremiah names their overweening pride as the cause of their ruin. They boasted particularly of their "terribleness," that feeling of hopelessness which must have gripped the enemy when he beheld the seemingly unconquerable fortresses on which Edom relied. Even if Bozrah (v. 13) had fallen and Teman was laid waste, there was Selah, or Petra, "the Rock," a flat-topped mountain some fifty miles to the south of the Dead Sea, slightly more than a mile long from northwest to southeast, and about one-half mile wide, rising out of the surrounding plateau almost perpendicularly to a height of 250 feet. On the summit of this mountain was the fortress of Petra, accessible only by a narrow defile leading upward to the city. Into the massive rock were cut huge cisterns for the storage of water and provisions so that even a protracted siege would seem hopeless. Yet their confidence in their security against attack shall deceive them. Even if they would make their nest as high as the eagle flies (cp. Obadiah 4), the Lord will overthrow them as completely as Sodom and Gomorrah.

3. Edom's Judgment will Come Unexpectedly, Vv. 19-22

19 Behold, as a lion comes up from the thickets of Jordan towards the strong sheepfolds, so I will suddenly expel him from it; and him who is My chosen one I will place over her! For who is like Me? And who will challenge Me? And who is a shepherd such as shall stand

20 before Me? Therefore, hear the counsel of the LORD which He has determined concerning Edom, and His plans which He has formed concerning the inhabitants of Teman: Surely they shall drag them forth as the little ones of the flock; surely their fold shall be amazed
21 at their fate. At the crash of their fall the land trembles; the sound of her shrieking is heard at the
22 Red Sea. Behold, as the eagle he approaches, and soars, and spreads his wings over Bozrah, and on this day the hearts of the strong men of Edom shall be as the heart of a woman in anguish.

V. 19. Unexpectedly will the Lord come up like a lion against the strong sheepfolds, the impregnable fortifications, and chase the inhabitants from the land in headlong flight. He will do that through His appointee. "Who will appoint Me the time?" rather, "challenge Me?" Jehovah is accountable to no one. He alone knows whom He will call.

Vv. 20-22. The "least of the flock" is not the subject, but the object of "draw out." Against the Lord even the strongest nations are helpless. Their land will be bewildered by the sudden turn of affairs (v. 21). Like an eagle (v. 22), soaring high and swooping down upon the unsuspecting prey, the Lord will destroy Bozrah.

VI. The Prophecy Concerning Damascus, Vv. 23-27

23 Concerning Damascus. Hamath is put to shame, and Arpad; for they have heard evil news, they are panic-stricken, at the sea there is 24 sorrow; it cannot find rest. Damascus is enfeebled, she has turned to flee; trembling has seized her; anguish and agony have gripped 25 her as a woman in travail. How unforsaken is the city of praise! 26 the city of joy! Therefore her young men shall fall in her open places, and all warriors be silenced on that day, is the oracle of the 27 LORD of Hosts. Then I will kindle a fire within the wall of Damascus, and it shall consume the palaces of Ben-Hadad.

V. 23. Hamath and Arpad are sometimes mentioned in connection with Syria and Damascus (cp. Is. 10:9). They were, however, two independent cities. Hamath on the Orontes, about 110 miles north of Damascus, was a Canaanite city (Gen. 10:18), one of the chief cities of the Hittites. It formed nominally the boundary of Israel (Num. 34:8; Joshua 13:5), "the entrance to Hamath," the valley of the Orontes. It was a part of Solomon's empire (2 Chron. 8:4; 1 Kings 4:21-24; cp. 2 Sam. 8:9f.). Later lost to Israel, it was regained by Jeroboam II (2 Kings 14:28). In 720 Sargon incorporated it into the Assyrian Empire (cp. Is. 10:9; 2 Kings 18:34; 19:13; Amos 6:2); once called Chamath Rabba, Hamath the Great, Antiochus IV (Epiphanes) changed its name to Epiphaneia. The modern name is Hama, still a flourishing city.

Arpad is mentioned in Scripture only in connection with Hamath (2 Kings 18:34; 19:13; Is. 10:9; 36:19; 37:13). It is identified with Tell er Fad, a hill with ruins about 100 miles north of Hamath, evidently a city of importance in the time of Isaiah and Jeremiah.

Damascus is today the oldest still existing city. According to Josephus, Damascus was founded by Uz, the son of Aram, the grandson of Shem (Gen. 10:22-23). Josephus, *Ant.*, I, VI, 4. Cp. Gen. 14:15; 15:2. Because of its position on the juncture of several trade routes, Damascus was a prosperous and flourishing city throughout the ages. Tiglath Pileser had destroyed it 735. Evidently it had recovered or begun to recover from this blow. During the Persian period the city had regained its prominence and maintained it ever since. Its population in 1942 was 193,912 (*Encyclopedia Britannica World Atlas*).

The praises of Damascus' beauty have been sung throughout the ages. Mohammed is said to have gazed, while still a camel driver, on the city and to have turned away without entering the city. "Man," he said, "can have but one paradise, and my paradise is fixed in

347

heaven." Dean Stanley, who records this speech in *Sinai and Palestine,* p. 497, adds: "There may be other views in the world more beautiful; there can hardly be another at once so beautiful and so instructive. 'This is indeed worth all the toil and danger it has cost me to come here,' was the speech of the distinguished historian [Henry Buckle], whose premature death at Damascus almost immediately afterward [1862] gave a mournful significance to his words." Other travelers have agreed with Stanley. This city of praise, "the city of My joy," as Jehovah calls it in appreciation of its beauty, shall "wax feeble," etc.; fall victim to Nebuchadnezzar's victorious army. "How is the city of praise not left," "unforsaken!" We take these words to be spoken in divine irony. What a fine unforsaken city shall you be, after I send the enemy to destroy you! While there is no historical record of such a destruction, here is the word of the Lord of Hosts! (V. 26.)

VII. The Prophecy Concerning Kedar and Hazor, Vv. 28-33

28 Concerning Kedar and the king-doms of Hazor, which Nebuchad-rezzar, the king of Babylon, smote. Thus says the LORD: Arise, go up against Kedar, and destroy the 29 children of the East. They shall take their tents and their flocks, their tent curtains, and all their wares; and their camels shall they take for themselves and shall shout at them: Terror round about! 30 Flee! Fly afar off! Hide deep, O inhabitants of Hazor! is the oracle of the LORD, for Nebuchad-rezzar, king of Babylon, has coun-seled a counsel against you and 31 planned a plan against you! Arise, go up against the tranquil nation, living in security, is the oracle of the LORD. They have no doors and no bolts, alone they dwell. 32 And their camels shall be spoils, the multitudes of their herds shall be a booty, and I will scatter to all the winds the people of shorn hair, and from all sides I will bring 33 their destruction. Then Hazor shall be the dwelling place of jackals, an everlasting waste; no man shall live there, and no son of man shall sojourn there.

V. 28. The Lord's judgment extends not only to the great world empires. It includes the desert tribes and their "kingdoms" ruled by sheiks. "Men of the East" (v. 28), the desert countries east of Israel. As their representatives two tribes are named: Kedar in the Syrian and Arabian desert, descendants of Ishmael (Gen. 25:13), dwelling east of the Ammonites, in villages (Is. 42:11), their princes carrying on extensive commerce with Tyre (Ezek. 27:21; cp. also Is. 21:16-17; 60:7). Of Hazor we know nothing more than our text tells us. We cannot even definitely decide whether it is a tribal name or the name of a city or some desert area. Many interpreters connect it with a Hebrew word denoting an unfortified city, or village, or settle-ment (cp. Lev. 25:31; Joshua 13:23; etc.), in distinction to the Bedouin or nomadic desert tribes.

"Arise ye, and go up." "Up, and at them!" This is the Lord's sharp command. He is preparing a Waterloo for the desert tribes, the "sons of the East" (cp. Gen. 29:1; Judg. 6:33; 8:10-11; 1 Kings 4:30; Ezek. 25:4, 10). As the city dwellers trusted in their strong walls, so the desert tribes relied on the wide-open spaces, the immense expanse of the desert, which made army expeditions against them very difficult and facilitated their own escape. They felt quite safe and secure even without doors and gates and locks and bars (v. 31). The prophet warns them (v. 30) as he warned Dedan (v. 8); for Nebuchadnezzar would carefully lay his plans, counsel with men expe-rienced in desert warfare, and succeed in rudely shattering their fatal assurance of imperturbable security. He will surround them (v. 32c); from all sides they hear the battle cry of the enemy. Terror round about (v. 29c)! Cp. Jer. 6:25; 20:10; 46:5. Their tents, their curtains, all their wares (v. 29), their flocks, their camels, their cattle (vv. 29, 32), are captured and driven away by the enemy. Those that escape the sword or capture are scattered "to every wind," in every direction (cp. ch. 49:5). On "them that are in the utmost corners," rather, "that have the corners of the hair cut off," cp. Jer. 9:26; 25:23. Only jackals howl where once the sons of the East dwelt, if not in opulence, at least in safety and satisfactory comfort.

The exact date of Nebuchadnezzar's campaign against the desert tribes is unknown. Josephus quotes Berosus, who prior to his report of the battle of Carchemish writes: "This Babylonian [Nebuchadnezzar] conquered Egypt and Syria and Phoenicia and Arabia." Evidently Berosus knew of an Arabian campaign, but he gives no further information. Volz writes: "Arabian tradition records that Nebuchadrezzar, tempted by the fabulous wealth of the distant commercial cities and caravan markets, undertook a campaign against Arabia. 'It was rather a predatory expedition than a regular campaign. His gain consisted in no more than immense spoils and an ephemeral sovereignty. The Arabians retained the remembrance of the conqueror who had afflicted them so severely, and Bochtnassar became a legendary hero, round whose person grew up a mass of romantic and fabulous tales' (Maspero, *Geschichte der morgenlaendischen Voelker im Altertum,* p. 497)." Volz, *Jeremias,* p. 420.

VIII. The Prophecy Concerning Elam, Vv. 34-39

34 What came as the word of the LORD to Jeremiah the prophet concerning Elam in the beginning of the rule of Zedekiah, the king 35 of Judah: Thus says the LORD of Hosts: Behold, I am going to break the bow of Elam, the mainspring of 36 her power. And I will bring upon Elam four winds from the four ends of heaven, and I will scatter them to all these winds, so that there shall be no nation to which the outcasts of Elam shall not 37 come! And I will cause Elam to tremble before their enemies and before those that seek their lives; and I will bring evil upon them, the fury of My anger, is the oracle of the LORD, and I will send the sword after them, until I have 38 made an utter end of them. Then will I set My throne in Elam, and from there I will destroy king and princes, is the oracle of the LORD. 39 In the end of the days I will turn the captivity of Elam, is the oracle of the LORD.

Grammatical Notes

V. 36. "Outcasts of Elam." The K'tib reads עוֹלָם instead of עֵילָם: everlastingly scattered, eternal outcasts, a very striking play on words. Yet the Q'ri, a number of manuscripts, all the versions, regard it as a copyist's error.

Elam is named first among the sons of Shem (Gen. 10:22). He was the progenitor of a powerful nation, dwelling north and east of the Persian Gulf; west of Persia, south of Media, east of Babylon. Its capital city was Shushan, also called Susa (Neh. 1:1; Esther 1:2, 5, etc.; Dan. 8:2), about 200 miles directly east of Babylon. In the time of Abraham, Chedor-laomer was king of Elam, had with the aid of his allies conquered the rich cities of the Valley of Siddim, and had subdued a revolt in a vast campaign described Gen. 14:1-11. For centuries the Elamites with varying success had fought with Babylonia and Assyria until Assurbanipal (668—626) succeeded in conquering them. Is. 22:6 the Elamites are named as allies or vassals of Assyria in the campaign against Hezekiah (cp. vv. 8-10), and Is. 21:2-6 the Lord calls upon Elam and Media to overthrow Babylon. After the fall of Nineveh (612 B. C.) the Medes subjugated Elam, and Cyrus embodied it in his vast empire.

V. 34. Jeremiah's prophecy was spoken in the beginning of Zedekiah's rule shortly after Jehoiachin's deportation.

V. 35. If the archer's bow is broken, the "chief," literally, the beginning and basis, the mainspring and mainstay, of the archer's power is broken. The Lord is getting ready to break the bow of Elam, which was renowned for its skilled archers.

Vv. 36-38. Jehovah, the God of tiny Judah, the real world Ruler, will set up His judgment throne (cp. ch. 1:15; 43:10-11) in this

351

mighty nation, hundreds of miles distant from Jerusalem, will remove its king and princes, appoint a ruler of His own selection, and scatter the nation to the four quarters of the earth. This prophecy was fulfilled by Cyrus, the shepherd and anointed of the Lord (Is. 44: 28; 45: 1), who incorporated Elam as a province in his vast empire. Elamites and Medians formed part of the army of Cyrus and aided him in conquering the Babylonian Empire (Is. 21: 2; Jer. 50: 3, 29, archers; v. 42, bow).

V. 39. In the New Testament era Elam also will participate in the spiritual deliverance and salvation of God's Kingdom of Grace (cp. Acts 2: 9), for Jehovah is the God not only of judgment, but of salvation for Jews and Gentiles.

IX. Prophecy Concerning Babylon, Ch. 50—51

CHAPTER 50

1. Babylon's Fall Is Israel's Deliverance, Vv. 1-10

1 The word which the LORD spoke against Babel, against the land of the Chaldeans, through Jeremiah 2 the prophet. Publish among the nations, and let it be heard, and raise a signal, let it be heard, do not conceal. Say: Babel is taken, Bel is put to shame, Merodach is dismayed. Her carved images are put to shame, the statues are dismayed. 3 For there arises against her a nation from the north that shall make her land a desolation so that no one shall dwell there; both man and beast have fled, have 4 gone. In these days and in that time, says the LORD, the children of Israel shall come, they and the children of Judah together. They shall weep while they walk, and they shall seek the LORD, their 5 God. They shall ask the way to Zion. Their faces are turned toward it: Come, let us join the LORD in an everlasting covenant which shall not be forgotten.

6 A flock of lost sheep was My people. Their shepherds led them astray; to the mountains they turned them; from mountain to heights they have gone; they forgot 7 their fold. All that found them devoured them, and their opponents said: We are not guilty, because they sinned against the LORD, the pasture of righteousness, and the hope of their fathers, 8 the LORD. Flee from the midst of Babel, and go out of the land of the Chaldeans; and become like 9 bellwethers before the flock. For, behold, I am arousing and leading up against Babel an assembly of great nations from the Northland, and they shall array themselves against her; from there she shall be captured. Their arrows are like those of a skillful warrior who re- 10 turns not with empty hands. And Chaldea shall become a spoil; all her despoilers shall have their fill, is the oracle of the LORD.

V. 1. "By Jeremiah," literally, "by the hand," see Jer. 37:2.

V. 2. As long as Babylon ruled the world, fear silenced the tongue of the conquered nations. Now there is no longer any need of such fear. Belu was the deity of ancient Nippur, the Sumerian Enil (Barton, *Archaeology and the Bible,* p. 199), and from primeval times one of the highest gods. When the city of Babylon gained the sovereignty, the local god, Merodach (Cuneif. Marduk, only here in Old Testament), was placed at the head of the Pantheon, and many features of the cult of Bel were transferred to Marduk. Bel became an appellative of Marduk, and finally one of his proper names. On the magnificence of his gigantic temple in Babylon, cp. Herodotus, I, 181—183. Excavations by Koldewey (died 1925) during 1910 to 1911 have partially uncovered the huge foundations of this great temple, the north wall of which measured 257 feet; the west wall, 278 feet; the main court, 102 by 122 feet. (Koldewey, *Das Wieder Erstehende Babylon,* p. 200f.) "Idols," a contemptuous word, something

353

formed, shaped; "images," literally, something rolled. The two words describe the huge tree trunks or stone blocks that had to be formed into likenesses of Bel-Marduk and were placed on rollers to be put into position (cp. Dan. 3:1ff.). The entire Pantheon is pictured as in a terrible uproar and fear.

Vv. 3-5. In this time the prophecy of ch. 3:14ff.; ch. 31 and 32 shall begin to be fulfilled.

Vv. 6-7. "Shepherds," the spiritual and political leaders; "mountains," where they could satisfy their carnal lust at the altars dedicated to heathen idolatry and immorality. Cp. ch. 3:1, 2, 6, 8, 9. Their "resting place," the sheepfold, was forgotten. V. 7 defines this resting place, or, as it is called, their "habitation," as the Lord, in whom alone they could find rest and peace for their souls. Him they forgot! Against Him they sinned! And the enemies used this apostasy from the Lord, of which Judah was guilty, as an excuse for their heartless, cruel oppression of God's people (v. 7).

Vv. 8-10. After the Lord has punished the apostate people, He prepares to deliver them from bondage by overthrowing Babylon. They are told to "remove" out of Babylon, to hurry back to their homeland (same word as Ps. 11:1). They shall be as the he-goats before the flocks, because for Israel's sake the Lord broke the yoke imposed by Babylon upon all nations (Jer. 25:17-28). It was the Lord who sent His servant Cyrus (Is. 44:28—45:4), who permitted all deported nations to return to their home countries.

2. Babylon's Shame Is Israel's Glory, Vv. 11-20

11 Though you rejoice, though you shout for joy, you plunderers of My heritage, though you gambol like a threshing heifer and neigh
12 like the stallions, yet your mother shall be put to deepest shame; she that bore you shall be abashed. Behold, she is the very last of the nations, a dry desert and wilder-
13 ness! By the wrath of the LORD she shall be uninhabited and shall become altogether a desert. Everyone that passeth over Babylon shall shudder and hiss at all her wounds.
14 Array yourselves against Babel round about! All you that bend the bow, shoot at her! Spare not your arrows, for she has sinned
15 against the LORD! Cry out against her round about: She has surrendered! Her supports have fallen! Her walls are razed! For this is the vengeance of the LORD! Avenge yourselves on her! As she
16 has done, so do to her! Cut off the sower out of Babylon and the reaper in the time of harvest! Before the deadly sword everyone turns back to his people, everyone
17 flees to his land. A sheep is Israel; lions have driven him away. At first the king of Assyria devoured him, and as the last one this Nebuchadrezzar, the king of Babylon,
18 has gnawed his bones. Therefore thus says the LORD of Hosts, the God of Israel: Behold, I am about to punish the king of Babylon and

his land as I have punished the
19 king of Assyria. And I will bring
back Israel to his fold, and he will
feed on Carmel and Bashan, and
on the Mount of Ephraim and
Gilead he shall satisfy his soul.
20 In those days and at that time,

is the oracle of the LORD, the guilt
of Israel shall be sought, and it is
no more, and the sins of Judah,
and they shall not be found! For
I will pardon those whom I will
keep as a remnant.

Vv. 11-13. The heifer calf, frisking about the threshing floor and eating its fill (cp. Deut. 25:4) is a suitable picture of carefree, satisfied joy. No matter how great the strength of the Chaldeans, no matter how boastfully they rejoiced (Dan. 5:1-30), their "mother," the nation personified, will be turned into a dreary wilderness.

Vv. 14-16. "Bend the bow," a reference to the Medo-Persian armies and their renowned archers (cp. ch. 49:35; 51:3-11). "Hath given her hand," most probably in pledge of surrender, because she sees everywhere the uselessness of resistance. "Sower and reaper." The rural population shall feel the woes and hardships of warfare even before the city dwellers. To a large extent these tillers of the soil were foreigners, deported from their homeland by Babylonian conquerors. They flee from Babylon back to their native lands, leaving the newly sown fields together with the harvest already reaped in the hands of the advancing enemy.

Vv. 17-18. While the enemies of Israel had been instruments of God, yet they had pursued their own selfish interests in self-aggrandizement, and now the Covenant God is ready to punish Babylon as He had punished Nineveh. Koldewey reports that the ruins of Babylon in many places were covered with forty to eighty feet of sand and rubble. (Koldewey, loc. cit., Foreword, I.)

V. 19. "Carmel" and "Bashan," the west and east Jordanland, where they will be satisfied with the spiritual and material blessings of the Lord.

V. 20. Another Gospel promise of rare beauty, stating the reason why v. 19 can be realized by sinful mortals. In the post-Exilic times another miracle of grace, the miracle of absolute forgiveness, will be made possible, the efficacy of which will be retroactive to all sins in the past (Heb. 9:15) and will last to eternity. The "inquity," the guilt of Israel, and his "sin," his many missings of the mark, will be "searched for." The root meaning of this word is "to dig, scrape, seek thoroughly." There are many that seek for the sins and iniquities of God's people (Job 1:9; 2:4-5; Zech. 3:1, 3; Rev. 12:10; Rom. 2:15). Yet in spite of all searching, there is no sin to be found. This is not

355

a mere "whitewashing." No, there is a "non-existence of guilt," for the Covenant God of infinite grace says: "I will pardon." Richly, daily, He will forgive whomsoever He will "cause to remain," to be one of the remnant. On the meaning of "pardon" see Jer. 31:34; Micah 7:18-19; Eph. 5:26-27. — Salvation *in toto* is a work of the Lord, earned and procured for and offered to all the world (Gen. 6:3; Deut. 30:19-20; Job 33:16-18; Is. 53:6; Ezek. 33:11).

---

3. Babylon's Power Destroyed, Vv. 21-28

21 Against the land of Double Defiance, arise against her and against the inhabitants of Pekod! Lay waste and devote her to death, is the oracle of the LORD, and do exactly what I have commanded 22 you. The noise of war is in the 23 land, and great ruin! How is the hammer of the whole earth broken and smashed! What a horror has Babylon become among the na- 24 tions! I laid a snare for you, and you, O Babylon, have been caught unawares! You have been found, and you have been taken, because you have pitted yourselves against 25 the LORD. The LORD has opened His armory and brought forth the weapons of His wrath. For this is a work which the LORD of Hosts has to do in the land of the Chal- 26 deans. Come against her from afar! Throw open her storehouses! Pile her up like heaps of grain! Destroy her utterly until nothing is left of 27 her! Slay all her bullocks! Let them go down to the slaughter! Woe unto them! For their day has come, the time of their punishment. 28 Hark! they are fleeing and escaping from Babylon in order to declare in Zion the vengeance of the LORD, our God, the avenging of His Temple.

Vv. 21-23. *"Merathaim," "Pekod."* Because *Pukudu* is the cuneiform name of an Aramaean tribe in Babylon, and *Marratim,* "sealand," is a cuneiform designation of southern Babylon (Fr. Delitzsch, *Wo lag das Paradies?* p. 182; Schrader, *Keilschr. u. A. Test.,* 2d ed., p. 243), many commentaries find in *Pekod* and *Merathaim* a reference to these geographical districts and a play on words. While undoubtedly there is here a play on words, one of the prophet's favorite figures of speech, the geographic reference seems rather doubtful. *Pekod* is inf. Qal of פָּקַד, to visit, punish. *Merathaim,* dual of a noun derived from מָרָה, to be obstinate, rebellious (Jer. 4:17; 5:23), means double rebellion or defiance.

The words, occurring only here, may have been coined by the prophet. The dual has the sense of "enough" and "overflowing," as in Is. 40:1. The dual *merathaim* does not mean exactly two rebellions, but superabundant, excessive defiance. *Merathaim,* defiance, refers to Babylon's sins; *pekod,* visitation, to God's judgment. The hammer that smashed the whole world into submission shall itself be broken, smashed.

Vv. 24-28. Suddenly and unexpectedly, only a quarter century after Nebuchadnezzar's glorious rule, Babylon was caught in the snare the Lord had prepared for this supercilious enemy. It was God's work, the Lord gave success to Babylon's enemies as He had given success to Babylon against Judah. "Cast her up as heaps" refers to the huge piles of rubble left after the destruction of the city (cp. v. 18b). The fall of Babylon is of special importance to God's people, and all fugitives are told to declare in Zion the vengeance of the Lord upon the Chaldeans because they destroyed His Temple (v. 28).

4. Babylon's Pride Humbled, Vv. 29-32

29 Summon multitudes against Babylon! Let all that bend the bow encamp round about her! Let there be no escape! Repay her for her deeds! Exactly what she has done, do to her! For she has been arrogant toward the LORD, the Holy
30 One of Israel. Therefore her young men shall fall in her squares, and all her warriors shall be silenced on that day, is the oracle of the
31 LORD. Behold, I am against you, O Arrogance! is the oracle of the Lord LORD of Hosts, for your day has come, the time of your punish-
32 ment. And Arrogance shall stumble and fall, and no one shall lift her up! I will kindle a fire in her cities which shall devour all that are around her.

V. 29. "Archers," A. V., rather, multitudes, רַבִּים; so also the ancient versions. The arrogant city shall be reduced to dust and ashes.

5. The Lord, the Redeemer of Israel, Sends the Sword upon Babylon Vv. 33-40

33 Thus says the LORD of Hosts: Oppressed are the children of Israel together with the children of Judah; and all that have taken them captive hold them in their grip; they refuse to let them go.
34 Their Redeemer is strong, the LORD of Hosts is His name. He will wholeheartedly espouse their cause in order to give rest to the land and to disquiet the inhabit-
35 ants of Babylon. A sword upon the Chaldeans, is the oracle of the LORD, upon the inhabitants of Babylon, and upon her princes, and
36 upon her sages! A sword upon her babblers! They shall become fools. A sword upon her strong men! They shall tremble with fear.
37 A sword upon her horses and upon her chariots, and upon all the foreigners in her midst! They shall be as women. A sword upon her treasures! They shall be pillaged.
38 Drought upon her waters, and they shall dry out. For it is a land of idols, and they are foolishly proud
39 of horrible things. Therefore desert animals will dwell with jackals, and young ostriches will dwell there. She shall be no more inhabited forever, and unoccupied
40 throughout the ages! As God overthrew Sodom and Gomorrah and all their inhabitants, is the oracle of the LORD, so shall no man dwell there, no son of man shall live there.

Grammatical Notes

V. 34. "Give rest . . . disquiet." Note the contrast, and in the original the play on words, הַרְגִּיעַ — הִרְגִּיז: two favorite figures of speech with Jeremiah.

V. 38. "A drought," חֹרֶב. The LXX omits the word; Lucian has "sword"; Origen in *Hexapla*, "sword." "Idols," אֵימִים, terrors, horrors.

Vv. 33-34. Judah's enemies forgot that Israel was the covenant nation of the Lord of Hosts, "their Redeemer." As such He will plead their cause, not by lengthy speeches, but by mighty deeds. He will quiet the world (Is. 14: 3, 7, 16; Zech. 1: 11) and disquiet Babylon. The policy of Cyrus was to gain the good will of the subject nations by permitting all deported people to return to their native land. On his edict see Barton, *Archaeology and the Bible*, p. 483 f.

Vv. 35-38. The Sword Song, a triumphant hymn praising God's judgment upon Babylon. The proud city will be deprived of all its supports, its staffs and stays. Its princes, its wise men, its "babblers," or soothsayers, its "strong men," its powerful armies, its horses and chariots, its "mingled people," the people attached to it, either as allies or mercenaries or enslaved exiles (on "mingled people" cp. Ex. 12: 38; Neh. 13: 3; Jer. 25: 20), its riches — all will vanish. One of the chief sources of its prosperity and power, its immense irrigation system, dating back to the time of Hammurapi, who legislated on it in his *Code*, §§ 53—56 (Barton, *Archaeology and the Bible*, p. 382 f.), will be destroyed by the Lord, either by the ravages of war, the sword, as some of the Greek editions read, or, following the Masoretic pointing, drought. The canals gradually silted up, and the life cord of Babylon was severed. Their graven images and idols are unable to help. "They are mad"; A. V. follows the M. T., they make fools of themselves; others point as to read: "they glory in." We prefer A. V. The highly cultured Babylonians still did not use their reason and wisdom for the high purpose for which they are given (Acts 17: 27). They had ample opportunity to find the Lord by their many contacts with the Lord's chosen people, but they preferred their own idols to the Lord of grace and mercy (Rom. 1: 18-23). The prophet calls them "idols," literally, "terrors," horrible creations of the depraved mind of man, cruel, bloodthirsty, immoral, lecherous, capricious, keeping their worshipers in constant doubt, fear, uncertainty as to their temporal and eternal welfare, horrible caricatures of the God of unchanging holiness and justice, of unlimited loving-kindness and grace.

V. 39. On this verse cp. Is. 13: 20-22; 34: 14. "Wild beasts of the desert," perhaps, wild cats; "wild beasts of island," most likely, jackals; cp. "cry," howl (Is. 13:22). "Owls," perhaps, ostriches. Babylon will no longer be the dwelling place of people, but of desert animals. On v. 40 cp. ch. 49:18.

6. Babylon is Destroyed by an Enemy from the North, Vv. 41-46

41 Behold, a people shall come from the north, a great nation, and many kings are stirring from the ends of 42 the earth. Bow and spear in their grip. Cruel they are and know no pity. The noise they make is like the sea when it roars. On horses they ride, arrayed like a man for battle against you, O daughter of 43 Babylon! The king of Babylon has heard the report, and his hands grow slack, distress grips him, anguish like that of a travailing 44 woman. Behold, as a lion comes up from the jungles of Jordan into the evergreen pasture, so I will suddenly come and drive them away from it. And him who is My chosen one will I appoint over her. For who is like unto Me? And who will challenge Me? And who is a shepherd such as shall 45 stand before Me? Therefore, hear the counsel of the LORD which He has determined concerning Babylon, and His plans which He has formed against the land of the Chaldeans: They shall certainly be dragged as the little ones of the flock. Their fold shall be amazed 46 at their fate! At the report of the capture of Babylon the earth shall tremble, and her cry shall be heard throughout the nations.

Vv. 41-43. The prophet applies to Babylon what he had threatened to Judah (ch. 6:22-24). "Many kings" is added (v. 41) to describe the complex nature of the huge army. Others translate: "mighty" kings. "Many" is used of great power and great number.

Vv. 44-46. Cp. ch. 49:19-21. Babylon's judgment shall be that of Edom. God is not a respecter of persons. Babylon, the world empire, is as a drop in the bucket before Him (Is. 40:15, 17), is responsible to Him, and will be cast off by Him like the small nations of Edom and Judah if it dares to oppose Him.

CHAPTER 51

7. The Holy One of Israel will Send His Winnowers Against Babylon
Vv. 1-6

1 Thus says the LORD: Behold, I am stirring up against Babylon and against the inhabitants of Leb-Kamai the spirit of a destroyer. 2 And I will send winnowers to Babylon, and they shall winnow her and empty out her land. For they oppose her on all sides on 3 the day of calamity. Against the archer let the archer bend his bow, and against him that takes pride in his armor. Do not spare her youths! Send to destruction all her 4 hosts, so that they shall fall mortally wounded in the land of the Chaldeans, and pierced through in 5 her open places. For Israel and Judah are not left widowed by their God, the LORD of Hosts, for their land is full of guilt against

6 the Holy One of Israel. Flee out of Babylon, and let everyone save his life! Let not destruction take you on account of their sin! For this is the time of the LORD's vengeance; He pays out to her due recompense!

Grammatical Notes

V. 1. "In the midst of them that rise up against Me," לֵב קָמַי, literally, the heart of My opponents, an *atbash* (cp. ch. 25:26, Grammatical Notes) on the word כַּשְׂדִּים, Chaldeans, designating them, i. e., Babylon, as the very heart of opposition. V. 2. "Fanners," M. T. points זָרִים, foreigners, instead of זֹרִים, winnowers, without materially changing the sense.

V. 3 presents textual difficulties. LXX omits the two "against." Syr., Targ., Vulg., and about fifteen Mss. read אַל, "not," instead of אֶל. The K'tib may be translated: Against him that treads, let the treader tread his bow; the Q'ri: Against him that treads (be) the treader of his bow. On the omission of אֲשֶׁר and the preposition governing a verbal clause, cp. Is. 65:1; Jer. 2:8; Ezek. 13:3; 1 Chron. 15:12; etc. G.-K. 155n. Since the K'tib presents a satisfactory sense, we prefer to retain it. On the Jussive in conditional sentences, see Driver, *Hebrew Tenses*, §§ 150—152. "Tread," the huge bows of the ancients had to be bent by means of the foot.

Vv. 1-6. "Raise a destroying wind." The Hebrew phrase is never used in this sense, but always: "arouse the spirit" of a destroyer. "In the midst of them that rise up against Me." See Grammatical Notes. The words designate Babylon as the very heart, the life seat, of opposition against the Lord, the Antichrist of the Old Testament, and a type of the Antichrist of the New Testament (cp. Rev. 17:5). The Lord will send winnowers against her (cp. ch. 15:7). "Bendeth the bow," a reference to Medo-Persian armies (cp. v. 11). In this manner the Lord will prove that Israel and Judah have not been forsaken by the Covenant God, the Ruler of the universe. V. 5b, "though" = "for," refers to the Chaldeans named v. 4.

8. The Golden Cup Broken, Vv. 7-10

7 A golden cup was Babylon in the hand of the LORD, intoxicating all the earth. Of her wine nations drank; therefore nations became 8 deranged. Suddenly Babylon falls and will be shattered. Wail for her! Apply balsam to her wound; perhaps she may be restored to 9 health! We were determined to heal Babylon, but she is not healed. Forsake her, and let every one of us go to his country, for her guilt 10 reaches up to heaven and is as high as the clouds! The LORD has brought to light our righteous cause. Come, and let us declare in Zion the work of the LORD, our God!

Vv. 7-10. Great Babylon with her riches, her culture, her architecture, her power, her successes (Dan. 4: 20-22, 30), represented indeed the *ne plus ultra* of human achievement. She was like a splendid golden cup "in the LORD's hand," since the Lord had chosen her as His instrument (ch. 25:15-38). Her influence was like strong wine, intoxicating the nations which idolized Babylon in spite of her cruel arrogance, her avarice, her selfish exploitation (Hab. 2:6-17). Because of her self-exaltation the Lord was ready to cast her off like Assyria (Is. 10:5-19; cp. Is. 14:4ff.). In their fatuous admiration of Babylon's power and wealth the nations sought to prevent her destruction, to heal her (v. 9), to restore her to her glory. Only when all efforts proved futile, did they leave her to her fate and return to their home countries. They did not understand the real cause of her unexpected (v. 8) and complete (v. 9) destruction. The prophet reveals it in v. 10: it was the avenging hand of God, vindicating His chosen people. He urges the believing Jews to return to Zion in order to proclaim "the work of the LORD, our God," the God of little, despised Zion, the Church of God, one of the many victims of Babylon's prowess, against which all other "gods" were helpless.

9. The Lord Summons the Medes to Avenge the Burning of His Temple, Vv. 11-14

11 Sharpen the arrows! Prepare the shields! The LORD has roused the spirit of the kings of the Medes; for He has planned to destroy Babylon. For this is the vengeance of the LORD, the avenging
12 of His Temple! Against the walls of Babel raise up standards! Strengthen the blockade! Set blockaders! Prepare the ambushes! For what the LORD has planned, He has also carried out, what He has spoken concerning the inhab-
13 itants of Babylon. O you that dwell beside great waters, mighty in riches, your end has come, the
14 measure of your gain! The LORD of Hosts has sworn by Himself: Even if I had filled you with men as locusts, they shall shout their vintage shout over you.

The mighty walls which seemed insuperable; the great waters, the commerce carried over the Euphrates and the rich harvests gathered from fertile lands irrigated by the stream; the multitudes of inhabitants, all together are powerless against the Lord of Hosts, the Universal Ruler, who has bound Himself by a solemn oath that the vintagers' song shall be sung ("lift up a shout") over her as the enemies trample her under foot as vintagers tread the grapes (cp. Is. 63:3). — "The measure of thy covetousness," the ell, cubit, of your "cut," "cutting," slicing off a huge profit by hook or crook (cp. Ex. 18:21; Jer. 22:17). The end has come for this "ell" also; the measure of her profiteering, her exorbitant taxation (Hab. 2:6 ff.), is full! Now comes the end! And it will come! Even though He has filled the city with people, their numbers shall not avail against the Lord's counsel!

10. Against the Almighty Creator Mankind and Man-Made Idols Are Helpless, Vv. 15-19

15 He who has made the earth by His strength and established the world by His wisdom, and by His understanding has spread out the
16 heavens — when He utters His voice, there is the noise of waters in the sky, and He causes vapors to arise from the ends of the earth; He creates lightnings for rain and brings the wind out of its cham-
17 bers. Stupid is every man with- out knowledge! Every refiner is put to shame by his image, for his castings are deceit, and there is no
18 breath in them! Vanity are they, ridiculous work! In the time of their visitation they will perish!
19 Not like these is the Portion of Jacob! For He is the Former of all the universe and of the tribe of His possession. LORD of Hosts is His name!

On vv. 15-19 see Jer. 10:12-16.

11. The Shattering Hammer Shattered, Vv. 20-24

20 You were a hammer, My weapon of war. I shattered with you na- tions; I shattered with you king-
21 doms; I shattered with you horses and their riders; I shattered with you chariots and their drivers;
22 I shattered with you men and women; I shattered with you old men and young; I shattered with
23 you youths and maidens; I shat- tered with you shepherd and his flock; I shattered with you plow- man and his team; I shattered with you governors and vicegerents.
24 And I will requite Babylon and all the inhabitants of Chaldea before your eyes for all the wrong they have done to Zion, is the oracle of the LORD.

At present Babylon is still a hammer smashing the nations, yet it is a hammer in the hand of Jehovah (Jer. 25:15ff.; cp. 51:7), who can readily cast aside or break the hammer. And He will do so because of Babylon's maltreatment of God's people. The hatred against God's Church brings on the ruin of nations and rulers. Though God uses wicked people to chastise the Church, yet they did that not to glorify God, but themselves, to wreak their vengeance on their enemies.

12. The Mountain of Destruction Destroyed, Vv. 25-26

25 Behold, I am against you, O Moun- tain of Destruction, is the oracle of the LORD, that has destroyed the whole world! I have stretched out My hand against you and will roll you from the rocks and will make
26 you a burning mountain. And they will take from you no cornerstone nor a foundation stone, but you shall be everlasting desolation, is the oracle of the LORD.

362

"Mountain," perhaps because of Babylon's high walls or its inordinate pride and ambition. "Mountain of destruction," same phrase as 2 Kings 23:13, translated "corruption"; the corrupting, destructive influence of Solomon's idolatry. In our passage perhaps both physical and moral destruction emanating from Babylon are intended. With His powerful hand Jehovah tears the towering mountain from its bedrock foundation and in the fire of His judgments reduces the smashed rocks to powder and ashes. Not a single particle can be found suitable for a cornerstone or foundation. Never again shall Babylon become the seat of an empire, and never again shall a new empire originate, be founded, at Babylon.

13. Babylon Is Like a Threshing Floor Being Prepared for Threshing
Vv. 27-33

27 Raise up a standard in the land! Blow the trumpet among the nations! Consecrate against her nations! Summon against her kingdoms, Ararat, Minni, and Ashkenaz; appoint a mustering officer against her; bring up horses like
28 bristling locusts. Consecrate nations against her, the kings of Media, the governors and all vicegerents, the whole land of his rule.
29 Then shall the earth quake and tremble, for the counsels of the LORD stand against Babylon to make the land of Babylon an un-
30 inhabited waste. The warriors of Babylon have ceased to fight; they sit in their strongholds; their strength has failed; they have become women; her dwellings are set on fire, her bars are broken.
31 Courier runs to meet the courier, messenger to meet the messenger, to report to the king of Babylon that his city is captured from end
32 to end, that the fords have been taken, that the marshes have been set on fire, and the warriors are
33 panic-stricken. For thus says the LORD of Hosts, the God of Israel: The Daughter of Babylon is as a threshing floor at the time when it is being trampled hard; a little while longer, and the time of harvest shall have come for her.

Vv. 27-33. The judgment upon Babylon is drawing near. As the Lord called the Babylonians to destroy Jerusalem (Jer. 1:11-16), so He summons the nations against Babylon many years before the actual occurrences. "Prepare" (vv. 27-28) = consecrate (cp. ch. 22:7). "Ararat," cuneif. *Urartu* (Gen. 8:4), the Armenian highland bordering on the River Araxes, north of Lake Van, extending from Mount Ararat in the east to Erzerum in the west. "Minni," cuneif. *Mannai*, between Lake Van and Lake Urmiah. "Ashchenaz," son of Gomer (Gen. 10:3), most probably in Armenia, north of the Mannai. "Captain" (v. 27), the *"Tiphsar,"* Assyr. *Tupsharru*, scribe, enlisting or mustering officer. "Rough," occurs only here, usually translated "bristly," referring to the wings of the locusts encased at a certain stage in a horny skin and sticking up on the backs; others, densely numerous. "Caterpillars," the licker, one of the stages of the locusts' development. The Medes are at the head of the invading army (v. 28). The "captains" here, like v. 23, *pechah,* governors of provinces; the "rulers," *sagan,* commissioners, vicegerents. At the approach of these semicivilized hordes the Babylonian soldiers become panic-stricken. They withdraw into the strong fortifications. Their power of resistance gone, paralyzed with fear, they see the houses of the city go up in flames, set afire by the firebrands hurled into the city; the bars, the gates, are being battered down. From all sides the messengers come to the royal palace, some from afar reporting that the marshes, dried up by drought, are afire, the "passages," the fords across the canals, have been seized by the enemy, cutting off all escape. Others coming from within the city announce the capture of the city gates, general panic ruling the city. The Lord is already preparing the threshing floor, the ground for which was trampled down about harvest time and the grain immediately threshed. Both harvesting and threshing are symbols of divine judgment (Joel 3: 13; Is. 41: 15-16; Micah 4: 12f.; Rev. 14: 14-20).

---

14. Israel's Complaint and the Lord's Reply, Vv. 34-40

34 Nebuchadrezzar, the king of Babylon, has devoured us, has browbeaten us, has set us down as an empty vessel, has swallowed us as a sea monster, has filled his paunch with my dainties, has rejected us,
35 driven us out, has purged us. My reproach and my flesh be upon Babylon! let the inhabitants of Zion say. My blood be upon the inhabitants of Babylon! let Jeru-
36 salem say. Therefore, thus says the LORD: Behold, I am ready to plead your cause and avenge you with vengeance, and I shall dry up her sea and cause her reservoirs
37 to fail. And Babylon shall become a heap of ruins, the home of jackals, a place of horror and hiss-
38 ing, uninhabited! Even though they roar like lions and growl like
39 lions' whelps, yet when they have become hot, I will prepare a banquet for them; I will make them drunk so that they shout with laughter and then sleep an everlasting sleep from which they shall not arise, is the oracle of the
40 LORD. I will bring them down to slaughter like lambs, like rams together with he-goats.

Grammatical Notes

In v. 34 K'tib has plural suffixes. K'ri calls for singular. We follow K'tib. V. 35 continues with the singular suffix.

Vv. 34-40. The Jews in exile complain bitterly to the Lord because of the indignities and cruelties, the depopulation of their land, the destruction of their national existence, which they suffered from Nebuchadnezzar. "Dragons," some sea or river monster. "Delicates," all that the Jews delighted in. The outrages inflicted upon me, my flesh consumed, my blood shed by him, be avenged upon Babylon and the Chaldeans (vv. 34-35)! The Lord promises to plead the cause of His people and to avenge them. "Her sea" and "her springs," reservoirs, refer to the mighty Euphrates, the means of her commerce, and to the innumerable canals and ditches crisscrossing the country, irrigating it, the cause of its fertility and its prosperity. All will dry up, the land turned into an arid desert. From their boisterous, drunken revelries they shall sink into perpetual sleep (cp. Daniel 5).

---

15. The Prison Demolished, the Prisoners Set Free! Vv. 41-46

41 How is Sheshach captured and the praise of the whole earth taken! How has Babylon become a horror
42 among the nations! The sea rises up against Babylon, she is covered
43 by the raging of its waves! Her cities have become a waste, an arid land and a wilderness, a land in which no man dwells, through
44 which no human being passes. And I will punish the Bel of Babylon and draw forth from his maw what he has swallowed. Then the na-tions shall no longer stream to him. Also the wall of Babylon shall fall!
45 Go out from her, O My people! Let everyone save his life from the fury of the anger of the LORD.
46 Let not your heart grow faint or fearful at the rumors heard in the land, when one rumor comes in one year, and afterward another rumor in the next year, and violence is rampant in the land, and one ruler opposes the other.

Vv. 41-46. On Sheshach see ch. 25:26. "Sea," "waves," denote the huge armies of Cyrus flooding the country and leaving it a desert forever. "Bel," "hath swallowed," a play on words, *Bel-bela.*" The swallower must disgorge what he devoured. Since the prison house is demolished (v. 43) and its walls are fallen (v. 44), the imprisoned people are free. Cyrus permitted them to return to their homelands. V. 46 is an admonition to the Jews not to be disturbed by conflicting rumors nor by the violent inner conflicts. The Lord's plan will be carried out!

---

16. The Nations Rejoice at Babylon's Fall, Vv. 47-49

47 Therefore, behold, days are coming that I shall punish the carved images of Babylon, and her whole land shall be put to shame, and all her mortally wounded shall fall
48 within her midst. Then heaven and earth and all that is within them shall rejoice; for from the north shall the destroyers come to her,
49 is the oracle of the LORD. As Babylon was eager to have Israel fall mortally wounded, so at Babylon are fallen the mortally wounded of the whole land.

The Babylonian gods together with their ardent worshipers shall be put to shame, while heaven and earth rejoice that Babylon is no more.

---

17. Flee from Babylon in Order to Escape the Horrors of Her Final Doom, Vv. 50-58

50 You who have escaped from the sword, go on! Do not stand still! Remember from afar the LORD, and let Jerusalem arise before your
51 mind! We are put to shame, for we have heard reproach. Shame has covered our faces, for strangers are come into the sanctuaries of
52 the house of the LORD. Therefore, behold, days are coming, is the oracle of the LORD, that I will punish her carved images, and in the whole land mortally wounded
53 shall groan. Though Babylon should rise to the heavens, though she render inaccessible her high fortifications, yet from Me shall destroyers come to her, is the
54 oracle of the LORD. Hark! a cry from Babylon and great ruin from
55 the land of the Chaldeans! For the LORD is the Destroyer of Babylon and turns to silence her noisy din. Though her waves roar like mighty waters and her tumult sound aloud,
56 there comes upon her, upon Babylon, a Destroyer, and her strong men are captured, their bows are broken, for a God of recompense is the LORD; He pays out to the
57 full. And I will make her princes and her wise men drunk, her governors, her viceregents, her soldiers; and they shall sleep an everlasting sleep from which they shall not awaken, is the oracle of the King, whose name is the LORD of
58 Hosts. Thus says the LORD of Hosts: The broad walls of Babylon shall be razed to the ground, and her high gates shall be burnt with fire. So the people have toiled in vain, and nations have wearied themselves for fire only.

V. 58 b is an adaptation of Hab. 2:13 with significant changes to indicate the sudden and complete frustration of all their hopes and labors.

---

18. Seraiah is Commissioned to Sink the Scroll in the Euphrates Vv. 59-64

59 The word which Jeremiah the prophet commanded to Seraiah, the son of Neriah, the son of Maaseiah, when he accompanied Zedekiah, the king of Judah, to Babylon in the fourth year of his reign. Seraiah was the quartermaster.
60 Jeremiah had written all the evil which was to come upon Babylon on one scroll, all these words which were written concerning Babylon.
61 So Jeremiah said to Seraiah: When you have come to Babylon, then see that you read aloud all these words,
62 and say: O Lord, Thou hast spoken concerning this place that Thou wilt cut it off so that there would be no one living in it, neither man nor beast, because it is to be an
63 everlasting waste. And when you have finished reading this scroll, tie a stone to it, and throw it into
64 the Euphrates, and say: Like this shall Babylon sink and no more rise because of the evil that I shall bring upon it, and they shall be wearied. Until here the words of Jeremiah.

Vv. 59-64. Seraiah, a brother of Baruch (ch. 32:12), was a "quiet prince," a prince of "resting place" (Is. 32:18), preparing in advance the royal quarters, a quartermaster. The purpose of Zedekiah's journey is not stated, perhaps he was eager to assure the king of his loyalty, or ask a favor, or was summoned to some festivity, or to explain the assembly of ambassadors at Jerusalem (ch. 27). "In a book," the numeral is added, one book; evidently ch. 50-51 are a compilation of all the oracles spoken by Jeremiah against Babylon. "Shalt see" (v. 61), rather, then see to it. He was to select an opportune occasion, perhaps in the company of a few trustworthy friends as witnesses, for the sinking of the scroll in the waters of the Euphrates. This was not a magic incantation, as Volz regards it (*loc. cit.,* p. 442) and on this account denies Jeremiah's authorship, but a symbolical act by divine command, foretelling the doom of Babylon, total destruction. Having sunk the scroll, Seraiah was to repeat the last word of v. 58: They shall be wearied! The final statement of v. 64 declares ch. 52 to be a later supplement.

X. Appendix

CHAPTER 52

The concluding chapter of Part II (ch. 52), in the form of an appendix to the entire book, once more tells the story of Zedekiah, the last king of Judah, the destruction of Jerusalem, and Jehoiachin's release from prison.

With the exception of a few changes this chapter agrees with 2 Kings 24: 18—25: 30; Jer. 52: 28-30 is added, while 2 Kings 25: 22-26 is naturally omitted in Jeremiah (cp. Jeremiah 40 and 41). Nebuchadnezzar's name is written with "n" in 2 Kings, with "r" in Jeremiah 52. In v. 10 the slaying of the princes is added; in vv. 19-23 a number of specific statements concerning the Temple vessels and pillars are made, not found in 2 Kings 24 and 25 nor in the chapters describing the building of the Temple (1 Kings 6 and 7).

We cannot determine whether this chapter was added by Baruch, or some other person, or by Jeremiah himself, who may have lived to see Jehoiachin delivered from prison by Evil-Merodach, the son and successor of Nebuchadnezzar, 562—561. According to one tradition, Jeremiah was slain by the Jews in Egypt (Jerome, *adv. Iovidianum* 2: 37; Tertullian, *adv. Gnost.* 8); according to a Jewish tradition, Nebuchadnezzar, after his conquest of Egypt, 568/7, transported Jeremiah and Baruch to Babylon, where Jeremiah died peacefully. (*Seder olam rabba* 26.)

---

1. The Capture of Jerusalem, Zedekiah Blinded and Deported, Vv. 1-11

1 Twenty-one years old was Zedekiah when he began to rule, and he ruled eleven years in Jerusalem. The name of his mother was Hamital, a daughter of Jeremiah of
2 Libnah. And he did what was evil in the sight of the LORD, like all
3 that Jehoiakim had done. For by the anger of the LORD, Jerusalem and Judah were doomed even to rejection from His presence. And Zedekiah rebelled against the king
4 of Babel. In the ninth year of his reign, in the tenth month, on the tenth of the month, Nebuchadrezzar, king of Babylon, came with his entire army against Jerusalem and encamped against her and built bulwarks round about against
5 her. So the city remained under siege unto the eleventh year of
6 King Zedekiah. In the fourth month, on the ninth of the month, famine became so severe in the city that the populace had no more
7 bread. Then the city was breached, and all the soldiers fled and left the city at night by way of the gate between the two walls, which lies close to the garden of the king (the Chaldeans had completely surrounded the city), and went by the
8 way of the Arabah. But the Chaldean army pursued the king, overtaking Zedekiah in the steppe of Jericho, while all his army was
9 scattered from him. Then they captured the king and brought him to the king of Babylon at Riblah in the land of Hamath, and he

pronounced judgment against him.
10 And the king of Babylon slew the sons of Zedekiah before his eyes and slew also the princes of Judah
11 at Riblah. Then he put out the eyes of Zedekiah and bound him with two fetters of brass. So the king of Babylon brought him to Babylon and kept him in prison till the day of his death.

2. The Sack of the City, Vv. 12-23

12 In the fifth month on the tenth of the month — this was the nineteenth year of King Nebuchadrezzar, the king of Babylon — came Nebuzaradan, the commander of the body-guards, who stood before the king
13 of Babylon, to Jerusalem and set fire to the house of the LORD and to the royal palace; and all the houses of Jerusalem and every
14 large house he burnt with fire. All the walls round about Jerusalem the whole army of Chaldeans, led by the commander of the body-
15 guard, tore down. But some of the poorest of the people, and the rest of the people remaining in the city, and the deserters who had deserted to the king of Babylon, and the rest of the people, Nebuzaradan, the commander of the bodyguard,
16 deported. But Nebuzaradan, the commander of the bodyguard, per-mitted some of the poorest in the land to remain as vintagers and
17 farmers. And the Chaldeans broke the bronze pillars of the house of the LORD, the bases and the bronze sea in the house of the LORD, and carried all this bronze
18 to Babylon. They also took with them the pots, and shovels, and the snuffers, and the sprinkling bowls, and the forks, and all the bronze implements which they used for
19 the service. The commander of the bodyguard also took the pots, the basins, and the snuffers, and the sprinkling bowls, and the pots, and the candelabra, and the forks, and the cups, the gold as gold, the
20 silver as silver, and the two pillars, the one sea, and the twelve oxen of bronze which were under the bases, which King Solomon had made for the house of the LORD — one could not weigh all the bronze
21 of all these vessels. The pillars: Each pillar was eighteen cubits high, twelve cubits in circumfer-ence, and their thickness was four
22 fingers, hollow. At the top was a capital of bronze, and each capital was five cubits high, and round about the capital there was lattice-work and pomegranates, all of bronze. And the second also had similar [ornaments] and pome-
23 granates. There were ninety-six pomegranates on the sides. Round about the capital there were one hundred pomegranates.

On vv. 12-16 see Jer. 39:8-10; 2 Kings 25:8-12.

On vv. 17-23 cp. 2 Kings 25:13-17.

V. 13. "All the houses of the great men," rather, every large house. The king gave special orders to burn all large buildings. Only small homes, if any, escaped the general conflagration.

V. 23. "On a side," רוּחָה, "windward," on the side. The meaning "side" for רוּח is established by Ezek. 42:16-20. Sidewise, on the side, or sides, were ninety-six pomegranates; perhaps twenty-four on each side, and one more on each of the four corners, making a total of one hundred.

369

3. Other Officials Condemned to Death, Vv. 24-27

24 And the commander of the bodyguard took Seraiah, the chief priest, and Zephaniah, the second priest, and the three guards of the sill. 25 He also took out of the city a eunuch who was an overseer of the troops, and seven men who were the king's personal advisers, who had been found in the city, and the secretary of the chief of the army, who enrolled the people of the land, and sixty men of the people of the land who were found 26 in the city. And Nebuzaradan, the commander of the bodyguard, took them and brought them to the king 27 of Babel at Riblah. And the king of Babel scourged them and put them to death at Riblah in the land of Hamath and deported Judah from its land.

V. 24. "Keepers of the door," rather, of the sill, Temple guards, whose duty it was to prevent any disturbance or desecration of the Temple (cp. 2 Kings 12:10; 22:4; 23:4; Jer. 35:4). This term has nothing in common with the "doorkeeper" of Ps. 84:10, which designates one standing at the sill, a constant attendant at the worship.

4. Various Deportations by Nebuchadnezzar, Vv. 28-30

28 These are the people whom Nebuchadrezzar deported: In the seventh 29 year 3,023 Jews; in the eighteenth year of Nebuchadrezzar, from 30 Jerusalem 832. In the twenty-third year of Nebuchadrezzar, Nebusaradan, the commander of the bodyguard, deported Jews, 745 souls; all souls, 4,600.

Vv. 28-30. This is not a record of all deportations of Jews, nor of the sum total of all Jews deported by Nebuchadnezzar, but the number of deportations not recorded elsewhere. The first occurred in the seventh year of Nebuchadnezzar's rule, 598, the year of Jehoiakim's death. After defeating Jehoiakim, Nebuchadnezzar deported 3,023 Jews as a warning against further rebellions. When this warning was not heeded, Nebuchadnezzar returned and deported Jehoiachin and more than 10,000 people (2 Kings 24:11-16; Ezek. 1:2) in the eighth year of his rule. The second deportation (Jer. 52:29) occurred in the eighteenth year of Nebuchadnezzar and consisted probably of the fugitives who had deserted from Jerusalem to the camp of the Babylonian army (Jer. 38:2-4) and other captives, whom Nebuchadnezzar sent off to Babylon when he raised the siege to repel Pharaoh Hophra (Jer. 34:21-22; 37:5-11).

The third deportation took place in the twenty-third year of Nebuchadnezzar, four years after the destruction of Jerusalem, after the Jews had left the land for Egypt (Jeremiah 41—44). The circumstances are unknown. The dates and the sum total of these three deportations, 4,600, also prove that neither the deportation in the third year of Jehoiakim (Dan. 1:1ff.), nor that of Jehoiachin (2 Kings 24:11-16), nor that after Jerusalem's destruction (in the nineteenth year of Nebuchadnezzar (ch. 52:12), is included in this enumeration.

5. Jehoiachin Released from Prison and Honored, Vv. 31-34

31 And in the thirty-seventh year of the captivity of Jehoiachin, king of Judah, in the twelfth month, on the twenty-fifth day, Evil-Merodach, king of Babylon, in the second year of his reign elevated Jehoiachin, king of Judah, and released 32 him out of the prison house and spoke kindly to him and placed his throne above the thrones of kings which were with him in Babylon; 33 and he changed his prison clothes, and he ate his meals in his presence all the days of his life. And 34 as for his provision, a regular allowance was granted to him by the king of Babylon every day according to the needs of the day, until the day of his death, all the days of his life.

Evil-Merodach (Assyrian, Amel-Marduk), the son and successor of Nebuchadnezzar, ruled two years, 561—559, and was assassinated by the priestly party, who brought about the accession of Nergal-shar-usur, his brother-in-law (cp. Jer. 39:3), who ruled 559—555.

371

The Lamentations of Jeremiah

LAMENTATIONS

The Lamentations of Jeremiah

1. Name

In Hebrew Bibles the first word, אֵיכָה, "Ah, how!" serves as a superscription. The ancient rabbis called it קִינוֹת, dirges, lamentations (cp. 2 Sam. 1:17; Amos 8:10; Jer. 7:29; 9:10; etc.). The LXX translated this term *Threnoi*, the Latin version *Lamentationes*. The author laments the horrible destruction of Jerusalem and Judah in five odes.

2. Authorship

Ancient tradition names Jeremiah as the author of the hymns. The Septuagint prefaces the book with the statement: "And it came to pass after Israel was led into captivity and Jerusalem was destroyed, that Jeremiah sat weeping and lamented with this lamentation over Jerusalem, and said." The Talmud places Lamentations among the Ketubim, between Song of Songs and Daniel, and a few lines later states: "Jeremiah wrote his book, Kings, and Lamentation." (Baba Bathra, f. 15, 1, Rodkinson, *The Babylonian Talmud*, Vol. 7, pp. 44—45.) The Targum begins its transcription: "And Jeremiah the prophet and great priest." All the ancient church fathers regarded Jeremiah as the author. The first one to deny his authorship was Hermann von der Hardt, who in a pamphlet edited 1712 at Helmstaedt attributed the five hymns to Daniel, Shadrach, Meshach, Abednego, and King Jehoiachin. Modern interpreters refuse to acknowledge Jeremiah as the author. Usually ch. 2 and 4 are regarded as the oldest hymns, composed shortly after the destruction; ch. 5, ca. 530; ch. 1, some time after the destruction (Bewer, *Lit. of O. T.*); between 520 and 444 (Pfeiffer, *Introd. to O. T.*); in time of Deutero-Isaiah (Sellin, *Einleitung*); ch. 3, the latest, 529 (Sellin); before 538 (Eissfeldt); "low literary level, theological meditation, similarity to Psalm 119, tend to tip the scales in favor of third century" (Pfeiffer). The reasons advanced vary.

1) Diction and style not that of Jeremiah. Dean Plumptre, quoted in *The Bible Commentary* (Vol. V, p. 578), writes in refutation of this argument: "In both we meet once and again with the picture of the 'virgin daughter of Zion' sitting down in her shame and misery (Lam. 1:15; 2:13; Jer. 14:17). In both the prophet's eyes flow down with tears (Lam. 1:16; 2:11; 3:48-49; Jer. 9:1; 13:17; 14:17). In both there is the same haunting feeling of being surrounded with fears and terrors on every side (Lam. 2:22; Jer. 6:25; 46:5). In both the worst of all the evils under which they are suffering is the iniquity of the

prophets and the priests (Lam. 2:14; 4:13; Jer. 5:30-31; 14:13-14). The sufferer appeals for vengeance to the righteous Judge (Lam. 3:64-66; Jer. 11:20). Finally he bids the rival nations that exulted in the fall of Jerusalem prepare for a like desolation (Lam. 4:21; Jer. 49:2)."

It is a cheap subterfuge to explain these and many other similarities in the two books by declaring that the author or authors of Lamentations were, of course, acquainted with the Book of Jeremiah and wrote in similar style. While Lamentations contains a number of words not found in Jeremiah, or found only in a different form, or which express an idea for which Jeremiah uses different terms, this does not prove difference of authorship. Must a writer always employ the same vocabulary in every book he writes? It is a well-known fact that poetry often deliberately employs forms and terms different from those of prose, and that rhythm, or meter, or both, necessitate the choice of a word or form differing from that usually employed. As we shall see, there are so many similarities in diction and style and such uniformity of spirit pervading both books that they far outweigh the differences in vocabulary.

2) Nor does its position among the Ketubim argue against its authorship by Jeremiah. It contains neither history nor prophecy and therefore was very properly placed among the Ketubim by the same rabbis who declared Jeremiah to be its author (see p. 375). The LXX inserted Lamentations after the apocryphal Book of Baruch, which they appended to the Book of Jeremiah.

3. Structural Form

The book consists of five poems, four of which (ch. 1—4) are alphabetic acrostics. In ch. 1 and 2 each stanza, beginning with the appropriate letter, has three verses; in ch. 3 the three verses of each stanza begin with the same letter; in ch. 4 each stanza has two verses. Ch. 5, also consisting of twenty-two verses, is not arranged alphabetically. This acrostic form is found also in Psalms 9 and 10 (two verses to each letter, incompletely carried through); Psalm 25 (ו missing, two ר instead of ק, ר; פ repeated in concluding verse); Psalm 34 (ו missing and פ repeated); Psalm 37 (ע omitted, צ taking its places and reoccurring after פ); Psalms 111 and 112 (half verse to each letter); Psalm 119 (eight verses beginning with same letter); Psalm 145 (נ missing); Prov. 31:10-31. Lamentations 2, 3, 4, the פ precedes the ע, while ch. 1 has the usual order. The sacred poets were not slaves of form, but made use of this formal scheme only as long as the sequence of the alphabet suited the sequence of thought.

CHAPTER 1

I. Lamentation over the Ruin of Judah and Jerusalem

1. The Prophet's Lament, Vv. 1-11

1 How lonely does she sit, the city once crowded with people! She has become like a widow, once great among the nations! The princess among the provinces has become 2 a bondmaiden. Bitterly she weeps through the night, her tears upon her cheeks. No comforter for her among all her lovers! All her friends have betrayed her, have 3 become unto her opponents. She has gone into exile out of misery and hard labor. She dwells among the Gentiles, unable to find a resting place. All her pursuers have overtaken her within the narrows. 4 The roads to Zion are mourning, for there are none coming to the festival assemblies. All her gates are desolate. Her priests are sighing; her virgins sorrowful; and oh! 5 what bitterness is hers! Her oppressors have become her head! Her opponents are happy. For the LORD has made her sad because her transgressions were so many. Her children have gone into cap- 6 tivity before the oppressor. All her beauty has gone from the daughter of Zion. Her princes have become like harts that cannot find pastur- age and flee exhausted before the

7 hunter. Jerusalem remembers in the days of her affliction and wan- derings all the pleasant things which were hers since the days of old, while now her people have fallen into the hand of the op- pressor, and there is none to help her. The oppressors gaze at her and laugh at the cessation of all 8 activity. Jerusalem has greatly sinned, so that she has become filthy. All that had praised her despise her, for they see her nude- ness. Even she herself moans and 9 turns backward. Her filthiness is in her skirts! She did not consider her end, and so she fell to the astonishment of all! Not one com- forter has she! Behold, O LORD, my misery, for the enemy has be- 10 come haughty! The oppressor has spread out his hands on all that was dear to her. For she sees Gen- tiles coming out of her sanctuary, those of whom Thou hast com- manded that they should not come into the congregation that is Thine. 11 All her people are moaning, seeking bread. They give their cherished possessions for bread to revive themselves. Behold, O LORD, and take heed! For I am being despised!

Grammatical Notes

V. 7. "Miseries," מְרוּדֶיהָ. The word is variously rendered, LXX "expulsion," others "abasement" or "persecution," etc. The most plausible derivation seems to be from a root רוּד, to roam, wander (cp. Jer. 2:31, not "we are lords," but "we roam"). The plural used here occurs also Jer. 3:19, for which passage Ges.-Buhl offers the translation "unrest, vagrancy," an ab- stract plural. Is. 58:7 the plural is used in the concrete sense of homeless people, roaming about without a home. We take it as an abstract in our pas- sage, her wanderings, roamings; com- pare the legend of the Wandering Jew.

Vv. 1-2. Jeremiah laments the cruel oppression of Jerusalem by the enemy. V. 1 presents three contrasts in the form of an ascending (populous city; great, renowned, among nations; princess among

377

provinces) and descending climax (solitary, widow, tributary). Night and day her tears flow down her cheeks. Not a single comforter among all her former lovers that courted her assistance or whose aid she sought. They have turned against her, have become traitors and opponents, cruel oppressors. (Cp. Jer. 27:3ff., Egypt and other neighboring countries, allies of Judah, with 2 Kings 24:2; Ezek. 25:3, 6; Ps. 137:7; Lam. 4:21-22.)

V. 3. "Because of," rather, "out of," the miseries of war, famine, and pestilence (Jer. 15:2-3), servitude, hard labor, and vassalage, high taxes, and tributes paid to Necho (2 Kings 23:33) and to Nebuchadnezzar, the cruel oppressors had removed them from their homeland into a strange land, where they were war captives, exiles. They dwell among Gentiles, far from the land of their heritage, God's own land, in a land where they could find no rest, disturbed by false prophets (Jer. 29:8-9), harassed by worries and anxieties, depressed by homesickness, surrounded by idolaters; no temple, no sacrifice; outcasts! And not the least cause of restlessness was the knowledge that their transgressions had brought on their destruction. Their evil conscience gave them no rest (cp. Jer. 2:19; 4:18). Their captivity is inescapable. The pursuers have overtaken them "in the straits," a figure of speech taken from the narrow passes or defiles which make rapid flight impossible, the fugitives falling an easy prey to the pursuing forces.

Vv. 4-5. "The ways mourn," personification. "Solemn feasts" (cp. Ex. 23:14-17), including such other assemblies as were called for on special occasions (2 Chron. 30:22). Lev. 23:2-3 the weekly Sabbaths are named first in the list of "the feasts of the Lord." Pilgrims traveled on all the roads leading to Jerusalem for these festivals (cp. Ps. 42: 1-4; 63:1-3). All these festival days and seasons were no longer celebrated at Jerusalem, for the people were gone and the city and Temple destroyed. On "gates" see Jer. 1:15, p. 28 f. The priests mourned, because they could no longer serve in the Temple; the maidens, because they could no longer sing their joyous hymns or play their instruments (Ex. 15:20; Judg. 21:19-21; Ps. 68:24-26; cp. Jer. 31:13; 33:11). "The chief" (v. 5), cp. Deut. 28:44b in contrast to 28:13. The enemy mockingly rejoices over the misfortunes Judah endured in divine judgment for her trespasses, while little children are forced to walk the long, weary road to Babylon by their hardhearted oppressors. How many perished on the way! Wherever the prophet looks, he sees heartbreaking cruelty and oppression.

Vv. 6-11. The loss of all her splendor. All her "beauty," pride, glory, splendor — gone! "Princes," see Jer. 1:18, have been taken captive or slain (v. 6). "Pleasant things" (v. 7), precious possessions, objects of delight, spiritual or material (cp. 2 Chron. 36:19), "goodly vessels," in homes and Temple. "Her people" (v. 7), named first, v. 1, gone! Her "helpers," conspicuous by their absence. "Sabbaths" (v. 7), literally, "cessations," *mishbatteha,* a play of words (of which Jeremiah is so fond) on "Sabbath." They had refused to keep the divinely appointed day of rest and cessation from labor (Jer. 17:19-27), now in fulfillment of Lev. 26:33-43; Jer. 7:34, a complete cessation of all activity in homes, business places, courts, Temple, domestic and foreign trade, had set in (cp. 2 Chron. 36:21). The silence of death and desolation shrouded city and country. "All that honored her," her admirers and adulators, gone! (V. 8.) Her comforters gone! (V. 9.) Once more, "her pleasant things" gone! (V. 10 a.) Her sanctuary defiled by Gentiles "entering in," literally, "coming out of" the Temple, carrying out the precious vessels and furnishings (Jer. 52: 17-23); Gentiles uncircumcised, who were not even permitted to be members of the congregation (cp. Gen. 17:14; Ex. 4:24-26; 12:47-48), much less to enter the sanctuary (Lev. 16:1-2; Num. 3:10, 38; 16:40; 18:7, 22), these Gentiles had laid their hands on the holy vessels, defiling them, had entered the Holy Place and even the Holy of Holies, desecrating them, and then they had burnt them. The Sanctuary, God's dwelling place (Ex. 25:8), the most precious possession of Judah, gone! What little of their material possessions they could carry with them, they had to give to the enemy for bread (v. 11) and water (ch. 5:4).

V. 7. "Miseries," see Grammatical Notes. They had loved to roam (Jer. 2:31). Now they are condemned to roam. In her wanderings, scattered throughout the earth (Jer. 9:16; 18:17; 30:11), afflicted and homeless Judah too late remembers "all her pleasant things," all her precious possessions she had in the days of old, gracious gifts of her Lord, to be cherished highly. She had despised both the gifts and the Giver. Now nothing remains but affliction and wanderings and grievous sins (v. 8), filthy sins, defiling her skirts (v. 9; cp. Jer. 2:34), manifest in spite of her self-righteousness, her formal worship, her hypocritical boasting (Jer. 7:4ff.), sins unforgiven. Stripped naked of all her splendor, only filth is seen (cp. Ezek. 16:1-43), filth so horrible, and nudeness so abhorrent, that not only her former admirers despise her (v. 8), but she herself moans and turns her back in shame,

379

aghast at her own ugliness. "She is removed," literally, she has become uncleanness (cp. Lev. 12: 2, 5; 15: 9; Lam. 1: 17).

V. 9. Judah had not "remembered her last end," had not believed the possibility of fulfillment of God's threats voiced already at the establishment of the Sinaitic Covenant (Ex. 20: 5, 7) and repeated throughout the centuries (Deut. 28: 15 ff.; Jer. 11: 1-17; 25: 1-11; etc.). Now she experienced God's veracity (Num. 23: 19; 1 Sam. 15: 29). "She came down wonderfully," literally, plural of same word used Ex. 15: 11, "wonders." As Israel's deliverance out of Egypt had been a divine miracle, so Judah's ruin is a wonder, inconceivable, beyond belief. The plural emphasizes the bewildering nature of Judah's destruction. In her sorrow she has no comforter. Forsaken! Therefore Jeremiah, keenly feeling Judah's affliction as his own, as the spokesman of the believing remnant and the teacher of all his people, appeals to the Covenant God to behold their affliction. "Magnified himself," has become haughty, overbearing. On this sense of "magnify" see Ps. 38: 16 (M. T., v. 17); 41: 9 (M. T., v. 10); Jer. 48: 26, 42. On the idea cp. Is. 10: 5-15; Hab. 1: 6-11, 15-17. And he closes his lament with the fervent petition v. 11b; cp. Luke 18: 13. "Vile," utterly despised and despicable.

---

2. The Lament of the City, Vv. 12-22

12 Is it nothing to you, all you that pass by the way? Behold and see if there be any sorrow like my sorrow which has been inflicted on me, with which the LORD has saddened me in the day of His 13 furious anger! From on high He has sent fire into my bones, discomfiting them. He has spread a net for my feet, He has turned me back, He has made me desolate, sorrowful all the day. Bound is 14 the yoke of my transgressions by His hand. They are knit together; they have come upon my neck. My strength has fallen! The Lord has given me into the hands of 15 those I cannot resist. The Lord in my midst has trodden down all my mighty men, He has called an assembly against me, to crush my young men. The Lord has trodden a wine press for the virgin daugh- 16 ter of Judah. For these things I am weeping, my eye, my eye flows with water, for far from me is a comforter, a consoler! My children are stunned, for the enemy 17 is too strong. Zion spreads out her hands. No comforter for her! The LORD has given command concerning Jacob that his neighbors are to be his oppressors. Jerusalem has become abominable among 18 them. Righteous is He, the LORD, for I have rebelled against His Word! Hear, all ye nations, and behold my sorrow. My maidens and young men go into exile! 19 I called to my lovers, but they repudiated me. My priests and my elders perished in the city where they sought food for themselves 20 to sustain their lives. Behold, O LORD, how oppressed I am! My spirit is troubled, my heart is perturbed, because I have so obstinately rebelled. In the streets the

21 sword slays my children; in the home, death! They hear how I moan! I have no comforter! All my enemies have heard of my trouble; they are glad that Thou hast done it, hast brought the day Thou hadst proclaimed. But they 22 shall be like me! May all their wickedness come upon them and afflict them as Thou hast afflicted me for all my transgressions! For great is my sorrow, and I am sick at heart!

Grammatical Notes

V. 17. "As a menstruous woman," נִדָּה = filthiness, menstrual uncleanness, Lev. 12: 2, 5; 15: 19f.; here defilement by idolatry and sin service.

V. 12. "Is it nothing to you?" literally, Not to you? אֵל is here used in the sense of "pertaining to," to be one's business, or concern (cp. 1 Sam. 23: 20), "our part," our concern (Ezra 4: 3; Micah 3: 1). The phrase is to be regarded as interrogatory: Is it not of concern to you? Do you not care? In her anguish, Jerusalem calls on all passers-by for pity and commiseration. Can they imagine a smiting more painful and shameful, a punishment more severe than hers? And the deepest stroke that pierced her was the stroke that Justice gave, was the fact that the God of the Covenant Himself had turned against her in the fury of His anger; that it was a smiting she had fully deserved.

V. 13. From heaven above He had sent the fiery bolts of His wrath penetrating the very marrow of their bones, leaving them hopelessly enfeebled, and on earth He had spread the nets for their feet in which the enemies caught them, from which there was no hope of escape.

Vv. 14-15. By His hand a yoke was harnessed upon them, composed of their sins twisted together, knitted together, unforgiven sins that rise higher and higher upon their necks, holding them in their clutch, weighing heavier every moment upon their conscience. (Cp. Ps. 38: 4f.; Ezra 9: 6.) In just punishment of their sins the Lord has surrendered them to the cruelties of an irresistible foe, irresistible not because of his strength, but because Judah has no longer that Covenant God on her side who had promised Lev. 26: 7-8; Deut. 28: 7, and threatened Lev. 26: 17; Deut. 28: 25. Note: In vv. 14 and 15 Kittel accepts the reading Jehovah (LORD), found in many Mss., instead of Adonai (Lord). "In my midst" according to position and accents is to be connected with "the Lord." It is repentant Judah speaking. Yet the Lord in her midst is not only the God of infinite mercy, but likewise the Lord of unalterable holiness and justice. He has rejected her "mighty men" who had forsaken the Lord and exalted themselves

381

above His Word and will. Therefore the Lord had called an assembly, a festival gathering (cp. v. 22; Lev. 23: 4), joyful not for Judah, but for her enemies; an assembly "against" her, to shatter her young men (ch. 2: 21 f.). He has trampled under foot as in a wine press the virgin daughter Judah, who was once the virgin pure and undefiled, a daughter loved by the Lord.

Vv. 16-17. These judgments of the Lord are the cause of her tears and unconsolable sorrow (v. 16). Yet she confesses that she had deserved to be punished because she who was to serve as an example of holiness (Deut. 4: 5-9; Lev. 11: 44) had become filthiness (cp. v. 8), "a menstruous woman."

Vv. 18-22. Judah acknowledges the righteousness of God and her own guilt. Yet the very fact that she, the nation so highly honored as to have the Lord dwelling in her midst, had rebelled against Him and lost her precious possessions, causes her wounds to reopen, her tears once more to flow in unconsolable sorrow (vv. 18-19). She is brokenhearted because of her rebellion and the cruelties inflicted upon her by an unrelenting enemy who, after slaying her people in the streets and in the homes, rejoices over the ruin the Lord had sent (vv. 20-21a). Yet still trusting in His justice, she appeals to the Lord to avenge the injustices inflicted upon her by the cruel enemy merely to satisfy his own bloodthirstiness (vv. 21b-22). This prayer is in keeping with God's prophecy (Is. 10: 12-21; Hab. 2: 5-17; Jer. 25: 12-14).

II. The Lord Is the Only Savior

1. The Lord's Severe Judgment, Vv. 1-10

1 How has the Lord in His wrath covered the daughter of Zion with a cloud! He has cast down from heaven to earth the glory of Israel and did not remember the footstool of His feet on the day of His 2 wrath! The Lord has devoured without mercy all the habitations of Jacob. He has thrown down in His fury the strongholds of the daughter of Judah, has struck them to the ground; He has defiled the 3 kingdom and its princes. He has cut off in the fury of His wrath every horn of Israel. He has drawn back His right hand before the enemy. There is a burning in Jacob as a flaming fire which de- 4 vours round about. He has bent His bow like an enemy, standing with His right hand like an opponent. And He has slain all that was delightful to the eyes. In the tents of the daughter of Zion He has poured out like fire His fury. 5 The Lord has become like an enemy. He has devoured Israel, devoured all his palaces, destroyed his strongholds, and heaped upon the daughter of Judah lamenta- 6 tion and lament. He has violently torn down His tent like that of a garden; He has destroyed His meeting place; the LORD has caused festival and Sabbath to be forgotten in Zion. He has repudiated in the heat of His anger both 7 king and priest. The Lord has rejected His altar; He has abhorred His sanctuary. He has surrendered into the power of the enemy the walls of her palaces. They shouted in the house of the LORD 8 as on a festival day. The LORD had determined to destroy the wall of the daughter of Zion. He stretched out the measuring line; He did not withdraw His hand from destruction. He caused rampart and wall to mourn, together 9 they languish. Her gates have sunk to the ground; He has destroyed and broken her bars. Her king and her princes are among the Gentiles without the Law; even her prophets do not find a vision 10 from the LORD. The elders of the daughter of Zion sit on the ground, are silent, heap dust upon their heads, have put on sackcloth; the virgins of Jerusalem bow their heads low to the ground.

Grammatical Notes

V. 4. "In the tabernacle" is to be connected with the following clause and a period placed after "to the eye."

V. 6. His tabernacle. שֹׂכּוֹ occurs only here; some translate "hedge," "fence," "enclosure," or "that which is fenced in"; others regard it as a variant of סֹך, hut, tent (Ps. 27:5; 76:3), or thicket (Jer. 25:38). Whatever its exact meaning, it is certain that the Temple is meant. "As if it were of a garden," כְּגַן, either, as the A. V., an abbreviated simile, referring to a hut or shed erected in an orchard, or, as Keil prefers, as a garden or orchard is destroyed when it no longer serves its purpose. The use of the term "violently taken away" favors the latter interpretation, since it is not the ease of taking away that is to be stressed, but the anger, violence, which prompts the destruction.

Vv. 1-10. The prophet almost exhausts the possibilities of language in describing the enmity, the fierce wrath, the hatred, of the

383

Lord, the God of absolute holiness. Nothing, absolutely nothing is spared. "All the horn of Israel," all strength, every means of defense, is cut off by the Lord (v. 3), and all that was pleasant to the eye (v. 4), on which her eyes feasted, all the precious possessions enumerated here and including all her clothing and fineries (Jer. 4:30; Is. 3:16-26) have been "slain" by the Lord, the adversary of Judah. "Slain" is used here in the wider sense of complete destruction (cp. Ps. 78:47). Zion (vv. 1, 4, 6, 8, 10), and Israel (vv. 1, 3, 5), and Jacob (vv. 2, 3), and Judah (vv. 2, 5), and Jerusalem (v. 10) destroyed, swallowed up, from the outermost ramparts and walls (v. 8) and gates (v. 9) to the habitations (v. 2) and palaces (vv. 5, 7), and even to His sanctuary (v. 7), His altar (v. 7), yea, His footstool, the Ark of the Covenant (v. 1). All given into the hand of the enemy, polluted, destroyed! Kingdom and king and princes (vv. 2, 6, 9), and priests (v. 6), and prophets (v. 9), and elders and virgins (v. 10), all rejected, polluted, despised by the Lord! His "tabernacle," His Temple, no longer serving its purpose, violently destroyed (v. 6). His "meeting places," rather "feasts," festival assemblies (same word as "solemn feasts" in this verse), destroyed by Him; and so completely that festival seasons and Sabbaths were forgotten, were no longer celebrated in Zion, where on every Sabbath and on every solemn feast crowds of people had gathered in the city and Temple. The Law, the *Torah,* is no more (v. 9). The specifically Jewish Law, which constituted the basis of God's covenant with Israel with its many ceremonial and ritual stipulations, was practically abolished with the destruction of the Temple, where alone the sacrifice, the purifications, the service prescribed by the Law could be carried out. The Lord abhorred His sanctuary (v. 7), defiled and desecrated as it was by idolatrous worship (2 Kings 21:2ff., 21; 23:4ff.), and hypocritical lip service (Jer. 7:3-11). Therefore He left this house (Ezek. 11:22-23), surrendered it to the enemies, whose shoutings, while sacking and destroying the Temple (v. 7), were no more offensive to the Lord than the idolatrous and hypocritical hymns and prayers of those who professed to be His people.

2. In Vain Are All Human Efforts at Consolation, Vv. 11-16

11 My eyes are spent with tears; my spirit is anguished; my liver is poured out on the ground for the ruin of the daughter of Zion, for babes and sucklings fainting away
12 in the city squares. They cry to their mothers: "Where is corn and wine?" while they faint away like the mortally wounded in the city squares, while their souls are poured out at the bosom of their
13 mothers. What shall I take as an example for you? To what shall I compare you, O daughter of Jerusalem? To what shall I liken you in order to comfort you,

O virgin daughter of Zion? For vast as the ocean is your ruin! 14 Who shall heal you? Your prophets have divined absurd falsehoods for you. They have not disclosed to you your iniquity in order to restore your prosperity; but they divined for you false burdens and 15 expulsions. All who pass along the road clap their hands at you. They hiss and wag their head at the daughter of Jerusalem. "Is this the city that was called perfect in beauty, the joy of all the 16 earth?" All your enemies open their mouths wide against you, hiss, and gnash their teeth. They say: "We have swallowed her up! Ah, this is the day we hoped for; we have found it! We have seen it!"

Vv. 11-12. In sincere sympathy with his sorrowing brethren and sisters the prophet weeps bitter tears. "Liver," like the bowels, is the seat of emotion. He is deeply moved at the scenes of anguish he beholds, particularly the slow, horrible death of starvation to which the innocent babes and sucklings must succumb. He hears their ever-repeated (imperfect) cry for food which ever remains unanswered (v. 12). He sees them lying on the street corners, abandoned by their despairing mothers; he sees others gasping out their souls at the bosom of their mothers, whose tenderest love cannot keep them from starving.

V. 13. "What thing shall I take to witness for thee," testify, say to you for your instruction and comfort? Search as he will, he cannot find any tragedy equaling the "breach," the smashing ruin, vast as the unlimited ocean, of Zion, a ruin beyond human aid. To him she still is the virgin daughter of Zion, no matter how filthy she has become.

V. 14. While Judah is guilty, one of the chief causes of her ruin are the false prophets, whose lying oracles encouraged the people to continue in their wickedness and hypocrisy. Frank exposure and reproof of their sins might have helped to avert the destruction. "Vain," lying, without foundation, deceptive, and "foolish," unsalted (Job 6:6), unsavory, insipid, silly; the two words are found also Ezek. 13:6-11, 14, 15, where the second term is used to denote "untempered" mortar, i. e., whitewash, which will not and cannot hold the stones together, cannot prevent the wall from collapsing. Folly to use whitewash for this purpose, and wickedness, if used to deceive people. Ezekiel 13 is the best commentary on our passage. "Banishment," literally, "expulsions," the plural is intensive; the prophet had threatened that they would be "driven out" of the land (Jer. 27:10, 15, same root as here). Luther: "whereby they preached you out of the land" (zum Lande hinaus).

Vv. 15-16. "A union of scorn, hatred, and exultation, . . . the intensity of which is shown by the heaping up of unconnected words" (*The Bible Commentary*). "The perfection of beauty," cp. Ps. 50:2 (Ezek. 27:3 used of Tyre, and Ezek. 28:12 of Tyre's king); "the joy of the whole earth," cp. Ps. 48:3 (A. V., v. 2). So men had called her, so God Himself had called her. In ridiculing this expression the enemies ridicule the Lord God of Israel. This profanation of God's holy name and city was caused by Judah's wickedness (cp. Ezek. 36: 20-21), yet it seemed to the Gentiles a proof that Jehovah was either too weak or too hardhearted to come to the rescue of the city of His Temple.

3. Only the Lord Can Help. Turn to Him! Vv. 17-19

17 The LORD has carried out what He had planned. He has fulfilled His Word which He decreed in the days of old. He has thrown down without mercy. He has let the enemy rejoice over you. He has exalted the power of your oppres-
18 sors. Their heart cried out to the Lord. O wall of the daughter of Zion! Let your tears run down like a stream day and night! Give yourself no rest. Let not the pupils
19 of your eyes cease! Arise! Cry out in the night, at the beginning of the watches! Pour out your heart like water before the Lord! Lift up your hands to Him for the life of your children, who faint for hunger at every street corner!

V. 17. While the enemies malignantly rejoiced because their plans and ardent hopes had been fulfilled, the destruction was due not to their power and cunning, but was the Lord's fulfillment of His age-old threat "commanded," decreed, Deut. 28:15ff., the long-delayed execution of which had now come.

V. 18. Therefore the Lord alone can help, and therefore their hearts, the hearts of the Jews, cry to the Lord. In a bold personification the prophet calls upon the very walls of Jerusalem, the heaps of ruin, to let their tears flow day and night, as long as they lie in ruins, to continue their pleadings to the Lord for reconstruction until He would hear. A similar personification as in v. 8; ch. 1:4; Is. 14:31. "Rest," פוגת, occurs only here, denotes the torpor or numbness following excessive grief. "Apple of thine eye," literally, the daughter of your eye (cp. Ps. 17:8), perhaps so called because the pupil is the dearest and tenderest part of the eye. Yet it should not be given any respite, not allowed to cease its anguished grief.

V. 19. The prophet's urgent plea that Judah call on the Lord in submissive, penitent prayer. Let "the beginning of the watches" (three night watches, sunset to ten, ten to two, two to sunrise) find you praying to the Lord, particularly for the innocent babes.

4. The People's Prayer, Vv. 20-22

20 Behold, O LORD, and consider to whom Thou hast done this! Shall women eat their offspring, their babes tenderly nursed? Shall priest and prophet be slain in the sanc-

21 tuary of the Lord? On the ground in the streets lie young and old. My virgins and young men have fallen by the sword. Thou hast slain them in the day of Thine anger! Thou hast killed them with-

22 out mercy. Thou hast asked as to a feast day my terrors round about. There was not one that escaped and remained in the day of the LORD's anger. Those that I had tenderly nursed and brought up, my enemy has consumed.

V. 20. The prophet teaches them how to approach God. Vv. 20-22 remind strongly of Jer. 14:17-19. They are to present their sorrows to the Lord, who, though just now manifesting Himself as the holy and just Judge, still remains unalterably the God of grace and loving-kindness (Ex. 34:6-7). If anyone, He can and will help. He is asked to consider that this is His people (cp. Ex. 32:11-13). His judgments have caused His people to sink below the level of heathen morality, to cannibalism. Shall that continue? Priests and prophets, called and anointed by Thee, are killed in Thy Temple! Young and old, male and female, even babes and sucklings hast Thou slain! Thou hast surrounded us with terror round about! (Jer. 6:25; 20:3, 10; 46:5; 49:29.) The terrors prophesied by the prophet (hence "my terrors") had now been assembled by the Lord in the concrete form of the enemies and the accompanying sword, and famine, and pestilence, and death — horrors called by the Lord as to a festival banquet (cp. ch. 1:15). Thou hast done this in the day of Thine anger! Jehovah, hast Thou forgotten Thy grace? Shall our children continue to be consumed? On this note of seemingly hopeless sorrow the prayer ends. Will the Lord hear?

The prophet has to do with a people, most of whom were impenitent, hardened in their sin. See Jer. 44:1-30. His first duty was to bring them to a knowledge of their wickedness and of the unalterable justice of God in His dealings with them. God, whose covenant they had broken, remains faithful to the stipulations of the covenant, and as He has fulfilled His promises even when they had not deserved it, so He now fulfills His threats by sending judgments harsh and severe, but long overdue. Humble yourselves under His mighty hand, which now punishes you and which alone can help. Surrender to Him unconditionally whether He kill or make alive (Deut. 32:39). Only in hearts that are contrite will the High and Lofty One that inhabiteth eternity, whose name is holy, dwell to revive the spirit of the humble, to revive the heart of the contrite ones, Is. 57:15.

III. The Mercy of the Lord the Only Source of Comfort

1. The Calamity Is So Great that No Sorrow Seems Adequate and No Comfort Possible, Vv. 1-18

1 I am the man who has seen afflic-
2 tion by the rod of His wrath. Me
He has led and made me walk in
3 darkness without light. Alone
against me He keeps on turning
4 His hand all the day long. He has
worn away my flesh and my skin,
5 broken my bones. He has fenced
me in; He has surrounded me with
6 poison and anguish. He has made
me dwell in dark places like those
7 dead forever. He has fenced me in
on all sides, and I cannot get out.
He has loaded me with fetters of
8 brass. Even when I keep on calling
and crying for help, He refuses to
9 hear my prayer. He has fenced in
my ways with hewn stones, and
10 my paths He has twisted. He is
to me like a bear lying in wait,
11 a lion in ambush. My ways He
has made crooked and torn me in
12 pieces and made me desolate. He
bent His bow and set me up as
13 a target for His arrows. He sent
into my vitals the shafts of His
14 quiver. I have become the
laughingstock of all my people,
15 their song all day long. He has
sated me with bitterness and has
16 given me wormwood to drink. He
has crushed my teeth with gravel
stones, He has pressed me down
17 into ashes. He has deprived my
soul of peace; I have forgotten
18 what blessings are. I said: Perished
is my strength and my hope from
the LORD!

Who speaks here? It is an individual, "I" (vv. 1-24), changing to "we" (vv. 22, 40-47), again to "I" (vv. 48-66). Keil quotes Ewald: "Who is this individual that laments, and voices his thoughts, and pleads, whose 'I' almost imperceptively, yet just at the right moment, changes to 'we'? O man, this is your own picture! All are now to speak and think as the speaker does!" It is not every individual Jew that speaks here. Nor is it Jeremiah weeping in bitter grief over the injustices committed against him by his countrymen, their mockeries, their insults, their persecutions, particularly his imprisonment in the dungeon (Jer. 38:6). It is Jeremiah as an individual member of the nation lamenting the ruin of the people and the city he loved. The sorrow that had come upon the nation he felt keenly and bitterly as his own sorrow, a judgment of God which sorely tried his faith, which, try as he might, he could not understand. Yet he speaks here at the same time as the divinely appointed prophet and shepherd of his people in order to teach them and future generations how to pray in times of agony and extreme anguish and heart-rending experiences. He teaches that lesson which he had to learn (Jer. 12; 15:15-21; 20:7-18), which Job, and David (Psalms 38, 143), and Asaph (Psalm 73) had to learn, to humble oneself under the majestic and mighty hand of the Lord of holiness and justice, to confess one's sinfulness and depravity, yet in believing contemplation of the compassionate loving-kindness of this same Lord to ask Him for His help.

Vv. 1-3. In his deep sorrow the prophet sees and feels only the rod of God's wrath. His way is wrapped in dense darkness, he cannot understand God's judgments (Amos 5:18; Job 23:9; 30:26). No matter what he began, God's hand was against him, frustrated every plan. Here he plainly speaks as the representative of his people.

Vv. 4-6. In days he has aged by years (v. 4; cp. Job 7:5; 16:8; 30:30). "Builded against me" (v. 5), as an enemy builds ramparts against a city. "Gall," a poison plant (Jer. 8:14; 9:15); "travail," anguish, agony. "Dead of old" (v. 6; cp. Ps. 143:3), eternally dead. (Cp. Is. 26:14: the wicked shall not live again, rise only to eternal death, Is. 66:24, with Is. 26:19: Thy dead men shall live.)

Vv. 7-9. "Hedged about," closed off the way with an insurmountable wall, weighted me down with heavy chains of brass, unbreakable. No possibility of escape! (Job 3:23; 19:8.) No answer to his cries (Job 30:20). V. 9a repeats v. 7a. "Hewn stone," carefully prepared, fitting close together, a well-made, strong wall. When he tried to look for a different way, he found himself in a maze, walking on paths leading he knew not where.

Vv. 10-11. Suddenly, like a bear or lion (cp. Job 10:16; Amos 5:19) lying in ambush, the Lord seized him and tore him in pieces. Vv. 1-12 a vivid picture of the last days of Jerusalem, the frustration of all their plans, their panicky efforts to find some means of escape instead of surrendering unconditionally to Nebuchadnezzar, as the Lord had time and again demanded Jer. 27:12-13; 28:14; 34:2-3; 38:17-18).

Vv. 12-13. He feels that God has become his opponent. "Arrow," a common metaphor for persecution, tribulation (Ps. 38:1-2; Job 6:4; 16:12-14).

V. 14. Jeremiah speaks as representative of the believing individual who was ridiculed by his people, the mass of whom disregarded and mocked all warnings and every warner.

Vv. 15-16. His food was bitterness, anguish, until he was sated, nauseated; his drink, wormwood (see Jer. 23:15) to the point of intoxication. "Gravel stones," grit, either a proverbial expression similar to Matt. 7:9, or referring to the grit of the ashes which filled his mouth, when he was pressed down into the ashes. Both expressions signify deepest humiliation and sorrow, cp. "My bread has turned into stone."

Vv. 17-18. Overwhelmed by the catastrophic destruction, he feels as if that dreadful curse of God (Jer. 16:5b) applies to him also. "Forgot prosperity." He no longer knows what good is, what it means to enjoy the blessings of life. Gone away, strayed, is his strength, his very vitality, his hope, his expectant waiting, from the Lord! His loss is named first, and "Jehovah" last. Yet the very mentioning of this name in the deepest depth of misery and hopelessness restores both hope and confident strength in the Lord. He experiences the truth of Prov. 18:10. To this Lord he turns in confident prayer (vv. 19-39).

2. Remembering the Unchanging Mercy of the Lord of the Covenant, the Believer Regains His Confident Trust in the Lord, Vv. 19-39

19 Remember my affliction and my wanderings, poison and anguish!
20 Whenever my soul remembers, it
21 becomes depressed. This I will call to mind; therefore I begin to hope.
22 The mercies of the LORD are the reason why we are not consumed, for His compassions never fail.
23 They are new every morning, great
24 is Thy faithfulness. My portion is the LORD, says my soul, therefore
25 will I hope in Him! Good is the LORD to him who waits for Him,
26 to the soul that seeks Him. It is good both to wait, and that silently,
27 for the salvation of the LORD. It is good for a man that he should
28 bear a yoke in his youth. Let him sit alone and remain silent, for He
29 has laid it upon him. Let him place his mouth into the dust, per-
30 haps there still is hope. Let him offer his cheek to him that smiteth him; let him eat his fill of dis-
31 grace. For the Lord will not reject
32 forever. For even if He afflicts, He also has compassion according to the abundance of His loving-
33 kindness; for His heart is not set upon afflicting and grieving the
34 children of men. To grind under foot all the prisoners of the earth,
35 to distort a man's judgment before
36 the Most High, to subvert man in his cause, the Lord does not ap-
37 prove. Who is there that speaks, and it is done, while the Lord has
38 not decreed it? Do not the evils and the good proceed from the
39 mouth of the Most High? Wherefore does man that lives complain? Everyone for his sins!

Grammatical Notes

V. 20 is a conditional sentence (cp. G.-K. 159c). The imperfect תִּזְכּר denotes the repeated memory, ever and again arising to disturb him, the absolute infinitive זָכוֹר the intensity of the act. Whenever the memory of my troubles grips me, I become depressed. שׁוּחַ does not mean to be humbled, but to sink, be sunk (cp. Prov. 2:18; Ps. 44:26).

V. 19. The four terms express the depth of his sorrow. "Misery" here in the sense of "vagrancy" (cp. ch. 1:7). "Gall" in the sense of poison (Deut. 32:32, 33; Job 20:16), capping the climax.

Vv. 20-21. The more I think of my sorrow, the deeper I sink into despair. "What can these anxious cares avail us, These never-ceasing moans and sighs? . . . Our cross and trials do but press The heavier for our bitterness" (*The Lutheran Hymnal*, 518:2). "This," i. e., the uselessness of constantly brooding over my losses, instead of thinking of the Lord, "I recall," I will bring back, "to my heart." "Therefore have I hope." The imperfect is nascent, I begin to hope, and gradually grow in hope, rather than lose myself and my Lord in useless lamentations.

V. 22. "Mercies," חֶסֶד; the singular, loving-kindness, grace, favor, unselfish, self-forgetting love; the plural used here denotes the manifestations or evidences of this grace. "Compassions," pity, רַחֲמִים, sympathetic love and kindness especially toward the helpless, destitute, suffering (cp. Ps. 103:13; Is. 49:15). Jeremiah employs this term in connection with the return of captive Israel (Jer. 12:15; 31:20; 33:26, verb form; 42:12, noun; and ch. 30:18), even of dwelling places standing desolate. God's "mercies" and compassions have no other origin than Himself, because He is the God of loving-kindness and pity, whose very name as He proclaimed it, whose Essence as revealed by Himself (Ex. 33:19; 34:5-6), is that He is "merciful," and "abundant in goodness," of great loving-kindness. God's mercy is motivated by itself, even as His compassion has no other motive than itself, in the fact that His mercy and compassion are the compassion and mercy of I AM THAT I AM (Ex. 3:14; cp. also Ex. 33:19b; 34:6). And just because He is I AM, His favor, His loving-kindness is unalterably the same, and His compassions fail not, never are at an end. In v. 22 His compassions are named as the cause and source of His mercies, while later His compassions are said to be due to the multitude of His mercies. Loving-kindness stresses the unselfishness, the selfless, loving consideration for others; compassion, the pity for the afflicted and helpless; both emphasize their voluntariness, their spontaneity, their utter disregard of any merit or unworthiness on the part of the person to whom they are extended. Therefore the prophet says that it is owing only to the mercies and compassions of the Lord that he and his fellow men are not consumed, are not at an end, that they have not ceased to be, but still have life and breath. He has pointed out the unworthiness of himself and his fellow men (ch. 1:8, 9, 14, 18), and will do so again (ch. 3:40-42). Yet now he sings the praises of the marvelous mercies and compassions of the Lord.

V. 23. Every morning ushers in new evidences of His loving-kindness and pity. Great, abundant, multiform is His faithfulness with which He carries out His promises. Picture the dreary situation

391

at the time these words were spoken! Every breath, every sip of water, every crust of bread, every stitch of clothing is regarded by the prophet as evidence of the ever new, inexhaustible mercies and compassions of the Lord.

V. 24. "Portion." The Lord gives Himself, undivided, I AM THAT I AM, to every individual. Can mortal, sinful man ask more? Ps. 73: 25-28. This gracious gift is the starting point, the foundation of our hope.

Vv. 25-33. "Good" comprises all that has been stated vv. 22-24; just as the noun "goodness" (Ex. 33: 19, same root) comprises all He reveals Ex. 34: 5 ff. Since this goodness is the portion of everyone who waits for, and seeks, the Lord (v. 25), it certainly is good for man to wait silently for the Lord rather than to grumble about His ways (v. 26). Therefore it is good for a man to bear his yoke in his youth, for under the training of the gracious and compassionate Lord he will early experience that even the greatest sorrow will teach him to become patient and hopeful (Rom. 5: 3-5) and to yield rich fruit of righteousness (Heb. 12: 11). Let him learn to suffer in silence and not to murmur against the Lord, who has sent the tribulation (v. 28); humbly bow to God's will, hoping against hope (v. 29). Even if he must suffer many injustices (v. 30), let him willingly submit (cp. Is. 50: 6; 53: 7). Vv. 31-33 motivates such patient submission. The Lord of unending mercy will not forever punish (v. 31; cp. Rom. 8: 18; 2 Cor. 4: 17); even in affliction He remains the God of mercy (v. 32); the Lord finds no delight in punishing (v. 33).

Vv. 34-36. "The Lord approveth not" (v. 36) is the protasis, the apodosis precedes it vv. 34-36 a. As the Lord is not a cruel taskmaster (vv. 31-33), so wrongs committed by men do not meet with His approval. "Approve," "see," here in sense of looking favorably, approvingly, as, e. g., Is. 53: 2; Ps. 22: 18; Prov. 23: 31. Cruel treatment of prisoners or captives (v. 34); injustice in legal proceedings, "before the face of the Most High," whose representatives the human judges are (Ex. 22: 28; Ps. 82: 6), v. 35; or any other subversion of the rights of one's fellow man (v. 36), the Lord will not approve. Others translate the last clause of v. 36: "will not the Lord see?" i. e., regard and therefore punish. The sense is not changed materially.

Vv. 37-38 are correctly rendered as questions in A. V. On v. 37 cp. Ps. 33: 9. No one can carry out his plans unless the Lord grants success. Both good and evil come by the Lord's decrees and are sent by Him for His own wise purposes (Is. 45: 7; Amos 3: 6 b; Jer. 18: 7-10).

V. 39 reverts to the thought of v. 22. Since that is true, why should a man moan and complain as long as he is alive, has life and breath, unmerited gifts of God's grace? He has deserved death and damnation (Deut. 27:26)! "A man for his sin!" If there is to be complaining, let it be for one's sin! This thought is carried out in the next paragraph.

3. The Prophet Urges His People to Return to the Lord in Sincere and Prayerful Repentance, Vv. 40-45

40 Let us search and examine our ways and return to the LORD!
41 Let us lift up our hearts to our
42 hands unto God in heaven! We, we have rebelled and revolted!
43 Thou hast not pardoned! Thou hast made a covering of wrath and hast pursued us; Thou hast slain with-
44 out mercy. Thou hast covered Thyself with a cloud so that no
45 prayer can pass through. Thou hast made us offscourings and refuse among the nations.

Vv. 40-42. Sins! (V. 39.) Not a pleasant subject for most people. Yet one that every man must sooner or later face. Therefore the prophet urges his people, every individual, not overlooking himself: Let us "search," literally, dig into, look for what is hidden from our eyes by our deceptive heart (Jer. 17:9), and "try," explore, so as to become thoroughly acquainted with the object, so used of exploring a city or country (Judg. 18:2; 2 Sam. 10:3; cp. Ps. 139:1, 23). Return to, עד, the Hebrew preposition includes arrival at one's goal; not stop after one half or nine tenths of the way is completed. Let us not be satisfied with lifting up our hands, with the uplifted hands let us lift our hearts in sincere, repentant prayer (v. 41). The emphatic "we" and "Thou" (v. 42) stress the causal relation. "Transgressed," revolted, "rebelled," were obstinate. The perfects describe the life of the nation as an uninterrupted obstinate rebellion (cp. Ps. 94:10; Jer. 7:22-28; 25:3-7). Therefore the Lord has not pardoned and could not pardon, because they rejected Him, His law and His Gospel.

Vv. 43-45. "Covered," made a covering (see Ps. 91:4), has enveloped Himself in a cloud of wrath, out of which His thunderbolts flash forth against the rebels in the form of pitiless pursuit and slaying (v. 43), and through which no prayers can penetrate (v. 44); neither the prayers of the people (Jer. 14:12) nor of His prophet (Jer. 7:16; 11:14; 14:11; 15:1). On pitiless slaying cp. Jer. 15:2-9; 16:4-5. "Offscouring," sweepings; "refuse," the abs. inf. used as a noun, objects of contemptuous rejection (cp. 1 Cor. 4:13), by divine judgment!

4. The People Plead for Deliverance from Their Cruel Enemies and for the Lord's Vengeance upon Them, Vv. 46-66

46 All our enemies open their mouths
47 wide against us. Panic and pit is
our lot, desolation and destruction.
48 My eye flows with streams of water
for the ruin of the daughter of my
49 people. My eyes overflow inces-
santly and will know no respite
50 until the LORD looks down and
51 beholds from heaven. My eye
makes my soul ache for all the
52 daughters of my city. Those who
had no reason to be my enemies
have hunted me down like a bird.
53 They have cut off my life in the
pit and have thrown stones at me.
54 Waters flowed over my head.
55 I said: I am lost! I have called
upon Thy name, O LORD, from
56 the depths of the pit. Thou hast
heard my voice! Close not Thy ear
against my sighing, against my cry!
57 Thou hast drawn near when I called
upon Thee. Thou hast said: Fear
58 not! Thou hast pleaded the causes
of my soul, O Lord! Thou hast
59 redeemed my life! Thou seest,
O LORD, the wrongs I suffer!
60 Judge Thou my cause! Thou seest
all their vengeful plans, all their
scheming thoughts to harm me.
61 Thou hearest their insults, O LORD,
all their scheming thoughts to
62 harm me, the whisperings of my
opponents, and their mutterings
63 against me all day long. Mark
them! Whether they sit down or
64 arise, I am their song! Pay them
in full retribution of all their
65 deeds! Give them blindness of
heart! Thy curse be upon them!
66 Pursue them in anger, and destroy
them from under the heavens of
the LORD!

Vv. 46-47 describe the contemptuous treatment. "Opened their mouths," cp. ch. 2:16. "Fear and a snare," cp. Is. 24:17; Jer. 48:43. "Desolation," tumult, noise, cp. Num. 24:17; Jer. 48:45. The two words combined denote crashing, smashing destruction.

V. 51. Mine eye "affecteth," same word as Lam. 1:22; 2:20, to do, act; to do harm, cause grief. My eye, either by what it is compelled to see or by its constant weeping, grieves, depresses my spirit "because of"; on this sense of ‏לְ‎ cp. Is. 6:4; Is. 53:5; Job 22:4. "The daughters of my city," the girls and young women, who were subjected to special shame (cp. ch. 1:4, 18; 2:10, 21; 5:11). The prophet speaks as the representative of the people.

Vv. 52-54. Once more Judah laments her pitiful condition. "Chased me sore," the term denotes a successful chase, hunting down (Gen. 27:3, 5, 33; Jer. 16:16; Lam. 4:18). "Without cause" connects with enemies (cp. Ps. 35:19; 69:4). "In the dungeon" (v. 53) cannot refer to the imprisonment of Jeremiah (Jer. 38:4-6). In the entire book Jeremiah never speaks of the personal wrongs he suffered from his fellow Jews, but of the sad fate of Judah and the Jews. "Dungeon" is a common metaphor for "grave," extreme danger (Ps. 28:1; 30:3; 7:16 [A. V., v. 15]; 40:3 [A. V., v. 2]). "Cast a stone upon me," rather, threw stones at me, the singular is collective; "cast upon," not to place a stone on the pit, as some translate, but to throw at me. "Waters" (v. 54), again a figurative term for overwhelming misfortune (cp. Ps. 18:16; 32:6; 69:1, 2, 15); in Jeremiah's pit there was no water flowing over his head; that would have meant a swift death; there was mire, into which he sank and from which he was extricated (Jer. 38:6). The believing Jews, addressing God, confess that they had no hope of survival, that they felt as if they had been cut off from God's grace. Yet it was the Lord who had sent this calamity. To Him they turn in penitent, hopeful, trusting prayer.

Vv. 55-63. Basing their petition on past experiences when they had called on God from lowest depths and God had heard their voice, they plead that God would not hide His ear from their sighings and cries (v. 55). Remembering that the Lord had come to their aid in answer to their prayer (v. 57a), remembering His promise (v. 57b) and the former occasion on which He had defended the "causes of their soul" which threatened their soul, their very existence, and had redeemed their life (v. 58), the life of their nation; and knowing that the Lord had seen and taken note of the wrongs inflicted upon them by the cruel hordes of the enemy (v. 59a), they appeal to Him to judge their cause. In vv. 60-63 they enumerate these wrongs. "Imaginations" (vv. 60-61), plans, machinations; "device," meditation (Ps. 19:15), mutterings, denotes the intensity of their plannings.

Vv. 64-66 the final appeal to repay their cruelties by destroying them from the earth. After all, the heavens are the Lord's. He is the Supreme Ruler and Judge in spite of all efforts to dethrone Him. Fulfill Thy threat against them, Thy promise to us (Jer. 25:12; 29:10; 50 and 51).

IV. Jeremiah's Hope for the Lord's Forgiveness

1. The Severity of the Judgment, Vv. 1-12

1 How dim has the gold become! How has the choice gold been changed! Holy stones have been thrown about at every street corner!

2 The precious children of Zion valued as pure gold, are regarded, alas, as earthen vessels, the work of the potter's hands.

3 Even the jackals present their breasts, suckle their whelps. The daughter of my people turned cruel like the ostriches in the desert!

4 The tongue of the suckling child cleaved to his palate for thirst; children were begging for bread, but there was none to give it to them!

5 They who had feasted on dainties perished in the streets; they who were carried on scarlet

6 resorted to a dunghill. The guilt of the daughter of my people grew greater than the sin of Sodom, which was overturned suddenly, untouched by any hand. Her

7 leaders were purer than snow; they were whiter than milk. Their bodies were ruddier than corals,

8 as a sapphire their figure. Darker than soot has their form become; they are not recognized on the streets. Their skin cleaves to their bones; it has become dry as a stick.

9 More fortunate were they who were slain by the sword than those slain by famine, for these pine away, pierced through, for lack of the products of the field. The hands of tenderhearted women have boiled their own children; they became their food in the ruin of

11 the daughter of my people. The Lord has vented His rage. He has poured out His furious wrath. He has kindled a fire in Zion, which has consumed her foundations.

12 Neither the kings of the earth nor all the inhabitants of the world believed that the oppressor and adversary would enter the gates of Jerusalem.

Vv. 1-2. The many contrasts throughout this chapter speak for its authorship by Jeremiah, whose prophecies are replete with contrasts. Vv. 1-2 three terms are used for gold, first the general term זָהָב; then, הַכֶּתֶם הַטּוֹב, the finest gold; then, פָּז, pure gold. Not only is gold darkened, the finest gold has changed so that there is no more any resemblance to its former beauty. "Stones of the sanctuary," rather, "stones of holiness," i. e., stones assigned to holy purposes, are, contrary to their customary valuation, poured out, scattered carelessly at every street corner. V. 2 establishes v. 1 as figurative and explains it. "Precious" refers to "stones of holiness," the children of Zion, set aside to be a kingdom of priests and a holy nation (Ex. 19: 5-6), "comparable to," literally, "weighed with," therefore, "valued like" pure gold. Now regarded and treated like earthenware, worthless, carelessly treated, its loss unmourned.

Vv. 3-4. The sad fate of the children (cp. ch. 2: 11-12). "Sea monsters," rather, "jackals," the wild, roving beasts of prey, give suck to their young. Judah's mothers are likened to the ostriches.

"The hens belonging to one cock deposit their eggs in common in a shallow excavation in the sand, dug by the male. Various contradictory statements have been made in regard to the part played by the two sexes in incubation, but there is no doubt that the cock alone undertakes this task at night. During the day incubation is necessary only in the cooler parts of the ostrich's range; elsewhere the eggs are merely left to the heat of the sun." (*Nelson's Encycl.*, Vol. IX, p. 113, *sub* "Ostrich.") While the stork is called *avis pia,* the pious bird, the ostrich was regarded as a symbol of maternal neglect and cruelty (cp. Job 39:13b-16). "Breaketh," v. 4, cp. Is. 58:7; Jer. 16:7.

V. 5. "Delicately," literally, "on delicacies" (cp. Gen. 49:20), dainties, the finest of foods. Now, deprived of their riches, they walk about the streets stunned. "Brought up," carried, supported (in their infancy), in garments of scarlet, costly clothing, now embrace, hug, "dung heaps," ash heaps, side by side with beggars, seeking a warm resting place. Their riches gone, they are reduced to beggary.

V. 6. "The punishment of the iniquity," rather one word, "guilt," "the punishment of the sin," simply "sin." "Stayed on her," literally, to turn in a circle, to turn round about, of the sword (Hos. 11:6), here of human hands; they did not turn about in the business of Sodom's destruction. In like manner Jerusalem's destruction was effected not by the turning of many hands, but by God's judgment (cp. v. 12).

Vv. 7-8. "Nazarites." נזר = to set apart, either by the special vow of Num. 6:1ff. or because of their position. Joseph is twice called נזיר (Gen. 49:26; Deut. 33:16), "that was separated," the eminent, the ruler among his brethren. We know too little of the Nazarites to regard such exuberant health and special beauty as expressed here by the ruddiness of their cheeks, the fairness of their complexion, and the stateliness of their appearance (literally, cut, outline, shape) as a special characteristic of the Nazarites. Many of these may have been poor people, and it is doubtful whether a few weeks or even months of abstaining from wine and every product of the grapevine would effect such a change in their general appearance as to be a characteristic mark. The description rather suits the elite, the "flower" of society, the leaders socially or civically. Now their fairness has turned to sooty darkness so that no one recognizes these princes and princesses of society as they walk through the streets like living skeletons (cp. Is. 3:16-24).

Vv. 9-10. Far better to die the swift death by the sword than to be pierced through, mortally wounded, doomed to die the slow, lingering death due to the lack of food, a pining away so torturing that even compassionate, tenderhearted women were so crazed by hunger as to forget their maternal affection and to cook their own children to still the all-overwhelming pangs of hunger (Lev. 26:29; Deut. 28: 53-57; 2 Kings 6:24-29; Josephus, *Jewish Wars,* X, 9).

Vv. 11-12. This horrible calamity was effected by God's fierce anger, a destruction incredible to all the world particularly since the marvelous deliverance in the days of Hezekiah (2 Kings 19:32-36).

2. Judah is Punished for the Sins of Her Prophets and Priests and for Placing Her Trust in Human Helpers, Vv. 13-20

A. The sins of prophets and priests, vv. 13-16

13 It was for the sins of her prophets, the iniquity of her priests, who shed in her midst the blood of the 14 righteous. Like blind men they staggered through the streets. They were defiled with blood so that no one could touch their garments. 15 "Away! Unclean!" men called to them; "Away! Away! Touch not!" As fugitives they also roam. The nations say: "They shall no longer 16 remain here!" The anger of the LORD has scattered them. No longer does He favorably regard them. They do not honor the priests nor respect the elders.

Grammatical Notes

V. 14. "Men could not touch." וּיְכְלוֹ is here construed with imperfect instead of infinitive with or without לְ.

Vv. 13-15. "Prophets" and "priests," murderers (cp. Jer. 26:7-14), by word and example seducing the people and leading them to destruction (Jer. 6:13-15; 23:11-15; Ezek. 13:10-16; 22:25-26), now wander irresolutely, groping their way, looking everywhere for help except to the right place (Jer. 26:4-9; 27:16-17); running blindly, headlong into destruction. So defiled were they with blood that men could not touch them. People meeting them apply to them the warning cry which lepers were to use if anyone approached them. Their own fellow Jews would shun them: "Out of our way, you unclean persons!" and when they fled into other countries, they would be like vagabonds, for no nation would permit them to settle down. "They shall not live here any more!" (Cp. Deut. 28:65-66.)

V. 16. "The anger (literally, the face) of the Lord hath divided," scattered, "them" (cp. Gen. 49:7), because He no longer regards them favorably. "They respected." The people among whom they dwell will not respect them, not even their priests nor their elders (Deut. 28:20).

B. The people's trust in human helpers, vv. 17-20

17 And we — our eyes still were worn out, looking for help in vain, in hopeful watching waiting for a
18 nation that did not help. They dogged our footsteps so that we could not walk in the squares. Our end was nearing, our days were finished, for our end had come!

19 Our pursuers were swifter than the eagles of heaven. In the hills they chased us, in the wilderness
20 they lay in wait for us. The breath of our life, the LORD's anointed, was caught in their pits, he of whom we said: Under his shadow we shall live among the nations.

Vv. 17-20. "As for us . . . failed." In spite of all the divine judgments still we continued to look, till our eyes failed, for our help! In vain! Their hope that Pharaoh Hophra would defeat the Babylonians, which had prompted them to break their solemn covenant (Jer. 34:8-22), proved to be futile. All their "watching," their confidence in Egypt, had been misplaced. The enemy returned, dogged their footsteps, so that it was no longer safe to assemble in the public squares because of the missiles hurled into the city from the siege towers. The end had come! Flight was in vain! No escape possible from so swift an enemy who was ready for us, whether we tried to escape into the mountains or the wilderness. "Breath of life" refers to Zedekiah. A kingdom's life depends on having a king. He was the Lord's anointed. We hoped that under the protection of the son of David, the divinely appointed dynasty, we would live as an independent nation. They trusted in man and refused to put their trust in the Lord and His Word. And so their kingdom perished, when its breath of life was taken in their pits, loaded down with chains, his sons slain, and then, a blind, sightless man, he was led into captivity to die there!

3. Salvation for Judah, Destruction for Her Enemies, Vv. 21-22

21 Rejoice and be glad, O daughter of Edom, living in the land of Uz! To you also shall the cup pass, you shall be drunk and be denuded!
22 Your guilt is past, O daughter of Zion! He will no more send you into exile! He will punish your iniquity, O daughter of Edom, He will expose your sins!

Vv. 21-22. A ray of hope illumines the dark night of hopelessness. The enemies, represented by Edom, the ancient enemy of Judah (cp. remarks on Jer. 49:7-22, and see Ps. 137:7), are ironically exhorted to rejoice and sing. Their joy will be short-lived. Also unto them, as now unto Judah, shall the cup of God's wrath come (Jer. 25:15ff.). In that long list of nations to be conquered by Nebuchadnezzar (Jer. 25:15-28), Edom (v. 21) and its border state Uz (v. 20) are also mentioned. Edom will have to drink this cup to its last bitter dregs, till she is intoxicated, reels, falls, stripped naked of all her power and glory (see Jer. 49:7-22). Then shall be at an end the guilt of the daughter of Zion, the true Church of God; no longer shall she be exiled! The Church of the New Testament, the communion of saints, will forever be united with her Lord. But the guilt of Edom shall be finally punished. God will uncover her sin, uncover, the opposite of "cover" by the atoning blood. The last remnant of Edom perished during the siege of Jerusalem in the early years of the Christian Church A. D. 70, 71. (Josephus, *Jewish Wars,* IV, 5; V, 6. 1.)

CHAPTER 5

V. The Prophet's Prayer for the Lord's Mercy

1. The Prophet's Sorrow, Vv. 1-18

1 Consider, O LORD, what has happened to us! Take note and ob-
2 serve our disgrace! Our heritage has been turned over to strangers,
3 our houses to aliens. We have become orphans, fatherless, our
4 mothers like widows. We must drink our water for silver, our
5 wood comes to us for a price. On our necks are our pursuers; we
6 are exhausted, obtain no rest. We have pledged ourselves to Egypt, to Assyria, in order to be satisfied
7 with bread. Our fathers have sinned. They are no more. We are
8 bearing their guilt. Slaves lord it over us! There is none to deliver
9 us from their hand. At the risk of our lives we bring in our har-
10 vest because of the sword of the wilderness. Our skin glows like a furnace because of the fever of
11 hunger. Women were ravished in Zion, virgins in the cities of Judah.
12 Princes were hanged by their hands; old men were not respected.
13 Young men carried hand mills, youths staggered under loads of
14 wood. The elders have left the gates, the young men their song.
15 Ceased has the joy of our hearts, changed to sorrow is our dance.
16 Fallen is the crown of our head! Woe unto us, for we have sinned!
17 For this our heart has grown faint; for these things our eyes are dark-
18 ened; because of Mount Zion which is desolate, jackals run about on it.

V. 1. It is impossible that God did not remember, but so it seemed to the prophet. He pleads with God to show by His actions that He realized what has happened to His people and to prepare to remove their shame.

Vv. 2-4. They have lost everything! Their land, their "heritage," turned over to foreigners, their homes to aliens (v. 2). Fathers and husbands are slain (v. 3). Water and fuel are taxed although both are "ours" (v. 4).

Vv. 5-6. They are cruelly oppressed. They are constantly pursued (imperfect) "on our necks"; they are feeling the hot breath, hearing the harsh commands of their oppressors all day long; worn out completely, they are allowed no rest. "Given the hand" in solemn pledge, particularly of surrender, servitude (see 2 Kings 10:15; Ezra 10:19; Jer. 50:15; Ezek. 17:18), in order to obtain food.

V. 7. "They are not," are dead. "Borne their iniquities." That applied to those who hated God (Ex. 20:5). Every individual sinner was to be punished for his own sin (Jer. 31:30; Ezek. 18:1ff.); but if children continued to walk in the footsteps of their wicked fathers and even excelled them in point of wickedness (Jer. 16:11-12), then their penalties will increase in keeping with opportunities neglected, precepts and commandments set aside, warnings and repeated judgments

401

deliberately ignored. Yet as members of a nation that is suffering the severity of God's wrath for long-continued neglect of His Word and will, the believing child of God will feel the agony and shame of the ruin just as keenly as, and at times more severely than, the unbeliever. Though the sting of punishment, God's wrath, has been removed, though the penalty is changed into wholesome chastisement (Heb. 12:6-11), yet the child of God finds it hard to rid himself of the sense of guilt. He cannot forget that he has contributed to the guilt of the nation, has deserved nothing but punishment. And his flesh rebels as fiercely against any suffering, call it penalty or chastisement, as the flesh of the unbeliever (Jer. 17:9; Rom. 7:18). Yet he learns to submit and humble himself under the mighty hand of God, even if he does not understand His judgments.

V. 8. The prophet continues to picture the severity of God's judgment. Many of those now lording it over them had been slaves, to whom Prov. 19:10; 30:22; Eccl. 10:7 applied; formerly underlings, now overbearing, bullying dictators. To such men the people of God were hopelessly surrendered by the Lord!

Vv. 9-10. At the risk of our lives we "gat our bread," we brought in our harvest (cp. on this phrase 2 Sam. 9:10; Cant. 8:11; Hag. 1:6), because "the sword of the wilderness," marauding Bedouin bands, roamed over the country to deprive them of their harvests (cp. Jer. 41:8). What little they saved was barely sufficient to keep them alive. Their skin "was black," glowed, like an "oven," a fire pot, because of the "terrible," rather, the flame, the heat of fever due to famishing.

Vv. 11-18. Particularly sad was the shameful fate of women and virgins (v. 11). Princes were hung on high poles or stakes, to which their hands were tied, a shameful (cp. Deut. 21:23; 1 Sam. 31:10, 12, after death), lingering death. Old people were no longer treated respectfully (v. 12). Young men were taken "to grind" (infinitive; cp. Judg. 16:21), the work of women or slaves. It may be better to translate: "Young men carried the mill," or "millstone" (noun, same form as infinitive). In either sense they were reduced to slavery, hard labor. Children, here in contrast to young men, boys, were loaded down with wood for fuel or war purposes (v. 13). No more assemblies of the old men, or elders, at the city gates, or of young men to make merry with music. Joy and every form of merriment has been changed to sorrow (vv. 14-15). So completely has the glory of Judah, the crown of their head, been removed by the hand of God because of their sins (v. 16). Their heart is sick with sorrow, their eyes are darkened, dimmed by tears, because of the loss of all these things

(v. 17), and particularly because of Mount Zion, the site of God's house, now a desolate heap, deprived of its glory, the sanctuary, while jackals have made it their domain (v. 18).

2. The Prophet's Final Plea, Vv. 19-22

19 Thou, O LORD, shalt throne forever! Thy throne endures forever
20 and ever. Why hast Thou forgotten us forever? Forsaken us for length
21 of days? Turn us, O LORD, to Thee, then shall we be turned.
22 Renew our days as of old! Unless Thou hast completely rejected us, art angry with us overmuch!

Vv. 19-22. Having poured out his sorrow, Jeremiah now turns to the Lord in a last fervent appeal. We have lost all Thou hadst given to us as our Covenant God. That has not changed Thee. Through all the catastrophic changes Thou "remainest," sittest, in the sense of "throne" (1 Sam. 4:4; Ps. 80:2; etc.), forever. Thou art the everlasting King, and Thy royal throne cannot ever be overthrown. "Under a sense of human frailty, the passing away of generations, and the falling of earthly thrones, it is a relief to the pious heart to turn to God and say: Thou, Lord, remainest forever." Cowles. (Cp. Psalms 90 and 102.) "Forget forever" (Ps. 13:2, A. V., v. 1; Jer. 15:18). For most Jews then living, the seventy years of exile (Jer. 25:12), fifty years after 586, were indeed perpetual, lifelong captivity. It seemed to them as if God had forgotten, forsaken them forever (cp. Ezek. 11:15). "Turn Thou us unto Thee," for then, and then only, shall we be turned (Jer. 31:18), and then only can we hope that Thou wilt fulfill Thy promise to bring back to Judah the exiles (Jer. 29:10-14) and the Temple vessels (Jer. 27:19-22) and renew us, restore to us, the peace and prosperity we enjoyed in the days of old. "But," here in the sense of unless, except (Gen. 32:26; Lev. 22:6; Ruth 3:18, the second "until"; 2 Sam. 5:6; Is. 55:10-11, "but"). "Utterly reject," the abs. inf. intensifies the idea of rejection. God is asked to restore Judah to its prior state, unless He has utterly rejected it. And such rejection would be incompatible with the promise (Jer. 27:19ff.; 29:10ff.) of Him who is I AM THAT I AM. The same sense would be obtained if we translate: For if Thou wouldst utterly reject us, that would be excessive wrath, because it would not agree with Thy promise. The concluding verse, therefore, is not a lament nor a cry of despair, but rather the final fervent appeal of a soul that pins all its trust on God's promise and its fulfillment, guaranteed by the fact that He is the Lord Jehovah, the Covenant God. (Cp. Jeremiah's fervent pleas, Jeremiah 14—16.)

403

Topical Index

H

Abbreviations

tribe, were brought to Alexandria by Ptolemy II Philadelphus (285—246 B.C.) in order to translate the Hebrew Bible into the Greek language. Its accuracy varies considerably.

Ms = manuscript.

MT = the Masoretic Text, the traditional (masora, massora = tradition) Hebrew text as edited by the Masorites, Jewish scholars at Babylonia from the second to the tenth century A.D., and at Tiberias in Palestine from the seventh to the thirteenth century A.D. These scholars sought to establish a correct standard text of the Hebrew Bible on the basis of the text as fixed by the Talmudists (200—500) on the basis of ancient manuscripts. After the decline of the Babylonian schools in the tenth century the school of Tiberias became the center of study of the Old Testament text and fixed the Masoretic Text as it has been generally accepted. The best modern edition of this text is that of R. Kittel (died 1929) and P. Kahle, 1929—1937. After the death of Rudolf Kittel, 1929, the publishers, Privilegierte Wuerttembergische Bibelanstalt at Stuttgart, asked two noted scholars, A. Alt and O. Eissfeldt, to continue the work so ably begun by Kittel. It is based on the Leningrad Manuscript dated 916 A.D., and now preserved at Leningrad. Fourteen Hebrew scholars aided in the editing of this Bible, in which a large number of Babylonian variants found in manuscripts recently discovered are given in the footnotes.

Q'ri = "read," the reading suggested by the Masorites in place of the written text.